a patriot's dream

Part I

j.k.blakely

for nancy
je t'aime

and
for those who sacrificed their youth,
property, families and lives,
who forged a new nation,
a beacon of liberty for all,
the united states of america.

Special acknowledgment and thanks to the Web's Wikipedia and other sites, and The World Book Encyclopedia for various factual information found in this novel.
All rights reserved. No part of this novel may be reproduced in any form.
© 2015, 2016

"the die was cast, the rubicon crossed"
(john adams…….april 1775)

Chapter I

White Carnation

*passionate peace brushed tranquilly, shield us from storms life brings
hear the trickle of the mountain stream, the rustling leaves of spring
journey as one about rapturous waters, blissful sea bathe us eternally
beneath the hush of our evening star, we immerse in precious serenity*

It seems only yesterday when I read his words for the first time, when I whispered those lines that autumn morn so long ago. Seasons have come and passed, a generation and more since then, yet my eyes still mist as they did on that day I first touched the ink of his words and felt the soft resignation of his soul. Oh, how I remember his tender voice whispering, "I love you, Andrea," how I long for his sweet lips, for the gaze of his tranquil eyes into mine. How I yearn to nestle beside him, my hand gently within his, his fingers caressing mine, to touch his skin, be near the beat of his heart.

He used to say my eyes were serene green pearls, yet the fall of time's sand ceases not for me, ceases for no one. My pearls have dulled with years, my locks now silvery grey, and the softness of my skin has vanished, succumbing to the ravages of time. The sun has risen thousands of times since those days, spraying rays upon a new century, a new epoch which seems so detached from then, yet memories of my Ethan ever stoke the flames of my heart. He is with me always, nestled upon my shoulder at dawn and tenderly stroking my cheeks when I rest for sleep each night. Transcending the years from another place, another time, my passions for Ethan flow just as intensely now as then. How I miss him so, how I still love him so.

The revelations of yesterday have ignited a smoldering past within me, and as my thoughts of Ethan simmer deeply, memories of yesteryear are being set free, mysteriously unleashed from so many secret places. The story of those days long past, memories of what truly happened, have begun to unfold from hidden rooms of my heart and mind, as if those cherished events were only moments ago. Some say we were unwavering in those days, those of my generation, women and men of the English Colonies as we were known back then. It was a time when courage was not just a stylish word, an ornate expression cloaked upon the notion of self, but an intransigent spirit engrained within so many, a daring quality surging the souls of righteous men.

It seemed common in those days for so many to risk so much for a cause greater than their own, dangerous deeds willingly accepted which could lead to loss of wealth, family and homes, and sometimes, life itself. Tens of thousands were spurred by an impatient restlessness back then, casting a spirited shadow upon all of us. The liberating pursuit of life and happiness was not simply an abstraction quilled upon parchment in those days, but an inspiring vision infused within the hearts and minds of audacious souls, the very essence of a daring generation.

Mystical explosions the day before had sprayed the dark above hundreds of ports, villages and towns, fires illuminating the stillness of a summer night with sparkling trails of blues, reds, yellows and whites. Horns blared and steeple bells rang, rejoicing sounds echoing the hills and fields north, south, east and west amid the beating cadence of distant drums, celebrations reminding thousands of the birth of an idea many years ago. Yesterday we reflected upon that pivotal day of a July long past, on those of my generation and the ones which came before. We cheered those who survived the war and remembered those who did not, of the blood spilled upon grassy hills and chilly snows, of the thousands of patriots resting all these years in lonely fields.

Yesterday was the fourth day of July 1826, and memories flourished from Savannah to Williamsburg and Trenton to the port of New York, from Lexington to Boston and Philadelphia to here, my village of Germantown. Fifty years have passed since that transcending day, two score and ten from our spirited beginning, daring hours forever quilled upon our nation's history. It was the unraveling of emotions swirling about all those things, intimate unions of entwining pasts, memories of my Ethan which kindled sensuous joys brushed with struggling sorrows, a time of arousing passions in my life.

We were so young in those days, those fleeting hours of July 1776, Ethan an impassioned twenty-five and I just twenty-six, while many were older and wise. It was a time when the candle for an entire generation seemed to have been set aflame by a magical fire, moments which blossomed from enlightened thought for over a hundred years. It was a time when the ideals espoused by spirited men resonated throughout, phrases which thrilled minds and emboldened souls, fundamental beliefs stroked upon parchment by the innocence of a feathered quill. It was a day when the poetic words of a man from the Colony of Virginia burst upon the conscious of every colonist, phrases polished and honed by an inspiring statesman from my Pennsylvania and a robust barrister from Ethan's Colony of Massachusetts Bay.

Yesterday had been a jubilant day, the fiftieth such day since that document by Thomas Jefferson, Doctor Franklin and John Adams had been approved by a collection of colonists gathered just south in Philadelphia. It was a sheet of tan parchment scripted of ideals, visions and hopes presented to dozens of men meeting in the sultry hall of our Pennsylvania Statehouse. Its meanings had been forged with Mr. Jefferson's quill and refined by Franklin and Adams, a document presented to our Continental Congress by their committee of five, a spirited revelation that our Thirteen Colonies were snipping their ties from the clutches of King George the Third. Our determined struggle against London was into its second bloody year by that fourth day of July, and that single sheet of parchment declaring our independence with resolve, inspired thousands while galvanizing our patriot cause.

It had been over thirty years since Doctor Franklin passed from our lives, leaving years for Jefferson and Adams to reflect upon our nation's past outside the doctor's wise peering eyes, hours to reminisce of their creation and ponder the truths of its lines. As those two patriots slowly aged with all the others of a dwindling generation, they seemed to represent the final pillars of our young nation, two colonists whose dynamics and duty forever altered the grateful lives of millions of women, children and men.

Then suddenly, as if by divine design, yesterday their lives were entwined a final time, for Thomas Jefferson and John Adams joined the thousands still resting in solemn fields, succumbing together to their mortal fate. They had reached the end of their inspiring lives on their most pivotal day, the Fourth of July, as if God had placed His hands upon our nation's soul and decreed it so, fifty years from the hour of what I and so many believe was man's most righteous moment, our daring cry for liberty.

Would our nation now founder, I painfully wondered, now that their hearts had fallen silent? Would the visions of those two patriot men and perhaps the hopes of my generation, and those yet to come, slowly drift from the flame sparked all those years ago and fade into darkness? No, such things must not be so! Our nation shall persevere! We've survived the loss of so many others, of General Washington and Sam Adams, Mr. Hancock too, and we will once again, for the ideals passionately quilled by that enlightened trio are more powerful than the visions of a single man.

Yet what happened yesterday still remains, Thom Jefferson and John Adams have gasped their final breath and dwell among us no more. The swirling storm of their passing has cast a grieving shadow throughout the old colonies this day, a gripping sense of loss at our hour of joyous celebration. Their deaths have awakened a nation which now strained to retain its patriot past, a traumatic event that has spurred my thoughts upon a journey for memories long stashed, savory moments quietly waiting to be plucked from my soul.

Reports of their fate had raced across a stunned nation throughout the night and into the warmth of this summer morn, the fifth day of July, words sweeping about the western frontier across the hills and fields to the sea, as if upon a frightening wind swirling of a solemn end to our beginning. They were accounts dashing through villages and towns of all the states by boisterous shouts of swift riders, younger men galloping snorting mounts north from Mr. Jefferson's Monticello in the hills of Virginia and racing south from Mr. Adams' village of Quincy on the shore of Massachusetts Bay. It was a wind that shattered the hearts of those who survived the war all those years ago, a wind which perhaps only those of my generation truly understand.

This July morn seemed as hundreds before which have bathed the eastern woods of Pennsylvania, and as I rock my chair upon the porch of my home here in the village of Germantown, I realize my step has slowed and the tenderness of my skin has creased and aged. It's just an old nicked chair, tired and worn as I these days, New Hampshire cherry cushioned with a tapestry of crimson roses. A thin maple stick with a curvy handle rests just to my right, a cane leaning to the side of my small oval table, an aging stick which someday will be laid to rest with my own mortality. As I peer to the leaves twisting the elms swaying along the lane, as my chair crunches with each creak, I wonder of my life, of what happened in the colonies all those years ago.

This has been my home for over forty years, and this porch my haven for reflection and peace, a cocoon peering south and west toward the frontier. It's a place I can watch the sun slide across the day and feel the cooling shade of nearby trees, while bathing in the smell of honeysuckle sweeping from a Germantown meadow amid a symphony of little chirping birds prancing about the leaves. I've come to cherish the aroma of the lane during a spring rain and the vision of dust swirling a summer day from a carriage's crackling wheels, and feel a brush of ease at the sound of hooves clumping the ruts and stones of the lane. This porch has been my sanctuary since the war, and now in my closing years, a place I ponder life while listening to distant children and the sounds of people rushing to some mysterious place.

I had wed Franz in my impressionable youth, and for several years lived five miles south in Philadelphia, then in the spring of 1781 we came to this precious little lot east of the square and began creating our home on Schoolhouse Lane. I remember how proud he seemed when his men embedded the final slats and stones after two years, completing this house shortly after our little son Benjamin became six, just months before the end of the war. Unlike most cottages and homes that rose about the village of Germantown in those days, dwellings of rocks and bricks, ours was mostly planks and timber sliced from nearby groves of maple, birch, oak and elm.

Three rooms fill the upper floor, the largest to the rear on the northeast side, a bedroom that had been for Franz and me many years, a room with a big window with dozens of panes peering to distant elms and the swaying grass of a nearby field. Two smaller rooms are nestled up front facing a manicured green lawn, each with a square-paned window that swings over my porch and gazes upon the ruts and rocks of the lane. A hearth of dark bricks and stones rises near the center of my home, a place for fires to warm each room, and a narrow hall leads to staircase steps descending to a foyer near the front door.

Just west of the foyer is where I once baked and steamed supper for Franz and little Benjamin, and now that I'm all alone, I might simmer a stew now and then when my aging temperament feels right. A staining brass spigot with a winged elm handle rises from a counter of grey stone beneath an easy oval window, and a white porcelain bowl with red dainty petals patiently rests nearby, awaiting a spray of Pennsylvania water. For many years an oil lamp had glowed just a bit right of that pump, glass of sapphire blue that now rests on a small round table of polished oak nudged into the far corner.

Running some eight feet long in the center of my kitchen, stretching toward the foyer from the northern panes, is a nicked maple table several feet wide. It was a place we'd gather with friends in the olden days, a table where during the hush of night, I sometimes hear tender whispers seeping from the past. Three maple chairs cushioned and slated line each side while an armed chair is nudged to each end, and upon the center of the maple sits an aging candelabrum, dark twisty wicks sprouting six tan candles.

Embedded along each side of that quaint oval window are several walnut cabinets with shelves lined by an array of kitchen things sequestered behind paned glass doors. Bronze molds for forming beeswax candles rest on a shelf along with dozens of oaken trenchers and spoons near crystal goblets and grey pewter mugs for ciders and ales, water and wine. Oblong plates have been stacked on lower selves since the war, porcelain dishes with dainty flowers of yellow and blue, and a gaggle of saucers and cups are neatly tucked nearby. And dangling from a silvery hook is a thin twisting rod with a sharp ashen trimmer, a dark iron snuffer of candles.

The stones of my cooking hearth consume most of the kitchen's east wall, with a sturdy mantel of knotty oak securely entrenched above blackened rocks and bricks. And an iron rod swivels from inside those scorched stones, its end crimped in a curvy hook for dangling pudgy dark pots simmering with stews of fowl and beets, corn and little beasts.

To the right of my front door, just east of the foyer and those climbing stairs, is a spacious room Franz designed for relaxing near a tranquil fire. Two delicately carved maple rocking chairs are set upon the polished oak slats near a pair of windows that peer upon my porch, panes with lots of squares for the sun's rays to streak to the fireplace stones rising near the rear along the western wall. A little round table has nestled between those chairs for over forty years, and a white porcelain lamp brushed with dainty little flowers always sits at the center of the oak. Similar tables have graced each corner of the east wall for years, both with a single candle rising from a dulling copper holder.

A large rug of thick twines weaved in greens, yellows, blues and browns circles near the hearth with a pair of cushioned chairs clinging to its edge, their paddled arms facing a little stack of birch logs bundled on the ashen bricks and stones waiting for winter's flurries. A cherry table with a lamp etched in glass of Persian blue sits between those two soft chairs, and a small brass box once home to the stained meerschaum of Franz's pipe rests near his old chair, its sweet tobacco smell still lingering the air.

Just right of the porch window, in the corner near those two rocking chairs, is mother's old spinning wheel, a treasure of daintily carved maple she gave me shortly after Franz and I wed. Oh, how I remember so many quiet hours during the war, so many struggling nights spinning strings and yarns for shirts and breeches, stockings, scarves, blankets and coats, and so many lonely years since. I cherish the serenity which has warmed my soul just seeing it nestled near the corner all these years, and wonder of those days so long ago each time I caress its slim threading hook and smooth tension peg, each time my fingers touch its slender spokes and tranquil wheel.

Beyond a thin elm wall to the rear of the room is an enclave tucked into the northeast corner, a place Franz once quilled cold numbers and phrases for business deals as the sweet aroma of meerschaum drifted the night air. Then after Franz died I slowly began to remove his merchant things, and when my aging body surrendered to the toils of climbing those stairs, I settled into that room for the waning years of my life. It's now my quiet little bedroom, a haven of the past and place I reach for Ethan in blissful dreams.

My quaint room has a modest dark door near the hearth, and just inside along the left wall is a nicked chest of walnut drawers. A slim bed cushioned of bundled cottons and wool is nudged into the far corner, with soft linen sheets, feathered pillows and a quilt stitched in yellows, tans, greens and reds. A large window with little panes is embedded into both east and north walls, and sometimes on stormy days I lie and watch the elms whipping in wintry winds or listen to spring rains dancing the sills.

A small tan lamp and thin dwindling candle are set on a little table of aging oak beside the head of my bed, and in the center of the wall right of the door hangs a special painting, a portrait of me brushed for Ethan before the war, when the world seemed innocently young. Sometimes, while lying on my bed and gazing to its walnut frame in the hush of night, to its greens, yellows and sapphire blue, those sensuous shades seem to eerily shift in the candlelight, as if mysteriously searching for a time long lost.

And now, on this warming morn the Fifth of July, 1826, I slowly rock in my cherry chair in the cocoon of my porch, a cherished haven all these years, and gaze to the summer winds while glancing to my winkling aging skin. It's a morning which began as so many before, with the scent of mountain laurels lazily wafting about the quiet breeze, a soft wind filled with the tranquil smells of baking breads, a morn soon to plunge into mystical waters swirling of the past.

As I nudged my toes with each swinging rock and a hush brushed the petals of scarlet roses sprouting about my porch, as little birds sang among the leaves rustling the elms swaying along the lane, I began to hear the muffled sounds of a galloping horse. The cadence of hooves pounding into the ruts and stones of Schoolhouse Lane grew louder with each passing moment, and soon a silhouette immerged from the summer haze, a lone rider blasting alarming crisp shouts.

A stringy brown mane was dancing his grunting mount with each dig of iron shoes into the lane, and an intriguing blue coat flapped about his body as he gripped and flailed the thin leather reins. With each rock I could see the intensity in his glare, a determined stare as he galloped around the lane's western bend, his weathered boots stuffed deep into stirrups amid a plume of Germantown dust. I watched with fascination as he dashed toward my porch, while dozens of startled women, children and men streamed from homes into the morning sun.

"They're dead!" the young man in dark breeches emphatically proclaimed with boisterous swivels and glares. "Mr. Jefferson is dead!" he shouted amid another thunderous clump, "Mr. Adams too! Yesterday! Thom Jefferson and John Adams are dead!" I watched in a stunned hush as his snorting mount rushed past at a dizzying pace, and listened through billowing dust as he continued to roar their fates. "They're dead!" he blasted as if in a mystical trance, gripping reins and flailing his arms with each thumping stride. "Mr. Adams! Mr. Jefferson! Both died yesterday, the Fourth of July!"

Then they vanished south around the bend in a dusty plume as quickly as they came, and soon his excited shouts faded as they galloped along the winding road to Philadelphia. I could feel an anxious unease begin to churn deep inside as I slowed my rock and grasped for acceptance of what I just heard, a shocking revelation spouted to hundreds of Germantown. And I watched in a numbing hush as women and men began to gather in a flowery meadow just off the lane, exchanging views of the stunning news.

I suppose most were grappling with their thoughts just as I, searching for understanding of what the passing of those two men would truly mean, of what might become of our nation upon the passing of the remnants of our founding generation. As I watched the throng assembling while struggling with my immerging grief, I began to hear muffled little stories being spewed from aging women and men, cherished memories of John Adams and Thomas Jefferson, of our colonial past being fancifully relieved.

I'd later hear that soon intriguing stories of those days were being recalled in taverns, homes and shops of towns and villages everywhere, fading memories being recited in little groups gathered about the square of Germantown too. Some were culled from family lore passed down by elders long gone, or fuzzy tales once whispered near a fire by greying uncles and aunts, mothers and fathers or aged patriot soldiers. They were now hazy memories and mystical beliefs of a trying yet special time, whimsical tales of a courageous uncle, daring brother or a proud villager or two. I suppose most were brushed with a tinge of truth while some were embellished with fancies, gripping stories whispered from my generation to the young of the colonies before and during the war.

As I rocked on my porch and gazed to the distant dust slowly settling to the lane, my thoughts began to wander to the colonies and the crown, to people I knew, to mother and father, to Franz. But most passionate of all are my memories of Ethan, and the story of our lives and what truly happened in those days began to unfold.

Ethan and I were of an immerging generation in those days, for we hadn't settled in the thirteen colonies from a place across the sea like our mothers and fathers, and so many before. We were born and reared here, in a new land they called the English Colonies, and looking back after all these years, perhaps ours was indeed, an impatient generation. Yet I suppose some now believe we were a generation that embarked on a journey that didn't really happen the way so many say, while others might whisper such things are simply fruits of whimsical stories. But it truly did happen, and happened this way.

Mother named me Andrea, in memory of her mother, and used to say it must be pronounced *Ohn-DRAY-ah*, and that my name would provide me with "calmness and courage wrapped by an aura of bold strength, just like mama." When I was young some would call me Andee, a name I was never fond of, and at times, despised, for to me it showed an appalling dismissal of my grandmother. But once childhood passed and I began to sprout an appealing shape, most began to call me by grandma's true name, even the jeering boys of Germantown. I've always felt close to her, and in a spiritual way am proud of keeping her legacy alive, and have always believed she's shrouded me with fortitude all these years, helping me survive the anguishing tribulations of my life.

I was born right here in Germantown, on a muggy Friday morn the third day of July, 1750, seventy-six years ago shortly after dawn in what was then known as the Colony of Pennsylvania. My heritage flows of Dutch, and in my earliest days, I discovered how to survive as an only child, often finding sanctuary in the hush of thoughts and dreams. The foundations of my core beliefs were forged by the teachings of our Society of Friends, and my understandings of life and God have been honed by my Quaker faith.

Others from the Netherlands were here in Germantown too, as well as from an array of nations across the sea like Ireland, Denmark and the Germanic principalities, and most prominently, the Kingdom of Great Britain. Some spoke the language of their native tongue, at least during their early years in the colonies, and I remember hearing Dutch and Prussian coming from many of the older ones when I was young. Yet most strived to acclimate to the essentials of English, words and phrases I and other children seemed to learn rather easily in those days, while the older ones like mother and father found it reluctantly challenging. But all realized that the king's royal governors and most doctors, merchants, barristers and tradesmen throughout the colonies relied upon English as the most dominantly fortuitous language.

Mother and father had sailed across the sea from Holland several months before I was born, disembarking in Philadelphia on an icy Delaware River dock, and within weeks settled here in Germantown, in a little cottage just a bit west. I remember father telling me tales when I was young about stories he heard about the Colony of Pennsylvania, in the years before he and mother severed their ties with the old country. He'd speak of lush forests, fertile fields and crystal streams, lands I'd later learn had been granted to William Penn by England's King Charles some seventy years before.

"It was a place they said was bathed of tolerance," father would enchantingly whisper on frigid winter nights bundled near a fire crackling in the hearth, "land for those who seek the freedom to live and pray as they choose." Mother always said she wanted those things too, "desperately so," not only for them but for me, their coming child, saying they wanted to escape the gloom of Holland that had shrouded their lives. They wanted to leave behind what they said were the prejudices of the old world, religious bigotry which had snatched the life of my precious grandmother.

When I was young, mother would tell me of the horrors of her mother's fate, events she insisted I know so I could understand who my grandmother truly was, so I'd realize the sanctity of my name. "She was a gracious woman," mother would say, dabbing a tear, "who wished to worship God as she chose, with her Society of Friends. She believed in the good of people, Andrea, and the simple, inspiring words of Jesus." I can still see the sorrow that would swell mother's eyes when she'd gasp and sigh, "I'm afraid it was your grandmother's righteous beliefs which stoked the ugly fires of a few in the Netherlands, wicked women and men whose hearts had chilled to stone."

"As icy winds swept from the sea over the village of Domburg," she'd say about the early hours of January 1750, "the soul of our village constable was gripped by a wintry hate." It was a village along the southwest rocks of the rugged Dutch coast, a place along the North Sea where mother and father shared a home with grandmother.

"Mama was snatched from our cottage, Andrea," mother once whispered while brushing a tear, "during a snowy flurry just after dusk the Sixth of January, and I never saw her alive again." After three frantic days of not knowing what had happened, not being told where she was or why, a pair of guards for the village constable wheeled my grandmother home as a light snow trickled the dark. "I was scared and wanted to scream," she said, "but all I could do was gasp. It was awful, Andrea. Mama looked so lonely lying on the snowy slats of that ugly cart, listless, wrapped in a crumpled blanket. Those two vicious men didn't say a word, just grabbed her in their devilish hands and carried her into the cottage, and with cold, lifeless stares, dropped her in a chair near the fire."

Mother and father would later learn that my grandmother had been whisked to a grisly stone gaol and confined in the darkness of a frigid room those anguishing days and nights, and left without food, water or a blanket too, for reasons neither the sheriff nor any village official would ever explain. And in the coming days and weeks ugly rumors began to swirl about despicable pain inflicted upon grandmother by the Domburg constable and a few wretched villagers, awful deeds intended to purify her Quaker soul.

Village elders ignored mother's sighing pleas for the truth of grandmother's fate, and to this day no one has ever come forward or been held accountable. The only words mother ever heard spewed by anyone of position came from one of those diabolical guards who carted grandmother home that dreadful night, contemptible words he sputtered near the village square in the days to come. "The old woman just gave out," he spritzed to the snowy stones, "just slipped away in her sleep." My grandmother was forty-two years old, and as of that wintry night, had come to the end of her life.

Father once said that the corrupted powers of a few in Holland had little people like Quakers by the throat, and that no matter how one struggled to find their way, the weight of that evil was merciless. After several agonizing weeks mother and father came to realize they'd need to abandon the country of their birth, would need to begin their lives once again in a far off place. With his merchant trade ties, father purchased passage on a sailing ship for a little bag of golden ducats they had scrimped and saved, then gathering a few cherished things, they sailed west to the English Colonies three thousand miles across the sea. "We knew we needed to leave Holland," he'd say, "escape the hatred and never go back."

It was the ugliness of intolerance, hatred of those perceived by ignorant people as being different, along with my grandmother's courage and spiritual beliefs, that caused my fortuitous fate of being born in my village of Germantown here in the colonies. "Your grandmother is part of you, Andrea," mother often whispered when I was young, "with you everywhere you go. Be vigilant and proud, and always, kind." Perhaps it was a yearning for her mother that instilled my own mother's need to keep my grandmother's memory alive, and in a special way, she is, flowing within me.

Mother was born in her mother's bed in a Domburg cottage on a wintry night twenty years before me, the Twenty-first of December, 1730, and liked to say she came into this world "as a spray of stars twinkling above the North Sea." And I remember how she'd tilt her head in an alluring way while whispering her name as it had been those early days, Gertrude Van den Berg, her voice in poetic song while gazing into the winds as if searching for memories.

She was a bit taller than most girls in those days, some six inches above five feet and perhaps a hundred and twenty pounds, and the dainty swirls of her sandy hair lazily swayed about her shoulders while gliding across a room when I was young. Mother's eyes were a sensuous blue that resonated truth when sparkling in the sun, a calmness which made me feel good, and there was always a tender blush of acceptance brushing her cheeks. She had a special aura of caring for those about her, a gentleness which conveyed a sense that every person has importance.

As most girls in those days, just as those in my own early life, mother stopped attending her Domburg schoolhouse when twelve or thirteen, a place which taught her crafty things for home like sewing, weaving and baking. And once here in Germantown, she mostly stayed close when I was young to care for father and me, and seemed to always be showing me the nuances of cooking tasty stews and making warm things with cloth, needles and threads. Although she cherished sewing garments and tending her home, she was rather eager to help a friend in need, and sometimes, would snip and stich for others of Germantown for a few helpful shillings and pounds.

When I was young, mother always seemed to have a sewing needle strategically pricked into the sleeve of her blouse or seam of a dress, as if waiting to be snatched and carefully thrust into the soul of unsuspecting cloth. And I remember gazing in a fascinated trance as she folded, snipped and stitched, and watching her on a snowy winter night years ago as she gingerly threaded father's nightshirt when I was six. "Come closer, Andrea," she whispered with an intriguing glance, gripping a gown of thin blue stripes, "watch."

I pressed closer to her chair near the flames of the hearth and watched as she nudged a slim needle trailing thin blue thread in and out of father's favorite nightgown, over and over again. "Softly, Andrea," she instructively whispered, "gently. Let the needle guide the thread. Here, see how smooth this edge appears, with soft twisting tugs? It's just a nice and easy running stitch. Come, I want you to try."

Her fingers began to gently guide mine with soft prances across the cloth, and as I pinched and tugged the needle and thread, she confided in a motherly tone, "There are many ways to mend, Andrea, but this special loop is the soul of sewing. Never forget this running stitch, for you'll use it all your life." I didn't just think of mother as the best seamstress in all the colonies when I was young, but as a sculptor or painter, an artist who seemed to escape to a wondrous place with each looping stitch. I'd watch her fingers effortlessly slide, as if she were brushing colorful oils across a canvas of life, and with each twist, tug and glide I could sense her wandering to a special place, perhaps to a medieval bluff high above the waters of the Meuse.

Father used to say he was born on a drizzly afternoon in the village of Domburg "as a dreary layer of roiling grey drifted from the sea," the Twenty-third of June, 1725. He was named Klaasz Karl Van Dijk by his father, a name mother once said intrigued her, and I can still recall her sputtering his stylish name when she thought she was alone on a spring afternoon. Many newcomers to Germantown, women and men who had also sailed across the sea from the Netherlands, referred to father by his entire name, while a few of the older ones knew him as Karl and some simply called him friend.

Perhaps a hundred and eighty pounds, father was a bit shy of six feet and rather confident some would say, and when I was a child he seemed larger than life, a vision which in a little girl's way, has remained with me all my life. His hair was trimmed in dark tan waves that flowed near his shoulders when he was young, thick curly locks which thinned and greyed through the years, just as most elders of Germantown. And father's eyes, so serenely blue, always brought a sense of calm to me, zaffre eyes which mother would confess at times, thrilled her.

I remember the stories father would tell when I was young, memories of how he toiled at various duties when he was boy to aid his family and enhance his fiscal lot, beginning at an impressionable age of nine. "Yet never," he'd proudly say, "did my string of little jobs interrupt my schooling," not only because that's what he insisted, but because his father was unyielding that his studies never be comprised.

Although he didn't always understand when his father would say, "You're going to move beyond those blasted loading docks, study your way, Klaasz, to a more robust life," he always respected my grandfather's dream. And in the fall of his sixteenth year father ventured northeast to the college in the port of Rotterdam, and for the coming four years, studied the nuances of the merchant trade. I can still hear father saying that his years in Rotterdam had changed his life, and although he didn't know it then, would provide mother and he the means to escape the sorrows of Holland for a new life in the colonies.

Father returned home to Domburg in late spring of 1745 and quickly found a position of promise, challenging duties that would allow him to expose the talents he reaped in Rotterdam. He viewed it as a coveted position in the merchant trade at what many said was one of the Netherlands' most envious shipping businesses, a place those of Holland knew as Geoctroyeerde Westindische Compagnie, while English investors across the North Sea knew it as the Dutch West Indies Company.

It was a company said to be involved with trading, selling and shipping various goods across the Atlantic, mostly to-and-fro little islands scattered about the Caribbean Sea and a slew of colonial ports like Charles Towne and Savannah, Philadelphia, Boston and New York. And I remember father explaining that sometimes he'd also trot his colt several miles southeast to his company's big warehouses in Middleburg, the same town where the Dutch East India Company had a gaggle of brick buildings along the square. He said they were a thriving competitor, a business with lots of similar goods stuffed in those buildings, a company most of Holland called the Vereenigde Oost-Indische Compagnie.

In a rather tender moment, mother once told me of the night she met father, "just days before Christmas, 1747," she said, after one of Domburg's more endowed women invited her to the village ball of music, dancing and supper. "I think it was a gesture of goodwill, her way of showing kindness to me for snipping and stitching several dresses that year." Mother would sometimes squint when sputtering about several of the village women she sewed garments for, saying some were rather dismissive, then soften her stare and confess, "But a few were different, Andrea, truly caring, and Gretchen was one."

I think mother said that melodies of Vivaldi, Handel and Bach serenaded those of the hall that wintry night, soft sonatas and quaint concertos strummed on gentle strings and serene nocturnes daintily tapped upon harpsichord keys. They were tranquil notes being played by some young and elder men of Domburg, passionate musicians who by day were shopkeepers, farmers, tradesmen and merchants, villagers exposing the hopes and dreams of women and men gathered that magical night.

She wore a delicate dress flowing indigo blue that kissed the shiny slats of the ballroom floor, and as Vivaldi's spring aroused the room, the eyes of mother and father passionately met. "It was a wondrous moment I'll never forget," she'd reminisce from time to time, "your father draped in a tan silken shirt ruffled with buttons of gold." He was standing hushed across the room as villagers sashayed about the floor, a crystal goblet brimming light wine cupped in the fingers of his right hand, and in a flaring black coat and dark blue breeches with tan stockings and gleaming shoes, "he looked so alluring," she said, "glistening in the candlelight. I secretly watched him for a moment, Andrea, then he twisted and peered across the floor in a sort of searching gaze, then in a mystical way, his piercing eyes latched upon mine."

They danced and talked for several tender hours that wintry night, and after courting through the spring, wed on a warm June afternoon and nestled by the sea in a Domburg cottage, inviting my grandmother into their home. Following the horror of my grandmother's fate, in the spring of 1750 father secured a fresh position in the colonies, then sailing on the schooner *Vryburg*, they disembarked on a Philadelphia dock after seven frigid weeks at sea. Father began his new duties for the Dutch West Indies Company in a warehouse along the Delaware River, and on a drizzling Saturday morn shortly before I was born, they stuffed tables and chairs, lamps, sacks and crates into a wagon and creaked some five miles north to our new home in Germantown.

As the sun's summer rays began to feel warmer on my aged skin, as I continued searching for memories of mother and father, remembering how different life was in the colonies in those days, an intriguing sound of hooves clumping the ruts and stones of the lane began pounding nearer. I could see a dusty plume following a hazy trot and creaking wheels, and watched as a dark buggy swayed closer to my porch with each roll. And as I curiously rocked and gazed toward the lane, all that squeaking and thumping came to a crackling stop when the young man pulled a mighty tug of the reins.

"Grandma!" he shouted, tossing thin leather straps and leaping to the dusty stones of the lane. "Have you heard? Has anyone told you?" It was my grandson Samuel, the only child of my only child, Benjamin. Samuel was now twenty-six, born in the spring of 1800 just months after the death of Mr. Washington, and much like his father, exerted an aura of confidence splashed with a tinge of boldness. And much like my Ethan all those years ago, he exudes independence brushed with compassion.

I watched as he dashed from the lane and scurried to my porch over the dewy grass, passing pink mountain laurels and crimson roses in his crackling bound up the elm steps. "Maybe you already know," he gasped in a hesitant tone as my chair creaked and rocked, "but I had to be sure. There are rumors, grandma, sweeping Germantown, saying Mr. Adams and Mr. Jefferson are dead."

"Yes, Samuel," I softly replied with a solemn nod, "I know." He shuffled to my chair and leaned, tapping my cheek with a gentle kiss, and as a warm hush shrouded the porch, memories of those two pivotal men, of the colonies and my Ethan, continued to caress my heart and soul. "A rider galloped by a half hour ago. I guess I'm in a little bit of shock, Samuel, like so many others I suppose, and maybe, a little numbed too. Come," I whispered, glancing right to the nicked oak of the rocking chair beside the little table, "sit with me for a while, please. Oh, Samuel, I'm so glad you're here. I think I need to talk, and tell you some things."

Just short of six feet with tender blue eyes, Samuel was perhaps more portly than most his age, and his soft sandy hair was usually twined and tailing down his neck. He lived alone a bit northwest of the town square, in one of the cottages of stone from the early days, and tended to drift toward me when stories of the colonies would swirl, as if he instinctive knew when something was important to me. He seemed to understand me, knew how I was feeling in an intuitive way, and knew how I felt about those two patriot men, of my passions for the olden days, for the colonies back then. And although Samuel may have been distant to others, perhaps emotionally protective in his own way, he always seemed to shed his armor when alone with me, exposing his precious sensitivity.

We nudged our chairs into gentle rocks and gazed to the swaying limbs of distant elms for a moment or two, and as the tranquil sounds of rustling leaves filtered about the soft summer breeze, emotions and memories stashed all these years began to swirl my mind and warm my heart. I glanced to Samuel and could sense his thoughts anxiously racing with each creaking rock, and as he patiently waited for my coming words, I could feel my passions suppressed for so long yearning to be free.

Visions of daring women and men began to flare, rekindling fires of the sacrifices and pride of courageous people, of unyielding resolve of so many in the colonies back then. Although memories have been held within all these years, with each pound of my heart they were now crying to be unleashed, a symphony of those trying days that's fluttered deep inside for over fifty years. With each nudging rock I could feel memories of Ethan struggling to break free, explode with the story of his life and the tale of so many brave souls who gave so much long ago.

As a warming wisp of summer wind gently brushed my cheeks, as simmering desires for Ethan's tender touch spritzed and clamored for release, I knew, on this July morn, I must surrender to the true passion of my life. While Samuel slowly rocked and waited for what was about to unfold, I knew what I would need to expose each patriot memory and lead me wholly to Ethan. With each breath I knew what would caress my heart and warm my soul, knew what had always whisked me to a century past, had always sailed me upon magical wings to a time I long for.

"Excuse me, just for a moment, Samuel," I whispered while reaching for my walking stick. "I'll be right back." I gripped my thin maple cane with wrinkly skin, and as Samuel leapt to his feet and swung the door, I slowly stepped into the foyer of my home and shuffled past that woven rug and fireplace stones, to my little room nestled in back. Then fixing my eyes upon the tiny knob of the small oak table right of my bed, I shuffled a bit more, and as Samuel patiently waited with each rock, I stooped and pinched that little knob with my fragile fingers, then tugged open the shallow drawer.

There it was, just a humble sheet of colonial parchment resting peacefully, a cherished gift from Ethan quilled to me on an October night long ago, words which have always twisted my soul while exposing his tender heart, sullen moments quilted in time. It had once just been a tan sheet void of passions, longings and tears, then Ethan's magical touch transformed its emptiness with precious words stroked in the hush of a lonely room by the flicker of candlelight. It's filled with stanzas oozing fanciful dreams, sentiments releasing his desires and hopes while taming horrid fears dwelling deep inside.

It's a tender poem quilled upon parchment creased and stained with regrets and tears, tattered edges I've folded thousands of times over the years. I keep Ethan's words near me each day, tranquilly resting in that little drawer or tucked in the pocket of my summer dress, or nestled inside the wool of a coat in fall, winter and spring. His lines comfort me while rocking in this chair on quiet days and lazy morns, words gently pinched in my yearning fingers or pressed to my tingling lips. Yet perhaps his thoughts calm me the most when caressing my memories as I doze during gentle spring rains, and his words always tame my anguishing fears during lonely flurries of wintry nights.

I've reread Ethan's words thousands of times, sensing the magic of his touch with each thrilling line, all the while caressing his dreams while imagining us gently entwined. I've shed so many tears to this tattered parchment too, drifting with visions of our sensuous moments upon each pressing kiss, wandering to a rapturous place we had found and few ever know. The world has spun a path strewn of frightened men during all these years since the war, angry men striving to silence those who espouse liberty and hope, yet every hour that's passed, every moment since those precious days, Ethan's passionate words have warmed my heart and inspired my soul.

I snatched the folded parchment from the shadows of that thin drawer and slid it into the right pocket of my summer dress, and with a tight grip of my walking stick, shuffled back to Samuel patiently waiting on the porch. Although the July morn was warming, I felt a chill race my skin, and settling to the slats of my cherry chair, I draped a soft shawl of knitted blue over my shoulders. And while Samuel rocked and gazed with an inquisitive stare to the distant elms, I nudged my fingers into the pocket of my dress, pinched the parchment of Ethan's poem and gently slid it to the rays of the summer sun.

"Grandma, are you alright?" Samuel caringly asked, slowing his chair to an easy rock. "What is that?" he quickly sputtered with an inquisitive glance as I unfolded the creases of Ethan's poem, then rested it to my lap.

I peered to the aging parchment pinched in my fingertips for a moment or two, then glanced to his puzzled gaze and said, "I'm fine, Samuel, really, truly I am. Please, just give me a moment." I could sense the questions swirling his mind as he stared to the tattering creases between glances to my eyes, then dabbing a tear, I whispered, "This is a poem, Samuel, quilled during the war. I want to read it to you, only, not just yet."

"Alright," he mumbled with a mysterious stare, "I guess I can wait. I'm just glad to be here, grandma, with you, on this incredible, yet sad day. But can you, will you, at least tell me who quilled that poem?"

"A man named Ethan," I softly uttered, "during an awful moment of war. I want to tell you about him, of others too. I want to tell you about the war, Samuel, so many things, and about the colonies all those years ago. But before I do, just give me a moment, let me quietly read these words to myself. Remember, I'll read this to you, I will, when the moment is right."

Samuel gently nodded and gazed to those swaying elms as I began to read Ethan's tender lines quilled on an autumn night so many years ago, and with each slide of my fingers upon his words, I could feel his passions explode. My thoughts began to drift to another time, and while reaching for precious memories, I could sense with a heavy heart the magnitude of what had happened the day before. After a few moments of a wondrous yet solemn journey, I finished the final lines of his longing words, pressed the parchment to my dress and gazed with Samuel to the leaves rustling in the summer breeze.

"Today is a proud day, Samuel," I whispered while dabbing my eyes, "yet a sad day too, for our country. What happened yesterday was a shock for many, especially the older ones of my generation. Oh, sure, we understood that someday they'd pass to another world, but I don't think we were truly ready, and when Mr. Adams and Thom Jefferson did, together, why, it seems surreal. Their deaths have spurred memories I've kept shuttered deep inside all these years, just as it probably has for many of my generation. Now the events of my life, what I remember of the colonies, of so many people from those days, your Grandfather Franz too, have been swirling my mind since I heard the news. But most of all, Samuel, what's truly coming to life from hidden rooms, are all the precious memories of Ethan."

"I'm young, grandma," Samuel timidly confessed with a caring glance, "not of your generation, but think I understand, at least a little, how you and your generation felt about those two founding men. I have fuzzy visions of you telling me things about patriots like them when I was a little boy, about things you'd seen in those days, yet I'm afraid I don't remember much. I want to know more of all those things you know, of the war, the times and people, and most of all, of that poet man, Ethan. Help me better understand, grandma, help my generation know."

"There's so much to tell," I sighed, "so many things you should know about those days. In a strange way, Samuel, their passing yesterday has sparked a feeling of urgency. I have this burning desire to explain to you what life was like when I was young, of our early colonial struggles, the war, of our lives, Ethan and me."

"I want to know all those things," he sputtered with an inquisitive stare to the dust dancing the lane. Then pressing to the slats of his chair, he softly added what I desperately wanted to hear, "I can stay all day. Tell me, grandma, tell me everything."

I gazed to the aging lines of Ethan's poem and softly stroked his tender words, then as so many times before, folded its tattering creases and slid the parchment into the pocket of my summer dress. And as a lonely cloud drifting toward the sea cast its shadowy tail upon my porch, shielding the warming July rays for a moment or two, my thoughts began to wander through the years to a time long past, back to the days before the war.

"I think, to be complete, be true," I whispered as we gazed into the summer winds, "I must begin with Ethan, of his early days, then the rest of my story will simply unfold. It was a time when he and I, all those of our generation, were known as colonists." As Samuel nudged his chair into an easy rock and stared to the rustling leaves, I brushed my fingers across Ethan's poem and closed my eyes, reaching for memories.

Ethan Francis Sheehan was born on a snowy Saturday night in the Colony of Massachusetts Bay, the day after Christmas, December the Twenty-sixth, 1750. I remember how he once said his mother had chosen the name Ethan because she thought it would bring him strength and shroud him with a spirit that was uncommonly bold, a title bathed with honor from ancient Israelite times. And his father had chosen Francis, insisting it had an aura of liberty befitting a free man, was a proper legacy for a Sheehan, a peaceful name cloaked with serenity bestowed from olden days.

Ethan's tender brown eyes always sparkled with a golden tinge whenever he spoke of those things, and as the years have passed I've come to understand how his name seemed to reflect the essence of his life. In a mysterious way, I think such meanings had bathed an entire generation back then, restless colonists who hadn't truly sought the turmoil that was to come, the struggle of war that would consume us. We were just women, children and men with hopes of life, who'd find ourselves thrust into the tempest of our times.

His mother and father had settled in Massachusetts Bay late in the spring five years before his birth, she having been reared in Scotland and he in a village across the Irish Sea. "Mom was born Elizabeth McCully," he once hushed to me, "on the fifth day of October, 1725, in the hamlet of Dundee." It was a little port perched upon grassy bluffs several miles east of Perth and northwest of St. Andrews, a fishing village on the icy waters of Firth of Tay along the North Sea.

Amid the pungent smell of crab, lobster and herring that wafted about the salty winds sweeping the slopes of Dundee, it seems sacks of course linens and tangy crates of marmalades and candies were shipped from its docks. Yet perhaps what thrilled tradesmen, merchants and seamen the most were the distilleries scattered about Scotland's eastern hills, secret places among groves of blackthorn and birch where tasty whiskies were bottled, jugged and corked. Ethan said scores of sacks, crates and bags bulging with Dundee spirits and goods were stuffed into the hulls of merchant ships in those days, then sailed to nearby ports and across the sea to the colonies.

"Mom was reared in the Presbyterian faith," Ethan once softly confided, "and like her mother before, began to toil as a village seamstress when only nine. She was kind of short too, not much above five feet, but at just a hundred and ten pounds with alluring brown eyes that gleamed in the setting sun, dad was rather charmed." Her hair was long for a girl of Scotland in those days, wavy auburn locks that kissed her shoulders and lazily flowed down her back, and some of the men and older boys would utter how she was vivaciously bonnie whenever she strolled near the docks.

I remember how Ethan's tone seemed a bit anxious when telling me about when his mother fled to Ireland, a prideful story sprinkled of hope, "for it was there," he'd say, "on that precious island that she and dad met." Then he'd quiver just a little when explaining about the troubles that began to simmer about the Scottish hills several years before he was born, frictions that at times spritzed to a boil near scores of hamlets and towns, including her village of Dundee. They were explosive eruptions like those some had seen during a fiery rebellion decades before, a defiant time Ethan said had been spurred by a shunned highlander yearning for a return of the House of Stewart.

Although they struggled to show loyalty to London during those troubled times, striving to keep their livelihood and home on the bluffs of Dundee, his mother's father and mother finally succumbed to the surging frictions, and in the fall of 1742, they fled Scotland. Just as hundreds had done to escape the rebellious fires erupting against the second King George in those days, they sailed down the shore of England and sliced the channel west to a new haven in Ireland. "They settled in Killorglin," Ethan whispered with a smile, "a fishing village on the eastern rocks of Dingle Bay. It was there in County Kerry, Andrea, on the southwestern shores of the island, where their eyes first met."

Ethan's father had lived in that fishing village all his life, having been born into his Presbyterian faith during a wintry drizzle on the ninth day of March, 1724, and christened Patrick Doyle Sheehan. "Dad was named after his father," Ethan proudly revealed, "Shane Patrick Sheehan. Granddad had battled against the English Crown with other excitable men of County Kerry some thirty years before, daring Irishmen willing to follow a courageous royal shunned by London."

They say that royal man was named James, a valiant warrior who once sat upon the throne of England before being tossed from London for what frightened people viewed were sympathies for the Isle of Ireland. "Dad said many on the island were attracted to the defiant stance by that former king," Ethan confessed, "Grandpa Shane too. They rallied to his wondrous notions of a free Ireland, and willingly took up arms against London's royal troops scattered about the island."

I still remember some of the enchanting stories Ethan would tell about his grandfather, especially his part in dreadful skirmishes of that earlier rebellion, like the decisive battle in the summer of 1690. Although it was valiantly fought by noble men of Ireland, they say the blood spilled near the River Boyne tolled the end of their dreams for liberty. "Although my granddad's quest had come to a dismal end, he stood proud with scores of County Kerry men at the surrender at Limerick, a village nestled along the waters of the Shannon in the emerald hills northeast of home."

Ethan's father was known as a vibrantly strong man in his early days, and standing just over six feet and almost two hundred pounds, Patrick Sheehan was a spirited farmer of hay for nearby ranchers and a tiller of grains, potatoes, beets and oats for several villages of County Kerry. I suppose life had always been a weary struggle for Irish farmers, particularly in those days for men like Ethan's father, for the fields were strewn with clumps of stone and swaths of rocks. And when such toils merged with the frigid winds sweeping from the sea, his father's work was exhausting.

Despite the obstacles and hardships, Ethan's father continued to till the soil of a farm that had once been freely owned by his father, and his father before, rocky fields which now belonged to traders and merchants loyal to the king in London, unkind men his father would say, hording the wealth of Killorglin. It was a farm which had been lost to men without souls during the fiscal woes that had scourged Ireland several springs before, yet land his father continued to till as generations before in return for a little cottage of stone and straw and a tiny pouch of shillings and pounds now and then.

"I guess dad was never the kind to discourage easy," Ethan once whispered near a tranquil fire, "and clung to his dream of tilling land his own. He talked of life away from County Kerry in those early days too, even hinting adventurous things like crossing the sea for the Thirteen Colonies. His hands may have been callused, Andrea, his skin cracked and worn from digging the land, but his heart was always determined. I think dad was just waiting for the proper moment in those days, patiently biding his time."

Then, as icy winds swept across the spritzing waters of Dingle Bay and whistled about the taverns, cottages, shops and docks of Killorglin on a Sunday morn of early December, 1743, that moment arrived, forever changing the life of Patrick Doyle Sheehan. "It happened right after the preacher's final words inside the chilly grey stones of Saint Michael's," Ethan recalled his father's story, "the village church near the rocks of the bay. She was leaning against an elm pew in what dad confessed was a rather flattering dress, warm sapphire blue, when she twisted and gazed to him. That's when it happened, Andrea, that very moment. Mom softly smiled, shyly, and snatched dad's heart."

They gently spoke for a while of easy things in the haven of a pew, and for the coming weeks and months saw each other out on his farm or in her father's home, and sometimes, in the glow of candlelight in a cozy corner of the village tavern, then married on a brisk afternoon the final Saturday of spring. Over the coming months they came to realize that the dream of Ethan's father for a life in a faraway place was one she also held, and as the frigid chills of winter began they both wondered of fertile fields across the sea where people were said to be free to be whatever they chose. And soon their mutual dream would lead them to a new land far from the old, a farm of their own in the American Colonies, a place where someday even the clutch of the king would fade.

After several weeks of anxious planning through that winter into spring, Patrick and Elizabeth Sheehan packed belongings and purchased passage on the tri-masked English vessel *Triumph*, a sturdy ship that had sailed into Dingle Bay from the tiny port of St. Agnes on the Celtic Sea. Along with some two dozen women, children and men of Irish and Scottish descent, they loaded chests and crates stuffed with goods, and grabbing bulging bags, boarded for the voyage to their dream. And as a chilly drizzle sprinkled from the grey that first Friday morn of April, 1745, Ethan's mother and father bid teary farewells and began their sail three thousand miles across sea.

After some six weeks of slicing the frigid waters and being tossed about the roiling spray, experiencing an uncomfortable nauseous ail from time to time, they sailed into the waters of Massachusetts Bay on a breezy spring afternoon, the Nineteenth of May. Ethan said the *Triumph* splashed anchor shortly before dusk at a dock of Gallop's Wharf, and as his father watched the ripples slowly circle into the harbor, they said a short gracious prayer to our Creator, thanking God for bringing them safely to Boston.

Within days his father had bargained with a Boston merchant for a little farmhouse on a spot of rich land, two hundred acres of colonial soil a dozen miles northwest, then assembled a snorting ox, a sturdy oak wagon and a pair of aging mares. They carefully stacked a few new things onto that wagon's slats, boxes of oils, lanterns and candles, and gathered their chests and crates of pans, cups, kettles and plates. They stacked six elm chairs and two small sentimental tables too, along with sacks of flower, grains and planting seeds and barrels of water, and their tattered bags stuffed with stockings and breeches, coats, shoes, dresses and shirts. And mingled among all those special things was a crate of fancy bowls and porcelain plates, and a dozen crystal goblets carefully packed before sailing from Killorglin to start a new life.

With their hopes now securely twined to the slats of their weathered wagon, on a brisk clear morn near the end of May Ethan's father and mother slowly rolled from Boston. With each dig into the road those aging mares tugged and pulled southwest through the narrows of the port's neck, then pivoted north on the elm slats of the old bridge crossing the waters of the Charles River, that ox tied by a thick hemp line grunting close behind. After clacking and creaking through the village of Cambridge, his father tugged the reins onto the ruts and stones of the Massachusetts Road, and as the sound of pounding hooves and crunching wheels echoed about the woods and farmers' fields, the Sheehans bounced and swayed to the village of Lexington several miles northwest.

They rolled into Lexington a bit after three that spring afternoon, and after resting their ox and mares for a moment by a tavern near the village field, they creaked and rolled another mile or so northeast to their new life along the dusty stones of the Billerica Road. Ethan once said that on that day the dream of his mother and father had finally come true, and that their new farm, that Massachusetts Bay land, would be the very spot his own colonial roots would someday firmly take hold.

I glanced to Samuel staring to the distant trees while listening to my story with each squeaking rock, then hushed for a moment to caress memories and gather my thoughts. Although it seemed my words had brought a sense of comfort to him, something which made me feel good, I sensed a strange unease simmering within, wondered if he was growing weary and wanted me to stop. "Are you sure you want me to go on, Samuel?" I nervously asked. "Maybe you'd like to go home, do other things? You know, this could take a while. Do you really want to hear it all?"

"Oh, yes, grandma," he quickly sputtered with a whimsical glance, "I do. If you were to stop now, I'm not sure I could forgive you. Please, go on, I want you to. I've got to know more about those days, and of this man, Ethan."

"Good," I sighed with relief. "There's so much more to tell about the colonies and the war, about me, about Ethan. I've already said some things of Ethan, and there's more, so much more. But first I think you need to know about other people and events, perhaps things about those these days only the old could know, things many have forgotten."

"Were you, oh, how can I say this?" he nervously blurted while fidgeting about in his creaking chair. "Were you in love with Ethan?"

My stomach began to twist in queasy knots as he snapped his inquisitive gaze from my eyes and peered deep into the warming morning winds, and as I watched the leaves rustling in the summer breeze, I wondered of the revelations soon to unfold. I hadn't planned on delving into such things just yet, had hoped my feelings would slowly be revealed as my story was told, yet I did want Samuel to know the truth. He needed to understand my past to know his own, and although I wanted to explain so many things about those days, I wanted to expose them on my terms, when the time was right. So hoping to assuage his curiosity for a little while, tamp his eagerness to know it all that very moment, I answered in a rather simplistic way.

"Yes, Samuel, I was," I sighed, dabbing a tear spilling my eye, "still am, and always will be. I'll tell you more, promise, about many things, only not just yet. We'll talk about it all, of Ethan, when the time is right."

I brushed my cheeks and reached for memories as we quietly rocked for a moment or two, and as Samuel gazed to the trees swaying along the lane, I could sense his imagination wildly wandering with fancies of youth. Then closing my eyes I could see Ethan as he was the first time we met all those years ago, enthralled with his studies near Boston, a sensitive man oozing life at a vibrant nineteen. Much like his father, Ethan was six feet tall and perhaps a hundred and seventy pounds, and his wavy locks kissed his ears in a sandy brown. He had a magical way of understanding me, and when his sensuous eyes gazed deep into mine he could see things no other could, my hopes, desires, fears and dreams, a peer that pierced my soul.

"Maybe I shouldn't ask, grandma," Samuel nervously muttered with a confusing squint, "or even have a right to, but what about Grandpa Franz? I mean, you say you loved Ethan, yet, you married grandpa? Maybe, you loved them both? What happened to Ethan? I don't understand."

I suddenly felt an urge to hide from my past, at least for a moment or two, for Samuel's questions sliced deep into the very essence of my life, and as smoldering embers flared I searched for an easy answer, something I knew didn't exist. "I understand your confusion," I whispered with a tinge of reluctance while grappling for the truth held deep inside for fifty years, "honest, I really do. But once you've heard my whole story, Samuel, I think it'll all become clear, promise. After I've explained so many things, exposed people and events from those days, you'll understand how our lives were molded all those years ago."

He pressed into the slats of his chair, nudged into an easy rock and stared into the soft distant winds as I slid my fingers back into the pocket of my summer dress and stroked the passions of Ethan's poem, rocking gently with each caress. "It was a long time ago," I whispered, "and now I'm grey, wrinkled and old. You know, Samuel, I've come to realize that life isn't brushed in a single shade, that most of the time there is no crisp line between bright and dark. We all have desires, hopes and dreams, lonely places to fill, and I suppose I succumbed to pressures that can weigh heavy early in life, and maybe, to my own limitations and fears. My life was a weave of needs I thought were important back then, wants spurred by my own weaknesses, and I failed to look deep inside, Samuel, grasp my dreams. After you hear it all, I hope you'll understand."

"Alright, grandma," he whispered with a caring glance, "I'll be patient. I'll listen to your whole story, promise."

"You know, Samuel, you're the last of our family, and today it just seems right to tell you so many things. Your Grandfather Franz was a good husband, a fine man, and I did love him. I guess back then, in a sad, youthful way, I was able to shun my feelings at times. I exchanged passion for acceptance and stability, and then one day, it was all gone."

"I never got to see grandpa, but I know you loved him. Everyone always said you did."

"There's more, Samuel," I confessed as my eyes misted with shame. "The truth is, I never had the same feelings for your grandfather as I had for Ethan. Oh, I loved your grandfather, but in a rather tame way, not like the passions that consumed me for Ethan."

"Yet," he mumbled in a puzzled tone, "you married Grandpa Franz."

"Yes, I did," I sighed, dabbing another tear, "and by dusk you'll know why, and hopefully, understand. God forgive me, Samuel, for I knew of my feelings before wedding your grandfather, knew long ago how my heart belonged to Ethan."

Samuel nudged his chair into a more robust rock as a beguiling expression brushed his face, perhaps his thoughts gripped by confusion and disbelief that his grandmother had once been a young woman struggling with conflicting wants, passions and needs. Whatever intrigues might have been swirling his mind, I simply watched as he peered to the swaying elms with a puzzled gaze, his fingers clasped about the arms of his chair, as if awaiting another aging revelation.

"There may come a time," I whispered in a motherly way, "when your mind leads you to one path, and your heart cries for you to walk another. I didn't know the truth of such notions back then, not really. No matter what happens, Samuel, stay close to your heart."

"Alright," he sputtered with a tender glance, "I think I understand." Then following a reflective moment or two, he inquisitively asked, "What happened to the two of you? Why didn't you, marry Ethan?"

"Patience, Samuel," I sighed, hoping to ease his anxiousness, "in time. Before I can really answer such a thing about Ethan and me, you need to know much more about those days, what it was like before and during the war, what happened in the colonies that changed millions of lives all those years ago. You're of a new generation, Samuel, living now in peaceful times, unscathed by the ugliness of that war, but things were so different back then. We had yet to become this wondrous nation, and I suppose life in the colonies really began to change around the time Ethan and I were born, when those of our generation were so young."

The July rays were filtering through the limbs of distant elms and dancing upon my mountain laurels and roses blooming near the porch, and as the summer morn continued to warm I could see little beads glistening Samuel's brow and trickling his cheek. "There's fresh water in a jug," I softly said as a wisp of wind tossed my hair, "in the basin of the kitchen, and goblets on a shelf behind the glass. Let's have some, Samuel, before I go on. Would you please fetch some water for us?"

"Of course," he quickly replied, snatching the door, "I'll be right back."

I could smell the soothing scent of marigolds scattered about distant hills sweeping up the lane in the warming breeze, and the sweet aroma of grains swaying in nearby fields began to stir memories. For a wondrous moment I thought I could hear colonial wagons crunching the dirt of Germantown lanes and creaking carriages clacking along the cobblestones of Philadelphia, and as I quietly waited in the summer winds, the howl of wilderness wolves seemed to mysterious filter from frontier. With each squeaking rock I wondered of the many things that took place when Ethan and I were so young, when colonists were beginning to grasp visions, hopes and dreams, and for a magical moment I could smell a tranquil colonial rain.

"Here you go, grandma," Samuel sputtered as the door closed with an easy click, scurrying me back to July, 1826.

"Thank you, Samuel," I whispered as he set my goblet to the little table. Then nestling to his chair, he nudged into a gentle rock, sipped a spot of water and clicked his crystal to the table. "Things were so different back then," I sighed, sliding my fingers to the pocket of my summer dress as our chairs creaked and rocked. "I don't think your generation could ever really know, Samuel, what it was like, and I suppose all you can do is imagine, wonder, how it truly was in those days so long ago." He rocked and stared to the leaves rustling in the distant elms, awaiting my coming words, and as I slowly caressed the passions of Ethan's poem, I began to remember the essence of it all.

There were no states back then, just colonies, and there weren't twenty-four of them either, not like now, with some thirteen million women, children and men in our union we call the United States. In those days there was no union, not even a nation, and there weren't twenty-four colonies back then, only thirteen, with perhaps a million or so colonists when Ethan and I were born. Our thirteen colonies, with some four million people by the first hours of the war, were not free and independent either, but beholding to the whims of England, to parliament and the king three thousand miles across the sea.

When Ethan and I were born in the middle of the last century, the crown of the English throne was worn by King George, not the first but the second, and our lands of the Thirteen Colonies stretched some fourteen hundred miles along the Atlantic coast. It was a land of forests, mountains and streams, hills and fields, farms, towns, villages and ports running from the Royal Colony of Georgia in the south to the northern reaches of the Colony of Massachusetts Bay, lands which in those days engulfed the wilderness of Maine. Looking back after all these years, some might say the colonies often behaved as if they were not aligned in any way, as if a small country of its own, rather than an integral part of a larger union like our nation is this summer day.

When I was young father once explained that each colony was established in one of three ways, and each was created under differing scenarios with intriguing names. He said some were viewed by London as a *royal colony*, lands firmly in England's grip, and others were called a *proprietary colony*, wilderness swaths controlled by someone selected under rules proscribed in an official grant from the crown. And there were a few known as a *corporate colony*, new lands governed by an adventurous company pursuant to a royal charter quilled by the king.

Yet no matter when, how or why each of the Thirteen Colonies was formed, by the years leading up to the war such distinctions had vanished, for each would evolve and all would become a royal colony. Each would become fully entwined to the idiosyncrasies of the English Crown, with each beholden to the intrusively consuming policies, acts and laws being spewed by London. Even after all these years I still recall the stories told by father, Ethan and others of my youth of how each swath of land had become a colony, of daring women and men who sailed with hopes, tales I shall never forget.

I *Virginia*: Father had said that the first of our thirteen colonies was Virginia, fertile hills and fields where some still believe England's first lasting settlement took root along a narrow river near the sea around 1607, some hundred and seventy years before the war. Daring men of the Virginia Company of London, settlers with a royal charter quilled by the first King James stowed in the hull of their vessel *Godspeed*, sailed across the sea with the *Susan Constant* and *Discovery*, dropping anchor at that wilderness river on a misty morn of spring. In honor of the crown they christened their little spot James Towne, and in memory of their newly deceased Elizabeth, father would say, a monarch some affectionately viewed as their Virgin Queen, they proclaimed the surrounding forests and streams to be Virginia.

Those first settlers had sailed from London with captains named Ratliff, Martin and Smyth, some hundred men and older boys adhering to the spiritual words of Robert Hunt, their voyager preacher. For many years colonial lore suggested it was Captain Smyth who inspired the settlers to quickly assemble a village from the abundant brush and timber, and that it was he who struggled to forge peaceful relations with a curious people who already lived about those Virginia lands, indigenous women, children and men most would refer to as Indians. They were tribal groups the settlers would come to know as the Nahyssan who hunted and fished about the nearby wilderness along the waters of that narrow river soon called James, and the Pawhatan who roamed north and south along the sea, or the Monacan and Manahoac who hunted about the inner hills of the Piedmont.

After several decades of settlers streaming into the colony, they began to experiment with a form of self-rule over their new land, forming what father said was an assembly they called the House of Burgesses. "Those settlers discussed important issues," he'd say, "and made policies and laws too," for what was then being referred to as the Royal Colony of Virginia. Yet soon, it seems their new mandates and rules were being reluctantly quilled under the intrusive influence of their colonial governor, a position many viewed as beholding to the whims of that Virginia Company of London.

I remember one of the stories I was told when I was very young was rather sad and confusing, a tale which to this day exposes the inhumanity of man, a vile sin I pray will someday vanish. It seems that about the time that assembly was taking hold, a new kind of thrift was beginning to evolve in the colony, not an enterprise of timber for ships, of hunting the forests or mining the hills, but a business of growing and shipping a plant. It was a product derived from the leaves of a Nicotiana plant, a commodity of sticky foliage most simply called tobacco.

Yet, it wasn't those Nicotiana leaves that caused my insides to twist in anguishing knots when I was young, but the parasitic system infused into the land by some of Europe and the colony back then to process those sticky plants. Father explained that as more people across the sea wanted to inhale the fires of those thriving tobacco leaves, along with an insatiable desire by some for more shillings and pounds, new ways were introduced to help expand wealth. It was a diabolical system designed by twisted minds to slash the costs of exhaustive labor and enhance the treasure of seemingly reputable men.

A new group of people to harvest those tobacco plants began to arrive in the colony, women, children and men with skin of a color unlike those of England or the principalities of Germany, or my Netherlands, Spain, Ireland and France. I remember my schoolmarm once said, "They looked different than the other settlers in the colony, with a darker pigmentation," a shadowy grey that seemed to provide those twisted minds with a "misguided justification for a wicked system of free toil." Among other horrific things, they were beginning to be known as Negroes, an innocuous phrase derived from Spanish, Portuguese and Greek forever to bathe people of another continent who were sailed across the sea unwillingly. "It was an unflattering term," she'd day, "which became fashionable in villages and towns sprouting about the Colony of Virginia."

There were ugly stories too when I was young, of how whole families of Negro women, children and men would be snatched from their African villages and farms and stuffed by Dutch and Portuguese men into the hulls of putrid ships and sailed across the sea to the colony. "They were now slaves," father once said, "viewed as property by greedy men who shackled them in iron chains, human beings stripped of the very thing your mother and I sailed across the sea for, freedom." They were not paid for their toils on vast farms, and as twilight descended the fields, were banished to the squalor of pungent huts. They were people who had harmed no one yet were being punished for the crime of having dark skin, and most would anguish in bondage for the rest of their lives.

After many years it seems new settlers from Ireland, Scotland and the principalities of Germany began to arrive to a colony which until then, was mostly comprised of women, children and men from England scattered about the hills nearer the sea. These fresh settlers ventured into the lands of a great valley and the Piedmont north and west, stretching the frontier with farms, villages and towns while expanding the tobacco trade further into the wilderness. Some would say that for decades the infusion of settlers into the Colony of Virginia was more rapid than any other colony for decades to come, expanding to comprise more colonists than any other for a hundred years.

Yet for me, and perhaps many of my generation, the Colony of Virginia will always be remembered as where some of the first cries of colonial discontent roared when I was young. They were robust arguments of patriot men that sparked the embers of what would ultimately come, words and deeds which not only stoked the flames of liberty in the decade before the war, but in the final hours of peace before the eruption of the guns.

II *Massachusetts*: Ethan once said his colony derived its name from indigenous people who lived near the sea many years ago, Native Americans from a tribe called Massachusett, a name that conjures native visions of a great hill by small blue hills, an area just south of what would someday be, the port of Boston. "At first they called my colony Plymouth," he liked to say, "founded some hundred and fifty years ago by righteous people from the Island of Britain." I'd later learn they were religious people called puritans by some or pilgrims by others, because of their wandering ways in search of a land to freely pray.

Father said they sought not only spiritual separation from what they viewed as religious suppression from those loyal to King James, but a complete detachment from England. It seems a hundred or so of those daring people stowed crates, barrels and bags of grains, clothes and other supplies into the hull of a ship brushed the *Mayflower*, and during a chilling morning drizzle of September, 1620, sailed west from the village of Plymouth in County Devon, on the southwest shore of England. Following what one would later say were several icy weeks slicing a harrowing sea, that group of determined people dropped anchor near a rocky point on what they'd soon call Cape Cod Bay.

They were said to have struggled to survive that fall and frigid winter of the coming year, and at times pondered abandoning their fledgling settlement and sailing in the spring back to England on their vessel still moored in the bay. Yet tales of their resolve resonate to this day, for rather than succumbing to the elements of those wintry months, a season of despair wracked by swirling snows, they prayed to our Creator and reached for the outstretched hands of indigenous people.

Those desperate puritans were said to have been helped by native women and men of the Mohican, Pennacook and Pocomtuc tribes, strangers who exposed their new voyager friends to various foods and crops. It seems they helped save their endangered lives those challenging winter months, showing those from England ways to trust the land, and in the fall the end of that trying first year, they all gathered near the waters of the bay for a tasty feast of crops, fowl and game. "We gave humble thanks to God that day," an aging witness would later say, "for our newfound friends, and for giving us the will to survive and showing us the way."

Although those settlers remained at their little enclave on the western rocks of Cape Cod Bay, it seems that after several years many began to seek new lands they hoped might be more hospitable. "Whole groups began carting their things northwest," Ethan once said, "some forty miles, searching for a more forgiving place, with most settling on the hilly soils of a small peninsula. It was there, Andrea, where a little village began to sprout, a hamlet they'd soon call Boston."

It was around then, perhaps 1630 or so, when England's new king, the first Charles, thought London should have more control over those newly settled northern lands. They say he granted a charter of rules to the increasing numbers of puritan villages, parchment which gave them the crown's blessing to expand further north and west into the wilderness of what London was now calling the Massachusetts Colony. It seems that for several years an array of freedoms slowly evolved in the new colony, a time an assembly of elected colonists was formed to administer their expanding lands, a spirited group that soon enacted a code of policies and laws they called their *body of liberties*.

Even though notions of freedoms and rights had been quilled to parchment in those days, after a while some say the roots of the colony, its puritan core, began to forget the ideals which had dropped anchor years before in Cape Cod Bay. "An acceptance of others began to dwindle," Ethan explained, "and many began to shun those who sought to pray in a differing way. Some of those early settlers sought to purge those they viewed as straying from puritan beliefs, urging them to seek refuge in some other colony."

Many began to flee as brutish puritan pressures continued to mount, new settlers now seeking the freedom of wilderness lands along the colony's frontiers in which to worship as they please. They stuffed rickety wagons and carts with humble things and escaped from the ugly cries, creaking, walking and riding with snorting oxen and mares to begin anew about the frontier, to create hamlets, villages and farms. Soon the forests north would come to be known as the Colony of New Hampshire and the wilderness still further northeast the enclave of Maine, a territory of the Massachusetts Colony, while the hills, fields and streams toward the south would become the colonies of Connecticut and Rhode Island.

It wasn't long before the English crown was worn by the second King James, and by the time the 1680s had come London had reconfigured the governing apparatus not only of Ethan's Massachusetts, but for the lands that all those worshipers had fled in their search for religious freedom. "The king had wrapped all those lands into what he called the Dominion of New England," Ethan once whispered near a flickering fire, "a title which didn't last very long," for just before the new century his colony escaped the dominion and insisted it be known as the Colony of Massachusett Bay. It was a daring separation that would come to be approved by the new King William and his bride Queen Mary.

In the decades leading up to the war Ethan's colony would govern itself through an array of tradesmen and farmers, shopkeepers, merchants, doctors and lawyers elected to an assembly to address fundamental issues of the day. Yet during those years the Colony of Massachusetts Bay continued to remain under what many would come to view as the oppressive authority of London, "and a string of unjust governors," Ethan would say, "loyal only to the crown." Many believe it was the casting of devious acts, policies and laws upon the colony that stoked the embers of rebellion in those early days, a repressiveness unleashed by the king, his parliament and royal governors.

III *New Hampshire*: They say that the eastern lands just north of the Colony of Massachusetts Bay was first viewed by an Englishman named Pring a few years before those puritans settled upon the rocks of Cape Cod Bay. He and his men had sailed north along the shore before pivoting inland up a short stream they'd later discover was called the Piscataqua by the native Abenaki tribe. Some would report that as their two vessels sailed the narrows of that river abutting the wilderness of what would become the territory of Maine, "we were curiously watched by scores of warrior men."

Said to be peaceful women, children and men of a greater Algonquian nation, the Abenaki tribe lived a subdued life with others of the Pennacook peoples in the forests, hills and fields along the river. They sheltered from spring rains and warmed from flurrying snows in wigwam huts of limbs, bark and skins, and hunted game and fished icy streams while toiling little patches of land sprouting yellow melons and tall stalks dangling green husks of corn.

Soon others from England followed, settling further west and north into the woods and hills of the wilderness, establishing quaint hamlets and little farms under the authority of parliament and King James. And within a few years, it seems that a special counsel for New England began to bestow vast swaths of frontier land to men who showed unfaltering loyalty to the crown. Father said some of those men were rather greedy, deceivingly eager men who were awarded for their loyalty with acres of wealth across the sea while never leaving London to survey their new lands.

Ethan once said he had heard disturbing stories about those greedy men when he was young, unflinching supporters of the policies of London, wealthy men like Edward Hilton, David Thompson, Johnny Mason and Ferdinando Gorges. "It was Mr. Mason," he liked to say, "who inspired the colony's name when he called his newly gobbled tracks of land, Hampshire, in honor of the county of his birth.

Along with women, children and men fleeing north from Ethan's colony to worship our Creator as they chose, for some forty years new villages, farms and towns continued to be settled by hundreds sailing across the sea from England. Then following decades of an infusion of those seeking land of their own and a taste of liberty, upon the stroke of the king's quill those swaths of northern lands were said to have merged with Ethan's colony. Yet within years, just before the new century they say, King Charles split the crown's lands once again, retaining Massachusetts Bay and granting those northern hamlets, streams and fields the royal title, Colony of New Hampshire.

I remember stories when I was a little girl that exposed how those who resided to the north of Ethan's colony were justly viewed as honest and decent people, a rural society brushed of civility with a chosen assembly in those days, tasked with resolving rather mundane colonial things. Ethan once said that the Colony of New Hampshire was brimming with spirited people who cherished a tranquil way of life, and that over the years they spread their creed amid the forests and hills stretching to the frontier. It was a land that would be settled by some fifty thousand colonists by those first hours of the war, a colony many would later say was governed for too many years by a repressive royal governor shackled tightly to the crown.

IV *Maryland*: Some say the Colony of Maryland was known in its earliest days as Terra Maria, a loyal expression of affection for the colony's namesake of Henrietta Maria of France, the bride of the first King Charles of England. Uniquely designed, the colony was ruggedly split by the waters of Chesapeake Bay that stretched south a hundred miles or so from its northern reaches, passing the mouth of a wide stream at the southern tip of its western shore. It was a stream called the Cohongarooton centuries before by natives of the Powhatan and Algonquian tribes, a river most settlers would soon come to know as the Patowmack. The northeastern bluffs of the Colony of Virginia edged the banks of that Patowmack River to the west, while the remainder of the lands of Terra Maria ran down the eastern shores of the bay, land strewn with rocky inlets and twisting streams abutting the tiny Colony of Delaware.

The hills and fields of Terra Maria were rumored to have been first explored by that English captain of the sea named Smyth, venturing from his nearby village of James Towne. Yet it seems it would be another two dozen years before a true European settlement would sprout along the Chesapeake, a little outpost erected by Willie Claiborne on the tip of a big island in the northern waters of the bay. Father said it was a spot on a narrow stretch of land soon known as Kent Island, a rugged settlement designed to enhance trade with natives of the Ozinie, Monoponson and Matapeake tribes. "It wasn't long before hundreds of new settlers arrived," he conveyed in a fatherly way, "and as more outposts were built and villages sprang about, those indigenous peoples were pushed out." For centuries those native tribes had peacefully hunted and fished along the rocky shores of Chesapeake Bay, and now they were being persistently nudged further west into the wilderness.

Some believe the first officious action by the English Crown to corral its authority over this new land happened a little after 1630, when King Charles quilled a charter proclaiming those lands surrounding the waters of Chesapeake Bay to be his. They say it was a document giving authority over Terra Maria to a man named Calvert, a loyal member of parliament bestowed with the title of First Baron Baltimore, a man known about London as Lord Baltimore. Yet, it seems that charter quickly passed to his son when the Baron mysteriously died, a royal son from County Kent who would affectionately be known as Little Lord Baltimore. It was a charter bestowing power for many years over lands that had been quilled to be Terra Maria-Anglice-Maryland, lands London would soon simply refer to as the Colony of Maryland.

One of the earliest settlements to sprout under that charter was said to be the southwest village of St. Mary along the Patowmack River, and for many years the colony's royal governor, that young Lord Baltimore, encouraged thousands of new settlers to sail the sea and carve new hamlets and towns about the shores of the bay. Although that little lord was rumored to be a religious man of the Catholic faith, some say he avoided the narrowness of other governors by seeking people of any faith to settle his new lands. "We invite people of all beliefs," he was heard to boast many times. "The Colony of Maryland harbors no biases, spurs thought and rains tolerance."

In the coming years it seems that each new royal governor was mysteriously known as a Lord Baltimore, and each spurred his people to grasp the reins of open governance by helping formulate and administer various policies and laws. And although some have said that for a time near the turn of the century London strove to intrusively immerse into the affairs of the colony, it was a trespass which eventually subsided, and in many ways, was ultimately subdued. For the remaining seventy years leading up to the war the sovereignty of the Colony of Maryland was said to be reserved to the royal governor and the women, children and men of the land about Chesapeake Bay.

V *Connecticut*: Exceeded in diminutiveness only by the colonies of Rhode Island and Delaware, some say Connecticut derived its name from what the native Algonquians had always called the land, Quinatucquet. It was a reflection of a phrase meaning upon-the-long-river, perhaps in reference to a stream slicing the colony, a river winding hundreds of miles south from the upper reaches of New England and merging with the waters of what they'd soon call Long Island Sound. "Some of the elders of Lexington," Ethan once said about his youth, "recalling their olden days, still called those lands the river colony," something traders of fur from my Netherlands had done years before.

It was a small land nestled along the chilling waters of the sound and bordered by what would become a trio of London's colonies, the wilderness forests of New York to the west, the watery meadows and streams of Rhode Island east and the hills and fields of Ethan's Massachusetts Bay to the north. They say that in the earliest days the lands of Quinatucquet were strewn with tribes of the Algonquians, with women, children and men of the Mohegan hunting and fishing the woods along that long stream, while natives of the Pequot were scattered about the banks of a river settlers soon called Thames.

I remember hearing tales when I was young of Dutch adventurers, and one about a sailor who discovered that long river a few years before those puritans landed on the rocks of Cape Cod Bay some hundred miles northeast. Some say Aerjan Block stumbled across the mouth of that Quinatucquet River near a rocky point in his vessel *Tyger*, then sailed a bit north with a few other ships to claim the lands for his Netherlands. Ethan said it would be another ten years or so before a true Dutch settlement appeared, a little fortified camp of twined timber sliced from the wilderness thirty miles north of the sound.

They called their little camp Fort Goede Hoop, a haven from wintry flurries and frightening natives, an outpost which in a few years would be called Good Hope by settlers of faith fleeing south from Massachusetts Bay. It wasn't long before those new settlers began to refer to their safe fort as the village of New Towne, only to change the name once again to Hartford, in homage to the English village many once called home.

One of those fleeing from the north was the puritan preacher Thom Hooker, a colonist Ethan said was from the village of Cambridge near Boston, a devout man who settled with other spiritual people in the hills about the village of Hartford around 1640 or so. They say his religious group was instrumental in quilling a document known as the Fundamental Orders of Connecticut, parchment extolling a series of rights for those of their emerging colony. Most believe it was intended to empower the settlers with the right to directly choose governing officials, and after the war some would view that decree as the first true constitution of rights, laws and principals quilled in the colonies.

New settlements continued to sprout about the colony for several years, little hamlets and towns sliced from the wilderness along wooded hills and winding streams. But after a decade or two it seems, London wrested control over the lands of the long river for the king, issuing an oppressive charter creating the royal Colony of Connecticut. From that moment forward they say, the colony began to slowly change from one which relied upon itself for crops, products and goods to one with an expanding gaze to the outside world.

Ethan once said that it was during those early years of the new century that the numbers of traders and merchants quickly grew, men exporting foods and grains to other colonies and shipping crates of colonial goods across the sea to London and other ports. And over the coming years the colony continued to transform, becoming a creator of homey things like ornate maple and walnut clocks and dainty things of silver and tin. Soon boats and ships were being crafted from the colony's swaths of timber by skilled carpenters too, and by the first shots of the war scores of elm vessels with two and three masts were departing its docks and slicing the seas.

VI *Rhode Island*: Although the smallest of our Thirteen Colonies, just twelve hundred square miles or so, the Colony of Rhode Island was known to some by the impressive name, Rhode Island and Providence Plantations. Nestled along the spray of Long Island Sound, with the Colony of Connecticut west and Ethan's Massachusetts Bay east and north, its lands surrounded the intrusive waters of Narragansett Bay.

Just as other colonies abutting Massachusetts Bay, Rhode Island was said to have been settled in the earliest days by scores of people fleeing prejudices espoused by women and men unwilling to tolerate those who wished to worship God in a differing way. And that bay, that wide swath of sea slicing north from the sound for some forty miles, was rumored to have derived its name from the native peoples who thrived about the surrounding hills and fields for thousands of peaceful years.

Some believe the first wanderer of Europe to sail along the colony's southern coast, the first to view the slew of little islands dotting the waters of Narragansett Bay, was a Portuguese explorer called de Cortereal. Yet others say all those isles, hills and streams were first seen by the seaman Giovanni da Verrazzano, an adventurous Italian from the village of Val di Greve south of Florence.

It seems that some two hundred years before Ethan and I were born, da Verrazzano had sailed the ocean for the crown of France and chests of gold in a daring search for a watery passage flowing through the colonies to a mysterious sea. And I remember a fanciful tale from my youth suggesting that when he first spotted an island in the bay, its rugged cliffs brushed by auburn soil, he proclaimed these new lands Rhode Island, honoring the Greek rock of Rhodes rising from the Aegean Sea.

Those first sightings seemed to fade into a misty haze, for it would be another hundred years before a village settled by people of Europe would take hold, a small enclave founded by a young theologian of the Protestant faith. They say his name was Roger Williams, a preacher from London who first sailed to the emerging hamlet of Boston before escaping the pressures of puritan believers. It seems he fled with his flock some forty miles south to worship freely, forging a new village he'd call Providence nestled along the northern rocks of Narragansett Bay.

I'd later learn that after several years a special commission granted legal rights over the lands to Mr. Williams and his people, then following another twenty years, perhaps 1670 or so, he and his throng of expanding settlers were granted colonial status with a governing charter by London. Now known as the Colony of Rhode Island, it was said to flourish for many years with herds of cattle and bountiful crops sprouting its rich soil, along with alluring ventures expanding about an array of inlets, islands and streams threading the waterway. It was a bay soon dotted with fishing hamlets and little ports, and docks with boats and ships being loaded with goods, crops, grains and meats for sailing to other colonies and ports across the sea.

Ethan once said he heard stories when he was young about things that began to happen in those early days, after all those ships sailed from the docks with hulls bulging of Rhode Island goods. "Other ships began arriving with sacks and chests brimming with shillings and pounds, jewels and colorful coins," he whispered, "expanding the wealth of merchants about the colony, men now grappling for power." It seems they were now delving into more temporal enterprises too, new paths of wealth in more secular trades like spirits and rum.

And there was a nauseous trade beginning to flourish with the guidance of a few with new found wealth, a disdainful venture some men shrouded by bigotry viewed as a way to expand their coffers with more shillings and pounds. It was a new type of commerce in those days, that shipping of shackled human beings into the colony from across the sea, an ugly trade of exchanging women, children and men with dark skin for money. It was a vicious scheme which flourished for some hundred years, a diabolical trade that would finally be mercifully stopped a few years before the war, but not until thousands had been bound in chains and traded on cold docks for silver and gold.

VII *Delaware*: The colony's northern edge rests just thirty miles southwest of my Germantown, a narrow strip of land nestled along the western rocks of what native Lenapes for centuries had called Poutaxat, waters settlers would soon know as Delaware Bay. Some say that this thin fertile land was first seen by an English wanderer named Hudson, an adventurer believed to have sailed the waters of the Poutaxat shortly before James Towne was carved from the wilderness some hundred miles southwest. It was a rich strip of fields and hills that would find its colonial name twined to the Englishman Thom West, a loyal man many knew as the Baron De La Warr.

It seems some twenty years would pass after Hudson's sail before an outpost would be sliced from the trees, a settlement of adventurous women and men that would rise by a rocky point jutting into the sea near the southern end of the bay. Yet they were not from the Isle of Britain like those sailing to the Colony of Virginia, but Dutch settlers from my Netherlands, daring people searching for a new life in a mystical land of Swan Valley, settlers who called their village, Zwaanendael.

Father once said those first settlers had been exposed to horrid acts of violence unleashed by savage tribes, mostly by warriors of the Lenape it seems, natives who dwelled in the woods along the banks of the Lenape Wihittuck, a wide river flowing south they'd soon call the Delaware. There were grisly stories too about bloody skirmishes between Dutch settlers and men of the Algonquian tribes, and ugly rumors that told of massacres inflicted by natives of the Nanticoke. After several years of dreadful attacks many of the settlers mysteriously vanished, weary people believed to have fled north to the forests of my Colony of Pennsylvania and wilderness havens west.

After several years of eerie calm, new settlers began to brave their way into the narrow lands along the waters of Delaware Bay, European people who sliced a new village from the northern woods. It was a hamlet carved from the wilderness by women, children and men of Sweden, a settlement near the mouth of the Lenape Wihittuck they named Fort Christina, a village that would be known as Wilmington in the decades to come. Soon hundreds more were sailing across the sea and settling into the woods north and south, along with a few fleeing their homes in Finland, adventurous people who began to call their land the Colony of New Sweden.

Yet it seems their claims to those settlements and waters were soon being challenged by various powers, and after several years their little colony was seized by determined Dutchmen who quickly renamed the lands, New Netherlands. Then around 1665 or so, control changed hands once again when the second King Charles of England snatched those lands for the crown. His agents were rumored to have vigorously procured those Delaware waters, hills and woods for London, grabbing every farm, port, village and town, a colony now administered by James, the Duke of York, the king's little brother already in control of a colony to the north.

The Duke would retain his reign for some twenty years, until such time London succumbed to pressures from the colony and allowed control of those Delaware lands to be transferred to Governor Penn of my Colony of Pennsylvania. Then after several years and countless pleas and missions to England, around the turn of the century Mr. Penn relaxed his powers over Delaware as that narrow strip of land was granted separate status.

Some began to refer to the embattled colony as a land reborn with a brush of autonomy, while others of an emerging generation grew to know the lands as the three lower counties. Although the Colony of Delaware was free to choose its own assembly, it seems the essence of power was loosely retained by my Colony of Pennsylvania, a challenging scenario that continued for many years until the first musket blasts of the war.

VIII *North Carolina*: I was told long ago that the first Europeans to view the shores just south of the Colony of Virginia may have sailed near a southern point as early as 1524, a sandy patch of rocks protruding into the sea most now call Cape Fear. Some believe one of those men may have been that explorer da Verrazzano, or perhaps Lucas Vasquez de Ayllon, a voyager for the monarchy of Spain some say established a tiny settlement along the colony's southern shore. It was a hamlet of ragged huts and docks, lore would recall, a small village that mysteriously vanished from horrid things like starvation and disease. Yet some would say that it disappeared at the hands of vicious warriors of the Natchez and Cherokee tribes.

There were several more attempts over the coming years to carve new settlements from the wilderness, ventures constantly at odds with an array of disapproving native tribes. One of those settlements sprouted on a little island along the northern coast, and was said to have been spurred by an English seaman named Raleigh and his crew. It was a bushy patch of rocky soil they'd later discover was home to natives of the Roanoke tribe, an outpost that would mysteriously vanish just as others had over the years.

Other attempts to conquer little slices of the land followed, and I remember one such tale when I was young of a conquistador named Pardo sailing for Spain. They say he and some hundred men sailed a tiny fleet along jagged southern rocks, then splashing anchors, rowed to shore and carved a path several miles west into the wilderness. It seems they stopped near a forested place they would soon realize was awash with women, children and men of the Waxhaw and Joara tribes, a lonely place where those gallant men quickly sliced maple, hickory and pine for a defensive shield of several forts. Yet awful rumors have lingered for years that those daring men were soon killed, grisly stories they were slaughtered by clubs, blades and spears of proud warrior men.

Although some came to believe that perhaps the wilderness was too virulent to settle, it nevertheless became land coveted by the English crown, and around 1630 King Charles granted those forests, streams and hills to a royal judge named Heath. Yet for reasons still a mystery after all these years, that magistrate was said to have shunned the king's will, failing to launch a viable surge to conquer those lands.

It would be another thirty years until a real settlement finally sprouted when a group of discouraged English women, children and men left their homes in the Colony of Virginia and ventured south into the wilderness, their carts and wagons brimming hopes and dreams. They creaked and rolled to lands some were calling the Province of Carolina, in reverence to the slain father of King Charles, and were said have created a rugged hamlet of cottages and docks along the sea near the waters of what they'd call Albemarle Sound.

In the coming years that entire swath of forests, streams and fields, wilderness that encompassed what would become the colonies of Georgia and North and South Carolina, was overseen by loyal men beholden to London. They say a bit after the turn of the century that powerful group of royal men succumbed to the will of England's new monarch, Queen Anne, and one by one loosened their ties to the land, allowing a strange calm to settle for decades. Then the second King George reconfigured the wilderness once again, granting a charter for the Colony of North Carolina out of the upper reaches of those woods and hills.

The colony remained beholden to London for the rest of its years, just as each emerging colony would in those days, a land ruled by a string of royal governors selected by the crown, and the numbers of its settlers would explode to some three hundred thousand by the first cries of the war. Small farms and fertile plantations would soon dot its lands too, rich soil sprouting an array of crops like grapes, rice and tobacco. And just as other colonies nearby, it would slip into the darkness of exploiting a race of human beings to increase its coffers, a wicked system of toiling Negro slaves that would survive the war.

IX *South Carolina*: The colony's origins are said to have mirrored its sibling directly to the north, having been granted its own royal charter by London decades before the war, lands split to become the Colony of South Carolina. Like several colonies back then, its lush forests, hills and crystal streams stretched hundreds of miles west into the wilderness, and its rocky shore of some two hundred miles was strewn with scores of little sandy islands. A winding river they'd call Savannah sliced along its southern edge, and the land just beyond those rushing waters would soon peel away to form the Colony of Georgia.

They say that the first real outpost was settled several years before the turn of the century when scores of women, children and men from England disembarked sailing ships near a rocky shore they'd soon know as Albemarle Point, a rugged place which jutted into the sea amidst several winding streams flowing from the wilderness. It seems that for several years a dangerous atmosphere existed between those settlers and an array of native tribes, and following many harrowing intrusions by warriors of the Yamasee and Cherokee, they abandoned their rugged huts and little farms, fleeing several miles north to the confluence of winding streams they'd call the Wando, Cooper and Ashley. "It was a place they felt safe," an elderly man once said. "And never wavering, they forged a little port out of the wilderness along the sea, a village they named Charles Towne, in homage to their king."

I still remember the startling tales when I was young of the violence that engulfed the colony in the first years of the new century, grisly stories not only of skirmishes with wilderness tribes which frightened me so, but of horrendous attacks from wayward men of the sea. There were tales of deadly raids unleashed upon settlers by vicious men sailing ships with ensigns of Spain and France, of bloody years of dreadful struggles many would someday say was a strange war fought in the name of London's Queen Anne.

There were ugly stories too of treacherous assaults upon the emerging port of Charles Towne by sailing men once loyal to the English crown, unscrupulous men who practiced ruthless piracy from the sea. And some say perhaps the most vicious of all was a villainous soul named Teach, an unprincipled man believed to have hailed from a village west of London, a mysterious seaman many colonists knew as Blackbeard.

Although London maintained its unyielding grip upon the colony for years to come, many would say that it nevertheless encouraged a loose style of self-reliance and governance, similar in scope to what was flourishing in its sibling colony to the north. Then in the spring of 1732 the boundaries of the lands were altered once again when the second King George tore away the colony's southern hills and fields to create the Colony of Georgia, leaving the Colony of South Carolina to fend for its own.

They say that during the years leading up to the war a steady stream of settlers slowly ventured to the colony, expanding to a hundred thousand women, children and men by the first hours of our struggle against the king. Many traveled from farms, villages and towns of the north such as the Colony of Virginia and my Pennsylvania, and all were eager to farm the rich soil, to grow an array of crops like those sticky tobacco leaves. And some of those colonists misguidedly embraced that evil system of indentured servitude, causing thousands of Negro women, children and men to toil their fields before, during and after the war.

X *New Jersey*: I'd hear fanciful tales when I was young about how the lands to the east of our Delaware River were once consumed by an array of Algonquian tribes, a coastal land they say the native Lenape had called Lenapehoking. It was a swath of merging tidelands and rich soil even back then, a land they say was first seen by a voyager from Europe some two hundred and fifty years before the war. Father always said it was that da Verrazzano who was the first to view the rocky shores of what would become the Colony of New Jersey, that seaman from Italy sailing north on his quest to find that mythical waterway west.

Yet it seems it would take another hundred years, around 1609 or so, before a new voyager would wander off the waters of Lenapehoking, a seaman paid sacks of gold by the Dutch East India Company and flying the red, white and blue ensign of the Netherlands. But the captain of the tri-mast schooner *Halve Maen* was an Englishman, that seafaring Hudson, also searching for that elusive river to another sea. Some say his ship sailed north along the colony's coast past a narrow barrier he'd quill in his log as sant hoek, a sandy bend with an intriguing hook near a stream soon called the Shrewsbury flowing into the blue waters of a bay.

Although there seems to have been little effort for years to forge lasting villages and ports, scores of settlers from the Netherlands were said to be sailing across the sea to these Lenapehoking lands. They were soon followed by women, children and men from Sweden, daring people bounding down planks along the colony's upper east shores in search of their dreams. At first the hopes of these new settlers appeared to be closely entwined, visions of carving their own farms from the wilderness, yet an ugly aura of tensions soon began to waft from the sea. They weren't frictions with native tribes such as other settlers had endured in other places, but increasingly perilous disputes between farmers of my Netherlands and Swedish traders encroaching for furs.

I remember aging stories of those two settling groups devising awful schemes against one another, each hoping to push the other into less hospitable, dangerous places, and soon those farmers had forced most traders into the wilderness north and west. In what many now view as an effort to grasp what they thought to be their lands, around 1660 many Dutch settlers were said to have crafted a rustic fort on western bluffs above a wide river, a crude settlement called Bergen that overlooked the waters flowing down to a harbor. It was an intimidating village of timber and stones, the first of what would be many settlements to rise in the colony in those days, a land where native tribes roamed amid Dutch and Swede settlers who'd soon call their colony, New Netherlands.

In spite of the efforts by those settlers to instill their authority over the forests, streams and fields of their Dutch colony, after many years it seems London deemed the moment ripe to act. Father said England suddenly invoked what some viewed as doubtful claims over the land, declaring it had been reserved for the crown over a hundred years before upon the voyage of the sailor Cabot. With that dubious rationale gripped in his royal hands, the second King Charles wresting control of New Netherlands.

The king proclaimed his newest conquest New Jersey, in honor of a big channel isle, and proceeded to give control of his new colony to his little brother James, who quickly handed that power to a pair of loyal men named Carteret and Berkeley. It seems the colony began filling with settlers from nearby colonies, along with women, children and men from places across the sea, caring people who simply sought to toil and worship as they pleased. I'd later learn many were Scottish Presbyterians and puritans fleeing the northeast, spiritual colonists searching for reform, along with scores from Christ Church and Quaker friends who prayed in meeting house pews like father, mother and me.

They say the western lands nearer the Delaware River, along with hills and fields in the south that stretched east to the sea, were being settled by thousands of people and Quaker friends of my Netherlands, while those of other beliefs were surging to the lands north and east. Then after many years of what most found to be an acceptable separation, London officially sliced the colony in two, handing Mr. Berkeley powers over the lands called West Jersey and Mr. Carteret over the east. Yet following several years of what the crown began to view as a cumbersome division, the lands were reunited to form the single royal Colony of New Jersey.

Although the colonists were allowed to choose an assembly with limited powers over rather trivial concerns, the fundamental power over the colony remained firmly in the clutches of royal governors loyal to the English crown, from Queen Anne to the trio of kings named George. During those years the colony thrived with waves of settlers sailing across the sea and woman, children and men venturing from other colonies, expanding to some three hundred thousand by dawn of the coming war.

XI *New York*: Some believe that it was the seaman da Verrazzano who was the first of Europe to sail the waters near the lands that would become the Colony of New York, while others have said it was that Englishman Hudson decades later who first sailed into the harbor in route up a river flowing south into the bay. For hundreds of years that wide rushing river was known as the Muhhekunnetuk by the Mohawk, Oneida and Seneca tribes, a majestic flow bound by great bluffs the Lenape, Montauk and Munsee knew as the river-that-flows-two-ways. Father once said that those early Dutch and Swedish settlers called it the North River, and while others preferred the name Mauritius, it was a river all would someday simply call the Hudson.

It seems the Dutch powers who had spurred Mr. Hudson's voyage were soon calling the bay and its array of islands New Netherland, along with the expanse of forests and hills stretching north into the wilderness. And soon scores of ships, their decks brimming thousands of settlers and their hulls stuffed with sacks, barrels and crates of supplies, began sailing into the harbor. They were farmers with wives and children in search of fertile soil for tilling hopes and dreams, trapper men too simply seeking to be free to gather their furs and pelts, and traders and merchants seeking chests of new wealth.

All the while, new outposts for bartering furs and goods were springing up along the river and the sandy fields and woods of a narrow pointy island thrusting south into the harbor. It was an innocuous patch of land where little cottages and huts were soon rising of timber and stones amidst rustic taverns and merchant shops. And quaint lazy inns for weary souls were dotting groves of maple, beech and birch amid acres of mayapple and ivy shared by hundreds of native Lenape who spoke of their home as Mannahatta, an island of many hills the encroaching Dutch would come to call Manhattan.

Others were settling along the western edge of another island just southeast of Mannahatta, spirited women and men building taverns, homes and trading shops on the tip of a strip of land some twelve miles wide and stretching over a hundred miles east into the sea. Scores of native Lenape and Munsee were said to peacefully roam its western hills and fields in those days, while hundreds of the Mohegan and Narragansett were rumored to till the soils further east. It was a rustic strip of land brushed in winter by a chilling breeze sweeping its rocks and trees, a stretch of sandy soil I often thought resembled a mythical claw jutting into the sea, a swath of land most would come to know as Long Island.

There were others too searching for dreams further north in the valley of the Muhhekunnetuk that flowed from the wilderness several hundred miles south into the bay. And within a few years they say, many of those frontier traders and merchants corralled their energies to promote their New Netherland, forming an enterprise they proudly proclaimed the Dutch West India Company. Soon a deluge of fresh settlers from England and my Netherlands, along with hundreds from various nations across the sea, began sailing into the waters of the harbor, many continuing north into the bustling valley of the Hudson.

As new farmers, merchants, trappers and traders settled some hundred miles north of the harbor upon bluffs of that rushing river, plush lands which had been home to native Iroquois and Mohican for hundreds of years, many of those from my Netherlands declared their little town Fort

Orange. It seems their wilderness hamlet of steeples, taverns, cottages and shops was named to honor their ruling House of Orange-Nassau across the sea, a rustic village that would come to be called Beverwyck. Yet following several years of scores of new Englishmen encroaching about those bluffs, their hamlet was changed once again to Fort Albany, a title soon whittled to just Albany.

They say that scores of new settlements like Fort Orange had begun to spring from the wilderness throughout the colony in those early days, but I suppose one of the more consequential was the village near the southern tip of Mannahatta, a settlement of timber and stone the Dutch in 1626 called Nieuw Amsterdam. It seems that after several years the traders, settlers, seamen and merchants of that bustling town sought to enhance their coffers by taking control of the whole island, and with a nod from across the sea, the colony's custodian finagled the isle's purchase for their Netherlands. Some say Mr. Minuit traded a bundle of goods worth just some sixty guilders to the befuddled Lenapes for their home of Mannahatta, quaint little tools, colorful fabrics and intriguing trinkets, sparkling goods meriting a tiny bag of shillings and pounds.

Over the coming years it seems that thousands more resettled in the colony, many of English descent from the nearby colonies of Connecticut, Rhode Island and Ethan's Massachusetts Bay. They were doctors and bakers, tradesmen and merchants, fishermen, farmers and lawyers creaking wagons and carts from the northeast, and they were fathers and mothers, sisters, aunts, uncles and brothers who sailed and oared across the waters of the sound to the rocky shores of Long Island, most bringing customs and ways rooted in British heritage. I remember tales of how many of those settlers began to trickle toward that thriving village on the tip of Manhattan, and how that merger of English and Dutch began to smolder.

It seems the position of Dutch authority was increasingly challenged by an awkward relation between its rule and the surging English settlers, dangerous frictions which simmered for many years until the summer of 1664 when the waters truly began to spritz. Deeming the hour right to snatch the colony for London, with a bold stroke of his royal quill King Charles proclaimed a new charter over the lands and declared his little brother, that Duke of York, the colony's royal governor. And soon a small fleet of royal warships sailed into the harbor and splashed its shackling chains into the waters, then thrust its iron guns at that village port on that land of Mannahatta.

"With menacing cannons latched to their elm decks," Ethan once said, recalling a thrilling story from his youth, "and their hulls bulging with hundreds of the king's troops, London's ships just bobbed in a foggy haze, never firing a gun or musket shot." It seems the fleet simply waited for the colony's Dutch chief to bend to the will of the king, and following several gripping days of threats, Mr. Stuyvesant surrendered New Netherland. "He placed the port and entire colony," Ethan whimsically added, "every field, grove, bluff and stream, every village and town, into the chalice of the English crown."

With the stroke of a quill and barrel of a gun the Netherlands relinquished its colony to England, and as dusk began to settle amidst a summer drizzle, London's new lands were now known as the Province and City of New York. It was a bloodless coup for precious lands that within a generation would be renamed the Royal Colony of New York, lands with a mighty river flowing into a harbor and hundreds of emerging hamlets and towns, including that thriving village on the Isle of Manhattan many would soon simply call New York.

Nudged south and west of the king's new possession was the Colony of New Jersey and my Pennsylvania, with Connecticut and Massachusetts Bay east, and further north off to the east were the disputed lands many called the New Hampshire Grants in those days. And some two-hundred and fifty miles north into the frontier, beyond the bluffs of the Hudson and the stringy waters of Lake Champlain, was a wilderness expanse Paris had proclaimed as New France. It was a chilly swath of forests, meadows, hills and streams, and a mighty river they'd soon quill the Saint Lawrence.

The Royal Colony of New York stretched hundreds of miles west into the wilderness too, nudging against two big lakes they'd soon call Ontario and Erie, and by the first musket blasts of the war some three hundred thousand women, children and men would settle throughout the lands. And just as other colonies before, it too would form an assembly of spirited men to address various concerns of the day, yet just as the others, it too was subservient to the whims of royal governors and the powers of parliament and the king three thousand miles across the sea.

XII *Pennsylvania*: When I was young father said that my colony had been inhabited by scores of native tribes for hundreds of years, and that it was only a few decades before he and mother sailed from the Netherlands that things began to change. Lenape warriors were said to have roamed the southeast near the rivers of Philadelphia and Germantown, while Iroquois villages of Seneca and Oneida thrived the interior mountains of the north, and women, children and men of the Shawnee hunted and fished about the wilderness toward the west. And rustic villages of the Eriez were said to be scattered about the forests of the northwest, while the tribes of the Munsee dotted the northeast frontier and the Susquehannocks roamed the southern hills stretching into the wilderness.

I remember old tales about a Dutchman who sailed up the waters of the Lenape Wihittuck, slicing the river north for the Netherlands from a body of water they'd come to call Delaware Bay. They say he was the first explorer from across the sea to venture up the river and land on its western bank in what would become my Colony of Pennsylvania, a wilderness some believe was first seen decades before by that seaman Verrazzano. Yet there were eerie stories of how that Dutchman mysteriously vanished with his crew before crafting a settlement, escaping with their lives during a spring rain, Lenape lore would say, never to return.

It would be another thirty years, father would say, perhaps 1645 or so, before true settlers would arrive near the remnants of a little native village, scores of Swedish and Finnish women, children and men who migrated up the waters of the Wihittuck, the river I've always known as the Delaware. "They were fearless people," he liked to say, "slicing timber to build their rugged fort of Nassau, then proclaiming the wilderness west and north the Colony of New Sweden for their crown."

Soon others daring arrived, many sailing from the port of Gothenburg across the sea, Swedish settlers who began to carve a new fortress from the wilderness along the bank of the river, a village they'd affectionately call Nya Gothenburg. It was a settlement that would thrive in the coming decades with traders and merchants shipping goods up and down the river, a port many years later Governor Penn would declare to be Philadelphia, a reflection of his Quaker faith bathed with notions of kindness and love of others.

For several years after the forging of their village of Nya Gothenburg, a mysterious calm was said to have descended upon the Swedish colony and its thriving port along the river, a tranquility aging tales describe as numbingly fleeting. Fighting soldiers and sailors began sweeping down from the northeast, invaders from the Colony of New Netherland who seized their little river port and surrounding settlements, grasping control of commerce and life for years to come. It wasn't until 1664 or so that the chains of that invasion were finally cast from the colony, when London conquered the Delaware River and its evolving port for the king, along with the wilderness west and north.

As the king had done in other places before, he assigned his little brother James ruler of the colony, an arrangement which lasted several years until the crown granted the lands to a spiritual man named William Penn. In his role as royal governor over London's vast new province, and with what father said was tacit support of the crown, Mr. Penn began shaping the lands in his own vision. One of his first decrees was to rename the colony Pennsylvania, out of reverence to the swath of forests that consumed the wilderness and to honor his deceased father, once a royal admiral in the service of the king.

Around the turn of the century, if I recall, the royal governor's appeals to those across the sea to settle in his lands had become rather emphatic, and mother once said that his early pleas to sail to his colony influenced my father even years after Mr. Penn's death. "He preached of freedom to worship," she explained when I was young, "and the opportunity to take part in governing our own lives, ideas that appealed to a growing number of women and men. It was those kinds of stories, Andrea, which spurred the dreams of many Quaker friends in our Netherlands. Then after mama died, why, your father and I knew where we belonged, here, in the colony of Mr. Penn."

I've heard stories of how he was instrumental in the framing of the first real constitution for my colony, an enlightened document, some say, that proscribed principles of governing. I think it was called a frame-of-government-for-Pennsylvania, parchment quilled in an understandable way that established procedures and rules which seemed to expand on notions hazily scribed in the colony's royal charter. It provided for an assembly of colonists chosen by colonists, an attempt to open governing to all the people, a daring ideal foreign in the colonies back then.

Over the coming years that document was said to have been altered many times, changes in rules, hopes and procedures, then shortly after the turn of the century a new foundation they called the Pennsylvania-charter-of-privileges was exposed. Although it continued to provide colonists with a say over policies and laws affecting their lives, most realized the true power over the Colony of Pennsylvania, an expanse of villages, forests, streams and farms and some three hundred thousand women, children and men by the first cries of the war, was firmly in the grasp of the king.

XIII *Georgia*: The final lands to complete the crown's thirteen colonies was the southernmost of them all, and in honor of England's new monarch, the second King George, beginning in 1732 was known as the Colony of Georgia. It was in the winter of that year they say, that the king quilled a governing charter giving authority over these lands to a member of his parliament and loyal general of his Royal Army, James Oglethorpe. Some believe that the crown was worried about encroachments from Madrid, and hoped the new colony would provide a haven between London's twelve colonies to the north and the sandy wetlands south, an untamed peninsula Spain's King Philip affectionately called La Florida.

London's thirteenth colony, a wilderness expanse of winding streams, forested hills and flowery fields, had been home to thousands of native souls for centuries, a mysterious land they say was first touched by an explorer from across the sea two hundred years before, a Spaniard known as de Soto. For years to come it seems it was vaguely claimed by the crown of Spain, a warm and humid land where women, children and men of Cherokee tribes hunted and fished the northern woods while native Creeks peacefully tilled little southern plots scattered about rose scented meadows.

There were intriguing stories when I was young of French adventurers also settling near the sea in those early days, intruding explorers who sought to expand their fledgling domain further south into those Spanish sands. They say King Philip, viewing those incursions as a threat to his lands, ordered his seamen and soldiers to construct a fort on a patch of shore near the northern rocks of his La Florida. Their Spanish settlement was impressively called St. Catherines Island, the first such village by seafaring explorers in the colony they say, a rustic fortress of timber and stones south of a majestic river flowing into the sea.

It seems the building of new settlements and forts of any kind in the colony dwindled as Spanish and French incursions into the land slowed over the years, then finally came to a hushing halt. And although London continued to declare its claim upon the land in the decades to come, including the crown's early decree approving settlement of the wilderness for the king, it would be another hundred years before England would grant a charter to that loyal General Oglethorpe.

I remember father once said the king's general had sailed from an English port on the merchant schooner *Ann* late in the summer of 1732, and after tossing about a roiling sea for some seven weeks, splashed anchor shortly before dusk near the mouth of that majestic river. Her hull was said to be stuffed with sacks, barrels and crates of vital supplies, and her deck was brimming with two hundred farmers and tradesmen, even a few dozen prisoners snatched from a stone gaol of London.

With the king's charter gripped in his hand, the general and those estranged men rowed to shore just north of where that Spanish fort once stood, a settlement which years before mysteriously vanished. And following what they say was a slew of anxious encounters with disgruntled warriors of the Yamacraw tribe, England's new settlers began to slice a new port from the coastal wilderness, a little village they'd soon call Savannah.

The Carolina hills bordered the Colony of Georgia to its north and the Spanish sands of La Florida were nudged against its southern fields, while its rocky shore kissed the sea for some two hundred miles and its wilderness in those days stretched west for hundreds more. The colony was said to prosper over the coming years with adventurous settlers from England and Scotland, as well as tradesmen, farmers and those seeking refuge from places like the Germanic principalities, and Switzerland and France. And although there were only a few thousand women, children and men tilling the fields and forging villages and towns before Ethan and I were born, there'd be over sixty thousand colonists by the first shots of the war.

Suddenly a warm burst of July air tossed my silvery hair, and I glanced to Samuel peering to the tips of distant elms swaying in the easy morning breeze, a whimsical expression dancing his face. Then slowing my pace, I slid my fingers back to the pocket of my summer dress, and as we rocked our chairs in a reflective hush, I caressed the passions of Ethan's poem and reached for memories stashed deep inside all these years. "Tell me more, grandma," he whispered amid the soothing rustle of summer leaves, "of your life in those days, the war, of Ethan."

Chapter II

Crimson Rose

So many years have come and passed, so much has changed, so many desolate nights. Despairing shadows had touched so many in those days, had shrouded my life, while the light of a new dawn had inspired so many, bright rays easing loneliness when so little seemed possible. A tinge of gloom had slowly flowed to my cup, and from those rising shades of changing haze I was rescued from the brim of an abyss, brushed by cherished rays of hope.

It was a time of rapturous happiness yielding too often to the wickedness of misguided men, to minds which seemed to have wandered from compassion far too long. I savor my wondrous memories and immerse within the waters of tender moments, and loathe the shrilling horrors of lesser men, the villainous waste of war. After all these years my thoughts wander to a life long ago, of emotions thriving upon the fruits of passions swirling wildly with joy.

My heart pleasingly pounds as I recall the euphoria of that night, all the while my soul cries with saddening pangs with the memories of the madness that's lingered all these years. Wintry flurries have begat spring petals many times since those days, yet when my aged eyes gaze to the glow of a gibbous moon dangling the dark I sense the mystical presence of another time, as if it were about to once again witness the carnage of that chilling night. When I glance to the heavens my thoughts drift back to the Colony of Massachusetts Bay, to soft specs of white settling upon the cobblestones of that Boston street, and remember how our joy was brushed with sorrow, of how a fiery fury had descended upon the snows that wintry night, the fifth day of March, 1770.

The sun ducked behind menacing clouds that wintry day as sporadic flurries dusted the port white, then slowly slipped beyond the colony's western frontier. I remember how the gleaming moon would appear in brief spurts amidst cracks and fissures roaming the sky, only to suddenly vanish behind strange dark creatures drifting over the sea. It was perhaps a quarter past eight when the moon seemed to hang above the port of Boston by a thin string of mysterious twine, its glow trimming eerie clouds wandering the night.

Its shine seemed so calm amid occasional bursts of stars, as if the moon had been placed at its spot for a special purpose that March night, beyond the squabbles of man to bear witness to the carnage soon to unfold. Or perhaps God had commanded it there to behold the gentleness of uncommon splendor, to beam its passionate serenity upon two young yearning hearts. Although the truth of such things are cloaked in mystery, for me its shine that night has remained awash with tranquil memories, and its quiet rays still gently tap the snows which had sprinkled Boston in a soothing white.

I lived in Germantown back then, with mother and father in those days, and was in special training to be a nurse, a healer of people, learning and gaining precious experience in Philadelphia five miles south. I was in the second year of four of training at the Pennsylvania Hospital built some twenty years before, a new kind of place of square paned windows and scarlet bricks father once said was the first in the colonies for ordinary people. I remember he'd tell me from time to time of how proud he was that I had thrust myself into what he viewed as a noble profession, a caring life away from the home, rather unusual for a young woman in those days.

And when a short pause in my nursing studies approached that winter, mother and father thought I should visit father's uncle Jason and wife Beatrice up in Boston, and I pleasingly agreed. Mother believed leaving Philadelphia for a little while might help calm my mind, and father said it would be good for me to get away after so many months of intense nursing, and both had hinted for weeks that Aunt Bea had quilled in many letters that they wanted to see me. I had always dreamed of visiting the port of Boston, maybe a bit intrigued by winter in a northern colony, and I suppose I knew the journey would be good for me. Yet I could never have imagined the magic my travels would unveil, nor have truly understood the caustic anger that dwells in people.

Father purchased passage for me on the *Dorchester*, a sturdy sailing ship he'd say to mother and me, solid and safe with three thick masts. Although mother seemed a little concerned, father believed sailing would be more exciting and a bit less challenging than creaking and bouncing some three hundred miles along the postal road through the port of New York. I still remember dashing up her springy elm plank after a teary hug from mother and father shortly after dawn the second Saturday of February, 1770, then sailing in an icy morning drizzle down the Delaware River from a rugged Philadelphia dock in route for Boston.

My private room they called quarters was rather small, and my narrow walnut bed with a plump feathered pillow and a pair of warm wool blankets was a bit rigid. I still recall the frigid winds whistling outside the tiny window above my bed and the blue waters that battered the Dorchester's bow, and can still feel the stinging chill that spritzed through little elm cracks of her hull now and then. And even though her crew seemed a rather rough lot, many from England and a few younger ones from Ireland, Scotland and my Netherlands, they treated me with courtesy, particularly a Scottish lad who shyly fumbled to ensure I was never in want of what I needed.

Over the coming four days she never slowed, slicing down the river and into the waters of Delaware Bay before escaping into the expanse of the Atlantic, and I can still see the Dorchester's sails bulging above the chilling sea as she cut north along the Colony of New Jersey. Then pivoting east with the brisk winds, she continued along the sandy south ridge of Long Island, slicing past little hamlets and towns with tiny docks and boats before sailing north once again, past the jagged rocks of the Colony of Rhode Island and up the rugged shore of the Colony of Massachusetts Bay.

On a chilly Tuesday morn, the Thirteenth of February, the *Dorchester's* bow sliced west through the spray of Massachusetts Bay and into the confines of Boston Harbor, and as tiny flakes drifted from the roiling grey to quickly vanish in the water, we moored on the port's eastside at a wharf they called Hitchborn. Several woman, men, and a few scurrying children, were gathered on the weathered dock, a little crowd anxiously waiting for a seafaring father or wayward son, or maybe a soothing chest of East India Company tea or a spirited crate of Caribbean rum.

I was standing in a cold breeze amid a light snow along what I was told was the port rail, bundled in my warmest wool coat and gripping the thin strap of a burlap bag stuffed with a few belongings, and felt so alone near the *Dorchester's* stern. I had never actually seen my aunt and uncle before that February morn, and what notions I had gathered were based on a fanciful portrait dangling a wall in our Germantown home and stories by mother and father. They had sailed for the colonies some forty years before, leaving Holland in search of what others had desperately hoped to find, a home in a new land where people could be free. Then my eyes suddenly grasp two huddled below on the wharf's rickety dock, my father's uncle and Aunt Bea waiting in the chill for me.

Uncle Jason was perhaps a few inches short of six feet and as of that wintry day seemed somewhat portly, for the bulge inside his belly would jiggle and bounce when he walked, boasted or haggled. Once a sandy tan, his hair was now a thinning grey, locks I'd soon discover he liked to stash beneath a fluffy wig he kept a powdery white while meandering about Boston's cobblestones, taverns and merchant shops. I quickly came to know he was a gentle, thoughtful man who adored my aunt, and I remember how he liked to tell intriguing tales when we'd gather near the hearth's flames after supper those winter nights. They were mostly stories about Holland when they were young or of Boston and their colony in the olden days, and a few were unsettling tales of that frontier war with the French some ten years before.

It seems in his youth he had been a printer in my Netherlands, and after they sailed to the Colony of Massachusetts Bay, he resumed his trade with a royal printer named Richard Draper. "I became an apprentice for him right away," my father's uncle would proudly say, "and have helped publish his Gazette and Boston Weekly Newsletter ever since." He said it was one of the oldest publications in the colonies, and although Uncle Jason had come to support Mr. Draper's unyielding loyalty to London, he was determined to be a free-thinker as well as a dedicated printer.

He was the elder tradesman of that newsletter by the winter of my visit, and after listening to his fanciful stories, I believe he knew just about everything that was happening in Boston, even of secret meetings and things some back then might have viewed as disloyal to the king. Uncle Jason seemed to know of events before they'd happen, even before most dockworkers, tradesmen, shopkeepers and lawyers, "and sometimes," he once said, "before Mr. Draper." I've often wondered if it was due to those things that he had expressed his desire that I not walk to the troubling sounds coming from the middle of town that March night.

Aunt Bea was a proper, delicately prim woman, and even at her maturing age was rather petit at some five feet and a casual hundred pounds. Her auburn hair curled gently to her shoulders, slightly bounced from side to side while shuffling about the home, and her tranquil style seemed to expose notions of intrigue when she was young. I remember how her eyes were pleasantly inviting, a glistening brown whenever she gazed to me amid the glow of candlelight, and how her demeanor toward others was always caring and kind.

During my short time in Boston she seemed rather content, finding true pleasure in doing simple things about her home, but most of all I suppose, I could see how she cherished her life with Uncle Jason. I quickly discovered that just as I, she loved to sew, delighting in snipping and stitching various garments like dresses, breeches and coats, and was always willing to help others meet those needs, even some down the hill at the printing shop. I still recall the sewing secrets she like to show, and how she touched me with her kindness while exposing wonders of life I had yet to know. I've always wished she and I had been together more in those days, for our paths would seldom cross, yet I'll never forget the tenderness she showed that winter so long ago. How I miss Aunt Bea so.

They lived in a rather charming home at 135 Beacon Street, a comfortable place along a path of crushed pebbles and little stones that rose up a slope they called Beacon Hill. It was a southwest rise on the Boston peninsula protruding north into the harbor, a peculiar strip of land bulging at its northern tip and stretching a mile or so south to the narrows. Their home of crimson bricks was a few blocks west of the cobblestones of King Street, and southeast down the hill were the snows of an expanse they called the common, while the waters of the Charles River could be seen a bit west and a short river they called the Mystic was shrouded by a misty haze in the distance northwest. It was a little stream native lore seemed to view with mystery, a river that ran just north of the peninsula of Charlestown thrusting east into the harbor, a pudgy patch of brush and sand with a little village and a few scraggly hills.

The front of their home peered mostly to the north across the stones of Beacon Street, and its red bricks of two floors were embedded with several windows with dozens of square panes, each edged by dark shutters that swung free in summer and closed like shields against the howls of winter. I remember how Uncle Jason kept them latched tight during my visit most nights, "to hold those bloody northern chills at bay," and how those wintry winds would tremble the panes with icy burst before sweeping down the hill. A pair of bedrooms waited on the second floor, just beyond maple stairs that hugged the southwest wall, and a curious little room extended from the ground floor at the rear, a homey place for special guests.

That intriguing room would be mine during my stay, a quiet place just off the expanse of the parlour and stones of the hearth, a quaint little room to sleep amidst the warmth of the fire. Even after all these years I can still hear the placid crackles of burning logs and sense the peacefulness which flared into my room each night, and sometimes, when I'm alone in my Germantown room, I can see the glow of those flickering flames casting tranquil shadows about that cozy room, bathing my dreams with soothing serenity.

I'd soon discover the colorful mornings that would spray through the panes of Aunt Bea's little oval window nestled upon the wall of her quaint kitchen, and would peer through the glass to the spire of Christ Church rising in the haze in the distance north. I remember how its white steeple seemed so inspiring each day, a slim tower piercing the Boston air from the stones of Salem Street, and how it helped bring a sense of calm to Ethan and me as it thrust into the darkness that cold March night.

"Many in Boston just say it's the north side church," Aunt Bea softly explained as we gazed through the frosty panes my first quiet morning. "Its' steeple has been reaching for the sky since before your uncle and I sailed here, Andrea, and has eight little bells that chime charmingly each Sunday. And sometimes, they ring on special occasions, when others think they should."

I can still see its stylish red bricks stacked in neat rows with bright mortar pressed between each, and the windows that lined each side, and remember the impressive square column that rose from the church steps. It was a crimson square topped by that white steeple, bricks with curvy little openings below that tower and dangling bells. A warming calm would surge my body each time I'd gaze through the kitchen window to the mist kissing that spire, a tranquil sensation which soothes to this day.

I soon learned that Aunt Bea and Uncle Jason didn't worship at that church, explaining how they preferred to gather now and then at Kings Chapel down the hill near the common, "with those who follow the tenets of Sandemanian beliefs." She said it was a rather mysterious faith which had splintered from the core of Presbyterians, a spiritual sect that came into prominence some forty years before by a reverend from Scotland. "It grew in scope after we settled here," she confided near the fire one night, "guided by a devoted man" she thought was named Sandeman who sailed to the colony from London.

"We believe in a simple life, Andrea," Uncle Jason added as we talked near the flames crackling in the hearth that night, "not much different than your father's Society of Friends. We also believe one must fear God, while showing reverence to the king." I remember how that view of my father's uncle seemed to cause Aunt Bea to cringe just a bit, beliefs which at times seemed bathed with loyalty to the crown. Yet I suppose most colonists accepted their ties to England back then, women and men more prone to refute than condone dissent of the king.

It was in their home that Monday night, beside the fire of the hearth that fifth day of March, 1770, when the bells dangling the steeple of that northern church and the chapel down the hill began to chime into the cold of the night. I can still feel the chills streaking my back with each eerie chime, a sensation which tugged me toward a mysterious path that would change my life. I could feel my heart thumping and pounding beside the snapping flames, intense beats foretelling feelings which, until that night, I had never known before, passions for a man that descended with the snows of Boston that night.

Aunt Bea was rocking easy in her cushioned maple chair near the hearth, and just left on the other side of a small table was Uncle Jason creaking in his, aglow in an aging lamp's light. I was peering to the fiery embers while prone on my tummy upon an oval rug weaved of yellows, tans, greens and reds, my cheeks warming by the crackling fire, and my chin was resting on a few feathered pillows snug beneath my chest. More pillows were stack in the corner by the door to my little room nearby, along with a few blankets Aunt Bea had knitted, folded yarns of greens, browns and blues.

We had just enjoyed Aunt Bea's supper of crusted rolls, roasted fowl and boiled beets, relaxing near the fire and softly sputtering of our winter day, talking of Germantown, Boston and what might come in spring. I could see little flakes gently falling in the dark outside the frosty panes, an easy snow settling upon Boston's cobblestones, shops, taverns and homes, dainty flakes dusting wintry limbs of oak, maple and elm in white. Then suddenly, the bongs of a distant bell began to chime among the crackling pops of flaming logs, rings which quickly attracted a multitude of surrounding bells, the most prominent coming from that chapel of the king down the hill near the common.

"That sounds like Christ Church," a concerned Uncle Jason said, "those first dings from the north."

As I snapped my stare to the snows sprinkling outside the south and east panes, Aunt Bea twisted a squint toward the windows and sputtered, "The harshest chimes seem to be coming from down the hill, nearer King Street. How strange, Jason, all this ringing on a Monday."

"I don't remember hearing so many bells either," he replied with a disturbing stare before quickly adding, "and I don't like it. Something is happening down there, and I'm not so sure it's good."

While shadows of flickering flames danced about the room, an eerie sound could be heard sweeping up the hill, muffled hoots and faint garbled hollers from what seemed scores of angry people in the distant dark east. "It sounds like a raucous crowd down the hill, by Queen or King Street," Aunt Bea, springing to her feet, excitedly surmised before gazing out the glass toward those erupting shouts and chimes.

I watched as Uncle Jason stopped his rock and gripped the arms of his chair, and for a few puzzling moments we listened in silence, wondering of the meaning of all those sounds, all those faint hollers, cries and bells which seemed to be beckoning the people of Boston to a troubled place. What's happening out there, I wondered, pushing myself up to my knees? What does it all mean? Aunt Bea and Uncle Jason nervously glanced out the window then gazed to each other's eyes, and for a moment it seemed he was somehow aware, in a printer's way, of what was brewing in the dark down there. And as I peered through the panes I could feel my insides twisting and churning, yearning to know why those chilling sounds were festering in the heart of Boston.

I could sense a strange compulsion gripping my soul as those enticing sounds drifted beyond the waters of the Charles to vanish in the night, a simmering curiosity draped with a compelling need to heed the cries echoing the dark. I leapt in my stockings as a little voice quietly commanded me to dash and see what was gathering outside, then rushing to the small foyer by the front door, I began to dress warm. Aunt Bea and Uncle Jason watched in a worried hush as I tugged and laced deer-skin boots without uttering a word, wrapped a tan wool coat about my winter dress and slid little buttons through loops, then bundled my neck in a yellow knit scarf. Sliding soft mittens over chilling fingers, I twisted a glance to their anxious eyes, then pressed a dark bonnet to my curling hair and snugged it tight with a twist of twine.

"Andrea!" Aunt Bea burst in a frantic tone. "What are you doing? Where are you going?"

"I have to go," I calmly replied as those faint sounds swirled outside. "I must see for myself, Aunt Bea, what's going on out there. I'll be alright, really. So please, don't worry. King Street is only a few blocks down the hill, and I've been there several times, with both of you. I won't be gone long, promise."

"Jason, do something!" she shrilled. "I don't like how this feels. Please, stop her!"

He nudged his chair into a stern rock as she stood quiet and anxious to his right, and I watched him silently stare to the snapping flames as if pondering my fate. Then he tenderly nodded to Aunt Bea as I waited at the door, a mitten near the latch, then twisted his gaze over to me and said, "Maybe you should stay here, Andrea, with us. Maybe that would be best."

"I'm sorry, Uncle Jason," I retorted in a respectful way, "to both of you, but I must go. Please, I must see what's going on out there. It's as if I have this divine compulsion to know, this wrenching curiosity. Please, don't forbid me from going. I'll be careful, I promise, and come right home."

"There are some extreme colonists up here," he pled in a fatherly tone, "pretty fiery, impassioned people some might say. They might be stirring the pot down there."

He glanced to Aunt Bea once again and quickly back to me, then confessed a few things he could no longer hold inside. "There was some talk today, at the shop, about some unsettling things, and rumors that a gathering of some kind could take place, maybe even friction tonight. I'm not sure you truly grasp our situation up here, Andrea. This isn't Germantown or Philadelphia, but Boston. The king's soldiers patrol the cobblestones, and there are colonists who defy the crown, want those royal troops to leave our town. So, you can see, Andrea, it might not be safe. Bea and I think it would be best if you stayed home, at least this night."

I tugged my mittens snug and reached deep inside for courage while looking caringly to their eyes, then with a resolute sigh, calmly said, "Maybe that's why I must go, Uncle Jason, because Germantown doesn't have such things. That's why I need to go, to witness what's really taking place up here. I'm sorry, Aunt Bea," I softly added with a tender gaze to her worrying eyes, "you too, Uncle Jason. I know you're just looking out for me, because you care and love me, and I cherish both of you for that. But I'm no longer a child, and tonight, I feel it's time I followed my own path. Please, try to understand."

"But, it's so cold out there, Andrea," Aunt Bea gasped in a surrendering way. "And you don't really know where you're going, not in the dark. Jason, please."

For a moment we just listened to the flames snapping in the hearth, and as Uncle Jason gazed into the fire, I couldn't help but wonder how he always seemed to hold me in a special place in his heart. He would attentively listen to me when others did not, and in a comforting way seemed to understand my feelings. "Let's let her go, Bea," he softly uttered while staring to the flames. "Andrea's right, she's no longer a child. Maybe it is time for her to see some things, as they truly are. Maybe she needs to witness what we here in Boston have known far too long."

"But Jason," Aunt Bea blustered before nestling back into her chair and reluctantly whispering, "Alright. Maybe you're right. We'll let her go, trouble or not."

"Be careful, Andrea," Uncle Jason insisted with a caring gaze to my eyes, "and come home soon. We'll keep the logs burning for you."

"I will, promise," I gratefully sputtered, tugging my scarf to my cheeks. "I'm not going far, just down the hill, just a few blocks. Thanks, both of you, for your understanding, for your trust."

They slowly rocked in the glow of the fire as I anxiously bid them goodbye, their eyes fixed to my every move, then snatching the latch, I swung the door and closed it tight as a wintry burst swept into the room. I bound down the frigid steps and rushed into the chill, dashing on the snowy stones of Beacon Street toward the faint shouts and cries east down the hill. My cheeks flushed with each step amid a sprinkle of dainty flakes, and as I hurried upon the thin layer of white, tiny stars popped in narrow fissures splitting the dark. And sometimes, when a gap spread just right, I could see that dangling gibbous moon bearing witness to the night.

The cobblestones of Sudbury waited at the foot of the hill, and as the robust sounds of that erupting crowd drew nearer with each chilling step, I could feel the strange presence of spirits roaming the dark shrouded the port's common. It was a grassy expanse off to my right scattered with maples, oaks and elms, a place where children frolicked and Bostonians strolled in spring, summer and fall, a shadowy field dusted white that March night. It was a place Uncle Jason said the king's soldiers loyally strutted their duty to the crown, an expanse where "those bloody redcoats think they can stomp our hopes," I once heard a disgruntled colonist say, "with their blasted muskets and damn royal boots!"

I quickly passed the shadows of the common and the dark haze of a distant pond Aunt Bea said believers once dipped those who strayed from their puritan faith, and as little flakes gently trickled, I pivoted to the stones of Queen Street. With each stride east I came nearer a throng coming from churches, shops, taverns and homes, women and men bundled in scarfs, coats, gloves and hats and spewing misty plumes. Soon I was shuffling with others toward those hoots, hollers and cries, and as the stones of Queen merged into King, I could see a disturbing anger spritzing from those gathering on the snowy cobblestones. I couldn't help wonder how unsettled so many seemed to be, as if that crowd was now a single breathing thing, an unruly horde swelling with angst near the center of Boston and the colony's statehouse, just a bit west of the harbor.

A sense of caution began to bathe my steps as I shuffled near the edge of the massing crowd, and slowing my stride, I could see groups of hollering men, unruly boys and a few pugnacious women converging outside a royal building. That's when I saw them, eight royal soldiers assembled in a row on the south side of King Street, and stepping left from the snowy stones, I stopped some sixty feet from that menacing line of troops. They were standing shoulder to shoulder and facing north into the surging throng, their royal backs to the bricks and slats of warehouses and shops. I'd later be told one of those places was the king's customs house, where colonial merchants, shippers and traders reluctantly paid shillings and pounds in taxes and duties to the crown.

Each soldier wore a scarlet coat and white breeches that vanished below the knees into dark boots speckled with snow, and black tricorn hats jutting toward the taunting crowd were pressed to their youthful locks. A long gun which frightened me so dangled from each shoulder too, brown muskets with bayonet blades thrusting into the chill of the night. And at the far tip of that royal line stood an officious soldier a step or two behind, a tricorn trimmed of gold covering sandy hair tailing back, and a sheathed sword dangled past bright breeches and dark boots from beneath a flaring crimson coat.

I first heard the term redcoat from Aunt Bea shortly after I arrived, or perhaps I had forgotten what some had sputtered in Philadelphia or Germantown in the months and years before, and on that cold March night I would hear many in that angry crowd blast disparaging names to London's soldiers. There were frightening shouts of "bloody king's men!" being spewed by Bostonians as I stood stunned off the cobblestones of King Street, and as specs of snow dusted the stones, I heard contemptuous cries of "bloody lobster backs!" amid heckling hollers of "damn redcoats!"

I watched from my distant haven as the vile shouts and unflattering cries seemed to spiral from control amid ugly phrases like, "to the devil, you blasted redcoats!", all the while those nervous soldiers and their royal captain stood cold and still. For a few precarious moments their expressions were stoic, as if chiseled from English stone, even as their eyes frantically snapped left and right into the glare of the fiery surge.

Soon the heckling crowd on the snows of King Street had massed to three hundred or so, and a bit before nine they began to increasingly push nearer those eight royal troops lined in a neat row outside the crown's customs house. It was now a throng of angry men and older boys spewing ugly threats while gripping slats of elm and limbs of oak, a taunting horde grasping bricks, stones and shards of ice as the king's soldiers stood their ground amidst misty plumes of scornful cries.

I could feel a frightening fear begin to swirl deep inside as the crowd surged nearer the king's line, fiery men and howling boys shouting contempt while wielding intimidating things. Some were now swinging sticks and flailing arms amid disdainful bursts of "bloody lobster backs!", and my stomach twisted in anxious knots with each emphatic "damn redcoats!" blast. As I stood off the snowy stones of King Street and gazed to the madness in a bewildered hush, I began to wonder if what was unfolding was real.

The angry shouts from the taunting crowd flared with each erupting moment, and I could sense my cheeks flushing as their eyes glared and faces crimpled with each contemptible jeer of "bloody redcoats!" All I could do was watch in a scared silence as scores of Bostonians pushed closer to those royal solders while flailing clubs, limbs and sticks. And some were now hurling dangerous things like ice, rocks and shells while blasting "go home, bloody bastards!", and others were tossing hard balls of snow and clumps of coal amid spritzing cries of "damn lobster backs!"

Suddenly a howling man bundled in a long tattered coat thrust a chunk of brick or shard of ice toward the king's men, whacking a young soldier near the end of that royal line above his eye. "Fire, you damn lobster backs!" that angry Bostonian blasted as a misty burst of spittle sprayed the night air. "Fire, you bloody redcoats!"

I watched with frightening angst as that royal soldier, a thin crimson stream trickling his eye and down his cheek, snatched his musket off his shoulder and aimed its barrel into all those erupting Bostonians. And while the king's captain stood still behind his line of eight redcoats, his sword lazily dangling and wits perhaps stunned, the rest of those royal soldiers reached for their muskets and pointed their muzzles into the surging crowd. From my haven I could see the king's line standing firm for a desperate moment, their nervous fingers twitching cold triggers, eight iron barrels now thrusting toward a mass of mocking and jeering.

"Hold your fire!" the captain excitedly demanded as the surging horde blasted taunting shouts. "Hold your fire!" he barked to his eight young soldiers as the flickering flames of colonial torches gleamed bayonets and barrels.

For several frantic moments it seemed the world had stopped its spin about the heavens, as if humanity had ceased upon the snowy cobblestones of King Street. I just stared at the intensifying scene as little specs of white drifted the night, gazing at the panic brushed across the faces of those young soldiers and the anger spritzing from the taunting crowd. It was then, during those frightening moments before the madness was unleashed, that our eyes enchantingly met.

It's been over fifty years since that March night, yet to this day the magic that thrilled my body when our eyes first met remains sensuously intact. The destiny of two lives was about to become passionately entwined forever, just as the mayhem of the hour was about to cast its brutish stain upon the colonies. It was as if we had been brought to that place by some mystical power at that precise moment that wintry night, and our gaze seemed to wrap our souls and bind our hearts forever.

Ethan was standing amid the crowd, no icy ball, stick, club or rock gripped in his hand, and just watching, not spewing curses to the king's men or blasting taunts of "bloody lobster backs." He was just there on the snowy cobblestones of King Street like me, a witness to the ugly event about to unfold, and was standing between two rather intriguing looking men some forty feet from me, nearer that redcoat line.

In a moment as fleeting as the flick of a flame he twisted right, as if he had mysteriously felt my gaze, then his peer pierced my heart. His brown eyes glistening with a tinge of gold drew me into him, and for a moment the pearl of my green eyes vanished deep into his sensuous stare. My heart was bursting passion I had never known before, and I wondered if such feelings belonged only in dreams or were the wondrous will of God.

We just stared in a tantalizing hush into each other's eyes for a moment or two, oblivious of what was about to explode on the snowy stones of King Street, and I could see a soft smile edge his lips as my gaze rushed through the chill with a tender kiss. His gentle eyes warmed my heart as joy surged my body, and for a moment the strain of Boston magically vanish for us, a precious moment that would forever ease my lonely soul.

Then within an instant our wondrous escape unraveled when the reality of that fateful March night burst upon the cobblestones. Ethan suddenly twisted toward the row of king's men as my stare shifted to the intriguing man who moments before had been standing just left of Ethan's shoulder. He was bigger than others with a complexion that was darker than most, a colonist they'd later say was the son of a mother of the Wampanoag tribe and a Negro father who once farmed a spot of land across the sea.

I watched as that daring man rushed through the shouting crowd toward those redcoats, flailing a thick stick of knotted pine before smacking a pair of those thrusting musket barrels. Then he tossed his club and lunged at another royal soldier, and as I gazed in a stunned hush, he wacked his musket and knocked that redcoat to the snowy stones. Wild taunts of "fire!" erupted from the surging throng, quickly followed by blasts of "damn you, fire, you bloody lobster backs!"

Still gripping his musket, that startled soldier leapt to his boots and gave out a curdling cry of "fire, fire!", and within a moment of madness the world I had come to know was shattered. Bursts of sparkling reds suddenly sprayed with plumes of grey from the king's musket barrels, explosions of tiny lead balls streaking into the fiery crowd, and as I watched with hundreds of stunned colonists, that royal captain, thrusting his sword into the smoky haze, dashed before his redcoat line and commanded, "Stop firing!" As quickly as those muskets blasted mayhem that cold night, a new kind of hush, an awakening patriot hush, descended upon the bloodied stones of King Street.

I could see Ethan still standing where moments before his tender gaze had pierced my heart, only now he was spinning and twisting to those about him as if grasping for understanding. I watched in a silent scare as women, children and men frantically scattered and others wandered about with aimlessly stares, and some with tears in the eyes simply fell to their knees upon the snow. A dreadful smell of burnt powder wafted the grey plume drifting above the street, and patches of cobblestones once dusted white were now spattered with grisly blotches of steaming red.

It was an awful sight that's haunted me all these years, a dreadful memory for every colonist who witnessed the crown's wicked deed on the cobblestones of King Street that night, gruesome visions that would dwell within Ethan the rest of his life. The blood of eleven daring men and elder boys had spilled upon the snowy stones of Boston that night, six who'd survive their defiant moment to carry their scares over the years and five who would succumb to those fiery musket blasts. Three would lose their life during those chaotic moments that March night and two would yield to their patriot fate in the hours and days to come, a courageous stand that would be etched upon the soul of every women, child and man throughout the colonies.

For several helpless moments all I could do was stare at those poor men and boys fallen upon the snow and watch scores of women and men wandering in a befuddled haze, many now beginning to disperse while some remained to aid those brave souls lying upon the stones. I had tended injured colonists before during my nursing training at the Pennsylvania

Hospital, and as I stared in a trembling gaze, I suddenly understood what I had to do. I knew I must stay with those courageous men and boys, tend to those with ghastly wounds trickling crimson to the snows, yet I'd soon realize my few years at the hospital had done little to truly prepare me for what I was about to encounter on those bloodied cobblestones.

"Help me," was a soft sigh I suddenly heard coming from somewhere in the scattering crowd, from a place where an ugly red was now pooling upon the snows of the stones. "Please, somebody," moaned another anguishing soul on King Street near the place where moments before the king's soldiers blasted muskets into the night, "help me."

I'll never forget the confused gazes brushed upon the faces of dazed colonists mingling about the spattered stones, nor the desperate cries of "no, God no!" of a small boy wailing on the far side of the street. I could see him kneeling on the stained snows with his little arms clinging to a listless man bundled in a bloodied coat, life oozing his chest from a steaming musket gash.

My moment had come to reach for the fallen, to tend to the wounded and help calm their fears as best I could, and in an instinctive spurt honed by my nursing training, I rushed to the anguishing sighs that had replaced the taunting cries. And in a mysterious twist of fate I've come to see as divine over the years, my path led to the man whose sensuous peer had pierced my soul just minutes before, a young man now holding that fearless seaman dying in his arms.

I could see the sullen eyes of the man I'd come to joyously know as Ethan misting as I quickly stepped, tears swelling as he quietly held the dark hand of that daring man who moments before had thrust defiance upon that redcoat line. Then glancing to that other intriguing man now standing stoic nearby, I slowed my step and watched in a numbing hush as Ethan comforted his fading friend in the closing moments of his life. I dabbed a tear as a sense of feebleness seemed to brush Ethan's face, a helpless expression as his friend gasp a final breath upon the snows of King Street.

An ugly steam was rising from a ghastly hole ripped into the chest of that man now limp in Ethan's arms, a caring man they'd say was the first and oldest of the five mortally felled by the king's men that wintry night. I'd soon be told that Crispus Attucks had once been shackled in bondage on a big farm in a colony to the south, toiling in fields without liberty or pay before fleeing his chains and sailing in a merchant ship to the Colony of Massachusetts Bay. Ethan would later whisper that Mr. Attucks soon found freedom as a seaman along Boston's wharf's and docks, and heeding the cry of spirited colonists earlier that day, was one of the bold men who stormed from the harbor and defiantly gathered on the cobblestones that March night.

I gazed to Ethan without uttering a word, then tugging the mittens from my fingers, settled to my knees on the snowy stones spattered in a gruesome red. That daring man's breathing had already fully withered, and pressing my fingers with a nursing poise to a cold still spot, I confirmed that his heart once pounding with life was now forever silent. I could feel a tear about to spill as I gazed across that poor man to Ethan's sullen eyes, and as a quiet chill brushed the stones, whispered, "I'm sorry."

He batted his eyes in a futile attempt to keep a spilling tear from trickling his cheek, then stared deep into my soul and uttered with a somber nod, "Thank you, miss, for caring."

"I'm so sorry," I sighed once again as Ethan gazed to the hand pressed in his fingers.

"Thank you," that other man standing stoic nearby added, "for your help."

"I only wish I could have done more," I softly said as he gazed down to that daring seaman, "wish things were different." I could see crimson specs dotting his bright breeches as he stood quiet with his hands warming in the tan pockets of his wool coat, and ugly stains smudging dark shoes.

My heart began to sigh as I snapped my gaze back to Ethan and watched a tear spill from his eye to the cold hand of his friend, and reaching for his arm I gently asked, "Is there anything I can do?"

As we quietly kneeled on the snowy stones for a moment or two, my fingers touching his coat in hopes of easing his pain, Ethan softly replied, "You already have." Then gingerly releasing Crispus' still hand, he dabbed an eye and tenderly added, "Thank you, for being so kind, for being here."

For a teary moment he just gazed to my eyes, then perhaps sensing how truly I cared, began to expose a few tender things swelling deep inside.

"I'm just trying to understand why, why all this happened tonight. I didn't know Crispus that well, not really, but believe he was a good man, who dared to show his courage. We first met a few years ago, in Lexington, yet I suppose Henry and I mostly saw him about the docks here in Boston. He was always friendly, and now here he lies. I guess I'm just a bit confused, and feel so bad, for those he's left behind."

"I think I understand," I whispered as that other man gazed down in a hush near his side, "know how you feel. You're so right, about those left behind. I wonder of the others here too, of what their families will be going through."

For a wondrous moment it was if Ethan and I were completely alone, that the other man and those rushing about the snows had vanished, as if the awful pleas for help and sighs of loss and pain drifting the cobblestones had mercifully been quelled. For a precious moment it seemed we were in a special place all our own, far away from the horror of mayhem and the dwindling crowd, two strangers now gazing with hope and passion into one another's eyes. I could feel my soul being pulled to his, and as I wondered of his kindness, of tears he had shed for a friend, I felt the urge to cast logic and doubt to the winds and escape with Ethan into the night.

"Let's cover this poor man," Ethan's friend suddenly uttered, gripping a tattered blanket a scurrying boy had just handed him. "It's the least we can do," he somberly added while spreading the wool over Mr. Attucks, "for such a dignified man."

Ethan let Crispus go as I slowly climbed to my shoes, his lifeless eyes no longer staring into the chill, settling his hair to a patch of specked snow as he gingerly rose from his knees. Dabbing my eyes, I gazed to the staining wool and wondered how fleeting life can be, how quickly dreams had been dashed that night on the snowy stones of King Street.

Suddenly the sighs, moans and pleas which had been wafting about the street intensified, becoming close, loud and real, awful sounds which moments before had been shielded behind some mysterious wall, and I quickly realized others still needed my help. I shuffled a step or two from the wool swaddling Mr. Attucks, and along with Ethan and his friend stood quiet for a moment, gathering our wits and taming our emotions amidst dozens of scurrying women and men.

"Again, miss, thank you," Ethan graciously uttered, reaching for my hand as we stepped away a little bit more, "for your kindness. I'm Ethan Sheehan." I can still feel the magic of his touch even after all these years, and the sensuousness of his hand. "This is Mr. Knox," he nervously added, nodding to his friend, "Henry. And you are?"

"Andrea," I anxiously whispered as his fingers aroused my skin. "Miss Van Dijk, Klaasz Van Dijk. But please, call me, Andrea." And as his eyes searched deep into mine, I nervously sputtered, "I'm truly sorry, about your friend."

"We know," he tenderly replied. "It shows in your eyes, Andrea, and in your touch. Please, call me, Ethan."

"Alright, Ethan," I whispered amid the scampering sounds of King Street.

"You've been very kind, Miss Van Dijk," injected Ethan's friend as my fingers slowly slid from Ethan's tender hand. "Thank you. And please, call me, Henry."

"I will. Please, Henry, I'm Andrea. I wish I could have done more for your friend."

As Henry bowed in a reflective stare to that tattered blanket spread upon the spattered snow, I snapped my gaze back to Ethan as he whispered in a wondrous tone, "You have beautiful green eyes, Andrea, like serene pearls."

"Thank you, Ethan" I shyly replied as my cheeks flushed. "It was nice, very nice to meet you, you too, Henry. Only, I wish it had been under different circumstances." I scanned the dwindling crowd for a moment and pivoted my thoughts to the waning moans and sighs, then peering back to Ethan, timidly added, "I'm a nurse, and need to go, help these people. But I want to come back, see you. Will you still be here?"

"Yes," Ethan quickly sputtered in an intrigued way, "I'll be here. I'm going to stay with Crispus, until someone comes for him. I can't leave him here alone on these cold stones."

"Of course," I hushed with a tender gaze to Ethan's eyes. "I'll be back, soon."

"I'm staying with Crispus too," Henry caringly insisted with a nod to Ethan.

"I'll be here, Andrea, when you come back," Ethan softly said with a sparkle in his eyes. "Maybe then," he boldly added in a nervous tone, "we can talk."

"Yes, maybe we can," I whispered while slowly stepping away and bidding both a gentle goodbye. "I'd like that, Ethan, very much. I'll be back."

Ethan fixed his stare upon me as I shuffled away, then gathered with Henry and others near the listless body of Crispus shrouded by that awful blanket on the snowy cobblestones. That's when I saw the hole near the lower seam of Ethan's coat, a frightful gash in the wool he'd later say was ripped that night by a redcoat musket ball.

I've often wondered what became of that lead ball. Had it continued its dreaded path to find another Bostonian shouting defiance to the king? Or maybe it danced across the cobblestones to shatter the panes of a merchant shop, or vanished into the snow? Ethan had skirted the wrath of the king that night, was one of the lucky ones surging about King Street, and in the years to come I'd pray for God to always keep him safe.

I gingerly stepped through the dwindling crowd wandering about wounded boys and men as little white specs began to trickle the dark, and with each stride took care to avoid the grisly scarlet patches scattered about the snow. I had been exposed to gruesome injuries before, yet the sight of colonists strewn about the cobblestones was troubling to bear. "You can do this, Andrea," I demandingly hushed, "you must!"

Nearer the colony's statehouse a bit toward the harbor laid a young man I'd later be told was just seventeen, a boy with misty puffs spritzing from his lips as I stepped closer, dropped to my knees and nudged to his side on the spattered snow of the cobblestones. A musket ball had ripped into his chest, slicing through his coat and lodging deep into his flesh, and as I pressed my fingers to the bloodying wool, I dabbed a tear and tried to ease his fears, "Shh, I'm here." His blue eyes just gazed to me in a frightened hush as my insides twisted with angry screams, yet all I could do was console as he struggled for life with each gasping breath. "Shh, I'm here.

Shh," I sputtered, brushing specs settling his brows, "and others will be soon."

In a desperate hope to stem the flow of the ugly crimson pooling beneath his back, I unraveled the scarf from my neck and folded it into a bundle, and with a tug of his coat, pressed it to the gash seeping to a ruffled shirt. A young woman then knelt to the snows and propped his head upon a soft clump of wool, then covered him with a quilt blanket as comfort from the cold. He was so young, with so many dreams yet to fill, and as he gazed with a forlorn stare, a tear spilled my eye as I wondered of the madness.

"Over here," I spritzed to a trio of scurrying men while pressing a bit harder and frantically adding, "Please, hurry!" They quickly bundled him in their arms, and with a furious dash across the snowy cobblestones, rushed his fading hopes into the king's customs house. He was laid to a table with others bloodied on that street only minutes before, colonists now being tended to by a pair of weary doctors who'd scampered to the blasts that night. I'd later hear that poor lad was Sam Maverick, a young man from the docks who had heeded the spirited cries earlier that day, and that he'd succumb to his grisly wound shortly after noon the following day.

For a solemn moment I watched candle flames inside the customs house glisten the frosting panes, a place now wafting with a simmering stench of death, then rushed to my right to a man face down upon the stones of King Street. His cheeks were pressed to the snow and a thin stream of smoky grey rising from his back was slowly swirling into the cold, a gruesome sight that sent a nauseous chill surging my body.

He was lying so still without misting a breath, and dropping to my knees, I could see a smoldering hole scorched into his coat, wool that had been sliced by a royal musket ball searing the mayhem that night. A sense of helplessness gripped my insides as I watched his dreams seeping to a crimson pool steaming on the cobblestones, and I whispered a tiny prayer while dabbing my eyes in the chilling night air.

As I kneeled in a solemn hush and gently brushed his hair in hopes of comforting his soul, a scraggly looking man a bit older than most began stepping close, a colonist who moments before was mingling with a little group sputtering in a rather taunting, royal way. He was somewhat gangly, with curly locks powdered white and bundled in a long deerskin coat, and stopping just beside me with a wag of his fingers, stood over that daring young man. I watched in silence as he pressed his boot to a shoulder without uttering a word, then was stunned as he rolled the listless body with an ugly thrusting jolt.

"I know this lad," he sputtered in a royal tone, "not too bright." And as he coldly added, "I think they call him, James," I gasped in horror to the sight of his eyes still open, staring up from the snowy stones into the chill of the night. "I'm afraid, miss," he puffed with an uncaring glare, "this boy is dead."

I dabbed my eyes and pressed my fingers in a nursing way to a spot of his neck, confirming what that dismal old man had uttered, then shuttered his gaze with a brush of my hand as a caring colonist spread a spattered coat over his body. As my knees chilled in the hush and snow I wondered of his family, of the pain soon to crush his father and the anguish about to consume a weeping mother. Someone would later say he was Jimmy Caldwell, a seafaring man a bit younger than me from a village along the waters of Cape Cod Bay, a daring man now forever at rest.

Brushing another tear from my cheeks, I crept back to my feet and rushed to another man lying on the snows nearby, his arms stretching from his body as tiny flakes gently settled to his closed eyes. He was perhaps a dozen feet from where the king's soldiers had aimed their barrels and fired their muskets, and as I dashed to his side my stomach twisted in frightful knots, for I could see he was no longer breathing. "Oh no," I whispered while pressing my knees to the cold stones. "Please, God, let him live."

A grisly red was pooling to the snow beneath his crumpled coat, and as I pressed my fingers to his frigid skin to confirm that this young man too was dead, the ugly smell of burnt flesh and wool wafted the air, another vile tale of a royal musket ball piercing a colonist's chest. They said he was maker of ropes in his father's nearby shop, a man about my age named Sam Gray, and some believe he had joined the surging crowd that night to settle a simmering score. As my knees quivered on the icy stones and those tiny flakes blessed his cheeks, all I truly knew that moment was that his life had come to an end, and as I quietly grieved at the young man's side, all I could do was whisper, "why?"

After a few somber moments a few men plucked Sam from the stones, and as I rose from the spattered snows and glanced about, there were still woman and men in little groups roaming about King Street. A few were finishing the care of the only young man still lying wounded, and others seemed to be milling about in a bereft daze. And I could see Ethan standing alone in the distance where he agreed to wait for me, the still body of Mr. Attucks no longer stretched upon the cobblestones. Then I watched as that last bloodied man was carried through the customs house door for care and mending, and wondered of his life as I stared at the flicker and glow of lamps and candles inside.

As I slowly stepped toward Ethan, listening to snow crunch beneath my boots and voices of wandering women and men, I glanced through the frosty panes of a customs house window just as that final man was laid to a table. Ethan would later say he was an honest man of resolute wits, a craftsman of leather who years before had sailed to Boston from a hamlet in Ireland with his mother and father. Patrick Carr was only thirty or so as of that fiery March night, a courageous colonist who would struggle to survive for some nine days before losing his battle with that royal musket ball.

"What a terrible thing, grandma," Samuel interrupted in a concerning way while gripping the arms of his chair and nudging into a more robust rock. "You've never spoken of that night, at least not to me."

"It was," I whispered as a wisp of warm summer air gently tossed my hair, "a frightening, horrid night, Samuel, at least in the beginning. Visions of those poor men and boys, and panicked colonists scrambling about the stones, are seared to my mind. I can still hear the awful sounds of those muskets blasting into the crowd, the screams of frightened women and cries of courageous men, things that today, seem unbelievable. Yet maybe the most daunting memory is of blood spattered about the snow, a grisly red spritzed upon white, a vision of life lost which haunts to this day."

Samuel continued to rock with a contemplating stare, peering to the distant trees swaying easy in the morning breeze, while I slid my fingers across the words of Ethan's poem nestled in the pocket of my summer dress, wondering of the mayhem and magic of that March night. With each caress I could sense the anguishing pains amidst the joyous passions of those days so long ago, and as memories slowly flowed from the parchment, I remembered the wondrous hours that followed the madness which had erupted upon the cobblestones of Boston.

"As awful as those moments were," I whispered, nudging my chair into a soft rock as Samuel gazed to the summer winds, "a defiant event some would call a bloody massacre on King Street, something magical would follow. It was the night I met Ethan. As tragic as that day was, it would become the most joyous of my life."

"What was Ethan doing there, grandma?" he asked with a puzzling stare. "Was he part of that angry crowd, that unruly mob?"

"No, he wasn't part of the anger," I softly explained. "Ethan was just there watching with his friend Henry, like me, just being a witness to it all. He wasn't gripping a club or throwing stones, shells or ice, wasn't shouting taunting things to those royal soldiers, but just trying to make sense of it all." Then glancing to Samuel gazing to the elms with a contemplating stare, I slid my fingers across the passions of Ethan's poem and comfortingly said, "Please, Samuel, be patient. You'll know so many things when my story is fully told, about Ethan and the war, your grandfather and me. You'll understand what it was like in the colonies back then."

"Alright, grandma," he calmly replied with a gentle gleam in his eyes, "I will, be patient, promise. I'll just rock and listen to your story. Tell me, grandma, about those days, the war, Ethan."

He pressed into the slats of his chair with an easy rock and gazed to the elms gently swaying in the summer winds, awaiting my coming words, and I closed my eyes and softly stroked the lines of Ethan's poem while listening to the leaves rustling in the breeze. With each slide of my fingers I could smell the musket smoke of that wintry night and hear the cries upon the cobblestones, and with each caress of Ethan's words, I could see his tranquil eyes and feel his sensuous touch.

Those eight redcoat soldiers and their royal captain had mysteriously vanished by the time I returned to Ethan, having rushed to a safer place amidst the panic their muskets had blasted upon the snowy stones of King Street. I'd later hear they had dashed within moments of firing into that raucous crowd, chaotic minutes when I and others were scurrying about trying to help the dying and wounded, escaping east to their barracks in an aging warehouse along the harbor.

Ethan was standing on a trampled patch of snowy stones in a sullen gaze at that customs house, and as I gingerly stepped amid an array of colonists milling about, I could hear a few spewing rather unflattering words about their royal governor. "Why, he's nothin but a murderin bastard!" a seafaring man angrily fumed into the chill, while some were spouting that the king's soldiers were "bloody cowards!" and other cursing things. Yet those stormy taunts seemed to fade as I stepped near Ethan's side, for that's when he twisted and gazed to my eyes, and tenderly said, "Hi."

"Hi," I hushed with a bat of my eyes before asking in a concerned way, "Are you alright, Ethan?"

"Yes, I'm fine," he softly uttered as mist spritzed his eyes. Then in a nervous, rather awkward way, he quickly added, "Henry walked over there, to the Green Dragon Tavern, as soon as Crispus was carried into the customs house. He wanted to talk with a few he knows over there, try to make some sense of this night."

"Oh," I whispered with a press of my hands to the sleeve of his coat before instinctively sighing, "it's alright, Ethan, I'm here."

"I'm glad," he confessed as his fingers softly touched mine. "Would you like to take a walk, get away from here, maybe to some warm place where we can talk for a while? This might sound strange, after all, we've only just met, but I feel I can talk with you. I won't be a burden, promise. You know, talking about what happened here tonight might be good for both of us."

I wanted to shout "yes" right then and there in the middle of King Street, before all those women and men still wandering about the stones, tell him there was nothing I'd rather do more at that moment. I wanted to scream "yes, yes, yes" into the chill, yet somehow doused my erupting passions, slid my mittens over my fingers and calmly pressed my hands to his. "I would like that very much," I whispered while gazing to his alluring eyes. "I'm visiting my aunt and uncle a few blocks from here, up the hill on Beacon Street. Would you like to walk me home, Ethan, and we could talk? And maybe, if you want, we could spend some time warming by a fire, and talk a little more."

"Oh yes, I do," he quickly replied as his cheeks flushed. "I'm so glad you feel this way, and want to talk."

He flicked some dark blotches and crimson specs spattered about the lower seam of his coat, solemn reminders of the mayhem which exploded that March night, then gently wrapping his right hand about my left, we began to step west toward the shadowy cobblestones of Queen Street. As his fingers comforted mine with each quiet stride, the suffering and carnage of the hour before began to mournfully simmer deep inside. They were churning feelings of grisly visions I had shoved to a dark corner of my mind while helping those daring boys and men, painful emotions about to burst from my soul.

My eyes began to swell with soft somber sighs and grieving tears slowly spilled my cheeks, and as I pressed my sorrow into my mittens, our stride stuttered and stopped. Without uttering a word Ethan spun and wrapped me in his arms, and as he tenderly held me near his heart, my sighs began to ease as my anguish was released. I felt so safe in Ethan's warming embrace that night, for he had tamed my despair and soothed my grief as little bits of snow drifting the dark brushed the cobblestones white.

After a few tender moments my soft cries began to subside, and gently twisting, I gazed to his caring eyes and whispered, "I feel so bad for those poor boys and men. It's heartbreaking, Ethan, and the ugly horror of it all, keeps swirling my mind. I don't know what to do."

I sighed and pressed back to Ethan's chest, and after swaddling me in his arms another moment or two, he tenderly said, "I guess, there's nothing anyone can do, not really, at least not now. But you're right, Andrea, it's like a terrible dream. You know, Crispus and the others felled tonight may not be the only victims of the king. Perhaps, in a strange way, we all are."

We comforted each other one more precious moment as a soft snow sprinkled the quiet of the night, then sliding his hands down the arms of my coat, Ethan whispered, "Come, let's go. Let's take you home."

He wrapped his fingers about my hand as we returned to a slow stride west on the stones of Queen Street, stepping ever further from the carnage of the night, and we whispered of easy things while strolling past the shadows roaming the common before pivoting up the snowy pebbles rising Beacon Hill. I could sense we were both a bit nervous as we talked, expressing views of this or that or exposing a trivial tale, and sometimes we just quietly walked in the wintry chill settling Boston, grappling with gruesome visions while wondering of our lives.

"I've only been in Boston a few weeks, Ethan," I confessed as we neared the peak of the hill. "I'm visiting from Pennsylvania, from Germantown, a village just a bit north of Philadelphia."

"I've never heard of Germantown," Ethan shyly replied while swaddling my hand. "But of course everyone knows of Philadelphia. I hope to go there someday."

"Our winters can get rather cold in Germantown," I nervously uttered as we neared the house, his warming fingers wrapping my mitten, "yet not quite like here."

"I'm a student," he shyly revealed as we stepped beyond the crest of the hill, "studying here in Boston. Well, not actually here, but over there, across the river in Cambridge. But I'm really from Lexington, a village about a dozen miles northwest."

"Maybe, someday, you can show me," I whispered as we reached the snowy stones leading to the house. "We're here, Ethan. This is where I'm staying."

"Yes, maybe I will," he tenderly sputtered amid the sound of crunching snow with each step of the stones. Then with a flick of the latch, I creaked open the door.

"Andrea!" Aunt Bea excitedly spouted, springing from her chair in the glow of the hearth as Ethan and I stepped into the foyer, escaping the cold. "Thank God, you're safe."

Uncle Jason slowly rose while staring to the logs crackling in the fire, and as Aunt Bea nervously tugged her saffron shawl draping her shoulders, Ethan and I stood bundled near the door. "We were worried, Andrea," he uttered in a fatherly tone, snapping a gaze to my eyes. "Are you alright?"

"Yes, I'm fine," I timidly replied with a brush of remorse. "I'm sorry, for having worried you." I tossed my bonnet, mittens and coat to the little foyer bench, then untwining and tugging my boots, carefully added, "Oh, this young man is Ethan. He was kind enough to walk me home."

"Thank you, Ethan," Uncle Jason gratefully uttered. "Please, won't you stay a while?"

"Yes, please do," Aunt Bea quickly chimed while motioning to the snapping flames. "Please, Ethan, take those damp things off, those wet shoes too, and warm here by the fire, both of you."

Ethan pulled his wool coat, with a tattered hole ripped by a musket ball and grisly stains near the seam, and gently laid it to the bench, then slid his snowy shoes from his stockings. And as I clasped his hand and we shuffled toward the fire crackling in the hearth, I brushed a tear from my cheek and blurted, "Uncle Jason, it was terrible. Men were killed by the king's soldiers tonight, some just boys, felled by muskets over on King Street. Oh, Aunt Bea, it was awful."

"Come," she whispered while caressing my shoulder in a motherly way, "it sounds so frightening, dreadful. But you're here now, Andrea, safe, both of you. Please, sit by the fire."

"Yes, let's," I spritzed to Ethan as the flames began to calm me. "This is my Uncle Jason, and his bride, Beatrice, my Aunt Bea."

"How do you do, sir," Ethan shyly uttered while snatching Uncle Jason's reaching hand. "I'm Ethan Sheehan. It's truly a pleasure to meet you."

"Jason Karl Van Dijk," he sternly replied in an accepting tone. "But please, just call me Jason. Sit here, Ethan," he gently added with a tiny nod right. "Bea, take my chair."

"Thank you, sir, but I can't do that. I don't want to take either of your chairs. Please."

"It's alright, Uncle Jason," I quickly blurted, "we want to relax closer to the fire with pillows, right there on the rug. Please, you two take your chairs."

"Yes, that sounds nice," Ethan softly said with a dash of relief. "Near the fire is good."

"Alright, since you insist," conceded Uncle Jason. "Let's sit with them, Bea, for a little while."

"It's very nice to meet you, Mrs. Van Dijk," Ethan nervously inserted while reaching for her hand.

"It's good to meet you, Mr. Sheehan," she comfortingly replied. "Thank you, for bringing our Andrea safely home."

"It was my pleasure," he sputtered while leaning and respectfully tapping his lips upon Aunt Bea's hand. "Please, Mrs. Van Dijk, you too, sir, please, call me Ethan."

"Have you known our Andrea long?" Uncle Jason quizzed as they nestled back to the comfort of their chairs and Ethan and I settled to the rug, snatching feathered pillows warming by the fire.

"No, I haven't, sir. We just met, tonight."

"Yes, just this evening," I quickly added, hoping to ease a tenseness lingering about my uncle's words. Then amidst the tranquil sounds of snapping flames and crackling logs a relaxing calm settled about the room, Aunt Bea and Uncle Jason snug in their chairs and Ethan and I nestling near the fire. "We met on the stones of King Street, Uncle Jason, just after those horrid musket blasts. Ethan was so kind, and when I asked, he willingly walked me home."

"We're so pleased you did, Ethan," whispered Aunt Bea.

"Yes, we're very grateful," Uncle Jason quipped after a glancing prod from his bride. "Thank you, Ethan. Now, you two stay right here, keep warm by the fire. Stay as long as you like, Ethan."

A gentle calm now bathed the room, Aunt Bea and Uncle Jason whispering to perhaps help Ethan and me feel more alone while we nestled on the wool by the fire. Ethan was stretched upon the rug with his stockings near the stones, his right elbow propped upon a feathery plump as flames nipped at his toes, and my legs were crossed as I sat by his elbow, my arms softly squeezing a pillow. We just gazed to the flickering flames amid the hush, and listened to the fiery snaps and cracks holding the wintry night at bay.

After several quiet moments Ethan softly pressed his left hand upon mine, and with each tender caress I could feel a mysterious serenity as we peered to the dancing fire. Then as if induced by some magical potion, our eyes snapped from the flames and fixed upon each other, his enticing gaze pulling me into him as sensuous urges surged deep inside. A calming expression brushed Ethan's face as his eyes seemed to confess contentment, and glancing to his fingers gently weaving about mine, he gazed to my longing eyes and whispered, "Thank you, Andrea, for bringing me here tonight. I love lying here, with you."

I remember the joy that thrilled me that moment, an arousal I had never felt before, and wondered of what our evening might bring while whispering, "I feel the same, Ethan. I'm so glad you're here." And as our fingers caressed we just gazed deep into each other's eyes, as if searching for some secret place in our souls.

"Andrea and I met near the customs house," Ethan nervously blurted in a shy way while twisting his stare to Jason and Bea, "not far from where the king's muskets erupted tonight." Then bashfully glancing to the fire for a moment, he boldly added, "Right after those redcoats blasted into the crowd, your niece showed such compassion. Andrea rushed to the boys and men bloodied on the stones, bravely tending to those wounded and dying on the snows. You can be very proud of her."

"Andrea," quizzed Aunt Bea with a worried expression, "you did those things?"

"Yes, she did," Ethan quickly said, as if he could sense I was trying to withdraw in a humble way, not wanting to dwell on the night.

"Yes, Aunt Bea," I softly admitted, "I did. But so did many others, Ethan too. I guess for me, it was just my nursing training, something I knew I had to do, that's all. Please, I'd rather not talk about it anymore, at least not tonight."

"It must have been terrible," Aunt Bea timidly uttered, "for both of you. Alright, Andrea, we won't talk about it tonight. You just rest."

"We're proud of you, Andrea," whispered Uncle Jason, caringly. "You can tell us about it, when you're ready."

"Thank you," I humbly sighed, "both of you, for understanding."

A solemn hush settled upon the room as Ethan and I returned our gaze to the flickering flames while his fingers entwined mine, and Uncle Jason and Aunt Bea pressed back into their chairs and reflectively stared to the fire. Then with a secret glance I could see an anguishing mist brushing Ethan's tender eyes, and wondered if he too was struggling just as I, grappling with grisly visions of that awful night. Although we had found each other only hours before, I felt compelled to reach for his heart and console his emotions twisting deep inside.

Suddenly Aunt Bea's clock atop the hearth's elm mantel shattered the quiet with ten rhythmic pings, flowery blue porcelain panging chimes which echoed about the house and vanished into the chill of the night. "Jason," Aunt Bea softly muttered, "let's go up, and leave these two young ones alone." As I twisted and watched them slowly rise from their chairs, she gazed to my eyes and caringly whispered, "You two stay here, Andrea, warm, by the fire."

"Goodnight," Uncle Jason gently sputtered while gripping a dim oil lamp, leaving the other to glow about the room, "both of you."

"Goodnight, Andrea," whispered Aunt Bea as they stepped up the stairs, her fingers gently held in Uncle Jason's hand. "Goodnight, Ethan. We hope to see you again, soon."

"Thank you," a twisting Ethan graciously replied, "both of you, for your kindness. Goodnight."

"Goodnight, Uncle Jason," I hushed as they reached the bend at the peak of the stairs. "Goodnight, Aunt Bea." Then looking to Ethan's eyes as the hearth's fire cast mysterious shadows about the room, I whispered with a passionate gaze, "Will you stay, at least for a little while? I don't want you to go."

"Yes, I want to stay," he tenderly uttered with a press of my hand, "very much so. But, are you sure it's not too late? Maybe I really should go."

"No," I imploringly spritzed, "no, it's not too late, don't go. Let's not think of time. Besides, Aunt Bea wants you to stay. Feel the warmth of the fire, Ethan? It's burning just for us. We can talk of whatever you want, for as long as you want, get to know each other. Maybe we can even talk about tonight. Like you said, Ethan, maybe that's something we need to do."

He snatched the pillow from his elbow and tossed it nearer the flames, then pinched mine from my lap and gently flipped it by his on the rug close to the stones. "I'm staying right here, with you," he sweetly relented while I reached for one of Aunt Bea's quilts. And as we stretched to our elbows toward the snapping flames, pillows tucked beneath our chins, I flicked the blanket about our backs as we gazed into the crackling fire. "I too would like to talk," he softly added, "of anything. You know, with each step on the cobblestones, and every moment here tonight, I was hoping you'd ask me to stay a while."

"Comfortable?" I softly sighed, tugging on the blanket just a bit while pressing my left shoulder into his right.

"Oh yes, very much so," he whispered, gazing to my eyes aglow by the fire. "This is so nice. No, this is, wonderful."

"Now, where should we begin?" I quipped in a playfully way, flicking the blanket gently with my stocking feet to warm our chilly toes.

"Your aunt and uncle are nice," Ethan confessed, gazing to the fire. "I feel very comfortable, so at ease, Andrea, here, next to you."

"I feel the same way, Ethan," I sighed, tenderly nestling to his shoulder. "Yes, they are nice, very kind. You know, Uncle Jason is my father's uncle, but to me, he's mine."

For a few quiet moments we just stared to the fire, our cheeks warming as our shoulders sensuously pressed with pillows beneath our chests, yet with each flickering flame I could sense an anxiousness, a tinge of uncertainty simmering in both Ethan and I. Then as if compelled by that magical potion, we snapped our gaze into each other's eyes, and for a moment he seemed to be searching for a mysterious secret as my heart passionately pounded for his.

"Your eyes, Andrea," he hushed as a flurry of cracks and pops leapt from the logs, "are so tranquil, a pretty serene green, like pearls I once saw in the waters of Cape Cod Bay."

"What a nice thing to say," I blushed, "thank you, Ethan. You know," I shyly added, snapping my glance to the flames then back to his prying eyes, "yours are pretty nice too, a peaceful brown, with a quiet golden hue."

We nervously returned our stare to the crackling logs for a moment or two before whipping our eyes back to each other's gaze, he back to my pearl green and me back to his alluring gold, and with each fiery flicker it was as if we our hearts were gently touching, perhaps enthralled by the snapping flames. As my skin tingled with a sensuous surge I broke our tantalizing spell with a quick peer to the fire, and tenderly pressing into his shoulder, sputtered, "I'm nineteen, Ethan. What about you?"

"Me too," he softly replied, "just last December, the twenty-sixth."

"For me, it's the Third of July," I whispered with an arousing nudge of his shoulder. "We have other things in common too, Ethan, like the love of a chilly night warming by a fire." Then as Aunt Bea's clock pinged the half hour, my thoughts mysteriously strayed toward a more dourly path. "What brought you to King Street Ethan? Why were you there tonight?"

"I'll tell you," he said while raising the right palm, "in a moment, promise. But first, show me your left hand."

He gently cradled my palm in his hands and warmed my skin with his tender touch, then sliding his lips and kissing my fingers, whispered, "You make me feel good, Andrea, comfortable, safe, as if I were home."

A sensuous calm surged my body while his cheeks gleamed with each snap of the flames, and as his lips tantalized my skin, I excitedly sighed, "This is so nice, Ethan. I know we've only met, but I feel the same. Your touch is so peaceful, feels so right."

As we gazed to the flames crackling in the hearth, Ethan softly kissing my fingers while I stroked his cheeks and caressed his hands, I think we both sensed something unusual happening that night. We could feel our passions flaring in a way I had never known before, and although we didn't truly understand, we both sensed the wonder of the moment and knew it was good. After all these years I've come to believe some things are simply what they are, and sometimes, special things erupt in our lives for reasons known but to God.

"Ethan?" I whispered as he aroused my skin. "Why were you there tonight?"

He peered to the dancing flames and breathed a few quiet sighs, intently staring while softly caressing my hands as if searching for a way to unravel a tangled story. "I had heard some things earlier today," he softly began, "intriguing rumors which piqued my curiosity, yet caused me to worry. Oh, maybe I should first tell you, I'm in my second year of studies at Harvard, a college just west of here, across the Charles River. I'm mostly studying laws and histories, of Europe and some of the colonies, a bit of theology now and then too."

"How interesting," I clumsily sputtered in a nervous way, "and so challenging. Even down in Germantown we've heard of Harvard College. Oh, I'm sorry, Ethan. Sometimes I talk can too much."

"Now don't you worry about that," he tenderly advised, gazing to my eyes. "I want you to feel free with me, Andrea, say whatever's on your mind, anywhere, anytime. Where was I? Oh yes. After classes this morning I rode back to Queen Street, galloping across the old bridge and up to Edes and Gill's Print Shop, not far from what happened tonight. When I'm not studying I'm apprenticing with John Gill and Benjamin Edes, printing the Boston Gazette and Country Journal, along with other colonial things. I guess I mostly edit stories and set lots of type, the little letters and marks to be inked, and sometimes when Mr. Gill deems it right, I quill some stories of my own, mostly just little bits of news. I like to express my thoughts with ink, Andrea, like to quill things, very much."

"Maybe someday, I can read something you've quilled," I whispered while caressing his fingers. "I've heard of Mr. Gill and Mr. Edes, from Uncle Jason sputtering after supper about opinions in their Gazette. Uncle Jason is a printer too, Ethan, has been for years for a Mr. Draper. Maybe you know of him? He prints a pamphlet here in Boston."

"I do know of him," Ethan confessed, pressing his lips to my fingers, "mostly just talk at the shop. I'd love for you to read some of my things, perhaps before you leave, Andrea, and you could tell me what you think. And maybe I can send some of my writings to you, down the postal road now and then."

"Yes, maybe you could," I whispered as his sensuous fingers entwined with mine. "I would like that, very much."

"Good, I was hoping you'd say that. Now, back to tonight. I heard some talk when I was at the print shop earlier today, about some kind of trouble a few days before, a noisy little ruckus around noon last Friday between a young roper and a few redcoats outside Johnny Gray's shop. Henry said it was Mr. Gray's son, Sam, one of the men felled tonight."

"Oh, Ethan, it's so sad," I sighed, brushing a tear and pressing my fingers back to Ethan's tender hands.

"Yes, it is," he somberly whispered, "and even worse, Henry said he heard that Sam might have started the whole thing. It seems he said some unflattering things to one of the king's soldiers strutting by the rope shop, after asking if he wanted a bit of extra work, something the soldiers often do up here. But many in Boston don't like it, Andrea, saying they're taking work from colonists, stealing our shillings and pounds. I guess when that redcoat replied he could use the extra task, Sam scowled and blasted a few unkind words about scouring a privy. Well, Henry said that soldier dashed across the cobblestones and shouted some pretty ugly things, then scampered and returned with a few redcoat friends. That's when the tussle really broke out."

"I think I heard Uncle Jason talking about that," I proudly sputtered, "with a friend on Saturday, a bit before supper. But then, did something else happen, maybe today?"

I could see Ethan's eyes beginning to mist as he caressed my hands and peered into the fire, and wondered of the daunting visions swirling his mind. "It's going to be alright," I whispered, stroking his skin. "We're here, Ethan, safe and warm."

He batted his eyes and breathed a bit of relief as our cheeks flushed by the fire, then brushing his lips over my hands, tenderly sighed, "I'm so glad I'm here, Andrea, lying by these flames with you." Then kissing my fingers, he peered back to the snapping cracks and said, "I was setting type this afternoon, for the coming Gazette, when Henry dashed through the door. You know, he's only a few weeks younger than you, and has a place of books over on Hanover, just down the hill. That's where I met him a few years ago, in his shop, when I began stopping by to browse his books, and we quickly became friends. We like to talk about events of Boston and Massachusetts Bay, other colonies too, like your Pennsylvania, and when he comes by the print shop, he'll delve into colonial concerns with Mr. Edes. But when he came in today, Andrea, his expression was ripe with caution, and in a secretive way, told me Sam was trying to marshal colonists to King Street tonight, hoping I might help spread the word."

"Sam?" I asked with a puzzling squint. "You mean, that poor ropemaker?"

"Oh, I'm sorry, Andrea," Ethan gently conceded, "no. Mr. Adams, Samuel Adams, a pretty spirited colonist up here, a man some say our Royal Governor Hutchinson despises the most. I told Henry I'd meet him on King Street around eight tonight, nearer the statehouse after my printing duties were done, and we'd just watch."

"But, why? What was the gathering about?"

"Although Mr. Adams would surely deny this," Ethan slowly revealed while tantalizing my skin, "I've heard he's pretty influential with our sons up here, the sons of liberty in Boston. Henry said Sam, that is, the sons, wanted to assemble a raucous crowd on the cobblestones tonight, to show our royal governor and the crown just how much colonists disapprove of London's intrusive policies and laws. You see, Andrea, the king's soldiers are everywhere up here, strutting their boots on the wharfs, stones and docks and snows of the common, and his tax collectors are viewed by many in rather unflattering terms. There are even rumors customs men are challenging merchants simply trying to bring goods into the colony, secretly I suppose, outside the governor's royal system, and some say the king's men are thieves, stealing our wealth with taxes and duties."

"We've heard rumors of such things," I whispered, pressing my cheek to Ethan's shoulder, "down in Philadelphia and Germantown, and I've read of rather daring things, a kind of resistance, taking place up here now and then. Why, it wasn't too long ago when the Pennsylvania Gazette and our Evening Post exposed the disapproval by many of Boston to the crown's use of intrusive royal documents I think they call writs. But you know, Ethan, I don't think many in my colony really understand what is happening up here, and until tonight, I didn't realize how dangerous it's truly become."

"There's more, Andrea," he sputtered while caressing my hands, "a lot more. Some of the king's soldiers show contempt for colonists of Boston and Massachusetts Bay, striving to intimidate woman, children and men simply wanting to live, and sometimes galloping in growling groups to nearby hamlets and towns. They're known to flaunt their bayoneted muskets in threatening ways when marching about, and spew spiteful, belittling words from their mounts. A few scuffles have exploded between colonists and those royal patrols too, not unlike that tussle on Friday with Sam."

We hushed for a moment and gazed to the embers sparkling in the dwindling flames and crackling snaps, and as Ethan caressed my fingers and made little arousing swirls about the palms of my hands, he whispered with a sensuous glance, "Your skin, Andrea, is so soft, and your pearl eyes, soothe me so. I feel so calm lying here with you."

"I like you too, Ethan," I confessed, gliding my fingers about his hands as the fire flickered and slowed. "There's still so much to talk about. Perhaps we could use a few more logs?"

"Yes," he uttered with a playful nod before crawling from Aunt Bea's blanket and scampering on his knees to a little pile of short knotty logs and thin twisting branches just left of the stones of the hearth. Then carefully tossing twigs and limbs to the pulsating glow of ashen logs crumbling to sparkling embers, he sputtered while scampering back, "There, that's better. Now," he sighed, nestling to me under our quilt, "where were we?"

"We were confessing," I whispered as our shoulders pressed and his sensuous fingers aroused mine, "how we like each other."

"Oh, yes," he softly replied as his caress thrilled my skin. "I do, and did, from the first moment I saw you."

For a few tantalizing moments we simply relished in the warmth beneath our blanket, quietly staring to the resurging fire and glancing to our eyes now and then. And as our sides pressed and the flames began to snap and pop amidst arousing desires, I could feel sensuous passions bursting deep inside.

"I heard another scuffle did happen today," Ethan calmly continued in the glow of the crackling fire, "shortly before dusk east on King Street. It seems tempers flared between a royal captain and a maker of wigs, over some dumb debt. Henry said the merchant had become rather provocative, spouting angry taunts that the king's soldier was a 'bloody laggard' for not paying a few shillings for dressing his hair. I guess a bit of pushing and shoving took place amidst wild shouts, some flailing swings too, then after breaking free of the struggle, that captain continued his strut toward the docks."

"How frightful," I whispered, "such anger and friction up here. Would you like some wine, Ethan?" I wishfully asked, pivoting our thoughts. "Uncle Jason showed me some bottles from France, and said it would be alright. I know he won't mind."

"Yes, that sounds nice. Maybe some wine will help settle our souls over what happened out there tonight."

"Good, I'll be right back," I snapped, crawling from our blanket and tiptoeing through the foyer into the dim glow of a little kitchen candle. Then filling a pair of Aunt Bea's crystal goblets from a bottle near that tiny flame, I rushed back to Ethan as eerie shadows danced about the room. "Thank you," he sweetly sighed, gazing to my eyes as I set our wine by the pillows, slid beneath the quilt and nestled to his side.

We snuggled to our pillows and peered to the flickering flames, the stem of his goblet gently pinched in his fingers and my wine cupped in mine. And as our cheeks flushed amidst tranquil crackles and pops, we slowly twisted our gaze to each other's eyes for an arousing moment or two, then he tenderly pressed his lips to mine. "Oh, Ethan," I passionately sighed, "that's so nice."

"Yes, it is," he whispered with another luscious slide. "Your kiss is like a dream."

We looked deep into our eyes as if in a heavenly trance, sipped a splash of wine and pressed our lips once again in the glow of the fire, then returned our gaze to the darting flames. I could sense Ethan's thoughts beginning to wander as a somber mist sprayed his eyes, and watched as he bowed his stare to the sparkling embers. "To Crispus," he reverently sputtered, "and those other brave men. May God bless their souls."

We softly clicked our crystals and sipped as the fire snapped solemn shadows about the room, ghostly images that seemed to portent things nobody could have truly known, at least not then, not that night. "Those are such fine words," I whispered, pressing my hand to his. "It's strange, Ethan. Although I morn for those poor boys and men, their loved ones too, I feel this immense sense of pride. They clung to their convictions, and showed such great courage."

"I hadn't taken a stand," Ethan softly confessed with a reflective gaze to the fire, "not really, hadn't come to a solid position about it all. I guess I haven't been sure about the disloyal talk, the simmering reluctance of obedience to parliament and the crown, at least not until tonight. Some believe we must show our loyalty, stop all this resistance talk, that all the colonies should encourage greater allegiance to London. They say all the royal soldiers here in Boston, throughout Massachusetts Bay, are here to help maintain our colonial way, protect our villages, farms and towns from wilderness foes along the frontier, and our ports from enemies across the sea. Yet others like Mr. Gill, Henry and Sam Adams hold different views, speak of true liberty and perhaps forging a new way someday, a way less obedient to the king."

Ethan caressed my hand as I pressed to his shoulder and tasted more wine, and while shadows flickered about the room, I could sense our intimacy bloom as he confessed feelings to me. Then pressing his lips to his goblet and sliding an arousing kiss across my hand, he continued to expose his soul as his sensuous fingers tantalized my skin.

"Not too long ago," he confessed, "Henry asked me to join his sons of liberty group, and I even attended a few gatherings, the last one over on the snows of the common. Some of the sons talked about what they view as the king's transgressions against the colonies, and Mr. Adams was there too, stoking the flames and lambasting London. I almost joined that night, Andrea, but couldn't, not with the uncertainties that kept tugging my soul. After all, we're all citizens of England, all the colonies, and our loyalties have always been aligned with the crown. But after these past weeks and months, and especially after tonight, I have my doubts. I'm wondering if straddling a neutral course is still proper, and now I wonder if those musket blasts on King Street have fractured a fragile trust in so many, have tainted any notions of loyalty."

"I feel like you, Ethan," I whispered amidst the snapping fire, "starting to wonder such things too. Many down in Germantown, my father and mother and their Quaker friends at our meeting house too, just stay quiet or proclaim allegiance to the crown. And there are doctors, patients and nurses at my hospital who say we must remain loyal to the king and his royal governors. But I've been struggling about all this, just like you, and now, after what happened tonight, after seeing those brave men felled on the cobblestones, my doubts are creeping too."

The flickering fire snapped darting flames of yellows, reds and blues about the stones and unleashed ghostly shadows about the room, and as Ethan's soft eyes allured mine, Aunt Bea's clock chimed eleven times. "Your touch," he whispered, his fingers strumming my skin, "feels so good. Just lying here with you, is wonderful. You bring contentment to me, Andrea, and although we've only just met, I'd be the gayest man in the colonies just holding your hand and gazing to the waters of the harbor from a crusty old bench, or lying with you upon a patch of the common."

I remember how thrilling his words were, and was amazed to realize how I too had such feelings, arousing emotions surging my body since we nestled by the fire. "You say the most enchanting things," I hushed, caressing his fingers and wondering of the magic dripping his words. "I feel those things too."

Overwhelmed by a daring urge, I leaned and sailed my fancies to some passionate place with a press of my lips to his, and after a few wondrous slides, we released our sensuous kiss. I reached and pinched my goblet and Ethan gently snatched his, then gazing to his enticing eyes, I softly said, "To us, Ethan, lying by this fire, to a future yet to unfold."

"Oh, Andrea," he whispered as wine dripped my lips, "how I love your kiss. Yes, to us, and many more nights." And as we nestled by the spritzing fire, I snuggled to his shoulder and listened to his story of what truly transpired that wintry day of March.

"Henry said that soon after that royal captain returned to his strut toward the water, a redcoat guarding the king's customs house dashed across the cobblestones and toward the harbor to confront that merchant. I guess he heard the taunting shouts of that wigmaker and felt compelled to help the captain, but was a wee bit late. Now fully enraged and gripping his musket, that redcoat began to blast ugly shouts to that wigmaker, enflaming things like 'you disloyal wretch' and 'dumb Boston bastard!' But that daring merchant held his ground, and exploded with a flurry of 'go home you bumbling redcoat' and 'bloody lobster back!'"

"Oh my, Ethan," I gasped. "What did they do?"

"Some said they saw fire spritzing from that royal soldier's eyes, and in a kind of wild rage, he sent our wigmaker tumbling to the snowy stones with a bash of his musket. Then suddenly a bunch of colonists cast their fears and rushed to the merchant's aid, a few spewing defiant shouts as that sentry scurried back to the haven of his customs house. I guess it was that scuffle, Andrea, and other tussles and disturbing events over the past weeks and days that spurred Mr. Adams to act, calling for colonists to gather on King Street tonight."

"What about some of the others I saw tonight?" I softly asked, sipping wine and nestling to his shoulder. "I could see some rather scruffy looking men, not shopkeepers or merchants, fiery men wielding sticks and hurling shells, stones and ice. Who were they, Ethan? What were they doing there tonight?"

Ethan stared to the snapping flames while I caressed his hand and kissed his fingers, then explained amidst the crackling glow of the fire, "Henry said Sam asked those men to be there, Andrea, having gone over to the docks a bit before dusk. By eight tonight some fifty seamen had heeded Mr. Adams' call, and gathered on the snows of King Street." Then sliding his lips over my skin, he gazing to my eyes and somberly whispered, "Crispus was one of those men."

We pressed our shoulders and quietly gazed to the spritzing fire, and as a dash of sorrow brushed Ethan's eyes, he tenderly said, "He was a kind man, Andrea, a gentle man the seamen say. Why do such things happen to good people? If only moments could be undone."

"I don't know," I whispered, caressing his pain with my fingers. "Maybe there is no true answer, Ethan, not really. Maybe some things are always in God's hands."

"Thanks, Andrea," he sighed with a twisting gaze to my eyes, "for listening. Thanks for letting me talk with you like this, letting me ramble, for caring."

"I want to listen," I softly confessed as his sincerity aroused my passions. "And you don't ramble, Ethan, but feel deeply, and mean what you say. You make it easy for us to talk."

For a moment I wondered if Ethan could sense my pining desires for him, wanting to reach and comfort him as we peered to the fire, for he was baring his anguish and sensitive soul that night. I began to marvel of the magic bathing our hearts as dancing flames soothed our thoughts while casting shadowy greys about the room, and wonder of the sensuous urges surging us. Perhaps it was fear or a youthful failing to deny, but looking back after all these years, I didn't truly understand the fires that were flaring deep inside. Yet I knew I wanted to be near Ethan, feel the beat of his heart and caress his skin, and to my wondrous surprise, his soul was yearning for me too.

Ethan lifted my fingers to his lips and pressed soft little kisses, sending my arousals swirling amidst the glow of crackling flames, and as he caressed my desires, that ornate clock atop the mantel pinged the midnight hour. The moments of our first night had come to a close while its ring sounded the first of a new day, chimes which quickly spurred a fear that our precious time might be over. I didn't want Ethan to go, and glancing from the snapping fire to his sensuous eyes, desperately hoped he too wanted to stay, talk of Harvard College and Boston, of his desires, fears and dreams.

"Ethan?" I timidly uttered as his lips thrilled my skin. "I know it's late, but I want, hope, you'll stay a little longer. We can talk about easier things, less daunting, more intimate things, if you want."

"I don't want to go," he whispered as his fingers caressed my hand, "but know I must, in a little while. I want to stay here, with you, Andrea, talk about things which matter to you, to both of us. I want us to talk open and free, and not worry if our words are just right. I want us to get to know each other, at least a little more, tonight."

"Oh, Ethan," I sighed, nestling to his shoulder as our fingers entwined, "I want those things too. Yet, before we talk do, and I hope you don't mind, after what happened tonight, I've got to know a bit more of what is happening up here in Boston. I've heard of troubling events and things in other colonies, over in Virginia and in Georgia too, but mostly just hazy stories and sketchy rumors, tales that seem rather placid compared to Massachusetts Bay."

"I'm afraid, Andrea," he sputtered with a tinge of weary in his tone, "what you saw here tonight has been brewing for some time, since all those royal soldiers came to Boston a few years ago. I've tried to ignore it, just tend to my studies at Harvard and duties at the print shop, but after tonight, things could spin out of control. I guess what happened on King Street was only a matter of time, and now, God only knows what will happen next."

"Sometimes, Ethan," I whispered while gently fiddling with his fingers, "I think I dwell in fantasy too much. I just wish a mighty storm would sweep these troubles out to sea. But that's not reality, is it, and I guess it never will be, not after this night. I suppose all I can do is just go home to Germantown, back to my nursing, live as best I can just like you, like all of us. Tell me about your school, Ethan, about your village of Lexington too. Tell me more about you."

"I left Lexington about two years ago," he confessed, sliding his lips to my fingers while gazing to the fire, "coming to Boston around the fall of 1768. I was just beginning my studies at Harvard College, Andrea, wanting to challenge my mind, learn about the world."

Ethan's words oozed sensitivity and his eyes sparkled with each snap of the flames, and as my desires flared with each press of his lips, he softly added, "My dad, Patrick, has come to know many here in Boston over the years, mostly due to his dealings with his tavern in Lexington. Maybe someday, Andrea, we'll go there together, visit dad at our Buckman Tavern. It was dad and our village printer, Mr. Giles, who made it possible for me to come here, live in Boston and study at Harvard College. They arranged my apprenticeship with John Gill and Mr. Edes at their print shop, ensuring of course, that it didn't interfere with my studies, and my boarding in Mr. Gill's house. I hope to finish my studies in two years, in the spring. Now, tell me about you."

My heart began to anxiously flutter knowing Ethan wanted to hear what I was going to say, for it meant that he cared, that my words mattered to him, and that made me feel good. "I've always lived in Germantown," I gently explained, gazing to the fire as he tantalized my skin. "I was born in our little home, Ethan, just months after mother and father sailed from the Netherlands."

"You must have been an awfully cute little girl," he teasingly quipped, kissing my hands and sliding his lips about my fingers.

"Mother does say I was a bit flirtatious," I playfully sighed, "in a rather frolicsome way. I have my precious grandmother's name, and sometimes, I wonder what she might think of me today. When I was little I wanted help others, and when I grew older, knew I wanted to help the injured and sick. For the past couple years I've been studying and training to be a nurse, at the Pennsylvania Hospital in Philadelphia. I like what I'm doing, Ethan, very much."

"I can tell," he whispered while snuggling to my side and making my skin tingle with sensuous little swirls, "can hear it in your voice, see it in your eyes. And it showed out there tonight, on the stained snows of King Street. It takes a caring person to want to help others like you do, a special quality I greatly admire."

"Oh, Ethan, your words are so kind. But I must admit, sometimes what I do can be rather sad, women and men with frightful fevers, injuries and ills, and children with smallpox and other dreadful ails. As trying as it is to watch someone wither, never to return to their home, there's joyous relief when another is nursed back to health. It makes my work, very rewarding."

"It must be hard to see those things, to know some won't go home, yet I think you've found a way to grasp the good that comes with easing their pain. And it must be so fulfilling when others are healed, in a sense, made whole."

"It is, Ethan, very fulfilling. And thanks, for listening, caring. It means so much to me."

For a few tantalizing moments we nestled upon feathery pillows beneath the quilted colors of Aunt Bea's blanket, our shoulders sensuously pressing in the glow of the flickering fire, and with each snap of the flames I bathed in a wondrous sensation. I realized Ethan wanted to understand me, and just knowing that comforted me that night, a soothing memory I've cherished all these years.

"Oh," I quickly sputtered as he caressed my hands, "I like to sew too, very much. I've snipped and stitched many things over the years, dainty bags and quilt blankets, breeches and stockings, scarves, dresses and shirts. It's a kind of escape for me, so relaxing."

I flicked our blanket over our stocking feet once again and tugged it nearer our shoulders, then revealed a few more things while reaching for his hand. "I love what I do at the hospital, Ethan, but it's sewing that's my true passion. Not only do I relieve some of the stresses of life when I snip and stitch, but I'm able to express myself in a fulfilling way by creating so many colorful patterns and designs with my needle, cloth and thread. In a way, sewing is my creative side, is who I really am deep down inside. And that, Ethan, makes me feel good, about myself."

"I think I understand what you mean," Ethan whispered as the crackling fire flushed our cheeks. "I can tell by your words how sewing makes you feel, and the sparkle in your eyes shows how you love it so. Maybe it even helps you in your nursing, brings a steady calm to your touch, like you showed on the cobblestones tonight, and when you consoled me. I feel those same kinds of things, Andrea, when I'm quilling words, expressing my thoughts. You know, I don't just help with a tidbit now and then for Mr. Gill's Gazette, but quill little poems too. And I've been learning a bit more about little passionate tales by reading intriguing poems from across the sea, like those by a man named Krasicki, from the Kingdom of Poland."

"Ethan," I sighed, pressing to his shoulder while squeezing his hands, "do you think we'll see each other again? You could touch one of my quilted treasures, and I could read one of your sweet poems. Oh, Ethan, I want us to. Do you think we will?

"Yes, I do," he whispered, kissing my fingers, "no doubt. We can while you're still visiting, then sometime later, hopefully very soon."

"If we believe enough, Ethan, keep hope, good things will happen. Don't you think so?"

"I do. Even after what happened tonight, the simmering uncertainty, I do."

We gazed to the dwindling fire for a moment or two as Ethan's fingers tantalized my skin, and watched as crackling logs collapsed to the sparkling embers and ash. "Who is that poet, Ethan," I whispered while gently lifting his fingers to my lips, "that man from Poland? I don't know of him."

"They say he has royal ties in his homeland, a prince of some kind, and his essays and poems are brushed with a Polish spirit of enlightenment, words just beginning to trickle into the colonies. I first read one of his poems at Henry's shop, printed in a London pamphlet, the Monitor if I recall, just one of a handful of copies sailed into Boston by a seaman from Ireland. His words are so passionate, Andrea, bathed of patriotism, convictions that seem to spring from his soul in an intriguing style I find appealing. I hope, someday, I too will be able to capture such emotions with my quill."

"I have a sense, Ethan, a tingling feeling inside, that you already do."

"That's nice, Andrea. I hope so. God knows I'm trying. Say, maybe you could read one of my poems tomorrow? I have classes in the morning and one early in the afternoon, then will be at the print shop until dusk. How about if I come by then, say, around six?"

I pressed my lips to his fingers and gazed to his yearning eyes, and as the dwindling fire snapped and sparkled on the stones, I desperately searched for words I hoped would not disappoint him so. Then I timidly explained, realizing there were none, "I leave tomorrow, Ethan, for Germantown. I'm so sorry, for both of us."

He batted his eyes and caressed my hands in a bewildering way, staring to the tiny flames spritzing the ashen embers, while I nudged my cheek to his, squeezed his fingers and softly said, "I don't want to go, Ethan, but must. I've got to get back to mother and father, to my nursing at the hospital. Uncle Jason is taking me to the coach house in the morning, then I'm off on the postal road for Germantown. I do want to see you again, very much so, and want to read your poems, but for now, it's just not meant to be. I'll quill to you soon, promise. Will you send me a letter, Ethan, with maybe a poem too?"

I could feel the dejection surging his body as he tugged my hands to his lips and gazed to the crumbling fire, and could sense his fraying hopes with each passionate kiss of my fingers. "I'm sorry too," he somberly whispered, "yet understand. I guess you're right, it just isn't meant to be, at least not now. Yes, I will, Andrea, send a letter and many more, along with a poem now and then too. I suppose until things change, we'll just touch each other with tender strokes of our quill." He just stared to the dwindling flames for a moment in a forlorn hush, then gazed to my eyes and said, "I don't want you to go."

"I know," I sighed as a mist sprayed our eyes. "But we'll quill letters, Ethan, and in our own private way, discover special things about each other. Our feelings and thoughts quilled to parchment will last forever, and we'll be able to hold them, read them when lonely, and touch each other all over again."

"Maybe you're right, but it won't be the same. I'm going to miss you, and fear I won't know what to do. We'll be so far apart. But I do hope, Andrea, our letters help, give us a sense of being together, at least for now."

"Oh, Ethan, my stomach has been churning all night about these things. I guess we'll just have to pray, and cling to hope. You know, we'll only be some three hundred miles from each other. That doesn't sound too bad, does it, Ethan?"

"It might as well be three thousand!" he sputtered with a frustrating gaze to the glowing embers and tiny flames. And as I held his hands and caressed his soul with tender strokes of my fingers, he softly added as his angsts eased, "I'm sorry, Andrea, you're right. That's not too far. But it is, disappointing."

"I know," I sighed as our fingers entwining, "I feel that too."

I could feel my heart pounding with desire as if it might leap from my chest at any moment, and as we nestled and gazed to the quieting fire, I wondered how such passion could become so consuming in just a few short hours. Why, only a day before the notion of we didn't exist, yet at that moment I knew my ways had magically changed forever. My soul was now bathing in serenity and my heart was erupting in a rapturous beat, and all because I was simply lying with a man from Lexington named Ethan.

What will mother and father say, I frantically wondered, we being friendly Quakers and he of Presbyterian faith, and what will others of Germantown think? "It doesn't make sense," came the doubting shouts from dark corners of my mind, "and hundreds of miles apart!" Yet amid my taunting pangs were passions spritzing from my heart, and at that moment I knew what I would do, knew I'd toss my fears to the winds and find a way to be near Ethan, bathe in our desires. And I wondered what would become of us in the months and years to come, wondered of the sensuous hours awaiting the rest of our lives.

"I already miss you," Ethan whispered, gazing to my eyes. "Damn, and it's getting late, almost one. But I don't want to go, Andrea, not just yet."

"You don't have to go, not now. The fire needs another log or two, and there's more wine in the kitchen. Stay, Ethan, a little longer."

I quickly tiptoed and filled our goblets as Ethan tossed a few more twigs and logs to the embers sparkling the stones, then uniting with pillows beneath Aunt Bea's blanket, we nestled in the glow of the resurging fire. Our fingers entwined as the tiny flames began to flicker and snap, casting wintry shadows about the room, and with each arousing caress we pressed closer, reveling in our precious moments.

"You said you were reared Presbyterian, Ethan," I softly said, veering to a more spiritual place while nestling to his side, "and since my ties are of the Quaker faith, I wonder how different we might be, how such beliefs are reconciled. My Society of Friends holds the teachings of Jesus rather close, of kindness and simplicity, and look to God as righteous and caring, while trying not to intrude upon the ways of others. I like those ideas, Ethan, and think showing compassion is a good thing. What do you think? I mean, what are your thoughts about faith?"

"I wish more people held your Quaker beliefs," he confessed while caressing my hands and gazing to the snapping flames. "Showing kindness and compassion, love and understanding are good things. You know, I've heard stories of Quakers up here too, some time ago, tales of little groups venturing into the Colony of Massachusetts Bay, simple people just wanting to tend their shops, farms and homes, just wanting to live and pray. But I guess others feared them, viewed them as threats to their puritan ways, so they shunned them until they just faded away, escaping to more friendly places."

"I didn't know those things," I sighed, warming his hands. "People can be rather vicious sometimes, Ethan, cloaking their cruelty in the name of God."

"Yes, they can. But that's not what I've known. Mom loved her Presbyterian church over in Lexington, Andrea, took me to services every Sunday when I was young too, yet dad was a bit indifferent to it all. I guess we both have drifted away over the years since mom's been gone, then after coming to Boston to study, my beliefs have continued to change. I've now been exposed to many theologies, differing religions and philosophies, various views of God and spirituality, and there's one they call Deism."

"I don't know of that faith, Ethan, that Deism. Tell me more."

"I've only read a little bit," he timidly confessed while sliding his fingers across my skin, "but I'll try. The name comes from Latin, and it's rather new, more philosophical I suppose than a true religion, more of ideas about God's role in nature. They seem to profess a belief in the goodness of Jesus, yet espouse a distrust of religion, suggesting too many have been corrupted by greed and superstition. I think they view reasoning and what they call laws of nature as being the true structure of God, not religions of men, and while most say Jesus was a wise man, they have doubts he's really the son of God. I'm sorry, Andrea, sometimes I get carried away. Do you want to hear more?"

"I do," I whispered, nestling to his shoulder and watching the snapping flames.

"I was hoping you'd say that," he softly said while caressing my hands. "I read that it's their belief that God, or as some say Nature's God, Father of Lights, Supreme Being or simply our Creator, formed the order of our universe then set it free, putting all the planets, galaxies and stars into motion, then backing away. I've heard there's an emerging flock of colonists leaning toward such views, some rather prominent like your colony's Doctor Franklin and others in Maryland and Virginia. Is all that true, Andrea? I don't know. I just think we should be kind to one another, don't you?"

"I do. Yet, like others, I suppose I have doubts about those kinds of things now and then, wonder of religions, but I still believe in the roots of my Society of Friends. Do you believe in God, Ethan?"

"I think so. I mean, I want to, hope so. I have this gripping conviction that only through God, and I like the name Creator, can any of us really be true to ourselves. But I must admit I've had doubts about Jesus, whether he really is the son of God or simply the wisest of men. I just don't know. Yet no matter what, I like to think our Creator exists, that there is a kind, merciful God who comforts us all during the challenges of life."

"I like to think of God that way too," I hushed as he pressed his lips to my hand. Then feeling a sense of relief knowing our beliefs seemed so close, I softly added, "Your willingness to expose these things to me, Ethan, your honesty, is so appealing."

A tranquil quiet settled the room as we watched the flames snapping and crackling the fiery logs, and after a moment or two my thoughts began to drift to the terrible plight of that man who died in Ethan's arms, and the shackling of so many innocent people. "What do you think about slaves, Ethan, about the thousands of Negro women, children and men who toil in the colonies? I mean, how do feel about the buying and selling of people, simply because of the shade of their skin?"

"I wish more colonists talked about it," he spritzed with conviction while nestling closer to my side. "I think it's vile, a wicked, diabolical trade reeking injustice."

"Some in Germantown say that trade is vital to the growth of the colonies," I confessed with disdain, "proper people, and I wonder of the wretchedness of their minds. I've heard Philadelphia merchants along the river docks rationalize that evil system too, suggesting it keeps our colonies competitive with those across the sea. Sometimes I wonder, Ethan, what God must think of our inhumanity."

"I think we feel the same way," he softly confessed while staring to the flickering fire, "and that, Andrea, makes me feel good, about us." Then pausing for a moment, he batted his eyes and added, "I didn't know much about Crispus, but heard he was once enslaved on a big farm somewhere in the Colony of Georgia, or maybe it was South Carolina, toiling fields sprouting crops like tobacco. Someone even said his father had been punished a few times by a lofty farmer, and that Crispus witnessed the final whipping of his father, hiding in the shadows when just a boy. Do you want to hear more?"

"Yes, as awful as that sounds, I do. I want to know about your friend, Ethan, want to know the truth of that dreadful trade."

"They say he hid amid brush and trees and watched as plantation men bound his father with twine, arms twisted behind his shirtless back, then with a fraying rope near a humble barn, dangled him by his hands from the knotty limb of an oak. I guess he had defied some fiendish rule, and for hours just hanged from that tree before dozens of weary women, children and men, Crispus' three little cousins and their horrified mother too. But before being unbound that sweltering day, his bare back was whipped into a sea of red by one of those haughty men lashing thin leather tails, and after cutting him down, he died in the arms of Crispus' aunt just as the sun began to fade. I long for the day, Andrea, when the evils of bigotry vanish with the souls of wicked men."

"Oh, my God," I gasped, cringing at the barbarity of man, "how cruel, that poor man. It must have been awful for Crispus."

"It was a few years later, when he was nineteen or so, that Crispus escaped from that wretched place and made his way north to Boston. I've heard he was taunted by some up here, Andrea, unkind people who feared those of darker skin, and some even tried to push him back to where he'd fled. According to an old tale, a few almost shackled him into the hull of a merchant ship and sailed him back to that farm, and all for a lousy handful of shillings and pounds. Yet Crispus persevered up here, beginning a life amidst the sea, and there's a rumor he was aided by some mysterious Bostonian, perhaps Mr. Hancock."

"It's so sad about his father," I sighed as Ethan tenderly caressed my hands, "ghastly. Yet, how Crispus managed to escape and start anew, is so moving. Whoever that mysterious Bostonian was, Ethan, showed daring grit."

"Yes, character and courage," Ethan sighed. "Maybe someday that whole vile system of slavery will be banished from the colonies. Maybe, someday, everyone will treat all people with kindness."

"Maybe," I sputtered with a dash of disbelief. "Yet sometimes, Ethan, I just don't know."

He wrapped his hands about my fingers and softly caressed my skin while we spoke of our youth, families and homes, and as we gazed to the snapping fire I could sense an evolving closeness that comes from the heart when speaking the truth. With each passing moment we slowly grew to know each other, revealing our hopes and exposing our fears, and with each passionate whisper and tender touch, his sensuousness bathed my soul. Although we didn't know what the future might bring, I knew that Ethan had a mysterious way of calming my despairs, a magical allure I wanted to hold.

For a quiet moment we sipped our wine amid sparkling embers and crackling logs, then set our goblets near the hearth's stones and gazed into each other's eyes, as if searching for a luscious treasure. "Tell me of your dreams, Ethan," I whispered while gliding my fingers across his palms. "What do you want in life? Where do you see yourself, in years to come?"

"Oh, maybe, I don't know," he shyly uttered with a reflective stare to the fire. "Maybe I just want a tranquil life, calm in which to quill things, discover the passions of life, to delve into the soul. Yet I often wonder just what those things really are, and sometimes think such things can only be found with a special other, that such things only dwell within the heart. I don't know. I guess I just don't want to settle for things, cling to what's convenient, slide into a life void of passion, a haven shielded by a stoic cold. Maybe, Andrea, what I really want, is to quill my dreams while immersed in serenity, a life of two yearning hearts bathed in absolute love."

"That sounds so beautiful," I sighed with a wanton gaze to his eyes. "I've never heard anyone say such appealing things, speak of love in such a magical way." As we peered to the fire and our fingers caressed I could feel my soul crying with desire, and wanted to believe such passion was real. Then wondering if our lives might truly become entwined, I wishfully asked, "Do you really think such love exists?"

"I'd like to think so, I hope so. I wonder of that calm place, where I'd be free to quill my visions and hopes without worrying about what the king or his royal men believe, a place where I could unleash my soul. They say Mr. Adams envisions a nation of our own someday, and there are others in the colonies with views like that too, men like Henry and some I know at Harvard College. It's their dream, a vision some mock, say is delusional. I guess if I were to find my absolute love, and have the liberty to quill my thoughts without fear, then that serenity I seek would follow, exposing my dreams. I wonder, Andrea, if maybe, such things could happen with you and me."

"Maybe," I whispered as our cheeks flushed in the fiery glow. "It's easy to see how much you love to quill, and your vision of serenity, is so appealing. Yet I wonder, Ethan, if such wondrous things can come true. I want to believe in that passionate place, where your tales and poems are free, but will the king ever let our colonies go?"

"I don't know," Ethan uttered with a sensuous glance, "I hope so, only not just to quill, but for you and me." He began kissing my hands with tender slides as we nestled with pillows beneath our blanket, and as my desires exploded by the spritzing fire, he softly asked, "What about you, Andrea? Tell me of your dreams, what you want in life."

"Your words have made me look deep inside," I sighed as he kissed my fingers, "to wonder of real things. I think I've always needed to feel secure, be accepted by those around me, and yet I have this secret, simmering desire for more. While you have your poetry, I have my sewing, and while you have your studies I have my nursing. In a way you and I want and have similar things, for I too dream of finding serenity, then holding it close to my heart. Your kind of passion, Ethan, that absolute love, sounds divine, and maybe someday, our time will come."

As flickering flames snapped eerie shadows about the room, that mantel clock suddenly chimed the chilling hour of two, and for a moment Ethan gazed to my eyes with gloom. "Damn," he frustratingly sputtered, "I think it's time for me to go. I've class early in the morning, in just seven hours. I don't want to go!" Then peering deep into my eyes and caressing my fingers, he tenderly added, "I want you to know, Andrea, meeting you tonight has changed my life. These hours with you have been wonderful." He pressed his lips to mine, and with each sensuous slide in the glow of the fire, my heart cried with joy.

We slowly released our lips after several tantalizing moments, then as a frantic chill raced my skin I passionately reached for Ethan and pressed one more luscious kiss. "Oh, Ethan," I sighed as mist sprayed our eyes,

"I'm so glad we found each other tonight. I love all the things we talked about, and will hold tight to the memory of us lying before the fire. I'll write soon, I promise."

I flicked the blanket as we rose in stocking feet from our warm haven into the cold, then quietly snatching two scraps of parchment from Uncle Jason's little table, Ethan and I quilled an address to send our letters, each a secure place. He stroked the home of Mr. Gill in Boston where he roomed with board while studying at Harvard, and I, desperate to cling to privacy and tame a simmering anxiousness, quilled the Pennsylvania Hospital in Philadelphia. With longing gazes we exchanged our tiny pieces then tiptoed to the foyer, and as the waning fire popped and snapped shadows about the room, I watched with misty eyes as Ethan slid my little sheet into the pocket of his breeches, laced his shoes, wrapped in the wool of his coat and pressed his tricorn.

I dabbed a tear as we stood hushed at the door, awkwardly grappling with the coming moment of having to say farewell, then wrapping my fingers about his hands while gazing to his sensuous eyes, I whispered, "Goodnight, Ethan."

"Goodbye, Andrea," he tenderly replied, pressing his lips to mine. "I'll miss you, very much, and think of you, every day."

"I'll miss you too," I sighed with a final slide before gazing to his misting eyes. "Quill me, Ethan, soon."

Suddenly the door clicked open with an eerier creak and an icy chill burst into the foyer, then as our misty eyes latched one final time, I watched in a teary hush as Ethan dashed into the Boston night. I pressed the door tight and quietly stepped to my little room, shuffling past our special place by those fading flames, then sliding my stockings and tossed my dress to a nearby chair, found solace with my linens, blankets and pillows. My thoughts were consumed of Ethan as I bundled in bed, and as tiny shadows roamed about the door, I wondered of the things swirling his mind as he scurried down the hill and scampered on the icy stones to Mr. Gill's house. I tried to envision each of his lonely steps through the cold, and wondered if he could still feel my lips and sense my passions erupting by the fire with each snowy stride on the cobblestones.

The grisly sounds of musket blasts on King Street would weave my thoughts as I watched the shadows of the dying flames, awful visions tamed by the wondrous memories of Ethan and me that wintry night. I pressed to my pillows and tugged the quilts to my chin and wondered of the intimate things we had talked of that night, and could still feel his body nestling with mine near the snapping fire, could still taste his lips, each sensuous kiss. And as I prayed for tranquil dreams of our first hours, sometime during the early moments of Tuesday, March the Sixth, I drifted to sleep in my little room. Although I didn't know it as of that precious night, I'd come to realize that Ethan had shattered my notions of life, that nothing would ever be the same.

After four days and three nights of creaking and swaying down the snowy ruts of the postal road I was back in Germantown, and for many days I found I couldn't quill a letter to Ethan. Looking back after all these years I suppose I was confused, didn't truly understand my feelings in those days, and perhaps was somewhat protective in my youth. Maybe I was afraid to accept or admit the passions burning in my heart, wary of quilling the truth of the fires burning deep inside. Yet, whatever fears I may have had were soon tossed to the anxious winds, for on the first Monday of spring, just three weeks from that magical Boston night, I received Ethan's first letter.

I had rolled in father's carriage to the hospital early that morning for training on special ways of healing, of readings and talks followed by several hours of assisting another nurse with tending to dozens infirmed and ailing. And as I swept through the door and stepped the oak slats of the hall toward my nursing desk, that's when I saw it, folded parchment propped against my tin of ink and cups of quills. With each click of my shoes my eyes peered with excitement, for I could see words of Boston wondrously stroked upon its upper creases, and fixing my stare to Ethan's letter, felt a surge of joy rush my body. At that very moment, the fretful feelings which had gripped my soul those waiting weeks suddenly surrendered to the passions swirling my heart, and I realized how truly I had missed my Ethan.

I quickly slid to the elm slats of my nursing desk chair, and as my heart pounded with arousing beats, snatched the folded parchment with my tingling fingers. Then glancing toward the hospital door to ease my anxious feelings, snapping my stare about the hall to ensure I was alone, I flicked its waxy seal, unfolded its creases, and began to slowly read Ethan's words.

"Dear Andrea," his tantalizing lines began, "How I've missed you so." I remember the rapture surging deep inside as I read his words, and how a sensuous serenity soothed my body knowing Ethan's feelings were unchanged, that he longed for me so. He quilled of trying things that happened in Boston in the hours and days after the musket blasts on King Street that March night, of pleasantries of his studies at Harvard College and duties at Mr. Gill's print shop too, and expressed tender words of his father in Lexington. They were the important things of his life, and although I truly wanted to know everything, my heart pounded wildly when he confessed his feelings about us near the hearth that night. "I was so content just lying with you," he confided, "nestling beneath our blanket, touching and talking in the glow of the fire."

As wondrous as his letter truly was, his final lines were the most precious of all, feelings from his soul about us that cold March night, poetic lines he quilled just for me and called *first night*. No one had ever written anything for me, and as my fingers caressed the ink of each word, I wondered of the artistic fires that passionately burned inside him. "Ever since that night, Andrea, my heart has ached for you. Then yesterday, during a chilly rain just before dawn, those feelings were consuming, oozing from my heart and dripping my quill. I miss you terribly, Andrea, and anxiously wait for your letter. Love, Ethan." I could sense his passion as I caressed each line, and feel our hearts wrapping as I read each thrilling word.

march moon gazes, scarlet coats, grisly royal muskets blaze
samuel and james, crispus, sam and pat, fearless and brave
daring cries spray the night, lives ooze boston cobblestones
echoes weep about the dark, tattered hopes, spattered snows

praying for souls, mending wounded, easing grieving hearts
her eyes caress, green pearls warm me, escape to our hearth
ghastly visions fade, consuming anticipation vanquishes tears
fanciful whispers, precious dreams, her touch calms my fears

andrea nestles beside me, desires flare amid snapping flames
shadows dance to crackling songs, fiery bursts tantalize, tame
two souls enticingly gaze, passions entwine, swaddle our night
embers aglow, emotions inflamed, caresses of sensuous heights

chilling crystals sprinkle panes, touching hands tingle tranquilly
andrea's lips stoke my desires, rapturous thrills arouse serenely

*longingly pressing amid spritzing flames, luscious kisses delight
passions bathe alluring dreams, hearts embrace our first night*

Chapter III

Lavender Lisianthus

Through all these years a gentle peace has comforted me with each memory of Ethan, a tranquil flow of tenderness which settles my soul, and has since those days so long ago. Although somewhat mystifying to me in those earliest hours, Ethan and I had uncovered a mystery few ever do, a wonderment that cries to be grasped tightly, a connection so preciously unique I have yet to fully understand. It was as if our souls had magically entwined, a twisting and churning magnificence, immersing within the essence of existence itself.

We seemed to be able to perceive each other without words, with a simple touch or gentle gaze, or with a passionate quill from afar. It was as if Ethan and I knew of the very emotions simmering within each, could sense our most intimate desires, comprehend the dreams our hearts pounded and cried for. Yet, perhaps the most amazing thing of all, after all this time, is that I feel the same joyous splendor this very moment as I did on that snowy March night in Boston all those years ago.

Ethan possessed a rare ability to emerge from the haze which at times can cast menacing shadows about our lives, and bring a focus upon the true nature of things, to perceive inner thoughts and core emotions in a clearer way than most. He once spoke of his times discussing colonial issues with seamen when strolling Boston's docks or with friends after studies in Cambridge, or with merchants at Mr. Gill's print shop or farmers in his father's Lexington tavern, saying, "we might not always agree, but they would know how I felt, and why."

He seemed to listen a bit more than others might too, showing an attractive attentiveness, displaying a real consideration for another's opinions and thoughts. And he desperately avoided indulging in unflattering embellishment or displaying an unsightly character of obnoxious verbosity, while believing it an unkind weakness to strike at an opposing opinion in an ugly way in an effort to elevate one's own purpose. Ethan was more introspective than most colonists I knew in those days, perhaps grasping a greater intensity of conviction, a confident shyness which would sparkle from his golden eyes. It was all those intriguingly caring things which attracted me so, an aura of serene understanding which pulled me deep into him.

As I reached and tugged the knitted shawl dangling my shoulders and glanced to Samuel rocking his chair, peering silently into the summer winds, awaiting my coming words, I wondered with a dash of sorrow of all the years that have passed since those turbulent days. So many who had witnessed the upheaval have since grown cold, relegated to the annuls of our colonial past, and I've slowed with the graying of old, memories vanquished to aging creases of my mind and soul. Yet, I have never ceased to feel Ethan's calming words and tender touch.

I nudged my chair into a softer rock and slid my hand into the warmth of my dress pocket, to the serenity of Ethan's aging poem, and as I gazed to the elms along the lane, their leaves dancing a soothing rustle in a gentle July breeze, I could feel his sensuous passions with each caress of his words. As so many times before, on lazy summer days and chilling winter nights, simply touching the parchment brushed my soul with a tranquil essence while unleashing wondrous memories of Ethan and our colonial past. I quietly rocked while Samuel peered to the distant limbs swaying in the morning summer winds, and with each slide of my fingers, my thoughts drifted to Ethan's first hours in the colonies back then, to the swirling fragrances of our generation before the war.

Ethan once said his mother had described the day he was born as "frigidly cold," that the sky had been cloaked with a dark layer of roiling gray that day, a steady stream of clouds that blotted the mass of stars twinkling the winter night. Flurrying snow had blanketed the icy fields and drifted about the ruts and stones of Lexington's roads that day, brushing his village and surrounding farms in a sea of white into the late hours of that Saturday night. Then in the chilling darkness on the day after Christmas, Ethan arrived a little before midnight, December the Twenty-sixth, 1750.

The reign of George Augustus was in its twenty-third year by that snowy winter night, a man who had been declared Knight of the Garter some fifty years before by his father's royal cousin, Queen Anne. It seems that throughout the years he had been showered with an array of important titles too, stylish monikers such as the Prince of Wales and the Duke of Cambridge and Brunswick-Luneburg, while some preferred to call him the Viscount Northallerton or Baron Tewkesbury, or Earl of Milford Haven. But as of that special December night most of Great Britain simply called him King George the Second, the royal monarch of Scotland, Ireland and England, the power over the Thirteen Colonies across the sea.

The serene sounds of violin strings and harpsichord chimes spurred by the wizardry of Johann Sebastian Bach had fallen silent across the nations of Europe just months before, when his vibrant cantatas and soothing concertos were laid to rest in a Leipzig field. And as those chilling flurries brushed the Colony of Massachusetts Bay white, Spencer Phips, the crown's royal governor, was in his second year of four of holding power for the king as of that December night.

The Sheehan farm was a mile or so northeast of Lexington, two hundred acres of colonial soil nestled just south of the road leading to the village of Billerica, a rustic little home where icy winds drifted the snows and howled against the window panes that wintry night. Yet the frigid air was being held at bay by sturdy farmhouse walls, and being tamed by a little bundle of flaming logs burning wildly in the colorful stones of the fireplace, spraying warmth about the parlor and two side bedrooms.

Patrick Sheehan, Ethan's nervous father, was anxiously pacing near the fire flickering about the hearth, while Ethan's mother Elizabeth was in her bedroom on the south side of the house, just right of the parlor, struggling to give birth to her only son. As she cried sporadic sighs amid painful moans while twisting about her bed beneath damp linens and blankets, Ethan's father shuffled upon the oak slats of the farmhouse floor as impatient shadows roamed about the room in desperate anticipation.

The tiny flickers of a lone candle and glow of an oil lamp flame did little to comfort her anguishing sighs, and as Ethan's father paced nervously near the hearth just outside the door, Lexington's only physician tended caringly to his mother. James Newman was not a real doctor, not like those of my Pennsylvania Hospital, but as Ethan once said, "Doc's our village apothecary," a mixer of medicines who did his best to mend sick and injured women and children, shopkeepers, merchants and farmers. And on that frigid winter night Doc Newman was donning the special hat of midwife, and with the help of Abigail, his dutiful assistant and cherished wife, was trying to calm birthing pains while bringing Ethan into the world. They were two of Lexington's more revered elders who had settled in the village after a spring rain many years before, just days after their Boston nuptials.

I remember Ethan confiding, "Doc had a rather distinctive appearance about him," saying he was a bit shorter than most in those days, "plump about his belly, with bushy-gray edging the back of his rosy cheeks and hair slowly twirling past his ears in thick white curls." The ruffled sleeves of his blue silken shirt were crumply rolled to his elbows as he shuffled about the edges of Ethan's mother's bed, and the skin of his wrists and hands, moist by steaming water, glistened in the glowing lamp and candle light. Although fifty or so as of that wintry night, his hazel eyes were focused and his hands were sure and steady, as if the passage of years had reverted to a more youthful life.

Several strips of clean white cloth dangled Abigail's left wrist as she comforted Ethan's mother's hand and passed needed things to Doc while holding the glow of the lamp a bit closer now and then. She was a little shorter than he and somewhat petit, and on that December night, her short graying hair curled down her neck as a bluish bonnet hung daintily at the shoulders of her winter dress. She had helped her husband with such caring duties many times over the years, and by that night had become affectionately known throughout Middlesex County as simply, "Abigail, Doc Newman's wife."

Ethan's father had frantically summoned Doc Newman to the farmhouse several hours before, and as Abigail and Doc tenderly comforted Ethan's mother, preparing to escort Ethan into the world, their weary mare strapped to a dark carriage waited outside amidst the flurrying snows of the night. Then it happened. As the winds howled the drifting fields and icy wisps brushed the window panes, as his grandmother's blue porcelain clock atop the hearth's mantel anxiously chimed the hour of eleven, Ethan's life began.

The story Ethan always liked to tell was how "Doc Newman gripped my ankles with his left hand, and dangled me by my tiny feet before the dim glow of the lamp." As Abigail soothed his watchful mother, dousing her sighs with soft brushes of cloth across her brows and skin, Doc rapped Ethan's bare behind with a slapping whap. "Mom said my tiny lungs flared," and as a tranquil fire snapped the hearth and the wintry chill swirled about the Sheehan farm, "I screeched an obnoxious cry into the December night."

Ethan was born in a place they say was first settled some hundred years before, plots of land about a dozen miles northwest of Boston, scattered groves of maple, pine, oak and elm surrounded by fertile fields, a place most soon called the Parish of Cambridge. It was an area viewed as ideal for tilling swaying hay and an array of grains, thousands of acres in the Colony of Massachusetts Bay that attracted adventurers from the port of Boston and throughout the Dominion of New England. Soon, it seems that parish was crawling with men speculating in what might become of those fields, purchasing acres upon acres with chests of shillings and pounds, gobbling rich swaths of the land.

Within a few years, as the numbers of colonists toiling new farms slowly grew, venturing merchants began to build a little settlement near the center of all those fields, and as the reign of Queen Mary drew to a close near the end of that century, those spirited women and men decided to call their tiny town, Cambridge Farms. Yet within a generation their little settlement was renamed Lexington, to honor a Lord of Parliament some believed, while others would say it was to bestow loyal sentiments upon a little village north of London.

Slowly the village expanded from its humble beginnings, with more colonists stuffing their belongings into wagons and creaking to its outlaying hills and fields to claim their own farms, and by that special day after Christmas in 1750 over five hundred colonists called Lexington's shops and farms home. And although the village continued to grow in the coming years, with Ethan's mother and father too, with new farms, cottages, merchant shops, taverns and churches, and Mr. Giles' printing shop, it remained a little village along the winding Massachusetts Road several miles outside of Boston.

The port of Boston was said to be home to over fifteen thousand colonists by that December night, and the numbers of women, children and men scattered throughout the Colony of Massachusetts Bay had swelled to some two-hundred thousand by then, a quarter of all those in the Thirteen Colonies. And by that wintry night, with its bustling harbor leading to the expanse of the sea, Boston was viewed by many as the hub of colonial political thought and cultural life, rivaled only by my Philadelphia.

But back in Ethan's Lexington, that bustling colonial world seemed so far away, and he once said his village "was a quiet escape, a sedate place" he cherished, galloping home now and then to visit his father at the tavern between studies at Harvard and duties at Mr. Gill's print shop. A spacious field sprouted in the center of his village, a few acres of grass that swayed lazily in warm summer winds, a field they called the green that glistened white in winter from flurries that blew across the hills from the frontier.

I remember how the golden glow of Ethan's eyes serenely misted when he once whispered about the blossoms which bloomed about the green in spring, of "dainty little petals flaring from the grass in pinks, yellows and blues." And I recall how his words seemed to drip with loneliness when he'd quill about young cockerels, hens and roosters dashing about the field, blasting annoying summer clucks as their tiny heads snapped. Or how he would confess of longing for home when exposing his desires to hear meandering cows mooing once again, or listen to the screeching bleats of goats scampering about the grass while munching disgusting clumps of cud in fall.

Surrounding that field were things commonly found in towns and villages throughout the colonies in those days, restful homes of brick and stone and little quaint cottages scattered amidst sprouting groves of maples, birch and pines. The village green seemed to be corralled by pitted roads and rustic lanes, tentacle streets nudging the grass of the field with names of Hancock, Harrington and Clarke. All the while the ruts and stones of the Belmont Road sliced south as Bedford Street darted north along the western edge of the field, and the narrow road to Billerica jutted past Ethan's farmhouse northeast.

Perhaps the most essential stretch of stony ruts was known as the Massachusetts Road, a vital path that cut through the colony from the waters of Boston Harbor. From Lexington it sliced west to the nearby hamlets of Lincoln, Concord and beyond, and to the east it wound through the villages of Menotomy, Medford and Somerville, coming to an end at a little settlement along the southeastern docks of the Charlestown Peninsula.

There were other amenities of Lexington that Ethan often quilled about too, such as the aging hut of the belfry "always on guard to summon the town," alerting the village and outlaying farms of celebratory news and dangers with its rings. There was a scattering of small shops too, like the general store infused with a chair for cutting hair and little tables for tea, including a place for postal packages and letters to come and go. "We have a shoemaker and blacksmith just like everywhere else," Ethan liked to reveal, as well as things other villages do without, "shops for our gunsmith and tinsmith, and a bricklayer too. And Doc Newman's apothecary shop, is just south of the green."

Corralled sheds to feed and shelter tired colts, fillies and mares was also in Lexington, not far from Doc's place, and there were steeples for the Church of England and Presbyterian faiths, two spires stretching for the sky, along with a little schoolhouse for a new generation and an inn for comforting weary souls. There were two places for farmers, strangers, shopkeepers and merchants to assuage their hungers too, taverns of Buckman and Munroe, havens to gather and talk of the colonial day with goblets, tins and mugs of rye whiskey, ale, wine and rum. Aside from his father's tavern in his later years, I suppose Ethan was most proud of Mr. Giles' print shop, where he published important notices and his Lexington Gazette, filled with simmering stories and inspiring opinions expressed by courageous men.

Ethan once talked of the homes too, and of one he viewed as perhaps the most revered by many near the northeast grass of the village green just off the stones of Hancock Street, a big yellow house on the south edge of the road to Billerica. It was a little parsonage when first made decades before for the Reverend Hancock back in the olden days, a man Ethan said was the grandfather of that kind merchant in Boston. It was a house on some eighty acres of fertile soil near the spire of Christ Church, a place where some believe Boston's John Hancock lived for several years when he was young after the shattering death of his father, a home where the Reverend Clarke and his family lived the night Ethan was born.

By that December night the little parsonage had expanded another floor, with a curving gambrel roof and an array of square-paned windows, several topped by quaint colonial gables. Ethan said some viewed it as an "impressive house" with several rooms scattered about each floor, a home built on a foundation of crimson bricks fired there in Lexington, with a wide column thrusting the center of the roof to form its lone chimney. And it seems that Susie Clarke, the reverend's bride, was some kind of cousin to Mr. Hancock of Boston, and for years to come after that wintry night, the reverend and she maintained the ministry while rearing a dozen girls and boys.

If I recall, a bit south of that house and along the edge of the village field was a shop called Duncan's Cordwainer, a place where the village shoemaker sliced, stretched and stitched leather into such goods as aprons, boots, leggings and shoes. They say that strange name came from a material called cordovan, refined goatskin of smoothly tanned leather found near the village of Cordoba somewhere in the southern hills of Spain. But here in the colonies such fine skins were rather scarce in those days, and it seems most cordwainer's like Mr. Duncan produced their goods from the rough hides of aging mares and wild game carted from the wilderness.

Ethan once said that Charles Duncan's cordwainer shop was actually a little place off the side of his three-room home, just right of the front door, and although he was forty or so by that December night, "he lived alone, a rather secluded life." He had learned his trade in a leather shop near the Charles River in Boston, not far from Aunt Bea's place, and standing an inch or two above five feet at some hundred and eighty pounds, with strings of graying strands that dangled past his ears from a scalp slowly balding, was viewed as rather portly. "He might have been a quiet, shy man," Ethan had whispered, "and kept his opinions to himself, but most in those days thought him to be perhaps the best maker of saddles in all of Middlesex County."

Although his Lexington shop was less sophisticated than those found in Boston or my Philadelphia, or the port of Savannah or along the harbor of New York, it never wavered from providing Ethan's village and the entire county with essential leather goods. And while the cordwainers of Boston and beyond were known to have an advantage of sailing more refined products into the colonies from across the sea, bags, boots, saddles and shoes from the ports of Sicily, France, England and Spain, Mr. Duncan's place was always stocked with his own vital things, goods for Lexington polished and displayed on an oak table nudged against the window of his shop.

Further south on the east side of Hancock Street was said to be the largest and most majestic home of Lexington, Jonathan Harrington's place, with bricks brushed white that seemed to glisten from across the green at twilight. A pair of red chimneys pierced its roof, thrusting for the stars, and with some twelve rooms and a maple staircase of elegant spindles that swept to the upper floor from an opulent foyer, it was known as lavishly stylish. An array of windows were scattered about its white bricks, their sparkling panes nestled between shiny dark shudders, and the home's wide front door of polished black opened to the stones of the road and the expanse of that Lexington field.

Nearby was the barn of Sam Burns, the village blacksmith, with a battered door of weathered slats that swung from sturdy rocks and bricks, and nestled some fifty feet in back was a little home with a pair of rooms hidden among a little grove of hemlock pines, their prickly branches drooping green needles. He was said to keep the Lexington farmers in tools needed, and could be seen almost any day pounding thin iron rims to stretch over the elm wheels of carriages and wagons. Ethan said he made what most blacksmiths did for colonists in those days, stylish andirons for hearths and unique decorum for embroidering homes, along with dark iron kettles and blades for plowing fields, iron hooks and fireplace racks, and axes, hammers and picks.

Just past the southeast corner of that Lexington field, near Danny Harrington's place and John Muzzey's home, was the village belfry on a shallow hill just south of where the stones of Hancock Street merged with the ruts of the Massachusetts Road. It was an odd looking oak hut, sliced and nailed square, with a small protruding tower that housed a dangling copper and tin bell. I remember Ethan said it had been cast in a London foundry some ten years before he was born, then sailed to the colonies and strapped with thick hemp twine to the elm yoke on that hill. It was a belfry those of Lexington felt passionate about, declaring it to be "ever vigilant," ready to warn the village and outlaying farms of approaching danger with each tug of its tattering rope, or give an echoing plea for colonists to gather with each ringing clap of its bell.

Close by to the west was the shop of Doc Newman, known by most of Middlesex County simply as "Doc's place," and dangling just outside the door from little black hooks holding tiny iron links was a thin blue board with *Newman's Apothecary* brushed in white. A little ceramic jar was painted to one side with a pudgy pestle protruding its top, and a slithering dark snake twisting about a thin rod was brushed to a small crimson oval. Oak slats lined the wall behind a gray counter of thick marble inside the shop, shelves that held special trade things such as delft jars colorfully glazed in a Boston earthenware shop or perhaps sailed to the colonies from a village port in my grandmother's Netherlands.

Ethan once confided that Doc Newman could be seen through the panes of his shop's twin windows reaching for a delft jar to devise an array of special medications for an injured farmer or ailing villager at any hour of night or day. "Why, just before dawn on a Sunday morning last summer," he said with a comforting glare in his eyes, "I glanced through the panes while galloping by the shop, and there he was, grabbing a jar and crushing a mixture of powders and chemicals with his little porcelain stick." It might have been a special chalk for a mother's heartburn or perhaps a concoction of calamine of zinc and oxides of ferric for an ointment or lotion to tame a farmer's skin. Or maybe he was crushing cinchona bark from an island of the Caribbean Sea, to help reduce a villager's fever, or was mixing yellowish powders with unique solutions to douse a merchant's pain with variations of caffeine alkaloids or numbing morphine.

Also stashed in his shop were ugly little things that some doctors at my Pennsylvania Hospital, and other physicians in those days, thought medically beneficial, slippery dark creatures that slithered about jars in milky solutions. Ethan said that near the far right corner of that marble slab was a bulky glass container filled with a mixture of fuzzy water, and darting in twisting motions about its haze were a dozen black leeches. They were short slimy annelid worms, waiting to be plucked by Doc Newman to perform their healing tasks in a wishfully mystical way.

And as many apothecaries in those days, his shop was more than just a place for concocting medicines by grinding and mixing. Lazily lining an oak shelf near a side wall was a slew of officious looking books laced in gold that detailed the apothecary trade, and scattered atop an array of cabinets, counters and shelves were goods found in most Lexington homes. There were quaint barrels filled with powders and spices and tins brimming of various oils, and nudged near little mugs and jars holding short thin sticks with tiny bristles were scuffed oak buckets stuffed with candles of creamy beeswax and tan tallow. Smoking pipes with stylish curves and deerskin pouches bulging tobacco were bundled near shelves stacked of knitted scarves and mittens, and a spray of dainty bonnets dangled from thin elm stubs in browns, reds, yellows and blues.

A little further west and a few hundred feet south of the Massachusetts Road was Lexington's little schoolhouse, hidden on the slope of a lazy hill, its elm slats brushed white. It was nestled among old birch and pines, and had survived in the shadow of one of the village's knottiest oaks for years, and dangling from a twisting arm by thick twine was a thin board of nicked elm. "I can still see it swaying in the winds," Ethan once quilled during studies in fall, "just a foot or so above the muddied grass, waiting for one of the children to swing in a cool autumn breeze or a refreshing wisp of spring."

Several weathered oak steps rose from the gravelly soil and trampled grass to the schoolhouse door, and four big windows with lots of square panes embedded the walls of each side. An inviting vestibule greeted the children just inside the door each day, a quaint foyer with short iron hooks dotting its walls to hang scarves and coats, little tricorn hats and dainty bonnets, a protected place to stash muddied shoes and scuffed little boots, and bulging cloth bags. A pair of rooms awaited the children on the other side of a creaking door, a left chamber for the youngest boys and girls and a right for those nearing the end of schooling, older ones soon to embark into the outside world.

I remember how Ethan described the desk placed to the front of each room near the northern wall, a modest oak table with three drawers running down each side, and how each had a nicked chair of worn slats with stylish spindles. They were the two desks and chairs from which Lexington's schoolmarm kept her watchful eyes upon the children, the place from where she tried her best to espouse knowledge upon each room. Little oak tables, stained and scuffed, were neatly arraigned in tidy rows in both rooms, and small slatted chairs were nudged to each for a dozen children or two.

Ethan said she would dash from one room into the other, spouting lessons and instructions to the younger ones from her left room desk before shuffling back to the older children patiently studying at their tables to the right. And sometimes, in a rather inconspicuous way, she would glide to-and-fro without uttering a word. "I can still see her," he once confided about days when he was young, "standing behind her desk with a piercing peer upon the rows of children, our eyes captured by the gaze of unchallenged authority. It was a stare, Andrea, which sliced a scare into the little ones."

Along the upper wall near the ceiling of each room, just behind both of her desks, hung a dusty frame housing a fading portrait of the English king, a discoloring image of the colonies' ruling crown. The canvas of each could be seen crinkling along its edges a little more each year, a painting of King George the Second when Ethan was very young, an image that would change to another George in the years to come. And dangling from a thin pine pole thrusting above the door near the corner of each room was an imposing flag of red, white and blue, London's ensign of the Union Jack.

Across the ruts and stones of the Massachusetts Road north of the schoolhouse was the Lexington Inn, an inviting structure rising along the southern grass of the village field. They say it was caringly constructed from village bricks and nearby elms by George and Cynthia Gables, a dream erected several years before that special December night. Known as a haven for sleepy travelers, wandering merchants or daring colonists searching for the frontier, it was said by many to exude an ambiance of home.

I remember Ethan quilling that the inn was one of the first structures seen by those approaching the village from the east, a comforting sight of two floors with a dozen rooms, all sheltered by a tapering roof. Four hearths of rocks and bricks were mortared to each corner, and thin trails of smoke could be seen spiraling from its chimney on gray autumn days and frigid winter mornings. Dark shutters edged an array of square-paned windows, and a bright door welcoming weary travelers opened to a patch of gravelly grass along the Massachusetts Road. It was a little expanse of dusty stones during summer and a muddied patch of slippery ruts during the rains of spring, a place for oxen and carts, horses, buggies and wagons.

A bit west of the inn was the Munroe Tavern, a spirited house along the northern edge of the Massachusetts Road where colonists on trotting colts or squeaking carriages could find relief, escape from their travels or toils of the day. It had been built years before on the southeast grass of that Lexington field near an unpleasant aroma that often wafted from the adjacent corrals of the livery stable, and since Ethan was young, had been owned by Will and Betsy Munroe.

"Their tavern had always been a place where farmers could moan and merchants could gripe about events of the day," Ethan liked to say, "a place where colonists could spew differing views with mugs of ale, goblets of wine and tins of rye whiskey or rum." From their quaint little home in back, nearer the grass of the green, the Munroes were said to sometimes hear emphatic voices spouting loyalty to the crown, spirited men in jovial exchanges with others expressing unflattering views of the king and his royal governor.

Still further west and a bit south of the stony ruts of the Massachusetts Road was a rustic barn with elm slats that tilted strangely, an aging gun and silversmith place known in Lexington as Ernie Wilson's shop. His hair had already begun to gray when Ethan was young, and they say he never wed, preferring to live a solitary life. He forged and molded an array of metal things in a little area just behind his shop, and slept each night in a tiny house that had once been brushed white. It was a weary little home with a pair of tiny rooms, a cozy place nestled among birches and elms that would sway wildly in chilling autumn winds and frigid flurries on blustery winter nights.

Most pistols, guns and muskets were dutifully sailed into the colonies from across the sea in those days, from various ports of England or France, and some were daringly smuggled out of view of the king's customs men to secret docks near the ports of Charles Towne, New York, Boston, Philadelphia and Savannah. Yet, Ethan always said that Ernie could make his own weapons, that he "knew his profession well," and possessed an array of knowledge about fixing those guns. And he had a reputation as a creative man with metals, molding tins and silvers into a slew polished works, and was rather good at carving woods for stocks while forging ores in his fiery bricks in back.

There were rumors when Ethan was young that Ernie had honed his vital trade years before in a tiny port north of Boston, perhaps in the village of Gloucester in the County of Essex some would say, and most viewed his talent of repairing a musket as almost wizardry. And when he wasn't fixing guns or forging a musket of his own, he could be seen hunched in a stained leather apron over a massive iron anvil hammering metals with mighty bangs, whacks and clacks. Or maybe he'd be pressed against his nicked oak bench, gently molding, tapping and shining sheets of silver and tin into dainty goblets and bowls, teapots and cups.

Several hundred feet south behind Ernie's place, near the trickle of a winding creek and the stones of the Marrett Road, nestled a little house of one of Lexington's "more colorful men" Ethan would say, a cottage for Israel Jacob, "the best maker of bricks in all of Middlesex County." Some believed he had once been chained for a trivial crime against the king, and a few of the village's taunting children unkindly sputtered that he had committed a gruesome act outside a village in the Colony of Virginia. Still other tales said Israel had once labored in a fortified camp for those deemed disloyal to the king, in a chilling stone gaol outside of Williamsburg.

There were even stories about an isolated place near the frontier many years before the war, in the western wilderness of the Colony of Massachusetts Bay, rumors of a penal colony forged in the forest outside a village called Housatonic. They were unfounded stories Ethan would say, wild conjecture that Mr. Jacob had learned his brickmaking skills in that dreaded place, hurtful tales Israel would emphatically deny for years. He had always declared that he honed his trade in his uncle's shop in a seaside hamlet along the waters of Cape Cod, and Ethan confided that his father always said, "Wherever the truth may rest, every man deserves a new chance."

The elder colonists said Israel arrived in Lexington during a wintry flurry in the last weeks of 1744, when he was perhaps twenty-three or four, with a wagon bulging sacks and crates stuffed with an array of strange iron tools. From the beginning most could see he was quiet and rather recluse, and his dark hair dangled scraggly to his shoulders when not bound by a thin reddish cloth whenever tugging and mixing sticks, leaves and roots with muddied soil and water from the nearby creek, making mounds of clay for bricks.

Ethan once said that when young, he would dash with other children after school to Mr. Jacob's place, and hiding among the brush and trees, "watch as he stuffed clay into a bunch of elm molds, forming scores of muddy little bricks that looked like soggy loaves of bread." It seems he would place those molds inside his barn to dry for a while, then scorch his infant bricks in the fires of his kiln, sealed in an oven beneath a layer of soil. The burning odor of ashen birch and oak would filter about Lexington for days as the flames of his kiln raged, firing his molds of clay into hundreds of hardy glazed bricks.

A bit further west sits the wheelwright shop of Sam Brown, closer to where the Massachusetts Road begins a slight right bend near the clumpy dirt of Bedford Street, a path that nudges the western edge of the village green before winding north for miles. Some would say he was a rather steady man for only twenty-six as of that December night, most believing it was due to the calming influence of his youthful bride Anna and the grounding of his young children, Christian and Kelly. "Dad always said that Sam's trade was vital to the colonists of Lexington," Ethan once quilled, "to shopkeepers and farmers alike, in all of Middlesex County." As in most villages and towns in those days, it was the skill of men like Sam, a craftsman creating sturdy wheels for carriages, carts and wagons, who kept essential goods and supplies moving about the colonies.

Mr. Brown was known to relish his duties, making ash and elm wheels while mending those already serving Lexington, tightly encasing those resolute wheels in thin iron rings forged and hammered by blacksmith Sam Burns. They were wheels large and small designed to survive the cobblestones of Boston and elements of nature, to overcome the icy snows of winter and the crushing rocks and stones along the colony's paths in summer and fall, and the muddied roads during the rains of spring. And from Lexington, those uneven paths led to the village of Billerica northeast and the hamlet of Belmont several miles south, Bedford a few miles to the north and Concord five miles west, and to Boston a dozen east.

Nearby, at the corner of the Massachusetts Road and the stones of Bedford Street, the doors of Henry White's shop and home swung open to face the southwest corner of that Lexington field. Not much older than his wheelwright neighbor, he and his wife Mary had arrived in the village just days before that December night, settling into the old Spencer place and quickly dangling a shingle proclaiming his cabinet shop. It was part of their four room home, a place Ethan had said was quaintly nestled amid a few maples and pines, and his woodworking shop was arraigned in a rear room off to the right. Within months he had unveiled a keen proficiency as the village carpenter, able to create an array of wooden things, and by Ethan's first day of school when he was very young, was known as one of the finer cabinetmakers of the county.

While Henry immersed in his woodworking trade, slicing and chipping pine and birch or dowelling smoothed pieces of elm, cherry, maple and oak, Mary had embarked upon a trade of her own, something rather rare for a woman in those days. On most summer, fall and spring days could be seen through the window panes baking cookies, muffins, breads and cakes in the bricks of her oven or simmering stews in a dark iron kettle or roasting little critters, fowl and game over the flames snapping the stones of her kitchen hearth. Ethan once heard a traveling merchant utter that she was rather pleasing to the eyes, and she was seldom seen without a colorful bonnet caressing the amber waves of her hair or an apron brushed with oils, powders and sweets wrapped about her dress.

"I can still smell the wonders she'd bake in that kitchen," Ethan once quilled in a letter oozing reminiscence, "a calming aroma which streamed through the open panes of her window, sweet scents that were whisked by spring winds across the grass of the green to swirl about the shops and homes. And on lucky days when I was young, those special smells would sweep the slope of our little hill, and bathe our schoolhouse."

Soon, and for many years, the tasty delights she conjured in the bricks and fires of her kitchen were not only soothing the souls of Lexington, but scores of farms like Ethan's, and nearby villages and towns. Women and men were said to creak their buggies from Belmont, Bedford and Lincoln for her baked treats, and tradesmen and merchants traveling west and east along the snows and ruts of the Massachusetts Road could be seen halting wagons, carts and mounts on the stones of Bedford Street. Most would dash to the aroma and exchange a few pence and shillings for warm muffins, breads or cakes, while some would halt for a brief moment to simply breathe the scrumptiousness filtering the window of her kitchen.

As pleasing as those aromas were, as dedicated to her baking as Mary was, it was the carpentry trade of Henry that brought fiscal stability of their home. Ethan once confided that he always seemed to be wearing his tricorn hat, and although he stood just five feet and a half, at two hundred pounds was known to be grappling strong. His shoulders were uncommonly wide, dominating his upper body, and his arms bulged beneath his carpenter's apron, deerskin that hung from the muscles of his neck to stockings stretching to his knees from stained scuffed shoes. It seems he had honed his skills in the Colony of Virginia a few years before, as an apprentice for a man named Jacob or Peter Scott, not far from the assembly house in Williamsburg.

Just like most carpenters in those days, they say that Henry always tried to craft his cabinets, desks, tables and chairs from timber of nearby groves, yet when needed, relied on logs of cedar, maple, spruce and beech sliced from the wilderness in the Colony of New Hampshire, hauled to Lexington in wagons and carts. Or maybe he'd choose a batch of timber chopped from groves of pine, hickory, ash or poplar in the Colony of Connecticut or Rhode Island, or cherry, walnut and birch carted from the eastern forests of the Colony of New York. But no matter the source, those of Lexington knew that Henry always considered the nature of his woods, how each might act in the snows of winter or chill of fall, or the steamy summer air, salty sea winds or drenching rains of spring.

Looking back after all these years, what Henry and other colonial tradesmen and merchants were beginning to do around the time Ethan and I were born, was seek goods and supplies produced and grown here in the colonies. Items of glass, woods, cloth and metals, even spirited delights like ales, whiskeys and rums, were beginning to be made closer to home by thousands in the colonies of Georgia, New York, Rhode Island and Virginia, my Pennsylvania and Ethan's Massachusetts Bay. No longer were goods simply being sailed across the sea to the colonies from ports of Sicily, Spain or Sweden, France, England or the Netherlands, a system of dependency that had shackled the colonies for over a hundred years.

Some would later say that it was in those earlier years, in the few decades before the war, that the ways of thinking for many colonists began to change. It seems there was a kind of shifting in attitude, a desire for colonists to have a freer hand to do things our own way, perhaps the way a child slowly slides to adolescence before snapping the bonds of home. "We began to look into our own souls," I remember a Germantown elder once say, "discover our own emerging culture, while slowly untwining our paternal reins that stretched across the sea to England and the crown."

I suppose it was around then that the colonies began to truly evolve, women and men searching for things more close to home, slowly forming a characteristic of delving inward that seemed to unify, of producing things here in the colonies for colonists. It was what some now say was an embryonic shift away from our ties to the king, an evolution those with gripping loyalties to London began to nervously fear.

Behind Henry and Mary's place was a field further west along the south side of the Massachusetts Road, a place where tall grasses swayed in summer winds and winter snows swirled among scattered birch, pine and elm. It was a field which slowly rose just beyond the nearby stones of the Harrington Road, a rutted path that sliced north and south at the base of the slope, and at the peak of that grassy rise was the highest point about Lexington, a place where the village's past rested in solemn silence. Several oaks and elms quietly peered upon weathered crosses protruding from the grass, a burying ground of etched stones corralled by snows and a string of white slats that December night.

"The aging markers sprouting from the summer grass seemed so cold when I was young," whispered Ethan while brushing a tear from his cheek that March night, "yet now, strangely, they bring comfort to me. They soothe those at rest, and in a mysterious way, are windows to the past, to vibrant lives now gone." It was the final resting place of settlers who had ventured from Boston long ago, daring people seeking a new life about the unknown hills and fields of Cambridge Farms, a quiet place for women and children newly entombed, a cemetery for precious fathers and mothers of Lexington. And as of that wintry night of 1750, it was a hushing place with little plots yet to be filled, snowy soils of a hill patiently waiting for the toll of colonial bells, for an immerging generation whose stories had yet to be told.

Down the slope of the burying ground hill and near the western edge of Bedford Street was an aging general store by that December night, the shop of Elias Cobb. It was built before the reign of the second George and peered upon the southwest edge of the village field, one of Lexington's earliest structures just north of the Massachusetts Road. And by the first moments of Ethan's precious life, it had also been declared by the colony's royal governor to be the postal home for the village.

Although the general store had some of the same things found in Doc Newman's nearby shop, it was brimming with much more, with an array of tools, goods and vital supplies needed by those of the village and surrounding farms. Yet, perhaps the most enjoyable aspect of Elias' shop were the few quaint tables with spindled maple chairs for villagers to escape a spring shower or the flurry of a winter snow, for women and men to whisper of trivial things while warming with a cup of steaming Dutch tea.

Perhaps fifty years old and a few inches above five feet, Mr. Cobb was said by many of the village to be a bit rotund by that wintry night. Ethan once said his hair appeared strange to the children of the school when he was young, "a stringy ring of gray that dangled from shining ridges, and the sides of his face sprouted snowy white whiskers," a beard that narrowed and spanned a sturdily cut chin. It seems he had been appointed postmaster for Lexington by the king's royal governor several years before, and most of the villagers knew how Elias was devoted to his royal duties, always ensuring the mail of letters, packages and sacks were properly routed about the colony.

Proudly displayed from dawn to dusk outside his store's front door each day was a large flag of England that twisted and flapped in the winds, a royal ensign tied with twine atop a pine pole near the stones of Bedford Street. Yet Mr. Cobb's ensign looked different than the flags dangling inside the schoolhouse, for it was an ensign most of Boston referred to as a maritime flag, a symbol of London's powers of the sea that others in Philadelphia and Germantown loyally called a meteor flag. I remember it was a royal cloth with horizontal stripes that alternated red and white, and had a canton of deep blue stitched to its upper inside. A couple crosses were embedded inside that blue square, and although I didn't know it back then, the red one was known as the St. George, a symbol of England's unity, and the other in white was for St. Andrew, in homage to the highlands of Scotland.

Known about Lexington for many years as a quiet, simplistic man, Mr. Cobb lived rather modestly in a small cottage behind his store, a tiny house procured for his use by Royal Governor Shirley years before. "It was only two little rooms," I remember Ethan once said, "with a narrow bed and a few nicked tables and chairs. And sometimes, in the late hours of a lazy summer night, I could see the flame of a lone candle flickering inside, glistening off the panes of his window."

A hearth of colorful stones smothered the north wall of his little home, a fireplace to soothe the chill of a winter night, rocks with thin iron rods protruding with tiny black hooks for roasting little creatures or simmering tasty stews from dangling kettles and pots. He was known to spend hours many nights rocking quietly in his oak chair as a crackling fire sprayed shadows about his little room, gazing through the glistening glass toward the darkness shrouding the village green while glancing to the flames now and then, perhaps taming his loneliness and wondering of long vanished dreams.

Behind the general store and a bit west, along the pebbles of the Harrington Road and a little north of the ruts of the Massachusetts Road, rose the steeple of Lexington's Presbyterian Church. It had been built from village bricks and groves of nearby elm during what Ethan said was a revival of puritan beliefs, a movement of religious furry said to have been ignited by a man named Edwards, a young minister from the village of Northampton some seventy miles to the west. "Mom would take me there when I was young," Ethan whispered to me that winter night. "She said it was a house of worship inspired by a great awakening, a surge of spiritual faith that had swept the colonies of New England several years before she and dad sailed to Boston."

There were aging stories about that revival whispered in Lexington when Ethan was young, several which told about an autumn day some fifteen years before Ethan and I were born. It seems Minister Edwards had journeyed to the village with an entourage of faithful colonists, most riding in creaking buggies, wagons and carriages, and by noon scores from Lexington and surrounding farms had joined them on the grass of the village field. "Doc said the minister jumped onto a crate near the middle of the green," Ethan recalled, "and cloaked in a dark robe that flowed to muddied shoes, began to spout spirited beliefs to a crowd silently mesmerized, pumping his fists and flailing his arms through the chilling autumn air."

He was said to have warned of the dangers of not believing, suggesting that a great fire would consume those without repentance, and in a moment of fiery passion bellowed that those on that field in Lexington, and all the colonies, were "sinners in the hands of an angry God!" It seems he preached in scores of villages and towns across the Colony of Massachusetts Bay in the weeks and months that followed, and the numbers of women and men heeding his cries and reaching for their bibles, surged. Through what some say was the minister's spirited determination, a generation of colonists in Middlesex County and beyond was reintroduced to a slew of resurging scripture.

Ethan said that for many years his mother's church of polished elm pews was ministered by a man named Whitefield, a spiritual man who had traveled from Boston with his family during the winter of '51. He was thirty-five or so and rumored to be rather loyal to the crown, and had studied theology at Harvard College before honing his faith with a Reverend Cooper at a church in Boston on Brattle Street, a little east of Aunt Bea's home on Beacon Hill.

He was a rather tall minister for those days, a little more than six feet and somewhat slim, with a trimmed beard and dark hair neatly cropped. "Mom always thought his homily well prepared," Ethan confided by the fire that March night, "intensely delivered with a splash of wisdom, and said his words brought her comfort each Sunday morning, listening from her special pew." And sometimes, it seems he displayed a ferocious emotion when spouting his guiding words, a fury the children had never heard, sacred passions the older ones had once seen bursting upon their village field.

Minister Whitefield had married Becky Wordsworth of Cambridge several years before, rumored to be the daughter of a loyal follower of the royal governor, and Ethan said they had a trio of little children by the December night he was born, Liz at two, Sarah at five and Jonathan at seven. They lived in the parsonage many in Lexington had helped build in the shadow of the spire a decade before, two floors of crimson bricks with quaint windows and a pair of chimneys along the stones of Harrington Road.

She was viewed by most as rather petit at some five feet, with soft eyes of light brown, and Becky's umber hair was usually hidden beneath a dark bonnet or tightly bundled in some contortioned sphere with thin twine. As expected of a minister's wife in colonial days, it seems she always donned a thick dress of black or gray, buttoned snug to her neck and flowing to the soils crunching beneath soles of dull dark shoes. And Ethan said she was passionately devoted to the minister, and was seen on most days tending to the grounds or polishing elms pews and shining glass panes.

Just a bit northeast of the steeple and along the western edge of Bedford Street was the Buckman Tavern, the other place in Lexington where colonists could satisfy their hungers while dousing fears and spurring hopes with ale, rum, rye whisky and wine. The older of the two village taverns, it had been dutifully sanctioned by the colony's royal governor some forty years before that December night, and for a sacred while had even served as a place of worship before the church of Ethan's mother was erected in the years of that great awakening.

I remember Ethan once saying that at times the tavern was even used as the village courthouse, "whenever the crown's roving magistrate for Middlesex County deemed it proper to hold court in town. And in those early days, it was the Royal Judge Henry Hanover." It seems he'd bound into Lexington in his squeaky buggy when the moment was ripe, settle into a corner of the tavern and proceed to resolve a dispute or two between merchants and farmers or conduct a trial of a colonist's disloyal malfeasance.

The proprietors of the Buckman Tavern in those days were Mr. and Mrs. McElroy, adventuring colonists named Nancy and James who had purchased the spirited place for several hundred pounds soon after they wed in Boston at twenty one, some thirty years before Ethan was born. Most thought Jim proportionally fit at some six feet, and by that December night of 1750, the hair waving over his ears had silvered and his mustache had grayed. It seems on most days he could be seen rushing about the tavern in light wool breeches and a tan ruffled shirt, with thin stockings that stretched from scuffed brown shoes to his knees, and a thin dark cloth was usually twisted in a bow about the bulge of his upper left arm.

Unlike the silvering gray of her beau, the golden glow of Nancy's hair still glistened as it did when she was very young, enticing locks she twined to a swirling ball when bustling about the tavern from dawn to dusk, hair which tranquilly flowed during the quiet of night. Wayward merchants and wandering colonists sipping spirits could be heard at times to whisper that she was "finely endowed," and the flattering hue of her greenish eyes was said to sparkle as she dashed about slats of the tavern floor.

They shared the duties of the tavern each day, and seemed to know without uttering a word what each might do or say. When not rushing about the tavern floor, Nancy was preparing various foods in the kitchen to the rear, bustling near embers cooking inside the bricks of the oven or hustling next to a fire burning the hearth, tending to roasting fowl or steaming kettles of stew. All the while James continued to satisfy the thirsts of men talking at tables or nudged to the barrel bar, colonists sipping whiskey, ale and rum, or perhaps a wine sailed to the colonies from some distant port.

As it had since its earliest days, the tavern looked more like a big home, with a dark front door brushed to a shine that opened to a wide string of red bricks imbedded into the soil, a short path to the stones of Bedford Street. A tall aging oak with twisting limbs rose toward the clouds just north of those bricks, its knotted arms smothered with leaves spinning wildly in a summer breeze or barren during the chill of frigid winter nights. And rising just east across the ruts of the road was another tall oak, its high spreading limbs casting shade at dusk over that Lexington field, a shadow that stretched toward the tavern door at dawn as the sun crawled from the sea.

The outside walls of the tavern's elm slats were said to be brushed in amber in those days, with an array of windows with lots of square panes lining both floors, and a small window just above the front door kept watch on the village field just east. A pair of crimson chimneys thrust into the sky near the center of the house, and a shallow third floor with a trio of quaint windows was nudged just below the tavern's angling roof, each crowned by an intriguing gable.

Just inside, a string of oak stairs hugged the north wall off to the right of the door, leading to the upper floor and several rooms where the McElroy's lived, a comfortable place brushed with passion above the tables and chairs scattered about the tavern floor. An array of colorful stones formed the fireplace consuming most of the tavern's rear west wall, and through a swinging door left of the hearth was the kitchen, near the end of the barrel bar. It was not only a place for preparing food for colonists of the village, but a kitchen for Nancy and Jim after the tavern door was latched tight each night. Yet the soul of the tavern remained on the oak slats of its spacious floor, a spirited place covered with an array of spindle-back chairs and round elm tables with lone thick candles.

Along the wall to the left of the front door was the bar of the Buckman Tavern, a thick slab of elm several feet wide and twenty long that had been sliced from a forest in the Colony of New Hampshire. It rested heavily on top of six oak barrels bound by wide iron hoops, big bulging jugs once filled with barley, malts and ales brewed in a Boston warehouse. An oil lamp etched in blue sat near each end, and just left of the bar was a table near the corner, a place where weary farmers and merchants could gaze through the window to the stones of Bedford Street and the expanse of that Lexington field. And off to the bar's right was the kitchen door, battered elm slats attached by little dark straps that squeaked with each swinging creak.

Ethan once quilled that the comforting smells of corn, berries, wheat and hay sprouting nearby fields would filter through the tavern's open panes on warm summer days, and the sweet aroma of azaleas blooming about the hills would sweep into Lexington upon the winds of spring. And when winter flurries whistled about the windows latched tight, icy winds that blasted snows across the stones of Bedford Street to brush the village green white, the flames snapping about the hearth would spray warming shadows about the room. It was a place where weary travelers could find refuge without disdain, a tavern where merchants and farmers could escape the wrath of winter and chilling fall rains.

A little north of the tavern up Bedford Street, hidden among some ash, pine and elms, was a small house for use by the village schoolmarm. It was a curious looking cottage built for the teacher of Lexington's children, and on the wintry night Ethan was born and for many years to come, was the home of Susanna Hutchinson. Ethan said she was only twenty by that December night, a young woman some of the children would uncaringly say was a spinster from Boston, someone Ethan always believed taught an array of subjects rather well while wrapping her quaint home with a dash of serenity.

Made mostly of white pine sliced from a grove several miles to the northwest, its dainty front door opening to the east was softly brushed in a tranquil red, and if not for the abundance of shrubs and trees, her little house would have a fine view of that Lexington field. A small window of six square panes peered east too, and a few more were encased along the south and north walls, while a fireplace of village bricks consumed the rear, a hearth with a thin iron rod that swiveled over the fire. An array of small tan rocks extended from the bricks into the pine slats of the floor, and a maple mantel about eye high was adorned by delicate little figurines. It was a polished shelf with a thin candle rising at each end, and patiently waiting at its center to chime the coming hour was an old porcelain clock of indigo blue.

A thick rug of braids circling in browns, yellows and greens rested near the hearth, and two oak chairs which rocked and swayed were nestled close to the bricks and rocks. A few maple tables polished round were pleasingly placed about her little room, each with a creamy candle rising from a copper holder with thin arching handles. And right of the hearth, near a few shelves and a flowery pitcher and basin, was a little nicked table, aging elm with four weaved chairs for Miss Hutchinson to dine, three more than she would dishearteningly need.

In the tranquil hours after dusk, when a hush had descended upon Lexington and her day of schooling village children was done, she'd nestle to a bed nudged in a little nook just left of the fireplace, sturdily stitched cloth stuffed with an array of soft cotton clumps and little woolen bundles pressed in a small frame of elm. Three feathered pillows always rested upon blue linen sheets smothered by a warm blanket quilted in tans, oranges, reds and greens, and an oil lamp usually glowed on a little oval table nudged beneath the window, glistening off the panes late into the night.

She was enticed from Boston around the time Ethan was born by the village farmers and merchants, tasked with teaching scores of children from ages five to sixteen, and soon it became clear that her style was effectively good. Ethan had said Miss Hutchinson's curriculum was rather varied, for she not only taught subjects for quilling and reading, numbers and histories, but many curious things about man and empires, as well as our earlier colonial days. "She would talk about present men too," he'd say, "delving into their evolving ideas, and discuss theories espoused by some across the sea, men she believed showed insight and wisdom." At times she'd invite a village merchant or tradesman to talk of their profession, of buying and selling, of woods, metals and printing. And as most schoolmarms in those days, she would make time for teaching the girls of homey life too, practical things like baking, sewing and chores, even ways of caring for the ill and mending injuries.

Mingled among bushes and patches of oak, pine and elm, several other cottages and homes were scattered just north along Bedford Street, a path that nudged against the stones of Hancock Street while winding several more miles north to the village of Bedford. It was a convergence of two roads along the northern ridge of that Lexington field, a spot some seven hundred feet from the Munroe Tavern near the southeast corner of the village grass, across the expanse of the green.

"Nathan Giles' house is just off the stones of Hancock Street, along the upper ridge of the field," Ethan whispered to me by the fire that March night, "on the eastern edge of the green, across the grass from the Buckman Tavern." It was his print and binder shop too, where he published his Lexington Gazette each Monday, a few parchment sheets that not only revealed little stories, but exposed the disgruntled pulse of Boston and Middlesex County. Ethan said the gazette also touched upon meddling policies of his colony's royal governor, along with evolving events in other colonies, and disclosed opinions about intrusive laws and acts declared by parliament and the king.

Forty-five or so by the wintry night of Ethan's birth, Nathan was rumored to have been reared in the village of Davidsonville near the rocks of Chesapeake Bay, and had come to Lexington from the Colony of Maryland seven years before. Ethan said that he was trained in printing and publishing by a man named Newsome in Baltimore, a colonist well known in the trade, having learned his skills from a Mr. Parks of

Williamsburg, a man some say published the first newspaper in the Colony of Virginia many years before.

Ethan said that Mr. Giles got the idea of going up to the Colony of Massachusetts Bay from Mr. Newsome, apparently telling him that Lexington was in need of a robust voice, suggesting that the village near Boston was ripe for establishing his own printing and publishing place. With a flourishing spirit and firm repertoire of his trade, Mr. Giles opened his shop along the northeast edge of that Lexington field, and soon his press was printing an array of things, including his beloved gazette. And there was a rumor in those days that his dream had come to fruition with the help of a man in Baltimore, or perhaps it was Philadelphia or Williamsburg, and some believed he may have received shillings and pounds from a colonial loyal to the royal governor in Boston.

The front door of his print shop opened southwest to the expanse of the village green, and the house of Minister Clarke was just east, across the stones of Hancock Street, while the spire of Christ Church was nearby and a bit north, along the Billerica Road jutting from the village past Ethan's farm northeast. Also his home, Mr. Giles' shop had two modest floors, with most of the first consumed by buckets of ink and stacks of parchment, and a big iron printing press. A quaint kitchen was nestled behind a fireplace and wall in back, where a dozen elm stairs rose to the quiet quarters for Nathan and Clara his wife. It was a comfortable space with dressers, rugs and a chair, basin and pitcher, lamps, candles and an old soft bed, and nestled near the window gazing over the village field, was a slatted maple chair and small polished desk.

The rear hearth of rustic stones warmed the shop while allowing Clara to simmer stews in an iron kettle dangling in the kitchen, stones that rose as a fireplace to ease the chills of their bedroom on winter nights, a hearth that vanished through the gambrel roof to thrust into the Lexington air. A pair of windows edged each side of the shop's front door, square panes extending into quaint little bays, and an array of smaller windows were scattered about each floor. Two of the upper windows that peered upon the village field donned dainty gables, colonial panes to witness the colors of dawn and the hush that settled upon Lexington each night.

Ethan once said that Mr. Giles had started his shop with only an agreement with the royal governor to print some officious colonial documents, but in the weeks and months that followed, several Lexington merchants began to pay shillings and pounds for an array of publishing services. And within a year or so he was printing many different things for scores of places throughout Middlesex County, for shops and merchants in nearby villages like Sudbury, Lincoln, Belmont and Concord, as well as an increasing number of colonists nearer Boston.

Aside from printing mundane documents and officious notices, Mr. Giles was selling space in his surging gazette for merchants to boast of services and goods, and his shop was always stocked with things to buy, like parchment sheets, tins of ink, sealing wax and quills. Stacked on shelves in his shop was an array of pamphlets and papers printed in villages and towns across Massachusetts Bay too, for villagers to visit and read, as well as publications from places like Charles Towne, Savannah, Boston and New York, and a few that had been sailed into the colonies from across the sea. I remember Ethan saying that some were rather old, daring insights about colonial disputes with the crown, along with a few tattered almanacs printed years before by Doctor Franklin.

Although he earned a living by printing new colonial rules to parchment, and sometimes to bigger sheets they called broadsides in those days, as well as an intrusive proclamation from the royal governor or an unjust law from parliament, Ethan always said that Mr. Giles' passion remained printing his cherished Lexington Gazette. "He relished the freedom he found with his Gazette, and loved to expose dubious actions coming from London or reveal colonial disputes with the king."

Ethan once described the complexities of how Mr. Giles' printing shop worked, explaining many of the nuances needed just to produce a single sheet of printed parchment, and from that moment on I viewed broadsides, papers, pamphlets and books in an appreciative light, realizing the inspiration required by such dedicated men. "There are many stages to the process," Ethan had said, "expanding from the idea to the need for hundreds of little pieces of type just to print a single page." They were tiny bits of iron marks and letters cast in an array of shapes and sizes, most having to be sailed to the colonies from foundries across the sea in England, the Netherlands or France. "It could take hours to set the type, Andrea, for one page, and the Lexington Gazette could have two, four or six sheets, each week!"

I remember how Ethan meticulously explained that each piece of tiny iron type had to be separated into little boxes by mark, size and letter, and because printing was pressed in reverse, each little piece for every word needed to be set backward. But Nathan had help in those days, for his bride Clara often assisted in the shop, particularly when many pages were needed for the Gazette. She might help by pressing hundreds of little type into position using what Ethan said was a composing stick, an iron rod printers used in colonial days to help secure words and lines into flat elm boxes. Then she'd twine those cases together forming a full page, locking the type into an iron frame secured to the stone of the printing press.

"That's when Nathan would spread his special ink," Ethan carefully explained, "a dark mixture of lampblack and varnish, then smooth it evenly with a mushy ball of deerskin stuffed with wool at the end of a short stick. Clara would carefully place a parchment sheet onto the type nudged in a cushy frame, then Nathan would grip the pressing handle tight, breathe deeply, and pull the plate down. He'd press the parchment hard, Andrea, on all those tiny iron pieces for a moment or two, squeezing so tight his cheeks flushed and knuckles turned white, then slowly release."

By dusk each Sunday every printed sheet of the Gazette had been clipped to a string of taut twine to dry, then gathered and arranged shortly after dawn the coming morning and distribution about the village by Mr. Giles, or one of the schoolhouse boys for a pence or two. Ethan said small stacks of the Gazette were always left at the general store and village taverns, while a few were placed at Doc Newman's place and most trade and merchant shops. And a little pile was always set on a maple table nudged to one of Nathan's bay windows, so villagers could come in to buy or simply read.

Regardless of the type of news or colonial events revealed in the Lexington Gazette, each printing was said to include a passionate opinion by Mr. Giles about some disturbing policy of the colony's royal governor, or unjust act of parliament or disgusting decree of the king. "His positions always seemed so bold," I remember Ethan saying with a dash of pride, "expressed without reservation or concern about what they'd think in the halls of London." It seems he simply didn't hesitate to expose his views even if they might be frowned upon by colonists in Boston or deemed offensive by the king's agents and royal governor, or others about the colonies unyieldingly loyal to the crown.

"We must be free to think and say as we please," Mr. Giles once confided to Ethan, "to print our views without the stench of royal interference or the fear of London's censuring condemnation. When those of power shackle colonists and the press from freely expressing ideas, or garnering information or exposing royal malfeasance, whether such threats come from the king in England or colonists right here, all liberty is doomed. Such oppression would cast our colonies adrift upon a sea of tyranny."

Perhaps it was those fundamental beliefs which motivated Mr. Giles to ensure that his Lexington Gazette was not only distributed throughout the village but to other hamlets and towns of Middlesex County, so colonists would be apprised of what he sometimes said was "disgusting nonsense" that wafted about the halls of London. Ethan said Mr. Giles also thought it was important to ensure that the opinions of colonists who spiritedly opposed facets of the crown were discussed in common places, where tradesmen, merchants and farmers tended to gather after the toils of their day. And in Lexington, such places were the taverns of Buckman and Munroe.

Aside from the village steeples, print shop and schoolhouse, the merchant shops, taverns, homes and trades, there were many other families in Lexington and scattered on farms about the hills and fields. John Parker and his bride Lydia tilled a hundred acres a bit northwest of the Buckman Tavern, just off the Harrington Road, and both had been reared in Lexington before marrying at the age of twenty a year or so before Ethan was born. Ethan once said they seemed rather fond of the Reverend Clarke and his wife, and were known to visit the parsonage on Saturday nights to discuss colonial issues, often with other villagers like Ernie Wilson, Doc Newman, Jon Harrington and Mr. Giles.

Although Mr. Parker was a fine farmer as well as an assessor for Middlesex County in those days, helping the colony determine the value of things, it seems he was also known as a talented mechanic with strange iron gadgets, and was often seen tending to such things for colonists in the village. But Ethan once said it was his skill with crafting wood that impressed others the most, some even saying he was the best joiner of his day, excelling at making cabinets, stairways, doors and moldings for Lexington homes.

Near the Christ Church was the Mulliken house, northeast of Mr. Giles' shop and the stones of Hancock Street, just across the Billerica Road from the reverend's place. Ethan thought the home of Samantha and Nathan was rather quaint, and remembered how their eldest child Joe, a few years older than he, would romp about the village green when Ethan was very young. And it seems their daughter Lydia was about two as of that special December night, with curling auburn hair that danced about her shoulders whenever chasing a dashing Joe about the grass of the field.

"Lexington sounds so, peaceful," Samuel politely injected, interrupting my thoughts while softly nudging his chair. "It seems like such a simple time, grandma, so much calmer than today, a slower pace that sounds, so appealing. I don't know, maybe, things were just less complicated then."

I tugged the edge of my shawl a bit over my shoulder and glanced to Samuel, then gazed to the distant leaves twisting in the warming summer winds while rocking my chair a little slower. Perhaps things really were a little calmer in those days, when Ethan and I were very young, or maybe, I wondered, after all these years it only seems so. Samuel glanced to my eyes then out to the elms gently swaying along the lane, as if patiently awaiting my coming words, and I slid my fingers back into my dress pocket and caressed the tender words of Ethan's aging poem. Oh, if Samuel only knew, I wondered, if we all would have only known, how calm the colonies truly were as of that special 1750 December night. If we had only known how our lives would be so drastically changed by the explosive events that would consume the colonies for years to come.

"I think I understand how you might believe they were calmer days," I softly said while rocking reflectively, "a more simple life. Maybe, Samuel, in an innocent way, they were. But I must say, looking back, I now see that our troubles were just beginning to truly simmer. Yet, I suppose when Ethan and I were born, those days were almost tranquil when compared to the volatile years soon to come, when everything changed."

"What do mean, grandma?" he quickly sputtered with a confusing squint. "I don't understand. The war was still over two decades away."

"Yes, Samuel, it was," I whispered. "But so much began to happen in the colonies the first years of our lives, and in the decade to come. Maybe, in a way, the true severity of what was yet to happen was somehow masked by an immerging discontent just beginning to brew throughout the colonies. It was an uneasy restlessness, Samuel, starting to grip an entire generation. Although we were royal subjects in those days, acceptingly so by so many, some were beginning to view loyalty to the crown with a brush of uncertainty."

"I thought the troubles with the king only began just before the war," he questioned with a puzzling stare into the summer winds.

"Oh, no," I sighed with a dash of disbelief, wondering what Samuel and those of his generation didn't know, "it all started much sooner, Samuel. Yet maybe, it only seems evident when looking back. The troubles were only beginning, rather slowly too, a complex web of disturbing events when Ethan and I were very young."

As Samuel stared intensely to a string of puffy clouds slowly drifting toward the sea, I wondered whether those of his generation could truly grasp what had happened all those years ago. Could they really understand the pressures that were beginning to simmer, have a true sense of the passions that were about to engulf so many in the years leading to the war? As Samuel watched those gentle clouds and my fingers caressed Ethan's words, I wondered if only those of my generation, and all the brave men and boys at eternal rest in the soils of forgotten fields, could really know. Maybe, only those who were there could true understand the fortitude that gripped so many colonists in those days, and comprehend the reasons why.

"There's so much I want you to know," I whispered as we settled our chairs into gentle rocks amid the sounds of leaves fluttering in the soft summer breeze, "so many things you need to understanding. I think what I'm about to tell you, Samuel, will not only answer many of your questions, of Ethan and me, your grandfather Franz, of the war, but enhance your sense of appreciation, for the spirited sacrifice of those days."

"I want to know, grandma, to understand. You were there, you know."

"Yes, I was there, Samuel, along with thousands of others, colonists who gave so much. But I suppose to tell it true, we've got to go back to the wintry hour Ethan was born, return to that frigid December night."

Samuel peered to the distant elms, staring toward what had been the frontier all those years ago, and I gazed to the mountain laurels in bloom just beyond the rails of my porch, dainty pink petals fluttering in the gentle summer winds. As we pressed to the slats of our chairs in silent rocks and my fingers caressed the passions of Ethan's words, I could feel his sweet touch, and remembered. Why did so many colonists, I wondered, women and men who had been citizens of the British Empire all their lives, colonists who had been loyal for over a hundred years, begin to take arms against their king? What kind of people does such a thing? I wondered of my Ethan too, of the challenges that would shape his life, and how he and so many others had become consumed with a spirited fire that raged deep in our souls.

I realized some of what I was about to tell Samuel would never be found on pages bound in some book, for such things are only seared upon the memories of those who witnessed it all. Perhaps most had already been revealed, and the only tales that remained to be told were the thin slices of fading memories of my generation, of the winkled and old. I wondered of stories stashed in some lonely box, aging tales quilled upon tattered parchment, of stories locked within the beats of a fading heart waiting to be banished to the grass of a village hill. As I reached for memories with each quiet rock, I could sense a determined need to expose the whole of Ethan's life, reveal all of what I knew about those days so long ago, about the war, before memories were silenced to my grave, vanishing with the winds.

Ethan had been born on two hundred acres of Middlesex County soil many of Lexington simply called the Sheehan place, an expanse of rocks, groves and fertile fields encircled by an array of farms as of that snowy December night. The farm of Cynthia and Andrew Beatty was nudged just west, a hundred acres of rolling fields amid a few patches of birch and elm. Ethan once said they were rather young as of that wintry night, just twenty-five or so, dedicated farmers with a son named Robert born the summer before, followed within a few years by Jonathan.

There were other farms too, like the Spoons place on the north side of the Billerica Road, two hundred acres of colonial soil tilled by Sarah and Alex, rumored to be her elder by many years. They had quietly wed in the Colony of Connecticut a few years before, and their daughter Francisca was only a few months old by that December night, born on the last day of spring. Just a little east was the smaller farm of Joe Hosmer and his bride Lucy, soils they had toiled for several years since their nuptials at the hopeful age of eighteen, and within the decade, they'd welcome little Dinah and Lavinia, followed soon by son Cyrus. And nestled along the eastern edge of the Sheehan farm was the Fiske place, a hundred acres south of the road that some said was the most fertile soil about Lexington. It was a rich expanse of birch, elm, hills and fields toiled by Benedict and Ethel his wife, and after a while little Hepsibah came along, a daughter born soon after that frontier war between Paris and London.

Ethan said that perhaps the most efficient farm of all was just south of his, three hundred acres of barley, hay, corn, melons and oats toiled by one of the only families of darker skin in Middlesex County. He had heard rumors when he was young of how Quincy and Josey Jafres were once forced to till a big farm in one of the colonies far to the south, Negro slaves shackled by the whims of soulless men. They had been forced to work the land for nothing, no pence, shillings or pounds, all the while hoping to someday till soil their own, dreaming of being free.

Then several years before that December night the Jafres miraculously escaped, finding their way north to the Colony of Massachusetts Bay in the hull of a daring colonist's sailing ship, and with the aid of a caring Boston merchant, purchased their dream for a few hundred pounds. The Jafres were now free, to choose their own path while gazing to the stars, to raise crops as they pleased while rearing a trio of children, daughter Jasmine and sons Booker and James.

Yet for me, what selfishly mattered most about Lexington was what was happening on the Sheehan farm during the closing hours of that chilling Saturday night, the Twenty-sixth of December, 1750. Ethan's journey through life was just beginning, with snows drifting the fields and frigid winds whistling about the windows and limbs of birch, elm and oak, wintry flurries dusting Doc Newman's carriage and the Sheehan house in white.

A weary mare stood in a frozen trance amid snowy flakes trickling past her ears, little specs that settled to the carriage's leather seat as her hooves slowly vanished in sparkling white. Just beneath the buggy's dark roof dangled a pair of lanterns along the upper reaches of each side, thin copper frames with etched glass encasing molten candles with curling wicks waiting to be lit for the short ride to Lexington for Doc and his wife.

Ethan once described their farmhouse as a bit smaller than most, a single floor with outer elm slats always brushed in his mother's favorite saffron yellow, with a sturdy entry door his father stained umber brown each fall.

Shingles of weathered birch layered a roof that rose toward its center, and near the rear a fireplace of colorful stones gently poked into the wintry air. Soothing glass panes adorned each side of the door latched tight that December night, and a few quaint windows were embedded about the rest of the house, each dotted by square panes with little white drifts nestling into tiny corners. And dark elm shutters were hinged to the side of each window, protective slats waiting to swing tight to hold the howls of winter and storms of spring at bay.

Dainty sprigs of holly were circled about the frames of the two front windows, colors twisted amidst thin twigs of green pines, pretty twines sprinkled with aging blossoms of pink rose and little crimson berries. A pair of turquoise lamps glowed from atop maple tables nudged beneath each window, their tranquil little flames fueled by whale oil carted from Boston glistening off the panes. And dangling near the center of each window was a tiny green cluster, twined mistletoe in homage of the Christmas season.

A spacious room filled most of the home just inside the front door, and off to the left was what would be Ethan's little bedroom, his father's den in the days before he was born. And a bit further east along that north wall, just beyond Ethan's little room and closer to the rear, was the area of their kitchen with a tan door that opened to the dark chill flurrying outside. A rustic counter was embedded along that kitchen wall, thick oak with a flowery jug and basin just below a window of several panes, a counter that pivoted a few feet right from the corner.

An array of elm boards lined the north and east kitchen walls, shelves displaying daily things like utensils for stewing and baking, little copper cups and pewter plates and mugs, and six crystal goblets Ethan's mother bought at the general store in Lexington. There was a stack of oak trenchers too, and some hidden drawers with tiny round knobs stuffed with little metal prongs and silvery forks, spoons and knives they hauled across the sea when they sailed to the colony several years before. And nearer the fireplace stones off to the right were a bunch of strange elm molds for forming tallow candles in tans, yellows and white.

A shiny cherry table sat just a bit right of the kitchen along the edge of a spacious rug, a wide wool circle in colorful braids that spread from the hearth about the oak slats of the floor. And a pair of thin candles rose from copper holders near the center of the table, their tiny curly wicks dark and cold, and pressed to its edges were four high slated chairs with sturdy weaved cushions.

The hearth consumed much of the rear eastern wall just off the kitchen, a place Ethan like to say his mother loved to cook, a fireplace of rocks and stones in oranges, browns and grays that began to narrow before vanishing through the roof. A thick elm mantel running the length of the hearth was fastened and tucked into the stones, with one of his mother's cherished candelabras rising near each end, three yellow candles thrusting from silver. A pile of logs sliced from nearby groves of birch and pine was nudged just right of the fireplace that December night, rocks and stones blackened over the years from ash and fiery embers.

Protruding from the inner left rocks of the hearth was a long dark rod with a tip that hooked, and dangling from that firm little curve by a thin handle was a bulging iron pot. Although cold and swung to the side that winter night, away from the snapping fire, it could be found over the years brimming with steamy stews on snowy winter days and chilling autumn nights. "I can still see mom flicking tasty seasonings into the kettle," Ethan once whispered as mist sprayed his eyes, "on stormy spring days or during wintry flurries, twirling a big spoon about her steaming pot. Then she'd lean, snatch a little nibble and smile, and give her simmering stew a few more fanciful swirls."

Nudged just left of the hearth on the oak slats of the floor was a small tin box stuffed with an array of little things to help bring flames to the logs, its thin dented lid clamped tight. It was a tinder box filled with tiny twigs and little flints, small gray stones and chippings of birch waiting to be struck, rubbed and sparked. And to the right of the fireplace stones was the Sheehan warmer, its thick copper disk resting to the slats of the floor and long oak handle leaning into the corner. Ethan once said he'd fill the copper hold with glowing embers on chilling spring, fall and winter nights, then gripping the thin handle and snapping the lid, with careful smooth slides warm the linens of his little bed.

Nearby, between that corner and his parent's bedroom door, was an aging spinning wheel Ethan's mother had purchased in a Boston merchant shop several years before. Thin strands of grayish wool dangled from its maiden posts on that December night, fuzzy threads that gently flowed down its spindled bobbin from the polished walnut of its wheel. And nudged close by, not far from the colorful braids of that big woven rug, was a little stool with a bluish cushion tied with thin loops of twine.

Two oak chairs with thick stylish legs were set to their proper place on the braids of the rug, each with tan cushions stuffed with tattered wool strips and little cotton clumps as they peered to the fire snapping in the hearth. And gently stashed in the southwest corner along that bedroom wall, near the lamp glowing in the window right of the house door, were several plump pillows resting upon a few folded blankets quilted in autumn colors, comforts to bundle with before a fire on blustery winter nights.

The door to Ethan's parent's room right of the fireplace was swung free during the final hours of that December night, a somewhat narrow room stretching the length of the house, with a pair of evenly spaced windows embedded in its southern wall. Pressed just below the panes of the right window was their bed, its head nudged near the glass, and an oil lamp glowed from atop a quaint oval table nestled in the corner. A similar table was set beyond the bedroom door nearer the other end of the room, polished maple with a lone candle, its little flame snapping shadows about the walls. Between those twin windows was a cherry cabinet sailed across the sea with Ethan's mother, a daintily carved cupboard brushed with little flowers, and a polished dresser with several maple drawers was nudged against the other wall by the door.

Hiding in the shadows was a small elm box that had been placed in the southeast corner of that room just a week before, a rather curious structure with slats and spindles that was to become Ethan's first little bed. It was a simple colonial crib with strange circular legs, thin disks of sliced elm to rock side to side, a miniature bed cushioned with a thick layer of soft woolen bundles. And as the final hour approached that night, a tiny quilted blanket his mother had snipped and stitched just weeks before waited for Ethan inside, along with a plump little pillow stuffed with soft feathers his father had plucked at a nearby creek from reluctant ducks frolicking about the icy waters.

I remember how Ethan's eyes sparkled when he softly confided, "Mom said that within the hour that night, before our clock chimed midnight, I was already dreaming in my little bed, snuggly wrapped from head to toe in that warm blue blanket. And each December when mom would recall that night, she'd whisper, 'you were so cute, Ethan, with smooth ruby cheeks and threads of brown hair that curled to your little ears. And your hands, were so tiny, with dainty little fingers.'"

Within moments after the hour of twelve chimed about the house that December night, Ethan's mother was finally resting easy in her bed, wrapped from the chill flurrying outside with linens and blankets. And his father stood quiet before the fire near the bedroom door, gazing to the flames between glances to his bride and newborn son bundled in his tiny crib. Abigail and Doc were standing before the hearth too, staring with a brush of contentment as the fire snapped about the stones, having finished several grueling hours of tending to Ethan and his mother. Gripped in Doc's left hand was a dark scuffed bag filled with special tools of his healing trade, little sponges and shards of cloth, small bottles of ointments and powders with tiny tan corks, and a scary array of silvery things like tongs and clamps, scalpels, needles and clips.

"Keep Liz calm tonight, Pat," sputtered Doc, breaking the hush while gazing to the fire, "and check little Ethan often. Keep him bundled up." Then with a concerned glance to Abigail standing patiently to his side, he cautiously added, "It might be a good idea to bring Ethan closer to the hearth too, move his crib into this room for tonight, and probably, the rest of the week. Keep him warm, Pat, close by the fire."

"Yes, Patrick," whispered Abigail concurringly, "bring little Ethan in here, at least for a few days."

"Alright, I will, tonight," replied Ethan's father while shuffling to their side. "Thank you, Doc, you too, Abigail, for all you've done for us, and on such a cold, dismal night. Thank you. I'll be in town to pay you, Doc, soon."

"It's what I do, Pat," uttered Doc Newman acceptingly, "Abigail too. But we appreciate your words, and you're welcome. Now, don't you worry about that payment tonight, just take care of Liz and little Ethan."

"That's right, Patrick," Abigail softly chimed, "you just keep Ethan and Liz warm, and don't you worry."

"I'll come out tomorrow," added Doc, "before supper, see how everyone is doing."

"Thanks, Doc," Ethan's father graciously replied, gripping Doc's hand before thanking Abigail with a gentle hug.

Stepping toward the farmhouse door, Doc and his wife donned their coats and scarves, gloves, bonnet and hat as Patrick tugged the wool of his coat, pressed his tricorn to his hair and dashed to the hearth, fetching a long twig with a little flame spritzing its tip. After a final gaze to the hearth's crackling fire and quick glance the quiet room off to the right, they stepped into the snow softly sprinkling night. As Ethan's father touched his fiery twig to the cold wicks of the candles, setting both lanterns aglow with little flames, Abigail and Doc climbed to the chill of their carriage seat, brushing at the white.

"You take care now, Patrick," uttered Doc while gripping the thin reins. And with a snap of the straps and spout of "get, get-get!" the buggy lurched into a creaking roll as hooves clumped in the snow.

Ethan's father watched as the buggy vanished into the wintry night, squeaking with each bounce on the snowy ruts of the Billerica Road to Lexington, then dashed back to the warmth of his home. He tossed his hat and coat near the door and untwined his icy shoes, then shuffled quietly toward the tranquil candlelight flickering softly in his bedroom. Snugging the blankets to the cheeks of his love, he leaned and kissed her tender lips, then shuffling toward the shadows of the corner, gently settled to a knee at that tiny crib. "Welcome to the world, little Ethan," he whispered, caressing the little curls of his hair. "Always know, I love you."

Chapter IV

Violet Gladiolus

George Augustus of Hanover had reached the age of sixty-seven during the year Ethan and I were born, and although he had occupied the British throne for nearly a quarter century by that 1750 wintry night in Lexington, some believed the king a bit slow to grasp the weight of governance, unwilling perhaps to ever-so-slightly ponder others' points of view. Yet some in those days believed King George the Second to be courageously brilliant, a monarch they'd say was unquestionably willing to lead his royal troops into battle.

Father once said there were others who found disloyal joy in mocking the King of England when the opportunity arose in those early days, spewing unsavory lies about his cerebral capacities, and some even accused the king of mimicking his Queen Caroline when purporting to espouse thoughts of his own. Still others perpetuated what Franz believed were vicious prevarications, that most ideas professed by the crown were surely uttered first by Prime Minister Pelham, or perhaps another of parliament or the elder statesman William Pitt.

Although the authority of the king was viewed by most to be absolute in those days, perhaps even thought of as divine, there seemed to be a brewing tendency in parliament to delicately exert an influence of its own, an embryonic sway acquiesced by the crown. All those laws, acts and decrees being contrived by parliament, intrusions finalized by the royal quill of the king, were not only altering the lives of millions of women, children and men on the Island of Great Britain, but increasingly intruding upon the lives of his royal subjects in the Thirteen Colonies, three thousand miles across the sea.

I suppose it was during those earliest years of Ethan's life, of my life and those of everyone throughout the colonies, when the twine that had loyally bound all of us to the English Crown for so many years began to slowly unravel. It was then, some would say years after the war, when our relationship with the king began to change in a distancing way, exposing an air of rambunctiousness by some questioning our loyal ties.

Embers glowing with discontent seemed to have been tossed upon each farm, port, village and town in those days, spritzing tiny flames of frustration about all the colonies about disturbing intrusions from across the sea. And if I recall, one of those inciting decrees espoused by London occurred that first year of Ethan's precious life, when the king and his parliament conceived what many believed was an ill-advised Iron Act. Some would later say it was an intrusive law cast upon our colonies to shackle our ability to thrive and create, while others came to view that act as the beginning of a painful fissure slowly oozing molten discord.

Even in those early days many colonists had come to view that Iron Act as simply intended to benefit loyal businesses in England at the expense of those in the colonies, for it terminated duties those royal industries had been paying for raw iron blasted over here. They say it was now less costly for those London companies to sail our colonial ore across the sea to produce metal goods in England, rather than allowing expansion of such trades right here in the Thirteen Colonies.

It seems that act also forbade our colonies from creating new factories for processing our own ore, as well as various tools needed to make iron goods, while insisting that the king's thirteen royal governors ensure each colony complied with London's new rules. And although most of our raw iron was said to be mined only in the colonial hills of Maryland and Virginia in those early days, many believed that the ships which sailed from our ports with hulls brimming ore, were perhaps the best hauls of all in the world.

Regardless of the varying opinions swirling the colonies, I suppose it was what many viewed as the unreasonable restrictions imposed by parliament upon our fledgling ore industry which aroused the ire of colonial entrepreneurs in those days, feelings which would cause embers of discontent to flare in the years to come. "The king and his parliament are conniving to destroy our industrious dreams," hundreds of merchants in the Port of New York, Philadelphia, Charles Towne, Boston and Savannah were said to have angrily bellowed. "We must find commonality among us, and oppose this disgusting nonsense coming from London!"

Looking back after all these years that 1750 Iron Act might appear innocently harmless, particularly I suppose, to Samuel and his generation, to those born long after the war, but to colonists reaching for dreams in those early days, it was viewed in a more disturbing light. When I was beginning my nursing training at the hospital many years later, just a year or so before that wondrous winter night when I first gazed upon Ethan, I remember hearing disgruntled merchants frustratingly saying, "What the king and his parliament truly meant by that wretched act, was to declare that colonists were not entitle to the same treatment as our brethren citizens across the sea in England."

They said it was as if we in the colonies had been declared less than those on the Island of Britain, for we were now forbidden from engaging in trades those in England could freely pursue. With a single stroke of the king's royal quill we had been relegated to an inferior position, prohibited from making common goods like iron nails for warehouses and little metal utensils for shops and homes, even plows for farms and sickles, knives and hoes. Some believed we had lost a slice of our liberty, and in a way a disheartening sense of subjugation began to take hold, a bitter odor that would waft about the colonies for years to come.

It wasn't long before King George and his parliament enacted more rules that were said to have caused many merchants in Ethan's Colony of Massachusetts Bay to become disgruntled, some even furious, when the crown instituted new regulations to limit the use of colonial parchment to pay for goods throughout New England. Ethan once explained that all four colonies were "forbidden from printing their own money," even if deemed necessary and proper for commerce, that their colonial assemblies and royal governors were prohibited from enacting laws for making or issuing their own scrip.

Although parliament called it the Currency Act, there were some in the colonies who preferred the less flattering phrase, "George's shilling dung," a restrictive law the king and his royal governors said was needed to stop the colonies from instituting policies harming England's merchants by decaying the value of London's pence, shillings and pounds. It seems many colonists in New England viewed parliament's reasons for that act as absurd, regarding it as an unjust erosion of our colonial rights, another preposterous intrusion into our colonial lives.

Yes, London had enacted some rather unpopular acts, policies and laws during the early years of my and Ethan's life, yet not all of the troubles beginning to simmer involved the brewing tensions between the Thirteen Colonies and the English Crown. Other disputes began to flare along the frontiers north and west, disturbing frictions simmering about the far reaches of the colonies that were being fueled by a foreign force. And although these rising tensions were mostly disputes between the King of England and the Crown of France over those wilderness forests, steams, hills and fields, the colonies were slowly being pulled into the fray.

It seems that some fifty years before, France had relinquished to England most of its holds over the northeast lands as punishment for being defeated in that quarrel many now call the War of Queen Anne. It was a wilderness expanse comprising the forests of New Brunswick and peninsula of Nova Scotia, along with an array of streams, mountains and bays, and a patch of land named Ile of Saint-Jean. It was a vast region most believed oozed sympathies for King Louis the Fifteenth of France, a wilderness harboring a troubling contempt for the British Crown.

They say Paris was determined to reclaim that vast region for their king, all of those northeast forests and streams the tribes of the native Inuit and Metis called Kanata. It was a wilderness many knew as the lands of New France, an area dotted with frontier villages like the fortresses of Montreal and Quebec. Yet, it seems King Louis also had visions of expanding further south and west, into the lands along the rocks of a few big lakes and the wilderness of the colonies of New York and Pennsylvania.

The surging incursions into those wilderness areas were said to include others besides soldiers of King Louis and French settlers and traders, for those of Paris had accumulated an array of indigenous allies, natives who had their own disputes with London. Thousands of Algonquians were believed to despise the policies of the English Crown, and many tribes of the Huron were rumored to hold an unsightly hatred for King George. Yet, in those days it seems London had corralled some native allies of its own, proud people like thousands of the Iroquois, along with a swelling cadre of spirited colonists seeking wealth, adventurers who coveted the resources abundant in the wilderness.

I'd later be told that soon both England and France were claiming that wilderness as their own in those months when Ethan and I were born, lands not only along the colonial fringes north and west, but the frontier from those big lakes down to the emerald sea west of Spain's La Florida. It was an expanse extending from the colonial frontiers of New York, Pennsylvania, Virginia, the Carolinas and Georgia to a mighty river many tribes knew as the Misiziibi, hundreds of miles west. And as Paris and London began to solidify their claims with an infusion of royal muskets, settlers and soldiers, each declared those lands for their king, a wilderness many were beginning to call the Ohio Country.

Some would later say that the friction between the crowns of England and France, troubles that would explode within a few years into an ugly conflict, truly began to brew in the hours before that December night in Lexington. There were stories that King Louis had been encouraging the Marquis de La Galissoniere, his loyal governor of New France in those days, to foster encroaching expeditions south and west into lands known to be within the purview of the British Crown. They say such ventures were not only to slice new outposts and forts in the name of Paris, but to become friendly with native tribes scattered about the wilderness.

It seems that around that time a few hundred French soldiers left the small fortress of Montreal under the command of an adventurist named Celoron, and within a week or so they crafted some little wilderness canoes and rowed further southwest along the shore of a big lake some called Erige. They had embarked upon an expedition into those coveted frontier lands, even carrying those small narrow boats several miles across the southwest fields and hills of the Colony of New York to the waters of a river the Allegewi natives of the Lenape tribe knew as the Welhikhane. From there they continued to row another hundred miles or so into the western wilderness of the Colony of Pennsylvania, where the river suddenly merged with the rushing waters of another wide stream the natives knew as the Menawngihella.

It was at that confluence where those two rivers formed a third that flowed southwest for hundreds more miles, a waterway the Seneca tribes knew as Ohiyo, a river most settlers were simply calling the Ohio. Although there was no true hamlet or village where those three rivers met in those days, there were rumors that a few rustic warehouses and huts belonging to the Ohio Company were scattered about the bluffs. It seems they were little frontier enterprises connected to the Colony of Virginia by the ruts and stones of a narrow road winding southeast through the wilderness, a fledgling settlement financed by some gentry colonists and merchants across the sea in London.

I remember father told me when I was young that it was on a rugged bluff above those three rivers that another expedition of French merchants and soldiers intruded several years later. He said they soon constructed an officious settlement in the name of their king, a rustic outpost sliced from nearby groves of oaks, hickory and elm those aligned with Paris soon called Fort Duquesne.

They say that Celoron and his Frenchmen continued rowing their canoes southwest on the waters of that Ohio River for several more days, then stopped their intruding expedition at the junction of another river the Algonquians had named for their Miami tribes. Those adventurists had sliced through wilderness that the colonies and London considered British lands, and along the way had thrust metal markers into the soil laying claim to the lands for Paris. There were disturbing stories too that Celoron's men had issued intimidating warnings to English merchants and colonial settlers in their path, to farmers and loggers, fur traders and speculators from the colonies of New York, Virginia and Pennsylvania, that the forest, hills and streams of the Ohio lands were now possessions of France.

Some believe that Celoron and his men also warned scores of native tribes encountered along their way of dire consequences should they continue to trade with colonists and English merchants, ugly threats they say were mostly ignored. Whether those peaceful natives were friendly with the English, French or colonists, it seems they nevertheless regarded the wilderness lands as their own, rich forest, streams and fields they believed should remain in their care. Yet, they were known to ally themselves in those days with whichever power displayed less belligerence and intrusiveness to their ageless claims, regardless of whether that power was London or Paris.

I think it was a few years later, perhaps when Ethan and I were only two, when those loyal to King Louis altered their earlier style of delicate warnings and embarked upon a punishing path, saying some native tribes of that Ohio valley had failed to heed their promised reprisals. It seems hundreds of fresh soldiers of New France unleashed an ugly campaign of shrilling violence against those who dared to defy the French Crown, an invading expedition into those lands with the help of native allies of the Ottawa and Ojibwa tribes. Now led by a man named de Langlade, that little French army followed the same southwest path deep into the wilderness during a chilling rain late that fall, slicing the river to a native village to confront its spirited chief Memeskia.

Some believe that it was during a lazy fog shortly after dawn at that tiny native village that the King of France began his brutal policy of ruthless punishment against those with differing points of view. Frightening stories would later reveal that within the hour that cold autumn morning many warriors and the defiant chief of that Piankashaw tribe lay silent in grisly pools steaming red, native men felled by blasting muskets or crazily sliced and bludgeoned to death. Fearful of retaliation from the English Crown, colonial settlers and vengeful native allies, de Langlade and his vicious band of killers quickly vanished northeast through the valley, escaping back to their haven of New France.

As horrific as that dreadful raid truly was, it seems that the thirst for blood by the soldiers of Paris and their native allies had yet to be quenched, for the following spring the governor of New France thrust another expedition into that Ohio valley wilderness. Some would later recall that this new invasion was perhaps gripped by a greater sense of purpose, a fresh intrusion most rational colonists described as "an affront to decency" for those who desired a peaceful resolution to the converging interests of Paris and London. They say that new French force of some two thousand men was commanded by an inspiring captain named de la Malgue, and along with scores of native allies eager to help enforce the encroaching lust of Paris, set out to defend what they believed to be forests, hills and streams belonging to the King of France.

Those invading actions were viewed by many colonists as dangerously provocative and seemed to cause panic in the souls of investors across the sea in London, as well as frontier speculators from several colonies like Virginia, New York and my Pennsylvania. Spirited merchants could be heard spouting that the French expedition was an "unacceptable intrusion into English lands of the American Colonies," an invasion that would in fact lead to an array of little French settlements about that Ohio valley, a string of fortifications garrisoned by soldiers of King Louis the Fifteenth. It seems their first outpost was erected along Presque' Isle Bay during the sweltering summer of 1753, a frontier fort on the southeastern shore of the big lake of Erie.

Fort de la Presque' Isle was rumored to look like a rustic oak box with thick pointy poles jutting from its walls into the air, a fort sliced along the northern fringe of a wilderness route leading into the depths of that Ohio land. It seems it had four square towers nudged to each corner too, timbered outlooks to keep a protective watch upon a little chapel for French soldiers and an array of barracks, and an infirmary for tending to the ailing and wounded.

Soon another fort they called de la Riviere aux Boeuf was sliced along a narrow creek some twenty miles south, as that determined French expedition continued to build outposts on its provocative incursion into the colonies of New York and Pennsylvania and the valley of the Ohio. They were intimidating actions said to escalate already simmering tensions along the frontier between the French Crown and its tribal allies, and the King of England and his native friends and colonies.

There were other disturbing stories too when I was young, frightful rumors about the slaughter of colonial settlers along the frontier by "savage native men," while some were said to vanish into the wilderness, "dragged into dens bathed of horror." They were dreadful stories about random killings, rumors that frightened even the older ones like mother as they spread from farms, villages and towns about the colonies, gruesome tales that haunted my dreams as winds howled the night.

I remember a story sweeping from the wilderness in those days about a young man from Londonderry in the Colony of New Hampshire, a village near the Merrimack River some thirty miles north of Ethan. They say Johnny Stark and his little brother Billie, along with an unsuspecting friend, were canoeing with spears, knives and dinged muskets for fish, fowl and game along a stream in the northern reaches of the colony's frontier, when their venture violently unraveled. It seems native warriors of the Abenaki tribe allied with the French Crown burst from the wilderness, capturing a terrified Johnny as little Billie escaped with frantic paddles of the canoe while screeching warriors bludgeoned the life from their friend.

Those warriors were said to have bound and dragged young John some sixty miles north through the wilderness to a forest near the French fortress of Quebec, and along with another colonist already tied to the trunk of a birch with twisting hemp, he too was twined and beaten. Yet, it was the rest of that horrible story that brushed my youthful imagination with hope while inspiring many colonists back then, tales about the torturous game those natives made those two captives play.

That young Stark would later say that he and Bart, or perhaps it was Otis or Burt, were forced to run between two columns of Abenaki warriors viciously swinging clubs and sticks as they raced down that torturous line. "Our skin would rip and slice," he determinedly recalled. "With each painful dash we left a spattering trail of red, and sometimes, our bones were heard to crack." They had been brutally persuaded to make that run under the threat of beheading, and young John would later tell how the whacks, moans, cries and cracks spewing from that gauntlet would echo about the woods as if from the depths of a ghastly dream.

But it's what happened next that gave hope to colonists that those frontier warriors aligned with France might not be as savage as rumored, that the natives struggling in the wilderness were brushed with a shade of fairness. While being threatened to make another frantic dash down that warrior line, it seems Johnny decided to grasp the reins of his fate, surprising his tormentors by snatching a warrior's bloodied club. With a determined glare in his stare he began to angrily swing at the slew of startled Abenaki men, thrashing that whipping stick defiantly about the air.

Stunningly impressed with his daring display of courage, the warriors halted their rage when their leader screeched and waved an end to their vicious gauntlet game, and as dusk settled upon the wilderness young Johnny and his bloodied friend were strangely accepted into the tribal fold. Then following what they say were weeks of discussions between Londonderry merchants and a few Abenaki men, the two were mysteriously released. For many years rumors suggested that Johnny and his friend were set free after an unsightly payment, released to their homes in the Colony of New Hampshire in exchange for an elm box stuffed with trinkets, shillings and pounds.

While those types of troubling events were taking place about the wilderness north and west in those early days, I was slowly becoming a young colonial girl in Germantown while Ethan was discovering his little world on his father's Lexington farm. Even though our villages seemed so far from those frightening things, Ethan once said that he could sense that maybe someday those wilderness clashes would slowly come closer to home. Yet, while those violent events continued to flare along the frontier in those years, and dispatches of their dangers were discussed in the halls of Paris and London, rumors of more pleasant things happening in the colonies were filtering about farms, ports, villages and towns.

A few of those rumors were of Mr. Franklin of my Colony of Pennsylvania, a rather respected man whom they say conducted many of his intriguing experiments about nature and life in Philadelphia. I'd later learn that his insightful theories and mysterious discoveries were well known throughout the colonies in those days, and it seems he had already developed a following across the sea in Warsaw, Amsterdam and London, as well with a few admirers known to sip Parisian wine along the River Seine.

It seems Benjamin Franklin was not from Philadelphia as I had believed when I was a little girl, but was born in a Boston cottage in Ethan's Colony of Massachusetts Bay in the winter of 1706. I remember how a few Germantown elders would sometimes say his birth was really the year before, as the old Julian calendar used to say, a system of dating changed by London to the Gregorian style when I was young. Ethan once said he was born on Milk Street near a church off King Street, and that his father was a tallow chandler in a quiet shop near the waters of Clarke's Wharf, making soaps, candles and other waxy things from the remnants of little animals.

The middle child of some ten siblings they say, Mr. Franklin began to expand his thoughts at the Boston Latin School when he was young, yet by the age of twelve or so had abandoned such formal learning. It seems he had become smitten with the trade of printing, and soon was apprenticing for his elder brother James, a colonial printer in his own right who was publishing news and events in his New England Courant.

Ethan said the Courant might have been the "first truly independent newspaper in all the colonies," and before long young Benjamin was quilling opinions for the paper, thoughts his brother declined to print. "That's when he began to expose a bold streak of independence," Ethan would add, "quilling letters from what in fact was an imaginary Bostonian," parchment sheets he'd surreptitiously sign as being quilled by Mrs. Silence Dogood. Her letters were said to espouse insightful opinions on an array of colonial things, and soon hundreds of colonists in and around Boston were reading the words of that curious widow printed in the Courant. They were drawn to what some said were Mrs. Dogood's daring assumptions sprinkled with spirited beliefs, and colonists could be seen discussing her notions with a splash of rum or sip of tea.

"But his ruse was uncovered by his brother," Ethan once whispered during a summer rain, "and that revelation seemed to cause their strained relationship to chill and splinter." It seems that soon young Benjamin deemed the moment ripe to leave the port of his birth, and shortly before turning eighteen, stuffed a bag with a few precious things and sailed to the

Colony of Pennsylvania on a Londoner's merchant ship, beginning anew near the Delaware River in Philadelphia.

Father once said that within weeks Mr. Franklin reentered the printing trade, continuing to hone his skills in various shops about Philadelphia, all the while quickly becoming acquainted with scores of women and men, along with an array of issues concerning the colony. It seems that within a few years he began to branch his interests once again, and was instrumental in gathering some artisans, tradesmen, printers and merchants into an influential group to discuss vital issues of the day. Soon, similar groups were said to have sprouted about Philadelphia, gatherings inspired by the colonial passions of Mr. Franklin.

They say that within a few more years he was volunteering for special colonial tasks too, eagerly delving into important things like helping to create a more proficient system of paths and roads to enhance the movement of packages, letters and bags to-and-fro villages and towns about the colonies. Yet perhaps his most cherished venture, I remember father would say, was his publication filled with an array of proverbial adages and phrases of wisdom he affectionately titled, Poor Richard's Almanac.

Although occupied by a string of divergent projects and interests through the years, perhaps his most intriguing indulgence involved the strange intricacies of the powers of electricity, a fascination that was said to culminate on a stormy afternoon in June, 1752. They say he had instinctively known that something special was happening when bolts would flash about the sky, that for years his visions had been brushed with notions of electricity, and that someday he would expose the connection between those two natural wonders. Father once said that Mr. Franklin's successful gamble captivated the colonies, jolting our imagination and causing a sensation to sail across the sea to councils of science and royalty in London, Amsterdam, Paris and Prague.

I heard stories when I was young that he had constructed a strange flying contraption in his study that spring, a kite of narrow elm sticks skinned by tan linen attached to a great length of twine. Wrapped about that thread was a stretch of latten wire, and dangling from that thin iron was a small latch key. They say that as a blustery storm began to brew about Philadelphia that gloomy June day, Mr. Franklin gathered his flying concoction and dashed to a grassy hill near the river. One witness explained that as the winds began to whip and droplets sprinkled his face, Mr. Franklin wrapped the end of the twine about his fingers, raised his kite and released the linen and sticks into the gusting breeze, setting his dangling key free.

"It leapt from his grip with a bursting jolt," that young witness would say, "darting left and right as it soared into the sprinkling winds of the billowing storm. He just stood there watching, gripping that twine for half an hour or so as that funny looking kite whipped about the breeze, until suddenly, a yellowish flash streaked across the sky. I saw the bolt whiz toward that swirling kite, and as if scripted by angels, with a thunderous clap it zapped that dangling key."

I remember father saying that Mr. Franklin's key had become consumed by an electrical charge, "just as he had predicted," and within days the exciting news about that mysterious kite was swirling about the colony. They say that by the final weeks of summer dispatches of Mr. Franklin's experiment, supporting his electrical theories, had not only reached hundreds of ports, villages and towns throughout the colonies, but had sailed across the sea in special courier satchels.

Revelations of his exciting discovery with kite and key were said to have been met with dazzling enthusiasm by those of science and intrigue, and soon others were confirming Mr. Franklin's findings with strange experiments of their own. Respect for his position was glaringly magnified throughout the colonies too, and in the coming months and years they say his reputation blossomed not only here in the colonies, but in ports, villages and towns scattered about Europe, especially in the councils of Paris and London.

It seems that with his surging reputation came more responsibilities too, and soon Mr. Franklin accepted an offer from the English Crown to hold what many would say was one of the most prestigious positions in the colonies. In conjunction with the postmaster of Williamsburg in the Colony of Virginia, Mr. Franklin was appointed by London to be Postmaster General for all the Thirteen Colonies.

I suppose many elder colonists in those days were not surprised by Mr. Franklin's impressive appointment, many saying he had been groomed for such a position for many years before Ethan and I were born. After all, it seems he had been postmaster for Philadelphia while struggling as the publisher and printer of the Pennsylvania Gazette, and during those days had become rather influential in the Colony of Pennsylvania. Particularly some believed, in addressing concerns with how best to ensure the efficient delivery of newspapers, pamphlets, packages and letters throughout the colonies.

I would learn years later that Mr. Franklin soon became instrumental in forming new postal roads, all the while ensuring existing paths were made better, trails like the postal road between Ethan's Boston and the Port of New York, a path first carved through New England decades before. They say he was uncanny at developing quicker ways for routing our colonial mail too, suggesting things like postal riders galloping through the night, an idea that sliced hours between villages, ports and towns. Special stones to guide weary riders and mark the miles were strategically placed along an array of postal roads as well, like the paths from Philadelphia to Dover and Williamsburg. Within a few years it seems those changes had created what father said was a "superior delivery system," one stretching over a thousand miles from the northern frontier of the Colony of New Hampshire to the southern hills of the Colony of Georgia.

Meanwhile, during those formative years when Ethan and I were so young, while those postal roads were being improved and troubles were brewing about the wilderness, colonists in my Germantown and Ethan's Lexington were going about their little lives, just as those in hundreds of colonial ports, villages and towns. Children were strolling to quaint little schools and mothers were simmering stews or spinning threads, snipping and stitching aprons, stockings and shirts, bonnets, blankets and breeches. Farmers were tilling their fields too, and men young and old were straining with sacks, boxes and crates on colonial wharfs and docks. And while tradesmen engaged in their crafts and merchants tended their shops, doctors and nurses mended the ailing and injured while barristers counseled colonists who had harmed another or unleashed the wrath of the crown.

Still others published stories about simmering troubles and colonial events, audacious printers exposing another encroaching policy of a royal governor or new intrusive act from London, or some unjust decree of the king. Some were said to quill with great passion about many of those things, inspiring opinions that seemed to spring from their souls when the moment was right, daring men expressing ideas in pamphlets and papers printed to parchment in hundreds of shops across the colonies.

Although Ethan and I were among the youngest in those early days, we would come to understand that most colonists simply sought their own way of life, grasp a path shown by their God, just as generations had years before the war. And those of my generation, little girls and boys in those days, seemed to exist in our own little worlds, away from the storms of life. We'd banish the thunderous changes echoing about the trees, escape to our own secure places awash with the sweet nectars of youth.

Ethan once told me of summer days outside of Lexington, of frolicking about a refreshing shower or basking in the heat that would clutch his Colony of Massachusetts Bay for what seemed endless days. And he'd whisper fondly too, of how he and children from nearby farms would escape their parent's ties, if only for a little while. "We'd dash to our secret place south of the Jafres farm," he'd say, "to the cool waters of a little creek, then amid a scattering of giggles and hoots, toss our shirts, stockings and shoes, and splash into the shallows of our stream."

I remember how he shyly blushed when confessing about a special little girl too, Francisca Spoons from across the Billerica Road, a year older who seemed effervescently wise. "Her eyes were so brown, Andrea, and her auburn hair dangled to her shoulders. I must say, I was smitten on those summer days, by a dainty girl of five. While the others were fetching tiny tadpoles, she and I would slowly wade to a secluded spot at a shallow bend near a knotty oak. Then Franci would take my hand, and we'd dive into a magical world. We'd open our eyes, Andrea, and for a few innocent moments, gaze to each other, then just as our lungs were about to betrayed us, she'd tap her lips to mine."

I can still see the mystical expressions that would bathe Ethan's face whenever he'd expose such tender secrets, and I'd wonder how he seemed to miss those youthful days, longingly so. "We'd play with old iron hoops too," he'd grinningly say, "from broken buggy or wagon wheels, all of us, rolling them about the road. And sometimes we'd gather and play nine pins, or maybe a scampering game of tag." They played other games in Lexington too, just like children throughout all the colonies in those days, even we little girls and boys in Germantown, innocent games like blindman's bluff and leapfrog, or simply racing about a field with legs ensnarled in sacks and bags.

He talked about gently gliding over the waters of that creek too, swinging on an elm slat hanging by thick twine twisted about the limb of that knotty tree. "We'd swing one-by-one, Andrea, sweep just above the water farther and faster, then leap and plunge into the creek. Sometimes, Franci would swing with me, and together, we'd splash into the water." There were moments too when the girls hopped about little squares lined by tiny stones on the road while Ethan and his friends, gripping thin branches with little hooks dangling thread, would wander to that creek to snatch a fish or two.

And on snowy winter days or when the rains of spring, summer and fall muddied the roads, hills and fields of Germantown and Lexington, of villages and towns throughout the colonies in those days, children would escape in the confines of their homes. Ethan said he'd spin a little whirligig about the slats of their farmhouse floor with a snapping flick of twine wrapped about his finger, or skim one his father's books, even reading a page or two. And just as thousands of little girls I suppose, I would thread a sewing needle and embroider special cloth or stitch a scarf or dress, or maybe mold waxy candles near a crackling fire, or don my little apron and help mother bake tasty muffins or stir a simmering stew.

Although most of the memories from our youth were bathed of preciously pleasant things, there was one Ethan recalled that was brushed by an ugliness that would sometimes emerge. Some in the colonies carried thoughts that struck at the very essence of innocence, ideas that would expose a darkness that dwelled within hearts to tarnish unsuspecting youth, even children of Germantown or Lexington. They were twisted notions planted into young minds by those with powers over little ones, a disturbing hatred brewed by the bigoted fears of wayward mothers and fathers, adults passing a despicable plague to beguiled children of a new generation.

I remember how Ethan would cringe when talking of Robby Beatty, about his age from the farm just west of his, an intimidating boy some of the children of Lexington tauntingly called crazy Bobby. "He'd spew vile things about the Jafres," Ethan once said, "hateful words about Negroes, of Quincy and his family. Robby was a bloody numskull, Andrea, spouting deplorable denigrations just because of the color of their skin. And I just knew, we all did, that he learned those disgusting things from his father."

Then when Ethan grew a bit older, when the bigoted words of crazy Bobby began to fade as the interests of the Lexington children changed, Ethan began spending more time browsing the books, pamphlets and papers his father had slowly assembled in their home. They were normally stacked in the little den his father made near Ethan's room, several piles on the slats near his father's desk, and many printings dealt with facets of Irish and Dutch, Scottish, English and French histories, with a few about our colonies. There were old dramas too, mostly by Englishmen like Shakespeare, Haughton and Shadwell, but the one which seemed to attract Ethan the most was a story quilled some fifty years before, a play called Cato by London's Joseph Addison.

There were rather carefree days as well, of Ethan simply strolling about their farm, sometimes with bare feet to feel the soothing richness of the soil while smelling the grains swaying the fields or the fragrance of gladiolus blooming about the hills. "On warm summer evenings I'd listen to a symphony of leaves," he once whispered to me, "the rustling of oak, birch and elm along the road, and sometimes at twilight, I'd just walk about the crops sprouting in rows." He talked of watching dusk settle over Lexington on quiet August nights too, of layering shades of yellows, oranges and reds creeping beyond the frontier as little stars exploded across the sky.

And when not studying in his chair at the Lexington schoolhouse, just a half hour stroll along the Billerica Road, or scampering about with little friends or wandering about the fields, Ethan would help his father till their farm wherever he could. Although rather thin and small in his younger days, so light he'd sometimes wonder if a blast of autumn wind might someday whisk him from the soil, he always strived to pull his own weight. "I wasn't very strong, Andrea," he'd humbly say, "and would struggle with the plough behind our smelly ox. I'd grip the handle and reins as best I could, then trudge the field while desperately trying to guide that crusty iron blade."

Ethan prided himself on being useful about the farm, and perhaps enjoyed the later days of autumn the most, when harvesting time would come. Although he'd say it was rather toiling work, he would smile just a bit when talking of bundling hay or stripping corn from gangly stalks on brisk fall nights. And when tasks became too much of a struggle for a young boy, even one as eager as Ethan, he'd fill an oak bucket with various grains and sprinkle tiny bits about a gaggle of chickens, a few dashing turkeys and some muddied sows squealing inside their pungent pen.

There were indoor responsibilities as well, chores Ethan's mother would kindly ask be done while teaching him an array of domestic skills when his father was not explaining the nuances of their tinderbox or showing him the proper ways of swinging an axe. "Mom showed me how to fire the hearth for cooking," he once proudly confessed, "and things about needles and threads, like special stitches for darning holes, rips and tears in stockings, shirts and breeches." Yet, when not wrapped in studies from school or consumed with home and farming chores, what Ethan truly cherished was simply lying upon a soft field of grass, lazily wondering of his life to come.

There was a special oak tree near the edge of the Billerica Road he once told me about, not far from the farmhouse, where he'd lie in a summer shade beneath sprouting limbs and wonder from where the tranquil winds had come. He'd link his fingers behind his hair and watch little clouds slowly drifting, puffs of gray and white that would magically change with his dreaming imagination. And on many evenings after supper, when his studies and duties were done, Ethan would rush to his precious spot near that tree and peer to the fading shades of the setting sun and first twinkles dotting the night, mesmerized by it all.

"He seems to have been, a kind of dreamer, grandma," uttered Samuel, softly snapping my thoughts, "or maybe, just more serious than most. It sounds like he could do what many would like, being able to shield his self from the struggles of life. You know, grandma, for being just a boy in those early years, it sounds like he had a strange insight about things, more so, than older ones."

"I think he was like that," I sighed, nudging my chair into a softer rock. "Maybe Ethan did view things different than most, Samuel, even at such an early age. I know that later, when we finally met, those things were some of the reasons he attracted me so."

We slowly rocked in a quiet hush and listened to the leaves gently rustling in the July breeze, and while Samuel gazed to the distant trees I could see a sparkle in his eyes, a special gleam that used to shine from Ethan's many years ago. Perhaps it was simply my imagination, a surging fancy to be near Ethan once again, yet I mysteriously sensed his presence amidst the glow of Samuel's eyes. "Ethan seemed to grasp the essence of life," I reflectively added, sliding my fingers across the parchment of Ethan's poem nestled in the pocket of my summer dress, feeling his tenderness with each caress. "It was as if he understood things better, knew what was right, important in life."

"You know, grandma," sputtered Samuel, glancing to my eyes, "I remember playing some of those same silly games when I was young, with little friends right here in Germantown. And as much as it pains me to admit, that same hatred in people who fear others who look different, like the bigotry spewed by that Robby, is still around."

"Oh, Samuel, how I wish it were not so. Why do people continue to treat others with contempt, simply because of the color of their skin? There are so many Negroes still in bondage right now, slaves laboring on farms of unjust men, and it's so wrong. I wish we could find the courage to end such evil right now, bury such bigotry deep in the soil."

"Do you think that will ever happen, grandma?"

"We can hope, Samuel," I encouragingly sighed with a tinge of lingering shame, "it just has to be stopped. But after so many years, maybe only God can bring that scourge to an end. At least we did bring a halt to part of it, no longer allowing ships to sail to our ports with hulls brimming Negro souls. It's a start, Samuel, a beginning of chipping away at the foundation of that evil system. Ethan always hoped that someday the color of a person's skin wouldn't matter, and once whispered with a dash of optimism, 'It's the inner essence of a person that matters, and that notion alone, Andrea, is what must bind our colonies together.'"

"I hope so too, grandma, but just don't know. There's so much powerful resistance involved, so much greed."

"I know, Samuel. But we've got to hope, like Ethan did. Maybe someday, compassion will grip everyone's soul."

"Maybe," Samuel uttered, nudging his chair into a more robust rock while peering with a doubting squint to the swaying limbs of the distant elms, their leaves fluttering in the summer breeze, "someday. You know, grandma, your eyes show how much you cared for Ethan, and your voice at times is joyous when recalling memories. Tell me more about those early days when you were so young, about the colonies. But most of all, grandma, tell me about Ethan."

"In a way," I whispered, caressing the passions of Ethan's poem, "those earliest days are when the views of many colonists began to slowly be brushed with evolving notions about who and what were truly were. And it wasn't just the older ones, Samuel, but many of the young like Ethan and me, untarnished little minds of thousands throughout the colonies."

As Samuel pressed to the slats of his chair and gazed to the distant leaves dancing in the breeze, awaiting my coming words while rocking a bit slower, I wondered how those early days had truly shaped my generation, molding ideas that would be carried into the years leading to the war. When I recall such things after all these years, I suppose many colonists had begun to view our connections with England in a differing light than the generations that had come before, and as the years slowly passed, our evolving thoughts and spirited passions simmered and spritzed until finally igniting into flames. Perhaps we were an impatient generation, yet inspiringly so, for we were colonists who sought to change not only the foundations of our lives, but those of generations to come.

I suppose it was in the fall of 1753, when Ethan and I, when so many were so innocently young, that those changes had truly begun, for it was during those days that the troubles simmering along the north and west frontiers began to boil. Those wilderness outposts created along the valleys, rivers and hills of the Ohio Country by the soldiers and tribal allies of King Louis the Fifteenth continued to draw the ire of the British Crown, while sounding frightening alarms throughout the colonies, particularly Virginia, New York and my Pennsylvania.

It seems that various merchants and investors of land may have been fueling those escalating tensions too, wealthy colonists and men of London who had growing financial interests in those wilderness lands. "They feared the loss of their vast investments," father once explained, "in the forests and fields, minerals and furs," and some were said to be frantic with thoughts of losing their wealth should the encroaching actions of Paris remain. Others seemed consumed with fears of diverging religions too, competing beliefs in God by the King of England and Catholic France, colonists worried about losing their spiritual liberties.

Whatever anxieties were simmering in those days, whether concerns of faith or losing prestige, land or power, father said it was probably a consuming fear of fiscal ruin which caused events to spiral from control, fears by wealthy investors in the colonies and London. It was that notion of doom sweeping from the frontier, and the belief that the army of France and its native allies had placed their treasures in peril, that many would say spurred powerful merchants in the Colony of Virginia to determine the moment to act had arrived.

Although it seems some of that colony's influential investors and merchants had close relations with the king's Royal Governor van Keppel, many were said to be more entwined with Robert Dinwiddie, his royal subordinate. They were rumored to have embarked upon a determined effort to persuade him that direct action to confront the French threat along the frontier was vitally prudent. "We must address the crisis in the northwest now," many were reported to demand, "or the King of France is certain to smell weakness in London. They'll expel the English Crown completely from the Ohio lands, along with our colonial interests."

After discussing all those vital concerns with an array of colonists and the royal governor, it seems Mr. Dinwiddie came to the same conclusion, that the French forces gobbling up the wilderness had to be confronted. Yet, they say it was decided that cannons and muskets would remain silent, that London would try to resolve its dispute with Paris through words with a single frontier commander. And in the fall of 1753 he summoned a young militia major for the Colony of Virginia, a man most agreed would properly convey King George's demands to Jacques Legardeur de Saint-Pierre, one of King Louis' frontier soldiers from the northern lands of New France.

Although their chosen major was only twenty-one as of that autumn, they say he had been reared in one of the more entrenched families of Westmorland County, a gentry-family with vast swaths of hills, woods and fields in the northeast sector of the Colony of Virginia. Yet, perhaps his intricate knowledge of the colony's lands made approving his role of leading that expedition more acceptable, especially his understanding of the western forests of the Colony of Pennsylvania and those disputed lands of the Ohio frontier. Although his selection may have had its doubters, they say most of Mr. Dinwiddie's group believed that young George Washington was the proper choice for delivering the crown's message into the wilderness.

One colonist recalled watching as Mr. Dinwiddie grumbled some instructions to Major Washington before creasing a sheet of parchment quilled with what were King George's demands, placing it in the major's hand and spouting, "Take this to that bloody French commander!" With the purpose of their mission firmly in his grasp, Major Washington was said to have assembled his small militia force, a group of daring men like Jacob Van Braam, a colonist well versed in French, and a surveyor named Gist from the village of Wills Creek.

Saddled atop a steady tan colt on the first Wednesday of November, Major Washington led his column of mounted men in a trot northwest from Williamsburg during a chilling morning drizzle. One witness would later say that he could tell by the glare in their eyes how determined they were to find that New France commander believed to be near a new fort called Le Boeuf, some three hundred and fifty miles into the wilderness. Stories would later reveal that toward the end of the month that colonial column finally reached the western frontier of the Colony of Pennsylvania, and as a blustery snow swept from the north, they created a camp along the waters of that Ohio River. They were now near Logstown, a tiny colonial outpost some twenty miles northwest of Fort Duquesne, the French settlement at the confluence of those three rivers.

Some believe that it was there, at their little camp along the river, that Major Washington and his militia encountered a band of Iroquois warriors of the Mingo tribe, natives known to hold sympathetic views of King George and his Colony of Virginia. A militiaman later revealed that his major parleyed with their chief, and as the tarpaulin of his tent buffeted with the chilling winds, it became clear that the Mingos supported the crown's plans. It seems that the chief confessed that his people were distrustful of the encroaching French, and expressed a slew of disdainful thoughts about all the outposts and forts they had carved from what he viewed as Mingo land.

Young Washington was said to have corralled the support of the chief and his warriors as planned, and shortly after dawn the following morning, the militia and its tribal friends began their challenging trek toward Fort Le Boeuf, some hundred miles north. They sliced their way through the wilderness across icy streams and snowy hills for several grueling days, and as a light flurry dusted the trees the second Tuesday of December, arrived at the French outpost shortly before dusk.

It seems Major Washington reported that he and de Saint-Pierre, well versed in the English language, dined alone in his quarters just inside the fort's south wall early that first night. Then shortly after supper, while sipping white wine from pilfered crystal goblets, the major presented Mr. Dinwiddie's letter to the fort's commander, advising of its' importance. It was a communique expressing the desires of King George and the royal governor of the Colony of Virginia, an unambiguous demand for the immediate withdrawal of King Louis' forces from the wilderness lands of the Ohio.

After slowly reading each line with a devious glare, a contemptible calmness brushed de Saint-Pierre's face as he creased the parchment and placed it upon a little table to his side. And as Major Washington stood quiet with his wine, the French commander gripped his goblet and stepped to the fire snapping wildly about the stones. "Intriguing request," he confidently conveyed with an impertinent peer. "No, Major Washington, I, we, shall do no such thing. On behalf of the French Crown, I must deny this demeaning threat, this unsightly ultimatum from your king."

"I see," young Washington calmly uttered while sliding his goblet to the table. "I must say, commander, your position is, disappointing. I'll report your views to my superiors." Pinching his tricorn and pressing it firmly to his hair, he bid de Saint-Pierre a solemn "good night," then snapping and shuffling in his boots, vanished into the chill.

Under a blue frigid sky the following December morning, Major Washington and his men climbed to their mounts shortly after dawn and galloped from the French fort of Le Boeuf. They returned to their Colony of Virginia through the wilderness, having been escorted southwest by their Mingo friends the first hundred miles or so, riding through chilling forests and icy streams amid wintry winds, before trotting the snowy ruts of the road into Williamsburg. The king's royal governor and Mr. Dinwiddie, along with scores of the colony's gentry, were rumored to have not only been disheartened by that French commander's refusal, but agitated by what many were saying was his defiant insolence.

It seems Major Washington also advised his colony's men that it appeared the French not only intended to remain garrisoned at Fort Le Boeuf, but seemed to be increasing in strength while thrusting further south along the frontier with wagons and carts bulging supplies. They say he also reported that King Louis' soldiers were continuing to construct outposts at strategic places about those three rivers, slicing new forts from the wilderness at places called Venango and Presque Isle, each brimming with provisions and troops.

Father once said that a disturbing sense of unease over the direction of those events began to sweep across the colonies of Virginia, Pennsylvania and New York, frightening feelings that were making their way to the colonies New Hampshire and Ethan's Massachusetts Bay too, and soon, to all the Thirteen Colonies. "People in some places were almost in a panic," he'd say, "many extremely nervous about what might happen in the coming winter and spring." It seems some of the older colonists remembered the previous struggles that had exploded along the frontier several times between Paris and London, the last a decade before in what they called, King George's War. And now, many feared that the crowns of England and France, along with their native allies, were barreling toward another deadly wilderness fight.

Yet, even though the frontier was said to be vitally important for several colonies, perhaps in what father would say was a narcissistic way, and King George and his parliament were determined to thwart these newest provocations by King Louis and his troops, each colony seemed to act as if it were a sovereign enclave unto its own. "We were English colonies," he once explained, "but not united in any way. We were thirteen separate groups, with each colony consumed with its own desires."

It seems each colony had its own distinct militia, with a structure of command tailored for its own needs, and each held selfish beliefs on how to address the tempest brewing in the wilderness. Thirteen differing strategies were being formed by thirteen royal governors, plans being developed with the aid of speculators of London and colonial gentry and merchants. Each colony was determined to uphold its own interests and views, and they say the Colony of Virginia intended to show the way, mustering its men as other colonies continued to simply talk of assembling their militias to make their own move.

While strategic discussions swirled about the assemblies of twelve colonies in the spring of 1754, the Colony of Virginia decided to act, and just as the fall before, Mr. Dinwiddie summoned that young soldier from Westmorland County. Having been promoted in the colony's militia, Colonel Washington was instructed to convince the French forces to abandon their positions on what was viewed as England's frontier, retreat north to their own lands of New France. Without the aid of royal troops from London, Colonel Washington assembled a modest force of some four hundred colonials, and in early May his militia began its march toward the northwest wilderness of the Ohio lands.

One witness would later recall watching the militia gather that spring morning and form two long columns with snorting mounts, each with muskets strapped over shoulders and most donning fur, tricorn or floppy hats. Then with crusted shoes and muddied boots stuffed into leather stirrups dangling saddles, they slowly trotted along the ruts and stones of the winding road from Williamsburg, close behind Colonel Washington. Although their destination was truly unknown by most colonists of the village, it seems some believed the militia was riding to the French fort of Duquesne at the confluence of those three rivers, an outpost now garrisoned by several hundred of King Louis' troops, along with scores of native allies and militiamen of New France.

I'd hear stories when I was young of how that colonial column was soon joined along the winding path by that Mingo chief and his fiery warriors, and for many miles through the wilderness that determined force met little resistance until the last Tuesday of May. Shortly after dawn, as a cool drizzle gently fell from a roiling gray, Colonel Washington and his men stumbled upon a patrol of some forty French soldiers and dozens of their native friends some fifty miles southeast of that French fort. It would later be told that those men had been dispatched from Fort Duquesne with orders not to engage, with instructions to initiate talks while avoiding a fight.

Unaware of their diplomatic mission and fearing a lethal strike, Colonel Washington was reported to have swung his sword into the spring chill while commanding his militia to attack, surprising King Louis' men. They say several French troops were mortally felled in the first frantic moments of hundreds of musket blasts, while dozens were sprawled about the trees with gaping wounds seeping life into the soil. After gathering his wits and surmising their frail position, the commander of the French suddenly ordered his remaining force to halt their fight as his distraught men tossed spears, knives and muskets.

However, it seems that fearing the approach of French reinforcements from Fort Duquesne, Colonel Washington was said to have cautiously dashed from those hallowed woods with his men, galloping a few miles southeast to a spring meadow. The militia quickly regrouped and began to construct a protective shield, a small encampment sliced from the nearby woods some would tauntingly call, Fort Necessity.

Although the militia had made a daring attempt to control its own fate, within hours the French troops Washington had feared materialized, a raging force supported by tribal allies that dashed from the wilderness. "We couldn't stop em," one of the militiamen would later say. "There was just too many of em." Unable to repel the surprising attack, Colonel Washington surrendered his position, handing the French force his sword along with hundreds of stunned militiamen. Yet, it seems the colonials were soon released by their Paris captors, mercifully allowed to return to their homes in the Colony of Virginia after Washington agreed to keep his forces from the Ohio Country over the coming year.

Some would later say that it was just a little skirmish in the wilderness, rather inconsequential when compared to gruesome battles which had taken place between the two kings along the frontier decades before. Yet, it seems that stories of Colonel Washington's debacle at that wilderness meadow would reverberate about the colonies, with disturbing dispatches of the French victory quickly sailing across the sea to Paris and London. I think it was then that many began to understand that the troubles brewing along the frontier were developing into a broader war between King Louis and King George, a pair of rival monarchs some viewed as obnoxious children tugging on mysterious twine spanning the waters of the channel.

"What about the other colonies, grandma?" interrupted Samuel with a gentle nudge of his chair. "What was happening in other places after that skirmish in the meadow? Did the Colony of Massachusetts Bay decide to jump in? What about Ethan's father and thousands of others? Were they beginning to feel as though they'd be dragged into that frontier fighting?"

I pushed my chair into a softer rock as Samuel stared to a string of dust swirling from the lane into the warming summer air, and wondered of the things he and his generation seemed so unaware, of our colonial history that was slowly being lost. And as I listened to the gentle breeze softly swirling about the distant leaves, I caressed the passions of Ethan's poem and reached for memories of those days so long ago, when Ethan and I were so young.

"I remember Ethan saying his father was toiling their farm that spring," I whispered while gently strumming the aging parchment and gazing to the rustling leaves, "just as he always was, just as most farmers about the colonies. And although his father was also in the Lexington militia, along with most men and boys from sixteen to sixty throughout the colonies in those days, their militia had yet to be called to muster."

"What about here?" Samuel inquisitively wondered. "What about the militias around Germantown and Philadelphia?"

"I was so young that spring, Samuel, yet strangely, remember so much. There were no gatherings of our Germantown militia, at least none that I had seen or heard, and father had never gone to drills before. I think it was like that down in Philadelphia too, at least that spring. But there were stories about some militias fighting hundreds of miles west, nearer our colony's frontier, and frightening rumors of more skirmishes near that Fort Duquesne. Yet those things seemed so far away. Most colonists back here, closer to the Delaware River, just went about their lives without dwelling too much on the sporadic troubles along the frontier."

"I don't understand, grandma. Didn't other colonies so something to address the dangers those skirmishes seemed to be exposing? What did the other royal governors do? Was the Colony of Virginia the only one to call out its militias?"

"I guess most colonies were just waiting, at least in the spring of 1754. Maybe it was because those skirmishes were seen by some as part of a fundamental struggle between Paris and London, not the colonies, with only a few colonists truly involved. Father said that at first those things were viewed by many as one king desperately trying to retain what he declared to be his rightful lands, while the other in Paris sought to dampen that wealth and power, make the wilderness his."

"But didn't you say some colonies did have interests in those lands? Like the Colony of Virginia."

"Yes they did, some more so than others, Samuel, those with investments in those wilderness lands. But I think most believed the core concerns involved the idiosyncrasies of the royals of England and France, and if I recall, most of the battles to come were fought with their loyal troops. Oh sure, some colonies would eventually send their militias into the fray, but most soldiers who fought those French had sailed across the sea from London. Some disembarked near here in Philadelphia, while others were said to have landed at Williamsburg, Charles Towne and the Port of New York, and more up in Ethan's Boston."

I paused for a calming breath of warm summer air and rocked a bit slower as Samuel continued to gaze to the swaying tips of distant elms, then sliding my fingers across the parchment of Ethan's aging poem, I reflectively added. "I think that some colonies wanted to find consensus on how to address the fighting flaring about the wilderness that spring, something that was proving rather difficult, what with thirteen differing views of things. Father said some wanted to find ways to coordinate colonial actions to douse the fires erupting north and west, rather than each colony striking on its own. Some even believed the colonies should form a special meeting of all thirteen to forge a united strategy to address the conflict brewing along the frontier, while discussing other interests, concerns and threats common to us all."

"What did the colonies do? Did they find a way to come together?"

"Yes, Samuel, they did, at least some of the colonies. Spirited men decided to meet up in the Colony of New York early that summer, at the village of Albany along the Hudson River, a meeting that also included chiefs of some tribes. It was sanctioned by the king and parliament too, as well as his royal governors, at least for a little while. Father later said they discussed several issues in common, concerns affecting all the colonies, especially the brewing conflict with the French. But not all colonies attended, Samuel, with only half sending men to discuss those vital things."

As Samuel gazed into the summer winds, awaiting my coming words with each rock, I caressed the ink of Ethan's poem amidst the tranquil sounds of leaves softly rustling in the breeze. They were soothing sounds as comforting now as they were when Ethan and I were so young, and as my fingers stroked his tender words, I could feel the memories of those days so long ago surge.

Some twenty delegates from seven colonies assembled in the village of Albany, a congress that also invited dozens of native chiefs from what they called the Iroquois Indian Confederation in those days. A few came to believe that the true reason for the king's approval of that meeting was to gain support of those tribes in his wilderness struggle against King Louis and his forces, hoping that somehow those warriors would ally with London, and thus, keep them from the clutches of Paris.

Ethan once told me in the days before the war that many came to believe that unforeseen consequences evolved from that colonial assembly in Albany that year, and in the eyes of parliament and the king, some disturbingly so. "They were things," he confided, "which would someday assist the unraveling of our loyal ties with the English Crown." Our colonies had finally begun to truly talk with each other, discuss common purposes, issues and concerns, and search for ways to coordinate colonial actions. In those early years, the crux of our common colonial concerns was what to do about the exploding frictions along the frontier. Then as the years slowly passed, our eyes shifted to the troubles brewing between the colonies and London.

It's been over seventy years since that conference assembled along the Hudson River some two decades before the war, yet for many of that generation, the men who attended and the accords that were forged remain clearly tucked in memories. Some still talk of how the chief of the Mohawk tribe spoke rather tough on behalf of his people, yet eloquently, and the colonists assembled discussed an array of things with insight and purpose. They were spirited men who represented the colonies of Maryland and New York, New Hampshire, Rhode Island and Connecticut, as well as my Pennsylvania and Ethan's Massachusett Bay.

The representatives from those seven colonies were said to have not necessarily sought to uphold some notion of colonial autonomy, but rather, strove to find ways to further the goals of the king while meeting the needs of both London and the Thirteen Colonies. Strangely, I still recall those men. Conrad Weiser, Doctor Franklin and his son William were there for my Colony of Pennsylvania while Oliver Partridge and Thom Hutchinson came from Ethan's Massachusetts Bay, and Theodore Atkinson and Meshech Weare spoke on behalf of New Hampshire. There was Stephen Hopkins too, from Rhode Island, and William Pitkin, Roger Wolcott and Elisha Williams of Connecticut. William Johnson, Philip Livingston and Royal Governor DeLancey came from New York, and young Ben Tasker and Abraham Barnes were there for the Colony of Maryland.

With the conflict brewing along the frontier entrenched in the minds of most delegates, the colonials meeting in Albany found a way to quill an agreement with the chiefs of that Iroquois confederation. Viewed by many as rather unique, it was hoped the treaty would spur peaceful relations between those tribes and the forces of King George and his colonies. Yet some would later say that the fruits of that agreement, as well as the results of the entire congress, were dubiously mixed at best, for many would discover that the tribes of that confederation were troubled with splintering loyalties of their own. Although warriors of the Mohawk tribe leaned toward London and the colonies, it seems others like the Onondaga were slipping into the sphere of Paris.

Even though flawed, that Iroquois agreement was viewed by many as an essential element of King George's clever efforts to halt King Louis' incursions into England's colonies, as well as the wilderness lands to the west the crown proclaimed as British. Yet the consequences for London of those diplomatic efforts, of that pivotal meeting in Albany, was a semblance of colonial unity, a threatening result which would slowly be rued in the years to come by each royal governor, parliament and the king.

Aside from that tribal agreement, those men in Albany were said to have discussed various governing methods which could bring the colonies closer by forming a more cohesive unit to address mutual concerns, and one of those methods spurring whispers of colonial harmony was called the *Albany Plan of Union.* Offered by my colony's Doctor Franklin, it encompassed a set of visions the delegates were rumored to have discussed into the late hours each night, until the plan was finally adopted amidst flickering candles in congress' waning moments. Father said it called for a single assembly for all thirteen colonies, a governing unit presided by a selected colonial delegate approved by the king, and within days quilled parchment sheets detailing the proposal were disbursed by swift riders to each colony's assembly and sailed across the sea to parliament in London.

They say the plan outlined an array of issues and concerns that the colonies would have greater jurisdiction to decide, not just left to the king and parliament, and that the colonial assembly would be run by a colonist with actual powers. He'd be known as the president-general responsible for ensuring proper relations with native tribes while monitoring the preparedness of colonial militias, and maintaining a fairer system of enforcing policies and laws affecting merchants and trade throughout the colonies. And the plan called for each colony to select its own representatives to that single colonial assembly, a grand council of unity entrusted with powers over things like duties, commerce and taxes, including maintaining a special army for all the colonies.

Although Doctor Franklin's plan was roundly supported by the men meeting in Albany that summer, a plan which seemed to arouse the spirit of tens of thousands colonists with hopes of more autonomy from the English Crown, it was nevertheless frustratingly rejected by the king and his ministers in London, along with each colony's assembly. While some believed the colonial assemblies were pressured by their royal governors to oppose the plan, and maybe some delegates thought it too great a threat to the king, looking back after all these years I suppose the plan's defeat simply exposed that many colonists fundamentally believed that continued loyally to London was best. Nevertheless, that plan shed light upon an emerging desire for colonial unity, a dream which would inspire thousands in the years to come.

A somberness began to twist deep inside as I felt the essence of those days so long ago, wondering what might have been, while Samuel just gazed to those swaying elms in a contemplating stare while rocking his chair, awaiting my coming words. What might today be like, had the king and our assemblies accepted that Albany plan? Would the war that would come in a generation, come to pass? Would thousands of colonists who sacrificed so much, patriots who lost their lives, have just grown old? Would we still be colonies of the English Crown, I wondered, faithful members of the empire, loyal to the king? Would Ethan be here this moment, listening to rustling leaves with me?

Even as a small child I could sense how the mood about Germantown, about all the colonies I suppose following that Albany congress, began to feel more gloomy, especially for colonists in the wilderness north and west where things continued to deteriorate. Disharmony between London and Paris, spurred by those intruding French soldiers and their native allies, continued to escalate through the coming fall, winter and spring. All the while English troops continued to sail across the sea to colonial ports as militias in villages and towns throughout the colonies began to polish their muskets and gather powder and little lead balls.

Shopkeepers and merchants, doctors, lawyers, tradesmen and farmers began to muster on village fields, colonists of Ethan's Lexington and my Germantown too, just as boys and men in villages and towns of several colonies. I suppose most colonists, even the young like Ethan and me, had come to realize that the war so many feared had finally come. It would be a bloody frontier struggle many would come to know as the French and Indian War, a violent fight that would surge across the sea to the fields of Europe for seven desperate years.

I remember Ethan once saying that his village militia began to hone its skills in the spring of 1755, not long after the final winter snow, drilling on the grass of the village field each Saturday afternoon. "I'd help dad hitch our mare to the wagon," he recalled in a boyish tone, "and the three of us would ride into Lexington. I'd nudge against the bench on my knees, Andrea, just behind mom and dad, and bounce with each twisting rut and stone as the wheels creaked down the Billerica Road."

He'd whisper how he anxiously waited for the coming of noon every Saturday to watch his father and militia march in rickety rows about their village field, twisting lines that would be thwarted now and then by a meandering cow or dashing goat, runaway sow or cackling hens. And as most little boys in those days I suppose, Ethan would sometimes dream as he watched, of howling warriors and French soldiers scattering to muskets blazing the frontier, while his mother would visit the general store for things needed on the farm. She'd gather various spices, candles and oils, and sacks of grains, flours and seeds, or maybe pretty fabric for a summer dress or sturdy cloth for stockings, shirts and breeches, supplies carted to the village from Boston.

Ethan described how the militia would drill shoulder to shoulder, strutting one direction before slowly shifting right or left in a pair of tortuous lines that resembled the road to Concord winding five miles west. And if I recall, he said that Doc Newman and Sam Brown, their village wheelwright, had a bit of military experience, and perhaps John Parker and Israel Jacob too. Yet, as with most militias throughout the colonies in those days, there was an untidy raggedness, for few of the men had seen formal training.

Only a handful wore what might be viewed of as a uniform of some kind, while most simply drilled in clothes they commonly used each day, whether farmer, merchant or tradesman. "But dad always dressed in his special marching clothes," Ethan would say, "a brown shirt loosely buttoned and baggy tan breeches that hung over stained stockings running from his knees to muddied shoes. And like Doc, a dark tricorn hat was always pressed to his hair, and both wore blue wool coats that flared short over their chests while dangling past the backs of their knees."

Some of the men and boys of Lexington's militia wore stained floppy hats, while others preferred pelt caps that dangled little fur tails of squirrel, raccoon or beaver, and some wore dark tricorn hats, a few trimmed in gold, while some wore none at all, villagers like John Muzzey and Ernie Wilson. Yet all carried his own long-barreled musket slung from his shoulder by a thin leather strap, flintlock fusils mostly brown or black that came from their village gunsmith or a Boston shop for a few shillings and pounds. And all had been hanging in homes for years, crusty iron barrels with nicked elm stocks dangling from farmhouse walls or fiery hearths.

Just as thousands were doing in villages and towns throughout the colonies that spring, the militia would assemble on their Lexington field each Saturday with muskets slung, whether the day was chilling, misting or ablaze with a noon sun. They were tradesmen like Henry White, Charlie Duncan and Sam Burns, along with George Gables of the village inn and their postmaster too. Lexington's two tavern men McElroy and Munroe also joined in drills on their field, and so did Nat Mulliken with his polished musket, a proud tinker who peddled little tin trinkets, copper kettles and iron pans, skillets and pots. And although ails and age limited his duties, Doc Newman mustered with the younger men too, a dark barrel dangled down his shoulder.

Ethan explained that his father was not the only Lexington farmer to gather for militia drills, proud men who were eagerly joined by others of Middlesex County. They were spirited farmers like Mr. Jafres next to Ethan's farm, and George Pratt, Alex Spoons, Andy Beatty and Peter Salem, a Negro from the village of Framingham a few miles southwest. Yet, of them all, Ethan always thought Mr. Parker was the most dedicated at drill, followed closely by the Reverend Clarke, Sam Burns and his own father.

Mr. Giles had been named captain of their militia, chosen by the village men to lead for his previous experiences several years before while serving for the crown in one of the king's little wars along the frontier. "Even then, he was the printer of our Lexington Gazette," Ethan liked to say, "and from the rear of our wagon, I'd listen to him bark commands to dad and the other men. He liked to say he was the 'publisher and sweeper of his printing shop floor,' a position that helped him ensure our little militia stayed in contact with others about the colony, especially, with Boston."

The Lexington militia dutifully drilled those weeks of spring, summer and fall of 1755, just as other militias throughout Massachusetts Bay and most of the colonies, each honing soldiers' skills for when they might be beckoned by the crown to handle a slice of the coming war. All the while, the frightening sound of musket fire was beginning to filter from the distant woods, hills and fields, eerie echoes sweeping from the wilderness, for it was during those months that smoldering embers began to flare. It was a time when a few colonist enclaves of the frontier and soldiers of Paris and London, along with their tribal allies, began to smell the stench of tattered flesh bathed by the crimson mayhem of war.

Although I was just a little girl in those days, stories that had swirled about the colonies remain seared in my mind, and there was one I recall from several months before about an English general dispatched to the colonies by King George. They say he had come to command London's army in the brewing war, and along with several Royal Navy ships and some two thousand royal soldiers, had sailed to the village of Williamsburg in the Colony of Virginia. Their hulls were rumored to have been bulging with iron cannons and muskets tipped with bayonets, along sacks and barrels of powder and lead balls.

Edward Braddock was some sixty years old when he strutted down an elm plank to a Williamsburg dock, "in a bright red coat and shining black boots," a villager would later say. "A tricorn hat embroidered in gold pressed his hair, and a sword dangled the side of white breeches." The orders of the crown's commanding general were rumored to be simplistic in words yet convoluted in deeds, to merge his disembarking men into a single fighting force with hundreds who had come in the months before. And his assignment was said to be bold, extinguish the troubles flaring about the wilderness from invading French soldiers and native allies, expunge London's enemies from the frontier.

The general assembled his soldiers within days, a force that would include Colonel Washington and several hundred militiamen from the Colony of Virginia, and with dozens of cannons behind snorting oxen, they began their grueling trek northwest toward the French forts scattered about the Ohio Country, marching three-abreast in a winding column into the wilderness. One of the men would say it was a scorching mid-summer day when they reached the frontier a bit south of those three rivers and Fort Duquesne, and there, General Braddock began preparing his force to attack. It was to be a daring assault upon some nine hundred French troops garrisoning the fort, an outpost believed to be augmented by hundreds of warriors scattered about the woods.

"The general's scheme was doomed from the start," a disgruntled militiaman would grumble years later, "a plan that adhered to the only tactics he knew, a style his bloody army had always employed on the fields of Europe." It was admitted to be an inferior method of battle once the fighting was done, long rows and soldiers nudging forward in dangerous lines with muskets ablaze, a fatal plan for attacking an unseen enemy waiting in the wilderness.

King George's force would soon discover that King Louis' men had become skilled in the fighting ways of their tribal friends, a warring method utilizing the element of surprise. The French were reported to have blasted their muskets from an array of hidden places, from the shadows of brush, rocks, fallen limbs and trees. And although some would later confide that General Braddock had been warned by Colonel Washington and his colonials about those things, militiamen who had been exposed to such frantic tactics from past wilderness frays, the general nevertheless pressed his frontal attack, a flaw forged by the old ways.

King Louis' force of French soldiers and loyal militiamen from New France, along with hidden warrior allies, suddenly dashed from the fort and attacked from the shadows of the wilderness, striking the soldiers of King George. Our colonials and London's men were viciously routed in a frantic struggle, a fierce battle that would claim the life of General Braddock. They say he was laid to rest beneath the bloodied grass of a nearby field, along with hundreds of royal troops and dozens of courageous militiamen.

The French garrison at Fort Duquesne had prevailed in what some were soon calling the Battle of the Wilderness, the first true engagement in a new war between Paris and London, a frontier fight that had sent dozens of King Louis's men to their grave. After a frantic escape from the massacre woods, the king's soldiers were said to regroup under the command of a royal colonel named Dunbar, or perhaps it was Meriwether or a young Thomas Gage, while Colonel Washington reformed his colonial militia. They say that the Virginian's only scars from that fateful day were a few tattered tears of his blue wool coat, remnants of the enemy onslaught he would ponder as the survivors retreated from the wilderness for the haven of Philadelphia, some three hundred miles east.

I remember other frightening stories of King Louis' soldiers and their tribal allies in those days, of horrific battles with King George's men along the frontiers north and west. There were disturbing rumors of French victories from that summer and fall at places like Crown Point, an outpost along the waters of Lake Champlain in the upper eastern reaches of the Colony of New York. And there was a gruesome fight along a rushing river hundreds of miles west at a fort the French called Niagara, a rustic outpost sliced from a narrow patch of wilderness between the big lakes of Ontario and Erie.

Yet there were other stories in those days too, reports which helped douse the earlier feelings of doom and gloom, hopeful rumors filtering from the frontier of successful fights by London's army and colonial militias. Some were even beginning to spout that King George's troops were "finally reversing the awful losses" of the summer and fall before, striking the French forces with daring attacks in various wilderness places. English soldiers were reported to have beaten back Paris' men in some remote outposts far to the northeast, and one rumor told of capturing an Acadia fort called Beaus'ejour, a settlement near the Atlantic in the lands of New France.

Soon, the wintry snows of 1756 began trickling the wilderness streams of spring, and as the months slowly marched through summer and fall, the confidence of the French bolstered by those earlier victories began to falter at the insistence of a determined Royal Army strengthened by hundreds of brave colonial militiamen. And some believed that King George's changing fortunes were taking place because of events across the sea in London, most strikingly I suppose by actions of new Prime Minister Pelham-Holles, known as the Duke of Newcastle along the River Thames.

Others in parliament were said to have contributed to the turnabout of events too, royal men like Henry Fox and the first Baron Grantham, and the elder statesman William Pitt. "It was at the urging of those powerful men," father once loyally explained, "that the king chose to strike the expanding French hard, declaring a state of war with King Louis." Some would later say that pivotal decision is what caused the conflict along our colonial frontier to split, spilling upon the fields of Europe too, for the remainder of the war.

It was around that time, Ethan once said, that his father's Lexington militia received an order from the new royal governor of Massachusetts Bay, Spencer Phips, instructing Mr. Giles to assemble his men for marching into the wilderness. It was an order that would change the lives of many men, instructions Ethan would later come to understand came directly from General Campbell, the king's new commander of all his colonial troops. Those in London knew him as the Fourth Earl of Louden, "a careful, thoughtful man" they'd say, a general those of the Colony of Virginia knew as their royal governor.

I glanced to Samuel once again, rocking his chair and staring to the swaying tips of distant elms, then gazed to my roses bathing in the sun, their crimson petals tenderly twitching in the soft summer winds. Those long ago days seem almost a dream, hazy moments from another's past, yet at times it's as though they're so real I can feel the sands of my youth caressing my toes and smell the aroma of berry pies baking in Germantown bricks. And although Ethan and I, all those of our generation, were so young in those days, he had a magical way of snatching memories of those months and years on the farm, a tranquil time he'd say, that was rapidly changing.

Ethan seemed to reach deep inside whenever telling me how difficult it was for his mother while his father was away with the militia, explaining the work involved on the farm and their limited coffer for essential things. And although Ethan helped his mother when he could, being so small and young, most daily toils had to be completed by her. Yet, she somehow found the time to earn a few shillings and pounds in other tiring ways, baking treats and breads now and then, but mostly snipping and stitching garments and such for those in the village perhaps too busy, young, injured, aged or ill.

I closed my eyes for a moment and breathed a calming breath, and even as the summer air warmly bathed the porch, petals and leaves, I felt a coolness eerily brush my aging skin. With a glance to Samuel still rocking his chair, I tugged my shawl a bit more about my shoulders and slipped my fingers into the pocket of my summer dress, back to the haven of Ethan's poem. How does a simple sheet of colonial parchment bring such calmness to me, I wondered? Perhaps it's a blessing that's always trickled from heaven, a spiritual brush from my Ethan. With each caress of his tender words I could feel his sensuous touch surge my body, and with each passing moment that July morn, the memories of those days so long ago warmed my heart and swaddled my soul.

"Sparkling dew had settled to the grass of our Lexington field," Ethan softly revealed about the spring morning of 1757 when his father and the militia marched west from the village. "Their muskets dangled shoulders as a cool mist filtered from the gray, Andrea, and the brush dotting the hills had just begun to blossom with little petals of yellows, pinks and blues. So many watched and waited with an anxiousness gripping their eyes, mothers and fathers, sons, daughters and wives bidding their solemn goodbyes."

The militia marched from the field in two columns as a gentle tear spilled Ethan's mother's eye, and began strutting on the ruts and stones of the Massachusetts Road toward the village of Concord. Leading the men was their printer Captain Giles, implementing the order delivered by a swift rider just days before, instructions refined by General Wolf, the king's regional commander. Ethan said the militia would march west across the colony, past the hills of Berkshire and Taconic peaks rising along frontier of Massachusetts Bay. And along with other village militias they merged with along the way, the colonials would continue into the upper reaches of the eastern wilderness of the Colony of New York.

I remember the grave tone of Ethan's words when he told me that story, and can still sense how his father's departure continued to tug at his soul. His voice slightly quivered when recalling how "a misty haze hovered about the hills when dad and our men strutted from Lexington that morning," and when telling me how the spring dawn seemed to "spray desperation upon the village." Then, as if exposing hidden emotions, he passionately added, "I was only six that spring morning, Andrea, perhaps the most somber day of mom's life, scary and sad for me too. Yet, I felt so much pride in dad."

It was a solemn scene being experienced in scores of villages and towns in several colonies, children, women and aging men helplessly watching as militiamen strutted toward the unknown lurking the frontier, colonists wondering if they'd hold their loves again. Even though most clung to pride in their militiamen, they watched as thousands of boys and men, Ethan's father too, marched toward a war few colonists understood. "Mom just gazed in a kind of hypnotic stare as dad and our men marched down the road, and when they vanished around the bend, a mist exploded about her eyes. While a hush settle over the village, Andrea, mom just stared, her cheeks trickling tiny tears."

What Ethan and his mother didn't know on that lonely spring morn, what few, I suppose, could have imaged, was that his father and their village militia would not return to Lexington for over two years. They had marched into the wilderness and would not be held by their loves until the leaves of oak, maple, birch and elm settled to the hills and fields in yellows, tans, oranges and reds during a late autumn chill of 1759. No one could have foreseen the changes that awaited, nor have fathomed the vicious battles along the frontier yet to come, and all Ethan and his mother could do, just as others, was watch as the days, weeks, months and seasons slowly passed on. At the age of six Ethan was now the man of the farm, the only companion to his mother, doing his best to help till the soils and keep up with chores, efforts that at times, he would say, were rather futile.

During those months his father was away at the frontier, Ethan began his studies at the little Lexington schoolhouse too, a time he began to delve into the writings of others, an interest spurred by their village schoolmarm. "Miss Hutchinson would read to us," he once told me in a pleasing tone, "from an array of special books she'd pluck from a case near her desk. I'd be mesmerized at times, Andrea, just listening to her voice as she unleashed intriguing stories for an hour or so after lunch, almost every day."

Ethan seemed to cherish her story telling in those days, and looking back after all these years, perhaps he felt a youthful attraction to his schoolmarm, for I remember him innocently saying, "She spurred curiosity in me, Andrea, made me want to rush to the village each day, delve into school. Miss Hutchinson seemed to always have a tender smile too, for all the children, a greeting which made me feel good." It was a period of Ethan's life when he began to explore the intricacies of dreams, stories, opinions and tales printed in an array of pamphlets and books, a time when he'd browse the bindings of her tiny library or peruse writings from his father's little collection on snowy nights.

"I'd find myself reading for hours on the farm," Ethan once whispered to me, "lying on our rug near the fire after dusk, nestled upon feathered pillows, devouring stories she let me take home from the schoolhouse. Or maybe I'd be at our little table while mom stirred a tasty stew simmering in the hearth, browsing one of dad's books of various histories by the flame of a candle." Yet, Ethan once confessed how at times he felt somewhat detached from the children at school, "because I read so many things, more so than others. They don't seem to have the same urge I have, Andrea, to discover what awaits on the coming page."

Perhaps Ethan was most attracted to books of the past, perusing printings of English, Greek and Roman histories stacked near his father's desk, while finding an intriguing attraction to the enlightened works quilled decades before by reasoning men. "I didn't always know what they were trying to say," he'd humbly admit. "I guess I was just too young back then. But the way each quilled phrases and beliefs, was enchanting."

I remember some saying that conceptions espoused by a few of those men, ideas which had been swirling the fields of Europe for some hundred years, tended to impugn the foundations of religious faiths. "What had been righteous beliefs by good men had slowly been usurped and corrupted," they quilled over the years, "and should fade from the heart. Such things should be replaced by a belief that from the logical mind will spring judicious holdings, bond society with reasoning bathed of enlightened thought." Ethan liked browsing those types of works in his father's collection, writings from men of England like John Locke, Thom Hobbes and Isaac Newton. And there was Francois-Marie Arouet too if I recall, an intriguing man those of Paris knew as Voltaire.

But it was the poetic play by Mr. Addison of London that seems to have appealed to Ethan the most, a story quilled decades before titled, *Cato, a Tragedy*. One of his father's favorite works, it was a tale of a Roman warrior Ethan found himself browsing many times on frigid winter nights when the Lexington militia was engaging French forces about the wilderness. Ethan once fondly said that it was an inspiring story of an aging soldier named Marcus Porcius Cato Uticensis, a daring tale of courage by Cato and his men willing to sacrifice their lives by standing against tyranny some two thousand years before. "They believed in personal freedom," he'd say, "in individual liberty, opposed to the chains of unjust men. And when that Roman Caesar demanded their souls, they clung to their dreams and resisted, fighting to their deaths."

Although Ethan always seemed so happy when revealing those stories of his earliest years, of the intrigues of a book or tale of school, I think his most cherished memories of those days when his father was away at the frontier, were the tender moments with his mother on the farm. They'd bundle near the hearth on brisk fall days and icy winter nights in the glow of a flickering fire, and warm beneath one of her quilted creations while nestling to a tiny pile of feathered pillows. "We'd whisper thoughts and things about our day," he'd say, "me telling of school or a new book, and mom revealing needed things about the farm or exposing a new rumor about the war. There always seemed to be a troubling tale, Andrea, swirling about the village of some battle at the frontier, and awful stories were reported in various papers too, like the Boston Gazette carted each week into Lexington by a disheveled old man."

Yet, I think he and his mother felt the most relieved, a joyous feeling perhaps brushed with an eerie gloom, when she'd read a letter quilled by his father somewhere in the wilderness. They were mostly recent tales bathed with hopes, and sometimes, they were aging letters his mother seemed to hold more dearly, keeping them close. Ethan once whispered how tears would swell her eyes when reading each line, and how the sorrow would trickle her cheeks while uttering his closing words.

"We'd stare to the snapping flames upon each pause," Ethan confessed with a misty gaze, "and even though I was rather young, I could see the loneliness brushing mom's face. There was a kind of desperation in her expression, an emotion that intensified in the glow of the fire. She missed dad, very much." At times they were lonely hours too, private moments when she'd hush a wish for his father's safe return, a silent prayer as chilling winds sweeping from the frontier howled about the night.

When events and weather were aligned just right, his father's letters were only a few weeks old, and other times, they were galloped into Lexington by a young swift rider after a month, maybe two. Each letter nevertheless brought relief to Ethan and his mother, a comforting sense that his father was safe and perhaps edging nearer, letters which always thrilled. Ethan once described them as a mix of passion for his mother and fatherly tales for a young son, letters which would eventually expose disturbing revelations of that bloody frontier struggle. They revealed the dangers Lexington's militia was encountering in the wilderness, and disclosed glimpses of exhausting marches and daring escapes, and sometimes, the gruesome horrors of war.

There was the battle at a distant outpost they called Fort Oswego, a frightening fight at a rustic settlement near the lake waters of Ontario in the northwestern wilderness of the Colony of New York. Yet, perhaps it was his father's words about a place near the shores of Lake George, in that colony's upper northeast, that truly exposed the realities of war, a shocking revelation which brushed fear across Ethan's mother face. It was a savage battle at Fort William Henry that exploded in the August heat that 1757, a vicious fight which sent horrifying chills through Ethan's body. They say it was another victory by French forces over King George, a defeat of some three thousand royal soldiers and hundreds of militiamen from villages scattered about the colonies of New Hampshire, Connecticut, New York and Ethan's Massachusetts Bay.

In spite of those harrowing tales, Ethan believed that his father tried to shield he and his mother from many of the unsightly things of war, delicately forgoing ugly details to quill about the men and their camps, the sleet and rains, the icy streams and snowy hills, the animals, birds and forests. He'd quill of doing well, he and all the men, and talk of how their morale was rather good, although faltering at times. "Above all," Ethan explained, "I think dad really tried to avoid dwelling on his fears, a dread which surely gnawed upon all the men, and shied from quilling of the horrors of those battles, somehow feigning an ease while stuffing his emotions deep inside."

Then an aberration struck during the summer of his father's second year fighting at the frontier, a letter of stained parchment exposing the carnage of that wilderness war. Ethan's father had succumbed to the truth, confiding of terrifying visions consuming his dreams along the frontier those trying nights, of the hour of pounding cannons and blasting muskets, of bayonets slicing life. They were revelations of the July 1758 afternoon when his Lexington men, along with thousands of the king's royal soldiers and militiamen from scores of villages and towns, and hundreds of native friends, merged amidst a clinging heat after thunderous rains in the northeast wilderness of the Colony of New York. They had trudged to the French bastion of Fort Carillon, an outpost of stony magazines, barracks and huts on the southern rocks of Lake Champlain, a portage viewed by most as strategic in the river valley of the Hudson.

The Lexington militia and thousands of colonials were now being commanded by the king's General Abercrombie, "an honorable soldier," Ethan's father had quilled, "who barked the disturbing order to attack, a command we'd soon discover was fatally flawed." Within moments the colonials began a mad dash toward the walls of the French fort defended by hundreds of militiamen of New France, their native allies and thousands of King Louis' men, a rushing thrust into deadly volleys of cannon and musket fire.

I remember how Ethan's voice quivered when recalling the words of his father's letter, of the horrors of that frontal attack, a mindless assault upon what was in truth an ugly stretch of timber, rocks and earth the French had massed just outside the fort's outer walls. "They had been ordered to smash that barrier," Ethan sputtered in a melancholy tone, "conquer and destroy at all costs. Dad and all those brave men had rushed into a hornets nest, Andrea, and found themselves frantically trying to survive the savage onslaught of hundreds of howling French soldiers and screeching warriors. It was a courageous assault, viciously repelled by King Louis' men."

Horrific rumors of that terrible battle had swept from the wilderness across the hills and fields to villages and towns throughout the colonies, frightful reports which by the later weeks of summer and first nights of fall were being talked about in taverns and shops of my Germantown. They say a thousand of the king's men perished that awful day, royal soldiers and colonials too, while hundreds had been maimed by musket balls and thrashing clubs, slicing spears and thrusting bayonets. The French force had defeated those of King George, a wilderness victory that cost Paris a hundred men with many more wounded, soldiers scattered about piles of timber and rock, oozing life into the soil. And although London's army was said to have captured scores of bloodied Frenchmen that day, they came at a mighty cost, for Lexington lost two its better men.

Ethan said that George Pratt was one of Lexington's finest farmers, and everyone liked his wife Abigail, and Sam Brown had been an integral cog of their village, one of Middlesex County's best wheelwrights who left behind Anna. Both had given their lives in the mayhem that awful day, and both left behind a pair of children who would never see their father again. Along with dozens of other brave men, they were buried shortly after the battle beneath the grass of a lonely patch, encased in the wilderness soil near a quaint little brook twisting through the woods, a quiet place amidst a grove of hemlock and birch.

If I recall, it was during the coming year that rumors would once again swirl about that French bastion, stories of another English force of royal soldiers and colonial militia commanded by a General Amherst. They say that new force surrounded the fort and assaulted King Louis's troops once again, French soldiers who one witness would later convey, "fought little before fleeing north into the woods." Fort Carillon had finally been conquered for the English Crown, a bastion of timber and stones rising at a waterway junction Mohawk warriors knew as Tekonteroken. It was a vital place now in the grip of King George's men, a frontier outpost they'd now call, Fort Ticonderoga.

Letters from Ethan's father also exposed the ordeals of militia life in the wilderness, of arduous marches through chilling fall rains and the brutal slices of summer's heat, while battling swarms of mosquitos. He quilled of rustic paths winding through woods, muddied roads with deep ruts cut by the creaking wheels of cannons, carts and wagons pulled by grunting mares and snorting oxen. They were arms, equipment and supplies tugged across soggy fields during spring showers and snowy hills during winter flurries, wagons and carts once filled with sacks and barrels of grains, powder and lead balls, provisions which slowly dwindled with each passing season.

Although Ethan held those frontier letters close to his heart, he also loved telling me of a special story about those days when his father was away, a cherished memory not of the war or words quilled by his father, but of a chilly night seared in his mind. In a way, I think it was a night which brought a guiding comfort to Ethan, not only during those moments he was a little boy, but for his remaining years to come. It was a memory that blossomed a few weeks before his father finally marched home from the wilderness, a blustery autumn night, the third Sunday of November, 1759.

"Winter had come early to Massachusett Bay," Ethan once softly reminisced, "icy winds sweeping the fields and howling about the trees, and that night, the snows swirled outside the house. I could see tiny white flakes brush the windows while hurtling about the dark, and the smell of the wilderness seemed to grip the chilling winds trying to slither inside through little cracks aside the panes. It was as though the wintry flurry battering the glass wanted to conquer our farmhouse that night, creep inside to destroy the tranquil flames snapping the hearth. But our home survived, Andrea, protecting mom and I from the wrath of the night."

Although just shy of nine as of that November night, Ethan seemed more emotionally ripe than most children his age. Perhaps he had learned too many truths of life while his father was away at the frontier, unpleasant things most girls and boys seldom discovered while so young. And maybe he had found the magic of caressing his own little soul, while whispering of so many things with his mother before a fire during those two lonely years, precious hours much like the moments of that late autumn night.

Ethan had just washed their supper plates and tossed more twigs and logs to the shrinking fire glowing upon embers sparkling in the stones of the hearth, and as the limbs began to crackle and burst with tentacles of red, yellow and blue, shadowy figures began to spray about the room. As they had on so many nights over those two anxious years, Ethan and his mother were now nestling with several feathered pillows on their hearth's wide rug, bundled beneath a blanket she had quilted months before. He was lying on his back snuggled in her arms, and for several precious moments they gazed into the snapping fire, silent in their thoughts.

His mother began to slide her fingers through his hair, as she had so many times over the years, slowly caressing his youthful dreams while taming his fears. "I'm going to tell you something, Ethan," she tenderly whispered as flickering flames warmed their cheeks, "words I hope you'll hold dear all your life. No matter what troubles may come your way, disappointments that might arise in your life, remember what I'm about to say. Never forget this truth."

Nervously wondering what she was about to reveal, Ethan could feel a chill rush his body while staring to the flames. "Your heart will speak to you, Ethan," she softly added with a gentle kiss of his hair, "and when it does, you must listen. Oh, you won't hear words, Ethan, but you'll feel its spirited plea. Listen closely, for it will never deceive you, and always remember, your heart is free."

Then gently twisting and gazing to his eyes, she cupped his cheeks in her hands and softly said, "It might not be easy, Ethan, to adhere to your heart, could even cause some pain. But you must listen, and have the courage to follow the path beating deep in your heart." She gave his lips a motherly kiss, and never again, spoke of such things. I can still see the mist spraying Ethan's eyes when he confided his memories to me, and remember how his passionate reflections exposed his tender vulnerabilities.

"Grandma?" suddenly chimed Samuel, halting my story as I dabbed a tear spilling my eye. "Are you alright?"

I rocked a bit slower and glanced to the mountain laurels gently quivering in the summer sun, and as another tear spilled my cheeks, I softly uttered, "Yes, I'm alright, just give me a moment. You know, Samuel, it's been over fifty years since Ethan first told me that little story, but for me, it's seems like yesterday. I can still see his eyes, teary, and each time I remember, sadness grips me."

"It's alright, grandma," he replied with a comforting peer to my misting eyes. "I think I understand."

"My hair might be gray now, Samuel," I whispered, dabbing a tear while gazing to crimson roses in bloom, "and my skin no longer pretty, but my memories are intact. I'm going to tell you something, and you might think me crazy. When I sit in this chair on my porch, I can feel Ethan's presence, and sometimes, his touch. It's as if he's right here, Samuel, at my side."

"I don't think you're crazy, grandma. But I'm not sure, I really understand. Maybe, someday, I will. Do you want to stop for a while, rest?"

"No," I defiantly sputtered in a grandmotherly tone. "I want to go on, feel it all. I want to remember, tell you the whole story."

"Alright," he tenderly uttered, caressing my shoulder while slowing the rock of his chair. "You know, grandma, I'm beginning to realize how right you truly are, that I do need to hear it all. So much has been lost about those days, and so much not understood."

"I think we need a bit more water, Samuel, before I go on. Would you fill our goblets, please, and fetch a roll or two from the counter? And if you'd like, maybe some of that berry pie too, baked just yesterday."

"I sure will," he excitedly sputtered, springing from his chair and grabbing our goblets before dashing through the door.

I pressed to the slats of my chair and nudged into an easy rock while gazing to laurels and roses in bloom, then watched a little string of white clouds drifting the summer sky. I wondered of all the Julys which had passed since then, as a tender breeze soothed my warming skin, and smelled the sweet scent of azaleas swaying in distant fields, just as they had so long ago. I wondered of how so much had changed since those days, and of how some things, never will. "Oh, Ethan," I whispered, "how I miss you so."

"Here we go," blurted Samuel as he spurted through the door and slid a porcelain platter to the little table between our chairs, a shiny plate with two crisp rolls of grain, a pair of silver forks and two thick slices of blueberry pie. Then I watched as he dashed back inside, fetched our goblets brimming with fresh Pennsylvania water, and rushed back to his chair as the door creaked close with a clack. "Now, where were we?"

"Thank you, Samuel," I whispered, pinching a fork and nibbling a bite of pie. "Come, have some, and I'll go on."

"Umm," he mumbled, leaning back into his chair and gobbling a few bites, "your pie, grandma, is scrumptious. There, I think I'm ready now. Tell me more about those days, about Ethan, and when his father finally came home from the frontier. What did that war do to the colonies, grandma? How did it affect Ethan's father and the Lexington militia, all the militias of the colonies?"

"I'm glad you like my pie," I replied with a pleasing gaze while nudging my chair into a soft rock and clicking my fork to the platter. "That frontier war changed the lives of so many colonists," I added amidst the sounds of rustling leaves filtering the warming air, "and not just those near the wilderness, but everywhere, Ethan's father too." As Samuel rocked easy in his chair and nibbled crumbs, awaiting my coming words, I slid my fingers into the pocket of my summer dress and gently caressed the parchment of Ethan's poem, reaching for memories of those days so long ago.

Ethan would later discover that the second assault upon that French bastion of rocks and stones, that wilderness outpost the English Crown now called Fort Ticonderoga, was the final battle his father and the Lexington militia would endure. Although that frontier war against King Louis the Fifteenth would not become a full British victory for four more long years, within months after that attack, the men of Lexington returned home.

The ragged column of Lexington men shuffled east into the village shortly after noon on a chilly Friday in late December, 1759, a weary militia strutting beneath a brisk blue sky on the snowy ruts of the Massachusetts Road. Just as thousands of militiamen throughout the colonies, they walked back to their taverns and inns, clients and patients, farms, trades and shops, back to their children, wives and homes, and some, back to the shadows of loneliness. All returned from the wrath of war, each forever changed.

"As mom dabbed her eyes," Ethan recalled of that exciting day, "I rushed to dad slowly walking the snows of the Billerica Road. He had a bit of a limp, Andrea, and his musket was lazily slung over his shoulder. I didn't know it then, but he had stuffed the scares from those wilderness battles deep into his soul, much like the others I suppose, militiamen grappling with visions of friends left behind in the soil of distant fields. They all had witnessed the savagery of war, Andrea, dad too, and it would haunt them every day, for the rest of their lives. I've always worried what must be swirling about dad's memories, and how those horrors must roar back to life in his dreams, cursing the night."

I remember Ethan saying how the coming year of 1760 was perhaps one of the happiest of his life, for his father was now home from the war and his mother graciously relieved, for his little family was made whole once again. And yet, as some things returned to their proper place, others would never be the same. Ethan's father had clung to a secret while away, not exposing the full truth of the war in his letters, hiding his wound. It was not an injury of memories and emotions that would gush from the shadows now and then, but a wound that would physically challenge every day.

It wasn't until his return to Lexington that the secret of his wound became clear, that Ethan and his mother would know the truth about the French musket ball that ripped the flesh of his upper right leg, tearing his thigh near the knee. "Although dad would never say, it almost cost him his leg, a wound mom and I knew, almost took his life." It was a vicious injury which would alter his walk forever, instilling a proud limp upon one of Lexington's militiamen, a badge of courage he'd strut with the rest of his life.

Just as thousands of other militiamen, Ethan's father would hold the horrors of war close inside, and rarely speak of colonial soldiers who had sacrificed their dreams for a cause some would come to doubt in the decade ahead. Yet it seems most in those early days believed it was a noble cause, a struggle against the French to defend King George's land, the colonies' land, our future, our frontier.

Although the battles against the French and their native allies in that frontier war had generally occurred far from colonial villages, ports and towns, away from Charles Towne and Savannah, Philadelphia, Boston and Williamsburg, Germantown and Lexington, the colonies had found themselves bound a bit closer. "That war gave us a sense of unity," some would later say, "binding us in a common defense of our lands," and it had provided many colonists with something that would someday haunt London, invaluable experience in the subtleties of war. From those days onward the colonies would understand the ugly truths of battle, and know of the requisite grit to persevere through the dreadful challenges of war.

Ethan had said that the early months of 1760 passed with a kind of tranquil ease about Lexington, and I remember a touching little story he told me about a Saturday afternoon in late September, intimate moments on the Sheehan farm. It was a memory which seemed to bring a sense of realism to Ethan, a story of a father speaking to his young son beneath a layer of roiling gray as the smell of distant rain lingered over the Colony of Massachusetts Bay. He and his father were nestled upon a special log lying near the Billerica Road, a rugged limb of knotted oak his father had dragged to that spot several years before. And now, sitting side by side, his father was ready to talk.

They just sat on that aging limb for a while and gazed in a hush about the lands of their farm, watching the autumn winds brush the fields spreading south, then gently settling his arm about Ethan's shoulders, his father tenderly said, "I want you to know, Ethan, how much I love you, your mother too. Why, it was the consuming thought of you two that kept me going out there, gave me hope in the wilderness all those months. God only knows where I might be right now, what might have become, had it not been for the two of you."

"I missed you too, dad," Ethan shyly sputtered, perhaps a bit nervous of just what to say. For a moment they quietly gazed over fields of swaying grains, then as a burst of autumn air tossed his tangling hair, Ethan softly added, "I know mom did too."

"You know, I was out there, Ethan, fighting a war," his father calmly admitted, changing his focus while twisting a bit and gazing to Ethan's eyes, "and I killed men, some just boys. They were men I didn't know, none of us knew, people with families just like me, men with sons like you." Then grasping for the proper words, he strummed his fingers through Ethan's hair and added in a tone that seemed to seep from his soul. "What we did out there, Ethan, in the wilderness along the frontier, we did out of duty to the colonies and the crown. We believed our struggle right. Do you understand, Ethan?"

"I think so," Ethan uttered, blinking his eyes and nervously glancing to the fields. "You had to kill those men, cuz they were the enemy, right dad? You and the others, our militia, fought because that's what was asked of you. It was your duty, right dad?"

"Yes, Ethan," he whispered while tenderly pressing his hand to Ethan's shoulder, "I think you understand. It was our duty. But most important, Ethan, it was right. We were protecting our way of life, our lands, in a way our farms and homes, from those who wanted to take them from us. Our militia was not only defending our Colony of Massachusetts Bay, but the futures of all the colonies. I know, these things can be confusing, Ethan, and it's anguishing to take another man's life, a man just doing his own duty too, a man we don't even know. But I guess that's what duty can mean, Ethan, and can be asked of any of us, at any time."

"I see," Ethan sputtered with a youthful nod while gazing to the gray roiling above the fields, wondering if he truly understood.

"You might be asked to do such things in your life, Ethan," his father added in a revering tone, "be called to grab your musket and fight for the colony, fight for reasons others will say are vital. I want you to remember this, Ethan. Before you commit, before reaching for that musket and marching to the horrors of battle, before you kill another man, search deep inside, think and reflect. Decide for yourself, if what you are about to do is right, that the reasons support your fundamental beliefs. Are loves at risk, is liberty in peril? Be sure your soul will be able to sleep at night."

"Alright, dad, I will. I promise."

"Good," his father uttered while caressing Ethan's shoulders. Then gazing to the fields and breathing a wisp of autumn winds, he boldly added,

"Your young, Ethan, but I think you're old enough to know. I want to explain a little about Fort Carillon, that awful fight against those warriors and French soldiers. You know, even though it's been some two years since that day, for me and the others, it happened yesterday. So many fine men lost their lives that day, like Sam Brown and George Pratt, and so many were maimed with gruesome wounds. None of us will ever forget."

They sat quiet for a moment or two, his father staring to the fields stretching beyond the farmhouse and Ethan watching a batch of dust swirling about a grove of distant birch and elm. They just listened to the leaves of the trees along the road to Lexington rustling in the autumn breeze, while Ethan waited for his father's coming words.

"I was with Sam," his father solemnly confessed, "crouched on our knees behind piles of rocks, fallen limbs and scattered trees in the woods near the fort's northern wall, with hundreds of other militiamen. Sometimes, we'd flop to our bellies, when musket balls streaked from French soldiers, blasts that would slam into trees and ricochet off rocks, sailing wildly about the woods. There were hellish howls too, from their native warriors screeching from hidden places. Sam and I just stayed there with the others, hunkered behind those rocks and trees, our muskets packed and ready, waiting for the order."

Ethan could sense his father drifting into some kind of strange trance about those gripping moments in the wilderness, perhaps struggling to reconcile that awful day in the Colony of New York. Then suddenly, his father just seemed to release memories that had been stashed deep inside, hidden in some dark secret place.

"For a few nervous moments, Ethan, a hush settled over us, and as Sam and I watched, mayhem exploded about the wilderness. I could see the fright in his eyes as he frantically uttered, 'Oh no!' before we leapt to our feet with hundreds of others after the command to attack was barked from the trees. We rushed into the smoking fray, racing toward that earthen mound outside the walls of that fort, and as Sam and I dashed, gripping our muskets amid feverish yelps and cries, a shout came from the woods, 'Go get em, boys!'"

His father's eyes began to mist as he stared to the grains swaying the distant fields, a gaze that seemed to peer into the depths of a horrific dream. "Sam and I quickly looked into each other's eyes," he stoically added, "and then, it happened. As we rushed into the billowing smoke amidst howling cries and musket blasts, Sam's life came to an end."

A little lead ball had ripped through Sam's forehead just above the right eye, streaking death blasted from a French musket from somewhere outside the fort's northern wall. It was one of thousands of tiny lead spheres frantically fired during that daring assault, a little ball that whizzed through the wilderness to strike its target with a ghastly thud.

"Sam never knew what happened," Ethan's father explained with reverence in his stare. "He just fell back onto a clump of muddied leaves, his musket falling silent at his boots. For a second, I couldn't move, just looked at the stunned gaze in his eyes. And his wound, Ethan, was gruesome, life oozing to the ground in a crimson pool."

As the battle raged about the wilderness, Ethan's father just stared to those lifeless eyes peering to the sky, all the while mysteriously oblivious of the muskets blasting from colonists and the king's royal troops, from French soldiers and their warriors. Then, as if awakened from a bewildered daze, all those streaking lead balls, thrusting spears and slashing knives, screams, hollers and cries, violently sprang back to life.

"Suddenly," his father proudly explained, "I knew what I needed to do. I gripped my musket and rushed back into the fray, dashing toward that bloody fort with all the other Lexington men. I think I killed two or three for Sam, Ethan, and then felt the thrashing pain burning down my leg. I survived that French musket ball, but Sam and so many others, George Pratt too, were laid to rest in a lonely field near a winding stream."

He dabbed an eye while turning his stare away from his young son, gazing somberly into the soft winds brushing the Lexington fields, then pressed his hand to Ethan's shoulder and whispered, "I've only told of these things to your mother, Ethan, and now, to you. I wanted you to understand the vicious truth of war, and to remember, cling to what your heart says is right."

"How will I know, dad?" Ethan inquisitively asked with a youthful gaze to his father's eyes. "How will I know when a war is right? How will my heart tell me?

"Have faith in yourself, Ethan, just as I have in you. If you search your soul, listen for the truth, you will know when a struggle is right."

Chapter V

Purple Pansy

George William Frederick arrived in this world amidst a cool London fog shortly after dawn the fourth day of June, a brisk spring morning of 1738. His mother was Augusta, a princess of the Germanic principality of Saxe-Gotha-Altenburg they say, and by that spring morning she had come to be known throughout England as the Princess of Wales. And his father was Frederick Louis of the House of Hanover, the eldest son of the then second King George, British royalty most simply knew as Frederick, the Prince of Wales.

Little George was soon baptized into the kingdom's Church of England by the Bishop of Oxford, dipped in the royal waters of Norfolk House along the cobblestones of St. James Square on the fourth day of July. There were rumors in those early days that for several years the king struggled to find an appreciation for his young grandson, a challenge some believed was spurred by the king's distaste for his son Frederick. It was an unflattering disharmony within the royal family which seems to have rapidly changed upon the untimely demise of the Prince of Wales in the spring of 1751, for now, little Prince George was only a heartbeat away from the English Crown.

Just as mountain streams trickle to the sea and rays of the sun spray across the fields each dawn, after weeks, months and years of Ethan's first decade had come to pass, change to the monarchy of England gripped London once again. In the chilling hours of an autumn morn, a Saturday like thousands for centuries that had come before, the history of a people was forever changed. After thirty-three years upon the throne, King George the Second expired to the pages of English lore, his being mortally betrayed as an icy drizzle brushed the stones of Kensington Palace and kissed the waters of the River Thames. The royal pulse of England had ceased shortly after dawn, October the Twenty-fifth, 1760, and a new king had ascended the British Throne. "Monarchs too find death," I remember hearing some morbidly whisper, "particularly kings who fail to understand the rights and dreams of man."

The young prince had been thrust upon the seat of power which for centuries had shackled minds and doused hopes of desperate peoples, while luring the unsightly greed of troubled men. At just twenty-two, England's new king, the third monarch they'd call George, had become the unchallenged ruler of Great Britain and its royal subjects, including some two million colonists three thousand miles across the sea. He would be exalted by most and feared by many, the king of an empire stretching the world, a monarch some in the colonies would uncomfortably believe must be appeased, colonists with tarnishing spirits willing to barter hopes for years to come.

As with most monarchs throughout the years, King George the Third was soon viewed by many as emphatically insistent that his ideas, positions and beliefs, including some spurred by loyal men of parliament, be intrinsically woven into the fabric of his Thirteen Colonies. And I suppose most colonists in those days thought it their duty to adhere to the will espoused by London, "after all," many would spout when I was young, "we are all English women, children and men, are we not?" By most accounts I guess we were, viewed as British citizens, and the colonies an inseparable entity of the empire.

Yet there were some in those days who were beginning to view the new king with a disturbing disdain, a contempt wrapped in a disloyal cloak, a simmering distaste for policies, acts and laws being espoused by parliament and the crown. Some in villages and towns throughout the colonies, spirited men of Boston and Williamsburg, Philadelphia, Dover and New York, Germantown and Lexington too, were once again expressing beliefs that colonists were being viewed by London as inferior to English citizens residing across the sea. Nevertheless, regardless of ones' position in those early days, it was becoming clear that King George the Third was now the exalted power of the throne, a truth which would remain long after the sun had set upon our colonial ways.

In the meantime, as the reins of power were being gripped by a new King George, a few of the final battles of that war lingering in the wilderness continued to take place along the colonial frontier. They were engagements which were followed by a period of relative calm, until finally, the war was declared done. One of those skirmishes occurred near one of King Louis' forts they called Levis, a bastion of timber, mortar and rocks along the river banks of the Saint Lawrence in the wilderness edging the Colony of New York, some hundred miles northwest of Fort Ticonderoga.

"It was a hellish affair," one of that colony's militiamen would later recall, a bloody skirmish most were soon calling the Battle of Thousand Islands. Father would say that it was perhaps the most costly battle of 1760, a decisive victory by London's General Amherst that many would come to view as instrumental in hastening the end of that lingering frontier war.

There were a few other fights too in the months that followed, smaller skirmishes near forts scattered about the wilderness, rustic outposts among groves of birch, pine and elm, little battles near icy streams, snowy forests and chilling hills and fields along the frontier. They were lonely places where rocky brooks twisted through the woods, sacred grounds where the lives of young French and English soldiers, colonial boys and men, warrior enemies and friends, were forever changed. They were ugly encounters where innocence was lost, where bloodied soils now swaddled the dead.

I remember a skirmish around the fall of 1762 that many believe may have dashed King Louis' dreams of wilderness expanse once and for all, a fight which seemed to have doomed his hopes along the frontier as well as his holdings in the northern lands of New France. It was a little battle those who fought described as "wrenchingly vicious," one of that war's final struggles they'd know as Signal Hill. It was then that a sense of the war's inevitable end swirled about the colonies as the leaves began to turn and winter flurries began, spirited optimism that swept to villages and ports, to my Germantown and Ethan's Lexington, exclaiming the defeat of the French in the far northeast.

Many were soon saying that King George had won the war, that the French surrender at Signal Hill to the British forces of Colonel Amherst, the frontier general's baby brother, was a mortal thrust into the heart of Paris. The demise of King Louis' wilderness hopes had finally arrived near the northeast port of Saint John's along the coast of Newfoundland, for the colonial war which had spilled upon the plains of Europe was about to end. It spurred the ultimate French defeat during the quiet winter of 1763, when the warring parties quilled their signatures to what they'd call, the Treaty of Paris.

"Most lives about Lexington," Ethan would confide a few years later, "in the village and outlaying farms, began to return to the way things had been, before the battles erupted along the frontier." I suppose even while those final skirmishes lingered in sporadic places about the wilderness during those first days of the reign of the new King George, we all began to emerge from the sacrifices of war. Colonists of my Pennsylvania and Ethan's Massachusetts Bay, all the colonies I suppose, had begun to slowly settle into what most were wishfully referring to as, normalcy.

Bricklayers and carpenters, bakers and blacksmiths went about their trades while farmers toiled their fields, and shopkeepers and merchants stocked their shelves, doctors tended to ailments and ills, and lawyers spoke for those who strayed. "Life was getting back to how it was before dad marched to the frontier," Ethan conveyed, "with dad doing his best on the farm, what with his aching leg, caring for mom and me. Yet even the pulsing pain that would surge when tilling the soil failed to dull the gratefulness spraying his eyes, a serene gleam which seemed to ooze from his soul."

The first months and years of that new decade seemed to portend a gradual shift in colonial attitudes as well, perhaps a slippery slide into what some would say was an increasing awareness of colonial issues, an evolving focus on what was important for all the colonies. Yet that sense of normalcy filtered about the colonies nevertheless, suppressing those earlier violent events along the frontier, and perhaps for those of my and Ethan's generation born some ten years before, at least those whose fathers returned from the war, life had not drastically changed. All the while, with each passing day, I had this strange notion of youth fading away, just as Ethan and thousands of others I suppose, and began to watch and listen to the changing winds swirling about the colonies.

It was a time which seemed brimming with anticipation, when optimism wrapped the lives of colonists north and south, a populace infused each passing year with women, children and men sailing across the sea from various ports of Europe. They say that the Colony of Virginia had more colonists than any other in those early days of the decade, some four hundred thousand if I recall, and that Ethan's Massachusetts Bay was close behind. My Colony of Pennsylvania was expanding with spirited people from across the sea too, bulging to a couple hundred thousand by July of my thirteenth year. Yet a few were said to remain pretty much the same in those days, like the Colony of Georgia, with the smallest population of some eighteen thousand women, children and men.

I think there were perhaps a few hundred colonists in my village of Germantown back then, mostly settlers from Germanic principalities and my grandmother's Netherlands, and if I recall, Philadelphia just south continued to thrive along the Delaware River docks. With some thirty thousand colonists in those early days, it was quickly being viewed by many as perhaps the most robust port in all the colonies.

Yet perhaps it was Boston up in Massachusetts Bay, home to some fifteen thousand colonists in those days, which was truly beginning to expand with dozens of sailing ships mooring weekly at its harbor wharfs, hulls brimming with sacks, boxes and crates stuffed with tons of spirits, foods and goods. Although many ports along our colonial shores continued to surge in the early years of that decade, places like Providence and Perth Amboy, Williamsburg, Baltimore, Charles Towne and New York, the most prolific docks shipping materials to-and-fro London were believed to be in Ethan's Boston.

Even though Ethan and I were still rather young in those days, I think we began to grasp the essence of events taking place about the colonies a bit better than others our age. Perhaps we just listened a little more when the elders talked or found greater meaning in what was being said, understanding stories and rumors swirling about the colonies, or at least we thought we did. And although Germantown was some three hundred miles southwest of Lexington, a village of some five hundred colonists by then, including an array of farms, Ethan's too, fascinating stories about things happening in his Colony of Massachusetts Bay found their way to villages and towns throughout the colonies, intrigues whisked by swift riders galloping the changing winds.

There were frightful rumors of a big fire said to have destroyed many things in Boston that first winter of that new decade, a flaming fury that consumed hundreds of warehouses, shops and homes while burning scores of sailing ships tied by thick twine to an array of wharfs and docks. And I think it was around that time when Ethan's colony began what some disturbingly would say was a comical shuffling of its governor chair, when three loyal men over a span of several months held that royal post for the crown.

I'd later hear that shortly before his demise, the second King George had grown disappointed in what he viewed as diminishing enthusiasm for positions of the crown by Royal Governor Pownall, replacing him with Thomas Hutchinson. Perhaps fifty at that time, they say he was a rather affable man from Boston, a colonist who had studied at Harvard College across the waters of the Charles and was an acquaintance of Doctor Franklin too, from their days at that colonial meeting in the village of Albany a few years before. Yet, Mr. Hutchinson's service to the crown was rather short, for within months he too was replaced by Francis Bernard, then the king's royal governor of the Colony of New Jersey.

They say Mr. Bernard was born across the sea in Brightwell-cum-Sotwell in the summer of 1712, a village in the County of Berkshire northwest of London, and that he had been appointed by the crown as royal governor of Massachusetts Bay several months before his arrival to Boston in early August, 1760. Ethan said he had been delayed by duties in the Colony of New Jersey, and had ridden up to Boston in a royal carriage that had bounced in the dusty heat along the postal road for over two hundred miles. Even though he was known as a loyal ally of parliament and the king, having for years been a royal administrator in the colonies, some in the Colony of Massachusetts Bay were said to soon view him with disdain, a governor who would rule for the rest of the decade.

I sighed and glanced to Samuel rocking quietly in his chair, his eyes shuttered tight as if trying to envision the nuances of my story, then gazing to the distant elms swaying easy in the summer winds, I longed for the days which had passed since then. As we rocked amid the tranquil sounds of rustling leaves, I wondered what might have been for those of the colonies back then, of the many things Samuel and his generation would never know, of all the years that had passed since I last touched my Ethan.

We calmly rocked our chairs with creaking slides while bathed in the comforting sounds of dancing leaves for a moment or two, and as Samuel watched a string of puffy clouds slowly pass high, perhaps recalling his own early days, I gently stroked the ink of Ethan's words nestled in the pocket of my summer dress. Then glancing to me while nudging his chair into a more robust rock, Samuel pleadingly whispered, "Grandma, go on, please. I've got to hear more, know it all." Snapping his stare into the warming summer breeze, he silently waited for my coming words, patiently.

I caressed the aging parchment of Ethan's poem as a burst of morning air tossed the silvery strands of my thinning hair, and with each gentle rock, the soothing scent of pink mountain laurels and crimson rose embraced the passions still gripping my heart. I reached for memories of those long ago days stashed deep in my soul, and with each slide of my fingers I longed for Ethan's thrilling touch, for one more press of his sensuous lips. Oh how I longed for those wondrous hours in the years before the war.

There were increasing rumors of agitating events sporadically flaring up in Ethan's Colony of Massachusetts Bay in the early days of the reign of King George the Third. They were stories which, once reaching hundreds of ports, villages and towns throughout the colonies, were beginning to disturb the semblance of normalcy many had come to know, rumors which began to stoke the smoldering embers of a simmering discontent. It was during those days that rumblings of disloyalty were beginning to swirl about the Colony of Virginia too, to villages and towns in the colonies of Maryland, Delaware and New York, restive sounds filtering through the Carolinas to the Colony of Georgia.

Views were being exchanged in Germantown and Philadelphia too, some supporting ideas from Ethan's Boston that were coming to be known as rather radical, while others seeking to tame the embryonic flames disapproved, calling for loyalty to the English Crown. I remember how father would spout after supper in those days that we must remain with the king, that as righteous colonists, we must never waiver from support of our royal governors and London. And sometimes, he'd say we mustn't align ourselves to either side, that mother, he and I must remain true to our faith.

I suppose father's views were mostly shaped by our Society of Friends beliefs, positions held by most Quakers of Germantown and Philadelphia in those days. Yet, perhaps they were not much different than many who just wanted to cling to the lives they had carved in the colonies, preferring to mesh within the royal system, not stray from the king. And some seemed to believe that the smoldering discontent would eventually grow cold and die, or just remain confined to the fringes of the Thirteen Colonies.

One of those agitating rumors began to sweep down from Ethan's Colony of Massachusetts Bay shortly after young George ascended the crown, disturbing stories swirling from village to town that fall of 1760, and the coming winter and spring. They called them writs of assistance, officious sheets of parchment Ethan would later say colonists of Lexington would spout contemptuous things, some angrily snapping, "That bloody Bernard is flaunting those writs and sapping our liberties!"

It seems Ethan's new royal governor had begun to expand the powers of the king's agents and customs men, insisting that royal judges issue to those men what some viewed as "unbridled powers" to search colonial warehouses, sailing vessels, shops and homes, even persons without restriction. Governor Bernard was causing hundreds of those writs to be flaunted about the colony under the guise of royal justice, allowing the king's men to search for whatever they and the governor deemed appropriate.

I remember hearing some say that an agent of London in possession of one of those writs had the power to search any person or place at any time, for whatever reason, a document without expiration that could be transferred from one agent to another. I suppose they were timeless warrants authorizing the search of colonists and their possessions for whatever purpose the royal governor and his loyal men defined, writs being employed by unscrupulous men for their own malignant purposes.

Ethan would later confide that those writs were soon being wielded mostly by the king's customs agents, in what Royal Governor Bernard was saying were efforts to "stop disloyal colonists" from circumventing what parliament called the Navigation Acts. Some colonists were being accused of not paying taxes and duties on sacks, boxes and crates of goods like teas, molasses, spices, wines and rums, goods the governor and his agents were declaring to be "contraband, which must be seized for the crown."

Sometimes after supper father would talk of those writs with merchant friends of Germantown, and I can still hear him passionately spout, "What happens in the Colony of Massachusetts Bay is not of our business!" He'd insist to mother and me, others too, that "our duty is to uphold the wishes of the crown, but if stew we must, we'd best utter nothing at all." Although many seemed to support the views of Ethan's royal governor, believing colonists must hold tight to parliament and the crown, opposition to those unjust writs and other disparaging things were beginning to immerge as a fiery issue in taverns, shops and homes throughout the colonies.

It seems that colonists were discussing the troubling events of Massachusetts Bay along the cobblestones of Philadelphia too, and in villages and towns across my Colony of Pennsylvania. They'd be heard boasting the righteousness of the king's writs while gripping the reins of colts, buggies and wagons along the stony ruts of village roads, or decreeing the folly of Ethan's royal governor while tipping mugs of ale at a tavern table or between grunts and moans while stacking sacks and crates on Delaware River docks.

Fiery discussions about those dreaded documents continued to brew as the wintry snows of 1761 began to flurry and swirl about the woods and hills, and soon a few daring colonists began to quill their disapproval of those writs in newspapers and pamphlets throughout the colonies, courageous men who refused to be silenced. One of those colonists, if I recall, to express his spirited resistance was a barrister up in Ethan's Colony of Massachusetts Bay, a thirty-six year old lawyer of Boston named James Otis.

He was said to have been born in the hamlet of Barnstable, a fishing village along the waters of Cape Cod Bay some sixty miles southeast of Boston, and after grooming his legal mind at Harvard College in Cambridge, settled across the river as a barrister to be reckoned with in Boston. Just as most colonists in those earlier days, Mr. Otis too had honed his beliefs in the English way, expressing legalese support that women, children and men of Massachusetts Bay, of all the colonies, were faithful subjects of the king.

Although his colonial duties were said to have first involved upholding the acts, policies and laws of parliament and the crown, including those enacted by the colony's assembly and declared by the royal governor, his views began to change shortly after that new decade began. It seems he started to hold beliefs which were contrary to the governor and the king, that his views were evolving toward those of a growing group of colonists beginning to question the wisdom of various things being espoused by London. Rumors of spirited speeches began to filter about the colonies, into Ethan's Lexington and my Germantown too, positions spouted by Mr. Otis that were brushed of resistance to the crown.

They say that soon after the colony's royal governor arrived in Boston that summer of 1760, he quickly became acquainted with Mr. Otis' legal reputation, and without reservation, declared him the colony's advocate general for the king's admiralty court. By the final days of fall in the first year of the reign of King George the Third, Mr. Otis had been propelled to the forefront of legal authority in Ethan's Colony of Massachusetts Bay, just a step behind Royal Governor Bernard. And within weeks, he was awash in the simmering opposition of shopkeepers, lawyers, doctors, merchants and printers to policies of the crown, Bostonians now disputing those writs of assistance in the court of the king.

Ethan once said his father sometimes sputtered to other farmers and shopkeepers in the village about the naivety of their royal governor, saying he was "bloody deaf to the surging opposition to those damn writs," and held wishful beliefs that Mr. Otis would vigorously defend their use. Governor Bernard was rumored to have been bewildered when he discovered that his advocate general had been slowly sliding toward the views of colonists, and dumbfounded when Mr. Otis began to agree that the governor's writs were "unjust." He'd say they provided the governor and the king's agents with "unbridled authority to infringe upon colonist, to search persons, property and homes without a whiff of probable cause or valid judicial review."

Unable to reconcile his positions with those espoused by Royal Governor Bernard, unwilling to fulfill his royal duties as advocate for the king, it seems Mr. Otis resigned from his officious colonial position, without oscillation or remorse. Within weeks he stepped into the swirling throes of opposition being voiced by spirited Bostonians, volunteering to represent their restless position without pence, shillings or pounds, advocating their displeasure of those unjust writs in the royal court of the crown.

Those judicious challenges were said to have culminated on a frigid winter day of 1761 inside the bricks of the colony's statehouse, just off the cobblestones of King Street. "Mr. Otis argued with royal lawyers before the crown's judge for hours," one witness would later say, "berating those intrusive writs before scores of supportive Bostonians." His oratory was rumored to have been brilliantly passionate, and with each passing hour of sparing with the king's men, defiant distain was said to flare from his eyes.

Some colonists would later say that the opposition to those writs in those early days may have been the first real signs of a crackling fissure between the colonies and London, opposition by Mr. Otis and others of Massachusetts Bay that would expand to other policies and rules proclaimed by the royal governor, parliament and the king. Yet the objections of discontented colonists apparently failed to alter the ways of Governor Bernard and the crown, for those reviled writs and new unjust intrusions into colonists' lives would continue for years to come.

While those challenges to London's authority continued to fester about Boston and Ethan's Colony of Massachusetts Bay, I remember hearing of other little acts of daring defiance fermenting about all the colonies. Nevertheless, I suppose the lives of most women, children and men on thousands of farms and in hundreds of villages, ports and towns continued mostly unabated as the chill of winter slowly gave way to spring. It had been a rather frigid winter if I recall, not only here in my Germantown but up in Ethan's Lexington too, with "snows drifting the walls of our farmhouse," Ethan would later convey. "It looked like white waves splashing upon our windows, and the thaw of spring came a bit late too. Dad had to wait until late April or early May, before tilling our fields for melon and corn, oats and hey."

Although Ethan was just ten as the seasons of 1761 began to unfold, he continued to be attracted to the thoughts of various men inked to the pages of pamphlets and books. By night he'd immerse in his father's tiny collection as he did when the militia was away fighting that frontier war, and by day peruse the intriguing volumes stacked on shelves behind Miss Hutchinson's desk at the Lexington schoolhouse. "I'd wake before dawn," I remember he once whispered to me, "many mornings that winter and spring, and just watch the dark slowly fade. I'd bundle with my blankets and pillow, Andrea, and just gaze through the frosty panes, watch a spray of colors crawl from the sea."

He told me of his mother's tasty tea too, brewed with honey each morning in her favorite blue kettle pot, and the eggs she would fry with crispy oat clumps in an iron skillet over embers of the hearth. "Then I'd tug my tan wool coat and wrap my neck with the scarf mom knitted the fall before, and pull my boots close to my knees, deerskin stitched with warm pelts of beaver. Mom would tap a kiss to my cheeks as I slid my fingers into my little wool gloves, then I'd sputter a goodbye before dashing into the cold. I can still hear the crunching beneath my boots as I rushed a mile or so down the snowy ruts of the Billerica Road into Lexington, and still see the children on the little hill beyond the village field, gathering in the distance near the steps of the schoolhouse."

Ethan usually arrived at his little schoolhouse a bit before nine, and after a few hours of lessons meticulously explained by Miss Hutchinson, she'd gather all the children for a while and read a story from one of her cherished books. "They were mostly of some adventure," he liked to say, "little dramas of mothers, fathers and children, or mystical stories of quaint animals or daring men fighting wars. Her voice was calming, Andrea, and she had a way of filling our little minds with fanciful visions of magical worlds."

I knew by the tender tone of his voice and sparkle of his eyes that Ethan's memories from his schoolhouse days early that decade brought a comfort to his soul. Yet, I think he was truly drawn to the writings of others, those he liked to read when alone and free. He continued to be attracted, even at his youthful age, to works most of the children viewed as convoluted or dull, writings perhaps intended for reflective minds, for people young and old reaching for dreams.

I think some of the works Ethan liked to read were those of a man from Ireland known as Edmund Burke, a statesman they say spoke to those of London and parliament rather well. Perhaps only thirty or so in those early days, it was his ideas about monarchies, of kings and queens that seemed to intrigue Ethan the most. Some would say his words were too tumultuous if I recall, an affront to aristocratic styles of the day, views others believed daringly bold. "He talks of mind over mystery," Ethan once said, "of intellect over superstition, of rational thought versus pious zeal. He has a patriotism that seems to burn from the soul, views I find rather refreshing."

It seems that many of the ideas quilled by Mr. Burke, or perhaps words he'd spout to those willing to listen about London, touched upon what he viewed as man's diminishing strength to resist the hardening of souls. Ethan said he talked about having the courage to confront things which must be opposed, and quilled about eternal truths, and in the coming years would tell a bunch of men gathered in the halls of parliament, "The only thing necessary for the triumph of evil, is for good men, to do nothing." It was a notion Ethan would say, was bathed in simplistic beauty.

There were writings of others too which caught the fancy of Ethan, little stories and pages of poetry he'd discover hidden in colonial pamphlets and aging books, passionate stanzas quilled by inspired men such as that Mr. Addison. Some were written by women too, and if I recall, a few of Ethan's favorite lines in those days were those of a women named Anne Bradstreet, or perhaps it was Maggie or Annabel, an imaginative girl born over a hundred years before in a village in the highlands of England.

She was said to have sailed to the colonies when young, settling with her mother and father in the hamlet of Newe Towne across the Charles River from Boston, a village that would come to be known as Cambridge. Ethan said it was her collection of poems titled *The Tenth Muse Lately Sprung Up in America by a Gentlewoman of Those Parts* which attracted him the most, along with another compilation of introspective words she named, *Upon the Burning of Our House, July 10, 1666.*

Yet, I think it might have been a poetic collage by a preacher from the village of Malden that appealed to Ethan the most, a little hamlet a few miles east of Lexington. They were lines quilled many years before by Minister Wigglesworth, "intuitive thoughts" Ethan would say, from a collection he called, *Day of Doom or a Poetical Description of the Great and Last Judgment.*

At the end of each school day, when the studies and stories were done, Ethan returned to his farm a few hours before dusk during fall, winter and spring. He'd stomp the ice or dash across the grass of the village field past Mr. Giles' print shop and Reverend Clarke's place, then crunch the snows or step the twisting ruts of the Billerica Road. Sometimes one of the other children, a farming neighbor, would walk with him along the road too, and they'd fling little stones or balls of snow at fence posts, squirrels and trees. "I'd watch the day fade from a field or that oak limb by the farmhouse," Ethan once said, "and knew I was home when I could smell mom's steaming stew, or a spritzing fowl or little roasting beast, an aroma that drifted from the panes and stones of the hearth."

Although winter's thaw came rather late to Ethan's Lexington and Colony of Massachusetts Bay, soon the sweet scent of magnolias, laurels and marigolds abloom in the fields filtered about the spring of 1761. And perhaps before Ethan was truly ready, the heat of summer had come and the changes of fall drew nearer. "The seasons were hard for dad that year," he distressingly confided. "His leg was always with pain, at times pulsating so, yet dad continued to tend to the needs of our farm, a challenge rather daunting even for healthy men. Doc Newman tried to ease the anguishing pain when he could, with mystical concoctions of ciders and powders he'd brew in his shop, then would remind dad in a hushing tone, that his wound had mended as best it would."

I remember how Ethan halted his words when telling me those things, perhaps trying to calm the unpleasant memories of his father's painful struggles with his wounded leg. Then he whispered with a brush of his eyes, "I tried to help, Andrea, whenever I could, mom too, but I was just too little. Looking back, I guess the exhausting drudge of each day was slowly taking its toll."

After a few quiet moments Ethan slowly raised his gaze to my eyes that day, and with a determined gleam dashed with a son's pride, he softly added, "But no matter, dad was up at dawn each day, except maybe Sunday. He'd make his way to the fields to flail seeds or grip the handles of his plow, till the land like farmers do. He always saw that mom and I had what we needed, Andrea, and that we were safe."

I think it was sometime during the first weeks of fall that year when a special postal rider galloped into Lexington with an officious notice for Ethan's father, folded parchment with the royal seal of the colony's Governor Bernard stamped in black. Ethan said it was a correspondence that substantiated an array of rumors that had been swirling about Massachusetts Bay and all the colonies in those days, stories about gifts of land for thousands who had loyally served the king in that frontier war. They were special grants of hills and fields for men of colonial militias, awards for fighting for the crown.

The governor's letter informed Ethan's father that the crown was giving him two hundred acres of virgin soil near the Mystic Lakes a bit east of their farm, in recognition of his "courageous service to His Majesty King George." Ethan said his mother was nervous about accepting such land and that his father seemed a bit reluctant, perhaps because he was leery about taking such a gift for just doing his duty, when other militiamen like Sam and George never came home. Yet Ethan was proud and told me so, and thought that in a quiet way, his father was too.

It was an expanse of hills and fields, acres of wild grass sprouting high amid groves of maples, birch and elms, and in spring petals of yellows, violets and blues blooming the meadow gently swayed in the breeze. Ethan's father now possessed four hundred acres of Middlesex County soil, but with his father's increasing limitations, notions of cultivating his new land would never take hold. Those acres which had been free for thousands of years would be spared from the plow, land Ethan liked to believe his father intended to give him someday, for his own little family. Yet, whatever visions his father may have held for those hills, groves and flowery fields, his dreams were about to be shattered.

I remember every word of Ethan's story as if told to me yesterday, a dreadful memory beginning on a chilly Friday morn shortly before dawn, the Thirteenth of November, 1761. Ethan had been warming beneath his quilted blanket for an hour or so, gazing through his window into the dark while listening to thin spindles of twisting azaleas scratching and tapping against the frosted panes. It was an eerily foretelling sound he'd say, rapid little clicks amid winds that seemed to have swept across the colony from some haunting cave along the frontier.

He pressed to his pillow a bit more and snugged the blanket to his chin while little bursts of cold air seeped through cracks and slits along the icing window, and as tiny specks of white dashed about the darkness, he could smell peril swirling about the snow. "I watched the night slowly fade," Ethan somberly conveyed, "and began to see dark layers of gray roiling about the morning sky. They looked blustery, Andrea, as if trying to keep the rising sun at bay." It was the first brush of winter, a chilling blow which seemed different to Ethan, sending an anxious shiver through his body that gripped his soul.

Soon Ethan could hear delicate noises about the hearth and kitchen table, comforting sounds of his mother preparing some kind of breakfast and his father sparking a flame to twigs and logs bundled on the fireplace stones. "That's when I crawled from bed, Andrea, and dressed for school like I normally do each Friday. After gobbling a little bowl of dried oats splashed with a dash of molasses carted from Boston, I watched dad vanish into the morning chill to hitch our mare to the wagon."

His father needed supplies from the general store in the village, and because of the snow now flurrying about the cold, thought it best that Ethan ride with his mother and he into Lexington rather than trudge through the wintry winds to the schoolhouse. It was half past eight and the fire was dwindling, when they donned their coats and scarves, boots, gloves and hats, stepped into the chilling fray and climbed to the bench of the wagon. "Mom snuggled close to dad," Ethan recalled, "with me just to her side, and with a snap of the reins we lurched into a creaking roll toward the Billerica Road. I pressed close to mom as we bounced toward Lexington, and watched flakes darting about before settling to a thin layer of white brushing the stony ruts of the road."

I can still see Ethan's sullen eyes when he recalled, "I'll never forget the whipping of those reins amid the clumping sounds of iron shoes pounding a path in the snow. With no canopy, those chilling winds were striking our faces, and I could see the snow, blowing a bit moist now, dotting mom's cheeks and clinging to her clothes." Upon reaching the general store just past the Buckman Tavern on Bedford Street, his father brought the wagon to a jerking halt with a tug of the reins near the western edge of the village field. "I leapt to the snow, Andrea, bid mom and dad goodbye, then dashed into the flurry past the Massachusetts Road and up the hill to the schoolhouse."

While Ethan rushed to begin his school day, his mother and father escaped the November snow with a dash into the general store, and as his father gathered supplies like oils and candles, tins and sacks of spices, powders and grains, his mother quietly nestled at a little table near the warmth of Mr. Cobb's dark iron stove. She gripped a dainty cup of steaming tea and watched her love gather an array of goods, a strange iron thing for farming too, while listening to the men banter in friendly chatter. Then after a little while she gazed east through the frosting panes of the nearby window, and in a silent stare, watched the snows swirl about the grass of the village field and brush the ruts and stones of Bedford Street white.

"Dad later told me how quiet mom was in the store that morning," Ethan whispered to me in a reflective tone, "and never did know why. I've always wondered what she was thinking, sitting there alone with her tea, silently watching the snow. Maybe the struggles of the farm were weighing heavier that day, or maybe it was a more somber thing, knowing that Sam Brown's children and widow were close by. I like to think she was simply caressing special memories, not sullen, wondering of unmet dreams."

Whatever thoughts and feelings his mother was experiencing that chilling morning, their wagon was soon brimming with bundles and sacks of supplies stacked and tied, and the mystical tea which had warmed her soul, was now cold. While Ethan was listening to inspiring things espoused by Miss Hutchinson at the schoolhouse, his mother and father climbed back into their wagon and bounced east along the snows of the Billerica Road, returning home amid wheels and hooves creaking and clumping in the blustery winds.

The supplies were quickly unloaded, either tossed into their weathered shed or carefully stacked near the candle of their cherry kitchen table, and as Ethan's father unhitched and rushed their mare to shelter, his mother began to quietly search for warmth. She quickly hung her snowy hat and coat, then tugging off her icy boots and gloves, hurried to press a pair of new logs to the glowing morning ashes. Soon little flames began to snap and flicker warmth about the room, and snatching a quilted blanket, Ethan's mother wrapped her chilling body and nestled to her chair.

A blast of frigid morning air raced into the room when Ethan's father escaped the swirling flurries and rushed back into the house, an icy surge that brushed his mother and caused the fire in the hearth to wildly flicker. He latched the farmhouse door tight with a quick swinging clack, then tossed his coat and things to the corner and joined Ethan's mother near the fire, nestling to the rug and snuggling to her legs. Although the room slowly warmed, his mother continued to chill, and as the snows zipping outside the frosting windows, she began to ache, shiver and quiver.

"I'm starting to feel strange, Pat," she sputtered, "not very good, kind of achy. But maybe this fire will help, warm the cold gnawing inside."

"You're warm, Liz," Ethan's father nervously blurted, pressing his fingers to her skin beading just above her brows, "too warm. I don't like it."

"Oh, I'll be fine," she wishfully whispered, perhaps grasping a notion both feared was untrue. "I just need to calm this chill, get warm here by the fire."

Ethan's father grabbed a couple more logs and piled them to the flames, then snatched another blanket from the corner and bundled his mother a bit tighter, and even though a soothing heat flickered from the fire, she continued to shiver with a chill. Soon a sweating fever had gripped the cold surging her body as a frightening pale now brushed her cheeks, and little beads began to trickle her brows while her arms and legs trembled.

It was then that his father plucked their copper warmer from the corner and stuffed it with glowing embers, then dashed into their bedroom and slid that heated disk about the linens covered by quilted blankets. He wrapped her in his arms and helped her to the bed, and as she pressed to the pillows, he bundled the blankets tightly about her and tenderly tucked her toes from the chill. Ethan said his father was at a loss of what to do, trying his best to keep her warm, while desperately tossing logs now and then into the snapping fire.

After several anxious hours, Ethan's father hitched their mare to the wagon once again, and at perhaps half past three, softly uttered, "I'm going into town, for Ethan." And as he tucked the blankets about her body and snugged them to her chin, he caringly added, "I shouldn't be gone long. The fire has plenty of wood, so you just try and sleep. I'll be back soon, promise."

"Alright," she whispered with a weary bat of her eyes. "Hurry home. I'll miss you."

"I will," he sighed with a tender squeeze of her hand before snugging the blankets about her shoulders. "I love you," he gently added, leaning and pressing his lips to hers. Whispering the same, she slowly closed her eyes.

She was calmly sleeping when they returned home, with a serene tinge in her pale glow, as if unaware of her dire position and oblivious to the whistling winds and swirling snow. "But dad had a strange nervousness brushed across his face," Ethan confessed some years later, "an ominous look, something I'd never seen. I remember he seemed lost in some mysterious world later that night while stirring a pot of steaming stew, and mom would wake for a cup of honeyed tea or sip of broth now and then. Dad was worried as he paced by the fire, and with each passing hour, mom seemed to slowly weaken."

Ethan and his father alternated tossing fresh logs to the fire throughout the night while snugging blankets to his mother's chin, and when his father would doze for a while now and then, Ethan would do his best to assuage her ailing needs. By dawn it was clear she was not improving, her eyes now a reddening dull brushed with a feverish tinge, and the skin above her brows was wet with agonizing beads as she twisted and turned amid chills, shakes and quivers. Ethan made sure the porcelain jug and basin near his mother's bed remained filled with cold water from their farmhouse pump or icy melting snow, while he and his father cared for her by the hour, comforting her eyes, forehead and cheeks with cloth dripping cool water. Yet throughout the day and into the night she continued to slide toward a frightening place, until finally Ethan's father knew the moment had come to fetch Doc Newman from Lexington.

The whistling winds of that late autumn snow had vanished by sunrise that Sunday morn, and the scraping scratches of those spindly azaleas tapping the frosted panes of Ethan's window had fallen silent. Ethan cared for his mother as his dad saddled his colt shortly before nine, and did his best to keep her warm while his father galloped into Lexington. Then as wavy layers of sullen gray slowly drifted from the frontier to the sea, and with Ethan's father high in the saddle in the lead, Abigail and Doc brought their buggy to a clumping halt just outside the farmhouse.

Ethan said Doc looked alarmed when he first saw his mother twisting in shivering discomfort beneath the linens and blankets of her bed, and his expression became rather somber as he began a slow, methodical examination. "I could see his bushy gray brows narrow with each squint as he touched her cheeks," Ethan recalled in a melancholy tone, "and he'd nod in a disturbing way when sliding his fingers down her arms and meekly probing her hands. He'd stare down to his little watch nestled to his palm while holding mom's wrist too, its thin silver lid flipped open while pressing his fingertips to her skin for a moment or two. Doc would close that ticking disk with a snap, Andrea, then rest his ear to the damp gown clinging mom's chest, listening to her waning heart with each struggling breath."

"She's burning up, Pat," Doc sputtered with a disturbing glance to Ethan's father and concerning stare to Abigail hushed near the foot of the bed. "We've got to cool her down, calm this fever. We could use more cloths, Ethan, and cold water. A few linens rolled with snow would help too."

After rushing for those cooling supplies, Ethan was assigned the duty of ensuring the flames of the hearth kept burning, all the while Doc, with the aid of his Abigail, struggled to banish the fever from his mother. And as they cooled her beading brows and brushed her feverish skin with strips dripping cold water, pressing linens stuffed with snow against her warming body now and then, Ethan's father caressed his bride's hands and kissed her cheeks while dabbing his eyes in quiet hope.

Ethan said he could sense the unease in Doc's eyes and see the dismay brushed across Abigail's face, and knew that his father's insides were twisting in frantic desperation. And he couldn't help but feel that Doc had witnessed such illness before, seeming to show an understanding that his mother's ravaging fever was not the kind of simple ailment which had touched many of Lexington and Middlesex County seasons before. With each passing hour that day, with each fresh wrap of snow and brush of cool water, with each new limb tossed to the fire and press of Doc's ear to Ethan's mother's chest, a frightening truth began to take hold.

"Her lungs, Pat, are struggling," Doc finally confessed in a wary tone. "They're just not working right. I'm sorry, Pat. With each breath, Liz labors a little more."

Ethan's father seemed to understand what Doc was trying to say, nodding in a forlorn way while Abigail silently brushed his mother's brows, and Ethan would confess some time later that although he thought he understood, he would come to realize he did not. With each glance to Doc's eyes Ethan seemed to know there was no mystical potion or magical healing powder stuffed in his little dark bag, and with each passing moment he sensed his mother's fate slipping into the hands of God.

Doc spoke with Ethan's father before leaving a little after dusk that trying night, confiding some anguishing truths while instructing him to keep Ethan's mother warm while easing her fever from the cold. "Keep the fire going, Pat," Doc caringly explained as he and Abigail donned their coats, gloves and hats, "and cool water ready too. And make sure Liz has some of the broth you're stewing. I'll come out tomorrow, early afternoon, Pat, and every day when I can."

"Thanks, Doc," uttered Ethan's father in a somber tone as a dazed expression rushed his face. "Thank you, Abigail, so much," he quickly added while guiding them to the door.

"I'm sorry, Patrick," she tenderly replied as they stepped to the cold draping the dark outside. "I'll pray for Liz, every day." Then with a glance back toward the snapping fire, she whispered in a motherly way, "Goodnight, Ethan."

"Thank you," spouted Ethan as Abigail and Doc climbed to their buggy and began their short ride back to Lexington along the snows of the Billerica Road. And with a farewell wave by his father, the farmhouse door clicked tight amidst a loneliness chilling the night.

For the coming five days Doc gripped his dark little bag and snapped the leather reins of his buggy, riding out to the farm each afternoon, and Ethan's father cared for his bride while comforting her with simmering broths and stews. And each night Ethan helped too, keeping fresh logs burning in the hearth while helping ease his mother with steaming cups of tea. All the while he never wavered from his studies, dashing to the schoolhouse each day at the insistence of his father, something his mother wanted too, for she told him so with tender whispers each night.

With each passing day they could see her spirit slowly fade, and each night Ethan's mother seemed to struggle a bit more with every breath as her strength feverishly dwindled. There was a disheartening gaze in Doc's eyes too when leaving the farm each day, and he'd always instruct Ethan's father to come for him should his mother's condition quickly shift for the worst. And during the lonely hours each night that awful week of November, Ethan would bundle with his blankets and pillow in the quiet of his little room, and hush teary pleas to heaven.

I remember how Ethan's eyes seemed to mist with a soft resignation when he told me of that brisk autumn day, the Twentieth of November, 1761, a chilling day that saw "an eerie calm settle over our little farm that Friday night, after Doc's daily visit." The winds which had whistled about the trees days before had vanished, and the night sky was glistening with millions of pulsating stars. And the little flame of the lamp beside his mother's bed was now casting daunting shadows about the room, its light bathing her feverish cheeks in a fiery glow as she struggled with each gasping breath.

"I was bundled beneath my blankets," Ethan had sighed with a dab of his eye, "my head propped to my pillow and dozing now and then, just gazing through the frosting panes to all those sparkling stars. The house was so quiet, Andrea, just the sounds of the crackling fire, and the light from the flames of the hearth was flickering into my room. Dad was with mom, sitting on the edge of the bed and holding her hand, comforting her, watching her so quiet. He wanted to stay close to her, be near her all the time, and wanted to caress mom's skin, calm her. I think maybe he was thinking of their life together, of their dreams, of what might have been."

Then, as Ethan watched a bright trail streak across the night sky, just as the mantel clock chimed eleven, his father shattered the hush that had settled upon the farm with a frantic cry, "Ethan! Hurry!"

Ethan could feel every muscle of his body tighten in twisting knots, then tossing aside his blankets, leapt from his bed and dashed past the flames of the hearth into his mother's room. "Dad was hunched toward mom and softly sighing, with his lips pressed to her hand. All I could do was stare, Andrea, couldn't mumble a word, and as confusion raced my mind, I shuffled to her side and grasped her other hand. Her eyes were closed, so calm, yet she struggled with each sighing breath as I sat to the bed and caressed her skin. For a moment I wanted to scream at the night, Andrea, curse the heavens, but as a tear trickled my cheek, all I could do was whisper, 'I love you.'"

His father gently dabbed beads from her brows and pressed his lips to hers now and then, and with each passing moment it was becoming depressingly clear that the battle Ethan's mother had waged for days was nearing its end. Her hair was nestled to her pillow and eyes were serenely shuttered, and as Ethan and his father softly caressed the skin of her hands, she wheezed a tender sigh and gasped a final breath. "That was it, Andrea, that was all there was. No symphony playing or angel songs in the air, no village chimes or ringing church bells, just an awful hush. Mom just drifted away, as if her flame had suddenly been doused by an eternal wind."

For a moment they just sat stunned, unable to move in a silent gaze, then Ethan's father pressed his lips to her lifeless hand and began to softly cry, while tears began to spill Ethan's cheeks amid aching sighs. Soon Ethan brushed his tears, leaned and gently tapped his quivering lips upon his mother's shuttered eyes, and whispered his love a final time.

Ethan had been ripped from his mother just weeks before reaching the age of eleven, and even though he was still rather young on that terrible night, he understood that the life he had come to know had forever changed. He said his father had somehow found a way to carry on, one step at a time, one breath after the other, showing a tough demeanor to the colonists of Lexington while grappling with the remnants of his shattered heart the rest of his life. It was a shocking tragedy his father struggled to move past, something Ethan said he never truly did, an unimaginable night Ethan and his father would never forget. "Dad cherished mom," Ethan explained, "and on that awful Friday night, I think he simply banished his emotions forever. The passion in his heart, Andrea, just seemed to die."

During the coming days Ethan's father maintained a stoical appearance while arraigning the funeral for Ethan's mother at her Presbyterian Church in Lexington, a service that would come to an end upon her final interment nearby, just southwest in the soil of the village's burying ground hill. All the while Ethan struggled to understand what was truly taking place those first few days and in the months to come, confiding to me once of his feelings of helplessness. They were desperate hours he'd say, a string of endless moments mired in a blur, when his life seemed suspended amid swirling voices attempting to console, sounds that seemed as if they were echoing from the bowels of a haunting abyss somewhere along the frontier.

A cold drizzle lazily fell from a roiling gray stretching from the wilderness to the sea that gloomy autumn morn, the fourth Monday of November, 1761, three somber days since his mother gasped her final breath. After a torturous night of dozing now and then, Ethan woke and twisted his gaze through the icy panes of his bedroom window, searching the vanishing dark for the courage to meet the dawn.

"I watched as the night slowly faded, Andrea," Ethan whispered of that awful morning his mother was buried, "and felt little bursts of a soft breeze slither into my room through tiny cracks. I just looked out that window and couldn't move, just waiting for the moment to dress that cold morning, staving off the hour when mom would be laid to rest on that Lexington hill. It was as if I were floating on those drifting clouds, all the while my heart was smoldering in thousands of pieces."

After a while Ethan and his father managed to muster enough strength to meet what awaited them that solemn day, each donning their clothes in the silence of their rooms, and as his father finished dressing in a somber quiet, Ethan nestled to the cushion of his mother' chair. Warmed in his boots and wrapped in the wool of his coat, he just sat hushed and stared into the remnants of the night's fire, wondering of the horror soon to unfold. Then, about half past ten, with his father now readied, they latched the door tight and climbed to the bench of their wagon, their disheveled mare patiently waiting in the chilling morning drizzle.

The snows of the days before were almost gone by that morning, and as his father flicked the reins and the wheels creaked, they began their daunting journey along the ruts and scattered snows of the Billerica Road into Lexington. "It was a terrible ride," Ethan had said with a distant stare, "the longest of my little life, with nothing but the eerie sounds of wheels and hooves digging into the road, and the smell of drizzle gripping the morning air. We didn't talk, Andrea, just bounced in a hush past fence posts, trees and barren fields, dad lost in memories and me reaching for meaning. All I could hear was the snapping of reins and the gentle whistle of wind, and those rhythmic sounds of hooves and wheels beneath the gray. It was numbingly, surreal."

They soon rolled past Reverend Clark's place and the king's church on the northeastern edge of Lexington, and after the wheels creaked along the northern ridge of the village field, his father tugged the reins and the wagon swung south along Bedford Street on the western edge of the field. Passing the Buckman Tavern and general store in a numbing silence, they pivoted west on the Massachusett Road with a tug of the reins, creaking up a twisting slope before tugging right onto the stones of the Harrington Road. His father soon brought the wagon to a halt in front of his mother's church some hundred feet north on the muddied ruts of the narrow road, bringing the sounds of pounding hooves and creaking wheels to a stop near the steeple rising into the drizzly gray.

"I could feel my stomach twisting ever more," Ethan said, "then dad snapped the reins a final time and we lurched with a crackling roll closer to the steps of the church. I wanted to leap right there, Andrea, run away, escape with my thoughts into the nearby hills, dash to a place where pain didn't dwell. But I knew there was no such place. So I just sat there with dad, waiting in silence."

Many of Lexington and surrounding farms were already assembled inside as the hour of eleven drew nearer, women and men who were fond of Ethan's mother, and perhaps some, she didn't even know. Weathered wagons, leathered buggies and canopied carriages lined the edges of the road in neat rows, while some were scattered on the mudded grass near the steps rising to the church. And dozens of colts, fillies and mares stood cold in the drizzle, perhaps wondering of finite lives and the sorrow waiting inside.

The church's twin elm doors were swung open as if waiting for Ethan and his father to walk through, and its bricks seemed to be luring them into the confines of its hallowed room, with all those colonists waiting in elm pews. Ethan could see a small empty space in the front row near the preacher's pulpit, two places for Ethan and his father near a narrow maple box he knew held his mother. It was a simple coffin with a trio of copper handles lining each side, a dreadful looking case set upon a white cloth dangling from a thin table, special linen with little crimson roses embroidered by a somber friend.

Ethan and his father slowly walked the aisle between all those colonists in a dreadful hush before shuffled right to their special place in the front pew, and as Ethan pressed to the elm and stared to that awful maple box, Minister Whitefield began stepping to his pulpit to express consoling words. While his father's gaze snapped from his mother's coffin to the preacher's flowing dark robe and back again, Ethan felt the glaring eyes of dozens clinging to him, women, children and men watching with hands neatly folded and emotions mercifully detached. And as he stared to that maple box, a grisly sight exposing eternal truth, he was consumed by tormenting sorrow.

"We gather this morning," the minister solemnly began, "to pray for the soul of our dear, Elizabeth Sheehan," and following a few more greeting words, he recalled some tender stories a few had shared about Ethan's mother and recited holy passages from the worn pages of an inspiring tan book nestled in the palm of his hand. "Dear Lord," he gently continued, gazing down to Ethan and his father, "bless Patrick and little Ethan with strength in the trying days, weeks and months to come, and please guide them, oh Lord, with patience and understanding."

He preached of reasoning wrapped with faith, expressing things like, "It's not for man to judge why such tragedy strikes, for only God truly knows," while acknowledging that Ethan's mother "was taken from this life, far too soon." They were caring words to help soothe anger, pain and grief, insightful phrases Ethan hoped might someday temper the sorrow of his tattered heart, spiritual notions which seemed to bring a consoling comfort to his father. "Dear God," he beseeched in the final moments while gazing to the crimson rose resting atop her coffin, "bless our beloved Elizabeth, and watch over Patrick and Ethan. Oh Lord, please bless all of us here this day."

Within a few anguishing moments Ethan and his father were slowly stepping behind his mother's coffin as six colonists gripped those copper handles and somberly walked between the pews and out the church door. As a cool drizzle softly fell from the gray that November day, a slew of Lexington women, children and men watched as those six caring men struggled down the stone steps before sliding the maple box to the slats of a special funeral wagon. In what Ethan said was a numbing gaze, he and his father watched an elderly man climb to its bench, his stringy gray hair dangling from a dark tricorn hat, then gripping the reins with a snap, the wagon lurched in a creaking roll down the muddied stones of the Harrington Road toward that burying ground hill.

As the pair of tan mares slowly wheeled his mother south and across the ruts of the Massachusetts Road, Ethan and his father, along with the preacher and those who had come to witness Elizabeth Sheehan's final day, stepped close behind, past patches of gravelly snow melting along the road. Soon that special wagon came to a clumping stop and all those people pivoted right, trudging another sixty feet toward a little fence up the mushy grass slope before gathering at a sacred place on that Lexington hill.

The village burying ground was a slightly rounded spot of an acre or so spread atop the hill, a solemn little cemetery surrounded by a quaint fence of short elm slats once brushed white. Weathered crosses of pine, oak and elm sprouted from patches of muddied grass and melting snow that awful day, and thin slabs of stone rose from the soil in scattered plots, some engraved with heavenly flowers and little angels. And all were etched with cherished names, caring words and fateful dates, each a bit of Lexington's past sleeping in sacred little places.

Near the cemetery's northern edge above the western ridge of the village, Ethan and his father joined the others beside an ugly narrow hole near a dreadful mound of soil. "My stomach was twisting in bundling knots," I remember Ethan whispering while dabbing a tear, "and a nauseous tension gripped my soul as dad and I stood hushed beside that awful hole. It was horrible, Andrea. For a moment, I could see myself tumbling, vanishing forever inside that grisly hole."

A mist continued to drizzle from the gray as Ethan gazed into the darkness of that gruesome hole, then he watched with his father and the others as those six men trudged through the cemetery gate and to his mother's grave. They had shuffled up the slope while holding those handles tight, a grip they gently released after lowering the box to a trio of thick slats placed across that hole. Ethan and his father stood in a numbing trance at his mother's casket straddling the dark, then gazing to the pair of leather straps stretched across that hole, the pain of what was about to unfold tugged their souls. As Minister Whitefield took his position at the head of that dreaded hole, uttering sacred words from his little book as he did shuffling up the hill, Ethan and his father bowed their heads with all the others.

His dark robe dangled his arms as he peered to the maple box for a moment or two, and between glances to Ethan and his father, uttered a slew of sacred words while strumming his fingers across the pages of his little book. I remember Ethan confessing that he was so distraught he could only recall a word or two, spiritual phrases that seemed to vanish into the hills with the autumn winds. He just stared to his mother's box while trying not to cry, grappling in a numbing daze with emotions swirling deep inside.

After a few more spiritual moments, Minister Whitefield nodded to four Lexington men and closed his little book, then Ethan watched with his father as each snatched an end of those leather straps and lifted his mother's coffin from the boards. As others tugged the slats to expose the ugliness below, those village men began to slowly lower the box into that awful hole. Amid ghoulish scrapes of leather straps and boots digging into the muddied grass, Ethan's mother, caressed by her crimson rose, came to rest in the Massachusetts Bay soil at the bottom of that grisly pit.

They tossed the ends of those straps down into the pit with a fatal flick, and as Ethan and his father gazed into the darkness of that hole with tears swelling their eyes, the gruesome thud of leather clacking against the maple swept over the hill. A deafening hush settled upon the burying ground as those who had come to witness prayed, while some hoped to understand the finality of death, a mortality they too would come to know.

After a few somber sighs, the minister opened his sacred little book once again and tapped his fingers to a special page, then gazed upon its words while gathering his thoughts for a moment or two. "I will lift up mine eyes unto the hills," he slowly began with a sweeping glance to dozens of sullen faces, "from whence cometh my help from the Lord, which made heaven and earth. The Lord shall preserve thy going out, and thy coming in, from this time forth, for evermore." Then peering to the distant hills amid the drizzly haze, he strummed another page and gently added, "Let my cry, come near before thee, oh Lord. Give me understanding, according to thy word."

Shuttering his holy book one last time, its tattering tan leather now gripped in the fingers of his descending hands, he glanced about and prayed, "Oh

Lord, bless Patrick and Ethan. Help them with their unbearable grief." Then gazing down to that dreadful hole and out into the gloomy drizzle, he tenderly added, "Elizabeth Sheehan was a loving wife, a caring mother, and a friend to those who now stand here before you. Accept her into your world, oh Lord, into the glory of heaven."

As the villagers stood hushed upon Lexington's burying ground hill, all eyes lowered in the drizzly chill with Ethan and his father to that dreadful hole, Minister Whitefield clutched his little book to his robe, gazed out to the hills, and began to preach a final prayer. "The Lord is my shepherd, I shall not want. He maketh me to lie down in green pastures. He leadeth me beside the still waters. He restoreth my soul. He leadeth me in the paths of righteousness for his name's sake. Yea, though I walk through the valley of the shadow of death, I will fear no evil, for thou art with me, thy rod and thy staff they comfort me. Thou preparest a table before me in the presence of mine enemies, thou anointest my head with oil. My cup runneth over. Surely, goodness and mercy shall follow me all the days of my life, and I will dwell in the house of the Lord, forever."

A hush bathed the hill for a solemn moment or two, then the villagers began to slowly disperse with the minister, some bidding a few caring words to Ethan and his father before shuffling past tilted elm crosses and slanted stone slabs and down the mushy slopes of that burying ground hill. But Ethan and his father stayed behind to dwell in their grief beside his mother's grave, unable to take their eyes away from that ghastly hole. Ethan would later say it was as if they were not ready to accept his mother's fate, weren't ready to leave her all alone in that maple box in the bottom of that grisly pit.

Then, as a chilling burst of drizzly wind brushed their cheeks, their quiet meditations were shattered by a pair of disheveled men clomping in muddied boots across the snowy grass, each snatching the long handle of iron shovels stashed to the side of that ugly mound. And as Ethan and his father watched in numbing silence, those men began to thrust their scoops and toss the soil into the hole, over and over again. Ethan said the dirt struck his mother's coffin with a ghastly clunk, and even though the sounds were almost unbearable, he and his father continued to silently pray for another moment or two, before hushing their final goodbyes. His father dabbed tears with somber whispers, and with a string of tiny sighs, Ethan sputtered his love before leaving his mother behind.

Ethan was just a step or two in front of his father as they shuffled through the burying ground gate and down the hill to the stones of the Harrington Road, and as their muddied shoes slid and scraped on little rocks and patches of snow, the ghoulish sounds of shovels scooping and soil clunking dwindled in the drizzly noon haze. And with each step toward the church, Ethan could see that some of Lexington had gathered inside, for several village women and the minister's wife had assembled a spray of food and drinks, tender mercies to ease the grief gripping Ethan and his father.

Long oak tables had been arranged just inside the doors and near a few pews toward the rear, thick slats covered with an array of roasted things like chickens, ducks and little beasts next to bottles and jugs, and cups, glasses and mugs. There were several birch bowls too, filled with boiled carrots, turnips and beets, and pewter plates were stacked near crusted rolls and crumbly goodies sprinkled with sweets. And just left of a curvy elm spoon protruding from stew steaming in a dark kettle, was another iron pot simmering with molasses and beans just as those baked in Boston.

"I could see that dad was pleased," Ethan tenderly recalled, "even though I knew his heart was broken. Maybe it was a way for him to escape from the misery of that day, or maybe it just gave him a little time to gather his wits. But I wasn't quite ready, Andrea, to let go of the pain, not just yet. I guess I needed to dwell on it all, a little longer. So when dad stepped into the church, to join his village and farming friends, I stayed outside near the door, just watching and listening, alone."

Nudged in the corner near the first pew, just inside and right of the church doors, Ethan could see dozens of pewter mugs and a gaggle of men near two oak barrels at the edge of a table, a narrow iron spigot thrusting from the bottom of each. He'd later discover that one was filled with cider concocted on the Hosmer farm near Ethan's place, and the other was ale brewed in a Boston warehouse on Foster's Lane, a barrel specially fetched by the Buckman Tavern for that day. And there was a smaller group of men sharing some kind of spirit from a dark jug, rye whiskey someone would say, stilled some twenty miles south in the woods outside the village of Medfield.

After a while Ethan's mingling fears subsided, and shuffling a bit inside to a safe place left of the church doors, he continued to listen and watch as the villagers enjoyed the spirits, food, cider and ale while talking of colonial things in little groups. He could hear soft chatter from a few women and men who'd glance to him now and then as he stood alone in his corner, colonists wondering of the tragedy of his mother while whispering of the sorrow gripping Ethan and his father. And he'd hear others speak of their own lives, of family dramas and challenges of hope, of intriguing tales and fanciful dreams.

Ethan watched as his father mingled too, shuffling from one little group to another with a mug of dripping ale and bowl of steaming stew, doing things Ethan hoped would bring a sense of calm to him. His father was exchanging ideas with farmers about the coming winter months and the type of crops they'd sow in spring, sputtering of mundane things like stalks, seeds and soils. And he discussed village things with Lexington men like Ernie Wilson, John Parker, Mr. Giles and Doc Newman, delving into more troubling things like the war lingering along the frontier, and disturbing policies and laws being forged by their new royal governor or parliament and new king. Everyone was whispering kindly things too, caring condolences to help ease his pain, and some ventured to pleasing tales about Ethan's mother, memories to help bring relief to the sorrows gripping his day.

After a while Ethan found the courage to shuffle closer once again, straying from the shadows of his haven to wander nearer his father and the others while snatching a grainy roll and a few tasty treats while listening to some whisper special little stories about his mother. They reflected upon her kindness, of how she was always willing to help with the needs of a colonist in the village or nearby farm, and how she liked to gather with some of her friends to snip, mend and stich blankets, shirts, dresses and breeches. They were soothing memories that helped relieve Ethan's pains, stories which seemed to magically resurrect his mother that day, if only for a few precious moments.

Meandering back to the haven of his little corner, Ethan nibbled his roll and watched his father shuffle off to a more secluded place near the preacher's pulpit to begin a lengthy discussion with James McElroy, the proprietor of the Buckman Tavern. Ethan wondered what was being said as his father's eyes squinted from a serious expression now and then, and somehow knew they were not talking about his mother, or that waning war or new king. He watched both sip from their pewter mugs while nodding from time to time as if they had found some kind of agreement, a discussion Ethan would later learn was of the nearby tavern, an accord that would come to fruition in the months to come.

It wasn't long before Ethan knew he needed to leave, for he was tiring of the effort it took just to watch and listen to so many mingling, knew he could no longer hide his anguishing emotions inside. "I started to feel like I was falling into a hole," he once whispered beside a fire, "and feared I'd burst into a childish cry right there in the church. I knew I had to go, Andrea, get away from all those people, knew I had to escape home. I guess I needed to be alone, needed to deal with my grief in my own secluded way." After explaining his feelings to his father who understood, saying he'd follow in another hour or so with the wagon, Ethan stepped back to the doors and spun to see it all one final time. He gazed about all those women and men, the pews, food, drinks and tables, then rushed down the church steps and dashed into the afternoon drizzle, strutting for the farm, alone in his thoughts.

He rushed past the Buckman Tavern and across the mushy grass of the village field amid a chilling breeze that smelled of distant snow, all the while struggling with images of his mother resting in the soil of that burying ground hill. With each scrape of his muddied shoes upon the snowy patches and stones of the Billerica Road, Ethan wondered how strange it was that the rest of the world didn't know. As he gazed to the wintry grey slowly drifting east, he couldn't help but feel it was somehow comforting his mother's soul, and with each weary step toward the farm, he wondered of the truths of life while grappling with the reality of how quickly hopes and dreams can be shattered.

Ethan immersed in the solitude of his room that afternoon, speaking only with his father for a while before bed, then bundling with the blanket his mother quilted years before, pressed his weary mind to his pillow. He gazed through the frosting panes as that awful day slowly faded, and watched with misting eyes as darkness shrouded the farm and the Colony of Massachusetts Bay. And he listened to those spindly branches fluttering outside his window once again, tapping the glass with eerie little clicks as tears trickled his eyes. Then sometime during the quiet of that night Ethan escaped from his consuming sorrow, drifting to sleep amid somber whistling winds.

An anguishing gloom wrapped Ethan each night from dusk to dawn for many weeks, a sullenness which squeezed his heart every day at the schoolhouse and when strolling home. I remember the pain in his eyes when he confided how much he missed his mother in those trying days, longing to hear her tender voice and feel her caring touch. Although the intensity of his grief began to ease as those daunting weeks slowly passed, he began to sense that the flame of his youth had been dulled to a tiny flicker, and began to believe that the fire in his heart would never glow as brightly again.

The days seemed to numbingly drift from one to other as Ethan and his father struggled to adjust their lives, continuing to do the things needed to survive, just as generations before. His father tended to the farm as best he could, and Ethan walked to school on the Billerica Road in chilling rains, swirling snows or beneath a soothing sun. And for many weeks into winter, caring colonists from the village and nearby farms came by to see how Ethan and his father were doing, many with a tasty dish or two. Ethan said Abigail and Doc rode out to the farm most Sundays, and always with a little kettle of chicken stew, and the McElroys usually dropped by each Tuesday with a pot of Nancy's boiled corn, turnips and beets, and sometimes with a berry pie or plate of cookies and treats.

Although kindness had been shown to Ethan and his father from many good people of Lexington, Ethan described the season of Christmas as somberly depressing, and felt his eleventh birthday had passed in an anguishing blur. Yet, as the days and weeks slowly crept on, as the frigid flurries began to blow across the hills and fields that winter of 1762, Ethan and his father found a way to carry on. "It was as though I was able to stuff things deep inside," Ethan once told me, "hide the past in a dark place, safe from my feelings, at least for a little while. But dad kept struggling, Andrea, much more than I. He couldn't seem to escape the truth of mom, something that tormented him inside, and after a while, I came to realize, he never would."

Then spring seemed to brush the Sheehan farm with a kind of resurgence, a respite from anguish which was gratefully received by Ethan and his father. The colony's streams began to flow with melted snow and flowers were again blooming in the nearby hills and fields, petals sprouting in shades of reds, blues, yellows and white, and groves of birch, oak and elm were awash in song of little birds prancing about the leaves rustling in the spring breeze. And their farm was escaping from the gloom too, a sadness that had hovered the fields since that awful November day, for the soil was once again seeded and tilled in hopes of an autumn harvest. Yet, with each passing hour Ethan's father began to realize the increasing struggles to meet the challenges of the farm, for the pains of his frontier wound were intensifying with each day.

Ethan once told me he also thought his father's desire to maintain their farm seemed to fade beginning that awful autumn day, confessing how his father began to dwell in a lonely place far from the farm once their dreams had been dashed that fateful November night. His father began to indulge in spirits a bit more too, sipping wine, rye whiskey and rum during the lonely hours of night from bottles and jugs stashed in his room. And at times, when Ethan was supposed to be sleeping in his little bed, he could hear his father uttering soft words to the flames crackling in the hearth. "He'd whisper about his day, Andrea, as if mom was right there, wrapped in his arms by the fire. After a while, I could him softly cry, sighing how much he missed her so, exposing his shattered heart."

With his father's physical inabilities and waning desires to properly tend to the farm now painfully exposed, the moment seemed ripe for dramatic change, and a week or so before the schoolhouse shuttered for the summer, his father decided to act. Upon the simple strokes of a feathered quill on the final Saturday of May, documents were signed and colonial deeds passed, and suddenly, the two hundred acres of the Sheehan farm belonged to the McElroy's of Lexington. Ethan's father had exchanged the farm for their village tavern, a quid pro quo transaction of the Sheehan land for the Buckman Tavern.

"I'd later find out that Jim and Nancy didn't want the land for tilling crops," Ethan explained, "but just wanted a home in the hills. They wanted a quiet place to relax and live, away from the bustle of the village. I guess it was to be their own spot of land, Andrea, to lie beneath the stars, rest peacefully for the remaining years of their lives, while dad and I were moving into Lexington, near the western edge of the village field."

Ethan and his father had bundled, stacked and twined the rest of their belongings onto the wagon shortly after dawn the third Thursday of June, 1762, and with a snap of the reins they began their ride with a creaking lurch down the ruts and stones of the Billerica Road into Lexington, his father's colt tied behind. The upper floor of the Buckman Tavern, above the barreled bar, kitchen, candles and tables, was now Ethan's living space, his bedroom nestled up front with panes facing the village field. And his father was now the proprietor of one of two Lexington taverns, a village house of spirits, foods, wines and ales. They had left behind the only life Ethan had ever known, abandoned a place crawling with memories, visions and pain, embarking upon a new life in the village, beginning anew.

Ethan's father had never had a true structured business, had never been responsible for a warehouse, inn or shop, but as a colonist who had indulged in taverns before, he believed he knew of the challenges that awaited he and Ethan. There would be the upkeep of the oak floor, of the bar, chairs and tables, and making sure they had plenty of supplies like candles and oil for lamps, mugs, goblets and plates, and spirited bottles, jugs and barrels. They'd need to maintain all the kettles, pans, skillets and pots too, for preparing food for villagers and traveling merchants, along with flours and spices, and vegetables, meats and breads. They were challenges Ethan knew they could meet, changes he believed would be good for his father too.

"The change seemed right," Ethan whispered near dusk one summer night, "and now, dad didn't have to experience the pains of his leg every day, trying to meet the needs of the farm. He could settle into an easier, less physical way of life, and maybe, find contentment in providing what many of Lexington wanted, a place to unwind with friends. I'd help around the tavern when I could too, after school, and Saturdays and Sundays, but most important I suppose, was that we were together, Andrea, and dad was no longer secluded out on the farm. He could talk with patrons and other merchants, and maybe, find peace in his life."

Ethan soon discovered what he could do around the tavern those first few months, youthful things like sweeping the colony's soil from the oak slats of the floor early each morning, and washing scores of forks, spoons and knives, cups, pans, pots and plates. He'd help prepare meals too, such as slicing and dicing turnips and beets, onions, cabbage, carrots and potatoes, sliding all into a steaming kettle, or toss another log to the flames of the kitchen's hearth for simmering stew or roasting little fowls and beasts. And sometimes on Saturday, he'd hitch their mare to the wagon and creak along the ruts and stones of the Massachusetts Road the dozen miles southeast into Boston, returning before dusk with an array of tavern things.

Having lived on the farm during his earliest years, Ethan hadn't really come to know too many elders of Lexington, but soon he and his father became acquainted with an array of colonists, including woman and men from outlaying farms and nearby villages and towns. There were others too, such as tradesmen and merchants traveling north and south through Lexington, or riding east and west to-and-fro Boston. They were hungry men Ethan would say, colonists willingly to exchange shillings and pounds for crusted rolls and steaming meats and stews, thirsty men wanting mugs of ale or tins of rye whiskey and rum. They'd talk of innocent things in little groups or with Ethan's father too, or voice concerns about events taking place about the Colony of Massachusetts Bay or over in Boston, or discuss an intruding policy of their royal governor or unjust act of parliament and the king.

And sometime that summer, or perhaps it was the first week of fall, the honorable Henry Hanover, the roving royal judge for Middlesex County, bounced into the village in his creaking carriage and held court in their tavern, resolving a spat between a nearby farmer and a merchant from the village of Bedford. Ethan once said the judge had a proclivity for rye whiskey, and could consume of stack of jonnycakes almost without breathing, and that upon each officious visit he'd remain for a while to discuss colonial issues with villagers like Doc Newman, Mr. Giles and Ethan's father.

It seems sometimes their discussions would get rather intense, delving into things like the war winding down along the frontier or the discontent many colonists had of those writs Royal Governor Bernard was using about the colony, especially over in Boston. Ethan said that the Reverend Clarke and John Parker would join them at times too, and maybe Andy Beatty and Mr. Hosmer when they'd stray from their farms. And every time, whether their discussions were taking place in late afternoon or into the night, Ethan's father would ask him to keep their tins, goblets and mugs filled with spirits, ale and wine.

One of those intense discussions took place a bit later that fall, "a lively debate" I think Ethan had said, one concerning his father, Mr. Parker and Nathan Giles, and officiously stirred by the roving Judge Hanover. Ethan had been in back washing and stacking saucers, trenchers and plates when he glanced across the tavern floor from the open kitchen door, seeking a better view and trying to hear what those four men were getting riled about. They were gathered about the round table in the southeast corner, just past the far end of the barreled bar and left of the tavern door, with spirited courage gripped in one hand while engaging in friendly chatter.

"The judge was sipping rye whiskey from his personal tin," Ethan recalled with a tender grin, "and Mr. Giles had a big cup of rum from a secret crate of Caribbean bottles I picked up for dad in Boston weeks before. And I remember John and dad were drinking ale that night, and can still see their pewter mugs dripping a stringy trail of white froth. It was ale from a barrel perched behind the bar, a blend of barley malts some say was brewed by one of the Adams men in a Boston warehouse on Purchase Street."

Ethan always said that corner table was his father's favorite spot, with plenty of space like others scattered about the room, a table with slatted oak chairs for colonists to gather and exchange tales and thoughts. Perhaps his father found that table pleasingly secure, being nudged into that corner, an ideal spot where he could watch patrons shuffling in while glancing east through the corner window to the village green. A flame flickered from a thick lone candle in the center of the table that night, a little fire that wildly twitched whenever one of the four men thrust his spirit into the air or a villager pranced through the tavern door. Similar little flames glowed on tables scattered about the oak slats that night, tiny flickers that could be seen through the panes from the darkness shrouding the village field across the stones of Bedford Street.

"Maybe," Ethan confessed, "I remember that night more than others because the sunset was so calming. It was clear and cool, Andrea, and the shades of yellows, oranges and reds just seemed to slowly fade, being engulfed by a dark sheet that crept from the sea. I stood outside the back door for a moment shortly after dusk, and just gazed to all those pulsating stars that night, then secretly listened and watched dad and those men from my little perch near the kitchen door."

"Yes, a writ of assistance is a powerful tool," the judge was heard to admit to Nathan, John and Ethan's father, "that I grant you. But it is a most requisite tool, which must remain at Governor Bernard's disposal. There can be no doubt, gentlemen, that those writs are essential for maintaining proper colonial order, and for protecting the interests of the crown while ensuring those of the colony."

"Surely, you jest!" blustered Ethan's father, gulping his dripping ale. "A tool for maintaining proper order? Order for whom? For the crown, I say! Writs do not to protect the interest of colonists."

"They're for protecting the governor," Mr. Giles sarcastically sputtered, trying to defuse, "and of course, his loyal friends. And let's not forget the king." Then with a glare to the candle's flame and taste of his rum, he seriously added, "I fail to see a colonial appreciation for those divisive writs. I must say, your honor, and do so with respect, many of Boston and Massachusetts Bay say to Mr. Bernard, parliament and King George, 'Damn those bloody writs!'"

"Without due authority to peruse persons and places," Judge Hanover royally retorted, "examine pockets, hulls and crates quickly, seize contraband when the moment ripe, London's agents would be rendered feeble. Our customs men must be allowed to enforce the king's rule, ensure the laws and acts of parliament are respected by all colonists, while upholding the policies of Governor Bernard. Writs must remain a viable tool," he confidently added with a sip of whiskey, "or smugglers will prevail. Such a notion, gentlemen, is not only disloyal to our king, but would invite colonial decay."

"I must say, your honor," injected John Parker, fidgeting with his mug of ale, "most of us are aware of such rationale in support of those writs. And while I respect your position, it is my belief that the power unleashed by Governor Bernard with those writs tramples upon the rights and liberties of colonists. Why, not even citizens of London are subjected to such folly. No, your honor, those writs must be abandoned!"

Ethan watched as the four silently sipped spirits in search of wisdom, and as they glanced about the tavern and back to the candle flickering about the table, Ethan's father scraped his mug of ale to the oak and boldly uttered, "I agree with Nathan and John, your honor, those writs are no good, should be abolished, not only in Boston and all of Massachusetts Bay, but in every colony! It seems to me, your honor, that we colonists should at least be treated like citizens in England, be afforded the same liberties, rights and privileges as the king's subjects across the sea."

"Jolly good, Patrick!" blurted Nathan while boldly glancing about the tavern before peering to Judge Hanover's eyes. "Oh sure, we understand the governor has legitimate interests, the crown too, and they have the power. But that does not make those writs right. Is it disloyal to believe colonists should be treated equal to those in England? I say, it is not."

"By golly, Nathan, that's right!" quickly chimed John with a tiny spritz of foam. "Those bloody writs are a damn dagger jabbing at our liberties!"

"Come now, gentlemen, please," Judge Hanover calmly insisted while sipping his tin, exposing a judicious style honed over the years. "I understand your sentiments, truly I do. But surely you see that the governor must maintain the crown's authority. The colony must have order, a functioning process with loyal procedures, and the governor must fulfill the will of the crown. Those writs you despise, gentleman, have been used for many years, and are viewed by London as a legitimate power of the king."

A hush once again settled over the table as the judge tasted more of his whiskey rye, and as the others gazed to the little flame dancing atop the candle, the judge added in what Ethan thought was an effort to appeal to sensibilities and assuage the grumblings of the table. "I too am a product of the Colony of Massachusetts Bay, have resided here all of my life, gentleman. I know of the passion in your words, and not as a jurist, but a colonist. Perhaps you and others view my position as one that must simply support the policies of our royal governor, without consideration of their consequences or dangers. That's simply not so. Various disputes about those things do surface from time to time, some with merit, but these writs are not one of those things. When properly used, their value is intrinsic. Most of all, I truly believe that we, as loyal colonists, have a duty to support the acts, policies and laws of parliament and the crown."

"Maybe that's true, judge," Ethan's father carefully replied, "most of the time, but not now, not with these writs. Why, it wasn't too long ago that Mr. Otis resigned his judicious position over this very issue, righteously so. As a Bostonian, as a colonist, he said no to the king's governor, refusing to uphold those writs."

"It does seem, your honor," reasoned Mr. Giles, "that individual rights, freedoms of colonists, are at the core of this whole thing. Don't those things have more importance than royal rationales for the intrusive use of those arbitrary writs? Don't you think so, Judge Hanover?"

"I have great respect for Mr. Otis," the judge replied with a dash of royal logic, "and appreciate your points of view, all of you. But just like you, we're all English citizen, British subjects under the jurisdiction of London. And although I respect the troubling nature of these writs, gentlemen, I hold unwavering support for the crown. I've sworn to uphold the laws and acts of parliament, the policies of King George and his royal governor, and shall continue to do so."

Ethan watched Mr. Giles nod in what seemed a disconcerting way while glancing about the tavern, then listened as he sipped his rum and uttered in a caustic tone, "Well, at least we have your appreciation. Maybe someday, your honor, you might see things more as a colonist."

John tipped his mug for a splash of ale with a disgruntled glare in his eyes, and with a tinge of boorish frustration, sputtered across the table to the judge, "Bloody Christ! I must say, your honor, in spite of the wrath of the crown, you must have..." Then suddenly he seemed to grasp the reins of civility and halted his angry words, perhaps sensing the unease of Mr. Giles and Ethan's father, or maybe, feeling the displeasure of the king. "I'm sorry, your honor," he continued in more reasoning tone. "At times, I get much too intense. Everyone is entitled to their opinion, and I value yours."

"Thank you, John," the judge replied in a judicious way, "for your spirited display of respect. I know we have differences, and I appreciate how you feel, how many colonists feel. I must say," he added in a friendly tone, clicking his tin to John's mug of ale and glancing to Nathan and Pat, "it is appreciated, refreshing too, to be able to sit here with you gentlemen, and exchange points of view."

"Hear, hear!" exclaimed Nathan and Ethan's father, followed quickly by John's, "That goes for me too."

"This is what I truly enjoy about your tavern, Pat," quipped Mr. Giles while tipping his rum, "colonists sharing thoughts, sometimes with passion, regardless of schooling, background or trade."

"Why, thank you, Nathan," Ethan's father graciously replied. "I think it's important for colonists like us, you too judge, to talk of such things, freely. And agree or not, walk away friends."

"I hope talking like this," added Judge Hanover with an eerie tone of trepidation, "discussing differences in taverns like yours, Pat, and throughout the colonies, will always be our preference."

Ethan's father raised his mug of ale over the candle's pulsing flame, then boldly exclaimed while glancing about the table, "To liberty, gentlemen, to the colonies!" As John reached with his ale and Nathan stretched with his cup of rum, the judge added while clicked his tin with the others, "To the colonies, and the crown!"

"Hear, hear, the colonies and the king!" Ethan heard being boasted about the table as they sipped their final splashes of whiskey, ale and rum. Then he watched as his father bid farewell to Nathan, John and the judge, and listened as they stepped from the tavern into the night, walking or riding home. Ethan finished his nightly chores and helped his father tend to a few lingering patrons for another hour or so, farmers and merchants whispering of trivial things while sipping ale at the barreled bar or tipping cups of rum at a table near the window just right of the tavern door.

Ethan and his father became increasingly familiar with their new life at the Buckman Tavern as the weeks carried on, his father becoming more comfortable with the ways of Lexington and duties of the tavern while Ethan delved once again into studies at the schoolhouse. Yet, Saturdays and Sundays were rather different from their days on the farm, for now Ethan had tavern chores while helping his father meet a few stray needs of villagers and travelers. Farmers, tradesmen and merchants came to the tavern searching for spirits and ales, and at times a meal of roasted fowl or steaming stew, while some simply sought to escape the tribulations of their lives, if only for an hour or two.

"Dad and I even went to mom's church," Ethan once tenderly explained, "at least sometimes back then, a bit more than ever before, and always before my tavern chores began on Sunday. In a way, Andrea, I think dad began to find some solace inside those bricks later that fall, a kind of peace which had eluded him the past year. Maybe I did too, just whispering little prayers in that same elm pew, while listening to the fiery words of Minister Whitefield."

When not delving into his studies or the intrigues of an enlightening pamphlet, paper or book, or helping his father with a slew of chores about the tavern, at times Ethan found escape from his young world lying upon the grass of his mother's grave, awash with memories atop that burying ground hill. Or maybe he'd spend his Sunday afternoon stretched in the shade of an aging elm near the tavern's back door, or strolling in the autumn breeze upon the swaying grass of the village field across the ruts and stones of Bedford Street.

Meanwhile, as the leaves that fall snapped and swirled with the cooling winds and a fresh year began just days after Ethan turned twelve, lasting changes were taking place about the colonies. Although the Lexington militia had returned from that frontier war several years before, some militias from chosen colonies had remained scattered about the wilderness with thousands of the king's solders, weary men waiting for that waning war to fall silent. Then soon those militias returned to their villages, towns and homes too, the horrors of battle etched in their souls, for during the first chilling weeks of winter that frontier war between Paris and London finally came to an end.

They called it the Treaty of Paris, officious parchment quilled along the waters of the Seine during a cold rain on a Thursday afternoon, the Tenth of February, 1763. Father once explained that several other powers of Europe had eventually tossed their armies into that war, not along our colonial frontier but across the fields of Europe, nations like Prussia and Portugal that aligned with King George of London, and Austria, Russia and Spain that supported King Louis the Fifteenth of Paris. But when the war was officially declared over, it seems that treaty was mostly signed by England and France, the two kingdoms that suffered the most along our colonial frontier, along with Spain which struggled to hold its southern lands near the colonies.

I remember the story Ethan told me some ten years later about that treaty, how he and several children, hearing the village bell madly ringing, dashed from the schoolhouse in a chilling breeze toward their Lexington field. "We ran to the grass, Andrea, along with dozens of colonists rushing from their trades, shops and homes, trampling upon the patches of snow scattered about the field. The banging ring of our belfry bell had now been joined by the one atop the king's church and in mom's steeple, exciting sounds that echoed the hills while summoning colonists to gather on the field, dad too."

A few of the villagers were engaged in prayer and some were singing merciful songs, grateful that the frontier war was finally truly over, and Ethan listened as a trio of women off to the right clutched hands while softly sighing. "Dad was watching from a distance along the western edge of the field," Ethan recalled, "just standing under the limbs of the big oak tree near Bedford Street across from the tavern. He just stood there, Andrea, leaning and listening to the joy on the field as the smaller children, who didn't really understand, gleefully dashed about the mushy grass."

Ethan had gathered with some of the older boys and girls along the southeast edge of the village field near the Munroe Tavern, and just gazed northwest toward his father standing alone in the distance beyond all the women, children and men erupting in joyous hoots and hollers amid ringing bells. Then he watched his father slowly cross the road and limp back into the tavern, returning with a few patrons to his haven of windows and walls, to farmers and merchants once again sipping rye whiskey, ale and rum.

That treaty signaled that the mayhem along the frontier was finally done, and early that spring all those dangling bells in thousands of belfries, churches and steeples exploded in song across the colonies. They were joyous claps whisked by the winds to towns, farms, villages and ports like my Germantown, and for a moment I thought I could even hear the muffled ring of the bell atop my colony's statehouse down in Philadelphia. Ethan said he later heard that colonists over in Boston had rushed to their cobblestone streets too, with hundreds gathering in celebration on the muddied grass of the common to release their joy with all the bells ringing in steeples about the port.

It seems that when Paris' minister quilled his name to that treaty, King Louis surrendered all possessions east of the mighty river his loyal soldiers knew as the Messipi, as well as his northern lands of New France. Each fort, settlement and outpost, every forested hill, field and stream, had been relinquished to King George the Third. Yet, in what some would say was a display of rare royal civility, the crown of France was allowed to retain its islands of Saint Pierre and Miquelon near the cliffs of Newfoundland, along with a pair of plots in the Caribbean Sea called Guadeloupe and Martinique.

Although I suppose most didn't truly understand what role the Spanish crown had played in that frontier war, when the minister for Madrid quilled his king's consent to that treaty's parchment, Spain lost its land of La Florida to King George. In exchange for his relinquishment of that coveted peninsula, they say London allowed King Carlos the Third to reclaim his lost Island of Cuba, as well the lands most knew as Louisiana further west, including its watery settlement of New Orleans.

I can still recall how a calming sense of relief seemed to settle over the colonies in the weeks and months following all those joyous bells chiming that treaty, and how a feeling of normalcy swept the hills and fields, if only for a little while. The frontier struggle was over and most colonial militias had finally returned home, yet thousands of London's royal troops remained in the colonies. They were young soldiers strutting in crimson coats and dark boots with muskets dangling shoulders who had sailed across the sea to defeat King Louis and his native warriors, royal soldiers now garrisoned in forts along the frontier, or soon, relieved to safer quarters nearer the sea.

During those calming months Ethan continued his tavern chores while perusing pamphlets, books and papers bundled at his schoolhouse or stacked in his father's little study upstairs in the Buckman Tavern. And as in months and years before, he continued to delve into the writings of spirited colonists and others across the sea, "enlightened men" he'd say, like Newton, Burke, Turgot and Locke. They were thoughts and theories being read by hundreds of colonists too, most older than Ethan and some young as he, inquisitive women and girls, boys and men in ports, villages and towns like Williamsburg, Dover and New York, Philadelphia, Boston, Charles Towne and Savannah, my Germantown and Ethan's Lexington too.

Ethan once said that some of those men spoke of freedom of trade and democracy, and others quilled ideas as fundamental as individual liberty, writings which inspired a growing cadre of women and men throughout the colonies while spurring his curiosity. He'd discover their writings in worn little books or tattered pamphlets which had been sailed across the sea by colonial merchants, or find their thoughts printed in publications gathered in Mr. Giles' print shop, in editions of the Boston Gazette and Country Journal or Annual Register, or his own Lexington Gazette. And Ethan's father always had a selection of printings in his tavern too, writings for farmers, tradesmen, shopkeepers and merchants to read when sipping alone or debate in little groups.

"What about you, grandma?" Samuel interrupted in an inquisitive way. "You've talked of Ethan and Lexington in those early days, the colonies and his poor mother too, but not you. What were you doing, grandma, when you were twelve and thirteen?"

I slowed my chair into an easy rock and glanced to Samuel with a dash of frustration brushing my face, for I wasn't quite ready to leave the memories of Lexington and Ethan. "I guess I was doing what most young girls did in those days," I whispered, "helping mother at home and tending to my schooling."

He nudged his chair into a more robust rock and looked to my eyes in a puzzling gaze, perhaps wondering of all the things yet to be told, while I peered to the tips of those distant elms swaying in the warm breeze. As we rocked in a calming silence for a moment or two, listening to little birds chirping in the rustling leaves, I slid my hand into the pocket of my summer dress and caressed the passions of Ethan's aging poem.

"Come now, grandma," uttered Samuel with a squinting gaze to my eyes, "surely there was more than that. What about those writings colonists were reading in those days? Did you see some of those too? Or maybe, your fancies were of other things in those days? Is that it, grandma?"

"I'd stroll to our village schoolhouse just like most children in those days," I confided in a weary tone while sliding my fingers across the tattering creases of Ethan's poem, "a place much like Lexington's I suppose. And like Ethan, I walked the half mile or so in all kinds of weather, brisk days of fall or a spring shower, even wintry flurries of snow. It was a little school on the southern edge of Germantown along the narrow road that wound down to Philadelphia, two rooms of red brick for children of the village and farms scattered about the hills. I guess we studied what most children did, and special things for the girls too, like styles and methods for baking, clothes and threads for stitching and sewing, and numbers too, for keeping track of shillings and pounds at home. But even in those earliest days, Samuel, my interests were shifting to medical things, to helping the infirmed, injured and sick."

"What about those writings, grandma, those pamphlets and books Ethan talked about? Did you read those things too?"

"I was young, Samuel, and unlike Ethan who truly delved into those things at such an early age, I loved to bake and sew, but mostly was fiddling with the notion of life as a nurse. But I did see some of those things, and remember rumors of opinions being espoused by various colonists, even some down in Philadelphia like Doctor Franklin, mostly just older things from his almanac years before. Some were beginning to quill ideas many viewed as brushed with a tinge of disloyalty, opinions being printed in Philadelphia's Evening Post or perhaps the Pennsylvania Gazette, views some thought to be rather satirical. I even recall how Mr. Franklin had a way of slicing to the core of disturbing issues swirling the colonies, a way of exposing the folly of acts, policies and laws being thrust upon all of us by royal governors, parliament and the king."

"I think I understand, grandma. You knew of those opinions being quilled by a few about the colonies, but your yearning was medicine."

"Yes, Samuel, I suppose that's right. It was around that time that I heard of the Pennsylvania Hospital down in Philadelphia, the one they say Doctor Franklin helped establish years before. Mother had a sewing friend in those days named Sarah Walsh who was a nurse at the hospital, and in the summer I turned thirteen, I rode down with mother and father to meet her. I'll always remember how kind she was, showing me about the hospital that day, and several other times that summer, letting me follow her around and watch her tend to patients' ailments and injuries. She was so encouraging, Samuel, and in a wonderful way, inspired me to reach for my dream of nursing."

"What a nice memory, grandma. I never knew. I'm so glad you shared that with me."

"Yes, it is," I softly replied, caressing Ethan's words while nudging my chair with easy slides. "There now, that's enough about me. Let's go back to more intriguing things about the colonies in those early days, to things of Ethan."

"Yes," he uttered, pressing to the slats of his chair and peering into the warming July breeze, "let's."

I closed my eyes and reached for another time as Samuel gazed to the distant trees, and with each soft slide of my fingers across the parchment of Ethan's poem, I searched for visions of how it used to be. The roses blooming about my porch smelled as they did in those days so long ago, and the summer winds gently tossing my hair were filled with an aroma that seemed to come from some mystical place hidden along the frontier.

And with each gentle rock and breath of noon air, my heart longed for the cherished hours of our colonial days and sensuous touch of my Ethan.

I remember that soon after our colonial lives began to slowly return to a semblance of normalcy that spring of 1763, disturbing rumors of turmoil along the frontier north and west began to once again swirl about the colonies. Only now they were troubles of a differing kind, not of those spurred by French soldiers of King Louis as in years before, but fires being sparked by a few tribes of their former native allies.

Frightful stories of gruesome skirmishes in those Ohio lands along the frontier to the west began filtering into Germantown and Philadelphia, and disturbing rumors from the northern wilderness near the big lakes of Huron, Ontario and Erie were sweeping across the colonies. They were native uprisings by disgruntled tribes lashing out against King George's soldiers and colonial settlers, savage attacks by warriors once passive when the lands had been controlled by the French. Some believed that those tribes had become increasingly dissatisfied with the manners of London's royal troops, disapproving of their methods of instilling England's predominance pursuant to that Treaty of Paris.

Father once said that for the first time "several tribes loosely banded to support a native cause," forming what some viewed as a violent fellowship to resist further incursions into the wilderness by the powers of Europe, and in the spring of 1763, the focus of their resistance was the English Crown. A trio of native groups was believed to be the foundation of the warriors sparking the escalating uprisings along the frontier, impassioned men who were mostly from the former lands of New France, natives learned in the language and ways of the Algonquian tribes.

Thousands of Ottawas, Ojibwas, Potawatomis and Hurons were rumored to roam the northern regions of those big lakes, natives believed to have engaged in intrigues and trade with the French before their banishment, and some who had mingled passionately with those of Paris, even wading into the waters of marriage. They were an assembly of tribes that some say were dumbfounded by the defeat of the French, an association now bewildered by what they believed was the crushing intrusion of King George's troops forcefully striving to control their fate.

Another native group had assembled in the wilderness some three hundred miles west of my Colony of Pennsylvania, warriors mainly of the Miami and Piankashaw tribes supported by hundreds from the Mascouten and Wea Kickapoo. They were rumored to have gathered in the forests of what some called the Illinois lands southwest of the big lake of Huron, natives believed to have been sympathetic for years to the troops of King Louis. And now, they were said to be disturbingly disenchanted upon hearing that the French had been tossed from the wilderness by soldiers of the English Crown.

The third group was said to be comprised mostly of tribes that wandered the wilderness about the Ohio lands in those days, an array of warriors from the Delawares, Shawnees, Wyandots and Mingos. Yet unlike the other native groups, this final band was thought to be less enthusiastic in its participation in the tempest brewing about the wilderness, warriors who had never truly discovered a brotherly bond with the departed French.

I would later discover that the tribes of that third group had actually migrated from the east some sixty years before, having fled from increasing frictions with Iroquois tribes as well as what they viewed as the encroaching English and French. Some said they had been allied with the banished forces of Paris for only a few years, and had done so not from some kind of loyalty to King Louis but in an effort to persuade King George and the colonies to let them return to their lands back east.

I suppose when those rumors of disgruntled natives began to sweep across the colonies from the frontier, most were unaware of a dominating leader trying to corral control and devise warrior strategy. Then stories began to seep from the wilderness about a native man said to arouse the tribes more robustly than any other, a warrior thought to be inspiring the efforts of those fiery groups surging toward an uprising.

If I recall, he was sometimes known as chief of the Ottawas, and thought to answer to the name of Pontiac, and was believed to have assembled a special group of tribes to discuss their mutual disputes with London and the king. There were frightful rumors too, that he had urged his warriors to emphatically resist England's attempts to dominate the wilderness, inciting his natives to lash out against the colonies and the crown, "force them from our rightful lands."

In the early hours of that spring the commanders of London's outposts and forts along the frontier, as well as the king's royal governors, colonial assemblies and colonists daring to settle further into the unknown, were hearing only vague stories of troubles brewing in the wilderness. They were disturbing rumors which had begun to sweep across the hills and fields to ports, villages and towns throughout the colonies, awful stories swirling about Philadelphia and Germantown of warriors gripping daggers, spears and menacing wampum belts.

In spite of those troubling warnings, it seems a confusing haze had descended upon our royal governors and colonial assemblies those crucial days, or perhaps it was simply an inexplicable failure to comprehend the dangers swirling the wilderness. And while those disturbing limitations garnered strength amid an absence of colonial coordination, stymying proper planning by the colonies and the king's royal commanders, those determined native groups unleashed their wrath along the frontier.

They say the English soldiers manning a wilderness fort near the western shore of the big lake of Erie had suddenly come under brutal attack by an array of warriors guided by that chief called Pontiac. Then soon and without warning, dozens more of the king's forts and colonial settlements scattered about the wilderness were struck by the fury of native men, including the outpost of Sandusky, some hundred and fifty miles west of Fort Detroit.

A dazed survivor would later recall how London's royal soldiers of Fort Sandusky were viciously overrun by a "band of shrilling Wyandots," and that the king's commander was captured and a dozen loyal men were butchered just after dawn. He told how some of the warriors savagely killed some trappers and traders too, "slicing their hearts from their chests as the men screamed curdling cries," and confessed how he and some of the fortunate ones watched from the woods as the natives burned the fort to the ground. The nearby fort of St. Joseph was soon destroyed by a ravaging band of Potawatomis, and in the weeks of May and June a string of forts hundreds of miles north named Miami, Quiatenon and Michilimackinac were torched by swarms of screeching Ojibwas.

There were encroaching rumors too of savage attacks still further southeast on an array of settlements and forts in the lands of the Ohio and western fringes of my Colony of Pennsylvania, outposts viciously captured or burned to the soil. Hundreds of Seneca warriors were also said to be thrashing colonial settlements scattered about the fort the French had called Duquesne at the confluence of those three rivers, an outpost King

George renamed Fort Pitt in honor of an English statesman and loyal London friend.

Yet perhaps the gruesome stories of what took place at the fort of Venango some seventy miles north instilled the most horrific visions in the minds of stunned women, children and men throughout the colonies, from my village of Germantown to Ethan's Lexington. "Those bloody savages tied the king's captain with twine," a witness would later say as he quivered and shivered, "then sliced his flesh and snapped his bones as he screamed for mercy." Some called it a brutal ritual that enticed the captain to quill a string of native grievances to a sheet of tattered parchment stained with spatters of crimson. But once he compiled that torturous list, those warriors bound him to branches and limbs and set him ablaze in a screaming sea of consuming flames.

But the mayhem didn't stop, for soon there were stories of fresh attacks against other wilderness forts like Le Boeuf near the lake waters of Erie north of Fort Pitt. The old French outpost was said to have fallen to hundreds of raging Seneca warriors near the middle of June, a bloody fight quickly followed by the capture of Presque Isle, the last fort to fall in the wilderness uprising that had flared since spring. Yet perhaps it was the utter horror of what happened at Presque Isle that stunned colonists the most, for we'd later hear that it was a brutal massacre. As dozens of the king's royal troops staggered from the fort in a drizzle early that warm summer morn, "frightened and weary soldiers tossing their muskets in surrender," a shaking witness would later recalled, they were attacked by hundreds of deceiving warriors, slaughtered by natives swinging, thrashing and slashing bloodying spears, clubs and knives.

Then as the weeks slowly passed that summer of 1763, rumors began to swirl that Fort Pitt had come under siege by swarms of the Delaware tribe, frightful reports soon followed by stories that renegade bands of Shawnee and other warriors were striking at colonial settlements further south and east. They were chilling rumors spurring fears that the native uprising was drifting from its isolation along the frontier, that the fires of the wilderness were spreading deeper into my Colony of Pennsylvania.

Grisly accounts of vicious attacks upon scattered colonial settlements began to sweep across the hills and fields of my colony, dreadful stories of innocent woman, children and men being brutally slashed and mortally beaten by roving warriors. I remember how some who survived told of "dashing into the woods for our lives," wandering about the trees in search of a haven or fleeing east to towns and villages like Lancaster, Milltown and Reading. And some escaped their frontier fate all the way to Philadelphia, straggling to the cobblestones with gruesome tales of unspeakable horror.

It wasn't long after those shocking stories began filtering east into Philadelphia and other villages like my Germantown, that we began to hear that the king's commander of his entire colonial Royal Army was devising a plan to counter the uprising in the wilderness. And I remember a disturbing story that a few soldiers on General Amherst's staff, desperate to quash the frontier violence, were concocting a diabolical scheme to defeat the warriors by making them sick. It seems they wanted a special group of the king's troops to expose those native men to a dreadful ill by secretly providing them with wool blankets infested with the plague of smallpox.

Yet father said that the general and some royal governors declined to engage in such a dastardly deed, deciding instead to cling to honor with a more civilized approach encased in military doctrine. And shortly after dawn on the final Monday of July, the general dispatched Colonel Henry Bouquet and some five hundred royal soldiers to march west three abreast, along with scores of colonial militiamen. Colonists were said to have rushed from their homes that summer morn to bear witness to those brave men strutting along Philadelphia's cobblestones toward the fray exploding about frontier, muskets slung from shoulders.

Following weeks of anxious silence, exciting stories began to filter into Philadelphia and Germantown revealing that warriors of the Delaware, Mingo, Shawnee and Wyandot had abandoned their siege of Fort Pitt to engage the king's soldiers approaching from the east. I can still hear the bells of Germantown celebrating the saving of the fort and defeat of those native men, and remember how relieved mother was to know that those warriors no longer menaced, having dashed into the wilderness north. Ethan would later say his Lexington belfry chimed in celebration too once the rumors had reached the Colony of Massachusetts Bay, as did the bells dangling in Boston and villages and towns across the colonies. They were victorious chimes proclaiming the bravery of my colony's militiamen and the king's soldiers at the battle many were soon calling, Bushy Run.

But those joyous feelings would soon pass when dire reports began to trickle to farms, ports, villages and towns across the colonies, terrifying stories being carried by swift riders from the Colony of New York. It was a revelation of ghastly deeds that would soon leap from broadsides and newspapers of every colony, from parchment of my Pennsylvania Evening Post to the Country Journal of Boston and Ethan's Lexington Gazette. Within days and weeks women and men in taverns, homes and shops throughout the colonies were being frightened by the accounts being reported in the Newport Gazette in the Colony of Rhodes Island, the Port of New York's General Advertiser, and the Gazette of Charlotte Towne down in the Colony of North Carolina.

They say it was a vicious battle on a narrow strip of land smothered by trees, a stretch of rocky terrain between the big lakes of Ontario and Erie near a thundering falls on a river the Iroquois knew as Niagara. It was a desolate place in the eastern shadows of the Colony of New York most had come to eerily call the devil's hole, a secluded patch the Ojibwa, Ottawa and Seneca had long ago discovered as a perfect spot for savagely trapping their foe. The Pennsylvania Evening Post would reveal that a hundred or so of the king's soldiers, supported by an array of wilderness men, were escorting a string of royal wagons bulging with vital supplies to a fort just north of the falls, when the mayhem began.

"Shortly after noon," the Evening Post revealed about that second Wednesday of September, "wandering warriors discovered the column of soldiers, carts and wagons led by Johnny Stedman. And within moments, hundreds of shrilling natives, with death streaming their eyes, viciously attacked our royal men." One of the wounded would later describe how the warriors leaped upon the column from high rocky cliffs and limbs of trees with crude tomahawks, spears and knives, while others swept over the king's soldiers from the shadows of the brush amid haunting yelps and cries.

Some eighty of the crown's men were said to have met their deathly fate that steamy afternoon, daring soldiers and colonists gruesomely mauled, hacked and sliced that summer day, while only a single warrior lay wounded. The Evening Post would later confess that the massacre at that hellish place was the most costly in human flesh of all the fights that had flared during those months of the uprising in the wilderness, a battle the lucky ones would forever recall as inconceivably brutish.

I think it was around that time, not long after the first chills of snow began to flurry late that fall of 1763, when women, children and men in hundreds of villages and towns throughout the colonies were starting to refer to that frontier uprising as a rebellious war led by that native chief Pontiac. And I remember how the many haunting stories of those vicious battles brushed a terrifying gaze across many eyes of Philadelphia and my Germantown, grisly stories that instilled a nervous fright in thousands in the Colony of Pennsylvania, especially deep inside mother and me.

Ethan would later confide that there was a disturbing fear beginning to simmer throughout his Colony of Massachusetts Bay too, that the warrior savagery aflame in the wilderness might soon sweep into his colony. Frightening thoughts of the frontier strife spreading further south and east was beginning to grip colonists everywhere in those days, particularly those of hamlets and towns isolated near the forests or on little farms in the colonies of Pennsylvania, New Hampshire, Virginia and New York.

If I recall, most of those wilderness skirmishes and battles as of the final days of that fall had involved brutal attacks by angry warriors against the royal soldiers of King George. But as the cold autumn breezes began to meet the coming wintry winds, disturbing rumors began to swirl of colonists gripping the reins of their own fate, forming their own little groups with muskets, powder and balls to defend their farms, villages and homes.

The Pennsylvania Gazette was soon describing those scattered bands of colonists as "misguided vigilante groups," fearless men determined to inflict retribution upon nearby native women, children and men rather than helping douse the warrior uprising further in the wilderness. They were said to prey upon unsuspecting natives who had in truth refrained from participation in the uprising further west, vigilante men who raided little native villages far from the frontier. And perhaps the most infamous of those colonial bands flared from the hamlet of Paxton, a little village along the eastern bank of the Susquehanna River some hundred miles west of my Germantown.

Some were disturbingly referring to those young men as excitingly inspiring, while father viewed them as dangerous boys from Paxton, and many described them as a frightening band of frustrated frontiersmen, pioneers of Irish, Scottish and Germanic decent who had abandoned their Philadelphia ties some years before. And some believed they were simply good and honest men who had traveled a bit further west to chase their dreams with brothers and sisters, wives and children, colonists who sought to slice new homes, farms and villages from the woods, live in harmony nearer the wilderness.

Rumors filtering east suggested that those angry men from Paxton had become disillusioned at what was said to be the ineffectual leadership of my colony's royal governor, John Penn, accusations which included the notion that his efforts to confront the dangers lurking along the frontier were dreadfully feeble. And following what one witness described as a "rambunctious gathering of dozens of furious Paxton men in the village's Crown Tavern," they agreed to organize a striking force for their hamlet's defense, a tiny army of fiery young men about to release sizzling frustrations upon an unsuspecting array of nearby native villages.

They were said to have exploded their punishing actions with delirious disregard of the true peaceful nature of the women, children and men who lived in those little native villages, tranquil people who had not participated in the acts of madness perpetrated by other tribes along the frontier. And I remember the frightening stories being told by riders galloping from the distant woods to Philadelphia and my Germantown, disturbing accounts of mindless mayhem dispensed by those inflamed colonial men.

I think it was during the first days of the new year when we began to hear grisly stories of what those young men did to a little Conestoga tribe living passively in a hamlet of rustic huts near Millersville, a village along the river some forty miles southeast of Paxton. Mother said that the natives of that little hamlet meant no harm to any colonist, calling them a benign, spiritual people who simply sought to hunt the woods, till the soil and fish the trickling waters of rivers and streams.

It seems that by the final hours of the old year those young Paxton men had come to believe that the natives of that Conestoga hamlet had somehow been in cahoots with the uprising tribes along the frontier. Gripped by murderous thoughts spurred by those bigoted delusions, dozens of those angry men galloped into the snows of the wintry night, approaching the sleepy hamlet along the river shortly before dawn. And as the natives began to wake with their rising sun, that band of frontiersmen thrust their madness upon the village, slashing flesh with shears and knives and blasting screams with little lead balls streaking from pistols and muskets. Some would say it was a satanic attack of ugly vengeance, a cowardly assault which viciously wounded dozens while sending several frantic women, children and men to their graves.

I remember how colonists north and south were appalled upon hearing of that brutal attack, and how rumors of disapproving contempt toward that band of angry Paxton men were soon swirling about my Colony of Pennsylvania, in Philadelphia and Germantown too. And there were stories that the colonists of Millersville, sympathetic to the plight of that native village, were contemplating some type of punishment against those Paxton men, while cries for retribution for that vile attack were being spewed from ports, villages and towns throughout the colonies.

I suppose it was those mounting pressures which caused my colony's Royal Governor Penn to try to stem the carnage and tensions brewing in the Millersville woods, for he soon ordered the local colonials to place the native survivors of that vicious attack into protective custody. The Pennsylvania Gazette revealed that they were secured inside the bricks of the village blockhouse a little north in Lancaster "for their own good," but that it wasn't long before the governor's plan was foiled by the wrath of those Paxton men. Amid horrific screams that chilled the winter night, those merciless men bashed their way through those bricks and beat, blasted and slashed the life from some two dozen Conestoga women, children and men.

Yet, for reasons bewildering to me and thousands of colonists who still remember after all these years, that murderous mob of Paxton men remained free to roam those western woods. As they continue their mayhem unrestrained, without limitation or effective resistance from our royal governor, that band of angry young men expanded in number and rampaging deeds. There were rumors of awful attacks on more and more little native villages, vicious assaults on peaceful people whose sole transgression was some ancestral connection with the rebellious factions of that wilderness chief named Pontiac. And as their thirst for native blood crept further and further east, hundreds of panicked natives began to desperately flee for safety nearer the sea.

Depressing stories began swirling about the colony during those first wintry weeks of 1764, frightful revelations that tribal women, children and men were beginning to stagger into Philadelphia. After walking in flurrying snows for days, entire native families were wandering into nearby villages, hills and fields too, some to the woods just south of my Germantown. Their clothes were said to be flimsy wraps that whipped and flapped in the chilling winds, and those without tattered shoes shuffled the snows behind creaking carts with soles bound by strips of fraying cloth.

Soon, there were frightful rumors that a few hundred of those determined Paxton men were galloping east from the woods, and most believed that their intent was to bring their terror to the native people who had sought refuge in and around Philadelphia. I remember father and some at our Quaker house saying those approaching men were cowards for wanting to harm innocent children, women and men, and many of Germantown and Philadelphia were angrily spouting that the viciousness must end. Then after many pleas by frantic colonists seeking a halt to the mayhem, our royal governor ordered several hundred of the king's soldiers to protect the people of those tribes and every colonist of Philadelphia from the madness of those Paxton men.

As that menacing mob of angry men galloped closer and closer, a growing number of colonists in Philadelphia and nearby villages and towns, mother, father and Germantown too, were becoming gripped by the notion that doom was descending from the west. And while that chilling gloom was frightening hundreds of women, children and men, rumors of a plan by Doctor Franklin, who had returned from London just the year before, began to spread. They say he was sailing back to England soon, to new duties as special agent for the colony, but before departing convinced Governor Penn of his little plan, including mustering Philadelphia's colonial militia in support of the king's troops.

Philadelphia was now feeling more prepared and secure to properly protect itself from those approaching men, and when that mob from Paxton galloped to its cobblestones that brisk winter day, they were greeted by what Doctor Franklin had insisted, reasonably calm men. And before any threat was spouted toward those innocent natives or fiery words were spewed between the governor's greeters and those angry men, Mr. Franklin was reported to have persuaded all to exchange any hostile intent for a rational discussion of options and remedies. It seems a few chosen Paxton men gathered just north of Philadelphia with the doctor and some of the colonial militia, the king's troops and a few of the governor's closest men, parleying in a little farmhouse along the road winding from my Germantown.

The minds of steady men were said to have prevailed in the farmhouse that frigid winter day, for after many hours of boisterous exchanges calmed by notions of civility, a reasonable understanding was found. The Evening Post would later reveal that in exchange for a cessation of the mindless mayhem against those native people, that Paxton mob agreed to have their grievances published and reviewed by the colony's assembly. With that meeting of the minds, the tempest that had swirled about the western woods before sweeping east into Philadelphia those wintry weeks of 1764 had finally come to pass, and the crisis spurred by those Paxton men was mercifully laid to rest.

The colonists of Philadelphia watched in an anxious silence as some three hundred Paxton men climbed to their saddles and galloped west into the woods and hills, back to their frontier homes, back to their children and wives. They were soon followed by hundreds of women, children and men of native tribes who had escaped the violence by trudging east through the snows, weary people hungry and cold returning with creaking carts to what remained of their rustic huts and tiny farms, their tattered hamlets and homes. I heard father utter that day how a "semblance of sanity had prevailed," and remember how calm seemed to settle over my colony's eastern lands once again.

Although the crisis spurred by those Paxton men had passed and the souls of their senseless violence had been laid to rest, the lingering embers of that native uprising continued to flare along the frontier now and then. Those rebellious strikes seemed to peak with an array of ghastly attacks on colonial settlements during that spring and summer of 1764, only now those deadly thrusts were no longer confined to the wilderness west.

Frightening rumors were sweeping into Germantown that April and May, ugly stories about screeching natives mauling innocent settlers in places like my colony's woods near Fort Loudoun, some hundred and fifty miles west of Philadelphia. There were other grisly rumors seeping northeast from the Colony of Maryland too, gruesome tales of savage attacks by shrilling warriors on colonists peacefully tilling their fields just seventy miles southwest of my Germantown, near a fort the king called the Cumberland.

Yet perhaps the most terrifying tales were of an attack by a band of crazed warriors from the Delaware tribe on a scorching July afternoon, grisly rumors that told of fiery natives rushing from the shadows of brush and trees to surround a little schoolhouse a mile or so from Fort Loudoun. "I could see the colors stroked on their faces as they smashed through the door," one of the scarred children who survived the savagery would later say. "All I could do was tuck into a little ball, and hide."

Amid desperate screams and horrific cries, those warriors proceeded to bash, bludgeon and slash the life from the young schoolmarm and a dozen innocent children, and as that poor little witness huddled in horror, they viciously sliced the hair from their heads and strung the dripping flesh from tomahawks, spears and knives. Then as quickly as those savages had come, they dashed wildly from their dastardly deed, vanishing into the woods with satanic madness flaring from their eyes.

As gruesome tales of that despicable attack swirled about Philadelphia and Germantown, there was an unflattering cry about the colony for justice, for some kind of reciprocity spurred by anguish or a compelling will to survive. Succumbing to those pressures soon after that massacre at the schoolhouse of Enoch Brown, our royal governor decreed that the crown would pay shillings and pounds for the scalps of warring natives. A bounty had now been bestowed upon the death of each wilderness warrior, an officious sanction of brutality unseen since the ruthless days of that frontier war.

It was around that time that the rumors of native carnage along the frontiers of the colonies began to mercifully subside, and once the first snows began to flurry in late fall those dreadful stories slowed to a trickle. The violence unleashed by warriors of that chief called Pontiac, as well as the death and destruction caused by an array of rogue tribes against the king's outposts and royal soldiers, against our colonial militias, farmers, settlers and traders, had finally come to a halt. The wilderness uprising had truly slowed to what father said was a "blessed stalemate," and prayers were being whispered across the colonies that the silence was a lasting peace.

Although the violence in my colony's western wilderness was winding to a close those final hours of 1764, many colonists had already decided to leave those fires behind, migrating back to the east. It seems that over those many months thousands of settlers had fled the slaughter of the frontier, seeking safer places in villages and towns nearer the sea, many creaking into Philadelphia with wagons and carts bundled and tied with precious things, colonists desperately searching to begin anew.

I remember that some returned with only a saddle strapped to a weary horse, and perhaps a sack or two stuffed with cherished things, while others less fortunate came shuffling back with desperation gripping their soul. They had walked many miles in scuffed shoes or worn muddied boots, most donning a tricorn or tattered hat and bundled in a ragged coat, all grateful to have survived. And some even wandered a bit further north into my Germantown, each with an undaunted desire to simply live.

In the meantime, while all those challenging changes were occurring along the frontier and in scores of ports, villages and towns, many in the colonies seemed unaware, or perhaps were too consumed by the native violence, to notice the effects of that wilderness uprising upon King George the Third and his parliament. "Not even Sam Adams was aware of all the decisions being made in London," Ethan once confided, nor did most royal men in Boston truly know that the crown had appointed a new commander for its Royal Army in the colonies.

Some believed that parliament had decided that General Amherst was to blame for the native uprising in the wilderness, saying his limitations had also caused the king's army to stumble in various colonial places, and having lost faith in their commander, relieved him of his duties by secret communique. He was quietly replaced by a general King George was rumored to view as loyally adept at diplomacy, an attribute thought crucial in bringing an honorable end to the dwindling troubles along the frontier.

Thomas Gage had been in America for almost a decade by the winter of 1764, and at the age of forty-four had become the absolute commander of all the king's forces in the Thirteen Colonies. They say General Gage had served under Edward Braddock early in that frontier war against King Louis, then accepted the position of royal governor of the northern wilderness of Montreal. And now, as his predecessor was sailing back to London stained of disgrace, he was the crown's top general for all the colonies.

He was said to have quickly acclimated to his new duties upon taking command as the frontier rebellion was winding down, and following many weeks of negotiations between the general's men and warriors of the uprising, a resolution to the violence was found. They called it a treaty quilled within the confines of the northern fort of Niagara near those rushing falls in the closing days of summer 1764, a final end to the mayhem some believe was brought to fruition by Will Johnson of the Colony of New York. Someone later said he was an émigré from County Meath across the sea in Ireland, and after years of transacting colonial lands, had developed an intimate knowledge of the native tribes.

It was a treaty General Gage hoped would bring an end to the uprising along the frontier of the northern colonies, a pledge of peace between the king's army and thousands of warriors from dozens of native nations and tribes. They had impressive names like the Six Nations of the Iroquois comprised of the Mohawk, Oneida, Onondaga, Cayuga, Tuscarora and Seneca, and a rival known as the Seven Nations of the Iroquois Confederacy, warriors from an array of tribes like the Mohawk, Abenaki, Huron, Onondaga, Algonquin, Nipissing and Ojibwa. There was a third too, from the lands about those big lakes if I recall, a group the treaty referred to as the Western Confederacy filled with warriors from the Iroquois, Wyandot, Mississaugas, Illini, Kickapoo and Shawnee.

Over the coming two years there would be several more treaties quilled between the warriors and London, each helping to instill a greater semblance of peace, agreements culminating in the summer of 1766 with what they called the Treaty of Fort Ontario. Although rumors of skirmishes flaring along the frontier would surface from time to time, rather trivial scuffles between renegade tribes and wilderness outposts, colonial farmers, settlers and traders, the rebellious flames that had been spurred by that fiery chief named Pontiac had, for all practical purposes, been agreeably doused.

Some five-hundred royal soldiers of the king's army were said to have perished at an array of wilderness outposts during that uprising along the frontier, while two thousand or so warriors from various tribes were bound to their graves. Perhaps the dearest cost over all those months was paid by colonists, with some four thousand farms and homes ravaged and destroyed while scores escaped with their lives to towns and villages east. Yet, it's the dreadful toll of hundreds of colonial settlers scattered about solemn fields that anguishes my memories the most, visions of innocent women, children and men still asleep in the frontier soil after all these years.

Although those treaties instilled a fleeting sense of tranquility about the frontier and throughout the colonies, thousands of the king's royal troops still remained at settlements, forts and outpost scattered about the wilderness. Most had sailed across the sea to fight the forces of King Louis in that frontier war several years before, while others had strutted to our colonial docks during the months that followed to help quell the native uprising flaring in the wilderness.

I remember how colonists began to talk about all those royal troops, many wondering if General Gage might reduce his forces along the frontier now that much of those wilderness lands, as proscribed by those treaties, were now within the purview of all those native tribes. Would the king's soldiers retreat east, perhaps as a display of respect for those warriors many wondered, esteem cloaked in embroidery? Or maybe, the general planned to sail thousands of his army back to their homes in England. The fate of all those royal troops was resting in the hands of General Gage in those days following that native rebellion, and what, wondered many, was he going to do?

They say that after several months of discussions by the general and his staff, along with contemplation by the king and his parliament in London, a fateful decision was finally made by General Gage. Many of the king's soldiers were to be removed from all those outposts, forts and settlements along the frontier, and relocated east to what the crown seems to have viewed as a few essential colonial ports. Soon some of the king's troops were marching into my Philadelphia and the port of New York, royal soldiers strutting in dark shiny boots with muskets slung from crimson coats, while most marched to new quarters scattered about the harbor of Boston in Ethan's Colony of Massachusetts Bay.

I think it was around that time when rumors of a royal decision made months before began to swirl about the colonies, an unsettling decree quietly espoused by King George in the fall of 1763. London called it a royal proclamation, a decree sure to stymie the dreams of colonial merchants, speculators and traders interested in those wilderness lands, a royal action which, now that the flames of rebellion had been doused along the frontier, suddenly became disturbingly relevant. Some believed that the proclamation's terms were unreasonably restrictive upon the colonies, saying they would "thwart the expansion of colonial goods and trade," and others said they would restrain those seeking to carve and till new homes and farms in the western hills beyond the frontier.

That royal decree was also said to have established a vast reserve for all those native tribes that had quilled their accent to those treaties, millions of acres stretching from the crown's new southern lands of La Florida to the northern reaches of the wilderness of Newfoundland. And perhaps most notorious of all, it created a new western edge of the colonies, a "boundary of limitation" many colonists would frustratingly say, a border some were soon calling the "dreaded proclamation line."

It was a divisive margin stretching from the south to the northeast along the western slopes of the mountains earlier Spanish adventurers knew as Apalachee, creating a vast expanse of sanctuary wilderness running hundreds of miles west from that dreaded line to the flowing waters of the Messipi. I remember that soon some royal governors were warning colonists wishing to settle upon those protected lands, claiming that those hills and streams, woods and fields were reserved for the native tribes. There were disturbing rumors too that colonists who had already staked their claims about those lands were being ordered to vacate their farms and homes, resettle to the east across that line.

Intriguing theories as to why the king had proclaimed such a repugnant decree began to swirl about the colonies in those days, convoluted conjecture and angry speculation being sputtered from Charles Towne, Savannah and Williamsburg to Philadelphia and the ports of Boston and New York, from my Germantown to Ethan's Lexington. "London is determined to restrict our freedoms," some were spouting in homes, taverns and shops, "restrain our possibilities by thwarting expansion west." And others were angrily spewing that the king's decree was "reprehensible nonsense! He intends to hinder our rights, and forever shackle the colonies to the crown."

There were colonists who sought to comfortingly support the crown too, suggesting rather loyally that the king was justified in his decree, much like a preacher protecting his flock. They believed that the colonial restrictions implemented by the crown, as witnessed by that proclamation line, were just a benevolent use of power to help bring stability to the colonies. "By ensuring those wilderness lands remain in the hands of those native tribes," many would loyally say, "the king shows his desire to quash the frontier violence once and for all. London just wants peaceful coexistence, for all of us."

In a way, those types of competing sentiments being feverishly discussed in ports, villages and towns throughout the colonies seemed to damper the notion of joy so many longed for now that the mayhem along the frontier had been laid to rest. And when coupled with the grumblings of resentment about those unjust writs still being inflicted upon colonists in Ethan's Massachusetts Bay, a disturbing odor of indignation was slowly filtering about the colonies. Although I was just fourteen in those days, I could sense a brewing unease over past loyalties beginning to settle upon the colonies, a contemptuous aroma simmering in the hearts and minds of earnest women and men.

I remember a precious story Ethan once told me of a chilling night during the first wintry days 1765, of his father and a few Lexington men exchanging friendly chatter about those fractious things happening about the colonies. He said it was a special night in the Buckman Tavern, "when I realized how I wanted to get involved in the intriguing trade of Mr. Giles' print shop." They were sipping mugs, tins and cups of ale, rum and wine at his father's corner table and talking about a story Mr. Giles printed in his Lexington Gazette, thoughts first quilled by Sam Adams for the Independent Advertiser over in Boston.

Ethan was tending to a few farmers and merchants while busy with late chores on the third Saturday of January, finishing his duties about an hour before shuttering the tavern door for the night. "I could hear Mr. Giles reading the words of his story to dad, Doc Newman and Reverend Clarke," he tenderly whispered, "boasting to a few others scattered about the room too, sipping rye whiskey and rum. It was pretty clear, Andrea, that those words of Mr. Adams were spurring Mr. Giles' passions, and stirring dad and the others too."

"That abomination King George calls a proclamation," Mr. Giles' was heard to spout, reciting the spirited words of Mr. Adams, "is nothing more than his latest attempt to hold the colonies in his iron grip. With the stroke of a quill, his highness seeks to kill the freedoms of his subjects in the colonies, deny us the very essence of liberty. And those bloody writs of his Governor Bernard are diabolical, intended to shackle our minds with royal intimidation while quashing colonial resolve. Yet those misguided actions only expose their folly, for every man, woman and child of the colonies are endowed by natural rights, and every heart is free to follow its dreams, adhere to the righteousness of He who dwells in heaven!"

"Hear, hear," sputtered an aging man across the tavern floor sipping ale at a little table near the fire snapping in the hearth, a greying colonist traveling from Boston to a village in the distant hills west.

"Bloody good, Nathan!" boasted bricklayer Israel Jacob, raising his mug of dripping ale as his belly pressed the edge of the barreled bar. "Bloody good!"

"Sam sure knows how to express his thoughts, choose his words," chimed Ethan's father to Nathan, Doc and Reverend Clarke as they pressed to the slats of their chairs at the corner table left of the tavern door. "He has a passionate way of exposing what many colonists feel, quilling what many have thought far too long."

"Yes, he does," spouted the reverend before adding with a tipsy sigh, "May the king's feet swell!"

"Wait, there's more from Sam," urged Mr. Giles, waving the parchment of his Lexington Gazette and sipping a splash of rum. Then resting the sheets to the table, he wearily added, "It's all right here, for anyone to see."

"Ethan," bellowed his father in a whispering tone while raising a hand toward Ethan busy gathering mugs, bottles and tins near the kitchen door at the other end of the barreled bar. "Please, a bit more wine for the reverend and rum for Nathan, and some ale for Doc and me. Thanks, Ethan."

He knew his father's wounded thigh was throbbing with pain a bit more that night, for he could see him secretly rubbing his breeches for the past hour or two. "Sure will, dad," Ethan quickly replied, rushing to the corner, gripping two mugs and dashing behind the bar to draw foaming ale from a Boston barrel. He could sense the inspiring words of Mr. Adams eerily wafting about the tavern as he slid the dripping mugs to the table, defiant thoughts that seemed to mysteriously hover above the little flames flickering candles scattered about the room.

Ethan dashed and snatched dark bottles of rum and wine from crates he had picked up in Boston, bringing them back to Lexington in their creaking wagon the week before. He said those spirits had been sailed into the colony by a local merchant without paying the king's duty, and unloaded from a sloop called the *Liberty* moored at a secluded dock, a vessel some believed was Mr. Hancock's. Uncorking each bottle with a twisting tug, Ethan filled the reverend's cup with French wine and Mr. Giles' tin with Caribbean rum.

"You have a fine son," uttered Nathan to Ethan's father in a flattering tone as Ethan, shyly surprised, topped his tin. "You know, I was talking with Clara just the other night, about how I could use a good man around the print shop. What would you say, Pat, to Ethan coming by the shop now and then, to help me with printing and publishing things? Of course, not to interrupt his schooling."

"Why, that's a splendid idea," Ethan's father proudly replied. "Ethan," he quickly added with an inquisitive glance to his eyes, "what do you think? You'd need to keep your studies up, you know, and the chores about the tavern."

"I can do those things, dad," he excitedly blurted, "keep up my studies and tavern things too, I promise. Yes, I want to help at the print shop," Ethan anxiously added with a glance to Nathan, "learn all I can of printing and publishing. I'll do whatever you need, Mr. Giles."

"I was hoping you'd feel that way, Ethan," uttered his father while supportively patting his hand. "I know how you love to quill, and have always been intrigued by the publishing trade. Well, Nathan," he sputtered with a twisting gaze, "it seems you have a budding printing man for your shop."

"Good!" belted Nathan with a confirming sip of rum. "I know you can do this, Ethan, and do it well. I've watched you over the years, seen you sprouting into a fine young man. Why don't you come by next week, say Friday, around four? How does that sound, Ethan?"

"Just fine, Mr. Giles," Ethan gleefully replied. "I'll be there. I want to learn all I can, of printing and publishing, and of your Gazette. I'll do whatever you need."

"I know you will," agreed Nathan as he tapped Ethan's hand. "There, now it's settled! You'll learn a great deal about the trade, Ethan. That I promise."

"Thank you, Mr. Giles. I'll always give you the best I have."

"I know you will, and truly, it's my pleasure."

"I'm proud of you, Ethan," his father caringly whispered as Ethan returned to his tavern chores during the closing hour that night. "You're a fine friend, Nathan," he softly said with a grateful glance. "Thank you."

Ethan was about to dwell into the expanse of a new world, a journey he once revealed he knew would expose a slew of inspiring horizons, and as he tended to his final chores that night, his heart seemed to beat with a greater pride while his mind raced of what could be. The reverend, Doc, Mr. Giles and Ethan's father resumed their talk for the rest of that final hour, and Ethan could hear sporadic cheers as more of Mr. Adams' enlightening lines of the disenchantment brewing in Boston were spiritedly spouted. They continued to discuss the disturbing policies of the royal governor and unjust actions of parliament and the king with each sip of ale, wine and rum, and grumbled of intrusive royal trends ominously simmering throughout the colonies.

Their voices would rise, Ethan would say, whenever a frustrating opinion was robustly expressed about polices, acts and laws implemented by parliament that past year of 1764. "They're overly intrusive acts," Mr. Giles was heard sputtering, "striking at the heart of our colonies. These are unjust policies and laws that amount to thievery of our colonial coffers, rules intended to shackle our liberties!"

Soon Doc Newman tipped a splash of ale and uttered a phrase that was becoming accepted by disgruntled colonists in those days, a poetic line I'd later hear was first declared months before by that barrister James Otis of Boston. I remember some believed his phrase rather incendiary, perhaps even disloyal to the king, while others viewed his words, "Taxation without representation is tyranny!" to be refreshingly pleasing, especially many of Ethan's Colony of Massachusetts Bay and those men sipping spirits in the Buckman Tavern that night.

Ethan said Mr. Otis first spoke that inflaming phrase to a gathering of curious Bostonians the summer before, a group of proud colonists wanting to formulate a united colonial response to the recent infusion of various laws being thrust upon the colonies by London. They say that soon after that meeting he also quilled an essay he called *the Rights of the British Colonies Asserted and Proved*, an enlightening observation printed by the Independent Advertiser in Boston.

Opinions like his were igniting the embers of a simmering discontent in those days, thoughts some believed flirting with notions of disobedience to the crown, beliefs that invited colonists of Massachusetts Bay and elsewhere "to cast the shackles of fear and grip the reins of resistance." His fiery ideas were said to inspire many of Boston and scores of villages and towns throughout the colonies, Ethan's Lexington too, to show their disapproval of the crown through peaceful fiscal actions. Soon, disgruntled colonists began to agree to not trade, buy or sell an array of products and goods sailed across the sea from England to the Thirteen Colonies.

One of parliament's 1764 acts was acquiesced by the royal quill of King George the Third earlier that spring as the fires of native discontent were dwindling along the frontier, a law Prime Minister Grenville called the Sugar Act. Some viewed it as simply a reduction of the six pence tax imposed upon the colonies many years before, a scheme to entice greater acceptance of that unpopular tax by reducing it to just three pence on sweet things like molasses. It was a tax London was now requiring on every sack, barrel and crate sailed into the colonies from non-English ports, such as the docks of French islands scattered about the Caribbean Sea.

Although some suggested that this new duty was only meant to correct existing flaws in methods used by the king's customs agents to properly collect his taxes, I remember that Sugar Act actually expanded the duty to an array of other imported things like cloth for sewing and indigo for ink, as well as sacks and crates of various wines and beans. Rumors were also swirling those months that the king's men were instructed to strictly enforce this new act, mandates that each agent collect the tax from every ship and dock throughout the colonies, especially in Ethan's port of Boston. There were disturbing stories too that the king's royal governors and agents now had the power to seize colonial property at will, without a semblance of judicious review.

The Pennsylvania Evening Post also revealed that parliament's new law increased two-fold the duty paid on colonial materials sailed to-and-fro England for refinement, and prohibited the colonies from sailing goods of timber to non-British docks while limiting the freedom of merchants to ship crates of rum to colonial ports. Some were beginning to say that London's Sugar Act, along with laws soon to follow, was a sneaky attempt by the crown to raise revenue from the colonies for its own selfish purposes, such as the burdensome debt accumulated by the king to fight the French in that frontier war.

"These unjust taxes are being placed upon our colonies," some were heard to spout, doctors and lawyers, bakers, tradesmen and merchants, "to replenish the king's coffers for the debt he incurred along the frontier against the French, and quelling that native uprising too." Still others wondered if London was simply forcing the colonies to pay for the cost of the king's royal troops manning wilderness outposts and forts, along with the thousands repositioned to the ports of Philadelphia, New York and Boston. Whatever the true reasons may have been, it was a crushing debt from all those things the Evening Post said had grown ten-fold, from seventy million pounds when Ethan and I were very young, to some eight hundred million by those first wintry days of 1765.

"King George just wants the colonies to pay its fair share," women and men more loyal to the crown were heard to insist in hundreds of villages and towns. "Why, didn't we benefit from his royal troop's battling the French and all those native warriors? And don't we continue to reap the rewards of London's soldiers protecting our frontier at all those wilderness forts?" Yet, as loyally persuasive as many were, I remember other colonists less supportive of the king and parliament, and all those new duties and taxes.

"Citizens of England across the sea do not pay such duties for the Royal Army's presence over there," Ethan once said Mr. Adams had quilled in a Boston paper. "That being true, why in the name of heaven are we of the colonies being forced to do so over here? No, my fellow colonists, no! Such nonsense is unjust!"

One of those other new laws imposed by parliament in those days was said to "infringe with a heavy royal hand" upon the fiscal structure of the colonies, new rules London innocuously referred to as the Currency Act. "Parliament and King George will stop at nothing," the Evening Post disapprovingly spouted the fall of 1764, "to coerce the colonies to conform to their distorted monetary views in a devilish effort to shackle our economic freedoms." Some also said that new act was intended to stymie the livelihood of merchants while punishing colonial trade, and others thought it might be the king's response to what some in London were disturbingly saying were questionable colonial currency practices.

Ethan would later say that many in his Lexington, Boston and Colony of Massachusetts Bay viewed that fiscal act as just another example of the crown's attempts to limit the dreams of colonists by placing increasing economic burdens upon the colonies. "By restricting our freedom to issue colonial currency," Mr. Giles printed in his Lexington Gazette, "the king seeks to strangle our merchants with unjust limitations while loyal enterprises thrive across the sea in London."

Although I was still rather young in those days, I could sense that what the colonies had done for many years had suddenly been forbidden, for by the stroke of the king's royal quill, we were no longer allowed to print our own colonial money. It was a suppressive act some were beginning to fear might threaten the very vitality of every colony, a fiscal limitation that could cripple the vigor of shippers, merchants, shopkeepers and traders while whittling the freedoms of colonial women, children and men.

Still other rules were implemented that year by the king, parliament and his royal governors, procedures viewed by some as "disruptive policies and laws intended to inflict colonial damage" by enhancing the crown's ability to collect duties and taxes while making it more difficult for merchants to thrive. One of those new procedures was said to shatter the established system for sailing goods, rules with disturbing nuances for increasing London's powers to enforce its hindering laws of customs and trade. "The king has moved our Admiralty Courts!" disgruntled merchants were heard to say upon discovering that hearings of seafarer complaints had been relocated hundreds of miles north, changed from colonial docks to the port of Halifax on the Island of Nova Scotia. "He may try to quell our rights," some would defiantly shout, "but King George shall never silence our spirits!"

Mr. Otis' inspiring phrase about the repressive nature of taxation and its innate relations with tyranny was being printed in newspapers throughout the colonies as the winter of 1765 began, not only in Boston and in Ethan's Lexington, but in the ports of New York, Philadelphia, Charles Towne, Williamsburg and Savannah, here in my Germantown too. Ethan once said that although he was only fourteen on that January night in the Buckman Tavern, he could smell an eerie scent of disillusionment wafting about the room as he listened to his father and those Lexington men. "It was a contemptuous aroma toward the English Crown, Andrea, a determined yet subtle defiance that seemed to flicker each candle while drifting into the night."

Looking back after all these years, I suppose most in the colonies clung to paternal loyalties to King George as that pivotal year began, while some were beginning to understand how infringements of our colonial freedoms were beginning to brew. They were disgruntled doctors and lawyers, tradesmen, farmers, preachers and merchants slowly being nudged from the crown upon the force of those subtle winds. There was discontent being printed in ports, villages and towns and talked about in taverns, homes and shops, forlorn feelings being quilled by young poets too. It was a colonial restlessness parliament and the king didn't seem to understand, an unease his royal governors failed to properly comprehend, embryonic embers smoldering amid spirited notions of liberty that would someday sweep across the colonies.

Chapter VI

Pink Ranunculus

Perhaps one of the more pleasing periods of Ethan's young life were those first serene days, weeks and months of 1765, for the years which had been so intimately challenging had passed, and the hours which had witnessed the spindly taps of a tearful melody had finally begun to fade with the wintry winds. Although a mere fourteen when that January began, Ethan had been consumed by loss and touched by a life most his age would need many seasons to understand. Yet, it was a new year, and the depressing pains of his heart had begun to ease as visions of what could be were being spurred by the spray of night stars and rays of a resurrecting sun.

"The doors of my life were starting to nudge open," Ethan once said, "and I began to touch ideas never before truly within reach, dream and hope of a life yet to come." It was during those winter days when the words his mother had once whispered to him on a frigid night began to swirl about his mind, inspiring thoughts of courage and dreams springing from a solemn place. "It was as if sweet little hymns were erupting inside," he'd say, "for I was beginning to finally understand what mom told me near the fire that night. It was then that I started to really listen to the cries of my heart, Andrea, and began to feel a gentleness soothing my dreams."

I remember feeling the weight of an array of things as I listened to Ethan so long ago whisper of those early winter days, of his hopes and losses past, and couldn't help but sense that in a strange way I too had touched such things before. Yet in those days I didn't truly understand the troubles simmering back then, not the way Ethan and others did, not the brewing intensities or how pivotal so many events were to become, and I suppose, few really did. Perhaps it was during those distant hours that the mighty clash of traditions and ties, futures and loyalties truly began, when engrained powers began to grapple with the fortitude of spirited men.

Looking back after all these years, I've come to see that the rebellious winds that would someday engulf the colonies had really begun to swirl that winter of 1765, and the spark of our liberation would only come to pass following several more years of what many would say was a cascade of troubling transgressions. It was a time when London's intrusive swells began to surge to our colonial shores more heavily, when the frightening winds of change began to whistle about the frontier and swoop across the hills and fields to every port, village and town throughout the colonies.

I think there was a sense of something special beginning to unfold in those days, of abstract notions of individual liberty being unleashed across the colonies that would forever change every women, child and man. Perhaps it was a rebirth of expectations of generations past, an awakening of dormant hopes and dreams subjugated by the crown too long, a flourishing of thoughts and passions in those days. There was an underlying tone of insurrection simmering about the colonies back then, a sense of tumult waiting for the proper moment to burst and banish London's House of Hanover from the colonies. It was a rebellious wave many would later say had been forged in the spirited souls of Boston men, a tide of discontent beginning to flow from the hills and fields of Ethan's Massachusetts Bay to the towns, villages and ports of all the colonies, from New York to Georgia and my Pennsylvania.

"What made that year so different from others, grandma?" Samuel gingerly interrupted while gazing to the twirling leaves of distant elms and rocking his chair. "I mean, the war was still ten years away."

A tinge of sadness gripped my insides as I once again realized that Samuel didn't really understand what was happening in the colonies in the years before the war. "Ethan and I were just fourteen when that winter began," I whispered while nudging my chair into a softer rock and sliding my fingers across the parchment of Ethan's poem nestled in the pocket of my summer dress. "But I remember it all, Samuel, oh so well. Just give me a moment, and I'll try to tell you what it was like back then." He rocked and stared to the distant trees, listening to the leaves rustling in the summer winds, and as I watched the little petals of my crimson roses flutter in the warming breeze, I softly stroked Ethan's passionate lines and reached for memories. "I've never told anyone these things, Samuel. But I want you to know it all, of Ethan and me, your Grandpa Franz, the colonies and the war." As I rocked and caressed the past, Samuel gazed into the afternoon winds and patiently waited for my coming words.

I remember the story Ethan told me of his first day at that Lexington print shop, a cold Friday afternoon, the Twenty-fifth of January, 1765, and how he had rushed home from school about an hour before to tend to his tavern chores, just like he always did. He swept muddied chunks of ice from the oak slats of the floor, brushed a few tables while snatching cups, mugs and tins, and washed a stack of plates and a kettle or two. Then around half past three the hour he had been anxiously awaiting finally arrived, the moment he'd dash to Mr. Giles print shop.

A layer of dark clouds was slowly drifting toward Boston and the sea as Ethan bid his father farewell and bound through the tavern door, rushing to a new world. He dashed across the snowy ruts of Bedford Street and toward the shop on the other side of that Lexington field, near Hancock Street and the Billerica Road leading to their old farm. And as he pranced across the wintry grass amid patches of snow, little white flakes began to drift from the roiling grey to dot the wool of his coat and brush fence rails and trees, settling upon cottages, shops and homes.

"It was there, Andrea," Ethan tenderly recalled, "in the middle of the village field, that I felt a strange compulsion to stop and look back. I could see dad standing at the tavern door watching me through the sprinkling snow, then he just waved, as if to wish me good luck. We both just stared for a moment, and then I rushed toward Mr. Giles' shop."

Ethan could see a thin trail of grey streaming from the chimney bricks and watched the trickling snow settle to the roof as he strutted across the field, and as he looked through the windows he could see that the Giles were home. Clara was upstairs dawdling about their room in a bright ruffled dress, and for a moment or two Ethan watched as she fluffed a few pillows and arranged a candle and lamp near the frosting panes of the gabled window. And through the bay window left of the door he could see Nathan busy doing what he loved best, finagling with parchment, ink and his beloved printing press. Although some of the elders of the village still called him captain from his younger militia days, Ethan said he looked very much the printer that day, wearing a light shirt and buttoned vest, with white stockings that ran from tan breeches to dark leather shoes.

Suddenly Mr. Giles instinctively glanced through the square panes of that bay window just as Ethan began to thump up the trio of oak steps and reach for the copper ring dangling the center of the dark door. "Come in, Ethan," Nathan bellowed with a greeting smile and swooshing swing of the door. "Please, step in from that cold. It's good to see you. I hope you're ready to learn a few things about printing this afternoon."

"Thank you, Mr. Giles," Ethan nervously replied, somewhat startled while gathering his wits. "Oh yes," he quickly added with a confident click of the door, "I'm ready to learn all I can. I've been waiting for this moment."

"Good! But please, call me Nathan," he insisted with a fatherly glance. "Toss your hat and coat over there, Ethan," he calmly added while waving his hand toward the pine pole rising near the slatted elm chair of his printers' desk, "then come here, watch what I'm doing."

"Yes sir," Ethan spouted in a respectable tone as he dangled his tan wool coat and dark tricorn hat from a thin pine finger jutting from that pole, then shuffled to Mr. Giles hunched over his printing press. "I mean, yes sir, Nathan."

He was busy setting type once again, hundreds of little iron commas, marks, dots and letters being tucked right to left, assembling each word and line into a big broadside page. "These little iron things are type Ethan, for printing a page of my next Gazette. I want you to just watch for a while, and before long, you too will be doing these things." After inserting a few more lines with an array of dark iron bits and sensing confusion brushing Ethan's face, Nathan snapped a glance and assuredly said, "Don't worry, I'll have you doing this before you know it, with ease, and twining these galleys tight. That's when we'll spread ink over the entire page, from that bucket over there, then lower this plate into position. With just the right pressure with that arm, Ethan, we'll hold a sheet of parchment against the galley tight, for a moment or two."

Although a sense of befuddlement gripped Ethan's insides as he watched, he somehow knew that the mysteries of the moment would eventually come to pass. "I see, Mr. Giles," he shyly replied, intently observing while trying desperately to control his quizzical looks, "I mean, Nathan. You make all this seem so easy, so smooth, effortless."

"Don't worry, Ethan. Before long, you'll find these things second nature. I assure you of that."

As Ethan watched in a hush he began to wonder of the expressive trade he was beginning to learn, of what such skills might mean for him in the years to come, for within weeks he'd be creating pages of printed words, transferring thoughts to parchment using a printing press stuffed with little iron things. Then he began to feel a mysterious sensation as he gazed upon each intriguing motion of Mr. Giles, an eerie feeling that at that moment he was experiencing his own reformation, from child to youthful man. "Thank you, Nathan," he boldly spouted as Mr. Giles reached for the short handle of a stick protruding from that nearby oak bucket, "for this opportunity. I'm truly grateful, and won't let you down."

"I know you won't, Ethan," uttered Nathan with a confident glance while gripping that stick and dipping its leather ball stuffed of cloth into the dark ink, "and you're welcome. It's one of the reasons I believe you'll do well, why I wanted to teach you my printing trade. You're like your father, Ethan," he added while brushing the squishy ball across the type, spreading ink over each iron line, "smart, with a quiet poise. But there's something else. You observe what's going on around you, listen to what's being said. I know you're still young, but I think you understand the troubles, concerns and ideas I print in my Gazette, and I know you are fond of the quilled word. Someday, Ethan, you might just find your own uninhibited thoughts printed on these pages."

"I see. You do?" Ethan bashfully replied while shuffling in his drying shoes and nervously glancing to the fire crackling in the hearth at the rear of the room. "Those are very kind words. Thank you."

"Yes, I do," he quickly assured before adding in a tone that seemed to suggest he viewed Ethan not as a boy of fourteen but a young printing man. "Do you remember those things your father was discussing with me and some others in the tavern last week?"

"Yes," Ethan timidly said, "I do."

"Those are the types of concerns this next Gazette addresses. I support Sam's disapproval of those acts and that proclamation, of those new taxes and duties, and those writs too, as well as James Otis' thoughts on those things. I'm asking that others support those positions too, Ethan, not only colonists in Lexington, but in Boston and throughout Massachusetts Bay. Oppose those unjust actions by our royal governor and London, that's what I say in this Gazette. Tell me, Ethan, what do think?"

"At first I didn't understand those writs," Ethan nervously said, "too young I suppose, when I first heard of them. But now, I think I know the damage they do, along with the king's proclamation and parliament's acts, not only here in Massachusetts Bay, but in all the colonies. I hear about those things in the tavern, like that night you were there, and have read some of the things said by Mr. Otis and quilled by Sam Adams, views printed in papers of Boston and by you here in Lexington. I may be young, but agree that those things are not good for the colonies."

"I do believe, Ethan," quipped Nathan, dipping that leather ball into the bucket and smoothly spreading more ink on the type, "that you and I will get along well. You know, someday, you'll quill thoughts of your own about those kinds of things, and we'll print them right here in our Lexington Gazette."

"I'd like to think so," Ethan uttered, "at least I hope so, someday. I have thought that maybe, writing of some kind, might be my future, along with the printing trade too."

"You're young, Ethan," he replied in a paternal way, "and time will tell. But I suspect that someday soon, you will truly know."

A hush soon settled upon the room as they eased into what seemed an appealing professional mode, going about the business of newspaper making. Ethan intensely watched his mentor's every move and listened as he sprinkled insightful whispers now and then, determined to consume each word and etch each moment upon his mind. He continued to shuffle a bit nervously too as Mr. Giles gripped and lowered that handle, and watched as the veins bulged from his neck with each mighty squeeze of the press. And once each parchment sheet had been properly printed he clipped them to a taut string of twine running the east wall, dangling each page to dry for the night.

Ethan once said that it was on that winter day when he began to sense that quilling his thoughts was his true passion, and although he enjoyed reading of theories, governance and histories, he somehow knew he'd someday reveal his feelings with a faithful quill. "I think it was right then, that cold afternoon, Andrea, when I felt those burning desires. It was as though I knew I'd discover how to expose the concerns gripping my mind and passions dwelling in my heart. I wondered too, if maybe, I'd find a way to discover the serenity searched for by so many."

Soon the chilling winds began to fade and the wintry snows of 1765 began to melt into the hills and fields of the Colony of Massachusetts Bay, trickle into icy streams winding to the sea, and the petals of spring were once again blooming about the meadows. Ethan continued his studies at the Lexington schoolhouse each day, and tended to his chores about the tavern most afternoons and nights. And without hesitation or delay he would dash to Mr. Giles' print shop after studies each Friday to further his budding apprenticeship, a devotion now consuming another evening or two and several hours most Saturdays, until a bit past noon. All the while, Ethan continued to peruse an array of pamphlets and books shelved at the schoolhouse or piled at the tavern, and devoured the latest newspapers of Boston always stacked at the print shop.

Ethan would read about colonial events and disturbing concerns in the Independent Advertiser on warming days and brisk spring nights, a Boston paper usually galloped to Nathan's print shop by a special rider, and read opinions expressed in other publications too, like the Boston Gazette and Country Journal whenever carted into Lexington. But I suppose he mostly consumed the things Nathan was printing in his Gazette, a paper that was distributed about the village most Monday mornings, reading each thought, line by line. And Ethan always made sure he read the specific words of Mr. Giles, absorbing his ideas about the issues swirling about Massachusetts Bay and all the colonies, along with the printed views of others from Boston like Sam Adams, Mr. Otis and a doctor named Joseph Warren.

There were other voices of concerned colonists in the port of Boston too, discontented men like that merchant John Hancock, as well as thoughts being espoused in other places by spirited men like Patrick Henry in the Colony of Virginia. I remember how each man was quickly becoming known to express disapproving views of those new laws and acts of King George and his parliament, and of his royal governors too enforcing those things with increasingly disturbing tactics. And when Ethan wanted to see and hear the simmering angst about all those troubling things, he'd settle into a secluded spot in his father's tavern and discover what truly dwelled in the hearts and minds of passionate shopkeepers, tradesmen, farmers and merchants.

I think it was around then, early that spring of 1765, when a rather compelling event seemed to disrupt the façade of tranquility that had brushed the colonies for a few fleeting months, a stunning misstep which galvanized the contempt brewing throughout the colonies. As if a natural flow from parliament's royal actions the year before, this new legalese from London ignited smoldering embers of colonial discontent which would sweep from the cobblestones of Boston to the docks of Savannah. King George the Third and his ministers called this new law the Duties in American Colonies Act, while many from the Colony of Georgia to Massachusetts Bay referred to this latest intrusion as the "unjust Stamp Act."

They say this new law wasn't the first of this type to be thrust upon the colonies by London, but rather the fourth of its kind, only this new act was viewed by many as the most despicable of them all. Perhaps its impact had been magnified by the recent litany of previous parliament acts, coming so soon after those laws over sugar and currency, and one known as the Quartering Act imposed upon the colonies just weeks before. Ethan once confided that his father and colonial merchants stewing with farmers and spirits in their Lexington tavern considered that new Stamp Act as fermenting angst, saying such things as it was "akin to placing bundles of kindling hay atop mounds of smoldering ash."

Although the king and his parliament were said to declare that the purpose of this new law was to spur economic growth throughout colonies, many from hundreds if ports, villages and towns, from Philadelphia, Charles Towne, Williamsburg, Boston and New York, my village of Germantown to Ethan's Lexington too, viewed this latest act rather suspiciously. "Why, it's just another means for London to take wealth from the colonies," many were heard to say, "to fill the king's coffers to pay for quartering his royal troops along the frontier and in our ports." Still others believed that this new tax was not to protect our colonies at all, but rather to uphold the interests of trappers, traders and speculators perusing the wilderness for London.

Yet perhaps what disturbed some colonists the most was a fear that just as those acts of the year before, this new Stamp Act was another veiled attempt to coerce the colonies to pay the crown's lingering debt incurred in its past frontier fights against the French and those rebellious warriors. It was a law, if I recall, that required an array of printed products made in the colonies to be done on parchment sailed from England, and every sheet was to be embedded by a royal stamp at a cost of shillings and pounds. And unlike most previous duties that were retained by colonial assemblies, it was a tax that was to be disbursed directly to London.

Although not intended to raise revenue for the king like that Stamp Act, I remember the recent Quartering Act, also imposed upon the colonies that spring, was viewed by many as unjustly intrusive. The Evening Post revealed that the crown was "insistent" that colonists provide some type of quarters for all the king's troops which had been repositioned from frontier forts to the ports of Philadelphia, Boston and New York. And although colonists were not being forced to open their homes to royal soldiers, many throughout the colonies viewed the act's intent as an affront to privacy, a trampling of property rights and unjust intrusion into our lives. Ethan once said that many in Boston were so incensed that some began to form spirited groups to express their displeasure, and that the pressure they placed on the royal governor caused him to move many of the crown's soldiers to the weathered barracks of Castle Island, a desolate patch of soil and rock in the waters of the harbor about a mile or so east of Boston.

All those policies and laws of the king and his parliament that winter and spring of 1765, perhaps most notoriously that despised Stamp Act, were being heatedly discussed throughout the colonies in those days, especially in villages and towns in the Colony of Massachusetts Bay, the port of Boston and Ethan's Lexington. And I remember a tale Ethan once told of a chilly Saturday morn early that spring when he dashed from the tavern a few hours after dawn, rushing through brisk winds to his duties at Mr. Giles' print shop.

"Good morning, Nathan," Ethan politely spouted, shuttering the door tight as a blast of spring air surged into the shop. And while Mr. Giles rummaged through an array of parchment sheets strewn about his desk and the flames of the hearth flickered, Ethan tossed his coat and tricorn hat to a chair and added, "I'm ready to do more printing, Nathan, finish this new Gazette."

"Damn that king!" Nathan sputtered in a whispering tone, perhaps not wanting to disturb his bride Clara quietly quilting a new blanket up in their room. Then without even a glance or twitch of his chair, he quickly added, "He's at it again, Ethan, his parliament too. They just seem intent on stuffing the colonies into a fiscal abyss."

"What do you mean?" Ethan gingerly asked, feeling the stress gripping the room. "What's the matter, Nathan?"

"It's this," he crisply replied, twisting in his chair while thrusting a finger to a sheet. "It's this notice from Governor Bernard about that Stamp Act, and what he and the king plan to do." Then snapping his head side to side, he added with a frustrating glare, "This is too much. We here in Lexington, Ethan, over in Boston too, cannot allow this to stand. Hell, this whole colony, all the colonies, must foil the crown's plan to shackle our lives with this nonsense. I say, no more!"

Ethan had only recently heard a few vague things about that act from some colonists at the tavern, and would later admit he mistakenly believed it was only a petty nuisance, a law that would not cause much trouble in the colonies. But that spring morning he'd discover his youthful folly, and gain an appreciation of why colonists must be properly informed. "What is that Stamp Act, Nathan, really?" he sheepishly asked while stepping closer to the desk. "I've only heard little bits about it, and must admit, I don't really understand."

"I think this whole mess will be a fine lesson for you," he quipped in a calming way. "Always know, Ethan, what those in power are doing. I'll tell you just what this truly is. It's an abomination, an outright exploitation of colonists' goods and property! What's worse, it's being imposed without a whiff of input from us. This Stamp Act is nothing more than a vile law imposed by an overbearing king and parliament, and if we don't stop this bloody nonsense, it'll begin crippling the colonies the first day of November."

Then strumming his fingers about another sheet and gazing to its lines, he twisted once again and began to recite a slew of disturbing things. "Just look at this, Ethan. That damn king and his bloody henchmen are insisting we pay this new tax on each sheet of printing paper imaginable, from a few pence to several shillings and pounds. All our officious documents will be affected, court records, licenses and contracts, along with papers for shipping goods and permits on all kinds of things, playing cards too. Worst of all, Ethan, London is trying to muzzle colonial opinions, strike at our cries for reason by insisting that every printer adhere to this new tax. Yes, the king wants to force every publisher of pamphlets and newspapers, my Lexington Gazette too, to buy the crown's special parchment emblazed with that bloody royal stamp!"

"What does all that really mean?" Ethan nervously asked with a tinge of youthful naivety. "What will it do to the colonies?"

"I think the impact of this act could be dangerous," he explained with a dash of apprehension. "If we remain silent now, if colonists allow this act to take effect this fall, I'm worried of the calamity that could follow. This bloody Stamp Act is being imposed without debate or consent by our colonial assemblies, and if we shutter our eyes now, do nothing to dislodge this new tax, why, London will simply thirst for more of our wealth and liberties. You know, Ethan, I think it truly does come down to what Jimmy Otis exclaimed last summer about taxes and tyranny, and what Jonathan Mayhew preached years before from his Boston pulpit, 'No taxation without representation!'"

"What do think the colonies should do?" Ethan daringly asked. "Do you plan to print something in your Gazette?"

"At this moment, Ethan, I'm not exactly sure what we must do. But I do know, whatever it might by, I'll express my thoughts right here in this Gazette, just as soon as that course is agreed. I'm riding into Boston within the hour to talk with others about this bloody act, then, Ethan, we'll know. Say, have you ever met Sam Adams?"

"No," Ethan nervously uttered, "I haven't. But I'd sure like to. Does this mean we're not going to work on the Gazette this morning?"

"That's right, Ethan, not this morning," he whispered while gathering a few parchment sheets scattered atop his desk, then folding and stashing each into pockets of his coat and vest. "I'm taking my buggy, and think you should come. It should be a fine learning experience for you."

Ethan could feel his stomach churning knowing he would soon meet a man he had heard so many intriguing things about over the years, a colonist whose views others always seemed to talk about in his father's tavern. His opinions had been printed in newspapers of Boston and Ethan's Lexington, in villages and towns throughout Massachusetts Bay and all the colonies, and now Ethan, at just fourteen, was about to meet him. "I think it'll be a fine experience too," Ethan replied in a shy yet excited way. "Yes, I want to go with you. I'll run to the tavern now, ask dad."

"Tell Patrick we'll most likely be at the Independent Advertiser," Nathan quickly advised, "at the print shop near the eastern docks of King Street."

"I will," Ethan anxiously replied as he donned his coat and tricorn hat, swung open the door and dashed into the brisk morning air as the door squeaked shut with a snapping clack. Shadows roamed the fresh grass below soft spring clouds lazily drifting toward the sea as he rushed across the field, and as he bound through the tavern door he could see his father busy behind the barreled bar, sliding dark bottles of French wine into square holes of oak shelves pressed against the south wall.

"Dad," Ethan blurted, rushing past a pair of strange merchants sipping ale at a table near the bar, "Mr. Giles wants me to go with him to Boston, ride in his buggy now. He wants to talk with Mr. Adams about that Stamp Act, and thinks it'll be a good experience for me. We should be at the print shop of the Independent Advertiser, near the docks by King Street. Is it alright if I go?"

"If Nathan thinks it's a good idea," his father replied with an agreeing glance before gripping another bottle from a crate of unstamped wine, "then yes, I want you to go. Just be back by supper."

"I will. Thanks dad!"

"You know, Ethan," confided his father with a caring glance, "Nathan and I talked about you starting at the print shop many times before that night, when we both knew the time was right. He believes in you, almost as much as I, and maybe, in you, he sees the son he never had. He wants you to reach for your dreams, Ethan, just like I do, he told me so, and if the printing trade is the way, then that's good. Someday, I think he'll be printing what you quill, maybe a little story you've created or thoughts on colonial things." Then sliding another bottle into the last empty hole, he pivoted his thoughts with a tinge of a smile and added, "I've met Sam a few times, Ethan, and found him intense yet affable, a smart, honest man. I think you'll like him."

"Thanks, dad," Ethan respectfully whispered, "for telling me those things. I'll listen to what Nathan and Sam say about that act, and learn what I can about the printing trade." Then glancing toward the tavern door and back to his father, he gratefully added, "Thanks for believing in me."

"I'm proud of you, Ethan," his father quickly replied with a tender stare to Ethan's eyes, "and so is your mother. Now go to Boston, find out what

Mr. Adams has to say. I'll see you around suppertime, and you can tell me all about it then."

"Alright, see you around dusk," sputtered Ethan as mist sprayed his eyes with memories of his mother. "Oh, there's Mr. Giles now," he excitedly added as the sound of creaking wheels came to a halt on the ruts and stones of Bedford Street. "So long, dad," he blurted while dashing from the tavern and climbing to the right cushion of the dark buggy's leathered plank.

The buggy lurched in the spring chill as Mr. Giles snapped the thin reins, sending his tan colt into an easy trot south past the general store before pivoting east onto the Massachusetts Road. Ethan confessed that he was a bit nervous as they rolled along the south end of the village field amid pounding hooves and the sounds of colonists stirring, and that Nathan seemed lost in thoughts of what Boston might bring as the buggy squeaked and swayed past the Munroe Tavern and Doc's apothecary shop. But as they passed the village belfry on the slope to the right Mr. Giles began to speak about the printing trade, and for the coming dozen miles he talked about newspapers and publishing while expressing views of the troubles brewing about the colonies.

They wound southeast along the ruts and stones of the Massachusetts Road for an hour or so through the villages of Menotomy, Medford and Somerville, before creaking through the narrows of the Charlestown Peninsula protruding into the harbor. Ethan could see the muddy waters of the Mystic River just north and the marshes of the Charles River a bit south, and as they rolled another half mile or so toward the village docks lining the southeastern rocks of Charlestown, he wondered of the trio of bushy hills rising off to the left. With skillful flicks and tugs of the reins, Mr. Giles finessed the buggy to an aging dock and the planks of a ferry, then they crossed the waters of the harbor a short distance to a northwest dock of Boston.

The waters of the Charles off to their right were eerily still and dark as they crossed, unlike the crisp blue of the harbor amid the brisk breeze of the sea, and Ethan said they didn't speak much while floating toward Boston. "We mostly just sat in the buggy, Andrea, listening to the cold water gently lapping against the slats of the ferry and watching white and grey gulls skimming the harbor and soaring in the spring winds. I could see the silhouette of distant islands too, shrouded by a haze, and watched as the trees, docks and bricks of Boston drew nearer."

A blanket of heavy mist had already lifted from the port when the buggy rolled from the ferry shortly after noon near a grassy rise they called Copp's Hill, a sacred place Ethan said some of Boston's past were lying in rest. With snaps of the reins they creaked east along the cobblestones of Lynn Street, passing several wharfs and docks jutting north into the harbor, then tugging right they rolled south on Fish Street past several more wharfs along the port's eastern docks.

Ethan said that soon Dock Square came into view, an expanse of warehouses and shops scattered along the edges of a swath of cobblestones lined by oaks and elms, and rising near the southern stones was a spirited place the colonists of Boston knew as Faneuil Hall. It was three floors of square-paned windows embedded in crimson bricks, an impressive building with a bell tower thrusting above a majestic façade. It seems it had originally been constructed by colonial masons some twenty years before, then after being consumed by the port's great fire, was rebuilt a few years before the end of that frontier war.

Rolling a bit further south past a long wharf at the eastern cobblestones of King Street, Mr. Giles tugged the reins and brought the buggy to a halt not far from the water and near the door of a little shop that printed the Independent Advertiser. "It looked more like a quaint house, Andrea," I remember Ethan saying, "just a single floor with a pair of rooms and a few windows, with lots of square panes overlooking the street. Mr. Giles said that Sam had once been the publisher of the Advertiser, but that he had relinquished most responsibilities by that spring to Daniel Fowle, an acquaintance of his departed father."

Ethan watched as Mr. Giles stepped from the buggy and wrapped the reins about an iron ring dangling an elm post near the edge of the street, then jumped to the gravelly cobblestones and followed him into the print shop, bounding up oak steps and through a squeaky door. There were a couple nicked tables with scuffed chairs near the far right of the room, and through an open door toward the left rear was a little office, all the while Ethan's eyes were fixed upon a man thrashing about a printing press. It was Mr. Fowle in a deerskin apron assembling an array of iron type for printing, the stained leather hugging his chest and dangling past his knees.

"Good morning, Daniel," blurted Mr. Giles as he and Ethan stood anxious at the door. "Daniel!" he blurted once again in a startling tone.

Ethan watched as Mr. Fowle jolted his spine and snapped a whipping glance over his shoulder, and with an expression splashed with relief, crustily hollered, "Nathan! Why, you old goat, what ja tryin to do, kill me? How are ya?!"

"I'm good, Daniel, real good. And you? Doing fine I trust?"

"Can't complain," he sputtered, pressing a few more iron bits into the galley before brushing fresh stains across the apron hugging his chest. "Actually, and maybe you've seen this too, orders have picked up this spring, what with all the concerns of what's going on around this colony. I must say, Nathan, printing is good."

"I want you to meet a young man from Lexington," insisted Mr. Giles with a proud wave of his hand toward Ethan standing to his side, "Ethan Sheehan. Maybe you know his father, Patrick, of the Buckman Tavern. Ethan's learning a great deal about the printing trade, Daniel, apprenticing with me at my shop, discovering what goes into publishing my Gazette. He'll be quilling his own things too, someday, we're sure of that."

"Why, that just fine," he spiritedly replied with an encouraging gaze to Ethan's eyes. "Good morning, or should I say, afternoon, young man. I have heard of that tavern, but not sure I've ever met your father. I just don't get into Lexington much anymore." Then stepping toward the door he greeted Nathan with a grip of his hand before reaching for Ethan's and adding, "It's always nice to meet an aspiring young printer, and a friend of Nathan, is mine. How are you, Ethan?"

"I'm fine, sir," Ethan nervously uttered in a respectable tone. "It's good to meet you too, sir."

"Please, Ethan," he quickly retorted while shuffling closer to his printing press, "call me Daniel."

"Alright," Ethan shyly replied with a timid nod, "I will. Thank you, Daniel."

"Now, tell me, Daniel," Mr. Giles inquisitively asked, "what are the good people of Boston saying about this latest nonsense from London? What are their views about this new act of parliament, and these bloody guidelines being spewed by our Royal Governor Bernard?"

"Oh, yes, that blasted Stamp Act. What I've heard, is that many here in Boston, throughout the colony too, don't approve of this new mandate, this consuming tax by the king. I think some feel trampled upon, downright besieged. I don't like it either, Nathan, not one bit!"

"I've been hearing those kinds of things around Lexington too, Daniel, sentiments gripping all of Middlesex County. I think you and I hold the same contempt for this bloody act. I'd like to talk with Sam about it, and was hoping he might be here."

"He was here, Nathan, a few hours ago, but didn't say where he was going. Wait, yesterday he said something about meeting a few gents from his old whipping post days over at the Green Dragon Tavern, around noon today."

"Thanks, Daniel, I'll try over there," he gratefully said as they gripped their printers' hands. "It was good to see you, and keep that Advertiser coming off that press." Then twisting to Ethan patiently listening at the door, he demandingly added, "Let's go, Ethan, to the tavern. It's not far from here."

"So long, Nathan," uttered Daniel, stepping to his press to once again immerse into a world of tiny iron bits. Then snapping his gaze back to the door, he cordially added, "Good to have met you, Ethan. Good luck with learning our printing trade, and with your quilling too. And whenever you're in Boston, please, stop by to see me."

"Take care," uttered Mr. Giles while stepping into the afternoon, followed by Ethan's, "Thank you, sir, I will," before strutting from the shop with a swinging latch of the door.

They climbed into the buggy with a snatch of the reins, and amid creaking wheels and clanking iron hooves, rolled along the cobblestones of King Street the short distance west to the Green Dragon Tavern. It was a place Ethan would later learn once belonged to a doctor who quilled disloyal pamphlets and papers about the king and the colony's royal governor during that frontier war. And although the tavern was now run by a sister named Abigail, there were rumors then that some mason men from the lodge of St. Andrews wanted to run that spirited place. There were other whispers too by that spring of 1765 that it was a place where disgruntled colonists gathered to express their displeasure with the crown, a tavern where Bostonians would vent their simmering angst with mugs of ale and tins of rye whiskey and rum.

Ethan once said that the tavern looked a bit like his father's in Lexington, a spacious place with a fireplace of crimson bricks rising from the middle of the rear, and quarters for living upstairs. A thin string of grey was twirling from the chimney into the afternoon air as they approached, and with each creak of the wheels Ethan felt a strange sensation, as if he were home. "Maybe it's just the aura of a tavern," he whispered to me near a fire one night. "I felt calm, Andrea, safe, as if it were the Buckman Tavern, and dad was there, busy behind the barreled bar."

"If Sam's in there," Nathan whispered with a tug the reins, bringing the buggy to a crunching stop on the cobblestones of King Street, "I want to talk with him alone for a moment. He doesn't know you, Ethan, and I want him to be at ease. So please, find a quiet spot at the small corner table right of the door, at least for a little while."

"Alright, I understand," Ethan youthfully replied as they climbed from the buggy and stepped to the tavern door.

Ethan followed closely as Nathan flicked the iron latch and swung open the tavern door, then shuffling inside, Nathan glanced to a round oak table off on the right and whispered as the door clicked tight, "There he is, Ethan, with those two men." Ethan watched as Nathan quickly looked about and breathed a relieving sigh upon seeing there were no royal soldiers in crimson coats indulging inside, young men known to spout unpleasant things about the colonies while numbing their minds now and then. "Over there, Ethan," he softly added with a nod toward the far right corner. "Take that table by the window, just past Sam's."

Some logs were aflame in the fireplace just left of a short barreled bar running the right rear of the room, and two men in muddied dark shoes, their bellies pressed to the bar, were gripping mugs of Boston ale that dripped foam to the oak. A dozen round tables of varying size were scattered about the slats of the floor, each with a tiny flame pulsating from a thick yellow candle, and Ethan could hear the faint muffled words of Mr. Adams and those two men as he quietly shuffled to his little corner table. Ethan sensed they knew he was there as he settled into a chair nearest the window facing the stones of King Street, and as Nathan stepped to their table, Ethan felt that those men were wondering just who he might be.

Although Ethan knew had had never met Mr. Adams before, nor the man directly across the table with his back to the tavern door, he wondered if perhaps he had seen the third man somewhere before, maybe a year ago in Lexington. A trio of tricorn hats were set on the table as each man gripped a large grey mug of Boston ale, one tan near Mr. Adams and one of indigo blue near the man to his left, and one black rested near the elbow of that man nearest the door.

"Nathan!" spouted Sam as crunching sounds neared the table. "Join us, please. It's good to see you."

"Yes, please do," the man to Sam's left spiritedly added.

"Sit right here, Nathan," the third man chimed with a wave of his hand to the chair on Sam's right. "It's good to see you again. We're discussing that bloody new law, Nathan, and would sure like to know what kind of thoughts are brewing out in Lexington. What are those about Middlesex County saying about the crown's new taxes imposed by that Stamp Act?"

"Thanks, Sam," Nathan acceptingly replied as he dropped his dark tricorn to the table, "you too Joseph, John. It's good the see the three of you. I just happened to come into Boston today to talk of these very things, discuss that act."

"Nathan," whispered Samuel while leaning close and glancing to Ethan in the corner, "didn't that young man come in with you? Who is he?"

I remember Ethan confessing that his insides "began to twist in nervous knots" when he overheard what Mr. Adams asked, and struggled with anxious breaths to calm himself knowing he was about to meet such a spirited Bostonian. He said he was "petrified of revealing a dim-witted youth" if he spoke, and just pressed into the slats of his chair and stared at the flame flickering on his table while snapping sneaking glances to those men off to his right.

"Yes he did, Sam," replied Nathan, peering toward the corner as Sam continued his twisting gaze and Joseph and John glanced over their shoulders to the little table. "That young man is Ethan Sheehan, of Lexington. Maybe you, and you too John, know his father, Patrick, of the Buckman Tavern."

"Yes, I do," Sam quickly sputtered. "He's a good man."

"I have met him, Nathan," snapped John with another glance to Ethan squirming in his chair. "Last fall I think, in his tavern, with Reverend Clarke."

"He's learning the printing trade with me at the shop," Nathan proudly advised the three, "and discovering firsthand what it's like to publish the Gazette. Ethan's an energetic, smart young man, and keeps up his studies while helping his father in the tavern. He has a keen interest in the troubles brewing about the colonies too, and came with me today to watch and listen, see what Boston thinks about that Stamp Act. And this should please you, Sam. He wants to be a quiller of words."

Ethan nervously twitched while listening to them talk, and tried to ease his mind by glancing through the panes to colonists, carriages and horses busy on the stones of King Street, or peering to the fire dancing in the hearth across the room. As he returned his stare to the little flame flickering the candle of his table, he could hear Mr. Adams twist in his chair and blurt "Thomas!" to the middle-aged barkeep bustling behind the barreled bar. "Please," he quickly added to Mr. Bartlett with an authoritative wave of his hand, "would you be so kind, fetch a mug of ale for my friend, Nathan. And bring something less spirited for young Ethan at the corner table. Perhaps a mug of cider would do."

Within moments Thom clanked a dripping mug of foaming ale near Nathan and slid one of spicy cider to Ethan's fingers, and as Ethan nervously sipped and gazed to his table's little flame, Nathan waved his hand and boisterously uttered, "Ethan, I'd like you to meet some men." Grasping for courage, Ethan tipped his mug quickly once again, slid back his chair and stepped to the four at their table, stopping between John on his right and Joseph to his left.

"Nathan's told us some fine things about you, Ethan," boasted Mr. Adams in an accepting way. "It's always good to meet a young man striving to earn his mark."

"Thank you, Mr. Adams," Ethan shyly replied while reaching for Sam's greeting hand. "It's a privilege to meet you, sir."

"The pleasure is mine, Mr. Sheehan."

"Ethan, I'd like you meet Mr. Hancock," Nathan politely interjected with a glance to Ethan's right, "and Doctor Warren."

"It's good to meet you, sir," Ethan nervously uttered, shaking John's outstretched hand before twisting a bit left. "Doctor, it's good to meet you."

"Nathan thinks rather highly of you, young man," the doctor pleasingly replied. "And now, I see why. It's my pleasure, Ethan."

"That goes for me too, Ethan," added John calmly. "The colonies need young men like you. Keep up the good work with Nathan."

"I sure will," Ethan muttered in a tone he hoped would mask the apprehensions fluttering inside. Then he graciously added with an appreciative glance to Nathan, "Thank you for your kind words, Mr. Hancock, Mr. Adams, Doctor."

Suddenly feeling desperate to escape to the haven of his corner table, to hide from the powerful aura resonating with each flicker as they began to talk, Ethan sputtered, "I think I'll rejoin my cider, Mr. Giles, listen from there until you're ready to leave." Then with a quick glance about the table, he added before shuffling to the safety of his chair and calming sips from his mug, "It was my pleasure to have met each of you."

He pressed to the slats of his chair and peered out the window while sipping cider and secretly listening to their words, four colonists becoming immersed in the ills afflicting Boston and their Colony of Massachusetts Bay. They talked of those recent laws of parliament and the crown, especially of that unjust Stamp Act, and were heard to mutter unflattering things of the king's misguided follies while discussing what the colony should do to display its discontent. And when Ethan described that day, he told me a little bit about those three men, of their passions and how they had come to gather in the Green Dragon Tavern that brisk spring day.

Ethan thought Mr. Adams was a bit larger than most, in a muscular way, and wore a dark wool vest that day, trimmed by a tan coat open at the chest. A bright shirt ruffled at the tips of each sleeve was snugged tight to his neck, and yellow stockings rose from polished shoes to tan breeches gripping his knees. And his hair was neatly cropped and curled just past his ears, locks fading from a soft brown to an intriguing silvery grey, and his dark eyes seemed to pierce the cool air of the tavern that afternoon.

They say he was born in Boston in late September some forty-three years before, one of a dozen children of his father Samuel and mother Mary, and was the elder cousin of John from the nearby village of Braintree. Reared in the puritan faith, it seems young Sam attended a Latin school for boys, and was said to have come of age along Boston's southeast docks. Ethan would later discover that Mr. Adams began studies at Harvard College when only fourteen, the first such school in all the colonies, and would earn his most prestigious degree in the spring of 1743. And there were rumors for many years that before he left those halls of Cambridge he quilled a provocative essay believed to have infuriated the colony's royal governor and others rather loyal to the crown, an inciting thesis some would say, brushed by the notion, "Whether it be lawful to resist the supreme magistrate, if the commonwealth cannot otherwise be preserved."

I suppose he would become known in his later years for espousing what those of London viewed as inflammatory opinions brushed with disloyal rhetoric, yet early it seems Sam simply ventured into more enterprising things, such as making malt with his father for brewing Boston ales and beers. But it was his thirst for knowing his colony's state of affairs that began to stir him the most, especially the actions of the king affecting Boston, and soon he was striving for a greater understanding of policies and law. There were various groups of colonists in those days too that tended to subscribe to his defiant points of view, merchants and others with an immerging interest of how their colony was being treated by the crown, spirited groups with intriguing names like the south-end caucus and that club he called the whipping post.

Ethan said Mr. Adams had ventured into officious functions for the royal governor too, having once served as one of the crown's tax collectors several years before that spring. There were even rumors that he tried to sway the colony's royal governor about disturbing issues swirling Boston in those days, using collected duties as a bargaining wedge from time to time. Then around the final months of that frontier war, they say he began to assemble women and men to express their frustrations at spirited gatherings, all the while he began to insist upon having his poignant opinions printed in papers like that Independent Advertiser or the Boston Gazette and Country Journal. Some viewed his letters and essays as disloyally defiant, opinions which spoke of colonial rights for Massachusetts Bay and all the colonies, words espousing ideas like fundamental liberties that were said to have inflamed the fury of Royal Governor Bernard and scores of officious men loyal to the king.

On the other side of that table, with his back to the tavern door, sat Doctor Warren, "a rather pedestrian looking man," Ethan would say, "a bit unpolished and somewhat philosophical, yet perhaps the most intriguing of the four." His was donning dark breeches like most men in those days, with bright stockings that vanished into scuffed black shoes, and his white linen shirt was a bit wrinkled beneath the wool of a greyish coat and vest. "The doctor's hair was well cropped, Andrea, resting to his ears in a sandy tan, and his eyes, a mysterious brown, seemed to cast a tranquil peer while expose the truth of his soul." Although he was the youngest of the four that day, he exuded a calming demeanor with his words, and his voice was brushed with a special quality of serenity.

He was born in the farming village of Roxbury in late spring just twenty-four years before, one of the earlier settlements to rise in the Colony of Massachusetts Bay, a hamlet on the southwestern narrows of Boston once known as Rocksberry. They say he was baptized in the old village church too, a place of worship made of pine planks and mortared rocks constructed by a slew of farmers over a century before. Ethan once said he could see the steeple when riding the southern road out of Boston, a spire rising on a lazy slope near a house once reserved for the royal governor along the Muddy River, a twisting thread of shallow creeks, ponds and brooks winding across the narrows to the waters of the Charles.

Then tragedy struck young Joseph much like it had Ethan early in life, for while in studies at the little schoolhouse in Roxbury, his father Joe suddenly died and his mother Mary was a widow. Some disparagingly said his father had fallen from his colt while trotting home from the Oyster Tavern, yet Ethan was later told that he had tumbled from an unsteady ladder while stretching for the fruits of his toils, gasping a final breath on the muddied soil of an apple tree. Undeterred at age fourteen, young Joseph continued to diligently study by the glow of a lamp each night until reaching his dream of attending Harvard College just across the river in Cambridge, receiving his degree with three dozen others in the spring of 1759.

It seems that soon Joseph Warren was teaching village children basic studies at his old schoolhouse in Roxbury while delving increasingly into his interest of medicine, and after a year or so embarked upon his own healing practice in Boston. Yet it wasn't long, they say, before he began to expand his interests into colonial things, joining the masonic lodge of St. Andrews and wading into the troubles beginning to brew about the colony. He was quickly becoming a regular at meetings sprouting about Boston, fiery gatherings organized by colonists like Sam Adams and Jimmy Otis, Bostonians becoming disillusioned by the actions of parliament, King George and his Royal Governor Bernard.

And just left of Sam at the table that day was John Hancock, the man nearest Ethan who seemed to exude a distinguished aura more refined than most colonial men. His breeches hugged his thighs in a deep blue, and his stockings of silken white seemed to sparkle while descending from his knees to glossy dark shoes. A stylish coat of indigo blue elegantly draped a light shirt that ruffled near his hands, and a thin string of golden twine was delicately stitched about each shiny button running to his neck. Although John's back was to Ethan that day, his brushed auburn hair flaring gently at the ears, each time he twisted Ethan could see a spirited glare in his blue eyes, a daring peer which seemed to show he understood the colonial changes drawing near.

Mr. Hancock was known to be a colonist of vast resources in those days, a man some believed may have been the wealthiest of Boston back then, and maybe, in all of Ethan's Colony of Massachusetts Bay. Yet his earliest days were said to have been humble, born the middle child of John and Mary in the village of Braintree during a wintry flurry of 1737. Ethan said that young John was known to scamper about bay coves and frolic about the village with Sam's little cousin, but at the age of seven his life was tossed to the winds when his father, a devoted preacher, succumbed to a wicked ailment few understood.

"Mr. Giles said it was soon after that," Ethan revealed, "that John came to live with his grandpa in Lexington, a few years before I was born. But after a while he was uprooted again, traveling to Boston to live with his dad's brother Thom and wife Lydia." It seems they had a home up on Beacon Hill, an impressive manor not far from my aunt and uncle just north of the common, a house disturbing rumors would later suggest was cared for by an indentured Negro or two.

His uncle was said to have been rather close in those days to an array of the king's men and the colony's royal governor, and with those loyal connections, was able to advance his merchant trade throughout the colonies of New England. He was known to ship a variety of products and goods across the sea from London, while sailing sacks, barrels and crates of colonial things like grains, fishes and rums from Boston docks in his own little fleet. Once in his new Boston home brimming of earthly things, they say young John began his studies at that Latin school for boys until reaching the halls of Harvard College, gaining his degree with nineteen others in the spring when Ethan and I were just three.

It wasn't long before John began to expend his energies in his uncle's shipping and merchant trade, even sailing to London during the first years of the reign of King George the Third, to expand their influence and enhance their wealth. But then in the summer of 1764 his life dramatically changed once again, when shortly after sailing back to Boston from England, his uncle died from a ravenous fever. In what some would enviously say was a "fortune bestowed overnight," John became perhaps the wealthiest man in the colonies when his uncle Thom bequeathed his bustling estate to his twenty-seven year old nephew.

Much like Doctor Warren I suppose, soon John began to delve into colonial issues simmering about Boston, even taking a seat on an array of port councils and a chair in the colony's assembly. Along with those new duties came an expanded relationship with many of Boston and throughout the colony, spirited men with similar distrusts of the intrusive polices of their royal governor and increasingly unjust laws from London. He was now discovering an entwining bond with colonists like Mr. Giles, Sam and that doctor, as well as Mr. Otis and Sam's young cousin John, and some Boston printers like Mr. Fowle, John Gill and Benjamin Edes.

I remember the glint in Ethan eyes when he told me of meeting those three men in the Green Dragon Tavern that spring day of 1765, of the eerie sensation that raced inside seeing how they seemed extraordinarily unique. "I guess they just displayed a special awareness of what was happening about the colonies," he confided, "more so than most in Boston, perhaps all the colonies, and their disapproving words of the governor and the king, of those newest laws and that Stamp Act, exuded confidence. It was as if each was endowed with a peculiar knowledge, Andrea, had a mysterious connection with ancient wisdoms, for they seemed to see things more clearly than most could understand."

"Please, Thom," a twisting Mr. Giles spouted to the barkeep, "we'll have some more ale." And as Ethan sipped his cider and humbly listened and watched from his corner chair, Mr. Giles returned his stare to the three and insisted, "Now, Doc, John, Sam, let's clear up some things about that Stamp Act. What are your true feelings about this, shall I say, rubbish, and what should we do about it?"

"Yes, Thomas," Samuel quickly snapped to the barkeep, "four more, and cider for Ethan." Then scanning the eyes of the table he boldly added, "Well, before we delve too deeply into that bloody act, I'd like to offer a few enlightening words some say Doctor Franklin once uttered."

The four hushed as the barkeep clanked fresh mugs of ale to the table before sliding another cider to Ethan, and as Doc, Nathan and John inquisitively gazed, Sam calmly raised his mug and said, "Gentlemen, please, join me." With fists thrust into the cool tavern air, each gripping pewter trickling foam, Sam glanced about the room and to the eyes of the three and uttered, "Doctor Franklin may have sailed for London months ago, but before departing, our Philadelphia friend exposed his wisdom with these comforting words. 'Ale,' he said, 'is living proof that our Creator loves each of us, and wants us, to be happy.' Drink up," he finished with a devious grin, "and taste the revelry!"

Ethan secretly watched as an expression of surprise brushed their faces at Mr. Adams' youthful joviality, and as the eyes of Nathan, Doc and John glanced to Samuel then each other, perhaps somewhat perplexed at his spirited gest, a comforting release seemed to brush each face. "Hear, hear!" the three suddenly boasted as all clicked their ale over the candle of the table.

"Enjoy, gentlemen," uttered Sam as their mugs clanked once again, "and be happy!" And while Ethan watched, they sipped a spot of courage to a colonial life slowly changing.

"As profound as your appeal truly was, Sam," uttered John, clicking his ale to the table, "I feel compelled to add a bit more cheer. Gentlemen, your mugs please." Then twisting an inclusive glance to Ethan hushed at his little corner table, he returned his peer to the other three and firmly added, "To that robust man from Pennsylvania. To his vigorous efforts on behalf of the colonies at expressing our discontent to the king and his ministers roaming the halls of London. Gentlemen, to Mr. Franklin."

"Yes, hear, hear!" chimed Doctor Warren.

Each man muttered, "To Mr. Franklin," while a few stray colonists about the tavern sputtered a gracious, "hear, hear," and as the four once again clicked mugs above the table, Ethan could see in their eyes the esteem each held for Doctor Franklin.

"Now, gentlemen," insisted Sam with a glance to John, Nathan and Doc, "let's talk about why Nathan came into Boston, the real reason we're here today. What to do about this latest bundle of nonsense from London, this bloody infringement King George and his henchmen call the Stamp Act. We know it won't be effective until fall, but in my humble opinion, the colonies mustn't wait. We must unite and act, gentlemen, in some way, against this intrusion in the weeks and months to come. I believe it vital that the colonies expose the truth of what's going on here, show London how much we colonists despise this despicable trampling of our liberties!"

"I've read some of your thoughts, Sam," Nathan supportively said, "and must say, you and I agree. Yes, I think the colonies should, must form a united front, show the king in clear terms our opposition to this act. Perhaps a coordinated assault in print, a display of our disapproval in the newspapers of Boston and throughout the colony, in my Lexington Gazette too."

"Yes, that's good," injected John without hesitation. "Why, I've even seen the intrusiveness of other policies and acts too, far too close, have experienced my own disputes with Governor Bernard and the king's customs men. I've heard of encounters by other merchants too, against colonists more loyal to the crown. I must remind you, gentlemen, these disturbing things are not isolated to our Colony of Massachusetts Bay, for there are similar reports coming from all the colonies."

Ethan quietly watched as John sipped a splash of ale and glanced about the table, then continued with a fiery determination in his tone. "In light of these other recent policies and laws, I'm very concerned that if this latest act is allowed to thrive unabated, the colonies invite further intrusions of our lives. Even though danger may lurk, this must be stopped! I support expressing our displeasures in an open forum, in papers and pamphlets throughout the colonies, and at the same time, gentlemen, devising a semblance of orderly resistance in all the colonies, especially right here in Massachusetts Bay. The colonies must not accept the fatal folly of appeasement, must not accept the whittling of our rights and liberties by parliament and the king."

"I concur with each of you," softly chimed Doctor Warren, glancing about the table before calmly adding. "And there's something else about this bloody act, a view I'm sure you'll agree. We here in the colonies are entitled to be treated just as those across the sea in England, for we are all citizens the same, and should hold like rights and liberties, particularly when it comes to duties and taxes. Should the colonies succumb to such treachery now, to this unjust Stamp Act, we will have accepted an inferior position in the empire while inviting more of the same. No, gentlemen, this must not stand!"

"Those are fine insights, Joseph," Sam agreeably uttered, "positions I'm sure each of us hold. What you say simply exposes the urgency we face, and spurs our desires to act."

"But there's something else we must consider," Doctor Warren hesitantly added while glancing about the tavern. "There could be dangerous consequences. Have we properly considered what actions London might take to counter defiance by the colonies to this Stamp Act, to King George? Things could spiral from control, turn rather ugly."

A hush suddenly gripped their table as if swept into the tavern by a mysterious wind, and while they pondered the ominous possibilities unleashed by Doctor Warren, a sense of the colonies' precarious position seemed to engulf the four. For a moment Ethan could sense that perhaps disturbing doubts were racing their minds, but then, as the flame of their candle flickered with that mystical wind, he could see the strength in their eyes. "It was as if a resolve had burst from their souls, Andrea, and at that moment, I could feel their burning determination."

Ethan watched as Sam pressed into the slats of his chair and gathered his thoughts for a moment or two, then leaned into the ridge of the oak and began to carefully express his words. "Your points are well taken, Joseph. In fact, John and I discussed those very things just a few days ago. We agree, and I'm sure Nathan too, those challenges must be given their proper due."

Then gripping his mug and straightening in his chair, Sam glanced about the table and continued in a secretive tone. "John and I, after talking with others here in Boston, good men like Ben Edes, Jim Otis and cousin John, have already been exchanging dispatches with other colonies by special riders. I must say, gentlemen, most agree with us, that this Stamp Act must be opposed, that this tyranny from London must be defied. I wonder too, what might become of our lives should the colonies from Georgia to Massachusetts Bay tamely submit to our royal governors and the king. I wonder of the darkness that would be cast upon us all, if we just timidly knelt to the soils and crawled. Never! Let consequences be damned!"

"Many may tremble, Sam," Nathan chimed with caution, "but yes, I agree. What's happening here is too vital to ignore. We have no true choice but to oppose, and to do so, the colonies must act together, unite as one."

"Well said, Nathan," John concurringly spouted while tipping his mug for a splash of ale. "I think those are our precise sentiments."

"I hope you gentlemen understand," Doctor Warren calmly added, "that I was merely pointing out the possibility of consequences. That's all. But you men know me, such things don't deter me, never have. I agree with you Nathan, John, Sam."

"Yes, of course we do, Joe," conceded Sam. "We know where you stand. And it's reassuring to hear such cohesiveness at this table."

"Just what do you two have in mind?" Nathan inquired with a quizzical look as Doc gripped his mug and listened with an attentive stare.

"I've always liked that about you, Nathan," confided Sam, sipping his ale, "straight to the point. Alright, one thing we in Boston believe is best, and I must say, most other colonies agree, is that we must ignore this Stamp Act. We propose to function as if that bloody act never happened, that's right, gentlemen, behave as though it was never imposed. Colonists will be asked to simply not abide its terms, and that means as many shopkeepers and merchants, barristers and our courts disregarding that damn act, doctors and printers too. We must refuse to buy the crown's specially stamped paper, and in doing so, we'll in essence shun payment of that bloody tax. We think colonists will be able to continue to function as they have, with our own unstamped parchment for benign things and officious documents like contracts, permits and licenses. We simply propose to ignore London, refuse to succumb to these unjust demands."

"What about the king's customs men," Nathan asked, "not only here in Boston, but in all the colonies? You know, Sam, they could get rather nasty."

"You raise a fine point, Nathan," insisted John in a logical tone. "Trust me, that very challenge has been discussed at length. Few in the colonies, and surely not Sam and I here, take that possibility lightly."

"I'm glad you brought that up, Nathan," inserted Sam, leaning back into his chair and gripping his mug tightly. Then glancing to John and across the table to Doctor Warren, he stoically added, "We've decided, and trust you'll agree, that if a customs man becomes, shall we say, insistent that colonists adhere to the terms of this Stamp Act, we may need to resort to ways that will help enlighten that agent as to our position. At times, it may be appropriate for colonists to provide some type of special instruction for those royal men."

"You mean intimidation, don't you, Sam," uttered Doc in a cautiously accepting tone, "and maybe, a bit of harsh inducement."

"Be what it may, Doc," sputtered Sam briskly. "Yet, I suppose that's pretty much true. Come now, we're not advocating violence, or inflicting harm upon the king's agents or others who cling to the crown. All we're saying is that it might be appropriate to ruffle a loyal feather now and then, for we know what's at stake here, know what must be done. If we let this pass unchallenged, blindly accept such things without as much as a tweak of our gait, why, we might as well stuff our remaining liberties into sacks and crates and surrender them to the waters of Boston Harbor!"

"You do have a delicate fancy with words, Samuel," Doc Warren sprightly replied, "and I must say, I find no fault in your passion. Yet, I'm still concerned."

"I'm a bit worried too, Sam," eagerly chimed Nathan. "Yet, I too understand, and support your point of view. I'm convinced as well, that acting collectively now is not a luxury, but what we must do. Right, John?"

"Sam, Doc and I have talked about these things with quite a few here in Boston, and I must say, support for Sam's views is abundant. Why, even Reverend Cooper has carefully preached such contentions over at his Brattle Street church. Most pretty much believe that effective defiance of this act can and must be done, not only here in Massachusetts Bay, but in as many colonies as possible. Many say they are prepared to do whatever is proper to ensure success of defying this act, whether boldly printed in pamphlets and newspapers or displayed on our port docks, and in warehouses and merchant shops. Yes, I'm with Sam, with the colonies."

"And you, Doc?" asked Nathan with an inquisitive glare.

"Like John, I'm with Sam, possible dangers and all, and will help do what I can to further our colonial interests. And from what I've seen here today at this table, we have your support too, Nathan, and that of your Lexington Gazette."

Nathan inhaled Green Dragon air and glanced to Ethan silently watching from his little corner table, then leaning to the oak and scanning the anxious eyes of his peers with a bold stare, he gripped his ale and said. "What I've heard this afternoon, gentlemen, is precisely what I had hoped I would when I came to Boston today. Have no doubt of my commitment. And as for Lexington and Middlesex County, I assure you, many will stand with you in Boston and those of like minds throughout Massachusetts Bay, in all the colonies. Gentlemen, you have the unwavering support of my Gazette."

"Splendid!" a jubilant John extolled.

"Our efforts aren't stopping there," Samuel quickly exclaimed. "There's talk of a more coordinated effort by the colonies, a more harmonious response sprouting from a single group."

"In the meantime," asserted John in a complimentary way, "each pamphlet and paper we bring into the fold will be invaluable, each providing a forum for our message to reach hundreds of villages and towns. Your Lexington Gazette is one, Nathan, and just as important as those here in Boston, like Sam's old Independent Advertiser and Ben Edes' Gazette and Country Journal. We're creating a pretty good rider system too, for getting information to flow from colony to colony, and that, gentlemen, can only help coordinate our thoughts and actions. I suppose if there were one area that is suspect, it would be how to pay for all these things. Well, John says that this is one thing I'm pretty good at doing, filling a coffer with shillings and pounds. And I'll do my best, to find more."

"I see," Nathan reflectively replied. "And so will Lexington and Middlesex County before long, that I promise."

"Excellent!" Sam quickly sputtered, gripping his mug for a spot of ale. "And while those things are taking place, Doc, John and I, along with others in Boston, will be helping to gather men from all the colonies into a single assembly, something many believe is vital if the colonies are to speak with a common voice. We think doing so might just compel King George and his parliament, his royal governors too, to heed our righteous concerns and repeal that bloody Stamp Act. Maybe, a united display of colonial discontent will rattle the crown and expose the dangers of its folly, and maybe, it'll infuse reluctance into those of London to never again impose such a wicked act."

"You have support for such an assembly?" a surprised yet intrigued Nathan asked.

"Yes, Nathan, we do," John answered before Sam, sipping ale, could reply, "from a variety of good men, like John Dickinson down in Pennsylvania, whose dispatch said his group of colonists is prepared to move forward with this assembly. We just received a message by swift rider from Robert Livingston's group too, in the Colony of New York, and George Wythe in Virginia quilled that his group is being corralled by a confident young man named Patrick Henry, a new member of their House of Burgesses."

"Now, that act isn't effective until the first day of November," added Sam in a tutorial way, "and we're confident our colonial assembly can be formed weeks before then, perhaps even as early as August or September. So we have a few months to garner support from colonists for that gathering, expose the folly of that Stamp Act and explain why it must be opposed."

"What do you propose calling this gathering, Sam," Nathan quizzically asked, "this colonial assembly?"

"Many want to keep it simple, Sam," John interjected quickly, "and I agree. Some suggest we call it, the Stamp Act Congress."

"That's good, John," replied Sam with a spirited gleam in his eyes. "I like it, and I'm sure most will approve as well. It conveys our reason for assembling in a way that not only colonists will understand, but so will the king and his royal governors."

I remember Ethan said that it was then, at that defining moment as the four were just about to click their mugs in homage to that coming colonial assembly, when the tavern door suddenly swung and a blast of cooling April air raced across the room to flicker each candle. They were the first soldiers of the king's Royal Army Ethan had been exposed to up close, and each had a musket dangling his crimson coat. The trio was a tiny part of the four thousand or so royal troops which had marched from the frontier to Boston upon the orders of General Gage, the king's overall commander quartered that spring in port of New York.

He watched from his corner table as they shuffled inside and stood quiet at the door in scuffed and muddied black boots, then one flicked the door shut with a snapping click as they glanced about the tavern. Ethan could see a pair of little guns tucked beneath the belt snugging one's belly, short iron pieces with curving handles Mr. Giles would later say were sixty-five caliber pistols. And as they brushed grimy specs from their coats Ethan wondered of those muskets hanging from their shoulders, dark barrels muzzled up and weathered elm stocks dangling near the tavern floor.

"For a moment they looked to John and Sam more intensely than the others," Ethan said, "as if they knew them from some other place, and although they glanced about in an intimidating way, I couldn't help but see how young they were, not much older than me. I couldn't help but wonder how those three soldiers were becoming involved in the concerns brewing about the colonies without truly understanding, three young men simply doing their duty for the king, and wondered if such a duty would ever be asked of me."

A dark tricorn hat rested upon each soldier's loosely cropped hair, and their coats flared over bright shirts and white breeches that vanished into those menacing boots just below the knees. Ethan and most colonists in those days would soon discover that the king's soldiers were simply known as regulars, just troops of London's army, in contrast to the men of our colonial militias. Yet there were others in the colonies that were beginning to view those royal soldiers roaming about the ports of Boston, Philadelphia and New York in more disparaging terms, referring to the crown's troops as blasted hatmen or lobster backs, or simply bloody redcoats.

They glanced about for another moment or two then clumped to a large round table in the southwest corner left of the door, scraping and sliding their muddied boots across the oak slats of the tavern floor. Ethan watched as each tossed his tricorn to a spot right of the darkened candle in the center of the table, then one by one carefully leaned his musket against the wall near the corner. They had placed themselves on the opposite side of the tavern from Ethan and the four, each flopping with an exasperating sigh into a slatted oak chair near the window facing the cobblestones of King Street.

"What can I get you boys?" asked Thom the barkeep after scampering to their table, a folded strip of white linen dangling his left wrist.

"Three mugs of that Boston ale!" spouted the more seasoned looking soldier with his back to the panes, as his two friends pressed into the slats of their chairs with a defiant gaze. "Please, sir."

As the king's soldiers settled in their corner, Ethan glanced to Nathan and his three sipping ale while in deep contemplation. "It was as if each table was suddenly gripped in a mysterious competition," Ethan revealed, "each group waiting for some mystical sign amid the silence of temperance, each wondering what the other might do. Then Sam, Doc, Nathan and John began to talk ever so softly, in a tone so low I couldn't hear, and within seconds those royal men struck a quiet discussion of their own. It wasn't long, Andrea, before Nathan sprang to his feet with a scrape of his chair."

"I'll be in touch, soon," spouted Nathan, bidding his colonist trio farewell before snapping a glance to the king's men in the far corner. "Let's go,

Ethan," he quickly added as Ethan, gripping his cider, listened and watched. "We've a long ride home."

"It was good to meet you, Ethan," Sam pleasingly blurted as Ethan stepped toward the tavern door. "Give my regards to your father."

"I will," Ethan shyly replied. "It was my pleasure to meet you, Mr. Adams."

"You take care, young man," chimed Doc Warren before glancing to Mr. Giles shuffling to the door and playfully adding, "Be good to this aspiring printer, Nathan."

"Perhaps we'll meet again, Mr. Sheehan," John suggested in an upbeat tone. "I do have a chance to ride to Lexington now and then, so perhaps then."

"Yes, I hope so," Ethan nervously replied as he reached the door, about to follow Nathan to the cobblestones of King Street. "It was good to have met each of you. I look forward to seeing you again."

That's when his eyes suddenly latched upon the glare of one of those three royal soldiers watching from the corner, and for a brief moment they stared to each other as if each sensed the strains of coexistence beginning to swirl about Boston. "He had a tinge of fright in his eyes," I remember Ethan saying, "perhaps of the tensions starting to simmer between the crown and colonies, a fear of the unknown which surged through my body too. Yet, in strange way, Andrea, we both seemed to understand." Then he spun with an anxious twitch and bound down the steps to join Nathan, pulling the tavern door shut with a snapping click.

They climbed back into the buggy and began to creak along the stones, and as they ferried the waters of the harbor and rolled across the Charlestown Peninsula, bouncing through its narrow neck on the ruts and stones of the Massachusetts Road on their ride back to Lexington, Nathan spoke of the daunting tasks ahead. He talked of the challenges of assembling that congress before the turn of autumn leaves, and of the supportive positions he'd print in his Lexington Gazette.

As Ethan listened to Nathan's ideas, plans and concerns, his thoughts wandered now and then to less stressful things, and as the rhythmic sounds of crunching wheels and thumping hooves echoed about the hills, he could hear spring leaves lazily rustling in the soft evening breeze. Little patches of clouds were drifting toward the dark creeping from the sea, and with each snap of the reins Ethan became mesmerized with the colors of dusk gently spraying the April sky. Then amidst the encroaching shadows he saw a dainty flower with little yellow petals sprouting among tiny stones near the road, and as he gazed to its beauty he wondered of the pending fury gripping Mr. Giles' words, wondered how that precious bloom, just as most colonists in those days, was so innocently unaware.

In the coming weeks and months Ethan would hear of events happening about the colonies from farmers, merchants and tradesmen in his father's tavern, colonists discussing those simmering troubles or simply escaping the tribulations of their lives with mugs of ale or tins and cups of rye whiskey and rum. And he'd stay apprised of those evolving events while continuing to learn the printing trade in Mr. Giles' shop, and read of such brewing things in his Lexington Gazette and the printings coming from Boston.

Colonists opposed to London's Stamp Act were beginning to robustly gather in various places about Boston, in a church just south of King Street or inside the bricks of Faneuil Hall, or perhaps in more intimate places like the room above Mr. Edes' print shop or the spirited confines of the Green Dragon Tavern. They were gatherings that Ethan once said reflected the brewing disgust of that taxing act, meetings spurring support throughout the colonies for that congress. Then in the first hours of summer that 1765, rumors began to sweep from Georgia to Massachusetts Bay, from Ethan's Lexington to my Germantown, that most colonies had finally agreed to gather selected men in the port of New York early in October, in a hall near the southern tip of the Island of Manhattan.

As details of that pending Stamp Act Congress were being discussed in secretive colonial places, I remember that supporting activities were also occurring throughout the colonies. The Pennsylvania Evening Post was calling one of those things committees for correspondence, small groups of special men being formed by colonial assemblies and spirited councils in ports, villages and towns, groups assigned the vital task of coordinating the flow of information to-and-fro all the colonies. If I recall, the first of these groups was formed in Ethan's Boston, with other committees sprouting about the entire Colony of Massachusetts Bay. And soon there were little groups springing forth in Charles Towne, Williamsburg,

Philadelphia and Savannah, in all the colonies from the Carolinas to Delaware, Maryland, Connecticut and Virginia.

Ethan once said that Mr. Giles, Sam Adams and Mr. Hancock viewed those committees as essential for corralling support for that congress and spurring resistance to that Stamp Act, or any other nonsense that parliament, the royal governors and King George might thrust upon the colonies to suppress our liberties. Just as important they'd say, those committees were entrusted to ensure that information and decisions arising from the group in Boston, from all the committees forming about the colonies, was quilled in a way easily understood and swiftly distributed among the hundreds of committees.

It was during that summer, late June or perhaps early July, when new rumors began to sweep north through my Colony of Pennsylvania to Ethan's Massachusetts Bay, stories he would later say were soon being printed in Boston and an array of village newspapers, including Mr. Giles' Lexington Gazette. With the schoolhouse shuttered for those summer weeks, Ethan was not only tending to his chores at the Buckman Tavern, but had seen his apprentice duties expanding at the print shop. And on this clingingly warm afternoon, he rushed into his father's tavern with a stack of freshly inked Gazettes bundled in his arms, just as he had every Monday that summer.

Colonial men were scattered about the tavern a few hours before dusk, shopkeepers, merchants, tradesmen and farmers escaping the toils of their day with elbows pressed to the elm planks of the barreled bar or gripping spirits in pairs and threes at an array of tables. Some talked of beans, corn and grains struggling to sprout or grumbled of roosters shattering the dawn, while others spoke of possible troubles brewing for merchants. Ethan could see a weary farmer from the village of Bedford too, sitting alone at a little table by the east window just right of the door, quietly sipping rye whiskey while peering through the panes. And some were anxiously talking of the simmering tensions spreading the colonies, including Ethan's father who mingled while filling cups, mugs, goblets and tins with whiskey, ale, wines and rum, discussions that increasingly drifted to that Stamp Act and the colonial gathering soon to come.

"I'm back, dad," Ethan spouted in a shy way, dropping the stack of fresh Gazettes to a little table left of the door as his father tended with things behind the bar. "This is the latest from Nathan's press, dad, and there's something here I think you'll want to see. It's about that Stamp Act, and things brewing in the south." As Ethan rushed toward the rear and the kitchen door to finish a few chores, passing a couple tired men tipping mugs at the bar, he hastily laid one of those Gazettes to the elm near his father. "It's this one, dad," he proudly added, tapping his fingers to the ink printed down the left side of the parchment sheet. "Nathan's helping me hone my style, and some of these words are mine."

Ethan once said that some of the things expressed by Mr. Giles in his Gazette reflected ideas Mr. Adams had recently exposed in the Independent Advertiser in Boston, along with bits and pieces of thoughts and rumors he had corralled from an array of special sources, such as less covert things being exchanged among the colonies and those sprouting committees. Yet Ethan always said the versions printed in the Gazette were mostly tailored for the colonists of Lexington and Middlesex County, with a tinge of input from Ethan now and then when Nathan was in a teaching mood and viewed the subject right.

"I say, Ethan," his father sputtered while scanning those printed words, before twisting to fill a pair of mugs with golden ale from the spigot of a Boston barrel, "this is rather good, and I think Nathan is right." Then sliding the mugs to a thirsty farmer and merchant with elbows pressed to the bar, he raised the parchment into the tavern air and proudly spouted, "Did you see this, boys, this latest Gazette? My son, right here, Ethan, had a hand in this. He's growing into a real printer, and a fine quiller of words."

A sense of panic began to rumble deep inside Ethan as a slew of eyes suddenly glanced, and with each piercing stare he could feel flashes of heat surging his body. "I'm glad you think what Nathan printed is good, dad," he shyly whispered with an embarrassing gaze, "and yes, some of it is mine." As his impulse to rush and hide gripped him tight, he quickly added, "I better finish my chores," then dashed through the swinging door into the safety of the kitchen.

"I think that's splendid, Patrick," spouted Lexington's bricklayer Israel Jacob, sipping wine alone at a table right of the tavern door. "It's bloody good to see boys gettin involved, knowin things happenin about the colonies. And learnin words likes that, why, it's bloody good! Nathan has a good man with your boy. You must be proud."

"I am, Israel," replied Ethan's father with pride in his step while gripping a pair of dripping mugs for two traveling merchants, colonists exchanging unflattering views of the crown at the corner table by the windows at the end of the barreled bar. "And thanks, for those kind words."

"Just speakin truth, Patrick," he uttered while scampering to the Gazettes piled left of the door, then scurrying back at his table. "Let's see what Nathan has to say about that bloody Stamp Act," he uttered for those of the tavern to hear while settling with his goblet and chair.

"Israel!" suddenly blurted Alex Spoons from his little table just right of the fireplace stones across the tavern floor, a spirited farmer whose fields were near Ethan's old place northeast of the village. "How bout we all hear this," he spouted while sipping rum with a rumpled looking man who helped till the farm. "Come on, Israel, read it aloud. Let's hear what Nathan has to say."

"Why, that's a fine thought, Alex," Ethan's father supportively agreed. "If you don't mind, Israel, we do all have a stake in this."

Hearing the words of Alex and his father, Ethan stopped sweeping colonial dirt and crumbly bits from the slats of the floor, then quietly swinging open the kitchen door, nestled to the corner near the end of the barreled bar. "I wanted to watch and listen," he told me, "gage the reactions of the men to what Nathan had printed, to what I had helped form. I wanted to see if they agreed to the ideas Mr. Giles expressed in his Lexington Gazette."

Ethan secretly watched as Israel laid the parchment to the table and gripped his goblet, and in what seemed a mysterious ritual to a lost love or imaginary king, raised his wine into the afternoon air for a moment, then sipped and nestled back in his chair. "Alright, I'll do just that," he calmly uttered as a curious expression brushed his face. "Maybes some of you, gentlemen, already knows these things, maybes not. Let's see what Nathan has to say."

An unusual hush descended upon the tavern as Israel pinched the edges of the Gazette, and with each man listening, eyes fixed and spirits in hand, he began to carefully read. "'Virginia takes action!' Nathan prints, then goes on to say, 'The assembly in the Colony of Virginia, with keen awareness of the shackling actions that King George and his ministers have taken against our Thirteen Colonies these past few months, has garnered unyielding opposition to the crown's most recent attack, that unjust Stamp Act. And in a righteous pursuit of remedies, a gentleman known by few beyond Williamsburg grasped their challenge this past May, emerging as a fresh leader of their House of Burgesses.

"'Patrick Henry is just twenty-nine, a barrister from the hamlet of Studley in the hills outside Richmond northwest of Williamsburg, and the newest member of the colony's house. Perhaps you remember hearing of this young man a year or so ago when he was a fresh lawyer in Hanover County, a legal hornet who gripped the reins of a parson's case and sparked a judicious war against the king and Royal Governor Amherst. With an eloquent style honed in the Hanover hills, Mr. Henry had the audacious spirit to dispute the nuances of the value of the colony's tobacco crop, proceeds siphoned by the crown to prop the king's church. He defiantly argued that colonists should have the sole right to set such a price, not royals roaming the halls of London.'"

Ethan watched from his little corner outside the kitchen door as Israel lowered the parchment and stopped reading, then glanced about the tavern and sipped more wine. Perhaps he just wanted to see if the men were listening, Ethan wondered, or maybe halting at just that moment was simply his taunting way of spurring anticipation. As Ethan nestled in his spot on the other side of the room, he could see an impatience beginning to brush the face of his father and the others, could sense their thirst building for more of Nathan's words.

"Well? Israel!" grumbled Joe Hosmer sipping ale at the bar, a farmer whose fields were near Ethan's old place. "What else does Nathan say?"

"Yes, Israel," a weary merchant chimed, "let's hear the rest."

"Alright, Israel," Ethan's father calmly uttered, "you've had your fun. Come on, please, continue."

"Alright, I will, just holds on a second," he confidently replied in a protective tone, tipping his goblet and pressing to his chair. "'Along with George Johnson,'" Israel continued with a gripping snap of the Gazette, "'Mr. Henry proposed five resolutions in opposition to that Stamp Act, bold statements those in other colonies will surely envy. With just enough allies assembled in the House of Burgesses, a quorum mysteriously missing a slew of members more loyal to the king, Patrick Henry ignited an enlightening debate. And once the yeas and nays had been tallied, the colony's defining resolutions were approved shortly after dusk the final Wednesday of May, 1765. They called their document the *Virginia Stamp Act Resolutions,* a courageous statement which reads in part:

> I) That the first settlers in the land now known as Virginia brought with them the same rights, liberties, privileges, franchises and immunities held, enjoyed and possessed by the people across the sea in Great Britain.
>
> II) That through royal charters granted years ago by King James, these Virginia colonists are entitled to the same rights, liberties and privileges as those born within the realm of England.
>
> III) That the only security against a burdensome taxation is for the people of the land of Virginia to tax themselves, for only the people of Virginia know what they can bear.
>
> IV) That the king's loyal people of this colony have without interruption enjoyed the immeasurable rights of governing themselves through laws passed with their own consent, with the approval of His Majesty, and these rights have never been yielded and have continually been recognized by the people of England.
>
> V) That because of these things, only the people of the Colony of Virginia have the right to lay taxes upon the colony, and any attempt to take away that right and power is an act to destroy not only British freedoms, but more importantly, the freedoms of Colonial America.'"

"Hear, hear!" exclaimed Mr. Hosmer as he stepped from the barreled bar to a chair at the little table just left of the hearth's stones. Then Ethan watched as his father brushed past to join Joe, each gripping a dripping mug of ale.

"Superb sentiments," Ethan's father quickly added while settling to a chair as Ethan listened from his nearby corner perch. "That Mr. Henry and his colleagues down there sure know how to press their words."

"To Virginia's House of Burgesses!" a spirited Alex Spoons exalted, thrusting his rum into the summer air as men scattered about the tavern joined his cheer.

Israel had raised his goblet too, having halted his reading to sip more wine as cheers erupted about the room. Then pinching the Gazette once again, he glanced about the tavern and playfully asked, "Well, do you boys wanna hear the rest of Nathan's story?"

"Damn right we do!" blurted Alex in a humorous tone from across the room. "Will you please, Israel, just read."

"Alright, alright," he sputtered in a friendly way, "since you asked so kindly."

"'After reciting the colony's resolves to his peers from a chamber railing,'" Israel continued to read as the men of the tavern anxiously listened, "'Mr. Henry was reported to have added some final spirited thoughts. He stood and gripped the lapel of his coat before those assembled, then thrusting a fist into the House of Burgesses air, boldly exclaimed, 'Caesar had his Brutus, Charles the First his Cromwell, and George the Third may profit by their example.' Then with a swooshing swing of his fist, he defiantly declared, 'If this be treason, make the most of it!'

"'As his words echoed about the chamber amid a spattering of cheers, one witness would explain, a few delegates more loyal to the king leapt to their feet with scornful shouts of, 'Treasonous, Mr. Henry, treason, treason!'"

Suddenly Mr. Spoons blurted, "Treason, hell!" from his table right of the fireplace stones, an emotional blast Ethan said was sure to have raced across the village field to swirl about the town. "I say bloody good, to that Mr. Patrick Henry!" he added as others joined with robust hoots while thrusting their goblets, mugs and spirits into the tavern air.

"Well said, Alex," injected Ethan's father in what seemed a calming, dutiful way. "It looks like we're all of the same persuasion here. I know most of us are not inherently defiant toward the crown, but on this Stamp Act, I suspect we are. Alright, if you please, Israel, let's hear the rest of Nathan's story."

"'But that spirit aroused by Mr. Henry began to soon fade,'" explained Israel as he continued to read, "'when determination by some began to wane and fear began to awaken in others. The House of Burgesses reassembled shortly before noon the following day without Patrick Henry, only now many of the men were less concerned about liberties than exposing the Colony of Virginia to the hath of the crown. And although this new gathering with more loyal men agreed in essence with most of the resolutions spouted the day before, it wallowed in caution and slashed that fifth statement from its final declaration.

"'In the final days of May the colony's assembly approved its revised document, calling their four statements the *Virginia Resolves*. Within days officious copies of quilled parchment were tucked into leather satchels and dispatched by special swift riders to the core committee of correspondence of every colony, and distributed to printers in hundreds of ports, villages and towns for publishing in a slew of pamphlets and papers. The Colony of Virginia has exposed its opposition to the king's Stamp Act, for all those of the colonies and the royals of London to see.

"'This humble Lexington printer is proud of Mr. Henry," Israel continued after a quick taste of wine, "and to know Sam Adams of Boston, and hope many colonists soon feel the same. And I'm proud to be involved, in my own little way, of expressing opposition to that intrusive Stamp Act, a defiance inspired by daring colonists like those of Virginia. I draw upon a few words of Mr. Adams recently printed in the Independent Advertiser over in Boston, thoughts which I suspect may help sprout awareness in all of us. 'Although those Virginia resolves are poignant,' quilled Sam only days ago, 'it is unfortunate that some men more loyal to the crown determined it proper to cast ignoble caution upon the valor displayed by Patrick Henry, a patriot I know as friend. Bostonians awake, and grasp the reins of liberty!'

"'This is my hope for Middlesex County and all of Massachusetts Bay, my plea to heed the words of Sam Adams and the resolves of Virginia spurred by Patrick Henry, and for every hamlet, village and town to support our noble cause. To allow this hour to pass in silent passivity, to numbingly accept this encroaching erosion of our fundamental rights, is to invite darkness to shroud the colonies. Join those daring to meet this moment with stern conviction, to come to the aid of this common cause, and support our gathering of patriots this fall in the port of New York. Our united cries from our Stamp Act Congress will cause the panes of London to shudder, and until King George strikes that dreadful act, we beseech all colonists to resist its unjust terms, defy that royal stamp and bloody tax. We shall never succumb!'"

Israel pressed the Gazette to his table, gripped his goblet and passionately exclaimed, "Well done, Nathan," while thrusting his wine into the afternoon air amidst a chorus of "hear, hear" being spattered about the tavern.

"Bloody good," Joe boldly uttered to Ethan's father. "Well done indeed, Nathan."

Ethan's father twisted and glanced to Ethan quietly watching near the kitchen door, and with an agreeing grin, sputtered a whisper only Ethan could hear, "I'm proud of you, son." Then twisting in his chair to face the others and Israel calmly sipping wine across the tavern floor, he boasted in a spirited tone, "Nathan did a fine job with his words, fine job indeed. Thank you, Israel."

"He sure did," Alex Spoons quickly agreed, "quilled them words real good. I agree, we colonists should defy that Stamp Act, and he's right about us supportin that congress they're puttin together down there. I think we all gotta think hard about these things, gentlemen, and realize what that bloody act will do to us here in Massachusetts Bay, in all the colonies. Yep, we gotta pull together."

"What did Nathan call that meeting in October, that assembly in New York?" asked Sam Burns in a shy way, Lexington's blacksmith quietly sipping ale at a table near the stairs to the right.

"The Stamp Act Congress," spouted a tidily dressed man gripping a cup of rum at a nearby table, an inquisitive elder traveling from the sea hamlet of Salem to the village of Concord five miles west. "I think it's a superb idea, something all free colonists should support."

"Ethan," whispered his father in a respectful tone while twisting in his chair, "would you fill the cups and mugs of all these fine gentlemen, please."

"I sure will," Ethan dutifully said, spurting behind the barreled bar to fill a big tin with Boston ale, then rushing about the tavern and topping each mug. And as his father chatted with his old farming friend Joe, an expression of fatherly pride brushed across his face, Ethan gripped a few bottles of wine, rye whiskey and rum and dashed about the room filling goblets, cups and tins.

"Thanks, Ethan," his father graciously said. "I don't know what I'd do without you."

Ethan said that as he dashed about the tavern that afternoon to pour more spirits for every man, his thoughts were consumed by the words Israel Jacob had read. And although he had helped prepare and was aware of the notions Mr. Giles printed in that Gazette, he was still captivated by Nathan's words and the moxie displayed by Mr. Adams and those Colony of Virginia men. Yet perhaps it was the fearless lines of Patrick Henry that moved Ethan the most, compelling words that gripped his soul while whispering of peril. "As Israel recited those daring lines," he softly confided, "I wondered of our colonial future, of the dangers lurking in the shadows."

That pivotal summer of 1765 continued until vanishing with the leaves of fall, with Ethan tending to his chores at his father's tavern and learning the printing trade more each day with Mr. Giles. While I in Germantown turned fifteen that July, and as in summers before, helped mother with household things like sewing and baking. I'd stitch father new shirts and darn wearing socks, stir spicy stews and roast little fowls and beasts, and bake crispy rolls and tasty pies and treats. And on warm starry nights I'd mold thin candles by a beam of the moon or mend a summer dress with gentle weaves of silken thread, or bonnets of yellow and blue.

It was during those summer days that Ethan also began striving to quill more intimate thoughts during quiet moments at the print shop or calming nights alone in his tavern room. He began to realize that what appealed to him most was the mystery of stringing words in rhythmic expressions, composing lines of poetry. Looking back I suppose it was his inevitable course, for he always seemed to view so much in a mystical way, perhaps delving into his soul more than most, searching for truths in life. Maybe it was his soft passion for simple things, the innocence of chirping birds, or the serenity he found amidst a whistling wind or trickling stream of spring.

Ethan once said that Mr. Giles had promised to print a few of his poetic creations someday, and that knowing that made him feel good, as if he had a special purpose in life. Yet he also knew that he was still wandering about his youth, that there was so much he needed to experience, so much he needed to learn of quilling visions, passions and thoughts. And he also believed his future would dwell somewhere in the printing trade, and he wanted to uncover the essence of expressing ideas with broadsides, periodicals, pamphlets and papers.

He began to increasingly dwell upon the intricate workings of Mr. Giles' print shop, on the array of various publications and details of producing the Lexington Gazette, and began to quill his thoughts and feelings upon little scraps of parchment, stuffing those intrigues into the pocket of his breeches. Then one day the coming fall that little collection came to fruition, for it helped him form some words and lines of passion. "I quilled my first tiny poem, Andrea," he sweetly whispered in a shy way, "by the pulsating flame of a candle that chilly autumn night. It was rather simple, just a few youthful stanzas, but they were mine, Andrea, inspired by things I was feeling."

While Ethan was expanding his skills and thoughts in Lexington that summer and fall of 1765, rumors began to sweep across the colonies and into my Germantown about a special group some spirited men had formed in Boston. There were soon stories printed in the Pennsylvania Evening Post too, reports I'd read when visiting mother's nursing friend at the hospital on Saturday afternoons or in the newspaper father brought home in those days. Then within weeks, new rumors began to swirl about more of those determined groups sprouting in ports, villages and towns throughout all the colonies, down in Philadelphia too.

Some say that most members of those groups were not the wealthier of the colonies such as doctors, merchants, lawyers or gentry, but were more laborious men like shopkeepers, tradesmen, dockworkers and farmers. Ethan once said that the first group of all was formed in Boston that summer, and had brushed itself with a rather innocuous name, calling their gathering the *loyal nine*. Along with other groups soon to sprout, those men of Boston tended to focus on arousing passionate opposition to that Stamp Act, while spurring distrust of London and the colony's Royal Governor Bernard.

It wasn't long before that Boston group, soon followed by the others forming in villages and towns that summer and fall throughout Massachusetts Bay and all the colonies, decided to alter its identity to more closely align with its defiant beliefs, changing its name to the *Sons of Liberty*. I remember how those groups seemed so secretive in those days, always dwelling in the shadows of privacy by meeting in secluded places or gathering in innocent ways that appeared rather harmless, and almost always after dusk. For in the years before the war, for colonists to assemble in such ways, to gather without the blessing of their royal governor, invited the wrath of the crown.

Ethan once said that he'd hear rumors all the way out in Lexington about meetings of the Boston sons, about gatherings after sunset on the grass of the common now and then too, at a spirited place near Hanover Square and the cobblestones of Essex and Orange. They'd meet beneath the spraying limbs of an aging elm sprouting from the grass near that corner, and engage in intense discussions beneath the stars about the latest actions of parliament and the king or unjust policy implemented by their scorned Royal Governor Bernard. Most emphatically I suppose, they'd rail against duties and taxes coming from London, and scheme to thwart the king's customs men and loyal colonists supporting the crown while always plotting ways to stymie enforcement of that despised Stamp Act.

Early in that fall there were some disturbing stories swirling about my Colony of Pennsylvania about that Boston group, frightening rumors of imaginary executions amidst the glow of ugly torches in the eerie mist of a late Saturday night. They say a mob of disgruntled sons tied cords of twine about the necks of a pair of stuffed dummies designed to represent the king's tax agents, then hanged those bundles of straw from a twisting limb of that aging elm. Some even said that just before midnight a gaggle of those inspired men began to whip those dangling dummies with a vengeance, as if trying to rid the colonies of a medieval ill with each thrash of hickory sticks.

As stories about that defiant hanging swept across the hills and fields into nearby villages and towns, many colonists began creaking into Boston in buggies and wagons or strolling the cobblestones to see and touch that mystical elm rising from the grass of the common. Ethan said it was just a tree like thousands across the colony, a white elm of deciduous Ulmus if I recall, no more than four feet thick with limbs sprouting high and wide. It was a simple tree with little purple petals blooming in spring and green prickly leaves smothering its limbs in summer, a blanket that had already begun to turn and fall in a spray of yellows, oranges and reds as of that autumn night, an inspiring elm Bostonians began to call their liberty tree.

Soon sons of liberty groups north and south were claiming their own liberty trees in town squares and village greens, watering each with the ideals flourishing in Ethan's Boston and draping inspiring banners and spirited lanterns from their limbs of elm and oak. I remember the special tree in my Germantown, knotted and twisted oak rising some fifty feet from the northeast corner of the village square, and can still see the thin pole twined to its bark now and then. Some of the boys at my schoolhouse said that when a tatted strip of yellow cloth was dangled from that pole, it was a signal for our small sons of liberty group to gather about the tree that night.

Our special tree in Germantown began to instill a tingling sense of colonial patriotism inside me in those days, just as all those other trees did for women, children and men throughout the colonies. I suppose those trees were becoming an inspiring symbol for the notions of freedom simmering the colonies back then, and each time I passed our Germantown tree in the wagon with mother and father or strolled by with a friend after school that fall, its vision would remind me of the spirited things taking place about the colonies. Even after all these years, I can feel how its enlightening limbs represented the notions of liberty brewing up in Ethan's Boston, ideals that were filtering down through all the colonies, a special tree that reminded all of us of what some viewed as the increasing infringement of our colonial rights by London.

Many sons of liberty groups were said to have catchy little defiant phrases in those days, yet there was one string of words most were spouting in villages and towns across the colonies, a demanding line created in Boston years before. They were printing its words on broadside sheets and stitching that line to colorful banners, and repeating that phrase on cobblestone streets and wharfs and docks, in taverns, churches and shops. "No taxation without representation!" could be heard erupting from spirited gatherings throughout the colonies from Georgia, Virginia and Maryland to New Hampshire, Connecticut and Ethan's Massachusetts Bay. It was a rebellious phrase father insisted never be spoken in our home, declaring such a thing disloyal to the king, a daring line I once heard Quaker friends opposed to that Stamp Act secretly whispering in a secluded corner of our meeting house.

Ethan once told me that the sons of liberty in Boston had a way of corralling the finest of men, colonists in positions to help promote its spirited agenda, daring merchants, tradesmen and printers like Mr. Giles of Lexington with his Gazette, and John Gill and Ben Edes with their Boston Gazette and Country Journal. By fall the sons of Boston were said to have over a thousand members, an array of enlightened colonists from young boys to older men, a group some believed was being guided by Ebenezer McIntosh, a shoemaker with a little cobbler's shop south of the common. Yet Ethan said Mr. Giles knew better, revealing once that the group in Boston was secretly directed by Sam Adams, with Mr. Hancock providing most of the shillings and pounds.

I think it was shortly after Ethan and I first met that cold March night all those years ago, when he confided in a letter about something he'd seen in those early days of the Boston sons, describing it as an "alarming Saturday" in those early weeks of fall. He revealed how a pair of merchants traveling to Boston from a village west of Concord had stopped at his father's Buckman Tavern around noon that day, hungry for some steaming stew and craving a tin or two of rum. "They were a few years younger than dad," he quilled, "and after talking with dad that afternoon in a secretive, hushing way, they told him about a gathering of Boston's sons that was to take place at the liberty tree on the common after dusk that night. I had never been to one of those meetings, Andrea, and desperately wanted to see what it was all about."

Ethan talked with his father about his desire to attend the gathering that night before discussing a few related things with Mr. Giles at the print shop, then saddled his tan colt Cato an hour or so before dusk and galloped southeast along the dust of the Massachusetts Road. Yet rather than ferrying across the harbor waters from the Charlestown docks, Ethan pivoted south through the village of Cambridge and across the Charles River on the weathered elm planks of the aging bridge into Roxbury, then dashed through the narrows north into Boston.

Night was slowly taking hold as Ethan trotted into Boston, and amidst the cadence of Cato's iron shoes clumping into dirt paths before scraping the cobblestones, he could see glowing lamps and flickering candles glistening against the window panes of tiny shops and little homes. And as he eased his trot along the southern edge of the common and slowly rode near the grass toward that liberty tree, Ethan could sense his thoughts wandering. He recalled inspiring words of Sam Adams and spirited printings of Mr. Giles, and remembered the intricacies of why many of Boston and Massachusetts Bay despised that Stamp Act.

"Mr. Adams advocated for respectful resistance," Ethan had quilled, "encouraging colonists to shun that act's unjust tax, and never shied from calling for defiance of other discouraging things coming from our royal governor and London. Along with Mr. Giles and others, he spoke of civility in action and words, sometimes using intriguing phrases like, 'Wits tame the hemlock of violence, soothing the bosom of resistance, at least until our liberties are attacked.'" Ethan supported such notions of persuasion in those early days, while despising the callous use of force, and confessed how disturbed he was of what he witnessed that night. "I saw an ugliness that dwelled inside a few Boston men, angry colonists spewing repulsively vengeful things, a madness that seemed to erupt from dark recesses of desperate men."

Ethan climbed from his saddle to the damp cobblestones near the common, and beneath a tranquil spray of evening stars, could see a few dozen sons of liberty men gripping flaming torches near that special elm. As he slowly stepped closer across the cool grass, he watched as some of those angry men twisted twine about a limb and dangled a cloth dummy stuffed of hay, its neck bundled tight in a grisly loop. Ethan would soon discover that amid defiling hollers and hoots they had hanged the caricature of Andy Oliver, the unfortunate loyal Bostonian who had been picked by Royal Governor Bernard to ensure compliance of the crown's Stamp Act.

But the hanging of that strange stuffed man from that liberty limb failed to slake the manic euphoria burning inside those men. As Ethan watched through the dark in a bewildering gaze, his insides now gripped by a frightening unease, he could sense that all those Bostonians had become a mob wielding pulsing torch flames. It was as if they had transformed beneath all those autumn stars from a group of concerned colonists into a mass of frenzied men, and in what Ethan described as a moment of scorching madness, they determined it their duty to unleash their remaining wrath upon Mr. Oliver.

Amid hoots, shadows, hollers and flames, one of the sons toppled that dangling dummy to the cool dew with a slash of the twine, and as an angry man tucked that bundle of straw beneath his arms, that mob of Bostonians, torches ablaze, began moving west across the mushy common toward the Charles River and the cobblestones of Kilby Street. Ethan nervously followed from a short distance in the dark until all those men finally reached Mr. Oliver's house, then watched as they huddled in a delirious circle upon the lawn of the governor's loyal friend. "I could see a man and women inside the bricks, Andrea, and some children too, their faces pressed to the panes in a horrified gaze. They just stared with fright in their eyes, bearing witness to the evil about to be unleashed by those inflamed men."

Tucked in the shadows of a nearby haven, Ethan watched as those Boston sons gathered and stacked branches and twigs before igniting it all with hateful flames right there on the grass of the tax collector's house, and in what seemed abandonment of colonial decency, began to shout vile disgusts into the night air. Then, as the glow of the blaze danced on the dew of the cobblestones and glistened off the glass of the panes, a trio of men dangled that body of hay over the flames as another sliced off its head with a crazed slash of a long curving knife. It was at that moment when Ethan realized that any semblance of civility had vanished into the night, and as the mob raged about the flickering flames, their sordid howls raced Boston's streets and swept into the hills across the river.

To Ethan's stunned surprise, he discovered that their lust for mayhem had yet to be satisfied, following those men as they strutted upon the cobblestones to the slopes of a nearby hill. He watched in a hushed gaze as they piled more branches and twigs in the shifting shadows then torched their angst into a fiery fury. "The mob seemed mindless by then," he observed with his quill, "men gripped in their own fears, grappling with lonely lives. They tossed what remained of that dummy into the fire, and as it flared into flames, the sons and others bellowed gruesome cries into the Boston night. I remember asking myself, Andrea, what they were so angry about. I wondered if perhaps, in a diabolical way, they believed they were not only destroying an image of the crown's agents, but King George and his royal governor too."

Although still rather young, not quite fifteen as of that fall, Ethan would later confide that he was appalled at what he had seen that autumn night, and vowed never to engage in such senseless acts. He seemed to understand that such abandonment of civility was in conflict with his soul, and hoped that in the months to come colonists would shun such destructive deeds when showing disapproval of the crown. It was in the weeks that followed that he began to truly wonder of just what kind of role he might play to address the troubles simmering about the colonies in the months and years to come. He somehow knew that the path he'd choose would be stroked with a quill, believing that his fate was not twined to the madness he had witnessed that night, but rested with the nurturing of liberty.

I remember the dreadful rumors filtering into Germantown about what the sons of liberty were doing up in Ethan's Boston that fall, and of stories of similar events erupting about Massachusetts Bay and other colonies. Frightening reports were being printed in Philadelphia's Evening Post and Pennsylvania Gazette too, revelations of things like the sons in the port of New York expressing their displeasure with that Stamp Act by torching crates of that special royal parchment. They were destroying the cherished property of men loyal to London too, such as the group that set Royal Governor Cadwallader's carriage ablaze as an eerie mist roamed the midnight harbor.

There were rumors of events like those happening all over the colonies, some tainted by mindless acts and others brushed with benign scripts of wit, stories of frustrated colonists gathering just south in Philadelphia and down in Charles Towne and Savannah, and over in Williamsburg in the Colony of Virginia. They were daring groups strutting muddied roads and cobblestone streets boasting spirited notions of freedom, with some expressing their displeasures while brandishing banners and signs taunting the king and his royal governors. One group of sons down in Dover were said to be insisting that London "scrap that bloody Stamp Act" while waving banners decrying it to be "the folly of England, the ruin of America." And others were venting frustrations of that impending tax by repeating what Boston had done, torching innocent dummies dangling liberty trees.

Still other groups preferred to dwell more closely into the realm of intimidation, actions father once said were "expressions of ignorant madness," and soon the Pennsylvania Gazette confirmed rumors about a series of mindless events that happened in ports and villages in several colonies like Maryland, Georgia, Delaware and New York. One witness told of an angry mob in the village of New Bern in the Colony of North Carolina, explaining how dozens of sons of liberty men were determined to express their disapproval of colonists who loyally supported the king and his Stamp Act. "They smashed the door of the crown's customs house," he nervously recalled, "and snatched a pair of tax collecting men from their chairs. I watched with others as they dragged em to the stones of the street, each frantically flailing his arms."

Several of those disgruntled colonists proceeded to brush those agents with a layer of pungent dark slime from a steamy oak bucket, while others with fury flaring their eyes tossed hundreds of colorful feathers over the goo from several big sacks, smelly rachis, quills and barbs plucked from scurrying fowl. "Then some of them sons began pushin and shovin them poor men to the cobblestones," that villager conveyed, "while others began tuggin and draggin them agents about the street as villagers taunted and jeered, women and children too." It was events like that, episodes of angry colonists unleashing unflattering desires without a semblance of empathy, events that seemed to spur more of the same in those days, that caused Ethan to question our colonial path, along with others like me. There was a stench that wafted the hours back then, an ugly odor that at times, I still smell to this day.

"Did Ethan join one of those groups, grandma?" interrupted Samuel with a squinting glance while nudging his chair into a robust rock. "Was he part of those sons of liberty?"

I could sense a disapproving tinge in Samuel's tone, as if someone from his youth had somehow strayed from their ways or even betrayed him, or perhaps he was simply struggling to understand things he couldn't possible know. "No, Ethan wasn't a son then," I whispered in a melancholy way while gazing to pink mountain laurels fluttering in the warming afternoon winds. "Not in those early days."

As Samuel peered to those distant elms once again, their gentle leaves twirling easy in the summer breeze, I pressed to the slats of my chair, and in a softer rock, explained, "Ethan was a peaceful, gentle man, Samuel, and disliked very much, those kinds of disturbing things. Yet, I must say, he once told me that in those early hours, before such events had occurred, he had thoughts of joining the sons. Just as many in those days, I think Ethan understood the reasons those groups were formed, and in a colonist's way, why some chose to express disapproval in such vile ways. But that wasn't Ethan. Oh, he wanted to do his part to help in the simmering dispute against the crown, against that Stamp Act, and knew those men of Boston were right, colonists like Mr. Otis, Adams and Hancock. Only, Ethan wanted to use his wits and quill."

"You know, grandma," Samuel replied in a reassuring way, "I didn't know Ethan, until today, yet it makes me feel good to hear you say that." Then pivoting his thoughts he curiously added, "Was Mr. Adams involved in the fiery things that night in Boston, when Ethan was there?"

"There were some rumors in those days that maybe he was, yet Ethan once said he hadn't seen him that night. Although it seems Sam Adams was rather influential with that Boston group, in a secretive way, with all the sons of Massachusetts Bay, Ethan always believed that he wouldn't condone such senseless acts. Could he spur a disgruntled crowd with his spirited words, incite colonials to decry London's acts? Yes, he could. Would he encourage the burning of property, the torture of people? I don't think so. No, Samuel, he chose to use words to encourage colonists to support that congress assembling that fall, to show disapproval of the crown and support for liberty."

"I want to believe you, grandma, yet I can't help but feel a doubt. Maybe I just don't understand what happened back then, don't know enough about those days, those years before the war."

"I understand, really I do, and have heard doubts from others before. Yet, Ethan believed Mr. Adams shunned those kinds of things in those days, and so do I. You know, Samuel, there were stories after the war that sometimes those who guided the sons didn't always have viable control of those spirited men, and sometimes, those groups would do things people like Mr. Adams didn't approve."

"Oh, I guess I hadn't thought of that. Now I know I need to know more, need to hear your whole story. Tell me, grandma, what happened in those days."

As Samuel stared into the July winds, waiting for my coming words with each rock, I slowly slid my hand into the pocket of my summer dress and nestled my fingers to the ink of Ethan's poem. No matter how distant those days have become, no matter the wrinkling of skin and greying of hair, the visions of those precious hours when Ethan and I were so young, always soothes my soul. My eyes began to mist with each caress of his aging words, and as I reached for memories of the colonies and the war, a tear trickled my cheek as my heart sighed for Ethan.

I remember how autumn of 1765 seemed a bit cooler than years past, and how the leaves seemed to snap their ties from summer a little sooner than before, sprays of tans, oranges, yellows and reds drifting to resting places scattered about the hills. It was during those October days when stories and rumors of that Stamp Act Congress began sweeping into ports, villages and towns, to thousands of taverns, shops, churches and homes. And there were tantalizing accounts and enlightening reports of that colonial assembly being printed in papers from Portsmouth to Savannah, Ethan's Lexington Gazette and my Pennsylvania Evening Post too.

They had gathered in a stone building most viewed as the village hall, an impressive structure mortared some sixty years before near the southern rocks of the Island of Manhattan, not far from Trinity Church. Slender windows encrusted both floors, dozens of square panes peering over the port of New York and the cobblestones of Wall and Broad streets, and a swath of stone steps reached toward a trio of elm doors. Ethan later confided that he once trotted past that hall during the war, and marveled how majestic its chimneys of red bricks appeared rising into the harbor air. But it was the open expanse above the entry doors that seemed to please his senses the most, a stately space embedded below an ornate façade amid white pillars of stone. They say aristocratic men would boast London proclamations from that perch, spouting royal embellishments to industrious colonists.

The Evening Post soon revealed that not all colonies chose to send delegates to that Stamp Act Congress, an act of timidity spurred by reluctance to display opposition to King George, parliament and his royal governors. And it seems that some delegates from the colonies which did send men chose to avoid boisterous expressions of discontent with the crown, deciding not to quill names to parchment or display vigorous opposition to that despotic act. The Post suggested that some colonies didn't want to antagonize London, fearing the wrath of the crown, and some wondered if their words and deeds would be construed by the king as disloyally treasonous. They were fears that should have been foreseen many would say, for most delegates were also members of their colony's assembly, gatherings which served at the whim of each royal governor and owed their loyal allegiance to England and the king.

"Four colonies balked at the final moment," declared the Post, reporting that only nine colonies decided to participate in our Stamp Act Congress in the port of New York, "for reasons that remain silent or unclear. Or perhaps the colonies of Georgia, New Hampshire, North Carolina and Virginia were suddenly gripped by London's intimidations or pounded into submission by the king's royal governors." I remember hearing unflattering rumors that those four colonies had been doused with a mysterious potion of undue loyalty, and others more frightening that suggested they feared what the crown might do to each colony, particularly to the participating delegates, and their children and wives.

Those special men from nine colonies assembled in that Manhattan hall the first Monday of October that fall, and over the coming nineteen cooling days, debated their response of opposition to the crown's Stamp Act. Those colonies and delegates had cast doubts and fears to the winds many would say, showing a colonial swagger by expressing a list of misgivings about that act, while revealing their colony's futile attempts to reverse the trespasses of parliament. Some would suggest that by simply meeting, our congress displayed to doubting colonists, royal governors and the crown that our colonies could boldly gather in harmony, and others said it was the first true display of colonial cohesiveness, even more so than that meeting in Albany a decade before. I suppose it mostly showed that most of the colonies were willing to unite to express displeasure of unjust laws being spewed from London.

Yet, a cautious emphasis of anonymity and secrecy seemed to swirl about that congress that fall, for the identity of each delegate was mysteriously missing from papers and pamphlets printed from Savannah to Williamsburg, Philadelphia, Boston and the port of New York. It would be months until rumors suggested there were twenty-seven delegates in all, and it would be much longer than that, if I recall, before the names of those daring men would be revealed, years after the war.

- *Massachusetts Bay*: James Otis, Oliver Partridge and Timothy Ruggles.
- *Rhode Island*: Metcalf Bowler and Henry Ward.
- *Connecticut*: Eliphalet Dyer, William Johnson and David Rowland.
- *New York*: William Bayard, John Cruger, Leonard Lispenard, Philip Livingston, Robert Livingston
- *New Jersey*: Hendrick Fisher, Joseph Borden and Robert Ogden.
- *Pennsylvania*: George Bryan, John Dickinson and John Morton.
- *Delaware*: Thomas McKean and Caesar Rodney.

- *Maryland*: William Murdock, Thomas Ringgold and Edward Tilghman.
- *South Carolina*: Christopher Gadsden, Thomas Lynch and John Rutledge.

Ethan would later say that his colony's delegate Tim Ruggles had been chosen by the other men to preside over that congress, and that Johnny Cotton from the port of New York had been retained for a few shillings and pounds to keep the delegates supplied with candles, quills, parchment and ink, while recording the minutes of the assembly. Though not a delegate, he was tasked with quilling the ideas, positions and debates expressed by the colonial men, and was said to perform his duties well, from opening monologues the morning of the seventh until the final words were spoken on the afternoon of Friday, the Twenty-fifth of October, 1765.

Yet, for reasons unclear all these years, it seems that much of those quilled records of that Stamp Act Congress were strangely misplaced, or perhaps as some would later suggest, destroyed. After all, it was known that some delegates, out of real or perceived fears, preferred that their views be secret, a position many believe caused most of their officious proceedings to remain shrouded in mystery. Nevertheless, it wasn't long before the essence of the debates and decisions being made inside the stones of that Manhattan hall began to filter from its panes and race the woods, hills and fields to hundreds of ports, villages and towns throughout the colonies. And on a chilly October day, all those intense discussions culminated in an agreement by that congress, an enlightening document of spirited words expressing their reasons for gathering and the position of the colonies.

They titled their document a *Declaration of Rights and Grievances,* sheets of parchment reported to address over a dozen disagreements our colonies had with London, areas of contention that congress seemed to corral into four core disputes. The Pennsylvania Gazette described this document as the "unshakable resolves of the American Colonies," an officious declaration which exposed simmering troubles, and printed a few of what it called the document's fundamental truths: *Use by royal governors of Admiralty Courts is abusive, because trial by jury must be a right for all colonists. *Colonists possess the rights of Englishmen. As such, we must be afforded the same rights and privileges as all Englishmen, just as those citizens across the sea in England. *Parliament does not represent the

colonies, because the colonies do not have representation in parliament.
*Only our colonial assemblies have the right to tax the colonies.

Even though that declaration was supported by most delegates, it seems that over the remaining few days before congress disbanded, those positions were also requilled into a trio of colonial petitions. The Gazette revealed that some delegates may have quilled their names while others did not, and that one petition was for King George alone, while the other two were intended for each house of parliament, Commons and Lords. Then in the final hours of October, after congress' candles and quills had dulled and stilled, copies of that declaration were routed by swift riders to the assembly of every colony. And most boldly of all, petitions were stuffed into leather satchels and sailed to London in the hulls of perhaps the very ships which only weeks before, had brought to colonial ports crates of the crown's despised paper and stamps.

Although some colonies were absent from that special congress that fall, I remember how disapproving sentiments of all the colonies to that Stamp Act were emphatically voiced from the rolling farms of Georgia to the wilderness woods of New Hampshire. And as colonists north and south began to hear the rumors of those three petitions sailed to London, as they began to read the defiant words of congress' declaration of rights and grievances being reprinted in pamphlets and papers throughout the colonies, the simmering disapproval of that dreadful act began to spritz to a boil.

Thousands of colonists were soon gripped by the boldness espoused by those men in that Manhattan hall, and by the first snows of winter thousands more were spurred to action upon reading the sentiments being voiced and printed by daring colonists such as that Mr. Henry in the Colony of Virginia and Mr. Otis and Sam Adams in Ethan's Massachusetts Bay. Women and men throughout the colonies were snatching the reins of resistance to that Stamp Act and engaging in little bits of opposition, flaunting the demanding tax of London's law by refusing to buy products and goods molded by the crown's special paper and those royal stamps. Ethan once said that it was then, perhaps for the first time, that the colonies had truly united to show its defiance of London, displaying in words and deeds its distaste of unjust intrusions into our lives by parliament and the king.

Perhaps not understanding the crux of that royal tax in those days, I found myself naively intrigued how such a feverish intensity could explode throughout the colonies over something like a little stamp. Although I would never hold one of those royal tools some say were delicately carved of mahogany or molded of polished bronze, never even see its regal print inked to some officious document, it seems they could be found in varying shapes and designs. Father said some were reflections of roses and others showed the king's crown and sword, and some were emblazed with special words like "America" or a phrase in French warning "Evil to him who evil thinks." And all reflected the pence, shillings and pounds surrendered by colonists for the privilege of paying that stamp tax to London.

Many chose to defiantly flaunt that tax by ignoring that Stamp Act, ordinary colonists like doctors, barristers and courtroom clerks, tradesmen, shopkeepers and merchants, and most of all, Ethan would say, those who printed vital news and spirited visions like Ben Edes in Boston and Mr. Giles in Lexington. There were rumors in those days too of colonists snatching crates of those stamps and the king's special parchment, then tossing them into the waters of harbors and rivers or casting them to their doom in fiery pits. And others in villages and towns throughout the colonies daringly showed disapproval of that act by refusing to participate in the trade of English goods like spices, linens and teas sailed to the colonies by merchants of London.

Yet one of the more troubling things happening as the new year began were the increasing clashes between colonists and the king's tax men. They were rumors of thunderous defiance being spread by swift riders and exposed in pamphlets and papers throughout the colonies, disturbing stories sweeping across the sea to the halls of London. But perhaps the most consequential of these events was the damage being inflicted upon the wealth of English merchants, loyal men simply striving to parlay their goods in the colonies. It was then, when things began to change.

Ethan once told me about something Mr. Giles printed in his Lexington Gazette in the first weeks of January 1766, shortly after his fifteenth birthday. "Mr. Giles and I were setting type for his story, when he gruntingly sputtered, 'the king's plans are dead.' He was about to publish a string of inciting thoughts, Andrea, ideas he and others in Boston, in all the colonies, had been waiting so long to print. And I remember his words so well, defiant lines spouting, 'King George is feeling our wrath. The rejection by the colonies of that bloody Stamp Act is taking a crushing toll upon London. Now, as this new year begins, parliament will soon surely fold.'"

The colonies' dispute was beginning to truly tarnish the coffers of London, for the opposition to that act by so many was thwarting the ability of royal governors to collect what the crown viewed as its rightful tax. Yet, I suppose more disturbing to those across the sea was that our concerted efforts were beginning to stymy the powers of the king and his ministers in their despotic attempt to enforce their will upon the colonies. "Parliament must recognize the error of its ways," Mr. Giles summed in his Gazette, "and King George must succumb to our colonies' righteous dispute. The time has come, to cast parliament's abomination to the ashes of history!"

The Evening Post would later suggest that one of the final displays of colonial disapproval of that fractious act, a personal appeal many believe spurred London's reversal, were daring words spouted by Doctor Franklin to a fidgeting parliament. "His reasoned dissertation was impeccable," reported the Post, "and his analytical plea for parliament to recognize the folly of its attempt to enrich the king's coffer with that unjust tax, was described by some as mesmerizing. 'In furtherance of pleasant relations with His Majesty King George,' he boldly advised the House of Commons, 'your loyal colonies pray for the repeal of this nonsense, this malignancy called the Stamp Act.'" Then later that spring rumors began to swirl about the colonies that the king and his ministers had surrendered, had repealed that divisive act on a Tuesday afternoon during a chilling rain, the Eighteenth of March, 1766.

I can still hear the ring of our Germantown bell and the faint dings filtering north through the woods and hills from Philadelphia early that May, wondrous revelations of parliament's repeal. I'd later hear that those bells rang from towers, steeples and halls in ports, villages and towns throughout the colonies for hours in those days, from Georgia and South Carolina to the colonies of Connecticut and New Hampshire, even the spirited bell dangling in Ethan's Lexington.

As joyous as those celebrations were over the demise of that dreaded act, the colonies' feelings of jubilation were soon doused by disturbing rumors that King George and his ministers had not repealed that law out of some sense of justice, but rather to enact more sinister things to enhance the powers of the crown. Ethan would later say that there was no mention from parliament that spring of what the Colony of Virginia had expressed in its resolutions, nor was there any semblance of recognition of what Doctor Franklin had so eloquently espoused. And he said Mr. Giles would sputter at his printing press that the colonial concerns quilled the fall before by our Stamp Act Congress had been ignored, silenced beneath the cobblestones of London.

"Parliament disparages the colonies once again!" exploded the Pennsylvania Gazette near the middle of May, a gloomy sentiment that was being printed throughout the colonies. "As the king's men in London pacified colonists in America by reversing that Stamp Act, they refused to acknowledge or disclose our righteous reasons for denouncing that despicable act. And at the precise moment of rescission, parliament issued a condescending claim that it maintains an unyielding authority to enact laws binding upon the colonies, declaring that the colonies remain submissive to the king."

"Whereas the continuance of the said act would be attended with many inconveniences," Charles Watson-Wentworth, the Second Marquess of Rockingham was reported to have spouted to a raucous parliament, "it also exposes the entrepreneurs of our kingdom to unhealthy consequences. Therefore, without the slightest surrender of His Majesty's powers, nor those of this parliament, the act is hereby rescinded."

I remember how some in the colonies were mockingly referring to Prime Minister Rockingham's words as "London's declaratory act," and how his oppressive attitude was seen by some as exposing the essence of King George's tyrannical lust for control over the hearts and souls of his subjects in the colonies. Some were also saying that such positions by the crown reflected London's true intent to someday enact other laws to shackle the colonies, actions sure to spur colonial passions for rights and liberties.

Ethan would later confide that when he learned of the prime minister's words in Mr. Giles' Lexington Gazette the first weeks of June, a swell of patriot feelings surged his soul. "I knew at that moment," he whispered to me, "that my youthful passion would flow in a poem." He called it *a roiling sea*, and although just eight lines of a pair of stanzas, Ethan said Mr. Giles remained true to his word, printing his little poem early that summer.

*parliament's unjust stamp stains our souls, shackles our freedom
liberty's sons rise, shout nay, courageous men petition a kingdom
these lands tis ours we say, american villages and towns, colonies
repress no more, release our thoughts, sever chains cast upon we*

*shield our rights from a consuming crown, heaven guide our way
tatter shutters of our eyes, rays of justice spray across our new day
providence brush our waters, bathe our souls in unyielding liberty
spur ideals with your righteous hand, protect us from a roiling sea*

Some would later say that 1765 was the year from whence our destiny began to erupt from some mysterious place, as if a radiant star streaking across the heavens. And although that Stamp Act had been banished by spring of the following year, its impact seemed to have slashed the remnants of colonial content, spilling the first drops of our spirit while casting a menacing shadow upon all of us. I suppose it was during those hours of my fifteenth year that the seeds of colonial unity had been planted into the soils of our fields, and the tilling of restless souls thirsting for liberty began to truly take hold.

Chapter VII

Scarlet Apple Blossom

The searing August sun had slowly faded from the hills and fields of Middlesex County, vanishing somewhere beyond the forests and Taconic peaks along the western frontier of the Colony of Massachusetts Bay. Gazing into the encroaching dark of tiny twinkles bursting across the 1766 summer sky, Ethan lazily peered into the emerging spray of pulsating stars, his fingers gently clasped beneath his hair, his mind calming with the cooling grass. From atop his lonely Lexington hill he swept his stare across the mystical depths of the warm night, and for a while watched a bright dot glowing above the sea, his mind reaching for its tiny rainbow rings in search of dreams.

He wondered of others who might be dwelling somewhere in the shadows of that endless expanse, perhaps strange young men gazing as he that very moment upon a faraway world, beings unable to feel the turmoil beginning to shudder our colonial soil. As he searched the night sky brushed of quivering lights spritzed dreams, the smell of melons sprouting nearby fields and the sweet scent of marigolds in bloom filtered about the village and up the slopes of his mother's hill. As a distant little beast howled the night, Ethan stretched beneath that sparkling spray and listened to the soothing song of leaves rustling in the summer breeze.

It was that spiritual rise of brush and grass just off the stones of Harrington Road southwest of his father's tavern, slopes which slowly peaked upon a serene plateau, a special hill with some elms and oaks keeping watch upon the village and its past. The white slats of that aging fence surrounded the edges of the soil and comforting grass, a solemn shield protecting villagers in eternal rest, its creaky gate loosely latched. And peeking in the northeast shadows just below the hill was the little cross atop his mother's steeple, reaching for the stars bathing the night.

Ethan propped his head off the soothing grass and glanced east down the hill over the village, to the darkness hovering his Lexington field and to candles and lamps flickering upon the glass of merchant shops. He could see a lone candle's flame inside a corner window of his father's Buckman Tavern, and marveled at the shades of yellows, oranges and reds dancing the panes of village cottages and homes. As he gazed upon the array of glistening glows, he wondered if their little flames brought calm to lonely souls, pulsating flickers to dine and reflect by, to douse anguishing troubles with numbing spirits by, wondering of the truths of life.

Suddenly the trotting sounds of a passing rider swept the darkness up the hill, iron hooves galloping east through the village on the ruts and stones of the Massachusetts Road toward the docks of Boston. Ethan rested back once again as the pounding slowly faded, pressing his hair to the cup of his fingers upon the cooling grass, then gazed to the mysteries dazzling the night. "That was always my special place, Andrea," he once whispered amid a soft summer rain. "I'm just able to ease my mind up on that hill, reflect on things, escape from the challenges of life, if only for a little while. Most of all, I suppose, I feel close to mom up there. I just talk with her, telling her things no one else knows. And sometimes, I'll just lie upon her grass and pray."

Stretched upon the moistening grass as a spec of sparkling white streaked across the night, Ethan could feel his heart pounding as his tan breeches crossed near the knees and his bare feet taunted the summer breeze. He watched that little star dash the dark, its thin trail stretching from the wilderness to the sea, and as it slowly vanished he wondered how it was so pure and free. "For a moment I felt I could snatch its sparkling tail," he confessed, "and then, it was gone. That's when I began to feel alone, my thoughts drifting to memories. It was as if mom was lying with me, and in a calming way, I could feel her touch. She was always so kind, Andrea, not just to me, but many, and had a magical way of understanding my feelings. I guess I missed her just a bit more that night."

Ethan entwined his fingers more tightly while gazing to the twinkling sky, and could feel his heart pound a little harder as a mist brushed his eyes and his soul reached for memories. Then a tear gently trickled past his ear and softly splashed to the summer grass, a release of loneliness he'd held inside perhaps too long, a youthful yearning for his mother. Although only fifteen on that summer night, he seemed to understand that releasing his buried feelings was a good thing, helped him touch the delicate truths of life, and as another memory dripped to the grass, Ethan gathered his thoughts and propping to his elbows. He peered down his chest past his breeches and over his airing toes, and beneath all those stars sparkling the night, gazed at the weathered stone thrusting into the dark. It was a thick sheet of white marble some two feet wide, a cold slab shaped and chiseled five years before in a mason shop near the eastern docks of Boston.

That chilling memoriam was surrounded by dozens of crosses and stones rising from the soil of that solemn hill that August night, a few tattered and listing, each expressing a tale of Lexington's past, of lives and passions lost. Ethan stared to the quiet marble protruding the grass near his feet, and as if in a hypnotic trance, gazed to the numbers and words etched into the stone glistening in the starlight. *Elizabeth McCully Sheehan* was tenderly chiseled to the face of that slowly arching slab, just above the caring words, *Loving Wife & Mother. October 5, 1725 - November 20, 1761.* And for a moment he stared to the little angels etched in the corners of the stone, their gentle wings guiding his mother home.

"I miss you, mom," Ethan whispered into the night, hoping she could magically hear. "I love you," he confessed upon her grave, his eyes fixed on those angels etched in stone, his pangs oozing into the grass. "It helps to come here, mom, be close to you, and just listen to the sounds of the night. You know, sometimes, it's as though you're lying right here, with me."

Then he stared to the stone as if it possessed some mystical power, gazing to the thin dark streams streaking from those angels and words as if trickling tears, and wondered of his life. "What is my destiny?" he softly asked, peering to silent wings. "Who am I to be? Is there a love out there, a passion so strong it's hard to breathe, waiting for me? Does such a dream even exist? What shall my days bring, mom, tell me?" Only the soft sounds of the village and gently rustling leaves could be heard brushing the hill, and as a solemn hush draped his mother's stone, he dabbed a tear and sputtered, "Oh, mom, how I wish you could talk with me."

He pressed his elbows deeper into his mother's soil and gazed to the spray of tiny spheres sparkling the dark, and felt a loneliness brush his soul as it had so many times on that village hill. A warm summer wind tossed his hair and kissed the crosses, grass and stones as faint sounds of the village hovered those hallowed slopes, a serene symphony that gently settled upon his mother's resting place. "I had been to that special spot many times before," Ethan tenderly revealed, "on misty days and quiet nights of spring, summer and fall, during the snows of winter too. But on that August night, Andrea, there was a mystical smell about the air, and I found myself wondering if mom could somehow speak to me. I wondered, maybe, she might find a way to touch my soul."

Ethan rested back to the solemn grass of his mother's grave, lying quiet and still, listening to the pounding of his heart beneath the spray of stars, then closed his eyes and searched for her touch. He longed to hear words she had spoken many years before, and as he snapped his gaze back into the night, he discovered her wisdom had dwelled deep within all along. "It was like magic," he confessed to me, "yet more spiritual, Andrea, as if an angel's wings had gently brushed my cheek. 'Trust in yourself, Ethan,' I could hear her words whisper to me, 'and find happiness in what burns in your soul. Do not fear the dark, for a wondrous love awaits you. Yet most of all, my little Ethan, have the courage to follow the path which beats in your heart."

I could feel Ethan's passion when he spoke of those things so many years ago, words which revealed how he missed his mother so, and sensed the depth of loneliness which at times gripped his soul. Although he had been with his father each day since his mother's final breath on that chilling autumn night, helping about the farm and tending to chores in their Lexington tavern, I could feel that his mother seemed to hold a precious place in his heart. Yes, he knew his father loved him, cared and listened to his concerns, but the feelings for his mother were different. Perhaps it was all those months she and Ethan were alone caring for the farm while his father was with the militia during that frontier war, a special time that twined them closer, a bond that would forever reach beyond her grave.

"Ethan seems to have been so passionate about things," Samuel reflectively uttered, interrupting my thoughts while nudging his chair into a vigorous rock, "and truly cared for his mother. What a tender story, grandma, he told you of that summer night on that Lexington hill. Did that night help him see things more clearly? I mean, it seemed so spiritual."

"I think, in a way, Samuel, it did. But, I suppose only Ethan really knows." As Samuel quietly rocked and gazed into the July breeze, I watched my petals of crimson rose flutter in the warming winds and caressed the parchment of Ethan's poem resting in the pocket of my summer dress. I desperately wanted to say my words just right, wanted to tell my story true, and with each gentle stroke of his passionate words, the memories of those days flowed. For a wondrous moment I could sense Ethan beside me, as if he were touching me, right here, on my porch.

"He once confessed," I softly added while rocking a bit slower and dabbing a tear, "that even as young as he was that summer, he felt his future was twined to a quill. But he'd admit, that he hadn't decided just what he wanted to write. Sure, he had begun to dabble with poetic lines, even quilling a few short pieces by that summer, only now he was delving much more into the trade of publishing and printing with Mr. Giles. His quilling skills were still being honed, and his expanding duties with the Lexington Gazette had exposed him to all the troubles simmering about Boston and his Colony of Massachusetts Bay, all the colonies back then."

We rocked easy in our chairs for a moment or two, Samuel in contemplation, peering to those distant elms swaying in the summer breeze, and I bathing in memories of my Ethan with each tender stroke of his passionate words. "You know, Samuel," I whispered in a reflective tone, "perhaps that night on that hill did help Ethan see things more clearly. He once told me that in a curious way, he felt a greater focus on what truly burned in his soul, and found he was slowly releasing youthful fears which at times shackled his spirit. Maybe he really was more inspired after that night, wanting to grasp the kind of life that was already unfolding, wanting to reach for his dreams. He wanted to know more of the printing trade while expanding his knowledge of enlightening views swirling about the colonies, and above all I suppose, he wanted to quill his ideas and feelings more truthfully, as if erupting from his soul."

"Do you think that night was a revelation of sorts?" Samuel asked with an inquisitive glance. "Or maybe it was a conversion in some way, an awakening of spirit?"

"I don't know, Samuel, maybe. Ethan seldom spoke that way about things. But he did say he felt freed to fully express himself after that night, without fear, as if inspired by the hushing whispers of his mother. It was soon after that night that he felt his studies would continue, and it was then that he knew he would forever quill. He confided to his father what had happened and revealed his desires, and told Mr. Giles about his printing dreams too. Maybe that's why, they were adamant that Ethan's wish of Harvard College would come true."

"Is that what happened, grandma? Ethan left the tavern, moved from Lexington to the village of Cambridge?"

"No, not that summer. I suppose Ethan was still a little too young for Harvard College, but he wouldn't be in two years. And when he did begin his studies in Cambridge, he would live across the river in Boston."

"Those two years must have seemed eternal for Ethan," Samuel compassionately uttered. "What did he do all that time, and what was happening in the colonies? And what about you, grandma, what were you doing in Germantown in those days?"

"Looking back, Samuel, after all these years, I've come to realize that those days were pretty calm from what would happen in the coming years, before the troubles between the colonies and the king truly began to boil." As Samuel rocked easy and waited for my coming words, quiet in his thoughts while peering into the warming afternoon air, I caressed the aging parchment of Ethan's poem and gazed to those petals quivering in the summer sun. And with each slide of my fingers across his tender lines, the memories of those days began to flow.

Ethan continued his youthful studies at the Lexington schoolhouse as the leaves of autumn sprayed the woods in rustic colors, and as they snapped their ties and the snows of winter began to flurry across the Colony of Massachusetts Bay, he continued to delve into ideas and visions waiting in papers, pamphlets and books. And as he turned sixteen and the frigid months of 1767 began, when not completing chores for his father at their Buckman Tavern, he was expanding his knowledge of the publishing trade at Mr. Giles' print shop. All the while, he continued to hone his emerging skills with parchment, ink and quill.

Ethan said that his days were consumed by fresh knowledge during those winter months, and as the snow of Middlesex County began to flow to the sea in icy creeks and streams of spring, he had already perused a slew of books stacked at the schoolhouse or upstairs in the tavern, printings oozing histories, laws, philosophies and theories. And there were the newspapers too, volumes of parchment piled in Nathan's shop or on that table left of the Buckman Tavern door, printings of the Lexington Gazette and other pamphlets and papers brought to the village from Boston by special cart, wagon or rider.

In the meantime, as Ethan's life unfolded a bit more each day in Lexington and mine slowly sprouted in Germantown, youthful lives finding their way, unpleasant things continued to flare about the colonies. Although that despised Stamp Act had been rescinded by parliament the year before, fresh rumors began to swirl about Philadelphia, Boston, Charles Towne and Williamsburg about troubles brewing in the Colony of New York that winter and spring of 1767, disturbances spurred by edicts from London.

The Pennsylvania Evening Post revealed that New York's colonial assembly was refusing to comply with that Quartering Act espoused by parliament two years before, and although resistance had been rather tame for many months, it was becoming disturbingly defiant. "The colonists of New York," reported the Post, "continue to reject the repeated requests of Royal Governor Moore to adhere to the wishes of London. They have once again courageously refused to succumb to the mandate of the crown, rejecting their governor's demands that the colony provide proper quarters for the royal soldiers of King George."

It seems that in an effort to coerce the Colony of New York to heed the mandate from the crown and satisfy its lust for control, the king responded to that colony's passive resistance with what the Post and others viewed as unjust vindictiveness. London was said to have suspended the right of that colony's citizens to gather to discuss vital colonial things such as that intrusive law about quartering, for in that spring King George had waved his royal quill and ordered that the colonial assembly be disbanded.

Reports of the crown's punishing action resonated with a nervous rancor from village to town in all the colonies, for if I recall, no colony had truly embraced that intrusive Quartering Act, and some believed that the king spared the other colonies because New York had shown such a rebellious defiance of that act. Ethan once said that Mr. Giles had printed, "London's reaction is a reflection of the crown's misguided nonsense," suggesting in his Lexington Gazette that the act was an "abuse of our colonial rights," and that the king's response was intended to "strike fear in the hearts of every colony."

There were other mischievous activities erupting about the colonies as the flurries of winter faded, actions father and others more loyal to the king viewed as dangerously disturbing. Some were spurred by angry women and men sporadically meeting to dispense their displeasure with the crown, while most were sparked by the hundreds of sons of liberty groups continuing to sprout about the colonies, spirited men gathering on starry nights beneath the liberty limbs of oak and elm on town squares and village greens, or in the shadows shrouding warehouses, wharfs and docks. They'd rail of perceived injustices being perpetrated against the colonies by London, or decry the latest intrusive policy spouted by their royal governor, and by that spring of 1767 all were expressing vigorous disapproval of the king's maliciousness toward the Colony of New York.

Ethan once confided that the small sons of liberty group in his Lexington was formed early that spring, just weeks after what he described as "prideful colonists acknowledging their Irish roots" with rye whiskey, ale and rum on the cobblestones of Boston and the port of New York. He said Mr. Giles was the force behind forging their village group, and that he expressed support of its spirited beliefs in the printings of his Gazette. "He always displayed enthusiasm for the sons in Boston, Andrea, along with scores of others forming across the colony, and used his parchment to appeal to shopkeepers, farmers, tradesmen and merchants throughout Middlesex County to support the sons. And if none existed in their village or town, he'd arousingly explain the reasons to form one."

I can still hear the reluctance in Ethan's tone when he whispered that he wasn't sure of his own position about the sons as of that spring, wondering if such gatherings reflected his true feelings, doubts which seemed to quell pressures to join the new Lexington group, at least for a little while. And maybe he also thought he was too young, even though there were others less his age joining the sons in Boston. Yet, he confessed how he knew he was leaning toward their beliefs and sympathized with core disputes so many were expressing against the crown. But then he'd whisper a little more, saying he couldn't seem to release visions of the madness he had seen erupt in Boston that night.

Unable to reconcile his thirst for enlightening beliefs about colonial rights and individual liberties with rumors and stories of brutish encounters happening about the colonies, Ethan gripped his youthful convictions and defied the encroaching pressures, shying from joining the Lexington sons. "I could feel my mind pushing me," he'd say, "pressuring me that spring to be a son, yet my heart shouted 'no,' telling me the moment wasn't right." While Ethan waited for the proper time, a wait which would last months and then seasons as he watched, read and listened, his father held true to his passions and joined his village sons that spring, without hesitation.

If I recall, it was a few hours after dawn on an April morning, shortly after a sunrise shower that Saturday of spring, and Ethan was busy tending to his tavern chores, just as he always did before dashing to the print shop around noon to set type for the Gazette. His father was shuffling about the floor arranging candles for several tables, while Ethan was scurrying about the barreled bar and wiping cups, mugs, goblets and tins. "Ethan," he father surprisingly sputtered with an inviting glance, "come with me. I want you to see this."

Ethan followed his father out the tavern door and to the muddied stones of Bedford Street, then they strode northeast across the mushy grass of the village field to Mr. Giles' print shop. "Dad had such a determined strut in his step," Ethan softly said, "something I hadn't seen since I was very young. Even the gimp of his leg seemed to vanish as we walked that soggy field in a strange hush. Then he gripped the latch real tight, and with a spirited burst swung open the door, and I followed him in."

"I'm with you, Nathan!" Ethan's father crisply spouted while stepping the oak slats toward Mr. Giles intensely quilling to parchment at his desk. "I've given your appeals great thought, and believe the cause just. Count me in, Nathan, as the newest member of our sons of liberty here in Lexington."

"Splendid!" a startled Mr. Giles quickly replied, leaning back in his chair and sliding his quill into an ornate cup at the corner of his desk. Then rising in his stained shoes and extending his hand, he pleasingly added, "I'm glad to hear that, Pat. We need you."

Ethan watched as his father uttered, "Thank you, Nathan," while snatching his hand in a sturdy grip, "I appreciate that. I see this not only as an honor, but my duty. And I want you to know, your sons can gather in my tavern whenever needed, anytime."

"That's 'our' sons, Pat," Nathan graciously said, "and thank you. We'll take you up on that." Then glancing toward the door, he pressingly asked, "What about you, Ethan?"

"I'm not quite ready, Mr. Giles, not just yet," Ethan anxiously sputtered in a shy way, sensing the pressures gripping the room. "But I want you to know, I'm with dad, and feel much like both of you. When the time's right, and I'll know it, feel it, then I'll jump in, join the sons. Until then, I just want to help this cause in my own way, here, in the print shop, Mr. Giles, with broadsides and your Gazette."

"Alright, Ethan," Nathan replied while nodding an agreeing glance to his father, "and we know you will, when you're ready. Yes, I think that's fine, we can sure use the help. There'll be plenty for you can do for the sons around here."

Ethan's father snatched Nathan's hand a final time and bid farewell, and as Ethan followed his father through the shop door, he stopped, spun and said, "I'll be back, in a few hours." Ethan marveled at the intense determination he had witnessed from his father that spring morning, and as they strutted across the mushy field back to the tavern, he knew that indeed, someday, he would stand with his father and Mr. Giles, with all the other spirited men, as a son of Lexington.

I remember that not all colonists expressed opposition to the crown or supported any resistance to London of any kind in those days, such as the words and deeds erupting in hundreds of ports, villages and towns by the sons of liberty, and how Ethan once said that not even in his Middlesex County was opposition to King George rampant. "Many wouldn't speak of such things," he'd say, "and strove to display allegiance to Royal Governor Bernard and the crown." I suppose the winds of obedience to London were quite shifting back then, with some of the three or four million colonists holding true to the throne and some gripping the reins of the simmering resistance. And some were choosing to shield their views from others, or perhaps feigning tendencies of loyalty while safely clinging to feelings of neutrality like mother, father and many at our meeting house in Germantown. Ethan confessed that such attitudes were perhaps prevalent among the two or three hundred thousand colonist of Massachusetts Bay in those days, as well as the six hundred or so farmers and villagers of his Lexington.

In the midst of such fluttering reluctance were special colonists willing to display a determined boldness that spring of 1767 and beyond, colonists such as Sam Adams, Jim Otis and Doctor Warren in Boston, along with others like Thom Lynch of South Carolina, Johnny Dickinson here in my Pennsylvania and Mr. Henry over in Virginia, Ethan's father and Mr. Giles too. It was that expanding group of patriot men that Ethan was soon to support with his quill, an intriguing group which would thrust forward without succumbing to fears of being cast as disloyal or reprisals from London. They were daring men readily delving into dangerous shadows dwelling the unknown, spirited men willing to express their views in pamphlets and papers, and propel our cause in secret gatherings in villages and towns throughout the colonies.

Within days of that Saturday spring morning Mr. Giles began to expound more deeply in his Gazette upon the arousing views of the sons of liberty in Boston and his new little group in Lexington, spurring many in Ethan's Middlesex County to awake to their stirring cause. Soon merchants, tradesmen and farmers from nearby hamlets and towns began to voice approval of the things he was printing in his Lexington Gazette, agreeing to views of the sons and notions that colonists be treated like those in England. It was during those spring days that some of the doubters in Lexington, in all the colonies, began venturing from the woods of indifference to wade into the waters of an embryonic cause spreading throughout the colonies, spirited streams flowing toward the ideals espoused by daring colonists like the sons of liberty.

Ethan once said that by early May many of Lexington had latched upon the reasoning of Mr. Giles and come to the support of the sons, villagers like gunsmith Ernie Wilson and bricklayer Israel Jacob, along with others like Johnny Parker and Nat Mulliken and his young son Joe. And by the closing days of spring Doc Newman finally joined, Billy Munroe too, and so did Reverend Clarke and most shopkeepers and tradesmen of Lexington, as well as dozens of nearby farmers like Joseph Hosmer, Andy Beatty and Mr. Fiske.

And by the first days of summer the Lexington sons decided the moment ripe for their group to declare its own spirited place to gather beneath the stars and sun, and chose a spot near a tree on the western edge of the village field, across the ruts and stones of Bedford Street and the Buckman Tavern. It was an oak which had been stretching for the sky for decades before Ethan was born, with little green acorn nuts that dangled its limbs in summer and tumbled to the soil in fall, a tree of chestnut Doc Newman liked to strangely call, quercus prinus.

Ethan liked to say that the crusted knobs dotting its grey ribs made that aging tree look as if it had been sculpted by some crazed artisan in a warehouse along one of the docks of Philadelphia, Boston or Savannah. Its creeping limbs spread high into the sky, crooked arms sprouting twisting twigs smothered by thousands of pointy leaves that wildly fluttered in the summer winds. And a stray limb or two crept low toward the village field, awkward looking arms that enticingly protruded near the grass for the younger ones to daringly climb, dangle and leap.

"I loved to gaze at that tree," Ethan once whispered to me, "watch from a tavern window or my bedroom panes as its limbs swayed in a stormy breeze. The leaves would spin in the spring, Andrea, and I'd wonder why such beauty had to surrender its colors each fall. And I'd lie on my bed on winter nights and listen to the winds howl, imagining its limbs dancing in the dark." It was Lexington's special oak, one which brought comfort to Ethan and seemed to protect the village, a chestnut his father, Mr. Giles and the sons had christened their liberty tree.

From time to time the sons of liberty in Lexington would gather beneath the limbs of that chestnut tree, and unlike groups in other ports, villages and towns, Mr. Giles' sons would stray from the shadows of secrecy and assemble now and then before God and the king. Ethan said it was as though neither Mr. Giles or his father, nor most of the other sons of Lexington, worried much about spurring the alarm of colonists more friendly to the crown, nor did they seem to fear meandering royal soldiers or the wrath of Governor Bernard. They'd just meet under that tree shortly after dusk, and sometimes, gather in his father's tavern.

One of those gatherings in the Buckman Tavern took place around nine the first Saturday of August, several hours after Mr. Giles dangled the sons' little yellow ensign from a thin elm pole just outside the tavern door, signaling those of the village to assemble inside later that night. Accepting the challenge of his father and Mr. Giles, Ethan did his part too, galloping that afternoon to farms of Lexington and Middlesex County to alert colonists of the gathering with spirits, wine and ale that night.

Shortly after the fading day dragged the silvery crescent of a summer moon beyond the frontier that warm night, perhaps a half hour before nine, Ethan watched as his father moved about the tavern from table to table in an anxious hurry, wiping each clean and glancing out the windows while tapping a little fire to unlit wicks with the flame of a candle. "I was sliding some goblets and mugs into neat rows on the little table near the end of the bar by the kitchen door," Ethan reflected, recalling that night, "and wondering of the troubles that seemed to be swirling about dad's mind. I had never seen him so nervous before, and could feel his anxiousness beginning to surge through me too, waiting for nine."

Soon some of the sons began to step through the tavern door, and as the hour of meeting drew near, most of Lexington's group had shuffled to a chair at a candlelit table scattered about the room or stood in muddied boots and soiled shoes at the barreled bar, an oil lamp glowing each end. While Ethan dashed about the oak slats filling goblets with wine and mugs with Boston ale, or cups and tins with rye whiskey and rum, his father was busy near the tavern door greeting each colonist as he pranced in.

Then Mr. Giles finally stepped into the tavern and mingled among his sons for a moment or two, bouncing between full chairs and tables until taking a place at the end of the barreled bar near the window facing the dark hovering their village field. Ethan watched as his father rushed to his favorite spot behind the bar, sliding a dripping mug across the elm slats to Mr. Giles before gripping ale of his own and leaning into the bar. Realizing most or all of the men had arrived, Ethan quietly slithered to a secluded little table near the fireplace stones and kitchen door.

Amid the glow of a little flame flickering about his haven, Ethan was now ready to watch and listen to the gathered men, witness what was about to unfold. And as Mr. Giles was readying to speak to his sons, Ethan snatched a shiny timepiece from the pocket of his breeches, a gift from his father for turning sixteen several months before. Then he snapped its thin lid tight, at three minutes past the hour.

"It's good to see each one of you men here tonight," Nathan spouted in a greeting tone, his back pressed to the edge of the barreled bar while scanning dozens of peering eyes. "Thank you, for coming on such short notice. Some of you may already know why I've called this meeting," he quickly added as Ethan watched and listened along with Jonas Parker and his cousin John, Doc Newman and Reverend Clarke too, "and the rest of you, are wondering why."

"We sure are, Nathan," Sam Burns jovially blurted. "So why don't you tell us, before our ale spoils from all the heat you're spewin about Pat's tavern."

Ethan watched as a smirk brushed his father and chuckles crept from others, amused little snickers that snapped what seemed a tension that had wafted the room. "Of course," Nathan playfully retorted, "you would know all about hot air, wouldn't you, Sam."

Nathan sipped a splash of ale, and with a serious glare in his stare, scanned the tavern once again and bluntly added, "It's those Townshend Acts you've been hearing about. Maybe you've seen my words in the Gazette, or read some of the disapproving things being printed over in Boston. We're here tonight, men, to talk about these blasted acts, this injustice thrust upon the colonies by King George and that bloody parliament, and what the sons should do about it."

"I was just in Boston," an engaged Jonas Parker spouted, "a few days ago, and heard some in shops and men on the docks talkin about them acts. They don't like em, not one bit. Some were sayin we should stop buyin all them goods coming over here from England, that maybe, we should just let them sacks and crates wither in the hulls of London's merchant ships. I even heard a few talkin of gettin together one of these nights and stringin up a stuffed dummy of that bloody Governor Bernard, then settin him ablaze from a limb on the common."

"I heard talk like that too," Alex Spoons added, the soil of his farm crusted to his shoes, "just this past Wednesday, up in Bedford."

"So have I," Nathan robustly replied, glancing about the tavern and peering to his sons' waiting eyes. "I've been to Boston many times these past weeks, talking with friends like John Gill, Ben Edes and Danny Fowle. And of course, I've held some pretty probing discussions with Jim, John and Sam. There's a solid opinion in Boston, just as with many of us here tonight, that these latest taxes and duties imposed upon our colonies by London, these unjust Townshend Acts, must go! As Sam said to me, they're nothing but a perverted leap into the past, an attempt by King George to saddle us with the same old revenue-grabbing gimmicks he's tried before."

"That's just what those Townshend Acts are," a spirited John Parker shouted, "and we need to do something about it, now! Maybe hitting those royals of parliament in their coffers is just the right approach. Maybe striking them in their golden chests of shillings and pounds is what's needed to rattle those greedy bastards in London."

"Something like that might be a bit rough," Ethan's father timidly retorted, "sure to cause those royals hardship. It could be dangerous too, for the colonies. But I say, yes. I support what John suggests."

"Pat has a valid point," a passive Doc Newman elegantly chimed. "Yet, I too like John's idea. It just seems the proper course at this time. Nathan, what do you think?"

"That seems to be the consensus in Boston too," Nathan reassuringly replied, "and pretty much the entire colony. Sam says there are groups in all the colonies planning to attack those acts in this way. Yes, I too support this plan. What do the rest of you men think?" he asked, glancing about the room. "We might not be able to stop all their goods, but we could slash deep into what colonists buy from London. Why, I just know thousands of women and children will do their part too, shying from using things taxed by those Townshend Acts. We just might be able to make those dunderheads in parliament see the ills of their ways, just like we did before."

"It might work, Nathan," the Reverent Clarke calming injected. "A plan like that just might show the crown how seriously we disapprove, while not falling into the misguided pit of violence. I think it's worth a try."

"So do I," Henry White quickly uttered, "I know of others too, who will stand with us."

"Anyone else have something to add?" Nathan invitingly asked as the men began to discuss the plan while sputtering of those Townshend Acts. "Alright, if nothing else, let's see the hands of those who believe the ideas espoused here tonight should be supported by the Lexington sons."

Ethan watched as each man with defiance in his stare thrust his hand into the tavern air, a glare which seemed oblivious of consequences lurking in the shadows roaming about the room from glowing and flickering lamps and candles. "Good!" Nathan blurted in a victorious tone while swinging his dripping mug before his sons. "Lexington has spoken. But we can't let it stop here. We need to spread this plan throughout the county, gentlemen, to every village and town, every farm we can."

"Hear, hear!" the men erupted while lifting their spirits into the summer air, enthusiastic bellows that swept across the stones of Bedford Street to swirl about the grass of the village field and the dark shrouding the steeples, homes and shops of Lexington.

"And soon," Sam Burns spouted from his chair, thrusting his goblet into the tavern air, "the repeal of those bloody Townshend Acts!"

"That's right," belted several sons inspired by daring words and spirits of ale, wine, whiskey and rum, "damn those acts!"

"Alright men, hold it down," injected Nathan Giles in a guiding way. And as a hush settled upon the room and the men gripped mugs, goblets, cups and tins, he boldly added, "May each man stay the course declared here tonight, defy the naysayers. To the sons of liberty!"

"To the sons!" they blasted, raising their spirits amidst pulsating candles.

From across the floor Ethan could see his father's lips utter those words before tipping his mug at the end of the barreled bar, and sensed a bit of pride surging Doc Newman as he rose from his table near the window right of the door, then strutted to Nathan and his father. "Those are fine words, Nathan, Pat," Doc declared with a sip of ale. "May that spirit thrive in the hearts and minds of every colonist." It was then, Ethan said, when a burst of warm air surged the room as Quincy Jafres stepped through the tavern door, a farmer whose fields were just northeast of the village near Ethan's old place.

"Sorry, Nathan, fors bein late," he sheepishly uttered while stepping toward Mr. Giles, Doc and Ethan's father huddled about the end of the bar. "Had to tend some ailin cows. I knows, I knows," he quickly added as some of the men scattered about the room twisted and stared, "I'm not a real member of your group, at least nots yet, but want to be. I want to carry my weight, Nathan, dos my part for Lexington, our colony. I want to be part of this, the Lexington sons."

"That's fine, Quincy," Nathan replied in a welcoming tone, "I'm glad to hear that. We need you. Go ahead, take one of those chairs. We've decided to do something about those Townshend Acts, Quincy, a plan that calls for us, all colonists, to stop buying things coming from London. Or at least, whittle away at what we do use."

"Good," he nervously sputtered. "That sounds real good."

"It's good to see you, Quincy," greeted Doc, words quickly repeated by Ethan's father as he stepped to show Quincy to a chair at the corner table just right of the bar. "Ethan," his father suddenly spouted with a gaze toward the kitchen door, "please, fetch a mug of ale for Mr. Jafres."

Ethan sprang from his chair and filled a mug with Boston ale from a barrel nudged behind the bar, then dashed to Quincy patiently waiting with his father at the table. "Here you go, Mr. Jafres," Ethan politely said, sliding the dripping mug to his hand near the flickering candle.

"Thank you, Ethan," a gracious Mr. Jafres replied, followed quickly by Ethan's father.

"Now wait a minute!" blurted Andrew Beatty, leaping to his boots at a table across the floor, near the steps rising toward Ethan room upstairs. "Let's think about this. Do we really want one of 'them' in our group? I say no, not here in Lexington, not even him. Why, what do you think other groups will think? No. I say no. No Negras in our sons of liberty. No!"

"You are way out of line, Andy!" Ethan's father lashed from behind the bar with a stare that seemed to pierce Mr. Beatty's soul. "What's the matter with you!"

"I don't believe I am," he boldly retorted, glancing about the tavern before defiantly peering into the eyes or Nathan, Doc and Ethan's father. "I'll bet there are others in this room, right now, who feel the same."

"That's enough, Mr. Beatty!" declared Mr. Giles, trying to defuse the tension gripping the room while discrediting the nonsense being spewed by that defiling farmer. "Sit down!"

I remember how Ethan said nobody moved from his spot, each man clinging to his position with piercing peers across the tavern floor, his father too, and how the little flames of every candle seemed to stop their flicker. Ethan slowly slithered back to his little table near the kitchen door as a hush shrouded the men scattered about the room, then slid to his chair and watched the expressions of all the sons. "I was trying to understand their sentiments, Andrea, each one of them, and sensed that some seemed to hold insulting views like Mr. Beatty." For a few moments all those in the tavern just gripped their spirits in silence, most bewildered by the vile they had heard, and some, perhaps reluctant to reveal a repugnant creed dwelling within.

As if strapped to an elm pole, Andy Beatty stood straight in dusty boots and glared across the room in a defiant stare, and as the others watched in an anxious hush, Mr. Giles slowly motioned for Mr. Jafres to remain calm in his chair, whispering not to confront the farmer he had known for years. Ethan could see an anger brushing Mr. Jafres eyes, an impatient glare tinged with a splash of fear, yet could sense an empowering courage simmering inside, as if Quincy had experienced such repulsive indignities too many times over the years.

Ethan would later confess that although he too was repelled by the wickedness spewed by Mr. Beatty, and for several moments controlled a youthful urge to leap from his chair and confront that Lexington farmer, all he could muster was the will to watch from his chair. It wasn't the first time he had heard such vile drivel, despicable thoughts from travelers in the tavern now and then and from Mr. Beatty's own son Bobby many times before. Ethan once whispered that at times he wondered where such decay came from, how colonists could founder in such intolerance, and wondered how long such diseased decadence would rumble about the hills.

"In spite of Mr. Beatty's, well, peculiar point of view," Mr. Giles, shattering the hush, boasted to the sons anxiously waiting about the tavern, "I say welcome, Mr. Jafres, to our Lexington group. I call upon all of you, every man here this night, to accept this fine gentleman into our sons of liberty."

Andy Beatty didn't move, just quietly stood across the tavern floor while slowly scanning the room, then gazed to Mr. Jafres watching and listening from his chair in a restrained silence near Doc, Nathan and Ethan's father gathered at the bar. "I don't have nothing against Quincy," Andy suddenly blustered in what Ethan would say was a beguiling tone. "Why, his farm's been next to mine for years. But let's be practical boys, it might not look good for us to have one of them in our group."

"One of, them?" Doc excitedly spouted, spritzing a bit of ale as he twisted in a frigid stare. "Why, you're nothing but a bloody bigot, Mr. Beatty!"

"Now you just hold off a minute there, Doc!" blasted Andy, clanking his ale to the table and wagging a scathing finger toward the bar. "I know you've been around here a long time, but don't you be gettin me all riled up, calling me names. I'm entitled to my opinion, just like the next man."

"Not in my place," Ethan's father courageously chimed, "not when it's cloaked in such filth. Not when it degrades a good man cuz you don't approve of the color of his skin. You're wrong, Andy, dead wrong."

As the men squirmed in their chairs or leaned against the barreled bar in silence, Mr. Giles quickly intervened in a grave yet calming tone, relieving the intensity gripping the room. "Yes, Andrew, you are entitled to your opinion, even if misguided. But so are Doc, Pat and I, and Joe and John over there, every man here. And so is Quincy."

While Nathan's words hovered about the tavern, Ethan's father spun right toward Mr. Jafres still quiet at his table. "As far as I'm concerned, Quincy," he expressed in a determined tone for all to hear, "you are as free as any one of us, to be part of this group. I welcome you to our sons of liberty. And never doubt, you're always welcome in my tavern, any time."

"Thanks, Pat," he softly uttered while deliberately rising from his chair, "you too, Nathan, Doc. For you fellas that don't know me too good," he graciously added while glancing about the room, "I don't like problems, never have, and don't wanna make none here. I feels I've gots just as much right as any to be part of this group, and that goes for you too, Andy. But, I'll abide by whatever you fellas decide." He glanced about the tavern once again and nodded to Nathan, Doc and Ethan's father, then settled back down in his chair and sipped his mug of ale, wondering of his fate.

"I see no reason," John Parker boldly spouted from his table right of the door, "why Quincy shouldn't be part of our group, none!" Then rising from his chair with a scratching slide, he raised his rum into the tavern air and snapped a piercing gaze to Andy Beatty settling back to his chair, then scanned the eyes of the room and added, "I support bringing Quincy Jafres into the Lexington sons."

"Would anyone else like to say something?" Nathan Giles quickly asked, anxious to resolve the debate once and for all. As the men glanced about, several uttering agreeing sentiments to John Parker's words, Nathan added, "Alright then, we'll put it to a vote. All those in favor of Quincy joining our group, say yea."

A resounding "yea" erupted about the tavern while three of the sons remained quiet in their chairs. Ethan watched as Andy Beatty stared at the flame of his table's candle and frustratingly tapped his fingers, while Charley Duncan and Ernie Wilson quivered nervously at a nearby table, the village cordwainer and gunsmith. "I could see the fume oozing from Andy's ears," I remember Ethan saying, "and the misguided loyalty in the eyes of the other two as they gripped their mugs in silence."

"And those who oppose?" Nathan added in a victorious tone.

"Nay!" spouted the three from their chairs, men unable to grasp the reins of humanity.

"Then it's settled," Nathan proclaimed, scanning the eyes of the tavern before twisting to Mr. Jafres at his table. "Welcome, Quincy, to the Lexington sons of liberty."

"Thanks, Nathan," Quincy replied in a timid tone while rising in his soiled shoes and glancing to the men scattered about the room. "Yous to Pat," he added as the naysayer trey squirmed in their chairs in a frustrating hush, "Doc and John, alls of you, for lettin me do my part. Yous can count on me, mys whole family, to support the sons and resist them Townshend Acts."

"We know you will, Quincy," Nathan replied for all the sons. "Any other items?" he added while scanning the room before glancing to Doc and over to Ethan's father behind the barreled bar. After a few snapping glances, sputtering whispers and straying stares, he wrapped up their meeting with definitive words, "We all know, gentlemen, what must be done to oppose those Townshend Acts. That's it for tonight."

I remember Ethan whispering how proud he was of his father that night, of all the sons but three during that first tavern meeting of the Lexington sons, and how he wondered whether that trio of misguided men would someday understand the error of their bigoted way. It had been a meeting which evolved into a tiny clash of societal confusion about all men, a gathering which at its core was a fundamental discussion of those Townshend Acts. As I caressed the parchment of Ethan's poem and glanced to Samuel peering to those distance elms, a befuddled expression brushing his face as to what those acts truly were, I realized some were confused in those days too. They were intrusive acts dictated by London that were despised by thousands of colonists back then, many who would someday come to understand, just as I, how those acts forever changed our colonial lives.

Rumors of those new laws had begun to filter about the colonies late that spring of 1767, and by summer the Pennsylvania Evening Post was referring to those intrusions by London in their more formal term, the Townshend Acts. It seems that in the absence of the ailing Prime Minister William Pitt that winter and spring, the king insisted that his fiscal wizard Charles Townshend lead parliament, his loyal Chancellor of the Exchequer. The Post revealed that unlike the aging Pitt, Mr. Townshend was less sympathetic to colonial views, suggesting he had a lustful yearn for colonists' property and would be the least likely of the king's men to mourn the passing of our colonial liberties.

Those Townshend Acts were in essence several laws quilled by parliament that winter and spring then approved by King George in the first days of summer, and if I recall, mostly consisted of what London named the Revenue Act, the Indemnity Act and the Commissioners of Customs Act. The Post explained that the revenue law was a "connivance to steal colonial money" by imposing a fresh slew of taxes and duties on goods sailed to the colonies from London, burdensome levies on products like parchment and paints, lead, glass and teas.

Some believed that the shillings and pounds siphoned from the colonies by London through those new taxes were to help pay the costs of garrisoning thousands of royal soldiers at outposts along the frontier and in the ports of Boston, Philadelphia and New York. And others disturbingly revealed that those funds would be used to wrest a greater degree of control over royal governors and colonial judges by paying those men directly from London. Ethan once said he had heard that the Revenue Act was also intended to bolster, in sinister way, the use of those dreaded writs of assistance so many in his Colony of Massachusetts Bay, in all the colonies, had bitterly opposed for years.

That Indemnity Act was said by some to be nothing more than a royal ruse to prop the fiscal position of a private enterprise called the British East India Company. "It manipulates the costs of crates of tea" they'd say, "to be more competitive with crates the crown believes are being smuggled into the colonies by Dutch and other merchants without paying those bloody duties to the king." And the Evening Post suggested that parliament's Commissioners of Customs Act was simply intended to enhance London's ability to collect all those taxes through the creation of a new board loyal to the crown, a commission scheduled to form in Ethan's port of Boston by the first snows of winter.

Just as those sons of liberty in Ethan's Lexington and throughout the colonies began resisting those Townshend Acts, unacceptable encroachments upon our colonial liberties many would say, daring colonists began challenging London's new laws in their own way. Some began to quill opposing views of those acts during those summer months into fall, and Ethan said that as the first chills began to sweep across the hills and fields, one of those colonists was Johnny Boyle, a young Boston pamphleteer from his Colony of Massachusetts Bay.

If I recall, he quilled his own pamphlet in a quaint house near the northeastern docks of Hutchinson's Wharf, a little publication he called the Journal of Occurrences in Boston. Not only were his thoughts reprinted in Mr. Giles' Lexington Gazette and other papers like Boston's Independent Advertiser and Mr. Edes' Country Journal, but throughout the colonies. Ethan said special riders with satchels stuffed with Johnny's writings were dispatched by the sons of liberty in Boston and galloped to printers throughout New England, while others rode to ports, villages and towns from the colonies of New York and my Pennsylvania to the Carolinas and Georgia.

I first read the spirited words of young Mr. Boyle in the Pennsylvania Gazette later that fall, lines which exposed thousands of colonists to what he and the sons of liberty were describing and calling for, the "non-importation of English goods." It was during those chilling weeks that their inspiring cry began racing throughout the colonies as if a wave surging from the sea, a plea sweeping the hills to taverns, homes, farms and shops that seemed to open the eyes of thousands of colonists to the deeds of London. It was a plea that gripped many of my Germantown too, a colonial cry to oppose those Townshend Acts and awaken the king.

Soon colonists in hundreds of villages and towns were heeding those pleas, women and men quietly showing opposition to the crown by refusing to release pence, shillings and pounds for items taxed by those Townshend Acts. There were many with a differing view too who remained loyal to the king in those days, colonists like father and friends at our meeting house who shunned such disloyal things. Yet it was around then that I began to see the loyal ties of some beginning to unravel, even a

Quaker friend or two of Philadelphia and Germantown, people who had for years clung to neutrality. They were colonists secretly leaning to the views espoused by Mr. Boyle and all the sons, a shift from London I found rather pleasing, Quaker friends like mother beginning to quietly support the pleas of the sons and think more freely.

There were others too who openly espoused the positions of the sons of liberty that fall of 1767, not only men like Mr. Giles of Lexington and Mr. Boyle and Sam Adams of Boston, but men throughout the colonies expressing their determined opposition to those Townshend Acts, such as Mr. Henry over in Virginia. And Ethan once said that all those men did those things at their own peril in those days, facing intimidating threats from royal governors and London. They were daring men who shunned those dangers, spirited colonists like John Dickinson in Philadelphia, a young barrister born in the Colony of Maryland some thirty-five years before.

Even though it seems he tried to keep his identity shrouded in secrecy, there were rumors wildly swirling in those days that some letters being printed in newspapers throughout the colonies were in truth those of Mr. Dickinson. They were a string of articles first published in my Pennsylvania Evening Post shortly before Christmas that 1767, several essays supposedly quilled by a mysterious farmer that voiced spirited opposition to those Townshend Acts.

Within weeks those opinions identified as *letters from a farmer in Pennsylvania* were being routed by swift riders to ports, villages and towns in all the colonies and being printed in papers north and south, from the Georgia Gazette of Savannah to Boston's Independent Advertiser and Mr. Giles Lexington Gazette. Those *farmer's letters* were being talked about in churches and homes, taverns, warehouses and shops, impassioned essays which sought to increase the awareness of colonists to what Mr. Dickinson and others believed was an "erosion of our colonial liberties, our rights as citizens of the British Empire." It was that secretive farmer's way of trying to persuade women, children and men to show their disgust for those acts being inflicted upon the colonies by London.

I remember that those farmer's letters were not Mr. Dickinson's first foray into the troubles brewing between the crown and the colonies, for he had been one of my colony's delegates at that Stamp Act Congress two years before. It was around then that he also quilled an intriguing essay spewing fiery insight about that disturbing act, an entreaty he innocuously titled *the late regulations respecting the British Colonies on the Continent of America considered.* And although I was only fifteen back then, I still recall how many of Philadelphia and Germantown marveled at his eloquent phrases decrying the unjust policies and laws being thrust upon the colonies by King George.

Only now, Mr. Dickinson's farmer's letters, extoling the rights of colonists and exposing the folly of parliament, were being stowed in the hulls of merchant ships and sailed across the sea. They were being published in newspapers of London and whisked across the waters of the channel for printing in pamphlets and papers of Paris. I'd later learn that his farmer's letters were being reproduced with a spirited preface quilled by Doctor Franklin, still faithfully tending his colonial duties in London of espousing the rights and virtues of the American Colonies.

In the meantime, as the wintry winds of 1768 began to sweep across the colonies, thousands had begun to heed the words of that Pennsylvania farmer and those other daring men quilling defiant beliefs in Dover and Williamsburg, Charles Towne, Boston, New York and Savannah. Although many continued to wade in the waters of neutrality or clung to loyalties to the crown, others were quietly gripping the reins of non-importation of English goods in defiance of those Townshend Acts. Those who dared were now refusing to purchase those products taxed by that act, a spirited posture that slowly began to whittle at the heart of parliament while depleting merchant and monarch coffers of London. And, not only were the sons of liberty and those quilling men inflicting royal damage with their determined deeds, but thousands of cunning women had grasped the challenge too, choosing to use other products and goods in their lives.

Mothers, girls, women and brides who normally ventured from their farms and homes to barter and buy things like cloth, spices, glass and teas sailed across the sea were now using smuggled items or colonial goods. All the while, an array of products was being shunned by thousands of merchants, tradesmen, doctors and lawyers, and printers in hundreds of ports, villages and towns. A spirited segment of colonists had united against those incoming English goods, refusing to pay the duties and taxes compelled by those Townshend Acts, a cry of non-importation that gripped women and men from Philadelphia to Boston, from Ethan's Lexington to my Germantown, even a few slyly consorting at my Quaker house.

Looking back, I recall that before those defiant actions began to truly take hold, before those farmer's letters began to sweep across the colonies that fall and surge across the sea that coming winter and spring, Ethan had accepted a new challenge. It was a greater role in the sons of liberty, not as an active member but in a supportive way, something which consoled his doubts and agreed with his sentiments of opposing those Townshend Acts. He told me that before Mr. Giles left the tavern after the sons' meeting that August night, and after discussion with Ethan's father, they asked and Ethan nervously accepted. "I agreed to ride into Boston the following morning, Andrea, with Nathan's quilled notes of the meeting, parchment advising the sons in Boston that those in Lexington had agreed to shun those English goods."

He said the gathering had disbanded an hour or so before midnight, and now only Mr. Giles was in the tavern with Ethan and his father. As Ethan hurried about dousing candles and brushing tables while gathering a slew of cups, mugs, goblets and tins, they mumbled secretive things near the end of the barreled bar and sipped a final splash of ale. And when Ethan tugged and latched the tavern door tight, his father suddenly uttered, "Ethan, come here for a moment, please."

Ethan dashed toward the kitchen door and tossed his damp cloth to a shelf, then carefully stepped toward his father and Mr. Giles sipping ale at the other end of the bar. "You know, Ethan," his father said in a reassuring tone, "Nathan and I understand how you feel, know you're not quite ready to join the sons, at least not actively. We both respect that."

"That's right, Ethan," Nathan calmly chimed, "we do."

"We also know how you feel about what we're doing here, with our sons," his father continued. "You heard the plan of non-importation we've decided to implement, and I think you support that kind of thing. And we know you agree with what Nathan prints in his Gazette, and the opinions in the papers over in Boston too. Isn't that right, Ethan?"

"Ya," he answered with a puzzling squint, "yes, I do."

"Well," his father quickly added, gripping his ale, "we've been thinking, that maybe, you'd like to get a little more involved. Oh, not in an official way, Ethan, or a defiant way. But in an important way nevertheless."

"What kind of way, dad?" he quizzically sputtered. "What do you want me to do?"

"We both feel you're ready, Ethan," Mr. Giles suddenly injected, "and would be comfortable in this small role. We think you'd make an excellent rider, helping with communications."

"That's right, Ethan," his father spiritedly added. "Taking a message between groups now and then, notes from meetings, that kind of thing. What do you think?"

"I want you to take a message for our Lexington sons, Ethan," Nathan quickly explained, "in the morning, and give it to a member in Boston. Now, if you don't want to, you don't have to. Just say so, Ethan, and we'll understand."

Ethan quietly gazed at the flame glowing the lamp near the end of the bar, trying to tame the anxiousness swirling his mind while gathering his wits, then glanced to Nathan and over to his father. "That's right, Ethan," his father calmly uttered, "if you're not comfortable doing this, we'll understand. Yes, Nathan is right, our sons could use your help, but only if you're willing."

"Just ride to Boston, that's all?" Ethan questioned in a nervous tone, his stare snapping between that lamp and their waiting eyes. "Take a message, nothing else?"

"That's right, Ethan," Nathan replied, "that's all. And maybe, if Boston asks, bring a message back."

Ethan glanced to his father who gave an agreeing nod, and as he slowly swung his stare back to Mr. Giles, an intriguing sense of adventure wrapped of duty began to surge deep inside. "Alright," he exclaimed without fear, "I'll do it. I want to do it."

"Excellent, Ethan," Nathan graciously spouted, "I'm so glad to hear you say that. Why don't you ride over to the shop in the morning, say, about an hour before noon? You can take my notes then, and be on your way."

"I'll be there, Mr. Giles." Then suddenly, as if compelled by some mystical compulsion, Ethan began to explain why his insides had struggled with the sons. "You know, it's not that I disapprove of the sons, its notions and cause, I don't. I wouldn't agree to ride, carry messages, if I didn't support your ideas. But I've struggled, dad, to reconcile this cause with some of the mindless recklessness I've seen and heard about, in Boston and all the colonies. Yet, I suppose for me, this is a way I can help promote its core beliefs, simply riding with words, your words Mr. Giles, and maybe, someday, with words of my own."

"I'm proud of you, Ethan," his father supportively said while tapping his shoulder with a few tender pats. "Now, I say, it's time for you get some sleep. I'll finish things down here."

"Thanks, dad, I will. Goodnight, Mr. Giles. I'll see you in the morning. Night, dad."

"Goodnight, Ethan," Nathan whispered. "And thanks, for being candid."

"See you in the morning, Ethan," his father softly uttered.

"That's quite a son you have there, Pat," Nathan confessed as Ethan stepped the oak slats of the floor and vanished up the stairs to the solitude of his room. "I sure see why you're so proud."

"Ya, I am. Say, let's have one more." Ethan's father snatched their mugs and filled them with Boston ale from that barrel behind the bar, then they whispered a bit more about the sons as the final hour of that August day slipped into the night.

Ethan said he bid his father farewell an hour or two before noon the following day, then saddled his colt Cato and galloped north on the dusty stones of Bedford Street before swinging east then down the ruts of Hancock Street along the edge of the village field. He could see Mr. Giles at his desk as he bound up the steps and a quill dancing his right fingers as he clicked open the print shop door, stroking notes of the sons meeting the night before.

"Good morning, Ethan," Nathan refreshingly spouted while quilling final thoughts with several slashes, dashes and dots before sliding his feather into the special cup at the corner of his desk. "You're just in time," he quickly added with a spin.

"Good morning," Ethan timidly replied as he stepped toward Mr. Giles blowing a few drying breaths upon parchment and ink.

"I want you to take this to John Gill," he said in a serious tone, "a printing man in Boston. He should be at his print shop, Ethan, at the corner of Brattle and Queen Street, just west of King. If you don't find him there he could be at the nearby Green Dragon Tavern, or even at home on Spring Lane, 362, a little southeast of his shop."

"Alright, Mr. Giles," Ethan confidently replied, "I'll find him. I remember the tavern, and think I've seen his shop before. I'll make sure he gets your message."

"I know you will. Oh, there's one more thing, Ethan. John prints that Boston Gazette and Country Journal with his partner Benjamin Edes, every week at their shop. They should be pressing a new edition today, if they didn't last night. I was hoping you'd bring a few back."

"I sure will. Is there anything else I should know before I ride? Want me to bring back anything else?"

"Just John's reply to my message, Ethan, something I'm pretty sure he'll do."

"Alright, I will."

"Thanks, Ethan," Nathan graciously replied while shuffling a few stray sheets about his desk before pinching the parchment of his sons of liberty message in his fingertips. "If you're unable to find John," he added, spinning in his chair toward Ethan, "leave this with Mr. Edes. If he's not at the shop either, or the tavern, his house is just a bit north on Brattle Street."

"Alright. Don't worry, Mr. Giles, I'll find one of them."

"I know you will, Ethan," Nathan calmingly agreed while creasing the parchment several times and sliding it into the safety of a small deerskin folder, securing it with tiny twists of its leather twine. "Your father and I have quite a bit of faith in you," he added, pressing that slim package into Ethan's outstretched hand. "Take good care of this, Ethan."

"I will," Ethan softly replied, raising his left boot to the elm chair just right. As Nathan curiously watched with what seemed a dash of pride in his eyes, Ethan slowly slid that special thin satchel deep into his dark boot, pressing it against bright stockings reaching to tan breeches. Then with a tiny nudge, he shoved it down just a bit further.

"That's good, Ethan, very good," Nathan uttered with a spryly nod. "Be careful."

"You can depend on it," Ethan assuredly replied. "I will." Then bidding Mr. Giles goodbye with a determined glance, he dashed from the shop and leapt to his saddle for the twelve mile ride to Boston.

With his boots snug in the stirrups and reins firmly gripped, Ethan snapped his heels into muscled ribs and Cato began a slow gait down Hancock Street along the eastern edge of the village field. The morning sun began to warm his cheeks as his colt trotted in the soft summer winds past John Muzzey's place, then Ethan tugged the reins left and galloped east on the ruts and stones of the Massachusetts Road, Cato's thick mane dancing and tossing with each thumping stride. Ethan could hear the pounding of hooves and rustling of leaves as they galloped past the village bell toward Boston, and with a glance over his shoulder amid sprouting oak, maple and elm, he watched Lexington vanish in a trail of dust.

As Cato trotted the Massachusetts Road through the villages of Menotomy, Medford and Somerville, galloping past grassy hills and farmers' fields, patchy groves and blooming meadows and the bushy narrows of the Charlestown Peninsula, Ethan wondered of those two printing men across the water in Boston. He had heard vague tales over the years from Mr. Giles and some in the tavern, and with each clumping stride he wondered who those two colonists truly were, wondered how John Gill and Ben Edes might mysteriously change his life.

From what Ethan had heard about those two men, he knew they published that Boston Gazette and Country Journal each week, a printing Mr. Giles once said was an early voice of opposition to the crown, and knew the royal governor viewed them as painfully antagonistic. They were known to print opinions which tended to cast a rather dim light upon the crown, letters and essays decrying acts, policies and laws spewed by the king, parliament and his royal governors over the years, and once proclaimed that despised Stamp Act to be "belligerent nonsense."

Ethan would later discover that Mr. Edes had always resided in the Colony of Massachusetts Bay, and spent his first twenty-two years in the village of Charlestown across the waters of the harbor. After a modest youth of experiences and learning, they say he traded his peninsula life for fresh opportunities in Boston, leaving behind his parents, siblings and home near the docks when Ethan and I were just four. And within months it seems he wed young Martha Starr, an enchanting woman rumored to be a distant grandchild of one of the founders of Harvard College across the river in Cambridge.

Mr. Edes was only some five feet tall, and Ethan said his cheeks were always blushed like reddish puffy balls, and his belly stretched his breeches and shirt while his eyes glared in a determined blue. Although his umber hair was beginning to show greyish strains curling near the ears in those days, he was usually seen donning an elegant wig powdered bright, a practice prominent gentry strolling the cobblestones of Boston, Charles Town, Philadelphia, Williamsburg and Savannah seemed to prefer back then.

In what Ethan described as mystical fate, John Gill was also born across the harbor in the village of Charlestown within months of his printing partner, and surely attended the same little schoolhouse near the peninsula's southern rocks on the Charles River. Some say that around sixteen he began to dabble in the printing trade too, tinkering with the creaky press in a little shop near the docks, and within a year or so rowed across the water to begin life anew in Boston. Mr. Giles said young John was soon a printing apprentice for Sam Kneeland, a spirited colonist who published the New England Journal in those days and once printed the Boston Gazette. Then in the fall of 1754 he married his mentor's daughter Stella and settled into an impressive house on Spring Lane, a brightly trimmed home of shiny panes and crimson bricks just a bit southeast of the cobblestones of King Street.

Ethan said Mr. Gill was a little taller than most, slim and perhaps just over six feet, and that his chestnut hair was cropped just above his shoulders and usually twined to a tail upon his neck. His youthful eyes seemed strangely sullen, a weary brown beginning to show thin strands of green, and when in the shop he always looked as printers did in those days, a stained leather apron snugging his shirt and dangling past his knees.

Although John Gill was known to support opposition to the crown that was simmering about the colonies in those early days, it seems at first his enthusiasm was somewhat timid when compared with his more vocal printing friend. After all, some would say, unlike Ben Edes, John had shied from joining a few of Boston's earlier groups meeting to assail laws and actions from London, gatherings like the old caucus club or now defunct loyal nine spurred by Sam Adams. Then finally awakened by the increasing encroachments flowing across the sea, Mr. Gill succumbed to his spirited passions to help form the port's sons of liberty.

It seems John and Ben first discovered a common passion for printing when Ethan and I were five or six, having met in late spring over mugs of ale in that Green Dragon Tavern, and as a hazy mist shrouded Boston that chilly day, they agreed to pool their shillings and pounds and open a shop on the cobblestones of Queen Street. They began to print business notices and merchant broadsides in their Edes and Gill Print Shop, and soon were publishing their Boston Gazette and Country Journal too, a paper the royal governor pressingly commissioned to produce an array of officious documents like royal proclamations and decrees.

In spite of that royal commission, as the years slowly passed they began to show their passion for independence, and by the hour of parliament's Stamp Act, their Boston Gazette was beginning to express a defying attitude Royal Governor Bernard was said to view as disloyal to the crown. And by that summer day of 1767 their shop was printing the enlightened thoughts of daring Boston men, spirited opinions of the sons and others which were disliked by those loyal to the king while exposing the folly of London.

It was a little past one that warm August afternoon as Ethan gripped Cato's reins and trotted past the shallow hills of Bunker and Breed's on that protruding peninsula, then clumping onto the elm slats of the Charlestown ferry, crossed the waters to Boston. Several of the king's Royal Navy ships were moored to docks and anchored in the harbor too, and through the haze shrouding the distant bay waters, he could see one of the crown's ships vanishing out to sea.

Copp's Hill rose near the rocks as they debarked and trotted southeast on the stones of Ferry Way toward Queen Street, and as Cato's iron shoes scrapped the cobblestones, Ethan glanced to the swallowtail vane rising atop the spire of Christ Church. Scores of colonists were strolling the port's lanes and creaking the stones in buggies and carriages as they trotted south on Prince Street that Sunday afternoon, and beneath a gaggle of gulls soaring about summer clouds, Ethan watched little vessels bob on the murky waters of the Charles River.

Ethan said they soon passed Mrs. Davies' Tavern on Hanover Street, a spirited house near the river's Mill Pond, then a bit past my aunt and uncle's place up Beacon Hill and near the edge of the common, they trotted east on the cobblestones of Queen Street. He could see the rusty bricks and impressive windows of his colony's statehouse in the distance on King, and after scraping the stones another block or two, tugged the reins tight near the corner of Brattle Street.

The shop was just to the left and looked to Ethan to be more like a house than a printing place, and the words *Edes and Gill Print Shop* were brushed in blue on a slat that dangled above the front door from dark thin chains. Several windows with multiple square panes adorned both floors, those of the upper shrouded by intriguing gables, a floor housing what Ethan would discover was a special room. It was a place that at times seemed hidden behind a mysterious door, a room where enlightened Bostonians gathered now and then to discuss a disturbing policy being imposed by Royal Governor Bernard or a new intruding mandate hatched in London.

Ethan slowed Cato with a gentle tug and eased to a stop, then leapt from his saddle and wrapped the reins about an iron ring dangling an oak post near the edge of cobblestones. As he bound up a few steps he could see two men through the panes of the left window, then flicking and brushing dust and bits from his breeches and shoulders, he snatched the latch and swung the door open. They were standing off to the left near a desk and stack of various pamphlets and papers in what seemed an intense discussion, and as Ethan shyly stepped to the slats of the shop and shut the door with a gentle click, they twisted with an intriguing glance.

"Excuse me, sirs," Ethan nervously uttered. "I'm looking for Mr. John Gill."

"Who might you be, lad?" the elder looking of the two calmly asked.

"My name is Ethan," he sputtered in an anxious tone, "Ethan Sheehan, from Lexington. I help Nathan Giles in his print shop, and have a message from him for Mr. Gill."

"That would be me," touted a confident John Gill while stepping with an outstretched hand toward Ethan. "A friend of Nathan's is a friend of mine," he gently added, gripping Ethan's fingers. "It's good to meet you, Mr. Sheehan."

"It's good to meet you too, Mr. Gill," Ethan shyly replied.

"Now, Ethan," he seriously asked, "what's this message from Nathan?"

"Well," Ethan sputtered while snapping an uneasy glance toward the younger man watching and listening.

"It's alright, son," assured Mr. Gill, sensing the concern in Ethan's tone, "you can speak before this man." Then with a swinging swoosh of his hand and glance back to that man standing steady at the desk, he added, "I'd like you to meet Mr. Revere, Boston's finest silversmith."

"Good to meet you, Mr. Revere," Ethan politely said, stepping to grip his outstretched hand.

"It's a pleasure, Ethan," he briskly replied. "Please, call me Paul. I've known Nathan for quite some time, a fine printing man, a good man."

"Now, young man," John intensely injected, "Ethan, what do you have for me?"

Ethan quickly scanned the shop and snapped a glance back to the door and windows, then stepping to a scuffed windsor chair nearer the printing press right of the desk, plopped his dusty boot to the maple and spindles. As those men curiously watched, Ethan reached deep into his boot and snatched the thin satchel, then unraveled its twisted twine and pinched the parchment. "Nathan asked that I give this to you," he explained with a brush of pride, handing the message to Mr. Gill, "or Mr. Edes, if I couldn't find you."

"Thank you, Ethan," John graciously replied. Then unfolding the parchment he began to read, and after several hushing moments, nodded to

Mr. Revere and said, "Lexington is with us, Paul, in opposing those Townshend Acts. Nathan says his sons will embark on a campaign in Middlesex County to reduce, and halt if possible, the purchase of those London goods. He quills here, Paul, 'To the devil with those bloody Townshend duties and taxes!'"

"That's fine news, John," Paul approvingly uttered while glancing to Ethan and back. "Let's see, that makes it some fifteen more towns just this past week."

"Paul," John quickly added, scanning the parchment for a moment, "we need to ensure that as many groups as possible, as many sons, know what we're doing here in Boston, and in other villages and towns, in Worcester, Taunton, Gloucester and Lexington. Ben, John and Sam want to make sure our messages reach not only all of Massachusetts Bay, but get to-and-fro all the colonies. We need to keep the sons informed, Paul, not only here in Boston, but in Charles Towne and Williamsburg, Philadelphia and the port of New York. We all need to know what's being talked about and planned."

"I've already talked with Johnny and Sam about it, Jimmy Otis too," replied Paul with a contented gleam in his eyes, "and think we have a pretty good system in place now. I've got riders throughout the colony, John, here and all the way down to Georgia, young men willing to gallop as swiftly as they can. I'll get this information out, depend on it, and ensure our riders return with information about what the other sons are planning."

"Excellent, Paul!" sputtered a pleased John Gill. "I do remember some of us touching on that topic some weeks ago." Then twisting to Ethan with that message still pinched in his fingers, he added, "I'd like you to take a response to Nathan."

"Yes sir, Mr. Gill," Ethan nervously uttered, "I sure will."

"Thank you, son," John graciously replied, shuffling to his maple desk and sliding to the tan cushion of the printer's chair, a comfort crafted in Williamsburg years before. Then nestling to its padded arms, he pressed Nathan's message to the desk, reached and dabbed a feathered tip into a polished tin, and began to stroke his reply to the back of the parchment.

While Ethan stood near Mr. Revere and watched Mr. Gill quill his special words, he could hear muffled voices coming from upstairs, and glancing to the rear of the shop he could see oak steps rising against the wall, a stairway that vanished into a ceiling and the door of a secret room. At first he thought it was two men up on the second floor, then it sounded as though it could be three or more, colonists in a spirited conversation shrouded in garbles and whispers. As Ethan watched Mr. Gill and snapped glances to the rear, he wondered what was taking place in that room atop those stairs.

"There's a big den up there," Mr. Revere softly said, sensing Ethan's inquisitiveness about the voices coming from upstairs, "a special place we call, the long room. When you see it, Ethan, you'll know why. It's a place more private, where we can gather now and then and talk about what's really going on here in Boston, around the colony. Those sounds are coming from Ben, Sam and John, John Hancock."

"That's right, Ethan," quickly inserted Mr. Gill with a glance to those stairs, "that's our long room. Maybe next time there'll be more time, and you'll be able to meet them." Then stroking his final word, he slid the quill to a cup of colorful feathers, carefully creased the parchment and placed it in Ethan's hand. "Take this back to Nathan, and give my regards to your father, a good man. And Ethan," he added with a paternal stare, "thank you."

"I'll take this straight to Mr. Giles," Ethan uttered, sliding the message inside that thin satchel and looping the twine, then stuffing it back into the safety of his boot. "You know my dad?"

"Yes, I do," John softly replied, rising from the leather of his printers' chair. "I've known your father for a while, Ethan. Pat and I have sipped ale and talked right here in Boston a few times, over at the Green Dragon Tavern. I've stopped by his tavern now and then too, when in Lexington to see Nathan."

"I didn't know," Ethan confessed as they gripped hands in farewell. "I'll give dad your regards, Mr. Gill, Nathan too. It was my pleasure to meet you." Then twisting with a departing reach, he added, "Good to meet you too, Mr. Revere."

"Yes, my pleasure, Ethan," Paul replied with sincerity, "good to meet you too. I trust we'll be seeing you again?"

"I'm pretty sure you will."

"Have a safe ride back to Lexington," John added in a fatherly way. "We'll see you again, I'm sure of it."

"Thank you, both of you," Ethan timidly replied while stepping to the door before suddenly spinning. "Oh, I almost forgot. Mr. Giles asked me to bring back a few copies of your latest Gazette."

"Of course, Ethan," John quickly chimed, glancing to a pile of Boston Gazettes stacked on the floor near his desk, "there's some right there. They'll be all about the port by tomorrow afternoon. Take whatever you need."

"Thanks, Mr. Gill," Ethan uttered, snatching a dozen or so and tucking them beneath his arm. "Goodbye, and again, thank you, both of you."

"So long," Paul whispered, quickly followed by John. "Be careful."

Ethan swung the door and closed it with a soft clicking tug, secured the Gazettes behind his saddle with a string of sturdy twine, then climbed atop Cato with a grip of the reins. Glancing down to that boot, he nudged his heels and began an easy trot toward the eastern docks on the cobblestones of Queen then King Street. Ethan wanted to ride back to Lexington on a roundabout way along the watery edge of Boston, and as they veered north then west amid the sounds of scraping hooves echoing about warehouses, homes, wharfs and shops, they trotted along the harbor toward the ferry for Charlestown.

Ethan said they passed several of the king's soldiers on that meandering ride, royal troops strutting about the docks near Faneuil Hall in dark tricorn hats and crimson coats or patrolling the wharfs in bright breeches and dark boots in little groups of twos, threes and fours. "But it was their musket guns, Andrea, dangling their shoulders which sent a chill through me, their muzzles thrusting up. I was nervous when glancing to those soldiers, most just gazing straight ahead, and surprised when a few nodded as we passed."

As they trotted along Boston's northern ridge, Ethan glanced back to Castle Island shrouded in the harbor mist, and for a moment thought he saw an array of the king's troops milling in the distant haze, tiny figures in red wandering about the stone walls of the island's fort. And as they approached the weathered planks of the Charlestown ferry he switched his gaze to the summer clouds stretching the frontier horizon, soft white wisps that would soon be shielding the setting sun in shifting shades of yellows, oranges and reds.

I remember Ethan confiding how crossing the harbor was always serene, and for a little while he'd escape his colonial life amid the whispering winds and the ferry's tranquil path smoothing the chilly waters. And he'd snap his gaze south too, to the expanse of the Charles River that narrowed in the distance to a stream along the southern edge of Cambridge, a quiet river that meander several miles northeast from some mysterious place near the village of Hopkinton.

They trotted past those Charlestown hills and through the peninsula narrows, and with a tight grip of the reins, galloped another dozen miles along the dusty stones of the Massachusetts Road through that trio of villages back to Lexington. With each pounding gait Ethan glanced to groves of maple, birch, oak and elm scattered about the meadows, hills and swaying crops of farmers' fields. And as the soft evening wind brushed his cheeks, he could hear little birds singing in the trees, tender chirps which, in a mysterious way, made Ethan wonder of what awaited his life.

He began to think of his small new role with the Lexington sons of liberty, of what that might expand to and mean someday, and wondered what the coming year, two or three might bring. Ethan found himself whispering for patience with each clumping gait and chirping song, understanding in a mystical way that at just sixteen, his young life had yet to unfold. And as they galloped closer to the Buckman Tavern his thoughts began to drift to what he had seen that summer day, to those two men in that Boston print shop, and realized that although he knew a bit about Mr. Gill, he knew little of the other one.

I remember how Ethan once said Mr. Revere didn't look much like a printer, at least not in the style of John Gill or Mr. Giles, but seemed a bit more unpolished and rustic, perhaps the way a silversmith was supposed to be. I think he described him as somewhat chubby, a little shorter than most with roundish cheeks, and his dark hair was neatly groomed close to his ears that day. His white stockings ran from tan breeches down to shiny brown shoes, and his loose vest exposed a belly pressed to a bright ruffled shirt snugged to his neck.

Ethan would soon discover that Mr. Revere had a shop on Fish Street near Clark's Wharf along the northeastern docks, and was known about Boston and the colony as a gifted silversmith, an artist in creating, etching and molding things like plates, trinkets and bells in copper, silver and tin, and cups and pots for tea. And although Ethan had only learned of his relation to the sons of Boston that day, he could clearly see that Mr. Revere was creating more than just metal things, that he was instrumental in devising a message system for not only the sons of liberty of Massachusetts Bay, but for all the colonies.

Ethan stopped at Mr. Giles' print shop after trotting into Lexington, handing him Mr. Gill's reply and leaving a stack of those Boston Gazette and Country Journals, and as the sun began to spray its setting colors beyond the frontier that day, he quickly galloped across the village field to the Buckman Tavern. He left a few of those Boston papers on the little table left of the tavern door, for his father and inquisitive patrons to peruse, and after tidying an array of tables and washing a slew of wares and plates, cups, mugs, goblets and tins, dashed to his room beyond the stairs. "I was tired, Andrea," he confided, "and so happy to be home, safe in my little room. There was a serene summer breeze that Sunday night, and after a while, I just drifted to sleep."

Those summer nights soon passed and Ethan returned to his studies at the schoolhouse that fall, to all those papers, pamphlets and books, and as the winds of winter began to blow, he continued to help his father at the tavern, learn more of the printing trade with Mr. Giles, and dash with a sons' message now and then. And shortly after his seventeenth birthday, when the first flurries of 1768 began to sweep across the hills and fields, he began to expand his duties at the print shop after school and Saturday afternoons.

All the while, King George and his parliament continued to suppress the colonies with those despised Townshend Acts, and the sons of liberty and other daring colonists in Boston, Lexington and beyond continued to shun those London goods. They were determined actions by spirited women and men, which when combined with the swelling discontent being quilled and printed in the ports of Boston, Philadelphia and New York, in Williamsburg and Charles Towne, enflamed the tensions simmering between the colonies and the crown.

Ethan once said that the sparkling embers of discontent were beginning to flare more intensely throughout his Colony of Massachusett Bay during those stormy winter weeks, and that the fiery strains between Royal Governor Bernard and the colony's assembly began to sizzle and spritz. Perhaps known more widely as a general court in those days, it was an assembly of colonists chosen by villages, towns and counties that would gather at the statehouse on King Street in Boston, an assembly controlled by the royal governor and a panel of his loyal men. Mr. Giles and Doc Newman were there for Lexington and most of Middlesex County as that winter began, while Sam Adams and John Hancock ensured that the spirited voices of Boston never missed an arousing session, two men rumored to be daggers in the governor's side.

While those disgruntled fires were flaring about the assembly of Massachusetts Bay and other colonies, the hundreds of sons of liberty groups continued to plea for resistance to those acts as increasing numbers of courageous colonists expressed their supportive views. And even though Ethan was now attending each gathering of Lexington's sons in an observing way, he continued to struggle with noxious rumors of callous violence tainting the cobblestones of ports, villages and towns throughout the colonies, Boston too. He began to wonder, if such troubling things would ever change.

Those disturbing stories were filtering into Germantown during those wintry weeks too, frightening rumors of rabid sons destroying royal property and taunting those loyal to the king. Father said that dozens of crazed men set fire to several stuffed dummies in the port of New York during a snowy chill near midnight, desperate sons who torched bundled images of Ethan's Royal Governor Bernard to show disapproval of his enforcement of those Townshend Acts in the Colony of Massachusetts Bay. Other sons were rumored to have released their wrath those icy nights upon some of the king's customs men too, assaulting their safety and defiling their homes near the southern rocks of the Island of Manhattan.

In spite of those kinds of disturbing stories swirling about the colonies, Ethan hushed his misgivings and continued to attend the gatherings of the

Lexington sons, finding a way to watch and listen while whispering before sleep each night to avoid such unruly things. Perhaps staying was a reflection of pride in his father, or a sense of respect for Doc Newman, John Parker and others of Lexington, or maybe Ethan wondered, it was an impulsive desire to belong, even when a few violently strayed. Yet I suppose most of all, Ethan knew he simply agreed with the core beliefs of the sons, their spirited views in opposing the king, and supported the ideas touted by James Otis and Sam Adams, his father, Mr. Giles, Ben Edes and John Hancock, views as to why those Townshend Acts were so destructive to the colonies.

It was during those wintry months that Ethan's apprehensions began to slowly crumble beneath his surging appreciation of the sons' passionate opposition to those London acts, and his desire to become more involved began to squelch his reluctant feelings dwelling inside. "Riding to Boston on special journeys," he once confided, "taking important messages for Mr. Giles, doing my part in enhancing communications for the sons, grew more and more appealing. And the notion of meeting such spirited colonists, Andrea, such daring men, touched a passionate core, stirring a fascination deep within."

He began to increasingly volunteer to carry special sheets of folded parchment for Mr. Giles, vital notes of his Lexington sons, stuff them in his boot and gallop to Boston for delivery to Mr. Gill or Ben Edes, and sometimes Mr. Revere at his silversmith shop. Soon Ethan was riding with messages to sons in other villages and towns too, galloping north to Bedford during a Saturday evening flurry or dashing west to Concord on a chilling Sunday morning along the snowy ruts of the Massachusetts Road.

As intrigued as Ethan was with his expanding riding duties as that winter of 1768 passed, I suppose he was most excited by his increasing involvement in the publishing trade. Mr. Giles was slowly adding fresh responsibilities to Ethan's printing tray, allowing him to help develop the designs for the Gazette and accepting more tidbits of Ethan's youthful views for printing now and then. His knowledge of the printing trade expanded with each display of trust from Mr. Giles, and his proficiency with pressing parchment sheets with iron galleys, type and plates was being honed with each passing day. And if I recall, Ethan wasn't just reconfiguring the views of Mr. Giles, or reprinting the beliefs of those in Boston opposed to those Townshend Acts, but the ideals of colonists like George Mason and Mr. Henry over in the Colony of Virginia.

I remember one of those special letters quilled in Boston was reprinted in Philadelphia's Pennsylvania Gazette later that February, views quickly printed in other pamphlets and papers throughout the colonies. It was a letter that seemed to ignite a fresh surge of support for the positions espoused for months by the sons of liberty, words that some were saying squeezed the hearts of the king's royal governors in chains of displeasure, especially Ethan's Governor Bernard. It was a sheet of parchment quilled in a candlelit room by Sam Adams that explained the righteousness of opposing the crown, a daring expression of defiance that was approved by his colony's assembly and circulated throughout the colonies by an array of swift riders.

The Pennsylvania Gazette exclaimed that his letter eloquently expressed colonial displeasure with those Townshend Acts, and that it reasoned with clarity why the sons of liberty were appealing for all colonists to resist London's guile of once again taxing our colonies without a whiff of representation. "Unite in common action against King George and his parliament," Mr. Adams defiantly pled, hoping the colonies might corral their opposition to the crown's "abomination of unjust taxation. We must express our righteous scorn of the king's loyal men in our colonies, royal governors pressing forward with enforcement of these despicable acts." I remember he also explained the methods unleashed by the sons in Boston and Massachusetts Bay to defy the duties and taxes imposed by those acts, while appealing with each stroke of his quill for the colonies to "band in thoughts and deeds for liberty!"

Ethan later said that Mr. Revere had organized the circulation of that letter throughout the colonies that February, assembling a slew of swift riders to gallop to hundreds of ports, villages and towns, and upon orders of the colony's assembly in Boston, dispatched special riders to deliver Mr. Adams' appeal to each colony's assembly. It seems Mr. Revere personally carried that letter to the assembly in the port of New York, inspiring scores of riders galloping from Boston, like the young tanner named William Dawes he'd later say showed daring enthusiasm. "I did my part too," Ethan proudly whispered one night, "riding printed copies to the sons in dozens of villages and towns. I even pressed Mr. Adams' words to several printings of the Lexington Gazette that winter and spring."

Soon a few colonial assemblies were overtly displaying approval of the positions espoused by Ethan's Colony of Massachusetts Bay, and some were courageously decreeing that many in their colony supported the pleas of Mr. Adams and the cries of the sons to unite in opposition to those Townshend Acts. "It is not only proper," they'd say, "but the duty of every colonist striving for individual liberty." I remember my Colony of Pennsylvania supporting those spirited men of Boston too as the final flurries of winter blew, a position Philadelphia's Evening Post said was increasingly appealing to the colonies of Connecticut, New York and New Hampshire. They were daring positions sure to stir the tensions brewing between the king's royal governors and our colonial assemblies, defiant postures father would declare "ungratefully disloyal" while fuming before the hearth with a goblet of wine after supper those snowy nights.

Then in the hours before spring, rumors of rising discontent across the sea in London began to spill upon our colonial shores, stories being spread by seaman debarking ships in the ports of Charles Towne, Providence, Newport and Wilmington, Boston, Savannah and New York, of fiscal pressures being brought to bear upon English merchants. There were disturbing rumors too of King George and his ministers becoming royally annoyed at the increasing news of colonial opposition to his beloved Townshend Acts, powerful men huddling amid the glow of midnight candelabras while scheming of devious reprisals to halt what the crown viewed as "misguided misdeeds of disloyal colonists."

It was around then that the king's minister responsible for the American Colonies, Wills Hill, the First Marquess of Downshire whom most simply knew as the Earl of Hillsborough, was reported to have decreed from the halls of parliament that our royal governors were to "suppress immediately" all support by their colonial assemblies of that "traitorous letter quilled by that scoundrel, Sam Adams." That royal order on behalf of the king was quickly followed in early spring by another, commanding Royal Governor Bernard to "dissolve forthwith" the assembly of the Colony of Massachusetts Bay should it "refuse to debunk that rebellious venom spewed by Mr. Adams." Yet for hazy reasons bewildering to this day, it seems Ethan's royal governor flinched in enacting a proper plan to implement the crown's desires, and whether spurred by reluctance to stir the tempest or simply a glimmer of colonial empathy, it was a delay some say allowed that appeal for unity to flourish throughout the colonies.

While the pleas of the sons of liberty for colonists to shun those Townshend goods were increasingly taking hold that spring, their policy of not buying or using those London things was being passionately debated in colonial assemblies by men who supported those defying views and those who loyally leaned toward the king. It was around then that I began to hear rumors of little colonial fleets sailing those tainted goods in the hush of night to secretive docks in the ports of Boston, Williamsburg, New York and Savannah, efforts to deny those Townshend duties from the crown. And just as they had some three years before, at the height of defiance to that Stamp Act, the king's royal governors and loyal colonists described those merchants as "disgraceful smugglers shirking their duty" to pay London's taxes. All the while, the sons and hundreds more like Sam Adams, Doctor Warren and George Mason portrayed those daring men as "colonists seeking justice for all Englishmen."

Ethan once told me about one of those secret vessels known as the *Liberty*, a seafaring sloop owned by Mr. Hancock that was seized in early June by agents of the king at a shadowy dock of Boston. "Dad said she had just sailed across the sea from London," he confided with a gleam of pride in his eyes, "and beneath a misty sliver of a midnight moon she quietly sliced the harbor with her hull stuffed with an array of Townshend goods. Mr. Giles always said, Andrea, that John never intended to pay the king one pence in taxes, not one shilling or pound for those things." It was a sloop he'd later hear was brimming with boxes and sacks of pulps, glass, ink and parchment, along with crates of French wine and Caribbean rum.

It seems the *Liberty*'s shipping plans were thwarted by Royal Governor Bernard that hazy spring night, stymied with the assistance of a mysterious Bostonian with gripping loyalties to the king or a wicked disdain for Mr. Hancock. Ethan said most believed it was a colonist with objections of the sons, and there were fuzzy rumors the informer may have been the boy of a Boston tinsmith. Yet I suppose most believed that the royal governor's good fortune was spurred by Richard Draper, a foe of Mr. Hancock and publisher of a loyal newsletter known as the Massachusetts Gazette and Boston Weekly.

The crown's customs agents were apparently alerted shortly after sunset, and as that slender ship skimmed the waters in the hushing hours near midnight, the governor's loyal men quietly slid into position. As the *Liberty* slowed and moored to a creaky dock at a weathered wharf along the harbor's southeast rocks, the king's tax agents sprang from the shadows and suppressed a surprised crew. The crown's men dashed upon her deck and confiscated all those sacks and crates of Townshend goods, and as several royal soldiers with muskets gripped manned the dock, they impounded that sloop in the name of the king.

Ethan said it was a week or so later that he first met that fearless Mr. Attucks, when he bound through the Buckman Tavern door shortly after dusk on a rare gallop through Lexington. Some of the men sipping spirits whispered that Crispus was a mix of Negro and native, suggesting that his mother was of the Wampanoag tribe down in Rhode Island. And Ethan would quickly learn that he was a worker of the docks as of that late spring day, unaware that he'd die within two years on the snows of King Street that chilling March night. "He was on his way back to Boston from Concord," Ethan remembered, "when he stopped at the tavern to rest his colt and wash down the dust of the Massachusetts Road."

After Ethan watched Crispus whisper with his father at the barreled bar for several secretive moments, he soon realized that Mr. Attucks was a member of Boston's sons, and with a mug of dripping ale taming his thirst, he began to reveal things that had happened to that sloop imprisoned at the docks. "He told dad and all of us that dozens of sons," Ethan confessed, "along with scores of colonists decrying Governor Bernard's unjust actions, had gathered near John's boat still shackled at Palmer's Wharf. They had rushed to show defiant support for Mr. Hancock and seething distain for those Townshend acts, blasting angry taunts at the king's agents milling about her deck and hurling scathing threats at royal soldiers stoically at guard on the dock. 'Release Mr. Hancock's goods!' Crispus recalled their shouts. 'Return his *Liberty*!'"

Crispus nervously explained that he was with other dockworkers a few hundred feet north, snatching, tossing and stacking sacks and crates from a merchant ship while listening to the howling crowd, when he and his men stopped to watch the swelling mob shouting an array of scornful jeers. They were shouts Ethan would later understand were intended for Royal Governor Bernard, rumored to be safe that very moment inside the bricks and panes of his royal house several blocks northwest. "Release Mr. Hancock's ship, you bloody Bernard!" they continued to demand, and as Crispus and his men watched in a riling silence, they blasted a little more, "Set his cargo free!"

"Them agents just stood their ground," Crispus recalled to Ethan, his father and a few farming men sipping rye whiskey and ale, "didn'ts budge on that there deck. Neithers did those redcoats. Theys didn't move, and nothin was released." It seems all those taunting demands and threats continued for another hour or so, then Crispus, his men and all those angry colonists watched as a fresh column of royal troops strutted to the dock. They snatched those guarding soldiers and customs men from their plight, and in rhythmic strides, marched north to the haven of Halsey's Wharf.

Ethan would later learn that despite the daring taunts of those determined women and men at the dock that June day, all the sacks and crates of Mr. Hancock's Townshend goods, products and supplies Royal Governor Bernard had declared contraband, were never to be released, and his *Liberty* would remain the property of the king. Yet, in a small way, those colonists had created a tiny victory, for within hours that late spring night all those soldiers and customs men were evacuated from the cobblestones of Boston by the governor, whisked in a royal vessel to the safety of Castle Island hidden in the shadows of the misty harbor.

It wasn't long before those of Boston and Massachusetts Bay, all the colonies I suppose, would discover that the events of that contentious June day, when combined with the troubles already brewing in Ethan's colony, infused a sense of panic in Royal Governor Bernard. It seems that shortly after dawn the following day he sailed a desperate dispatch to London advising of what he described as "rebellious events" while pleading for the crown to send more royal troops. "We must bring an end to this disloyal unrest," he was rumored to quill, "ensure parliament's laws and the king's will are adhered to by all colonists." Then in late July or perhaps early August the *HMS Romney* of the crown's Royal Navy, a menacing warship with a trio of masts and some fifty iron guns shrouded by an early morning haze, sailed into the waters of Boston Harbor.

"Her complement of royal soldiers was rather slim," Ethan would later confide, "and she mostly just floated in the harbor, her royal anchor dropped a few hundred yards off the northeastern docks of Boston. Mr. Giles said that the sole purpose of that ship was to intimidate the port and help Governor Bernard maintain his grip on the colony." It seems she just kept her cannons pointing toward Faneuil Hall, to Boston's homes, steeples and shops, and every day the crown's Union Jack lazily dangled at twilight and wildly fluttered in the afternoon winds. King George and his parliament, and their royal governor too, were determined to hold their powers and enforce those Townshend Acts.

Despite the pressures being brought to bear by the crown and its royal governors upon Ethan's Boston and Massachusetts Bay, upon all the colonies that spring and summer of 1768 in their efforts to enforce those acts and silence our colonial assemblies, discontent continued to brew. Although many in each colony's assembly remained loyally twined to the king, a growing number of colonists were finding the defiance espoused by those of Boston to be righteously just. And following what the Pennsylvania Evening Post described as "divisively arousing debates" in every colonial assembly, each colony would come to align their fate with the Colony of Massachusetts Bay by opposing those Townshend Acts and rejecting the subtle threats of royal governors. Unity over discourse had been chosen by the colonies that summer, and the ugly intimidations spewed by the crown had been spiritedly rebuffed.

As those types of tensions simmered about the colonies, especially in Ethan's Massachusetts Bay, and after many weeks of Royal Governor Bernard's inability to persuade his colony's assembly to renounce the views espoused by Mr. Adams in his defiant letter, the king's governor pounced. Succumbing to what many believed were mounting pressures from London, in early August Governor Bernard dissolved his colony's assembly.

The Evening Post revealed that reaction to the governor's "misguided belligerence" was swift in Boston and throughout the colony, spurring a greater vigor in colonists to oppose those parliament acts and deprive the crown's coffer of all those duties and taxes. Once docile women and men in hundreds of villages and towns were suddenly invigorated, Ethan's Lexington too, refusing to buy or use those Townshend goods. And thousands once quiet throughout the colonies began to grasp the defiant ideals espoused by the sons of Massachusetts Bay, particularly colonists in the port of New York. "Someday, even a blind king discovers a flame," blasted the Post, "and maybe, on that day, London will understand it will not be allowed to run roughshod over the colonies. Hear our righteous pleas, King George, and repeal those bloody Townshend Acts!"

Yet those rational pleas from reasoning colonists seemed to fall silent upon royal governors unable or unwilling to mend, and as the leaves began to turn and the defiance of spirited women and men in Massachusetts Bay and all the colonies rooted deeper into our colonial soil, royal hearts across the sea continued to harden. There were disturbing rumors too in those autumn days of royal governors dispatching unflattering reports of disloyal events to London, desperate men quilling for more help. Then soon we began to hear that the crown's new Prime Minister FitzRoy, the young Duke of Grafton known as Augustus Henry and sometimes Earl of Euston, approved increasing brute power in the colonies. "Demand such a force as you deem appropriate," his dispatch to General Gage was rumored to read, commander of all the king's forces in the colonies, "to quietly quell the rebellious voices of Boston."

It was the second Saturday of October, Ethan would later recall, as a chilling morning mist hovered Boston, when a fleet of Royal Navy warships could be seen slowly slicing toward the harbor from a distant haze shrouding the sea. And by three that autumn afternoon, hundreds of Bostonians would witness what seemed the entire English Army strutting to the docks of Burrough's Wharf. The Evening Post later revealed that over seven hundred of the king's troops debarked that day, two regiments of royal soldiers from the northern port of Halifax descending to the cobblestones of Boston. They had come with bayonetted muskets to Massachusetts Bay by order of the king, spry soldiers in black boots and crimson coats assigned to help Royal Governor Bernard enforce those despised Townshend Acts while subduing the spirited ideals gripping a growing throng of colonists.

"I was there that afternoon, Andrea," Ethan once confided, "watching from the docks of Hunt's Wharf just west, when all those soldiers marched down those planks into Boston. I remember wondering how young they looked, not much older than me, and how each seemed so eager. They stepped from their ships in a long single column, each with a musket strapped about his shoulder, then quickly assembled on the dock in dapper rows of three. For a while I thought the lines of tricorn hats strutting from the decks of those ships would never end, and for a moment wondered of their intensions, just as hundreds of others I suppose, and how long those redcoats would remain."

Rumors of those intruding troops filtered about the colonies and into Philadelphia and Germantown for weeks to come, stories with fanciful descriptions of how those royal soldiers looked strutting from the docks to the cobblestones of Boston that autumn day. Some sputtered that their hats were innocently trimmed with thin braids, a royal ruse of pleasantries marching to our colonial soil, and some feared their menacing boots that scraped and stomped the port's stones. Perhaps I was a bit too young in those days to truly understand the meaning of their arrival and stay, or maybe I simply chose to ignore, for I had a vision of beauty in their crimson coats flaring bright shirts, their red tails dangling dark boots and white breeches.

Yet Ethan seemed to understand their true nature in those days, perhaps more so than many others, for he was slowly immersing into the tempest increasingly stirring about Boston and Massachusetts Bay. And perhaps he was a bit wiser than I and the youth of our day, able to sense the severity of what might come. Or maybe women, children and men in distant ports, villages and towns, colonists like father, mother and me in Germantown, believed in a misleading way that we were safely detached from the troubles brewing to the north in Boston.

Ethan would later confess that as he watched those royal soldiers gathering at the docks that day, he found that his stare was fixed to the muskets dangling their shoulders, their muzzles thrusting into the autumn air and silvery blades glistening in the sun. They were long guns with dark iron barrels and brown wooden stocks, muzzle-loading flintlocks that would instill a sense of fear in me and so many others in the years to come. Even Ethan confided that he too felt an eerie premonition swirling his soul at the sight of those guns that day, a grisly feeling of death dripping the tips of those shiny bayonet blades.

Looking back after all these years, I suppose those royal soldiers who strutted to the cobblestones of Boston that October day were not much different than young men in the colonies that fall, Ethan too. They were older boys and younger men from ports, villages and towns of an island across the sea, hamlets and farms in England much like those scattered about the colonies from Georgia to New Hampshire, Delaware and Virginia, my Pennsylvania and Ethan's Massachusetts Bay. "They're just loyal boys doing their duty to the crown," father would say, "frightened soldiers far from home," from villages in England's north like Edinburgh, Lancaster, Lincoln, Nottingham and York, from Oxford, Plymouth, Hastings and London. They were royal soldiers unsure of what their youthful adventure would entail, troops strutting into the unknown, a place no one could have truly imagined in the months and years to come.

Yet soldiers they were with allegiance sworn to King George the Third, young men who, at the behest of General Gage and on behalf of the crown, were now performing their royal duty in Boston. Soon they were patrolling the cobblestones and docks in pairs or clusters of four, six or eight, and others with muskets strapped to shoulders were standing guard at Governor Bernard's place, or protecting buildings of the crown like the customs house collecting duties and taxes for the king. And others donning tricorn hats and crimson coats were displaying their presence in a more stylish way, parading across the grass of the common with muskets slung to show all of Boston that the king and his governor intend to maintain colonial control.

There were other disturbing stories too filtering into Germantown that fall, revelations of obnoxious royal soldiers confronting colonists with spurts of debasing words or intoxicated shouts, verbal assaults many soon came to believe were intended to antagonize and degrade. Some of the king's men also had a propensity for physically lashing at Bostonians simply stepping the cobblestones or strolling the common, wharfs and docks, while others seemed to delight in scuffling among themselves after dusk or spouting unflattering tales spurred by whiskey, ale and rum. I even heard that General Gage, having moved his quarters from the port of New York to Boston in the early days of winter, had placed a pair of the king's iron guns during a light snow near the eastern docks of King Street. "He's trying to intimidate the colonists of Massachusetts Bay," some would say, "and with the blessing of that bloody Governor Bernard, has pointed those iron barrels toward the bricks of the statehouse."

Ethan was just a boy, a young man of seventeen that summer and fall of 1768, and as all those troubling things were being unleashed upon his Boston and Colony of Massachusetts Bay, and I suppose, in essence, upon all the colonies in those days, he was grappling with thoughts of what his life would become. "I was at the Boston docks that October day," he'd later confess, "because of my future. It was the reason I found myself witnessing all those royal soldiers disembark." And then he told me of the Saturday in July weeks before, a hot summer night that changed the course of his life.

Ethan said he had just finished his duties at the print shop shortly before dusk that day, having set the final iron bits for Mr. Giles' opinion piece urging colonists of Middlesex County to shun those Townshend Acts, when he walked home to the Buckman Tavern across the grass of Lexington's field. A pair of dusty men was at his father's favorite table by the corner windows left of the tavern door, weary farmers sputtering of heat, soil and crops while sipping from mugs dripping Boston ale. Mr. Giles was already in the tavern too, talking with Ethan's father at a small rear table near the fireplace stones right of the kitchen door. Ethan could see they were engrossed in deep discussion as he bound into the tavern, and as he stepped the oak slats toward their table, they twisted and hushed with intriguing stares.

"Ethan," his father calmly uttered with a soft flick of his hand, "over here. Please."

"Sure will, dad," he replied while stepping easy toward their chairs. "I finished setting the type, Mr. Giles," he quickly added with a snapping glance.

"That's fine, Ethan," Mr. Giles graciously said, "Thank you." Then sipping a spot of ale and glancing to Ethan's father gazing down to his mug, he spiritedly added, "I think your father has something he wants to say."

"That's right, Ethan, I do. Please, sit down."

Ethan could feel his insides twisting in a gripping knot as he slid to the oak slats of the table's third chair nudged against the wall, and could sense panic surging from his toes to flushing cheeks wondering what was about to unfold. Then he breathed an easing sigh and pressed back into the slats of the chair, and with his eyes glancing left to Nathan and right to his father, he gripped its arms and waited.

"We've been talking, Ethan," his father slowly began, shuffling his mug of ale between his hands near the flickering flame of the table's candle. "You've told me, many times, that you want to continue your schooling, study more of histories, theories and laws, read the words of others from here in the colonies and across the sea. You want to improve your own quilling too." Then he hushed for a moment and sipped a dash of ale, glanced to Nathan gazing to that pulsating flame, then back to Ethan's waiting eyes. "Do you still want those things, Ethan? Do you still want to continue your studies?"

"Oh, yes," Ethan quickly confessed with fluttering glances between his father and Mr. Giles, "I sure do!" He could feel those anguishing twists slowly subside, and amid a surge of youthful anticipation, meekly added, "I can't remember not wanting that, dad. Yes, I still want those things."

"I was hoping you'd say that," his father softly uttered with a pleasing tap to the table. "You have a place, Ethan," he calmly added, clicking his mug against the pewter gripped in Nathan's outstretched hand, "at Harvard College, and begin just before fall, if you still want it."

Ethan stared in stunned silence to his father before glancing to Mr. Giles and back, and could hear those two farmers across the room grumbling about the grueling toils of their summer fields, and for a moment felt a sense of euphoria grip his soul. "Well, Ethan?" his father insisted, shattering Ethan's trance. "What do you think?"

"You know I've always wanted this, dad," Ethan softly said, crawling from his quiet shell. "I don't know what else to say, except, yes, I want it."

"We both know that, Ethan, and have for several years. Now, it's officially settled. Congratulations, Ethan."

"But, dad," Ethan questioned with quizzical glances between his father and Nathan, "how did you do this? What, who, how did this happen? It's so difficult to get a spot at Harvard. And the cost, dad. How did you do this?"

"Nathan and I have been talking about this all year," his father insightfully revealed. "We know how you feel about it, Ethan, and so do others, not only here in Lexington, but in Boston too."

"That's right, Ethan," added Nathan with a steady stare and tap of fingers to the pewter of his mug. "Your father and I have discussed this with some in Boston, men who've offered to help."

"You've already met John Gill," explained Ethan's father, "at his print shop. Well, we've been talking with him for quite some time, Ethan, usually in Boston. And after he met you a while back, he wanted to help. Just like Nathan and I, he thinks that with the proper education you'll have a pretty good future in the printing trade, with pamphlets and papers, and with your own writings too. Why, after Harvard, Ethan, you'll be able to do whatever you want."

"I never knew," Ethan shyly uttered while gazing to the flame dancing the twisting wick. "I don't know what to say."

"I believe in you, Ethan," his father caringly replied, staring to the depths of Ethan's eyes, "and so do others. There are good people out there who want to help, and Nathan and John are two of them."

"That's the truth, Ethan," Nathan quickly chimed, "we do. And I must say, John is not one to feign his words. He truly wants to help."

"He's already talked it over with his partner too, Ben Edes," Ethan's father anxiously added, "and both want to provide quite a bit of what you'll need for four years of Harvard studies. They'll pool some funds from their print shop, Ethan, handle most costs, and they'll make a place for you at their shop too, helping them with things you've already begun to learn from Nathan. Of course, keeping up with your studies is what's most important, but then, you already know that. Well, what do you say, Ethan?"

"It's quite an offer, Ethan," Nathan whispered with a sip of ale, "quite a challenge too, and what an opportunity."

"There's something else, Ethan," his father quickly injected. "Mr. Gill has agreed to provide you full board, a room and meals, while you study for four years. You know, Ethan, living in Boston, in his house, might just give you a new perspective on many things, and I think you'll like the independence. Oh, I almost forgot. They plan to pay you a stipend of shillings and pounds too, for your duties at their print shop."

"You know, dad," Ethan softly confessed while dabbing the corner of his eye, "ever since I was little I've wanted to study somewhere, and mom always thought it should be right here, at Harvard College. Now, it can come true. Yes, I want to do this, dad, and agree with all those things." Then with a timid glance to Nathan and back to his father, he added, "I promise not to let you down, either of you. I'll keep up my studies, and do my best for Mr. Gill and Mr. Edes. Thank you, dad, Mr. Giles."

"You're welcome, Ethan," Mr. Giles uttered in a fatherly way, "and glad I could help. Now, you just study those books over there, and become the man God wants you can be."

"Yes, Ethan," his father added with emotions surging his tone, "become what you can be, want to be in this life, but most of all, be happy. Your mother would be so proud of you, maybe more so than I right now. We'll talk more tomorrow, Ethan, or maybe later tonight, after I've shuttered the tavern."

"Alright, dad," Ethan shyly sputtered while rising from his chair with a scraping scratch. "I think I'll take a little walk," he softly added, feeling an anxious flutter deep inside. "I won't be gone long. I'll wrap up my tavern chores before bed, promise. Goodnight, Mr. Giles."

"Goodnight, Ethan. Why don't you stop by the shop tomorrow, if you want. I have some new, rather interesting printing techniques we can go over, some fresh type settings too."

"I just might do that," he replied with a grateful glance, "thanks, Mr. Giles. I'll see you soon, dad," he quickly added, strutting across the dusty slats of the oak floor and dashing into the lazy twilight through the open tavern door. The colorful spray of a cooling dusk was fading beyond the frontier as Ethan stepped toward the dark shrouding the path of Bedford Street, and as little twinkles exploded across the Lexington night, he gazed to the calm settling upon the village field. He scanned an array of candles and lamps glowing windows of shops and homes in oranges, yellows and reds, and as he stepped to the shadows roaming the grass and glanced to the symphony of pulsating stars, he wondered of the things his father said, of Harvard College and possibilities, of what his life would become in Boston.

As the chirp of dancing crickets and hoot of distant owls tranquilly brushed the Lexington night, Ethan could eerily sense the eternal pull of his mother's hill. Amid all those twinkles and sounds he stepped through the dark down the village field to the stony ruts of the Massachusetts Road, then pivoted southwest through the shadows and up the grassy slope of that burying hill. A gentle summer wind smelling of farmer's fields and sweet marigolds kissed his cheeks as Ethan creaked through the cemetery gate, and quietly sneaking past solemn crosses and somber stones, he knelt to the cooling grass swaddling his mother's grave.

"I miss you, mom," he whispered to her lonely stone. Then glancing to the stars sparkling the night, he gazed back to her little angels and added, "I have something to tell you. I'm going to study at Harvard College, mom, for the coming four years, and live in Boston. I wish you were here, wish we could talk." He bowed and stared to the solemn grass for a moment or two, and as the soft summer breeze hissed the trees, he softly said, "You'll be with me, mom, while I'm away, right here where you always are, safe in my heart."

Ethan later said he stayed on his mother's hill for an hour or so that summer night, pondering his future while hoping her spirit might calm the anxiousness swirling his soul, and as he wondered of the lasting changes about to grip his life, his worries began to ease. Then suddenly, as his knees pressed the cemetery soil amid the serene sounds of Lexington, a thread of sparkling white slashed across the starry night and vanished in the dark shrouding the sea. I remember the tear in his eye when he confided that fiery streak was a heavenly sign from his mother, showing his future would be shaped just east in the port of Boston and hamlet of Cambridge.

"He left Lexington as those troubles were truly beginning to brew in Massachusetts Bay?" Samuel inquisitively asked while nudging his chair into a softer rock. "Ethan left his father and the tavern behind, for Boston, for Harvard College? He wasn't concerned?"

I glanced to Samuel in a grandmotherly way and rocked a bit slower, then gazed to the leaves gently rustling in the noon breeze and remembered what Ethan once said. Yes, he had fears at times of the unknown in those days, especially being so young, yet never wavered from his dream of Harvard. I guess Ethan never doubted the spirit of his mother, or the guidance of his father. "He did have concerns, Samuel," I whispered while caressing the parchment of Ethan's poem nestled in the pocket of my summer dress, "just as many colonists did in those days, me too. But he was resolved to choose his own path, even in the face of the simmering frictions between the colonies and London. Ethan would often say, such things were out of his control."

"I see," sputtered Samuel in an impressed tone. "Ethan seems so insightful at an early age, rather courageous too. I guess he was just a determined young man." I glanced with an agreeing nod and brushed a tear trickling my cheek, and as I softly stroked the words of Ethan's aging poem, Samuel gazed to my misting eyes and caringly asked, "What about you, grandma? What were you doing in those days? What were your goals and dreams?"

"Yes, Samuel, I had goals in those days," I sighed while dabbing a tear, "dreams too. Even though I was eighteen that fall of 1768, with immerging notions of life, I still knew I had so much to learn. I suppose mother thought I might find contentment in sewing, a seamstress of some kind, and liked to show me new fabrics and stitches for quilting blankets and sewing dresses and coats, breeches and garments with needles, cloth and thread. Yet, she and father also knew of my desire to help the injured and ailing, a dream I had been nurturing for the past few years at the Pennsylvania Hospital with mother's friend Sarah. By that fall, Samuel, I knew I wanted to help comfort and mend colonists as a nurse."

"I guess I never really knew those things," he confessed while gazing to crimson petals quivering in the summer sun. "Oh, maybe I did hear little bits years ago now and then, but not much. Yet, I did know you'd train to be a nurse, but how, where and when?"

"You know, Samuel," I calmly reflected, "looking back, it almost seems magical that Ethan and I would begin our search to discover our way at the same time, hundreds of miles apart. He too would soon turn eighteen, and just as he had finished his early studies at his Lexington schoolhouse, I too completed mine in Germantown near Mr. Deshler's old place. He was beginning new studies that fall, Samuel, in Cambridge, and I was just starting my nursing training in Philadelphia."

"How, grandma," Samuel excitedly asked with a youthful glance, "what happened?"

"Father had a friend in Germantown in those days, Doctor Schmitz, and when he wasn't tending to colonists up here, he'd take his buggy down to the Pennsylvania Hospital in Philadelphia, maybe two, three times a week. I guess he was good friends with Doctor Bond back then, a man father said was an acquaintance of Mr. Franklin, and knew Sarah rather well. Father spoke to Doc Schmitz sometime in late spring, and after what he said were delicate deliberations, he agreed to help open a training spot for me at the hospital. That's how it happened, Samuel, how my official nursing truly began. In early fall I started riding down to the hospital five or six days a week, and over the coming four years trained with several special nurses while learning as much as I could from a slew of medical books."

"I never knew, grandma. It sounds exciting, fulfilling for you, and in such unsettling times."

"It was, Samuel, it truly was."

As he rocked and peered to the distant elms swaying in the warming breeze, I gazed to petals of laurel and rose bathing in the summer sun as an uneasy calm surged deep inside me. I nudged my chair in an easy rock and slid my fingers across Ethan's tender words, searching for cherished memories, and as a tear trickled my cheek, I reached for the colonies and the war, for those days silenced so long ago by unforgiving winds.

Chapter VIII

Blue Delphinium

Anxiousness rumbled deep inside as Ethan gazed through the open panes peering to the quiet in the moments before dawn, Saturday, the Third of September, 1768. He was lying in his room where he had been resting since the gibbous moon had first glistened off the glass near midnight, dozing now and then, his hair pressing his feathery pillow and blue linen sparingly spread about his body lazily sprawled upon his bed. A warm summer breeze brushed of sweet scents softly wisped through the windows, square panes swung toward a dawn soon to creep upon the dew dripping grass of his Lexington field. For hours he had struggled to ease his mind and escape to sleep, to release the apprehensions gripping his soul of what the coming weeks and months would hold, only to succumb to feelings of dread tainting hopes through the night.

A soft haze lingered low over the village field as the dark edged toward the frontier, and bright little stars began their dutiful fade as night slowly surrendered to the fiery sun creeping from the sea. Ethan nudged a bit deeper into his pillow and gazed to the spray of thin clouds stretching the horizon, misty layers gently swirling as if brushed upon an emerging canvas of zaffre blue in sprays of yellows, oranges, reds and whites. And as Ethan watched the night's final twinkle and gazed to the morning rising over his village of Lexington and Colony of Massachusetts Bay, he knew it would be a day he'd never forget.

It was a morn unlike any other in his young life, for Ethan's cocoon of Lexington was about to crack and splinter with the dawn, exposing him to a colonial world which, in many ways, was still a mystery. Hushing strolls about his village field in the solitude of a summer night or an autumn morning chill were about to become memories, at least for a little while, and the gripping slopes of his mother's hill would be left behind. Ethan was about to unravel the ties which twined him to his earlier days on the farm, leave his home with his father and chores at the Buchman Tavern, his duties at the print shop too, begin anew a dozen miles southeast at Harvard College in Cambridge and across the waters in Boston. Although he would only be a short gallop from his father, and knew he'd visit many times in the coming months and years, Ethan wondered if the village of his birth would ever again, truly be his home.

A dark cloth bag was pressed in the corner by the door and bulged of breeches, stockings and shirts, along with a few special items like that story of the ancient Roman Cato, Mr. Addison's play gifted to Ethan by his father just hours before. Ethan was about to begin his Harvard studies in only days, the following Monday morn, and could feel the anxiousness churning inside while lying on his bed, gazing to the dawn while snapping nervous glances to that bulging bag. He knew what he was doing was right, knew he wanted to begin a new life, yet was grappling with fears of forging his own way. He had stuffed things he'd need over the coming days into that bursting bag in the moments just before midnight, and now was waiting for the moment to depart, bid farewell to the only world he had ever known.

Ethan slowly raised his head off the pillow, propped to his elbows and gazed to his bulging bag once more, then scanned his little haven in a melancholy way, knowing what was about to come. He rolled from his bed a bit before eight and quickly donned stockings, breeches, boots and a bright shirt, then gripping the thin leather straps of his bag and giving his room a final glance, Ethan hushed a departing whisper and bound down the stairs to the tavern floor. Hearing clicks and clanks coming from his father busy in the kitchen to the rear, he rushed across the oak slats toward the end of the barreled bar, tossing his bulging bag to a chair near the door. Dashing in, he could see his father doing what he always did on a Saturday morn, gathering an array of things while slicing a freshly roasted hen, readying for a new tavern day.

"There're some rolls over there, Ethan, and a few boiled eggs in that bowl," his father energetically offered, pointing his right hand to a shelf beneath the open panes of a kitchen window, his shiny fingers gripping the handle of a carving blade dripping tasty hen. "Mornin, Ethan. Please, set those things right here. I'll whip us up a little sandwich, and make a few of this tender chicken too, for your ride to Boston."

"I sure will, that sounds great, dad," Ethan graciously uttered, fetching that birch bowl of eggs and oval porcelain platter of crusted rolls, then placing them to the oak beside his father slicing and picking juicy hen from its bones. "Morning," he softly added, sliding to a high-slatted chair at the little table nudged against the wall near embers still sparkling on the hearth's stones.

"Manage to sleep, Ethan?" his father asked with a caring glance. "I hope so. You've a long day ahead of you."

"Not too well, dad," he sputtered while watching his father pivot from carving tasty fowl to shelling and slicing four boiled eggs. "I guess I was a bit anxious about today, staring out into the night, counting stars. I did manage to doze now and then."

"I understand," his father replied, carefully arranging thin slices of egg on a pair of golden rolls baked the day before by Mary White, the village cabinetmaker's wife who created breads, cakes, pies and other tasty treats for the tavern over the years, "I really do. It happened to me too, many times at the frontier. Here you go," he proudly added, sliding a plate to Ethan and another toward an empty chair.

"Thanks, dad," Ethan whispered as each, now settled in his chair, began to feast on a breakfast of eggs and rolls.

"Ethan," his father seriously uttered with an intense stare while brushing crumbs to his plate, "I want you to remember, always, this is your home. You'll only be a few miles away, and when you feel the need, why, you just ride right back here, anytime, during the week after classes, Saturdays and Sundays too. You can always stay the night, Ethan, and gallop back early, get back to your studies, to duties at Mr. Gill's print shop. Just know, I'll always be here."

"I know, dad," Ethan sighed with a soft gleam in his eyes, "thanks. It helps ease my nerves, just hearing you say those things. I don't yet really know how much free time I'll have, but I'll get back as often as I can, promise." Then pressing back into his chair and watching his father finish his roll with a brush of his plate, Ethan wondered how his father would truly survive without Ethan doing his tavern chores and fetching supplies, moving and stacking barrels, sacks and crates. "Dad, are you sure you'll be alright?"

"Now don't you worry about any of that," his father insisted in a reassuring tone. "I've some good friends here, you know that, and when needed, for a few shillings I'll fetch one of the lads from the schoolhouse to help with things. You just stick to your studies, Ethan, and don't worry about the tavern. Show those fellas at Harvard College, John Gill too, all of them in Boston, the fine young man you truly are."

"Alright, dad," Ethan uttered with a tinge of relief, "I won't worry, and you know I'll do my best. You know what else, dad? I think Mr. Gill and I will get along fine."

"Good," his father exclaimed as he scraped his chair on the oak slats and snatched their empty plates, clacking them to the counter. "Don't forget, Ethan," he quickly added while gripping that dripping blade, carving a bit more of that tender hen and stacking slices to a trio of crusted rolls, little sandwiches for Ethan's journey east, "I'll be in Boston from time to time too, for tavern supplies. Hopefully, we can visit then."

"Sure, dad, I'd like that," he replied as his father bundled those three tasty rolls inside a white linen cloth, then tied its corners with knotty twists and tossed it to Ethan. "Thanks, dad. You know how I love your chicken sandwiches. I'll be right back," he quickly added, dashing through the kitchen door. He grabbed his dark bag of items and clothes, then rushed back through the kitchen and out the rear tavern door to saddle his colt for the ride to Boston, securing his bulging bag and bundled rolls close behind with a string of sturdy twine.

Soon Cato's thin reins were dangling a hitching post near the dusty stones of Bedford Street, not far from the tavern's front door, and Ethan's father was outside to bid his son farewell. "It looks like everything is tied pretty good," his father nonchalantly uttered, "knotted down and ready to go. I'll miss you, Ethan," he whispered, stepping to the road and tenderly wrapping Ethan in his arms. "I'm proud of you, son," he softly added while nudging a bit back and gripping his shoulders, "and so is your mother. Take care."

"I will," Ethan hushed as a mist brushed his eyes. "Thanks, dad, for everything. I'll miss you too. I'll get word back soon, let you know how I'm doing."

"That sounds fine, Ethan," his father calmly said before tugging Ethan close once again. "We'll see each other soon."

"Bye, dad," Ethan sighed with a departing hug before spinning and leaping to his saddle, his tan leather boots digging deep into the stirrups. With that bulging cloth bag and bundled linen twined close behind, Ethan flicked his heels into Cato's sides and began an easy trot down Bedford

Street, along the western grass of the village field. Then as if compelled by an irresistible impulse, he twisted to see his father watching from the tavern door, then gave him a little wave as his father tapped his fingers above his eye. They just gazed to each other for a moment or two, then Ethan twisted once again and rode away.

As Cato trotted east on the little rocks and ruts of the Massachusetts Road along the southern edge of the field, his father stood quiet at the tavern door watching Ethan gallop past the Munroe Tavern and Doc Newman's place in the distance, perhaps adrift in a swirl of memories. The day was still a bit cool, with a thin layer of grey now flowing from the frontier toward the sea as the sun continued its rise shortly after nine that September morn. I remember Ethan confiding how quiet it was with each trot, as if he and his father were the only villagers yet to stir that day, and how peaceful it seemed as a few cows meandered about the grass and roosters dashed about the field, a serenity that spurred a sense of loneliness.

Ethan galloped past Lexington's bell dangling in that hut on a slope south of the road, and along the path lined of birch, oak and elm near the southeast edge of the village, he twisted in his saddle and looked back, gazing past trees, shops and homes to the top of his mother's hill. He could see the elm that towered over her stone, majestic limbs which cast a tranquil shade upon her grave, and with a tear trickling his eye, whispered a soft farewell. Then he twisted once again as Cato's iron shoes dug into the Massachusetts Road, and with a tight grip of the reins, continued his morning ride to Boston.

I remember Ethan saying that it wasn't long before a sense of melancholy began to grip his soul, a nauseous feeling of desperate panic realizing he was truly leaving home. "I just dug my boots into those stirrups, Andrea, gripped the reins tight and spouted to the morning, 'Calm down, Ethan, calm down!' while sputtering over and over, 'everything's going to be alright.' After a while, just before reaching the edge of Menotomy, after a few more sprinting gaits down the Massachusetts Road, that frightening fire began to subside, vanishing into the woods."

With each clumping stride through the villages of Menotomy, Medford and Somerville in his ride toward the narrows of the Charlestown Peninsula, Ethan could sense that desperation flare deep inside now and then, and with each digging gait into the ruts and stones he wondered of the life he was about to find. "Maybe," he'd whisper as colonial dust billowed with each stride, "I'm too young. After all, I'm only seventeen." Yet, while doubts and fears lingered within, he still believed he was ready for the challenges that waited, that the time was truly right, and he clung to the notion that he was never really alone, that his father was close in Lexington and his mother dwelled in his heart. And in a relieving way, he seemed to know that he wasn't the only one struggling with such anxious feelings that September morn, for other young men too were in route to the halls of Harvard College.

Ethan was to meet Mr. Gill that afternoon at his print shop, then ride to his house nearby and discover the nuances of those strange surroundings, settle into his new home. But as he neared the peninsula narrows he wondered of the place his studies were to begin in only two days, and feeling a surging urge to scan those college grounds, tugged Cato's reins right and galloped amid maple, birch and elm down the road to Cambridge. As he trotted through the village he could see the dome of Harvard Hall shining in the late morning sun, its thin copper vane swung into the wind, and from a nearby hill the Harvard Yard grass came into view, and the waters of the murky Charles slowly flowing in the distance east and south.

Cato's trot slowed on that easy rise overlooking Harvard's buildings and grounds, then tugging the reins and coming to a stop, Ethan gazed upon the yard's expanse of green lush grass that rose to a sloping knoll near campus structures of mortar, windows and bricks. They were buildings no more than five floors high for study and quartering young colonists nurturing their dreams, and a short slatted fence stretching the eastern edge of the yard seemed to distinguish toil from pleasure. From his quiet perch Ethan watched a dark carriage slowly circling the grass on a narrow path, tiny stones crunching beneath plodding iron shoes and creaking wheels, and could see scholarly caricatures of professors and young men meandering about the grounds in fours, pairs and threes.

Ethan once told me that in his first weeks of study he had yet to truly understand the intrigues of Harvard College, but would soon discover a history that only enhanced its allure. Some stories were revealed by those who once stepped its halls, revered students from its past who visited now and then, and others were spawned by studious men who had been teaching on the grounds for years. But the more fanciful tales, he'd say, were recalled by aging colonists residing in the village of Cambridge.

It seems the land was first settled some hundred and forty years before by spiritual people rowing across the waters from Boston, women, children and men in search of a place to worship as they pleased. They were a small group of daring colonists refusing to succumb in those days, determined people who soon molded a little village they'd call, Newe Towne. Then a few years later, perhaps 1636 or so, a special school for higher learning was granted to the village by the crown's men in the Colony of Massachusetts Bay, an institution most referred to as the College of Newe Towne. It was a name that would soon conflict with that of the village, for within a year or so it seems the founders of Newe Towne, inspired by scholarly halls across the sea, renamed their quaint little hamlet, Cambridge.

"But it's what happened a year or so later that truly changed the fabric of learning," Ethan would proudly say, "when the preacher John Harvard was buried on the Charlestown Peninsula, after a painful struggle with consumption." They say he was a respected young minister when he died during a late summer rain, and that the colonists of Cambridge were stunned to discover he had bequeathed much of his estate to the new college, a gift that included hundreds of books of his cherished collection. It was in the spring of the following year, Ethan said, that the village renamed their precious school Harvard, a distinction designed to enshrine his memory.

Ethan rested high in his saddle and gazed to his future from atop that slope, and as a pleasing sensation surged his body while peering to his school's windows, grass, mortar and bricks, he twisted and snatched one of his father's tasty rolls. As he gripped the reins and slowly nibbled, he felt inspired at the sight of those special halls and plush green yard, and as a soft breeze brushed his cheeks, anticipation of what was to come teasingly swirled.

He described the building to the far left as rather quaint, just one story on Harvard's northern edge, a small church of crimson bricks and white trimmed windows they called Holden Chapel, mortared some thirty years before. It didn't have a steeple like most in those days, and its intriguing door was topped by a triangle roof that kept watch upon the grass of the yard, as if holding despair and petulance at bay. And a little back to the right was Hollis Hall, a majestic building with six chimney stacks and thousands of bricks, four floors with dozens of rooms and an array of square-paned windows.

Off to the right and a bit south rose the bricks and panes of Harvard Hall, "the core building on campus," Ethan would say, the lone library housing a massive array of pamphlets, papers and books. He said it had been destroyed by a mysterious fire, then rebuilt a few years before through the efforts of determined colonists in Cambridge and Boston. And there were rumors that its resurrection had also been spurred by preachers spouting fiery sermons of faith and retribution, spiritual men like the aging Minister Whitefield.

Harvard Hall was two stories of rusty bricks lined by dozens of windows with scores of square panes, all topped by that shiny dome and weathered vane, an inspiring building which aroused a sense of enchantment while captivating students' souls. Its westerly end kept watch upon the grass of the yard, and its grand façade gazed toward the waters of the Charles in the distance southeast. And I remember Ethan saying that a few elders of Cambridge would spew fanciful tales of seeing wisdom ooze from beneath its elegant elm doors, mystical goo that would spill its stony steps during an eerie howl of a wintry night or serene hush of a spring morn.

A little closer to the river were the four impressive floors of Stoughton Hall, its glass rows of square panes lining an array of scarlet bricks, windows searching for truth fluttering about the village fields and Harvard grounds. An intriguing door swung to the west, while yellow gables shrouded the upper panes and several chimneys reached for the noon sky. And from his saddle Ethan could see a mysterious clock perched atop the hall, and for a moment thought he could hear its thin iron hands clicking ominously over the colonies.

Running to the southeast nearest the Charles was perhaps the grandest of them all, an inviting array of gables and glass, mortar and bricks they called Massachusetts Hall. A quad of smokestacks rose from a tapering roof blanking four floors, a pair thrusting each end, and its majestic doors swung toward the bend of the river. Ethan said Mr. Phipps' farm was just to the east, a place where goats and cows roamed near the swampy lands jutting into the Charles, fields where crops swayed along the river in summer and fall.

Ethan finished his final bite and sat quiet in the saddle, his fingers pinching the reins and hands resting upon its worn leather horn, and from his lazy knoll peered toward the distant Charles while scanning that farmer's fields along the river. Then gazing to the virtuous bricks of his Harvard College, he thought he could hear the faint sounds of hooves digging into that gravely path and carriage wheels crushing its tiny stones, and as he watched colonists lingered about the yard, he wondered what the coming months and years would bring. "How will those halls prepare me?" he whispered to the noon breeze. "What will I become?"

As the September winds rustled the Cambridge leaves and fluttered his hair tailing from his tricorn hat, Ethan scanned that grassy yard a final time, all those bricks, panes and chimney stacks, that dome's tarnished vane too, then nudged his heels into Cato's sides and tugged the reins. They galloped north to the stones of the Massachusetts Road, then scampered east through the peninsula narrows to the Charlestown docks past those quiet hills. "I wanted to get to that ferry," he said, "get to Boston and Mr. Gill's print shop. I wanted to see his home, Andrea, get to my room on Spring Lane. I wanted to start my new life."

The early afternoon sun was now banished behind a layer of grey stretching from the frontier to the bay, and as they crossed the waters of the harbor and Cato clumped from the ferry near Copp's Hill, Ethan could feel his anxiousness truly brewing. He listened to his colt's iron shoes scrap the cobblestones as they wound along Boston's northern edge and down its eastern docks, clacking past a slew of wharfs and that port square before pivoting west on the stones of King Street. Bostonians were strolling the streets and docks or creaking along the cobblestones in buggies and wagons, and several patrols of the king's soldiers were strutting in twos, fours or eights, and as Ethan passed the statehouse he could see carriages, colts and mares tethered outside the Green Dragon Tavern.

King became Queen just beyond the tavern at Cornhill Street, and across the stones to his left was the port's courthouse near the corner of Brattle, and just up on the right was Mr. Gill's print shop. "The upstairs window was closed," Ethan would say, "its shutters buttoned tight, but through the downstairs panes I could see a few men in the shop. Two were talking off to the side, and one was busy near the printing press." Ethan climbed from his saddle at the edge of the stones and slung the reins about an iron ring dangling an elm post, then brushing dust and specs from his breeches and shoulders, he rushed up the steps, swung open the door with a snatch of the latch, and slowly shuffling in.

Ethan had never seen the middle-aged pair standing near two desks off to the left, and when he clicked the door shut, they hushed and glanced before twisting and resuming their whispery discussion. He didn't know the third near the center of the shop either, a somewhat portly yet impressive man busy setting type at the printing press, and just watched as he gripped a stick from an oak bucket and brushed a layer of dark ink to hundreds of iron bits. Although Ethan had yet to meet Mr. Gill's partner, the man spreading that printing goo seemed to fit the description Mr. Giles once expressed of Benjamin Edes.

His dark hair flowed just beyond his ears in scraggly strands greying with curling twists, and a tanned leather apron, blotted and stained hanging about his neck, was snugged over his shirt and breeches by a thin string of twine looped behind. "I think it was his belly," Ethan recalled with a fondly smirk, "that gave him away, bulging just like Mr. Giles said. And when he leaned into the press, squeezing his stomach to the stones, I knew he had to be Mr. Edes."

Ethan stood in his dusty boots at the shuttered door for another moment or two, wondering why his entrance was being uncomfortably ignored, and while the men near those desks continued their soft talk, the portly man draped by that sullied apron remained absorbed in his printing press. "Mr. Edes?" Ethan shyly uttered toward the man inking type. "Mr. Edes?" he questioned once again with courageous spunk. "Excuse me, sir. Are you Mr. Edes?"

"What?" snapped that printing press man as he glanced with a twist. "Oh, I'm sorry," he politely added, "didn't know you were there. This needs to be printed today, and I can get pretty involved. What can I do for you?"

"My name is Ethan," he nervously replied, glancing to the secretive pair now curiously watching, then back to that printing man, "Ethan Sheehan, from Lexington. I'm really looking for Mr. Gill, and thought you might be Mr. Edes?"

"I am, son," he quickly confessed, his belly no longer squeezing the press. "I'm Benjamin Edes. You must be our young Harvard man."

"Yes, I guess I am. I met Mr. Gill a while back, and now, am glad to meet you, sir. I thought I'd get settled in before studies begin this Monday, and was told Mr. Gill expected me. I was hoping to see your shop a bit too, before riding to his house, settling into my room."

"John's told me some good things about you," he said, easing Ethan's concerns, "and so have others." He brushed his hands across his apron, snatched a little stained cloth from a tiny hook and wringed his fingers, then stepped to Ethan and calmly added with an outstretched hand, "It's good to meet you, Ethan. I'm John's partner in all this. I'm sorry, but John's not here right now. He should be home, where he normally is around noon each Saturday."

"I'm pleased to meet you, sir, Mr. Edes," Ethan nervously replied. "And thank you, for this opportunity you've given me, you and Mr. Gill. My father is grateful too."

"After all of the good things I've heard about you," he confided, "from John and Nathan, your father Pat too, I've developed a good feel about this, knew you were the type of young man we like to help. Of course, we do expect a strong work ethic, Ethan, with your studies and here at the shop, and are confident that's just what you'll do. Please, call me Ben."

"Thank you, Mr. Edes," Ethan shyly replied, "I mean, Ben, those are kind words. I'll do my best here, and with my studies, that, I promise. I've been helping Mr. Giles at his shop for quite some time now, and look forward to learning as much I can of printing and publishing from you and Mr. Gill. I won't let you down."

"I believe that, Ethan, we both do, and it's rather pleasing to hear you say those things. Let me know if there's anything you need, anything else I can do."

"Thank you, sir, Ben, I will."

"Good," he replied in a calming tone before nodding and motioning right with his hand. "Come, I want you to meet these two men," he quickly added, stepping toward those desks with Ethan close behind, his dusty boots scraping the oak slats. "I think you'll find commonality with these fine men. This is Mr. Barrett, and Mr. Wingate. Gentlemen, I'd like you to meet Ethan Sheehan. He starts his studies over at Harvard on Monday, and will apprentice here at the shop during his stay."

"It's good to meet you, Ethan," replied the elder looking of the two while snatching Ethan's greeting hand. "Please, call me Sam. I think you'll find your experiences at Harvard pretty challenging, yet gratifying. And I'm sure John and Ben will keep things interesting for you here at the shop. I wish you the best."

"Thank you, Mr. Barrett," Ethan uttered in a sheepish tone.

"Those things go for me too," Mr. Wingate chimed with a friendly grip of Ethan's hand. "Most around here call me Paine. It's a pleasure to meet you." Then with a jocular glance to Mr. Edes, he added, "Just don't let this surly newspaper man bully you around the shop."

"I won't, Mr. Wingate," Ethan shyly sputtered. "It's good to meet you."

"You know, Ethan," Mr. Edes spiritedly injected, "these men, perhaps two of Boston's finest legal minds, were once in your position. That's right. They were young students at Harvard, Samuel finishing some twelve years ago and Paine a few years behind. And both learned a printing thing or two during their studies, right here in this shop."

"He's right," gushed Paine in a reassuring way, "so we know what you're looking at. If you find yourself struggling a bit with your studies, Ethan, I'd be glad to help. Sam and I have an office off Marshall's Wharf, just east of here near Kilby and King."

"That goes for me too, Ethan," Samuel caringly added, "anytime."

"Thank you, both of you. Your offers of help are reassuring."

"John and I were thinking, Ethan," Mr. Edes explained, "that it might be easier if you had a few days for all these changes to settle in before starting here at the shop. You know, get acquainted with John's place first, your new room, while easing into your studies. How about if you start helping around here a week from now, say, next Saturday?"

"That sounds fine, Mr. Edes," Ethan replied with relief, "I'd like that. Yet, I just might stop by the shop over the coming days to look around, get a better feel."

"Sure," Ben easily agreed. "Now, I'll bet you'd like to get over to John's place," he added, rubbing ink from his fingers with that stained cloth, "see your room, get settled."

"Yes, I sure would. My things are outside, twined to my saddle."

"Good. Just ride a block east on Queen Street then south on Cornhill near the First Church steeple, and Spring Lane isn't far. Go a little east, Ethan, toward the harbor, and you'll see John's house up on the left. You can't miss it, two stories of bright trims and red bricks, and a little upstairs perch looking west toward the river."

"Thanks, Mr. Edes," Ethan graciously replied with a farewell grip. "It was a pleasure meeting you, Sam, Paine," he added with a shake of their hands. "Hope to see you soon."

"Oh, Ethan," Ben quickly said, "my place is just a bit north, 708 Brattle Street. Feel free to stop in when I'm not here. You can meet Martha and the children, and we can talk."

"Thank you, Mr. Edes. I'd like that."

Ethan stepped and opened the shop door with a snatch of the latch before spinning and bidding the three goodbye, then with a tug and click, bound down the steps to Queen Street, untethered the reins and climbed to the saddle. The sounds of Cato's hooves scrapping the stones filtered about the bricks, shops and homes, and as they clacked past the steeple to the gravel of Spring Lane, he could see that perch of Mr. Gill's house near the peak of a shallow hill. The distant bluffs of Dorchester came into view as they trotted up the slope, grassy heights to the southeast with little cottages nestled amid brush, oak, rocks and elm. And as Ethan gripped the reins, he could sense a protective gaze being cast upon Boston by those spirited bluffs.

The pounding of Cato's iron shoes into the pebbly path seemed eerily foreign amid the hush engulfing Spring Lane, and as Ethan stared to that balcony facing west, he marveled of how the bricks of Mr. Gill's house were so mysteriously red, how the white trimming the glass seemed to have been freshly brushed just days before. He could see a pair of windows on the bottom floor and two rather lengthy ones running the edge of the upper perch, a balcony enclosed by a thin bright rail extending from a modest glass door. A tapered roof ran the length of the house, a crystal disk nestled high in its crevice, and a pair of chimneys thrust toward the September grey, their crimson bricks rising near its center. And although he was unable to see, another perch extended the east's upper side, its glass doors peering to the harbor and sea.

A shiny dark carriage sat motionless on the lane not far from Mr. Gill's front door, and as Ethan trotted near he could see its bench was padded by fine black leather, and its wheels had been newly trimmed with Connecticut iron and its spokes were of polished elm. An elegant canopy of dark stained hide was stretched about a thin hardy frame, a haven from flurries of winter and fall, from piercing summer rays and fresh spring rains, and dangling from its lead posts were glass lanterns etched and trimmed by copper rims. "It was the most striking buggy I had ever seen," I remember Ethan said, "even more so than Doc's back home, and was all latched tight by an array of splendid brackets and fittings."

Standing stoic between protruding elm-traces was a sturdy young gelding, his nostrils flaring now and then, with a white stripe running tan hair from his nose to bristling ears. Ethan thought he seemed at peace in the shade of the drifting grey, bathing in the soft afternoon breeze flowing off the harbor, his mane resting lazy. He seemed to be keeping watch upon Mr. Gill's house, windows and bricks mortared by a settler years before, then purchased by John for a pouch of shillings and pounds during that frontier war.

Ethan stopped Cato with a gentle tug and leapt from the saddle near the rear of the carriage, tossing the reins about a nearby iron loop, then untwining his bulging bag and tasty rolls, he gazed to the 362 tacked in dark numbers just right of Mr. Gill's door. With his bundles of belongings and tricorn now pinched in his fingers, he stepped the twisting path of embedded stones toward a pair of solid doors freshly brushed white. A spiraling column rose to each side beneath a Romanesque façade, elegant tan pillars oozing strength and stability, and polished brass handles and golden rings awaited Ethan's knock of the door.

With each nervous step Ethan could feel the anxious flurries fluttering inside, and after grappling for calm with several deep breaths, he grabbed one of those dangling rings and rapped four easy taps. Following a quiet pause for a moment or two he knocked a few more, then watched the door swing open with a twisting click.

"Ethan," greeted John in an enthusiastic tone, "it's good to see you! I knew you were riding in today, just wasn't sure when. Please, come in."

"Thank you, Mr. Gill," Ethan replied, his heart still fluttering as John snatched his things and set them to a chair just inside. "It's good to see you too."

"Ethan, please," he insisted, closing the door with a nudging click, "call me John. This is your home now, at least for a few years. I want you to feel comfortable."

"Alright," Ethan shyly replied, feeling his anxiousness ease as he glanced about the foyer. "I stopped by the shop on my way, thought you might be there, and talked with Mr. Edes for a moment. He sure seems like a kind man. He introduced me to a couple of his friends too, a Mr. Barrett and Wingate."

"Ben *is* a good man," he concurred, "and so are Paine and Sam, Harvard men, like you. Why don't you have a look around, Ethan," he added while twisting and beginning a slow gait up the stairs running straight back in the center of the house, "make yourself at home. I'll be right back."

As Ethan watched Mr. Gill bound up those stairs he wondered if he had been dozing or just lazily lounging that afternoon, getting ready to grasp his day, for over his breeches he was wearing a banyan striped yellow and white, a sleeping gown that hung to his feet. There was a long linen hat dangling from that chair left of the door too, a nightcap tipped with a little fuzzy ball which just moments before donned his greying hair. Ethan found himself quietly chuckling deep inside as John rushed in stockings up those stairs before dashing right into his room, and wondered if such was the way colonists of Boston dressed Saturday mornings into afternoon.

It seemed a rather large house for one man, and as Ethan stood in his dusty boots near the door and scanned John's home, glancing back now and then to that long cap dangling to Ethan's tricorn, bag and bundled rolls, he wondered of the people who had dwelled within its bricks over the years. Then he thought of Mr. Gill's bride Stella, a dainty woman he had wed during that frontier war, and how Mr. Giles said she took her final breath some two years before in a bed just up the stairs. Ethan said it was smallpox, that haunting dread mother called red plague, and wondered how the sorrow of her death seemed to shroud Mr. Gill the rest of his days.

For a moment Ethan's thoughts drifted to his mother's final hours on the farm that chilling autumn night years before, and as he closed his eyes and recalled the pain while clinging to memories, he wondered how melancholy Mr. Gill must have been all those lonely nights. Then snapping from his sorrowful trance he glanced about the foyer once again, and wondered how organized things seemed to be, objects properly arranged, windows gleaming, tables and chairs perfectly placed. And the tantalizing scent of alluring smells filtered about the house, soothing aromas of simmering stews, roasting beasts, and baking treats and breads.

Ethan began to slowly venture further into the home, glancing inside the core room of the house to the right of those stairs, a gathering place scattered with an array of tables and chairs, then shuffled to the door left of the foyer and peeked into the kitchen. Its walls were brushed a spring yellow, and a wide round table of polished maple, with several webbed chairs tucked tight, was set near the door. A pair of windows gazed south upon the pebbles of Spring Lane while an array of square panes peered west toward the Charles River, and six thin white candles rose in the center of the table from a silver candelabrum glistening in the daylight.

A long counter of oak slats for preparing meals lined the western wall beneath several dark cabinets with shiny glass doors, and the opposite wall was consumed by a cooking hearth of colorful stones, a fireplace mortared in rocks of black, tan and red. Deep pots and shallow pans hung from little hooks protruding the stones, and a pudgy dark kettle dangled from an iron arm above sparkling embers spritzing fiery tentacles. "I could see the stained handle of an oak spoon sticking out of that bulging pot," Ethan confided, "leaning against its dark rim in the steam of simmering stew." And a pair of quaint little windows was embedded along the rear wall at the north end of the kitchen, near a sheltered walkway running to the right beneath those rising stairs, a shadowy tunnel leading to an elegant dining place.

As Ethan stood hushed at the kitchen door and glanced to all those culinary things scattered about the room, an impressive figure slowly shuffled from the shadows near the rear, a woman stepping from what Ethan would discover was a little pantry stashed behind a small door near the corner of the west wall. "She was older, Andrea," he confessed, "maybe forty or so, and had a pair of crusty oblong loaves tucked beneath her arm, and a bundle of colorful leafy plants dangled her fingers." He watched as she carefully set those foods to the counter across from that steaming stew, still unaware he was standing quiet at the door.

Ethan would say she seemed to have indulged in her tasty dishes perhaps a bit too much, for she was rather plump at only five feet or so, and her azure-blue apron, now spotted and stained, was snuggly tied about a rotundish waist. A tan bonnet was pressed to short strands of dark curling hair, its thin twining strings dangling past ears to dark puffy cheeks gleaming from the fiery stones, and as Ethan watched, she glided about the slats of the kitchen floor as if a spirited leaf fluttering in a soft autumn wind. Her tan wide dress was loosely fastened near a shadowy neck, worn rumpled cloth flowing to the tips of scuffed brown shoes, and her crumpled sleeves were rolled to her elbows, exposing rosy palms, black hands and dark wrists.

She was employed by Mr. Gill as the keeper of the house, a position Ethan would soon learn she had fulfilled since those final trying months of Stella's abridged life, tidying and dusting the rooms, washing shirts, linens, and breeches, and preparing an array of foods. When not seeing to Mr. Gill's things, she lived in a small home on Tremoni Street with Wilmont her husband, a little house of pine and brick a bit west near the common. And aside from most Sundays she had performed her duties faithfully, just about every day for the past few of years.

Ethan continued to stand quiet at the door as she gripped a thin carving knife and sliced and diced those roots of onion, celery and carrots before slashing strange looking potatoes into little chunks. He watched as she scooped and mixed it all in a big cedar bowl, then spun and slid those colorful pieces into that steamy kettle, and wrapping her fingers about that thick spoon, began to stir her simmering stew. She'd spin and flick secret spices into her brew now and then too, leaning and tasting from the shallow cup of that spoon, then following a few more twirls and sips, she glanced to Ethan at the door, as if she'd known all along. "Yous must be

Mr. Ethan Sheehan," she uttered with an easy stir. "Well, son, is thats you?"

"Yes, it is," Ethan bashfully replied in a startled tone, grasping for composure while shuffling a step or two through the kitchen door. "I didn't mean to be hiding, and am sorry if I frightened you, watching like that. Please, forgive me, mam. I'm just waiting for Mr. Gill to come down from upstairs, and thought he was alone. I'm just looking around, mam."

"Thinks nutin of it, son," she jovially spouted. "I'm Mrs. Hetchings, Sarah Hetchings. But yous just call me Sarah," she invitingly added with another twirl of that spoon. "Come in, son, closer. Lets me get a good looks at ja."

"It's a pleasure meeting you, Miss Hetchings," Ethan shied while stepping nearer the table.

"It's *Mrs.* Hetchings," she playfully retorted. "Buts likes Iz says, just calls me Sarah, nutin but Sarah. It's fine ta meets ya, Mr. Ethan." Then snapping a quick glance and stare, she gave her stew another swishing stir or two, and added, "Yous younger lookin thans I expected. Fine complexion too. But it don't looks like you been eatin inuf, Mr. Ethan. Yous mighty thin."

Ethan just stood near the table in a shy hush, feeling as though he didn't really know what to say or do, and just watched her slide that spoon about the kettle in magical swirls. "I've been keepin for Mr. John going on three years now," she suddenly revealed, gazing to her twirling stirs of steaming brew. "Since before his blessed wife passed, God rests her soul. I sure hope ya likes stew, Mr. Ethan, little hen shards and tiny beast chunks, lots of greens n roots too. Yes sirs, Mr. Ethan, we gonna have plenty of stew arounds here."

"I do, Mrs. Hetchings," Ethan softly replied, sensing his bashfulness slowly easing. "I mean, Sarah. Your stew has such an appealing aroma, smells delicious."

"Good, and thank ya, Mr. Ethan," she said, slicing the tip from a crusty loaf and dipping it to the stew for another tasty test. "But this here batch ain't quite ready, won'ts be for a couple hours. I thinks yall like it here, Mr. Ethan," she comfortingly added with a motherly glance, "not just Boston, but here, in Mr. John's house. He's a fine man. And ya won'ts be able ta say ya weren't fed good neither. Why's, I'll puts meat on them bones. Yous ready for Monday, Mr. Ethan, for school startin?"

"I think so," Ethan answered with hope in his tone. "At least my classes are all set. And finally being here helps, with a couple days to settle in."

"That's good, Mr. Ethan," she supportively replied, spinning and shuffling between the counter and kettle while swirling that spoon and tasting now and then. "Yous just get settled in, makes ya self at home." Then as if seized by a need to express feelings that had been simmering for months deep inside, she stopped and twisted, and with a puzzling gaze, reflectively said, "Seems so manys in such a hurry these days, Mr. Ethan. Iz just don't know. Yous young ones scampering so fast to gets somewhere, do sumptin, whats, Iz don't know. Some older ones too, in a frightful hurry. Peoples just seem to be wantin to change things, maybes too fast, faster than ours Creator planned. Yous one of them young ones, Mr. Ethan?"

Ethan found himself a bit startled by her poignant reflections and scrambled for an answer to her enlightened probes, and although he had never before viewed our generation in such an anxious way, he wondered if her words were insightfully right, a notion he seemed to instinctively resist. "I guess I never really thought about those things, Sarah, at least not in the way you describe. I don't think I am. I'm just trying to do my best. That's why I'm here in Boston, to study at Harvard, learn of life. But you know, Sarah, maybe, in a way you're right. Maybe we are in a hurry, and haven't taken the time to realize it."

"Yous sounds like a pretty smart boy," she softly confided with a stir and calming glance. "And ya knows what, Mr. Ethan? Iz don't thinks yous are, one of them people in a hurryin rush. No sirs, yous seems like a good, God-fearin young man. Yous goin ta do real good here in Boston, Mr. Ethan, evens better in them studies overs there across the river. Yesim, yous are."

"Why, thank you, Sarah," Ethan shyly replied with a sense of relief. "You've made me feel more at ease about it all, with such kind words."

"Awe, it's nutin but the truth, Mr. Ethan," she confidently uttered while brushing crumbs and colorful slithers and bits from the oak slats of the counter into that cedar bowl, "but yous welcome anyways." Then twisting and thrusting fingers toward the foyer, she quickly added, "Yous room is just left at the top of the stairs. I think yall likes the room, Mr. Ethan. Has a fine porch lookins out toward the river. Mighty pretty sunsets froms up there, soothin to yous soul. When ya stands out there, looks over yonder, and yall see the tips of trees sproutin the common. Wilmont and meez lives rights close by, just a smidgen south. Yous beds all ready, Mr. Ethan, and there's water in the basin, cleans washin towels too."

"Thanks, Sarah. I do love the sky at dusk, all those calming colors."

"Yous go right ahead, Mr. Ethan," she insisted once again as he shuffled to the kitchen door, glancing to those stairs and gathering room on the east side of the house, "makes yas self at home. I thinks ya'll likes that room over there, lots of windows. Bright for readin all them Harvard books."

"I hope to see you later, Sarah," Ethan softly confessed. "I think I'll get better acquainted with that big room, then see my room upstairs."

"Yes, yous do that, Mr. Ethan," she spouted with a caring glance. "Weez can talk later."

Ethan stepped from the kitchen door and glanced up the stairs, wondering when Mr. Gill would return, then shuffled through the foyer into that gathering room, its sliding doors hidden within the wall. The room was brushed in light blue and elegantly trimmed in white, and just left of the door was an impressive fireplace of crimson bricks that vanished into the ceiling. A polished elm mantel was embedded in its bricks, and smooth grey stones crept from the hearth into shiny slats of the oak floor. And hanging to each side of the fireplace was a large colorful painting of a lush green forest and winding stream, each canvass encased by an opulent frame.

An ornate porcelain clock was set to the middle of the mantel, a precious timepiece sailed across the sea by Mr. Gill's mother many years before, an heirloom that once chimed the moments in a little village north of London during the first hours of the second King George. Ethan said it was shaped like a bluish egg with a quad of tiny legs, and he could hear its thin dark hands ticking and chiming through the night. And on the hearth's base of greyish stones were two brass arms for coddling burning logs, andirons that seemed in a mystical way, to hold the loneliness of night at bay. Thick shards and short chunks of timber were bundled in a rustic wrap just right, and a small tinderbox was set nearby, tarnished tin stuffed with tiny rocks and bits of iron, cloth and straw patiently waiting for the first chilling flurries of fall.

Ethan scanned the expansive glass embedded in the eastern wall across the room from that fireplace, a pair of gleaming windows with an array of square panes that peered toward the harbor and sea. And he glanced left to small oval windows at the rear of the room near Mr. Gill's fine dining table, and right to a pair of multiple panes keeping watch upon the distant bluffs of Dorchester and gravel of Spring Lane. Then he gazed to an instrument of shiny cherry propped upon elegant legs near those southern windows, to an enchanting musical box he'd soon discover could resonate with the most intriguing harmonic chimes.

It was a harpsichord crafted in the village of Williamsburg in the Colony of Virginia some hundred years before, a rhythmical marvel of the spinet design that was sailed to Boston when Mr. Gill was just four. A polished frame encased dozens of leathered quills that would tap thin iron strings upon the command of narrow walnut keys brushed dark and bright, an alluring board of some sixty short slats tailored for a passionate woman's delicate fingers. And a short quaint chair was nudged just beneath those enchanting keys, shining cherry cushioned by a bronze satin wrap awaiting the soothing sounds of yesteryear.

Ethan stepped to that slender long box and softly touched its tender shine, then gently brushing his fingers across those walnut keys for a moment or two, sensed a loss of cherished years now solemnly at rest. He gazed to that row of little black and white slats and wondered of those who had once exposed their soul with each passionate press, of the serene notes Stella might have tapped long ago. And now he wondered if those lonely keys simply rested quiet in the desperate hours of night or reflective rays of the morning sun, somber slats longing for the sensuous touch of precious dreams.

Slowly shuffling from those silent strings and row of keys, Ethan stared the length of the room toward the twin panes in the rear, to an area which had been invitingly configured to be Mr. Gill's refined dining place. A long walnut table sat upon a colorful rug running east and west, an oval of thick woolen twines spun in shades of yellows, tans and reds, and eight stylish chairs cushioned of auburn brown were pressed to its edge. Several thin candles rose from a polished candelabrum near each end, and a chandelier sprouting sparkling crystals and little candles dangled over the center of the table by the glistening links of an elegant chain.

Nestled near the fireplace and angled close to the bricks was a pair of maple chairs with flowery cushions and tan padded arms, and a small round table was set perfectly between. It was a special table made by Mr. Gill's father before sailing from England years ago, and on most nights was lighted by a stylish lamp of sapphire blue, its crystal base filled with oil from a whale that once roamed the sea east of Nova Scotia. And just a short distance behind, set between those two impressive windows along the east wall, was a sturdy case of polished oak lined by an array of shelves climbing to the ceiling, slats smothered by pamphlets, papers and books.

Beneath the window just right of those shelves was an elegant desk carved decades before from elm carted to Boston from the northern reaches of the Colony of New Hampshire, a scholarly desk with a short thick candle set to each upper corner. Ethan said Mr. Gill always kept a stack of parchment sheets on that desk, along with an ornate cup stuffed of colorful quills near a tin brimming dark ink. A tan printers' chair was always pressed to its center too, nudged between drawers with tiny knobs lining each side, and on many days, rays of the dawning sun would spray through the panes to kiss the tables, chairs, quills and bricks.

As Ethan stood near that gleaming harpsichord and scanned the room, wondering of studying at that desk during a spring rain or reading a Harvard book before a wintry fire, his thoughts were dashed by a jolting cry. "Ethan." spouted Mr. Gill as he bound down the stairs. "Ethan?!" he bolted once again, poking a glance into that gathering room. "I'm sorry for taking so long. Well, Ethan, now that you've had a look around, what do you think of your new home?"

"I like it, Mr. Gill, very much," Ethan shyly replied. "I met Sarah too, in the kitchen for a moment. She seems like such a pleasant woman, so kind."

As Ethan stepped closer to Mr. Gill near those fireplace bricks, Sarah suddenly came into view across the foyer at the kitchen door, ringing her fingers with a stained cloth. "Iz thinks Mr. Ethan will likes it here just fine, Mr. John," she unabashedly blurted. "Yesim, just fine!"

"It's good to hear you say that, Sarah," a pleased Mr. Gill quickly replied, now dressed in his usual printing shop shirt, stockings, shoes and breeches. "And thank you for taking such good care of Ethan while I was away." As she vanished into the kitchen to resume her keeping chores, he spun toward Ethan and compassionately said, "I know this isn't Lexington, Ethan, not what you're used to, your father and the tavern, but hope you'll grow to be comfortable here, come to think of my place as your home. You know, Ben and I are proud to have you here, Ethan. We want to help make your studies at Harvard as productive as possible, and your stay in Boston, tasks at our shop, pleasantly interesting."

"Thank you, Mr. Gill," Ethan uttered, "I mean, John. I'm very grateful, and your words do help me feel more comfortable. I'll do my best, and just know things will work out fine."

"I'm glad you feel that way, Ethan," he calmingly replied. "We know you'll do your best." Then twisting and glancing to the kitchen door, he spouted, "Sarah, keep your stew simmering for another hour or so, please. Ethan and I will be gone for a while."

"Yesim, Mr. John," she shouted, shuffling back into view, "Iz sure will. Yous twos takes ya time. These meats and carrots, them potatas, onions and greens, needs a bit more stewin anyways. Don'ts you worries none. Oh, Iz be leavin shortly, Mr. John, arounds four."

"That sounds fine, Sarah. And don't you worry about a thing, just leave the stew simmering in the pot. Ethan and I will dish up when we get back. Thanks, Sarah."

"Yesim, Mr. John," she graciously sputtered, scurrying back into the kitchen, "Iz do just that."

Ethan suddenly rushed through the foyer to the kitchen door, and peaking toward that steamy pot, softly said, "That goes for me too, Sarah, thanks, for such a fine smelling stew." As she twisted with a contented glance, he graciously added, "And thank you, Sarah, for your kindness. You've made me feel welcome."

"Awe, yous welcome, Mr. Ethan," she humbly replied. "Now, yous just let me know when yous needs sumtin, anythin. Oh, and feels free to eats whatsevers here, meats and stews, breads, muffins and pies, anythin, Mr. Ethan."

"Thank you, Sarah, I will."

"Come on, Ethan," insisted Mr. Gill, patiently waiting near the front door. "I want you to come with me to the shop, just for a little while. I'll show you some things. But how about first, you take your things to your room, just left up the stairs."

"Alright, I sure will," Ethan quickly agreed, snatching his bag and bundled rolls and scampering up the stairs before looking back to see Mr. Gill vanish into the kitchen. Gripped by a curious urge, Ethan twisted right and glanced about Mr. Gill's room, to walls brushed a soft sea green and trimmed in white. A dozen glass panes along the east wall were framed in shining maple, a pair of doors leading to a little perch peering toward the distant harbor, and just left of those panes was an aging desk, its oak edges nicked and worn. Across the floor on Ethan's right were a pair of soft chairs set near the fireplace stones, and nudged beneath two windows gazing upon the pebbles of Spring Lane was a plump bed smothered of blankets and pillows. And atop a chest of nearby maple drawers, was a damp blue towel crumpled beside a flowery basin.

Ethan spun and shuffled to his room left of the stairs, and as he stood hushed at the door, sensing a soothing aura while gripping his bag and rolls, he wondered of the room that was to be his home for the coming four years. Its inviting walls were a turquoise blue, and like Mr. Gill's, were molded bright, and as Ethan scanned the room he could smell Sarah's simmering stew oozing the oak slats of the floor through tiny cracks and fissures. A fragrance of the sea was filtering into the room too, flowing with a gentle breeze outside several windows and past the balcony's glass doors swung open to the river.

A bed with several fluffy pillows was tucked beneath twin windows imbedded along the north wall just inside the door, and its mattress of bundled cottons and fabrics was covered with linens and a blanket that lazily dangled past its edges. Another blanket quilted in tans, greens, yellows and reds was neatly folded and stretched over the foot of the bed, and a pair of little oak cabinets pressed the wall on each side, a thick candle on the far stand and a lamp of crystal blue on the one nearest Ethan. A quaint hearth rose along the east wall just left of the door, and a pair of dark cushioned chairs were set to each side of a small maple table with a trio of thin candles, all patiently waiting for fiery flickers to tame the coming chills of winter.

A stylish desk was nudged near two windows peering south toward those Dorchester heights, a desk Ethan would say belonged to Mr. Gill's mother when she was a child north of London, and from the door he could see parchment sheets stacked left of a crimson lamp. There was a little tin cup brimming with dark ink set to the upper right, its thin lid snugged tight, and nearby was a porcelain mug stuffed with an array of feathery quills. And more windows were imbedded along the west wall too, multiple panes set to each side of the balcony doors, and a maple chest with little knobs and several drawers was pressed to the wall just right of the desk. A little stack of tan towels rested beside a flowery bowl atop that chest, a colorful basin with an ornate jug filled by Sarah with colonial water just an hour before.

Ethan felt calm as he glanced about his new room, the day streaming through the windows and salty harbor breeze wafting about, those soft blankets and pillows bringing a sense of ease. Even that aging desk seemed to draw him into the room, and those glass doors swung toward the river were tugging him to the balcony. Ethan dropped his bag near the hearth and nudged those rolls to a chair, and stepping across the oak slats to that alluring veranda, inhaled a deep breath of sea air. Then leaning and pressing his palms to the iron rail beneath the afternoon grey, he slowly scanned the cobblestones and bricks of Boston, its steeples, shops and homes.

"I could see the distant waters of the Charles," Ethan once whispered, "and the tips of pines, oaks and elms reaching for the grey from the grass of the common. I could even see the chimney stacks of Harvard and Stoughton halls across the river through the afternoon haze, and several tiny cows grazing the fields of Davy Phipps' farm. It was all rather tranquil, Andrea, and as I listened to the faint sounds of bustling along the north and east docks, I truly began to realize that coming to Boston, to that room in Mr. Gill's house, had been the right thing for me to do."

Ethan inhaled another breath of sea air and glanced about the port one more time, then leaving that perch open to the breeze, spun and stepped back through his room, shuttered the door with a tugging click, and bound down the stairs to join Mr. Gill waiting in the foyer. They bid Sarah a final goodbye and climbed to the cushion of the carriage, and with Ethan's colt still secured to that hitching post, Mr. Gill flicked the reins and the buggy began its crunching roll down the pebbles of Spring Lane. As they twisted northwest along the cobblestones of Cornhill and past the steeple of that church in route to the print shop, Mr. Gill pointed and explained Boston things amid the creaking and clacking of wheels and hooves along the stones of Queen Street.

Once inside the shop Ethan found that those two Harvard men were no longer there, and neither was Mr. Edes, and glancing about he wondered if perhaps they had ventured up the stairs to that secluded place they called the long room. He wondered if Mr. Edes was quilling some secretive thoughts about those Townshend Acts up in that room, yet didn't know and was wary to ask, or maybe he was talking with other Bostonians about some other nonsense being spewed by their royal governor, parliament and the king.

Mr. Gill didn't seem concerned, just discussed with Ethan the crux of his duties while explaining a few special procedures and functions, many things Ethan had already been exposed to in Mr. Giles' Lexington shop. Ethan was shown to his small desk too, aged oak nestled among stacks of parchment near the left rear corner not far from those stairs, and after a while, they talked about Ethan's schedule. Mr. Gill was adamant that Ethan's printing duties not interfere with his Harvard studies, and soon they agreed on a few hours after classes on Tuesdays and Thursdays beginning at five, and several hours each Saturday starting at noon.

"Good," exclaimed John Gill, "looks like we've got these things settled. You be sure to let me know, Ethan, if these hours cause any problems. We can always juggle your schedule around. After all, it's your studies at Harvard that truly matter."

"I think this schedule is more than reasonable," Ethan confidently replied. "But I will let you know, Mr. Gill, John, if it becomes too much of a struggle. I promise." Then feeling his curiosity beginning to truly flow, Ethan glanced to the stairs climbing the rear wall and gingerly asked, "What's in that room up there, beyond that door?"

"Come on, Ethan," John surprisingly spouted, "I'll show you." With Ethan studiously strutting close behind, Mr. Gill gripped the elm rail and bound up the steps to the closed white door. "We call it, the long room."

Ethan watched as John creaked open the door with a gentle twist of its copper knob, and as they slowly stepped into the warm and stuffy room, he could see a long table and many chairs scattered about the dusty slats of the floor. There was no Mr. Edes, nor those two Harvard men, just a bunch of oak chairs with weaved cushions and high backs pressed to the east wall left of the door, across the room from a fireplace consumed by colorful rocks. Several soft chairs cushioned in yellows and tans were nudged near the hearth, and a few small maple tables with thin candles were strategically positioned about. And only a single large window allowed the day to filter in, multiple square panes waiting to witness colonial disputes that would someday erupt near those cobblestones of Queen Street.

Yet it was the long table gobbling the center of the room that spurred Ethan's imagination, thick slabs of dusty maple several feet wide and a dozen long, an intriguing table surrounded by a gaggle of those high slatted chairs. For a moment his thoughts raced with images of fiery Bostonians gathered to discuss colonial things, of spirited men spouting of unjust intrusions by London, of sons of liberty men devising plans to confront those despised Townshend Acts or other infringing laws being unleashed upon the colonies by the crown.

"Well, Ethan?" John softly uttered. "What do you think? It's not much, but is awfully private, and we prefer it that way. Sam and I don't normally use the room for printing things, but we do sometimes come up here to talk about delicate issues for our Gazette and Country Journal." As he watched Ethan seemingly absorbed in the nuances of that table, gazing to the shadowy light spraying from the window upon the dusty maple, he added in an intuitive way, "Perhaps it *is* more of a meeting room, Ethan, a secure place where colonists can gather to discuss rather sensitive things. Some of the men like to say it's our room of equilibrium, where royal injustices are exposed and ways to rebalance the scales conceived."

"I like the room, Mr. Gill," Ethan softly replied while scanning about, "intriguing. I can see why Bostonians like to gather here. I was wondering if maybe, it would be alright for me to use this room now and then. Not for anything secretive, just for study, when not being used by anyone."

"I don't see why not. I'll try to let you know when it's not available, and maybe you can tell me when you need it. And if you like, perhaps you can study up here with a colleague or two from Harvard."

"Sure, I'd like that. Thanks, Mr. Gill."

"We just want you to feel comfortable, Ethan," John caringly said while reaching for the door, "feel at home. Now, unless you've something else on your mind, I do believe we're done here for today. What do you say we ride back home."

"Alright," Ethan uttered, about to step down the stairs with Mr. Gill close behind. "I think I'm pretty settled with what we've discussed. Yes, let's go."

Ethan said Sarah was gone for the day by the time they creaked up the hill to Mr. Gill's house, and confessed that her simmering stew was almost as tasty as his mother's. Then after they talked in that harpsichord room for an hour or two, he retired up the stairs just as the September sun began to vanish beyond the frontier. "For a while, Andrea, I just browsed about my room, lighting a candle and trying to find a feeling of comfort. I stood out on that little veranda too, watching the day slowly fade."

Soon he disrobed and washed at the basin, then crawled to fresh pillows, linens and blankets in a desperate attempt to sleep, only to find the coming hours fraught with rolling, tossing and turning amid the strange sounds swirling the Boston night. "I'd press deeper into my pillows as the hours slowly crept by," he said, "listening to distant howls, croaks and hoots, to eerie rustles and creaks, watching the dark roam about the room. I'd snap my tiring stare out the windows now and then too, gaze out the open balcony doors and wonder of my new life."

At times he'd wander to memories of his mother and their years on the farm, to his father in Lexington and his room in the Buckman Tavern, and as the soft night winds gently kissed the waters of the harbor, he could feel the dew on the grass of his village field cooling his feet. And somewhere after midnight he dozed for a moment or two, drifting to youthful dreams of walking about the fields of their farm and wading in the shallows of his creek. Then just before waking once again, he'd smell the sweet scent of a spring meadow, and remember the joy of being bundled in his mother's arms.

Ethan would wander to frightful places too, to swirling dreams of his mother lying cold in her grave atop that Lexington hill, her gentle eyes gazing to his through a ghoulish haze. They were visions which would eerily change to his father desperately grasping for the passions of his past while struggling about the tavern, searching for his love's cherished touch while grappling with a sullen heart. Then Ethan would awake and wonder of the unknown while staring with each tossing turn into the dark, and as the aroma of the sea filtered about his room, he'd listen to the clock in the gathering room singing each hour, chiming the past and the hopes of morrow.

The following dawn was Ethan's first true day in his strange new world of Boston, just twenty-four hours before his new life at Harvard College would begin, and I remember how he once said he felt as though it was the final day of his youth. He wanted to see every nook of his new port home, exhaust the day strolling about the cobblestones, and could sense a surging desire to scrape his shoes upon each street and walk along the harbor's wharfs and docks. He wanted to feel every wisp of wind and smell the sea, hear each sound, every clank and creak that first Sunday of September, 1768.

A layer of wavy grey smothered the noon sky, stretching from the woods, hills and fields of Middlesex County to the hazy spray of the sea, and as Ethan stepped from the door of his new home, he could feel the mugginess begin to seep into his clothes. The shine of his leather shoes would slowly dull as he stepped west down the gravel of Spring Lane to the waiting cobblestones, and his bright shirt fastened snug to his neck would soon loosen with neatly rolled sleeves. And as he descended the gentle rise in thin white stockings and tan tight breeches, warm little droplets began to bead his brows while the cloth of his shirt began to cling to his skin.

He could see the sandy stones of King's Chapel in the distance near the grass of the common at Tremont and School streets, an intriguing church with impressive columns rising before its entry doors, and with each step he wondered of the shapely bell dangling its stubby tower. Although it was first built with Massachusetts Bay elm some eighty years before during the reign of London's second King James, Ethan would discover it had been firmly enhanced with those chiseled stones when he and I were young.

Soon Ethan shuffled right onto Cornhill, his soles sliding and scraping the cobblestones, and strutted north toward what most would say was the heart of Boston, the convergence of King and Queen. As he stepped the stones he glanced left to the spire of another aging church, a spiritual place of pine, mortar and bricks some fondly knew from olden days as the port's first meeting house, erected over a century before. He stopped at the corner and glanced left down the stones of Queen Street for a moment, toward Mr. Gill's print shop, then snapped his gaze east down the cobblestones of King Street toward the crimson bricks of his colony's statehouse. "I couldn't help but stare to its splendid angles and bends," he once said, "and even though I'd seen its stylish tower, windows and bricks many times, I hadn't really looked. It was beautiful, Andrea, unlike I'd ever seen before."

The colonial men of his colony's assembly would meet inside those stately bricks, and its three floors strewn with gables and panes gazed down upon the stones of King Street, while its majestic tower rose some fifty feet toward the grey. The east end of the colony's house peered toward the harbor, its balcony doors swinging to the water, and the other of stylish windows, smooth columns and intriguing doors looked west toward the print shop. And imbedded in those bricks and stones or perched atop its white tower were crystal spheres sheltered by golden wings and mystical animals, royal beasts listening to the thin hands of a clock slowly ticking the final years of London's rule.

He crossed the cobblestones and began an easy walk east toward those statehouse bricks, then snapped his gaze right as he passed the Green Dragon Tavern and stared to the doors of the crown's customs house on the south side of King Street. I remember Ethan said it was a rather mundane building nestled among brick stores and pine shops, a building much like others in the ports of New York, Williamsburg, Philadelphia and Savannah, a place where the crown's men collected taxes and duties in shillings and pounds from colonial tradesmen, doctors, lawyers and merchants. And as he slowly stepped the stones he gazed to a pair of the king's soldiers standing guard outside the door in dark boots, tricorn hats and crimson coats, young loyal men with bayonetted muskets dangling shoulders.

Further east near the harbor Ethan could see a quaint little structure at the corner of Kilby Street off to his right, a unique array of pine and bricks styled like homes near the common. Dangling above the door by thin iron links was a short white shingle scripted in blue gently swaying in the warm afternoon, a barrister's sign declaring the office of John Adams, cousin of Sam. Although he had never met John, a man many would say was dedicated to the public good, Ethan said his reputation as an unflinching barrister brimming legal prowess was already firmly established. And softly swaying across the cobblestones of Kilby was another shingle, a sign announcing the law office of those two Harvard men, Wingate and Barrett.

Ethan stopped to rest for a moment at a long wharf at the eastern edge of King Street, leaning to an elm rail of a creaking dock along the water. He gazed into the afternoon haze at dozens of vessels moored by thick hemp twines or anchored in the harbor by big dark chains, and watched as several of the king's Royal Navy ships floated easy or slithered in the water, their Union Jack ensigns lazily flickering in the breeze. And he watched sweating colonial men tugging, tossing and stacking scores of boxes, sacks and crates to-and-fro sailing ships and merchant boats amid the menacing glare of patrolling redcoat soldiers. They were strutting in pairs or intimidating groups, he'd say, their royal boots pounding and scraping the docks and stones as if ordered to instill a disturbing fear of the crown.

It was during those respite moments that Ethan realized he wanted to circle his new home of Boston about its edge, continue walking north along its eastern docks and west toward that Charlestown ferry, then south along the Charles River in route for home. "I just wanted to get a better feel for everything, Andrea, see things close, and smell the sea air."

Ethan regrouped his thoughts and spun into the gentle breeze, slowly walking along the harbor near that big square of merchant shops and the windows and bricks of Faneuil Hall. As the warm winds brushed the waters and kissed his cheeks, he glanced to the expanse of that hall and wondered of all the boisterous debates that had occurred inside over the years. He imagined disgruntled colonists gathering on brisk spring nights to denounce unjust laws being quilled in London, or passionately decrying on cool fall days the intruding policies of Royal Governor Bernard.

The afternoon grey was slowly beginning to stray into artistic bunches and fluffy sprays, and as Ethan strolled north he wondered of the beauty of the sun's rays glistening the water or gleaming off windows in mystical streams. And as he scraped the stones of Fish Street near Halsey's Wharf and the alley of Bell, he glanced to the sign of a tradesman he knew, a board scripted in red upon a sea of blue dangling in the breeze above a modest door. It was the workplace of the sons of liberty man Ethan had come to know in Boston, that young rider he once met near Mr. Gill's printing press, and the sign reading *Revere's Silversmith Shop* was swaying in the winds.

Ethan would later learn that Paul's home was close by on Wood Lane, not far from Salem Street and the narrow spire of Christ Church, a unique pine house stained a pale tan with an array of shutters and windows dotting both floors. He said its roof was rather steep too, and a few windows were strangely designed like precious gems etched in diagonal frames. And within days of beginning his studies, Mr. Gill would reveal that the majestic house on nearby Middle Street was the home of Thom Hutchinson, the colony's royal governor when Ethan was just nine.

Gentle winds tossed his hair as he walked amidst the smells of the sea while scores of squawking gulls gracefully circled teetering masts or skimmed the waters in daring swoops and dives. They were alluring visions and sounds tainted now and then by the stench of a fisherman's catch helplessly piled on docks in pungent stacks, smells that would mercifully escape into the muggy air beginning to cool with a refreshing breeze sweeping in from the sea. Ethan continued his stroll past the eastside wharfs of Burrough's, Scarlet's and Hutchinson's before pivoting west on the cobblestones of Lynn Street along the port's northern edge, slowly walking toward the Charlestown ferry near Copp's Hill.

All the while little groups of the king's men were patrolling the docks or strutting upon the cobblestones in pairs, fours, six or eight, loyal soldiers with muskets slung marching about in royal coats, boots and hats. Ethan strove to avoid the crown's troops as he walked, glancing away from their stares and strolling closer to the water when the sound of scraping boots drew near. Although rather intimidating to watch, with dread seeming to echo with each strike of their boots, Ethan confessed that he knew they were simply doing their duty for the king, nothing more, nothing less. There were scores of buggies bouncing and squeaking along the cobblestones that Sunday afternoon too, colonial women, children and men being pulled about the port by fillies, colts and mares, sounds which calmed Ethan's soul with soothing visions of Lexington.

Near the docks of Verin's Wharf Ethan glanced left to the spire of that north church reaching for the clouds, a steeple housing a pair of copper and tin bells molded in London some thirty years before. Then snapping his stare right he saw a little elm bench nestled in the shade of an oak rising from a patch of grass near rocks spilling into the water, a quaint bundle of weathered slats latched to a pair of barrels once dripping Boston ale. "It was a spot that looked so peaceful," he said, "a place oozing serenity, enticing me to rest. I just sat there for a while, Andrea, gazing about the mist spraying off the harbor, feeling the winds, listening to the rhythmic flow."

He shuttered his eyes amidst the screeching cries of playful gulls diving for tiny sea treats, and listened to the tranquil sounds of the water gently splashing the rocks, wharfs and docks. For a moment he pondered what Sarah had said, wondering if he truly might be, one of those colonists in a hurrying rush. Then gazing about the harbor, to those graceful wings soaring with the winds, he could feel doubts beginning to creep inside, suspicions he desperately wanted to douse. "Just be yourself," he whispered, trying to calm his nagging thoughts. "Study hard, Ethan, do your best, and let the truth play out. That's all you can do."

The salty air was soothing to Ethan's soul, and gazing across the harbor with thoughts of what might come, he wondered of all the new things gripping his life, his new home and room, Mr. Gill's print shop, and the challenges of Harvard starting in just one day. And as he peered to the distance beyond a gaggle of sailing ships, their masts tilting and swaying with the waters and winds, he could see little figures scurrying about a spot of land jutting south into the harbor. They were colonists on a shore dotted with what seemed tiny vessels along little docks, merchants and fishermen hustling about warehouses, huts and shops.

Across the harbor in the distance northwest was a point of rocks protruding south, splitting the waters into a narrowing inlet northeast and a tiny bay merging with the waters of the Mystic River flowing from the west. It was a short, murky river that Ethan said began at its namesake lakes northeast of his Lexington, a rather shallow stream which slowly flowed southeast to the northern edge of the Charlestown Peninsula before surrendering to the harbor.

The eastern rocks of that peninsula seemed so serene that Sunday afternoon, and as Ethan gazed west through the misty haze to the village of Charlestown, he wondered of the rickety slats of its elm ferry that would take him across the water on his ride to Harvard in the village of Cambridge each day. And he peered to that trio of shallow hills too, to the grassy slopes of Moulton's near the peninsula's northeast tip, to the higher rise of Breed's toward the village, and to Bunker Hill a bit further west nearer the peninsula narrows. As Ethan gazed to those hills he had seen many times on many rides from and to Lexington, he wondered how tranquil they seemed from that Boston bench in the lazy shade of an oak.

He breathed the sea and scanned the harbor for another hour or so, soaking in all those serene visions and sounds, and as his skin began to cool from a northeast breeze, Ethan realized the moment had come to abandon his haven. He rose from his barreled bench and bid farewell to his patch of grass shaded by those twisting limbs, and as the waters lapped against the rocks, he continued his westward stroll along the port's northern docks. The king's soldiers were still strutting in boots as hooves clanked and carriage wheels creaked, and with each step and glance about the harbor, shops, wharfs and homes, he listened to the scraping of his soles upon the cobblestones of Lynn Street.

Ethan stepped past the wharfs of Ruck's and Freeman's, and the boatyards of Baker's, Hunt's and White's, all the while gazing across the water to the shallow slopes of those Charlestown hills as he passed a group of patrolling soldiers. Pivoting south near the stones of Hudson's Point and strutting past more docks, he wondered of the weathered slats of that elm ferry that would take him across the water the very next day, a ferry he'd ride another four long years. Then striding southeast past the bend of Copp's Hill, he continued his meandering stroll near the waters of the Charles toward his new home on Spring Lane.

He could see a long narrow dock stretching into the river at a place they called Mill Pond, and near the stones of Prince Street was a short road that sliced through the swaying grass of an expansive field, a rustic path Ethan knew he'd take. He stepped that worn track toward the white pine of what he'd discover was a quaint chapel for those of the Baptist faith near the streets of Back and Stillman, and with each stride he was coming to realize he was establishing the route he would normally take on his daily ride to and from Harvard. Soon the cobblestones merged with those of Middle then Hanover, and off to the right on an alluring corner was Mrs. Davies Tavern, a spirited place where colonial men in Sunday shirts, shoes, breeches and hats were vanishing beyond its beckoning door.

Across the stones at the corner of Hanover and Union was an intriguing shop, and as Ethan stepped closer and peered through the windows, he could see bunches of books scattered on tables and stacked against walls, and hundreds of volumes lining a slew of shelves. *The London Book Store* was brushed in blue across the glass, and although its door was latched tight that Sunday afternoon, Ethan now knew he had a place to discover an array of papers, pamphlets and books. And even though the cobblestones of Union would lead Ethan southeast toward Cornhill then Spring Lane, he kept a southern pace on Hanover, passing Wings then Brattle and the gravel of my aunt and uncle's street rising right up Beacon Hill. Then near the western bend of Queen Street the common came into view, that expanse of pines, oaks, grass and elms he hadn't truly touched since that night of madness two or three years before.

"I had forgotten how deep and wide the common truly was," he said, "stretching southwest from the cobblestones of Queen for maybe a half mile or so to the waters of the Charles." If I recall, Tremont Street formed most of its eastern edge, running south to the corner of School near the stones of King's Chapel, the spot where Ethan said he stopped and gazed west across the expanse of the field. "I watched all those limbs and leaves swaying in the breeze, and not far from that liberty tree, Andrea, stared into the haze toward the river."

Yet I suppose what truly became etched in Ethan's mind is what he saw on the grass that day, hundreds of the king's men strutting upon the common, and stepping to a quiet place nearer that special tree, he secretly watched as his stomach twisted and churned. They were stomping across the grass just a short distance away, companies of Royal Army men drilling about the field in a trio of matching boxes. Their crimson coats tailed to the rear, and as they marched about in dark boots and hats, in bright shirts and breeches, he stared to their shouldered muskets, their glistening bayonets thrusting toward the afternoon sun.

He could see a pair of royal sergeants strategically placed about each bunch, one in the lead barking commands and another near the rear, both with a light flintlock fusil musket strapped about his shoulder. And standing stoic near each marching box was an officer Ethan wasn't sure was a lieutenant or captain, three royal men with curving sheathed swords dangling their sides. Their eyes were fixed in fervent stares upon their strutting men, redcoat soldiers dancing to the cadence of those sergeants blasting commands, ardent glares in search of the slightest betrayal of royal temperance.

Ethan remained hushed near the limbs of that liberty tree for a half hour or so, watching and listening to all those soldiers drilling in perfect unison upon each insistent shout. And as they snapped left then right, darting and spinning while strutting across the grass to-and-fro, he wondered of their names and what English village each young soldier called home. But it was the threatening behavior of those three officers that sent a chilling shiver down Ethan's spine, for each kept a hand firmly gripped upon the handle of his sword as if waiting to brandish those deadly blades, attempting to intimidate every Boston women, child and man.

Soon Ethan discovered he was no longer the only colonist watching all those royal soldiers, for many Bostonians had meandered toward the edge of the grass with a bewildering concern in their stare. Ethan could sense a frightful unease swirling within each women, child and man, and wondered of the distraught that seemed to be brewing inside as they stood quiet in gaze. Or maybe, he wondered, they had assembled just to watch the king's soldiers gracefully maneuver, perhaps hoping kindness and empathy would prevail in the months and years to come.

But as a thin blanket of grey once again stretched from the frontier to the sea, Ethan could see the dreadful truth in the eyes of many of those Bostonians, and he realized for perhaps the first time, that the divide between the colonies and London was truly expanding. Then glancing about the hushed crowd and breathing a whiff of sea air, Ethan scanned those strutting soldiers a final time then spun, resuming his journey to the serenity of his room as scruffy plump squirrels dashed about the grass and frolicking little birds chirped about the trees.

I suppose the apprehensions simmering about Ethan's Boston and Colony of Massachusetts Bay that fall of 1768 were in a way being felt in all the colonies in those days, even down here in Philadelphia and my Germantown. Yet, despite those spritzing concerns, Ethan said he found a way to suppress as much as he could during those autumn weeks, releasing such troubling things to delve into Harvard studies. He managed to pivot his thoughts away from the brewing tempest, at least for a little while, and begin to absorb enlightening ideals printed in pamphlets and books and espoused by spirited men.

The layering grey of the day before had vanished by dawn that first Monday of September, and as Ethan slowly woke from his swirling dreams, he gazed out his western windows. Although his first class was to start at nine that brisk morning, every student had been instructed to assemble at eight inside the bricks and panes of Harvard Hall. He pressed to his pillows a final time and watched the night's last star slowly fade with the day, and as the sun began rising from the sea, he rolled from his bed with an anxious burst, then hurriedly washed and dressed.

Ethan snatched the last of his father's little rolls and quietly rushed down the stairs, and after strapping a saddle to Cato a bit before seven, climbed to the stirrups, snapped the reins and nervously trotted away. He listened to his colt's iron shoes scrape the cobblestones as they rode north near the Charles River, and could feel the morning rays warming his neck as they crossed the harbor on the worn slats of the ferry. Pressing his tricorn hat firmly to his hair, Ethan galloped west through the Charlestown narrows and pivoted south along the road to Cambridge, dashing toward all those assembling in Harvard Hall.

Soon the hall's little dome sparkling in the morning sun came into view, and as Ethan galloped closer he could see several buggies rolling along the pebbles ringing that yard, while groups of young men strolling toward the hall mingled about the knolls and grass. Empty carriages lined the edges of that path and a slew of horses were tethered to a string of rails, rings and posts, and from the distance those fillies, mares and colts seemed made of stone, standing stoically still.

Near the northern edge of the campus yard Ethan tugged the reins and climbed from the saddle, then wrapping those leather straps about a hitching post near the slats of a short picket fence, he began a timorous stride toward the hall. "Good morning," he nervously sputtered to a pair of young men who quickly returned his greeting. "Morning," he shyly replied to another gent while strutting a grassy slope toward the hall. Ethan knew he tended to be a bit withdrawn, and with each step he somehow understood he would need to release those shackles, and prayed that over the coming weeks and months his confidence would slowly improve. I remember he said he was there to learn, expand his horizons, and realized he would need to find a way to scuttle his youthful timidity, banish those internally spurred limitations.

The cherry shelves smothered with thousands of papers, pamphlets and books had been removed from their spots and pressed nearer the Harvard Hall walls, leaving an expanse for scores of young men to assemble. Bounding up the stone steps leading to the door and shyly strutting into the hall, Ethan could see and hear faculty men pointing left and right while calmly spouting instructions, diligent men arranging each class into four distinct groups.

The most mature class, seasoned men scheduled to earn their diplomas in the coming spring of 1769, was assembling to Ethan's far left along the upper reaches of the north wall. They were gathering near a platform erected in the front of the hall, a stage pressed below big windows peering east toward the distant fields of Mr. Phipps' farm. Still standing just beside the west-end door, Ethan watched another group massing along the southern wall to the upper right near that stage, students who'd finish their studies in the spring of 1770. To his left nearer the door was the class of 1771, colonial boys assembling along the north wall, and gathering just off to his right were the new students of his class of 1772, young men like Ethan beginning a new life on the grounds of Harvard College.

I remember Ethan said there were a hundred and eighty-four young men gathered in the hall that Monday morning, each with different hopes and dreams, and thirty-nine were from that class of 1769. He'd come to know a few of those older ones too, studious men like Ebenezer Bradish from that village of Cambridge, Johnny Williams, Ben Wadsworth and George Wheaton from Boston, and Jacob Jewett from the hamlet of Chelmsford a little north of Ethan's Lexington. Some were from other colonies too, like Elijah Fletcher from the village of Derry up in New Hampshire and Nathaniel Webster from Providence, a port forty miles south in Rhode Island.

There were thirty-four students in that next class, with the youngest rumored to be Hezekiah Taylor from the fishing village of Newport in the Colony of Rhode Island, and Willie Hutchinson, said to be the oldest, was from the town of Nashua up in New Hampshire. Palsgrave Wellington and Jon Newell were from Boston and Jacob Burnap came from Braintree just a bit southeast, and Ethan said that Benjamin Chadwick of Plymouth was known to spew fanciful tales of strange fish off Cape Cod Bay. And Sam Osgood's family lived in the northeast village of Gloucester off the waters of Cape Ann, Johnny Winthrop was from Marblehead near Bakers Island,

and Amariah Frost called Fall River home, some fifty miles south of Cambridge.

The largest group assembled that morning consisted of sixty-three for the class of 1771, some Ethan would come to know, like the youngest named Ebenezer Allen from the village of Bedford just northwest of Lexington, and Abraham Watson from the nearby hamlet of Lincoln. It seems Gad Stebbins was already home, having been born right there in Cambridge, and Jedidiah Estabrook's father had a shop near the docks of the Charlestown Peninsula, and Sam Plummer, John Frothingham and Crocker Sampson were from Boston. Many came from further places too, like James Bowdoin of Brunswick some hundred and fifty miles northeast in the wilderness exclave of Maine, and William Cheever from the port of New London in the Colony of Connecticut and Moses Hale from nearby New Haven along the waters of Long Island Sound.

And there were forty-eight assembled that day for Ethan's group of 1772, many older than he, yet some just sixteen like Oliver Wellington Lane from the northern village of Haverhill. I remember Ethan said Paul Whitney's farm was near the village of Worcester some forty miles west, and that Thom Burnham, John Eliot and Sam Tenney were from Boston, while William Fisk had been reared a few miles south in Dedham. Some were from other colonies too, like Johnny Shaw from Dover up in New Hampshire and Sam Cook from the village of Warwick in Rhode Island. Ethan said that after a few months he knew many of them, and some developed a sense of camaraderie by forming studious little groups that evolved into enthusiastic sessions of dialog and debate.

By eight all the students had gathered into their respective class, and as Ethan nervously joined his group amidst a swelling of whispers and chatter, anxiously shuffling in his shoes while shyly glancing about, he wondered of the nuances of each young man. Some talking and mingling were rather short with bulging bellies while others like he were taller and slender, but most simply blended into their group in a conforming way. Many were twined to families from England and some were of Ethan's Irish and Scottish decent, and a few were from my Netherlands or a strange Germanic principality, while others were from ancestries rooted in colonies like Delaware, Georgia and Virginia. Yet as Ethan scanned the hall he came to realize that everyone was more alike than different, for just as he, they had gathered that morning with hopes of expanding their minds with enlightening theories.

Ethan stood hushed and listened or nervously fidgeted for what seemed endless moments, staying rather quiet and reserved while looking left and right with anxious little twists, snapping glances behind now and then. He once confided how he struggled with a sense of not belonging, speaking only if someone started with a word or two, and even those exchanges were rather harmless, short little utters of names and maybe the village from whence they came.

Just to Ethan's right was a student who seemed as lost as he, shuffling in shiny dark shoes and staring south through an array of square panes toward the distant Charles River and the nearby bricks of Massachusetts and Stoughton halls. Standing perhaps six inches above five feet, he appeared to be one of the younger ones assembled that morning, a rather chunky lad Ethan would soon discover was only sixteen. As Ethan gazed toward the Charles, that young man slowly spun, then stretched out his hand and shattered their silence, "Good morning. I'm Benjamin, Benjamin Loring, from Concord. And you are?"

"Morning," Ethan timidly replied. "I'm from Lexington, Ethan Sheehan. It's good to meet you, Benjamin."

"Well, Ethan, it appears we're neighbors," he confidently spouted as they released their greeting hands. Then in a style uncommon for someone so young, he quickly added, "I'm going to study ideals springing from Europe, governments and theories, philosophies too, things like that. What about you?"

"I'm thinking of histories," Ethan confessed as his sense of unease began to calm amid Benjamin's youthful candor, "literature too, mostly European, and judicial structures, law. I also want to delve into some political theories, not just from across the sea but from here in the colonies, and maybe some philosophies too."

"How interesting, Ethan," young Ben softly uttered. "I suspect we'll see each other in several classes."

"We just might at that, Ben," Ethan replied in a tentative tone. "That would be fine with me."

Ben then twisted and greeted another member of their class as Ethan spun a bit left and exchanged some simple greetings with a nearby trio of fellow first year men. Samuel Haven was tall and thin at seventeen like Ethan, a student who came to Harvard to study the histories of civilizations from the old countries. Myles Whitworth was the same age too, only slightly taller and a bit more bulky, a rather studious chap who said he wanted to learn of theologies, of our Creator, man and universe. And at twenty-one Josiah Badcock was a little shorter than Ethan, a determined student who declared he wanted to be a lawyer, a barrister of English law with a colonial twist, and learn all about what he said society referred to as common.

While Ethan watched and listened to the chatter of his new found friends amid the swelling sounds of scores of students, his gaze was suddenly snatched by the intriguing movements of a curious man stepping the platform rising near the eastern wall across the hall. He was shuffling a bit slow with a view over all those assembled, then stopped and stood hushed before an enchanting high-back chair of greenish cushions and polished maple they called Jacobean, a royal chair with ornate pommels perched atop shiny posts. And on the wall above the windows close behind was a glossy plaque with the words *Veritas Christo et Ecclesiae* delicately carved into cherry, an intriguing phrase Ethan would later learn was Latin for proclaiming the veracity of Christ and church. A more modest shingle dangled just below with *Veritas* etched into silver, a secular plea to always search for truth, a creed Ethan and his young class would soon understand oozed from the soul of Harvard College.

Ethan said that man was an inch or two shorter than he, and although he looked rather plump standing at that chair, thick dark hair curling in greying strands beyond his ears, his steady shoulders suggested colonial strength. His facial features seemed more dominant than most, with chiseled cheeks and lips clamped tight, as if desperately trying to contain enlightening words about to be spewed about the hall. A bright silken shirt was snugged to his chin and ruffled down his belly, and a scholarly robe loosely twined about his neck flowed over his shoulders to dark dull shoes. Ethan found himself staring at that curious man, standing at his royal chair and scanning the hall, and within a moment was joined by all those assembled, new friends Josiah, Benjamin, Samuel and Myles too, all awaiting his words in a gazing hush.

"For you first year lads," he began in a clergyman's tone, "welcome. My name is Edward Holyoke. For lack of a more humble phrase, I'm your president here at Harvard College." Then with a sweep of his arm from beneath his draping cloak, he studiously added, "And for you other gentlemen, welcome back. It's good to see you again. I welcome all of you this day to Harvard, to the start of our new academic year."

Ethan would come to learn that Mr. Holyoke had been coupled to Harvard College in various ways for some sixty years, having obtained his first diploma at age sixteen around the turn of the century. It seems over the coming years he earned a further degree while toiling in various studious roles for the college, before leaving to delve deeper into his faith as an eager pastor in the fishing village of Marblehead northeast of Boston. But then he returned to Cambridge some fifteen years before Ethan and I were born, accepting the presidential robe and beginning his quest to align his college's studies more closely with the ideals espoused by enlightened men. And for some three decades it seems Harvard's focus slowly shifted from being swaddled in religious theologies to an array of more secular things like analytical principles and philosophical theories, to literature and law, science and history.

Yet, it was Mr. Holyoke's emphasis upon debate that would come to attract Ethan the most, intriguing discussions they called exhibitions, planned gatherings to express ideals, notions and positions. He said they were intense dialectics, and usually began with a speech by a colonist Mr. Holyoke invited to Harvard, perhaps a printer like Mr. Edes or a Boston merchant, or a member of the colony's assembly. They were impassioned debates about the increasing concerns simmering throughout all the colonies, particularly Ethan's Massachusetts Bay.

Ethan said President Holyoke lectured that morning for an hour or so in a rather eloquent style, closing his gripping oration with what Ethan and his four new classmate friends would later describe as a pleasing slice of wisdom. "These are times which shall challenge a young man's capacities," the president calmly espoused in an ominous tone, "and undoubtedly stretch the limits of your own imposed bounds. These are times, gentlemen, which shall compel one to act with caution and care, moments to be pondered deeply. May our Creator be with all of you throughout this coming year and beyond, and may each of you expand your mind while furthering your sense of empathy, a spiritual compassion bathed in the waters of humanity."

He stopped and scanned all those peering eyes of the colony's future, all those young impressionable minds, then dismissed each class for the rest of the day with a few final words. "I hope each of you will spend the remainder of this day not only in anticipation, but cloaked perhaps, in a bit of reflection. Know they self, gentlemen, and you shall know your reason. I suggest you use these hours wisely, for classes truly begin upon the dawn of morrow."

With that closing line Ethan's Harvard day was over, and bidding a farewell to his new friends Benjamin, Samuel, Josiah and Myles, he returned to Boston in a steady trot past that trio of grassy hills and easy glide across the harbor on the Charlestown ferry. As the morning sun gleamed off the waters and glistened off windows of the port's warehouses, homes and shops, his thoughts seemed consumed by the vision of all those students gathered in the hall, and the elegant words of Mr. Holyoke. With each scrape of Cato's iron shoes he wondered of the challenges of Harvard and duties of the print shop, and was gripped with the notion of expectations by so many, of his father and Mr. Giles, John Gill and Mr. Edes.

He knew he'd be on the grounds of Harvard College a great deal three days each week, with English studies nine to ten, literature of Europe for over an hour before noon and studies of political thought from one to three, each Monday, Wednesday and Friday. His less consuming days would be each Tuesday and Thursday, with theories of the stars, galaxies and planets nine to eleven, and parliamentary procedures immersed in British law from noon to half past two. And he knew he wanted to arrive in Cambridge by seven each day, so he could study early each morning amidst the hush all those papers, pamphlets and books of Harvard Hall. "I thought it might do me good," he'd say, "be a welcome change from reading by the fire in Mr. Gill's gathering room, and studying into the night at the little desk of my room."

Ethan once said he took his responsibilities at Mr. Gill's print shop rather seriously too, never late for his duties after class most days and Saturday afternoon, a dedication he strayed from twice each week, preferring to focus solely on studies each Monday and keeping Sunday his own. It was his only day to stroll about Boston as he chose, walk about the cobblestones and common or wharfs and docks while gazing to the waters and smelling the sea, and sometimes, straying to the Green Dragon Tavern for a mug of ale or two. Or maybe he'd saddle his colt Cato late Saturday afternoon and gallop home to Lexington, spend the night with his father in the tavern before dashing back to Boston by dusk of Sunday.

As Ethan listened to hooves clacking stones on his trot back to Mr. Gill's home that Monday of September, 1768, he wondered of all the challenges awaiting him over the coming four years, and from time to time could feel disturbing doubts creep into his soul. "Then my mind would wander to mom resting up on that hill, Andrea, to her maternal strength, tender touch, and I'd hear those guiding words she whispered so long ago. It was during those reflective moments, Andrea, when I knew things would be alright."

Chapter IX

Purple Anemone

𝕰than's studies at Harvard College and apprenticeship at the print shop of Mr. Edes and John Gill began rather smoothly that fall of 1768, and as the days and weeks passed he found himself growing increasingly comfortable in his new haven on Spring Lane. It was a somewhat restricted, secluded life which seemed to protect him from the angry discontent simmering about the colonies in those days, as if he were shielded from the smoldering embers by some mysterious glass. The English Empire was entering its ninth year of the reign of King George the Third, a monarchy which seemed unwilling to see the resentful flames flickering ever more intensely across the sea. Or maybe it was a crown blindly dithering, simply unable to empathize with a peoples' righteous indignation, while parliament lusted for more intrusive powers over the empire's citizens in the American Colonies.

The expression of London's hegemony over the colonies remained in the grip of the king's royal governors, loyal men like Ethan's Francis Bernard and John Penn in my Colony of Pennsylvania, or Mr. Wright down in Georgia, Horatio Sharpe just south in Maryland and Norborne Berkeley in the Colony of Virginia, the Fourth Baron Botecourt. And while an increasing distaste of the crown's encroaching policies and offensive Townshend Acts was being experienced by an expanding array of colonists that fall and beyond, London responded with what many had said was arrogant indifference. More soldiers in crimson coats were sailed across the sea to patrol the cobblestones of Boston and drill upon the grass of its common, a vivacious field beginning to decay from the intrusive weight of King George.

It was during those tenuous times that sentiment for those rather secretive plans for colonists to stop importing and using English goods, first espoused by the sons of liberty in Boston months before, slowly increased with intensity that fall and into winter of the coming year. Yet, the cries of that surging resistance was beginning to expose a creeping divide not only in Ethan's Boston and Colony of Massachusetts Bay, but in every village, port and town throughout all the colonies. A deepening fissure continued to emerge between those who opposed London's expanding powers over the colonies, a suffocating influence over each women, child and man exemplified by parliament's dreaded acts, and colonists who viewed opposition to the crown as fundamentally disloyal. And as that simmering tempest continued to fester, others foundered in the waters of indecision while seeking to wrap their souls within the fleeting solace of neutrality.

I remember how that splintering within the colonies, an expanding divide not only in hundreds of villages and towns but in each colony's assembly, was exposing an intriguing labeling of those with differing views. Colonists who leaned toward opposition to the crown, those who railed, printed and quilled against those Townshend Acts and other unjust policies and laws being spewed by London, were being called Whigs. Some at the Pennsylvania Hospital were saying such things as "Whigs speak common sense, and uphold the notion of individual liberty," while others taunted them with disparaging remarks like "disloyal ingrates."

Ethan said young men at Harvard, and I suppose schools throughout all the colonies, were beginning to discuss such divisive things before groups of others too, confessing that students were debating various Whig ideals in campus halls or under protective limbs rising near the river, and sometimes, at a little tavern table in Somerville, Boston or Cambridge. And although mother and father would whisper disapproving things about Whigs in our Quaker meeting house, there were others of Germantown and Philadelphia who were attracted to their points of view, men willing to dispute the crown and women heeding the pleas of the sons, shunning those Townshend goods sailed from London.

And on the opposite shore of the spreading divide were those we called Tories, faithful colonists who leaned toward support of parliament and King George, women and men who breathed loyalty to the crown. "They seem rather rational," a doctor at the hospital once secretively said, "but tend to hold tradition more favorably than liberty. I don't understand," he added with a concerned glance down the hospital hall, "why those bloody Tories support the crown's suppression of our freedom, the taking of our property at the whim of the king."

The splintering of loyalties was increasingly flowing across the colonies in those days, sweeping across every farm, port, village and town from the frontier to the sea, differing views pitting neighbor against friend, mothers and fathers against daughters and sons, brother against brother, Tory against Whig. Yet I suppose most frightening was that our simmering Whig sentiments were pitting thousands of colonists against the king. Still, there were those choosing to remain silent, scores of farmers, tradesmen and merchants, doctors, printers and lawyers determined to evade the brewing tempest, including mother and father and their meeting house friends.

"That's what it was like, Samuel," I softly confessed, nudging my chair into an easy rock, "those final months of 1768. Ethan began his Harvard studies and I my nursing training at the Pennsylvania Hospital, while the colonies were slowly fracturing." For a moment Samuel just peered into the summer breeze, as if searching for a taste of the colonies with each rock, and I wondered how the dawn's rays seemed to spray in so many troubling directions in those days. It was a time when the winds sweeping from the wilderness were swirling with a fragrance of Tory or Whig, or the scent of blind indifference.

"What about Ethan, grandma?" Samuel finally asked with an inquisitive glance. "I know you touched on some of those things, but I'm not sure about Ethan. How did he feel about the changes taking place? I mean, at least that fall, what were his views? I'm a little confused about you too, grandma. Where did your sympathies lie?"

"I wonder, Samuel," I whispered, slowing my rock amid the gentle rustle of distant leaves, "if your generation, any generation, can truly understand what it was like back then, what it meant to oppose London in those days." He twisted his stare back to the warming breeze, perhaps wanting to know, trying to imagine, while I slowly slid my fingers across the parchment of Ethan's poem nestled in the pocket of my summer dress. "It was so different then," I softly added as my skin tingled with each caress, "so many dangers, Samuel, for those defying the king. I suppose the pressures were just beginning to bloom in those days, tensions that would have a lasting effect upon so many, the old and the young, colonists like Ethan and me. For thousands about the colonies, it was a time when the twine binding the foundations of what we had always known, began to slowly unravel."

"Maybe you're right, grandma," he admitted with a youthful glance, "but I want to know, need to know."

"I know you do," I whispered, closing my eyes and softly stroking the words of Ethan's poem as Samuel anxiously rocked, staring to little petals of rose fluttering in the afternoon sun. The aroma of baking bread filtered about the air, an alluring smell that reminded me of those days when I was so young, and with each caress of Ethan's tender words, memories flared of a time when life seemed so docile at dawn only to rush toward the tempest dwelling the dusk. I could see the years now etched upon my skin as I opened my eyes and watched pink laurels quivering in the breeze, and wondered of the troubles and pains so many endured in those days. I could sense the same desires that gripped my soul in those years too, feel each sensuousness slide of Ethan's tender lips, and desperately wanted to be consumed by his rapturous touch once again, if only for a magical moment.

"Ethan wanted to concentrate on his studies, Samuel," I slowly explained with a twisting glance, "at least those first few months, and tend to his print shop duties. But he once told me it became increasingly difficult to ignore events of Boston, to not get caught up in discussions about unsettling things happening about the colonies. Many students showed support for the contentions of Tories while others were leaning toward the views espoused by a growing number of Whigs, and little campus groups were beginning to read and debate beliefs printed in papers like Mr. Gill's Boston Gazette. Ethan just tried to keep to his studies amid the swirl of all those things, not supporting any one group, but with each passing week it became increasingly difficult. He knew his sympathies aligned with those of the Whigs, Samuel, for deep down he knew he opposed the encroaching powers of parliament and the king."

"But what does that mean, grandma? Did Ethan just keep his views to himself, stay quiet about those things?"

There was a tinge of youthful confusion in Samuel's voice, as if Ethan had somehow betrayed some imaginary expectation, yet I knew Samuel's questions would be answered as he listened to the rest of my story. And I could see the bewilderment in his eyes as he gazed to the swaying limbs of those distant elms, a stare that seemed to thirst for knowing how things truly were in colonial days. "Ethan did talk with others, Samuel," I revealed in a resolute tone, "eventually, not unlike many colonists, young and old. You'll see these things for yourself, once you hear my whole story."

"Oh, I see, alright. What about you, grandma? How did you feel about those things?"

"Ethan and I saw so many things in pretty much the same shade," I whispered, dabbing a tear trying to trickle my cheek. "Sometimes, Samuel, things lurk in an array of colors, or perhaps linger in shadows of grey, and sometimes an issue is fundamentally clear, either black or white. Once you know more of what really happened in those days, I just know you'll understand those shadows and shades. Then you'll know what Ethan and I came to believe, understand why we chose the path we'd take."

"I think you're right, grandma," he sheepishly replied. "I guess, sometimes, I want things in too much of a hurry, and need to slow down."

"Oh, Samuel," I gently sputtered, glancing to his caring eyes, "don't you worry. Remember, I too, was once young. Back then, my days were consumed with nursing training, watching and listening to those assigned to help me at the Pennsylvania Hospital, fine nurses like mother's friend Sarah, and devouring medical books. And even though Ethan and I had yet to meet as of those final weeks and months of 1768, I still recall so many things he'd later whisper to me." I hushed for a moment and dabbed my eyes amid the sounds of leaves rustling in the breeze, then softly stroked the tender words of Ethan's poem and gazed to petals of crimson rose fluttering in the summer winds. And Samuel peered to the distant trees while nudging his chair into an easy rock, and with a gentle gleam in his eyes, patiently waited my coming words.

Ethan once said that he formed a studious friendship with those four young classmates he briefly met that Monday morning in Harvard Hall, and soon that fall they began to quietly meet after classes to study and discuss assignments. And it wasn't long before they'd talk about other things too, mostly the troubling concerns brewing about Boston and all the colonies. "We'd muster beneath an elm near Mr. Phipps' farm," he explained, "or maybe on a few logs over by the river, and discuss our subjects and colonial issues rather intensely. Sometimes I'd just listen, Andrea, when the others were bantering about this or that, and just watch the fallen leaves dance the grassy slopes in the cooling breeze. And when the chilling autumn rains came, when wintry winds and the smell of flurries drew nearer, we'd gather inside the library hall and talk amidst all those pamphlets and books."

All five soon came to realize they held similar points of view about an array of colonial things, and seemed to agree more or less with the opinions of spirited colonists being expressed in rumors and papers. And they came to believe that discussing the intricacies of their studies, along with the nature of troubling events erupting about the colonies, would help them improve their understanding of assignments while preparing each for the outside world.

Myles Whitworth was from Salem, a little sea village several miles northeast of Boston, and Samuel Haven came from Milford in the Colony of Connecticut, a town a few miles west of New Haven on the waters of Long Island Sound. And Ben Loring was from the village of Concord five miles west of Ethan's Lexington, while the elder of the group, Josiah Badcock, had never lived anywhere but Boston. They first gathered just southeast of the halls near aging elms along the Charles River, assembling later that fall on a few scorched logs that had been mysteriously arranged by young students many years before. Ethan said that through the misty haze of that chilly day he could see the stone tower of that royal chapel rising across the river near the common, and liked to tell me of the tantalizing smells of the sea that wafted about the harbor.

The autumn afternoon was cooling when they gathered for the first time on the second Monday of November, mustering just a bit after three beneath a thick layer of roiling grey that smelled of the season's first snow. Each secured a strategic spot about those mysterious limbs, and following a few words about their intriguing surroundings they began to discuss the reasons for meeting then and in months to come, agreeing to focus on studies and colonial concerns. And as they talked of their group's purpose and exchanged various ideas, Ethan watched Josiah lazily drag the tip of a long twig through mushy grass of the soggy soil.

"I think we should have a name," Josiah suddenly surmised with a tilting gaze, "something of an identity." Then following a moment or two of puzzled glances and twists, he softly added, "How about if we call our little group, the 'river council'?

"Um, that's not bad, Josiah," uttered Myles. "Or maybe, how bout, the 'Cambridge five?'"

A hush descended upon their rustic haven as they stared and pondered, Josiah and Sam gazing northwest to the Harvard bricks while Ben, Ethan and Myles peered east across the Charles. And as Ethan stared through the chilly haze to little homes on the slopes of Beacon Hill and that liberty elm rising in the corner of the common, he remembered something he read years before in a pamphlet in Mr. Giles' print shop or a book at his Lexington schoolhouse.

"Wait," Ethan calmly sputtered, trying not to impugn Josiah or Myles as all twisted with attentive stares, "maybe, there's even something better. I once read about a special little group down in Philadelphia, oh, some forty years ago, tradesmen and merchants, lawyers and printers, colonists assembled by Doctor Franklin. If I recall, they'd get together and talk about concerns affecting Philadelphia back then, issues of government, royal and colonial, and dabble in philosophical theories and societal norms. I guess they were looking to improve their own lot too by enhancing the port's vitality, even striving to expand the horizons of every colonist by forming the port's first library with hundreds of pamphlets and books."

"How interesting, Ethan," Samuel supportively chimed. "What did they call their group?"

"It might sound strange," Ethan cautioned while scanning the gazing eyes of his friends, "but they went by the name 'junto.' Oh, I guess some of Philadelphia called them the apron club or something like that, but they liked to say they were the junto."

"Junto?" Ben sputtered in a puzzled tone. "What's a bloody junto?"

"I think its Latin, Ben," Ethan eagerly replied, "or maybe Spanish or Greek, and means something like a community faction or little political group, people who gather to talk about important societal things."

They snapped their stares among themselves for a moment or two, listening to the autumn winds whisk about leafless limbs as the waters of the Charles gently lapped muddied rocks and stones. "I like it," Myles emphatically said. "They must have been political intriguers, rather shrewd thinkers. Yes, junto has a mysterious ring about it, don't you think? I say we use it. After all, if it was good enough for Mr. Franklin and his friends, it should be good enough for Harvard College, for our little group."

"It does have a rather intriguing sound to it," injected Sam with an enchanted stare, "in a secretive way. And its meaning fits. I say Myles is right. We use it."

"I like it too," Josiah quickly insisted. "It's mystical. I think junto fits us well."

"Ben?" Ethan inquired, twisting a bit into the cooling winds. "What do you say?"

Ben clasped his hands and glanced to the others anxiously waiting, then nodded in agreement and confidently said, "Doctor Franklin has been a respected colonist for many years, perhaps the most in all the colonies. I think he'd be honored to have our little Harvard group go by a name he and his fellow Philadelphians thought of so much. Yes, junto sounds fine to me too."

"Then it's settled," Ethan spouted with a slap to his thigh while all glanced in agreement, "we now have a name."

"Nice going, Ethan," Josiah uttered as the others nodded pleasingly, "that was a fine suggestion. Now, let's get this first meeting of the junto here at Harvard underway."

I remember the sparkling pride brushing Ethan's cheeks when he first whispered that story to me all those years ago, and how a tinge of mist would spray his tender eyes whenever recalling his Harvard days. Their little group began to meet on those rustic logs for several weeks thereafter, sometimes early before studies but usually on a Monday after Ethan's final class, and when the flurries of winter began to blow they'd assemble at a secluded table in a corner of Harvard Hall.

Then in December Ethan and his junto friends decided to meet away from the Harvard grounds, gather at a public space somewhere across the river in Boston. He said it was mostly Josiah's idea, thought it would be nice to be among colonists, maybe listen to what they were saying about colonial issues while sipping ale from a Boston mug. And it was Ethan who suggested they gather a bit past six at the Green Dragon Tavern that coming Saturday, just down the street from Mr. Gill's shop.

That Boston night was fraught with chill as Ethan scurried about to complete his printing duties, glancing now and then through the frosting panes to see little white flakes gently settling to the cobblestones of Queen Street. He was stuffing tiny black type just before six in a frantic effort to ready the galleys for the coming edition of the Gazette and Country Journal, while Mr. Edes was quilling inspiring lines to a rumpled sheet at his desk. And although Mr. Gill was still at home enjoying a supper of stew and crusted rolls, he'd soon return to complete the Gazette, inking galleys and pressing parchment late into the night.

"I'll be leaving now, Mr. Edes," Ethan reminded his mentor, tossing his stained apron to a thin nail protruding from the wall behind his desk. Then snatching his tan coat from the back of his chair, tugging the wool and fastened it down his chest, he pressed his tricorn hat to his hair and hurried across the oak slats to the door. "The type is ready, Mr. Edes," he advised, "and the bucket is topped with ink. I'm off to the Green Dragon Tavern, to meet some Harvard friends."

"Very good," Benjamin uttered, glancing toward the door while sliding his quill through a tiny hole in the lid of a small tin of ink. "Thank you, Ethan. You know, we both think you're doing a fine job here, and you've done your duties diligently all week. Enjoy your friends, and your Sunday."

"Thank you, Mr. Edes," Ethan graciously replied while gripping the latch of the door. "You have a good evening too. I'll see you on Tuesday for sure."

"Yes, of course, Tuesday," he said, spinning in his chair and reaching for that quill. Then as he began to ink thoughts to a sheet once again, he quickly uttered in a fatherly tone, "And keep up those studies, Ethan!"

"I will," he promised, dashing into the chill.

Little flakes continued to gently drift from the cold engulfing the Boston night as Ethan stepped east along the north edge of Queen Street toward the cobblestones of King and the Green Dragon Tavern. He watched carriages slowly creak and listened to hooves clanking stones brushed by a thin layer of white, and with each slide of his shoes he wondered what the colonists of Boston were doing in homes that quiet night. Perhaps they were snuggled in blankets taming fiery desires near a flaming hearth, or feasting on tasty stews or roasted meats.

He could see several soldiers as he neared the tavern, royal troops at the crown's customs house across the cobblestones of King Street. Most were meandering along the edge of the stones while a pair stood stoically at guard outside the door, muskets strapped to each man's shoulder. "I would snap a glance," Ethan said, "but didn't stare, just kept stepping closer to the tavern. And as I passed without uttering a word, I thought I could hear mocking whispers."

They were some of the hundreds of royal soldiers that had sailed to Boston several months before to do their part in helping the king's governor and customs men enforce those despised Townshend Acts. Ethan once said that by that December night many colonists of Massachusetts Bay were referring to those men as regulars, simply soldiers of the crown's army, while others spurred by their crimson looks, were calling them redcoats. Yet it seems a growing number of Bostonians preferred to use more disparaging terms such as bloody bastards or lobster backs, names that were slowly coming to be heard along the docks and in homes, taverns and shops. He said there was an evolving contempt for the king's men emerging in Boston, a type of scornful sentiment that was beginning to spread to other villages and towns across Massachusetts Bay, a spirited bias that was slowly drifting throughout all the colonies upon disgruntled winds.

Ethan strutted past those gazing soldiers in an unflinching pace, and as the snow gently fluttered to the cobblestones, he bound up some boards to the shuttered door of the Green Dragon Tavern. He grasped the tarnished latch and swung the door open with a squeaky push, then quickly shuffling in as little flames burning candles on tables flickered in a burst of chill. Josiah, Samuel, Benjamin and Myles were already gathered with mugs of ale at a big round table off to the right, close to a few smaller ones nudged near the frosting panes peering upon King Street.

"Ethan," Samuel spouted from his chair facing the door, "over here. We've been waiting for you. It's about time you unshackled yourself from that printing press."

"Be right there," Ethan uttered with a determined shut of the door as he snatched his tricorn and brushed the night from his coat while glancing about the tavern. Wide candles were burning on the larger tables, their flames flickering tiny shadows about the room, and smaller candles were on the others, little pulsing fires glistening off goblets, mugs and panes. And a pair of matching lamps was set to each end of the barreled bar right of the fireplace to the rear, their wicks glowing brightly amid crystal of azure blue.

Over a dozen other men were in the tavern that night, some engaged in what seemed rather serious talk at a big table near the corner windows left of the door, and a few were sipping spirits at a smaller table nearby. And others were over to the right at a little table nudged into the corner near Ethan's junto friends, white foam dripping mugs gripped in their hands, while a pair with their backs to the room were leaning into the slats of the barreled bar, not far from the flames snapping in the stones of the hearth.

They were mostly dockworkers, tradesmen and merchants closing out their day, proud men gripping goblets, mugs, cups and tins filled of wine, ale, rye whiskey and rum. Ethan had met Thom the barkeep a few years before, and would watch him dash around the tavern that night tending to the men scattered about the room. But it was the pair leaning into the barreled bar that quickly grasped Ethan's attention, for they were not tinsmiths, lawyers, doctors or printers, nor farmers from the fields of the Colony of Massachusetts Bay, but rather two of the king's soldiers who had sailed across the sea just months before.

As Ethan stared to those two soldiers and untethered the buttons of his coat, he wondered if just hours before they had been drilling on the snowy grass of the common or been standing guard at the customs house across the stones of King Street. And he wondered if at that moment they were trying to taste a slice of normalcy in life, sipping ale before retiring to quarters in a seized warehouse or in that aging fortress on Castle Island nestled safely east in the harbor. Their crimson coats covered smirched light breeches and hung low to dark muddied boots, and their black tricorn hats rested nearby on the slats of the bar while their iron muskets leaned against the fireplace stones just left. Ethan would later discover they were royal grenadiers garrisoned in Boston with a regiment the king called his Twenty-ninth of Foot, and said they talked in a whispery tone with each sip while glancing about the tavern now and then, as if to see if anyone was watching or listening.

Ethan snapped his stare from those two soldiers and stepped right toward the table of his four junto friends, then gestured to Thom behind the bar pouring ale from the spigot of an oak barrel into a pair of pewter mugs. "Thom," he spouted in a courteous way while dropping his hat to the table and nestling to the slats of the chair just left of Samuel, "how about a mug of that ale, please." Myles was to Ethan's left and Josiah was across the table near Benjamin, and those two redcoats, several feet behind at the bar, were pretty much in Ethan's unobstructed view.

"Hope I'm not too late," Ethan muttered in an apologetic way as Thom slid a mug of dripping ale to his fingers. "I came as soon as I could. Thanks, Thom," he quickly added, placing a shilling to his hand. "Well, I suppose I have some catching up to do."

"We've been talking about something you might find interesting, Ethan," informed Josiah with a sip of foaming ale. "Oh, I suppose it has been a few months since it first appeared, but we thought it still pertinent, Ethan, worthy of a junto discussion."

"What do think about that statement our colony's assembly circulated about the colonies earlier this year?" Samuel enticingly asked, dangling a printed copy on crumpled parchment near the candle. "You know, Ethan, that letter they say Mr. Adams quilled. We're trying to decide if that letter was too defiant, or whether it was just right."

Ethan gripped his mug and twitched a bit in his chair as the others pressed back into their slats with anticipation, then sipped a little ale while desperately recalling details of what thousands of colonists surly remembered. "It's been awhile," he hesitantly replied. "I'm not really sure one way or the other. What have you fellas been saying?"

"We're somewhat divided, Ethan," inserted Myles, "leaning either way."

"Let's take another look at just what this letter says," Samuel boldly suggested, "go through it slowly. What do you say?"

"Yes, let's," Benjamin uttered, glancing about the table as Josiah, Ethan and Myles quickly agreed.

"Good," Samuel concluded while pinching the parchment near the table's flickering flame, "it's unanimous." Then tilting his head and angling that crumple sheet near the candle, he began to read what he perceived to be powerful portions of Mr. Adams' letter. "'His Majesty's high court of parliament is the supreme legislative power over the whole empire, and His Majesty's American subjects, who acknowledge themselves bound by the ties of allegiance, have an equitable claim to the full enjoyment of the fundamental rules of the British constitution.' Well, gentlemen," Sam asked, stopping and pressing back in his chair, "what does that means? Do we agree?"

"I think what he's saying," answered Myles, gazing to Samuel across the table before scanning the others' eyes, "is that the colonies are loyal to the crown, that we're bound to the king, and that parliament has the legitimate right to enact rules for governing the colonies. I suppose he's right, that we are subject to the powers of London. After all, we are British citizens, the king's subjects."

"I understand what you're saying, Myles," Josiah rationally injected, "yet, I'm not so sure I fully agree. Remember, it's three thousand miles to England, and takes weeks, sometimes months for ideas and positions to sail back and forth across the sea. Maybe the distance is too great between the colonies and London. And we still aren't truly represented in parliament, no one to cast a true vote in upholding our colonial interests. Maybe the time for creating our own laws, our own policies and rules, is drawing nearer. Maybe we should govern ourselves."

"Ya, that could be, Josiah," Myles spiritedly retorted. "But I must say, we've always been subjects of the English crown. And remember, it was the king's soldiers who not long ago came over here to defend our wilderness lands against the French and their native allies, protect our colonial interests and lives along the frontier from King Louis. Doesn't that mean we owe much to the crown, to parliament for doing those things? Doesn't that mean the colonies should pay these new duties and taxes, show loyalty to the king?"

"Those are both fine views," injected Ethan, glancing to Josiah and Myles, "but maybe, there's a more neutral position somewhere. Maybe the colonies would have a greater acceptance of the crown, parliament and their laws, if we had more autonomy. That is, give our colonial assemblies true powers to negotiate with London, freely discuss issues like duties and taxes with our royal governors. Give us a greater degree of control over our own lives. Would the king and parliament accept such changes? I don't know. I guess, time will tell."

"I have my doubts, Ethan," Ben calmly said, "and think I lean toward Myles. After all, we are British citizens subject to the crown, and have been for over a hundred years. My dad even fought with our militia alongside the king's troops in the wilderness against the French, just like yours did Ethan, yours too Myles. It seems to me that what many colonists seek is to simply be treated the same as citizens across the sea, have the same rights and privileges here as they have over there."

"And that might the problem, Ben," suggested Samuel. "It's those rights that colonists seem to be losing, or maybe, we never really had some of them at all. Now, let's see what else Mr. Adams expressed in that letter. 'It is essential,' he goes on to say, 'an unalterable right in nature and engrafted into the British constitution as a fundamental law, ever held sacred and irrevocable by the subjects within the realm, that what a man has honestly acquired is absolutely his own, which he may freely give, but cannot be taken away from him without his consent. That the American subjects may therefore, exclusive of any consideration of charter rights, and with a decent firmness adapted to the character of free men and subjects, asset this natural and constitutional right.' Alright," Sam uttered, scanning about, "what's Mr. Adams trying to say?"

"That the colonies shouldn't be saddled with duties and taxes," Josiah excitedly chimed, "imposed by royals thousands of miles away in London, when not one colonist is in parliament to represent, speak for the colonies. I think he's saying what Ben and Myles suggest, that all we want is to be treated the same here as citizens in England, that the king respect our rights. And I guess that means, among other things, that only a colonist can consent to the taking of his property, not the ministers in London. I support this view."

"Maybe so, Josiah," inserted Myles in a strange adversarial tone, "but isn't the rule of a monarch, if nothing else, absolute? Isn't the power of a king to rule his subjects paramount to the life of his crown? And isn't that true, regardless of whether a body of water separates his subjects from his throne, or whether his people are represented in parliament or some other constituted assembly?"

"Possibly, you might be right," Ethan said, sliding his mug with a click to the table. "And maybe, Myles, those are how things are right now, realities that Mr. Adams and a growing number of others seek to change. His letter seems to suggest that certain rights are fundamental, and therefore should prevail over what I think he views as antiquated absolute powers. Yet his thoughts seem tempered, for he says that we only seek rights already afforded those across the sea. Maybe Mr. Adams is just asking that the powers parliament and the crown have over our colonies be carefully reconsidered, perhaps reduced. I find his ideas appealing."

"I just don't know," Benjamin sputtered with a questioning squint. "Such thoughts could be viewed as a bit radical, maybe even dangerous. Even while I find myself sliding a little each day toward his views, they worry me."

"Alright you guys, let's move on," Sam insisted in a professorial way, "delve further into this letter. This segment seems to deal with those Townshend Acts, and reads: 'That the acts made there, imposing duties on the people of this province, with the sole and express purpose of raising a revenue, are infringements of their natural and constitutional rights, because, as they are not represented in the British Parliament, his Majesty's Commons in Britain, by those acts, grant their property without their consent.'"

"I think he's right again," blurted Josiah, spritzing the table's flame with a light spray of ale. "The colonies shouldn't be made to pay a tax without its own representative agreeing. And I'm not sure if Mr. Adams' letter addresses this directly, but there's something else, something I've been hearing from others. Some say we shouldn't be forced to pay duties and taxes to pay for feeding and housing the king's army over here, those barracked about Boston and down on the Island of Manhattan, or anywhere else in the colonies. If London wants to take our property in taxes and duties, then our shillings and pounds should be used to provide essentials for the colonies, better postal roads and docks for our ports, not to raise revenue to pay for his soldiers."

"That's a good point, Josiah," Sam calmly agreed, "makes a great deal of sense."

A rare hush descended upon the table for a moment or two as Ethan sipped the final spot of ale from his mug, and scanning the others with a tilt of his head, he could see they had tasted their final drops too. "Thom," he sounded while waving a hand toward the barreled bar, "how about five more ales over here, please." Then amid a flickering candle, he glanced about the table and softly said, "These are on me."

"Thank you, Ethan," uttered Myles, quickly followed by the other three. "Now, Sam, go ahead. Let's hear the rest of that letter."

As Sam held that crumpled sheet near the candle once again, Myles leaned toward the flame and slyly motioned for the others to join. "Don't' look, but I think those two redcoats over there," he softly whispered as Samuel, Ethan, Josiah and Ben stretched their necks, "have been trying to listen to what we've said. Judging by their demeanor, I think they disapprove of Mr. Adams' letter. I've seen them mumble and sneak glances back now and then, especially when we voice supportive views."

Sam snapped a fleeting glance to the backs of those soldiers leaning into the bar, while the others pressed back into their chairs and snuck a look or two. "Here you go boys," uttered barkeep Thom, sliding foaming ale toward each hand before snatching their empty mugs, "enjoy."

"This should take care of it, Thom," Ethan whispered, dropping several shillings to his hand. "Thanks."

"Here's to us," Samuel proposed as each raised his mug toward the flame, "to our junto club."

"To our junto club!" the others spouted in unison as all clicked dripping pewter mugs.

Samuel sipped his ale and leaned into the table while motioning for Ethan, Josiah, Benjamin and Myles to come closer, and as a restive hush settled upon their table once again, he boldly whispered in a defiant way, as if hoping the king's soldiers would hear. "I say to the devil with blooming lobster backs! Let's forget about them, and hear the rest of Mr. Adams' letter."

Ethan said he could feel his stomach twist with an anxious cringe as Samuel's contentious words slowly faded amid pulsating flames, for he feared he may have purposely sought to spur an unpleasant exchange with the crown's redcoats. Yet, apparently those two soldiers didn't hear, and the five junto friends simply gripped their mugs and pressed back into their chairs. And as Ethan snapped a nervous glance or two toward the barreled bar, to the pair of royal soldiers still whispering and sipping ale, Samuel held the parchment near the candle and began to read.

"'They have also submitted to consideration,'" he continued with the words of Mr. Adams, "'whether any people can be said to enjoy any degree of freedom, if the crown, in addition to its undoubted authority of constituting a governor, should appoint him such a stipend as it may judge proper, without the consent of the people and at their expense. And whether, while the judges of the land and other civil officers hold not their commissions during good behavior, their having salaries appointed for them by the crown, independent of the people, hath not a tendency to subvert the principals of equity, and endanger the happiness and security of the subject.' Well," Samuel uttered, pressing the parchment to the table and gripping his mug, "any thoughts on this?"

"I suppose," Ben boldly replied in an uninhibited way, "I mean, maybe, what Mr. Adams is saying is, if the colonies don't have true authority over the pay of royal governors, over colonial officers and judges, then their allegiances toward the colonies could erode. They'd be beholden to London, not the colonies, and their decisions could easily run afoul of our interests."

"That's makes sense, Ben," insisted a robust Myles, "and just might be true. Yet, if the crown is to maintain control of its empire, inspire loyalty from its kingdom, shouldn't it have the right to choose those who perform duties throughout the kingdom, in places like here in the colonies? Shouldn't the king have the right to maintain authority through things like payment of wages for royal governors, judges and such?"

"Not at the expense of our liberties!" Samuel spouted, surprising Ethan and the others with an intenseness that caused their flame to flutter in a tizzy. Then perhaps wanting to ease the anxiousness surging about the table, he added in a calmly way, "I mean, if we lose the freedom to secure our wellbeing, our happiness, what Mr. Adams seems to be implying, then have we not lost the essence of life itself? Why, the colonies could slowly slide into a medieval darkness, an oppressive abyss,"

"I think there's a lot of truth in what you say, Sam," Ethan enthusiastically chimed, "and Mr. Adams' letter seems to point that out. I suppose, for me, I think if we don't have control of our own authorities, then we, the colonies, have lost the fundamental right to determine our own destinies. Command over our property, dreams and lives, over the very foundation of happiness, could vanish."

"Josiah?" a concerned Samuel asked. "You've been a bit quiet for a while. What do you think about all that?"

Josiah gazed to Samuel's eyes before snapping a cautious glance over his shoulder toward the two crimson coats nursing Boston ale at the barreled bar, then undaunted, tilted his mug and downed another splash of froth. "I think I understand what Mr. Adams believes," he replied, "and heard what you guys have said. I must say, it seems unwise for colonists to remain silently obedient, not object in some way, to what looks to be an attempt to suppress our rights. I guess I side with Mr. Adams."

"Me too," injected Myles with a dash of timidity. "But, have we given enough thought to the cost of objection? Oh, don't get me wrong, I'm leaning to the views in Mr. Adams' letter too. It's just that, it has a sound of disloyalty, a defiance that could spur a degree of peril. Yet, even so, I can't help but feel his positions right, can't help but feel that maybe, the time has come to toss caution to the winds."

"What about you, Benjamin?" Sam inquired.

"Myles has some fine points," Ben replied while snapping glances about the table, "there are costs to defiance, peril dangling somewhere out there. I agree with the sentiments I've heard here tonight, yet smell a scent of danger."

"I think each of us, Ben," Samuel confirmed with understanding, "even Mr. Adams and others too, know of such dangers and hear the caution in your tone. Yet, I'd say each of us here tonight still believes such things right, and falls somewhere on the side of Mr. Adams." Then pinching the parchment in his fingertips once again, he dangled that letter near the candle and recited its closing words. "'These are the sentiments and proceedings of the Massachusetts Bay house of assembly. And as the enemies of the colonies have represented them to his Majesty's ministers and parliament as factious and disloyal, of having a disposition to make themselves independent of the mother country, our assembly has taken occasion in the most humble terms, to assure his Majesty and his ministers that with regard to the people of this province, and of all the colonies no doubt, the charge is unjust. This house cannot conclude without expressing its firm confidence in the king, our common head and father, that the united and dutiful supplications of his distressed American subjects will meet with his royal and favorable acceptance.'"

Samuel laid the parchment to the table and gripped his mug, and after a moment of reflective silence, confidently uttered, "The closing words of Mr. Adams seem to say that our colony, that all the colonies, remain loyal to the king. I think this letter clearly expresses our desires to remain twined to the crown, but in perhaps a more just way. He suggests that what we simply seek are the same rights and freedoms afforded the king's citizens across the sea.

"Yes, I think that's about right," Ethan eagerly agreed, "and must say his final thoughts have helped alleviate some of my initial concerns. Yet, even so, taking his letter on a whole, in a way I can see why parliament and the king viewed Mr. Adams' letter as threatening. I heard some say London's ministers were calling it disloyally distasteful, and that's why the king soon insisted that our royal governors thwart their colonial assemblies from endorsing his letter. Regardless, I support the colonies' views."

"Ben?" quizzed Sam while scanning the table. "Myles, Josiah? Does anyone have a differing view?"

"I would have liked to have seen more of a notion of separation from parliament," Josiah boldly replied, "greater emphasis on enhancing our colonies' abilities to make our own laws, decide our own taxes and duties, determine our own fate." Then pressing to the back of his chair and tipping his ale, he glanced over his shoulder to the king's soldiers leaning to the barreled bar and inhaled a frustrating breath of tavern air. "After all," he spiritedly boasted, "how much of this bloody nonsense are we colonists supposed to take!"

"I know what you mean," Myles timidly agreed while nervously glancing to those crimson coats, "truly I do. I support Mr. Adams' letter, but must say, with caution."

"That's pretty much how I feel too," added Ben, fidgeting in his chair and tapping his mug.

As those sentiments filtered about the tavern amid shadows roaming about the room from logs snapping in the hearth and little flames flickering candles, the five pressed back into the slats of their chairs while Samuel slid Mr. Adams' letter into a pocket of his coat, parchment creased with a trio of folds. "This was a rather enlightening meet," Ethan proudly suggested, shattering the hush while lifting his mug toward their candle, "a pretty good junto talk, don't you think? And the ale was rather pleasing too."

"Yes, I think so too," quickly chimed Myles, "inspiring. And I like your place, Ethan, this tavern. Perhaps we'll do this again."

"My sentiments as well," Samuel added, downing more ale. "I'm glad we discussed that letter too, positions that we all know are crucial. Yes, let's do, meet here again, soon."

Then as if under an hypnotic spell, the five junto friends raised their mugs a final time into the tavern air as Ben inspiringly spouted, "To our next meet here, at the Green Dragon Tavern," an arousing toast quickly agreed to by the others. They finished their ale and clicked their mugs to the table, then pushing back their chairs with scratches and scrapes, tugged on the wool of their coats, donned tricorn hats and began stepping toward the tavern door. And as Ethan twisted with a few thankful words to Thom the barkeep, he could see that those two redcoats were now watching with their backs against the bar, contempt gleaming from their eyes.

"Bloody blinking dopes!" the huskier of the two boisterously whispered in a tone that seemed intended for the junto five to hear.

Benjamin, Josiah and Myles slowed near the door while Samuel and Ethan stopped, then spinning daringly with shoulders squared and arms stiff down their sides, they simply stared across the tavern into the glaring eyes of the two king's men. Ethan said they were tightly gripping their mugs with intimidation brushed across each face, and that the four just gazed to each other without uttering a word as those scattered about the tavern watched in an unsettling hush. And while they stared amidst flickering candles and hearth flames snapping shadows about the room for what seemed endless silent moments, Benjamin, Josiah and Myles nervously watched from the door.

"What are you two bloomin dopes gawkin at?" the husky one spouted with a contemptuous grin as both rolled their shoulders and straitened their slouch, mugs still gripped in their hands.

Ethan and Sam didn't utter a sound, just stood their defiant ground with an intensity their junto friends had never before seen, and the four simply continued to silently stare into each other's eyes as if preparing for a medieval joust. "My heart was pounding, Andrea," Ethan would whisperingly confess, "racing wildly, and I could sense the tension snapping across the tavern from soul to soul. Yet somehow I found a way to understand that our fiery emotions needed to be restrained, knew that intellect must prevail." Although he and Sam seemed to know that prolonging the brinkmanship might cause the simmering embers to spark and flare, they nevertheless held their ground and glared across the room, perhaps infusing a sense of their undaunted will into the king's men. And after another anxious moment or two, Sam and Ethan nodded to the crown's soldiers with a chivalrous tilt, then spun and strutted behind Benjamin, Josiah and Myles through the tavern door into the Boston night.

The five young Harvard men bid their farewells and quickly dispersed, with Ethan walking a short distance south then east through the chill back to his room, and as his soles scraped snowy stones he thought about what had just happened in the tavern that night. He confided how nervous he had been glaring into the king's men, perhaps even a bit scared, and often wondered from where his daring defiance had come from. And as he stepped through cold up the slope of Spring Lane toward the bricks and panes of Mr. Gill's house, he gazed into the darkness in search for answers of what had silently propelled him, only to see tiny flakes drifting the night and gently kissing his cheeks.

Although Ethan struggled to truly comprehend what had transpired in the Green Dragon Tavern that night, he realized that what his junto group had talked about was perhaps just as consequential as the tensions unleashed by the crown's two soldiers. He knew he leaned toward the views Mr. Adams espoused in that letter, ideals of equity and liberty, and soon began to feel a strange wrenching inside when hearing the emphatic pleas of loyalty to London coming from colonists about Boston, Massachusetts Bay and beyond, Tory cries increasingly opposed by a growing number of daring Whigs. And in the coming weeks and months he began to feel a nauseous angst that soon he might be compelled to choose his course, and wondered whether he would find the wisdom and strength to accept the challenge. Yet he also believed that our Creator would someday show him the way, and lead all colonists upon the righteous path.

Ethan continued his studies at Harvard and duties at the print shop as autumn succumbed to wintry chills those final days of 1768, and his little junto group continued to meet now and then before the fall studies came to an end three days before Christmas. "We'd muster in our library hall," he'd say, "on days of blustery snow, or maybe in a quiet classroom or other warm place. We even got together at Mr. Gill's shop the final Monday before Christmas, up in that secretive long room, then finished our discussion that night with ale at the Green Dragon Tavern." And during those final weeks and months the king's soldiers continued drilling upon the snows of the common, or strutted in menacing boots about Boston's cobblestones, wharfs and docks in patrols of twos, fours, six or eight, muskets slung from shoulders.

With his studies now silent for several weeks, Ethan saddled Cato and galloped home to Lexington on a briskly clear Friday morn of late December, leaving behind his duties at Mr. Gill's print shop and little room on Spring Lane. He had relinquished the bustle and pressures of Harvard and Boston for the serenity of his village, at least for a little while, and for the coming twenty-nine days would wrap his body, mind and soul within the comfort of his father and warmth of the tavern, and the tranquil solace of his mother swaddled by the soil of her hill.

Ethan said he cherished helping his father those wintry weeks at the Buckman Tavern, even tending to tradesmen and farmers the day he turned eighteen that Monday of December, and always found time to visit Mr. Giles at his print shop now and then. And sometimes near dusk or during an early morning chill he'd bundle in his coat, hat and boots, and in the quiet kneel at his mother's grave, or maybe just stroll about the stones of the roads or snows of the village field.

"It felt so good to be home, Andrea," he once whispered, "to be near dad and mom, so many tranquil things, dad's shoes scraping the slats of the tavern floor and the nearby smells of Mary White's baking, even the clanking sounds filtering from Sam Burns' blacksmith shop. I can still hear dad talking about colonial things with patrons too, or the toils of tradesmen and struggles of merchants, while watching each sip whiskey, ale, wine and rum from goblets, mugs, cups and tins." They were feelings and smells, sounds and sights which seemed to bring a needed balance to Ethan, soothing his mind and soul.

Farmers talked of crops they'd plant in spring and merchants would discuss newfangled things they'd seen down in New Haven, or over in Worcester or Boston, and sometimes, nearer the lazy hours of night, Ethan would listen to unflattering spouts about the unjust taxes and duties imposed by those Townshend Acts. He'd watch his father gather with

Lexington men like Reverend Clarke and Doc Newman, John Parker, Joe Hosmer and Mr. Giles, and listen from behind the barreled bar or beyond the kitchen door as they discussed various Whig positions, sons of liberty things too, and talked about their increasing disgust of thousands of royal soldiers meandering about the ports of Boston and New York.

Yet perhaps what Ethan truly cherished the most were the simple things he had missed from his village, the aroma filtering about the tavern of a little beast roasting in the stones of the kitchen hearth and the smell of fresh snow settling to trees, fence rails, shops and homes. I remember he told me of the first flurry of the new year, of how he could hear Nuthatches chirping about the snows of his village field or dancing the leafless limbs of distant maple, birch and oak, serene trills that flowed with the icy winds through tiny cracks near his bedroom windows during the hush of dawn or chill of night. And sometimes during the quiet of an afternoon he'd nestle with a quilt upon his bed, his hair lazily pressed to pillows while gazing through the panes, and watch little flakes daintily drift from the grey.

He liked to say his village of Lexington was in a way detached from the stresses of Boston and outside world, at least so it seemed for Ethan in those early days, a life spared of the tensions slowly encroaching Boston and other ports scattered about colonies. But in a disturbing way he was now beginning to sense how those divisive troubles were truly nipping at the heels of his Middlesex County, disturbing winds blowing more intrusively to villages like Lexington and scores of other hamlets and towns throughout the Colony of Massachusetts Bay, to other counties like Worcester, Bristol and Essex. He once whispered how those frictions between the colonies and London had crept into the hills and fields before, yet now, in those early days of 1769, they were beginning to enflame a simmering discord more than ever before.

Not only could Ethan sense those simmering frictions beginning to sweep more intensely across the hills and fields of Massachusetts Bay, but he could see their fiery affects each time he visited Mr. Giles at his print shop. "Just as he had for years," Ethan said, "Mr. Giles continued to print the thoughts of colonists in his Lexington Gazette, spirited Whigs like Doctor Warren, Jimmy Otis and Mr. Adams." There were also others quilling and boasting opinions that opposed the rules, policies and acts being spewed by parliament and King George, his royal governors too, persistent men from the Colony of Virginia and the ports of New Bern,

Charles Towne and Savannah, determined colonists like Simon Boerum in the port of New York and Thom Wharton of my Philadelphia.

I suppose it was during those wintry weeks when Ethan began to truly realize that those of Lexington, and the women and men of ports, villages and towns throughout all the colonies, were beginning to thirst for greater understanding of the contentious troubles brewing in places like Boston. I think he could sense the depths of the simmering resistance while bundled beneath blankets those frigid January nights too, lying in the dark while listening to spirited Lexington men exchanging ideas amidst flickering candles down in his father's tavern room, opinions spurred with mugs of ale and tins of rum.

Ethan's visit to Lexington had been bathed with a tranquility he quickly realized how much had been missed, and as the days of the new year slowly crept by, he increasingly cherished each moment that passed. And on the third Saturday of January, 1769, he saddled Cato once again, and as a gentle snow settled upon the village shortly after dawn he exchanged tender grasps and words with his father, then galloped to Boston east through the chill. "I resettled back into my room at Mr. Gill's house," he confided while brushing a tear, "just a few days before classes resumed at Harvard, and returned to my duties at the print shop most days after class, Saturday afternoon too." Ethan delved back into his studies that winter and spring, and from time to time gathered with his junto friends to discuss the complexities of their assignments and the frictions continuing to brew about Boston and the colonies.

While Ethan returned to his normal routine of Harvard classes, junto friends and the print shop, and studying by the flicker and glow of candles and lamps up in his little room during the quiet hours of night, the troubles about those Townshend Acts continued to brew. Tensions between colonists and the crown simmered and flared in Boston, seeping to hundreds of villages and towns across the colony and into the halls of Harvard College, fractious disputes about those duties and taxes being heatedly discussed in that secret room at Mr. Gill's print shop too. And the sons of liberty continued to assemble in the shadows, spirited men gathering in dimly lit rooms as the king's soldiers patrolled the cobblestones and docks of Boston, or huddling in the dark beneath the limbs of that special elm within hours of the crown's men stomping their boots into the snows of the common. Ethan once said he could sometimes sense the tensions spritzing almost moment by moment that winter and spring of 1769, and see the expanding divide between London's soldiers and a growing number of Bostonians.

I remember hearing stories in those days of those disturbing things too, rumors sweeping into my Germantown and the hospital halls down in Philadelphia during my nursing training that winter and spring. There seemed to be more and more people in my Colony of Pennsylvania supporting the positions of the sons too, I suppose in all the colonies, pleas to shun all those Townshend goods coming from London. And some colonists preferred to keep their discontent shrouded in shadows of secrecy, while others daringly cast caution to the winds.

Yet many colonists continued to have a differing point of view, woman and men who thought it despicably disloyal to flaunt the authority of the king, a position pitting Tories against Whigs, while others like mother, father and our Quaker friends continued to cling to notions of neutrality. Even after all these years I can still see father sitting near the fire, sweet scented smoke spiraling from the bowl of his stylish pipe and billowing about the room, and hear him spouting of the folly of resistance to London. "If one feels even a tinge of disloyalty to King George," he'd grumble while nibbling his meerschaum bit oozing a hazy cloud, "then one should stay hushed, crawl into the shadows of silence!" Mother would simply cast an appeasing nod while fidgeting in her chair, then cautiously look to me with a sympathetic stare.

I could sense my sympathies evolving quite differently than father in those days. Perhaps it was my youthful naivety, an adventurous urge that seemed to brush my generation, or maybe I had a keener acceptance for Whig points of view. Or maybe I was able to hear the sons' cries for freedom more clearly than father, righteous pleas for liberty that some instinctively knew was truly in peril. Perhaps many colonists like Ethan and I began to untwine from the norms preached by entrenched men, respectable colonists like father, and began to reject the comfort of a fading past instilled by those of a more loyal generation. It was as if a tiny flame had been lit in the hearts and minds of a new breed of colonists, an embryonic resistance inspired by fundamental rights that was beginning to swirl about the colonies upon enlightened winds.

Even so, I can still feel the desperation that would seep into my soul from time to time that winter and spring of 1769, a fear of the unknown that would swirl about my dreams, and for a while found myself shielding my views from others, especially mother and father. There were also times I tried to deny my own feelings, stuffing them into some safe place deep inside, beliefs I'd come to release once my heart began to beat freely. Perhaps I simply wanted to protect mother and father in those days, from colonial pressures that were surely to come, and maybe I was selfishly shielding myself from scrutiny while training at the hospital. Yet soon I came to accept my beliefs, and began to quietly support shopkeepers and merchants of Germantown and Philadelphia who dared to display disapproval of those despised Townshend Acts. They were colonists actively supporting the pleas of the sons from Ethan's Boston, women and men now shunning all those English goods, a conviction of resistance that was slowly flourishing throughout all the colonies.

As the embers of that emerging resistance smoldered and flared among a growing number of spirited women and men, discussions about Mr. Adams' letter that had been circulated about the colonies many months before continued to rage in our colonial assemblies. They were heated debates between Whigs and Tories about how to respond to the escalating opposition by royal governors to the notions espoused in that letter, hostility spurred by London. Then in late May rumors began to swirl of a document quilled by the House of Burgesses in the Colony of Virginia, a defiant statement being discussed in churches and taverns, homes and shops throughout the colonies, Ethan's Boston and my Germantown too.

The Pennsylvania Evening Post called it the *Virginia Resolves*, a declaration many would say was mostly quilled by George Mason from the County of Fairfax, one of the assemblymen tasked to create the colony's response to London's Townshend Acts, a group that included that spirited Patrick Henry and Richard Henry Lee of Westmorland County. The Post reported that those resolves were introduced to the Virginia assembly by Colonel Washington, commander of the colony's militia during that frontier war, and explained how the declaration railed against those Townshend duties and taxes as well as the "deplorable reactions" by the king and his royal governors to Mr. Adams' letter.

Adopted by the colony's assembly within hours, it seems those resolves asserted that the power to lay duties and taxes upon the Colony of Virginia "rested solely in the hands of its elected assembly, not in the halls of London," while condemning parliament's role in censuring the positions espoused by Massachusetts Bay in that "righteous letter." The House of Burgesses further declared that Virginia strongly disapproved of the crown's intent to sail colonial malcontents across the sea for trial in London, suggesting among other things that "colonists must be judged by colonists." Although some were saying those daring resolves espoused rather dangerous positions, it was a declaration repeated in similar fashion by the assemblies of other colonies before the year was done.

The Evening Post soon revealed that the royal governor of the Colony of Virginia quickly responded to those defiant resolves in what it described as "a Tory fury," for by the wave of his royal wand the Fourth Baron Botetourt determined it proper to silence the House of Burgesses. "The king's governor demanded Payton Randolph appear in his royal chambers," printed the post about the barrister from Williamsburg, the leader of the colony's assembly, "then proceeded to reprimand and scold before declaring it his 'duty in the name of the king, to immediately dissolve that rebellious house of rabble.'"

Angry rumors were swirling about Philadelphia and Germantown about what the Baron Botetourt had done to the Virginia assembly, and there were unflattering whispers denouncing his actions as "bloody royal paranoia," while still others suggested that he was simply a loyal henchman consumed with pleasing the king's ministers in London. Yet it seems there were some in the Colony of Virginia refusing to kneel and grovel at his royal feet, daring men such as a few from that House of Burgesses who defiantly cast his scolding threats to the winds. There were inspiring rumors that a group of the colony's assembly began to secretly gather in the shadows of various places, courageous men meeting in secluded halls or spirited rooms like the Raleigh Tavern in the village of Williamsburg.

"So while all those troubling things were brewing, grandma," Samuel interrupted with a puzzling glance and robust rock of his chair, "while those frictions were escalating in the Colony of Virginia, up in Boston and maybe here in Philadelphia too, Ethan simply clung to his studies and you to your nursing training? It must have been hard to do that, difficult for both of you, and I suppose for so many others throughout the colonies."

"Looking back, Samuel, after all these years," I softly replied, gazing to those distant elms, "I guess it was for Ethan and me, for many. Yet, in a strange way, it wasn't. I mean, most of us knew of the troubles brewing, but they were fires that seemed out of our control, at least for those young like Ethan and me. Sure, I kept training at the hospital, and Ethan stayed true to his studies and print shop duties. We just went about our lives, like most I suppose."

For a moment we simply rocked and listened to the leaves rustling in the warming breeze, and as Samuel gazed into the afternoon winds, I slid my fingers back into the pocket of my summer dress and caressed Ethan's tender words. "Remember, Samuel," I whispered with a glance to his peering eyes, "Ethan and I were not yet twenty, with years and years awaiting our lives. Even though there were disturbing troubles simmering about the colonies, tensions I must say that were spurred by London, Ethan and I, and I suppose thousands of boys and girls, young women and men, thought it our duty in those early days to cling to our training and studies. Like so many of the young, we were simply reaching for our future, trying to find our way."

"Do you mean that you and Ethan," Samuel questioned with a squinting gaze, "and thousands of your generation, simply chose to look the other way? Is that what happened, grandma? Young people just clinging to their own lives?"

"Oh, Samuel," I sputtered with a bit of disillusionment, realizing he may never grasp how truly different life was in those days, "it wasn't as simple as that. Sure, I suppose some chose to look inward, to not see, find it safe to be neutral, but most did not. Those troubles were flaring all around us, and being discussed in villages and towns everywhere, in the hospital and Harvard halls too. Yet many of us simply carried on with our lives, farmers tilling fields and colonists tending to taverns, shops and homes, and some like Ethan and me, studying and training. All the while, Samuel, those rising tensions with London, frictions between Tory and Whig, were inescapable, always on our minds, regardless of whether young, old or otherwise."

"I'm sorry, grandma," Samuel timidly replied, "I should have known better. I guess as I listen and know more, I'll better understand. I want to know what it was really like in those days, what happened in the colonies, and know of your life, grandma, and Ethan's."

"It's alright, Samuel," I comforted in a motherly way, "I'm proud of you."

Samuel rocked and gazed to those distant elms softly swaying in the summer breeze as I slowed my chair and caressed the parchment of

Ethan's poem, and as a tranquil hush brushed my petals of crimson rose, I wondered of the things Samuel and his generation didn't know of those days so long ago. "I know you want to hear what I have to say," I whispered, glancing to his wondering eyes, "and hope you'll sense the same pride as I, for those of my generation."

"I know I will, grandma," he replied with a caring glance.

"Oh, Samuel, just hearing you say that, makes me feel so good." As he rocked with wonder, thoughts reaching for the summer winds, I gently stroked Ethan's tender words in search of his sensuous touch, reaching for memories of life so long ago.

Ethan completed his first year of studies as June of 1769 came to a close, and I soon finished my first year of nursing training at the Pennsylvania Hospital down in Philadelphia. He returned to Lexington for several weeks that summer to once again help his father at the tavern while rejuvenating his soul upon the soil of his birth, and on many nights watched from the grass of his mother's grave as dusk settled upon the village. I remember he said he had galloped from Boston just a week or so after the disturbing death of President Holyoke, and by the time he returned to his campus halls a few weeks before fall, the reins of Harvard were being wielded by John Winthrop, a professorial man from the studious class of thirty-two.

While Ethan passed his summer days in Lexington and I in Germantown with mother and father when not training at the hospital, lives bathed of normalcy, the tensions over those Townshend Acts continued to simmer and brew. Sentiments of resistance to those duties and taxes were steadily flourishing, all the while the increasing cries to shun those London goods continued to sweep from the frontier to the sea, to hundreds of farms, ports, villages and towns throughout the Thirteen Colonies. The sons of liberty continued to meet in all the colonies too, even in Ethan's father's tavern or beneath that special tree on the grass of their village field.

It was during those summer months, if I recall, when I first heard the intriguing rumors of a new style of clothes, of coats and stockings, dresses, breeches and shirts not snipped and stitched across the sea in England but sewn with cloth and thread right here in colonies like Virginia, Georgia and New York, Ethan's Massachusetts Bay and my Pennsylvania. Colonists were in deed heeding the sons' pleas to forgo those Townshend goods from London, and by the flicker and glow of candles and lamps, daring mothers and daughters, young women and brave wives had discovered a way to defy the crown. They were snipping colonial cloth and stitching an array of things, garments that were coming to be worn by courageous women, children and men.

Then later that summer or perhaps early fall, I finally saw what some of those clothes truly looked like, bright shirts and floppy hats being worn by women and men about Germantown, and breeches clinging the thighs of some doctors and patients at the hospital in Philadelphia. They were garments sewn in the shadows of seamstress shops or by secret candlelight of homes late at night, and each had a little square patch stitched to its outer side with *homespun* scripted in dark thread. Ethan said he encountered his first while riding home to Mr. Gill's house after classes in early fall, when he saw a colonist wearing a light coat strolling near the common, a small patch stitched to its upper back. It was an inspiring slice of cloth that would come to pit Whig against Tory and symbolize a sense of unity for colonists disputing the king, a little tan patch that displayed support for that defiant letter and spirited pleas of the sons.

Mother and father viewed such things in a rather unyielding light, often mumbling accusing phrases like "unsettling disloyalty" while untwining from the toils of their day near the cold stones of the hearth after supper those nights. While they preferred to straddle that fence of indifference with many of their Quaker friends, just as others of Germantown and Philadelphia, I found my spirit struggling to loosen the hold my faith had upon me all of my life. And sometime during those changing days I began to feel my core sliding toward the cries of all those liberty men, could sense my beliefs slowly aligning with the sons of Philadelphia, Boston and beyond, perhaps not much different than how it had been for Ethan. I could feel an anxious twinge deep inside tugging me toward supporting their pleas, and wondering how, in my own little way, I might quietly become involved. Then on a peaceful morning in the summer of 1769 my twisting search came to an end, for amid the mystical chime of steeple bells, I found my proper path.

During those months of spring, summer and fall, mother, father and I attended Sunday services down in Philadelphia now and then, riding our buggy five miles south on the winding road through the wooded hills to the Quaker meeting house not far from the Delaware River. And on one of those lazy mornings of August, I wandered near a faithful group of girls nervously whispering about two women of their meeting house, dutiful Quakers rumored to be secretively sewing batches of those defiant clothes.

I'd soon discover that one of those women was Lydia Barrington Darragh, a rather regal looking woman about mother's age. She'd later tell me she was born across the sea in a little village on the eastern shore of Ireland, then shortly before Ethan and I were born, sailed to the colonies with husband William, a clergyman's son from Dublin. The second woman was Elizabeth Griscom, a proud girl not much younger than me who liked to boast now and then that she was born "during the first moments of the first day of 1752" in a cottage along the river right there in Philadelphia. Yet as the years carried on I'd hear unflattering whispers that she had actually been born a bit east in the Colony of New Jersey, in the village of Collingsworth they'd say, or some other dubious place.

Perhaps spurred by those whispering girls, it wasn't long before I also heard rumors that they would meet to sew now and then at Lydia's place on Charles Way not far from the hospital. Or they'd stitch those things in the quaint home Elizabeth shared with her mother and father at the corner of Arch and Bread streets, a little place of bricks, mortar and pine near that Quaker meeting house just northeast of the colony's statehouse. Each time they gathered they'd snip and stich homespun hats and shirts, coats and breeches from colonial thread and cloth, and as I began to understand more of their quiet activity, I realized I knew how my thirst to become involved would be satisfied.

Then after a week or two one of the older girls at the meeting house, a rather quiet young women who'd help comfort patients at the hospital now and then while visiting a nursing friend of her mother's, introduced me to Lydia following a Quaker service. She was kind from the first moment we meet, showing interest in my words and confiding her feelings rather freely, and I knew Lydia and I would become friends. And as I was bidding her goodbye to return to Germantown with mother and father, she carefully invited me to her home to help Elizabeth and she "snip and stich new seeds." I agreed, meeting them to sew homespun things for the first time after supper the last Sunday of August, 1769.

I still remember how Lydia would confide that she was almost a nurse, having been a midwife in Philadelphia for many years, and would proudly tell of William's tutoring and teaching of boys and girls in their homes, yet always confessed that her passion was sewing. Gentleness seemed to radiate from her brown eyes that shined as if speckled with gold, and standing just a bit more than five feet, she was elegantly petite with smooth rosy cheeks. She always seemed so stylishly dressed too, and gracefully moved as if sliding to the notes of a gentle nocturne, and when her dark hair was not daintily tied or wound beneath a bonnet of yellow or blue, it softly flowed over her shoulders. And even though she was rather protective of her inner thoughts and desires, particularly when strangers edged near, she would express herself easily around those who cared, precisely with emotion and intellect.

Elizabeth seemed to sparkle with an essence of life, displaying a youthfulness that somehow beguiled a maturity that reached beyond her years, especially when escaping from colonial troubles with Lydia and me. I remember how she possessed an uncanny ability to envision the importance of things that others might never understand, and how thrillingly talented she was with needles, cloths and threads. And over all these years she'd confide many times that snipping and stitching helped her survive the hardships of the war, made her feel worthy of our cause, and in a solemn way, kept her alive.

A bit shorter than Lydia and rather trim in those early days, Elizabeth's skin was tenderly smooth and seemed to glow amid a flickering candle or bat of her brown eyes, and her auburn hair gently flowed when we gathered to snip and sew. It wasn't long before she and I became rather close friends, in many ways the sister I never had, and I can still hear the first words she ever uttered to me all those years ago, "Please, Andrea, call me Betsy."

If I recall, at the beginning of our first August night, Lydia explained to Betsy and me that William was away for a few hours with some teaching friends a little south at the Tun Tavern, or maybe it was the White Horse Inn, a daunting ferry ride across the river. They were each so courteous and polite that night, instilling a sense of ease and making me feel comfortable, and before we even began to speak of homespun things, before arranging needles, cloths and threads, they made me feel truly accepted. I'll never forget how they introduced me to the spirited realm of fermented tastes, and with trusting kindness, welcomed me to their little group.

Although most at our Quaker meeting houses, and perhaps mother and father, might refer to such a thing as wickedly appalling, I found what we were about to indulge in rather exhilarating. I remember watching in a youthful gaze as Lydia slowly poured what I'd soon discover was chardonnay wine, filling three crystal goblets from a stylish decanter, and as we sewed she'd pour a little more. We talked and laughed while threading homespun garments that night amid the flickering glow of a lamp and candles, an ambiance that pleased our souls, then around nine, after we'd snipped and stitched the final touches to a bundle of breeches, hats and shirts, Betsy playfully sipped and said, "I hope we don't run out of this sweet wine."

Lydia snapped a frisky glance to Betsy and me, rose from her couch and snatched the nearby shaft of a silver candelabrum, and by the flicker of three little flames, led us to a shuttered door in a darkened hall near the kitchen. "I think we'll be fine, Betsy," she quipped, twisting the brass knob and creaking open the door. "Well, Andrea," she softly added with a mischievous grin, "do we have enough for sewing?"

I could see dozens of dark dusty bottles laying within little squares of slatted oak, their thin corked necks protruding along the left and right walls, and in the shadows were dozens more waiting in the rear. "Oh my," I gasped with widening eyes, "there must be a hundred here."

"More like two," Lydia proudly proclaimed, "some reds, but mostly whites. William brings them home by the crate after dusk now and then, carefully placing them in this room. I think they're unloaded on secret docks along the river, without duties being paid, and that's why William quickly hides them here. They're from across the sea, Andrea, mostly from villages of Spain and France. Feel better, Betsy?"

"Now, Lydia," Betsy sputtered with a soft tap to her hand, "you know I was just kidding. I just wanted you to show all these bottles to Andrea."

"I've never seen so much wine," I confessed, scanning the bottles and glancing to Betsy and Lydia. "Mother and father would be aghast. I guess you're right, we won't run out tonight."

"Let's get back," Lydia whispered, tugging the door shut with a creaking click before leading Betsy and me back to our gathering room, to cloths draping chairs and needles stuck into soft silken balls, their eyes dangling strings of colorful thread. Some logs were piled to andirons on the ashen fireplace stones, pine and elm ready for the flurries of winter, and three crystal goblets waited on a table near those breeches, shirts and hats.

As we would for years to come after our first meeting, Betsy, Lydia and I continued to sew until after ten that night, all the while whispering about life with each cut, fold, snip and stitch. We talked of personal things like family dynamics and desires, passions and secrets, perhaps a little less that first night and more intensely over the coming months as we became more trustingly comfortable, and discussed medical things and nursing strides, and lots of intrigues of sewing. Yet perhaps the most intense moments came when we'd talk of rumors of the mounting frictions up in Boston and other places throughout the colonies, and of the troubling things being done by the king, his ministers and our royal governors.

Soon a contenting ease began to evolve among us, and we discovered a friendship that would flourish a bit more every time we'd gather to expose our feelings and thoughts while sewing homespun things. It was that sewing that brought us together that first night, gave us a sense of purpose and reason for years to come, and knowing those things made each of us feel good. And although we knew what we were doing could be viewed by Tories and others as disloyal to the king, perhaps even dangerously treasonous, we knew that creating all those homespun clothes would help our Whig cause. Believing it right to support the sons' pleas for liberty, Betsy, Lydia and I would meet many times after that first August night, mostly once a month after supper on a Sunday, and defiantly stich those special garments while talking and sipping wine.

I began my second year of nursing training at the Pennsylvania Hospital near the end of that summer of 1769, and Ethan had returned to his room on Spring Lane, to his second year of Harvard studies and duties at Mr. Gill's print shop. Ethan once confided that the tensions of Boston had somehow increased while he was away in Lexington that summer, and I can still see his anxious expression when he confessed that things continually got worse that fall and into the coming winter. "It was as if the entire port was steaming," he said, "like one of Sarah's stews frantically bubbling. An uneasy sense of discontentment was not only simmering along the docks, Andrea, or in dark secret rooms like that one at the print shop, but in the eyes of once tranquil colonists strolling along the cobblestone streets or snowy grass of the common. You could feel the tension rising between our royal governor and Bostonians, between colonists and the king's loyal troops."

He explained how troubling episodes of redcoat soldiers spouting unkind words to colonists were increasing, boisterous encounters spurring disparaging retorts from a growing number of angry Bostonians. And as those stirring exchanges continued to stoke the fires of contention, some of the king's loyal troops were causing those embers to flare by padding their lot with menial work about Boston, taking little jobs away from colonists for fewer shillings and pounds. Ethan said they weren't the best type of jobs, nor was the fiscal gain much, yet it was work now no longer available for a colonist to care for his family. When combined with all those taunting exchanges, it seems the resentment and distrust continued to flare, and soon the air about Boston was beginning to waft with a smell of danger.

There were fresh rumors too swirling about all the colonies as the autumn leaves began to fall, disturbing stories related to that letter of Mr. Adams that had been circulated about the colonies months before, rumors that raced through Germantown and the halls of the hospital down in Philadelphia. The defiant stance of the sons against those Townshend Acts continued to spur frictions between colonists who supported those Whigs and Tories who clung to the crown, tensions now gripping the king's royal governors in all the colonies. And soon the Pennsylvania Evening Post began to reveal that festering frictions were increasing in the northeast once again, in Ethan's Colony of Massachusetts Bay.

Following what the Post said were months of debate in that colony's assembly that spring and summer, along with secret gatherings of spirited colonists in churches, taverns and homes, and shadowy little rooms above printing shops, some Bostonians decided to clearly express their defiant sentiments. Various thoughts espoused by colonists like Jimmy Otis and Sam Adams concerning their royal governor had been printed in Mr. Gill's Boston Gazette and Country Journal too, disparaging remarks that expressed colonists' weariness over his antagonistic policies to collect the king's duties and taxes as called for in those Townshend Acts. "We colonists of Massachusetts Bay," the Whigs of Boston defiantly declared, "have determined the moment ripe to act in accordance with our rights, and humbly petition King George the Third for redress. We urgently appeal that His Majesty's Royal Governor Bernard be relieved of his duties, be removed from power over our Province ever more."

It seems that for weeks those demanding sentiments simmered in Ethan's Massachusetts Bay until a muggy morning of August, 1769, a summer dawn that saw the culmination of the bitterness that had been brewing for years between Bostonians and their royal governor. Ethan once said it had only been days since he returned from Lexington when he first heard the joyous shouts echoing about the cobblestones, "Governor Bernard is gone!" He had finally succumbed to colonists' pressures that had engulfed his royal tenure, and perhaps, some would say, exhausted the patience of the king, and quietly resigned, replaced by Thomas Hutchinson, the Boston man who had reigned over the colony a decade before.

The Evening Post later revealed that within days Mr. Bernard boarded the king's warship *HMS Dublin* moored to a dock at Burrough's Wharf, and by noon that summer day set sail for London. Ethan said he was in Mr. Gill's print shop when the celebrations truly exploded, when women, children and men began dashing from shops and homes to race east on the streets of Queen and King toward the water to bid a mocking farewell. "I stopped pressing type to the galley," he confessed, "and Mr. Edes tossed his apron to a chair, then we stepped to the cobblestones to watch and listen to the joy erupting about Boston."

For hours after the king's ship sailed toward London that afternoon, Ethan said just about every bell dangling steeples of Boston clapped an endless string of rapturous dings, dongs and rings as trumpets blared amid musket blasts, joyous sounds that swept the hills and fields to nearby farms, villages and towns, his Lexington too. And after finishing his duties at the print shop early that summer evening, Ethan stepped the cobblestones of Queen Street to the grass of the common as dusk sprayed its colors across the western sky, and listened to waning releases of glee filtering about Boston.

"Many with torches had gathered on the common," he later revealed, "and as the sun slipped past the horizon, I just watched their flames flicker and flare. Women, children and men were massing on the grass near that special elm tree, Andrea, and some were tossing strings of petals about its limbs, flowers of white, purple, pink and red. They were decorating the tree with scraps of parchment and little candles too, and a few were even singing. It was as if all of Boston was releasing years of frustration, I suppose the whole colony too, and maybe many were hoping that calmer, happier days waited in the weeks and months to come. Yet, as I watched and listened, Andrea, I wasn't so sure, and felt a twisting unease."

Yes, the contentious royal governor of Ethan's Colony of Massachusetts Bay for the past nine years had been disgracefully summoned back to London, replaced by a loyal subject who more closely resembled one of the colony's own. Yet hundreds of the king's soldiers remained in Boston to roam the streets and docks or strut on the grass and snows of the common, an abomination that continued to spur angst among colonists opposed to the unjust acts of parliament and intrusive policies of the king. Unsettling exchanges between Bostonians and those redcoats continued to erupt too, unruly quarrels and events that were being exposed in pamphlets and papers like Mr. Giles' Gazette in Lexington and Mr. Gills' Boston Gazette and Country Journal, frightening stories and rumors that were filtering about the colonies, here to Germantown and Philadelphia too.

Ethan once whispered that as the weeks of autumn passed and the wintry winds began to howl across his Colony of Massachusetts Bay, secretive encounters in the print shop began to increase with each chilling rain and flurry of snow. "It seemed like more colonists were coming into the shop," he softly revealed, "to whisper things with Mr. Edes or quietly chat with Mr. Gill, and more and more they'd gather around that maple table up the stairs in that long room. I knew they were talking about an array of disturbing things affecting Boston, and sometimes all the colonies, and could hear their muffled voices rising with tension now and then." And he told me about a Saturday night in December, perhaps a week before Harvard studies ended and he galloped home to Lexington and his father once again. Ethan was in the shop setting type with Mr. Gill, getting things ready for another printing of the Boston Gazette, when rumors swirling that day suddenly became uncomfortably real.

Mr. Revere was in the shop that night, the silversmith who forged an array of sons of liberty riding routes and galloped special messages to villages and towns for the sons now and then, leaning back in a spindled chair near Mr. Edes quilling at his desk. Ethan said Paul had come to the shop to talk of colonial concerns as he often did Saturday nights in those days, usually after Ethan had already left for the day, and with his shoes propped against the elm of that desk, was scanning last week's Gazette while exchanging views with Mr. Edes about skirmishes rumored to have taken place in Boston that day.

As he pressed the final bits of iron type into the galley with Mr. Gill, Ethan could hear Paul and Ben sputtering about a scuffle on a street just a bit northwest of the print shop a few hours before, an unruly brush between a cabinetmaker and some of the king's soldiers. "Josh had been at Mrs. Davies Tavern," Paul revealed, "with a few merchant friends, tipping splashes of rye whiskey and rum, when those bloody redcoats attacked. They say he was minding his own business, Ben, just walking back to his shop near the Charlestown ferry, when a gaggle of those damn soldiers, blasting insults, dashed across the cobblestones to assault poor old Josh."

Witnesses would later say they were shouting ugly things to Josh like "bloody wood shucker," while others said a few of those soldiers were spewing vile taunts too crude for a colonist to repeat. Then after exhausting their challenged vernacular over several frightening moments, two or three royal soldiers began to pummel Mr. Baker with flailing fists, tumbling him to the cobblestones of Ferry Street. "That's when they really exposed their cowardly ways," Paul explained with fiery eyes, "thrusting their bloody boots into Josh's shoulders, arms and ribs."

Soon Mr. Gill joined Paul and Ben at that elm desk, and as Ethan finished setting type he listened as the three discussed another disturbing event that happened a day or two before. John described it as distastefully appalling, a story which spurred many about Boston, Tory and Whig, to feel a sense of violation, uncivilized behavior even those who clung loyally to the crown condemned.

Ethan said Sarah Tufts was perhaps thirty and fondly known as a shy, kindly woman, dedicated to her work while preferring to avoid strangers, and each night she cooked and tended for her father in their cottage near King's Chapel, things she had done since her mother died of fever years before. After spending that December day dutifully toiling in a flower shop along the river near Copp's Hill, she did what she had done since she was young, walking home shortly before dusk along the cobblestones and snowy grass of the common.

She was bundled in mittens, boots and a dark wool coat, with a yellow scarf wrapped about her neck, and a blue bonnet looped and twined below her chin pressed her sandy hair. One witness would later say that as she stepped across the eastern edge of the common sprinkled in white, a handful of the king's soldiers rushed toward her with devilish deeds on their minds. Just the hour before they had been drilling about the expanse of that Boston field, strutting with scores of other royal troops in muddied boots, tricorn hats and crimson coats, and as they puffed and clanked toward Sarah, dark muskets clung to their shoulders.

Some believed Sarah could sense them rushing close as she steadily stepped across the common toward home, then could hear iron clinks and royal boots trampling the snowy grass as they scampered nearer. "Hey fellas," the lead redcoat was reported to have blustered, "lookie here, it's one of them Boston bitches we've been hearin so much about!" And as that gaggle of misguided soldiers kept pace while swarming close to her back, another despicably blurted, "Well, Boston lady, is that what you are, just a dumb colonial bitch?"

"Sarah didn't bat an eye," that witness proudly said, "didn't glance left nor right, didn't look back, just kept walkin in a confident stride along the edge of the common." And in what some described as a moment of uncommon rationality, those young redcoats stopped their menacing taunts right there on the snow, standing and staring in a befuddled hush. Perhaps stunned by her defiant courage, they just watched as she ignored their repulsive words and just kept walking south toward home, keeping pace past that special tree to the cobblestones.

Ethan said that as Mr. Gill, Paul and Mr. Edes continued to discuss those disturbing events, as well as others from days, weeks and months before, he just listened while finishing the setting of type for that Saturday night, then hung his stained apron to a nail on the rear wall behind his little desk. It was now a few minutes before eight, and as Ethan tidied a few stacks of parchment and readied to leave, a burst of chill rushed through the room as the shop door swung open. He watched as a young man snapped the door closed with a creaking thud and strutted to the three gathered about Mr. Edes' desk, then lazily plopped into a spindled windsor chair.

He had seen him a few times in the shop before, usually for just a moment or two after studying during the week, and although Ethan had seen him walking the cobblestones from time to time too, they had never truly met. And he had heard some at the print shop say he owned the little bookstore near Union and Hanover across from Mrs. Davies Tavern, a shop Ethan had seen many times on his rides to Harvard, yet had only briefly once stopped and browsed.

He seemed about Ethan's age, with light linen socks that ran from tan breeches down to polished brown shoes, and his dark deerskin coat was untethered, exposing a bright ruffled shirt that was snugged to his chin and fanned at the wrists. His auburn hair was loosely cropped and twined to a short tail, and his eyes were sullen and dark, as if exposing age beyond his years. "As soon as he sat down," Ethan said, "he began talking with Mr. Gill, Paul and Mr. Edes about some of those disturbing events. And as they discussed those things and I readied to leave, John and Ben would snap a spirited glance to me now and then."

Ethan nudged his little desk chair and tugged the wool of his coat over his arms, then pressed his tricorn hat to his twined hair as Mr. Gill invitingly spouted, "Ethan, I'd like you to meet someone."

"Be right there," he nervously uttered, pressing his tricorn a bit more while nudging parchment sheets into a perfect stack upon his desk.

"I'd like you to meet Henry, Henry Knox," John snapped with a lazy slide of his arm as Ethan stepped to the four gazing from Mr. Edes' desk. And as Henry studiously rose from his chair, Mr. Gill gently added, "Henry, I'd like you to meet Ethan Sheehan."

"It's good to meet you, Mr. Sheehan," he graciously said with an extended hand. "Please, call me Henry."

"Alright," Ethan uttered as their hands confidently gripped. "Call me Ethan. It's good to meet you, Henry."

"I've seen you here before," Henry confessed, "just briefly, only you've always been pretty busy with your printing duties, or studying books. And I think I've seen you passing on the street now and then."

"I guess I do get busy in here," Ethan said before quickly quipping, "thanks to John and Ben. I've seen you on the streets before too, and in your bookstore a while back, when I stopped to browse for a moment on my ride back from Harvard. I remember you were rather busy, tending the questions of two admiring girls."

"Yes, that's it!" he proudly blurted, as if just resolving the most pressing issue of the day. "I remember. Those two young women were swarming me with a slew of literary inquiries. I think you came in, looked around, for just a moment, then vanished."

"Yep, that was it, Henry. I'm glad we've finally been able to talk."

"Yes, indeed."

Ethan would later discover that Henry and he shared some things in common such as both were born in the Colony of Massachusetts Bay in 1750, only Henry in Boston a few months earlier on the Twenty-fifth of July. And both grappled with the traumatic experience of losing a parent at a young age, for Henry's father, a sailing captain of the sea, expired from a mysterious illness when Henry was just nine. Yet unlike Ethan, who continued schooling in Lexington following the agony of his mother's death, Henry soon drifted from formal studies to earning shillings and pounds, helping his mother meet their needs.

It seems he started with simple toils about Boston warehouses and docks, and around twelve began a more appealing position as a clerk in a shop of books near Freeman's Wharf. Then after three or four years his fortunes were rumored to have suddenly changed upon the demise of one of his mother's distant cousins, a rather obscure colonist who, for reasons Henry was never sure, bequeathed him a few barrels of shillings and pounds. Some say that windfall is what inspired Henry to buy his own shop across the cobblestones from that tavern by the river, a place he'd call, the London Book Store.

"You remember Paul," injected Mr. Gill, "don't you, Ethan?"

"Of course," he quickly replied, gripping Mr. Revere's greeting hand, "but it's been a while. Good to see you again, Paul."

"I guess it has been some time," he agreed, releasing his grip. "Good to talk with you again, Ethan."

"Ethan's from Lexington," Mr. Gill added with a glance to Henry and reminder to Paul, "learned the printing trade from Nathan Giles. Now he's in his second year over at Harvard, and staying at my place during his studies. Why don't you two stop by the house some evening, and we can all talk. And don't forget, Sarah brews the best stew in Boston."

"Yes, I remember," Paul uttered to Ethan. "You even did some riding for us, some months back." Then glancing to Mr. Gill, he added, "Thank you, John, that's a fine invitation."

"Yes, John, that goes for me too," Henry said with an agreeing nod before twisting toward Ethan. "We'll have to get together sometime, Ethan, talk about printing and books, perhaps with mugs of ale. What do you say?"

"Sure," Ethan said in a slightly shy way, "that sounds fine. I do have a rather busy schedule though, what with studies and duties here at the shop. But maybe we just could, say on a Saturday night sometime. I'm a bit partial to the Green Dragon Tavern."

"We'll do that, Ethan. I'll stop by the shop, maybe next week."

"Good. Thanks, Henry."

Suddenly the shop door creaked open and a burst of chilling air swept through the room, and two confident looking men dressed rather stylish shuffled in. As Ethan watched the door click shut he wondered if he had seen either before, perhaps from a distance on the street or somewhere along the docks, yet wasn't sure. They just stood hushed and stared to the five gathered about that printer's desk, then one slyly motioned with a brush of his hand for Mr. Edes to join them.

"Good evening, Ben, John," the shorter of the two eloquently greeted. "Good to see you too, Paul, Henry."

"Good evening, John," spouted Mr. Gill, "you too, Jim." Then twisting in his chair with a wave of his hand toward Ethan, he kindly added, "I'd like you to meet this other young man, Ethan Sheehan."

"It's nice to meet you, Mr. Sheehan," John replied, followed quickly by the taller man, "Good evening, Mr. Sheehan."

"Good evening, sirs," greeted Ethan sheepishly, not quite sure what to say.

Mr. Edes quickly shuffled some rumpled parchment to the side of his desk, then rose from his chair and uttered, "I'll be back soon, John," before stepping toward the two hushed at the door. "Excuse me, Henry," he politely added with a slow spin, "Paul, Ethan, I've some business to attend."

Ethan watched as Mr. Edes huddled with those stylish men and whispered with little leans and twists before all three spun and stepped toward the rear of the shop past the bricks of the printing press. And as he watched them slowly clump up the stairs and vanish into the bowels of the long room, listening with the others as the door's iron clasp clicked tight, he twisted with a puzzling gaze to Mr. Gill.

"Who are those men?" Ethan anxiously asked with quizzical glances about the three.

Henry and Paul quickly looked to each other as if wondering how Ethan could not have known, yet John Gill seemed to understand in a fatherly way that there were others in Boston, and throughout the Colony of Massachusetts Bay, who may not recognize either man. "The shorter one," Mr. Gill patiently explained, "is Sam's cousin, John. Maybe you've seen his office, Ethan, near the water by the long wharf. He studied at Harvard, you know, just like you."

"Yes, I've heard of him," Ethan shyly replied, "just hadn't seen him before. So that's John Adams. I've seen his shingle outside his office, on my walks about the docks, and did meet Sam for a moment once, several years ago. John seems, well, rather intense."

"The other man is Jim Otis," Mr. Gill gently added, "and like John is a barrister too, just like his father. Maybe you've read of his defiant positions against the crown and our governor from time to time, especially a few years back. Jim's opposition to those taxes from London was quite intense, and his disputes with the governor over those writs were gripping. He studied at Harvard too, Ethan, some ten years before John."

"Of course, yes, I sure have," assured Ethan quickly. "I've just never seen Mr. Otis before. I guess neither looks much like I thought he might. I must say though, they're rather revered by students over at Harvard, most of the professors too."

"Many say, and I agree, Ethan," Mr. Gill proudly added, "that they're two of the finest barristers in the colony, men who never shy from voicing their Whig views. Don't be surprised if you see them in here again, that is, when you're not too busy with printing things or studying. But I suppose they do come by mostly during the day when you're at Harvard, to talk with Ben and others about troubles brewing about the colonies, especially here in Boston. I'm not sure why they're here now, but have a feeling it has something to do with those disturbing things Paul and I talked about tonight."

Soon the four gathered about that printer's desk disbanded for the night to return to the normalcy of their lives, all the while John Adams, Ben Edes and Jimmy Otis continued their spirited discussion up in the seclusion of the long room. Ethan said Mr. Gill stayed in the shop to finish preparations for printing his Boston Gazette and Country Journal late into the night, and Henry and Paul disappeared north into the chill amid the lonely sound of soles scrapping the cobblestones. And Ethan walked back to Mr. Gill's house upon gravel and stones speckled white, back to the serenity of his room.

It was shortly after nine when Ethan stepped the stairs to his room, only moments after the chimes of the clock resting upon the mantel had faded in the darkness of that gathering room. Sarah had sparked a few logs in his bedroom's hearth before leaving that day, something she'd often do on wintry Saturday nights, and Ethan could feel the warmth of tiny flames as they snapped shadows about the room. He splashed cool water from the basin about his face and brushed little drops dripping his cheeks with a soft towel, then tossed his breeches, stockings and shirt to the chair of his desk. And glancing to a few books neatly stacked near parchment sheets, he shuffled to his bed to escape the day, nestling with blankets, linens and pillows.

Clasping his fingers beneath his hair and pressing into his feathery pillows, he gazed through the frosty panes of the balcony door into the tranquil chill of the night, envisioning the scattering of yellows, oranges and reds glistening Boston windows from the flicker and glow of candles and lamps. The colors of dusk had vanished behind wintry clouds hours before, an icy spray that slowly succumbed to the dark that wrapped the colony in a hushing cold, and while staring through the glass, his thoughts swirled of the troubling stories that had been told. And as the waning flames snapped lazy shadows about the room, he wondered of what those three men might have been discussing up in the long room that December night.

Intriguing images of those two men swirled Ethan's mind as he dozed upon his pillows now and then, hazy visions of James Otis and John Adams patiently standing at the shop door. He could see Mr. Otis in a dark wool coat and ruffled shirt buttoned close to his chin, lavender cloth that flared over his fingers, and sandy hair that curled past his ears and brushed the edges of roundish cheeks. Yet perhaps it was his height that struck Ethan the most, exuding a slim firmness that seemed to cast a dominating shadow upon the rather plump curves of Mr. Adams.

As Ethan's thoughts lazily flowed with the soothing sounds of soft wintry winds, he remembered some words he had seen months before in an aging pamphlet on a dusty shelf of Harvard Hall. It was a line spoken by Mr. Adams some nine years before, shortly after witnessing Mr. Otis rail against those writs of assistance so beloved by Royal Governor Bernard. Ethan said Mr. Adams had been in the colony's statehouse that day, and listened to each word boasted by Jimmy Otis about the strangling powers of the crown, and when asked what he had heard was rumored to say, "The oratory of Mr. Otis was the first scene of the first act of the opposition to the arbitrary claims of Great Britain."

As Ethan dozed amid hazy dreams, as he restlessly twisted, tossed and rolled about his linens, pillows and blankets that night, he wondered too of how little he truly knew about that barrister Mr. Adams. He was smaller than Mr. Otis he'd say, rather portly too, yet Ethan thought he seemed to exude a distinguishing purpose brushed of confidence, a boldness infused with a confusing dash of apprehension splashed of impatience. Not much taller than five feet, Ethan could see his puffy cheeks brushed in shades of rose as Mr. Adams stood at the shop door that night, and his tan hair that was starting to thin and recede curling the tips of his ears. There was a pudgy bulge beneath the wool of his dark coat too, a roundish protrusion that caused his ruffled shirt to sag from his belly and jut from his breeches.

Ethan would later learn John Adams was born in the village of Braintree just southeast of Boston on the last Sunday of October 1735, and that his great-great grandfather had sailed from England to the Colony of Massachusetts Bay some hundred years before. "His father was John too," Ethan would say, "a humble farmer, and his mother Susanna was from a hamlet southwest of Boston older colonists still call, Muddy River."

His aptitude for learning was said to be rather unique, even at a young age, and shortly after finishing his studies at Harvard College at nineteen, John accepted a position as schoolmaster for the children of the village of Worcester dozens of miles west of Boston. It seems that while wading into the waters of teaching a new generation, he also pursued what he'd later confess was his passion of becoming a lawyer, his love of the law, learning the required legalese through the mentorship of a local barrister named Putnam.

After a few years he was said to have been admitted to the colonial bar, then returned to Braintree and opened an office of the law, and some six years later married a young women he'd passionately describe as "my precious Abigail," a distant cousin from the nearby hamlet of Weymouth. Ethan said that soon after the birth of their son John Quincy, a year or so before Ethan began his Harvard studies, John and Abigail moved their growing family to Boston, where he quickly dangled his barrister shingle just off King Street near the water.

A warming wind suddenly brushed my cheeks as I rocked my chair in a solemn hush, then glancing to Samuel peering quietly to those rustling leaves, his chair creaking with each rock, my thoughts began to reach for my own recollections of that fall and coming winter. The Thirteen Colonies seemed to be changing so quickly in those days, contentious events affecting the lives of some four million colonists from Georgia to New Hampshire, frictions also entwining the struggles of over half a million Negro children, women and men, some free from shackles yet most enslaved.

I remember the rumors swirling the colonies during those first wintry weeks of 1770, of simmering tensions spurring unsettling events in an array of villages and towns, such as the explosive clashes up in the port of New York. The Pennsylvania Evening Post revealed that sons of liberty men had been igniting dangerous confrontations with scores of the king's soldiers over those divisive Townshend Acts, angry colonists blasting defiant hollers and taunting shouts on the cobblestone streets of the Island of Manhattan.

Frictions continued to brew in Ethan's Colony of Massachusetts Bay too, most profoundly in Boston I suppose, where embers of discontent would sporadically flare between the port's fifteen thousand colonists and the king's loyal soldiers, now perhaps three thousand strong. Ethan said that with each passing day of that new year an increasing number of colonists grew more disgruntled about all those redcoats drilling on the snows of the common and strutting about the cobblestones, wharfs and docks. And support for the sons' defiance of those Townshend Acts continued to flourish in Boston too, opposition spreading more intensely to villages and towns throughout the colony, including Ethan's Lexington. Spirited woman and men were forming new little groups pledging to defy the powers of London, colonists agreeing to shun crates of those English goods like parchment, glass and tea.

I glanced to Samuel once again still peering into the summer winds, then gazed to the distant leaves twisting in the soft July breeze and remembered all those troubling things from those days, and wondered of the frightening events yet to grip the colonies that would forever change the path of my life. I shuttered my eyes as a warm breath gently tossed my silvery hair, and as I rocked easy, slid my fingers back into the pocket of my summer dress to caress the aging parchment of Ethan's poem. With each gentle slide across his tender words I could feel his arousing passion, a serenity that was beginning to be brushed by an unsettling sense of impending change. For I also knew, it was during those wintry months that the simplicity I had come to know in my life was about to become wrapped by emotional complexity.

With each caress my thoughts raced to the closing hours of 1769 and the early days, weeks and months of that new year so long ago, to memories of a time when two distinct men would descend upon my life from two diverse places. I'd embark upon a journey with one that was cultivated by the wants and pressures of others, and in my own disturbing way, perhaps gripped by norms beyond my control, a journey I'd willingly accept by timidly surrendering to my frightened frailties.

I would sail with the other upon mystical wings to a serene place few even know exists, a sensuous garden beyond the petty winds of greed and spite, a journey with a young man who would cultivate my heart and soul. Yet it was a place I would someday come to understand could only truly be nurtured by a woman able to reject the desires and pressures of others, and willingly listen to the beat of her heart. For I'd come to know that only those with the courage to abandon the comforts of security would be able to walk the magical stones of that mysterious path, a wondrous road I'd mistakenly believe was shrouded by banishing winds.

As I softly touched Ethan's poem I could feel the passionate embers deep inside begin to flare, a fire which many times I'd suppress with logic and deceit in those days, stashing such emotions into a haven box. I suppose in those years I had found a way to douse my cravings with reasoning, casting desires to a hidden place to tantalize my dreams. And now, with each caress of his tender words, my aging memories continue to magically unfold.

Soon after the first snows had swept across the hills and fields of my Colony of Pennsylvania and settled upon the cottages, shops and homes of Germantown that December of 1769, I was introduced to a colonist down in Philadelphia. He was a determined man whom someday I would wed, a man who would become Samuel's grandfather. And as unimaginable as it seems after all these years, within weeks I'd meet another in the Colony of Massachusetts Bay who would consume the passions of my heart, a man I'd first touch on that exhilarating yet bloody March night of 1770.

"Your father and I want you to meet someone," I remember mother calmingly say up in my bedroom in late December. "He's from Philadelphia, Andrea, and we think he'd be a nice match for you. His name is rather impressive too, Franz von Handel." I could feel an anxiousness grip my insides as a hush quickly swirled the room, and I just sat with a befuddled bat of my eyes trying to grasp the true meaning of what mother just said.

"Your father knows his parents," she continued with a dash of tenacity while nestling closer to me, "good Quaker people, Andrea, faithful worshipers at Philadelphia's meeting house. He's in the merchant and shipping business with his father, 'von Handel and Son,' one of the best in the colonies I'm told, with a big warehouse and boats along the Delaware River." Mother twisted and stared into my eyes, and surprisingly told me I was to attend supper at the von Handel home with her and father on the eve of Christmas. Then gazing just a bit deeper, she whispered in a stunningly suggestive way, "Should you marry this man, Andrea, you'd have fine things the rest of your life. That would make your father and me, truly happy."

On that night before Christmas I'd discover that Franz was ten years older than me and had never wed, and lived alone in his own spacious home near the corner of Chestnut and Ninth, several blocks west of the colony's statehouse and a half mile from the Delaware River. He told me his father and mother had come from the village of Zaandam near the port of Amsterdam, having sailed across the sea to Philadelphia some thirty years before, and on a frigid Friday morn, the Fifth of February, 1740, he was born during a wintry flurry in a little cottage near the river. And he proudly proclaimed he had finished his schooling at the College of New

Jersey several years before, some forty miles northeast in the village of Princeton.

Franz was a bit taller than most in those days, just an inch or two less than six feet, and appeared strong and slim, filling his stockings, breeches and shirt rather hearty that night, something he'd say was honed during his youth in his father's warehouse. His eyes seemed a bronzy brown in the candlelight during supper that eve, while his sandy hair flowed easy to his ears, and his trimmed dark beard gave him an appearance mother said was distinguishingly gentry.

Although I knew little about Franz on that December night, I would soon come to realize he was rather smitten with me, for we began to see one another several times each week in a courtship that seemed shrouded by affluent pressures. I remember how he strove to gain my affections, wooing me with things like stylish dresses from England and France and dainty scarves from Spain, and elegant shawls from little villages along the waters of the Mediterranean Sea. From the very beginning it was as though Franz reveled in displaying his wealth, exposing a willingness to drape shillings and pounds upon me, and with each passing day I found myself realizing what mother had whispered to me that December night. I remember the unflattering desires for more that began to infuse me, and looking back after all these years, how beguiled I was to believe the importance of such things. They simply stoked the flames of my youthful cravings, and spurred more of mother's opulent reasoning.

As Franz showered me with all those alluring things, he was also sliding into what I'd slowly discover were caring emotions brushed of intimacy, feelings he'd soon confess as love, something that never truly evolved within me. Yet I began to selfishly realize in my own youthful way that I needed him, for he seemed to fulfill what mother insistently conveyed to me that wintry night, even while the passions he was displaying were not erupting inside me. Over the years I've come to reluctantly admit that my emotions toward Franz were mostly brushed by comfortable feelings of companionship, a principled sense of safety he bought to my life, an aura of security mother and father had always desired for me. He would be able to provide me with a charming position in Philadelphia life, and was of our Quaker faith too, things important to mother and father and enticing to a young woman wrapped by naivety.

As our lives began to slowly entwine those first weeks of the new year, I began to sense a restlessness stirring inside me. It was an uncomfortable pressure that seemed to be building from all the nursing training which had consumed me for close to two years, a sapping feeling compounded by conflicting emotions twisting inside about Franz who had suddenly walked into my life. I could sense that I needed to calm the swirling winds, and knew my anxiousness was becoming apparent to mother and father too, and felt a need to rejuvenate in a safe place, at least for a little while. It was then plans were made for me to visit father's uncle in Boston, spend a few weeks that winter in the Colony of Massachusetts Bay with Aunt Bea and Uncle Jason, and perhaps, find that sense of peace that was eluding me.

After mother received their letter from Boston saying they were delighted to have me visit, I boarded the English vessel *Dorchester* during a chilly drizzle soon after dawn on Saturday, the Tenth of February, 1770. We sailed down the river from Philadelphia to the waters of Delaware Bay before escaping into the Atlantic on our journey to the Colony of Massachusetts Bay, and as she sliced, pitched and rolled through the icy waters, I gazed the roiling sea and wondered what awaited my three week stay. Then shortly before noon on the second Tuesday of February, as little specs of snow gently drifted over the port and settled to the harbor, the *Dorchester* dropped its thick iron chain into the waters at a Boston dock. I had arrived at a strange yet enchanting place, and soon would meet a shy student of Harvard College, an enticingly sensitive young man named Ethan Francis Sheehan.

Chapter X

Red Iris

𝕿hose few weeks in Boston that winter of 1770 forever changed my life, and the violence of that chilling Monday night, the Fifth of March, spurred a simmering resistance in thousands of ports, villages and towns while staggering the consciousness of the Thirteen Colonies in a way few could have imagined. Over a half century has passed since my journey to the Colony of Massachusetts Bay, yet I can still smell the sea filtering about Boston that wintry night, still feel the brush of cold upon my cheeks and see the grisly steam rising from life oozing upon the snowy cobblestones of King Street. It was that March night which brought Ethan into my life, exposing a magical path bathed with his sensuous serenity, an impassioned ecstasy which continues to caress me to this day. It was a transcending night which witnessed the crackling of musket fire and spilling of spirited courage, blasts which silenced the dreams of five brave men and challenged our colonial soul.

After all these years the gruesome images of those men remains seared in my mind, visions of frigid eyes silently peering into the trickling snow forever etched in the souls of every colonist, especially those gathered on the cobblestones of Boston that bloody March night. It had been a Monday not unlike thousands before, with a gibbous moon that seemed to dangle from a silken thread amidst shadowy clouds and a thin tower rising from the statehouse. It was a defiant night when spirited shouts were crushed by royal muskets shattering lives with little lead balls, solemn moments when colonists tossed indecision to the winds to join our immerging cause, when the hearts of five daring men inspired every colonist searching for liberty.

Soon after my return to Germantown the Pennsylvania Evening Post revealed the names of those fearless men, referring to each as "a patriot, an inspiration to every Whig colonist." The Post first exposed the honor of Crispus Attucks, the oldest and first to fall that bloody night, a Negro man who toiled the docks and sailed the seas, followed by the young seaman James Caldwell and the studious Samuel Maverick, both just seventeen. Samuel Gray was said to be twenty-one and known about Boston as a "hardheaded brawler," an excitable young man who twined hemp into rope in a shop along the eastern docks. And Patrick Carr was a fine tradesman of leather and rumored to be a bit more cerebral than most, a spirited Irishman born thirty years before in a fishing village on the Mizen peninsula of County Cork.

I've heard some say over the years that our colonial struggle against King George the Third in essence began that cold March night on the snows of King Street, and that maybe, those five brave men were truly the first casualties of the coming war. I suppose it could be so, especially for every woman, child and man on the cobblestones of Boston that night, colonists like Ethan and me, and the thousands of our generation who shall never forget their selfless sacrifice. Yet they were simply five men who, like so many others, sought to live beyond the shackles of London's increasing oppression, determined colonists pining for the taste of true liberty while defiantly glaring into the abyss. Perhaps the Evening Post expressed it best when it suggested that those men had in fact become, "The faces of a new spirited breed of colonist, five daring souls destined for the ages."

My memories of that March night are brushed with conflicting emotions, of twisting anger and patriot Whig pride, gruesome visions and calming passions, for it was during those frightful moments on that Boston street that my eyes also first gazed upon Ethan. And even though we were together for only a short while that snowy night, sipping wine, caressing and whispering before the enticing fire of Aunt Bea's hearth, I could feel a longing for Ethan's sensuous touch while preparing to leave for Germantown the coming morning. We had found each other for just a brief moment in our young lives, yet the emotions I was feeling were real, passions swirling amid an unsettling confusion twisting inside. For I realized I was already involved with Franz in Philadelphia, a man mother continually insisted was the proper match for me. And when entwined with my youthful desires for acceptance, an unflattering need for conformity, it was a notion I'd reluctantly come to believe.

A gentle snow was sprinkling the Colony of Massachusetts Bay when I left Boston a few hours after dawn on that first Tuesday of March, 1770, dabbing a tear as I left Ethan behind. Yet, unlike my journey north on the icy waters of the sea, my return to the Colony of Pennsylvania was by an intriguing carriage on the postal road slicing southwest through the colonies. It was a rather rustic coach with splattered patches of muddied snow, and as a chilly breeze eased from the sea, I bound into the carriage for my four days ride over some three hundred miles back to Germantown. The driver was a shaggy looking man sitting at his station on a board wrapped by dark hide up front and high, an aging colonist bundled in a thick rumpled coat sprinkled with little bright bits. He just gripped the leather reins with wrinkled gloves and silently waited in the cold, a bushy grey beard warming his cheeks, and his silvery hair dangled his ears from the dark fur of a scraggly hat.

I nudged to the far right of the rear seat and shyly nestled to the cushion next to a quiet woman and man, and found myself looking forward into the eyes of two other men. Amid a nervous hush I gazed through the little window just right of my eyes and looked to Uncle Jason and Aunt Bea protectively watching near the door of the Massachusetts Bay and Colonial Stage Line, then softly waved a lonesome goodbye. And as I gently pressed my bonnet against the carriage and gazed to Aunt Bea's teary eyes, that lonely looking man with the bushy grey beard snapped the reins and the coach lurched forward. The wheels began to crunch little patches of snow while creaking along the gravely cobblestones, and as eight iron shoes clanked the Boston street toward the snowy ruts of the postal road, I gently waved as our misting eyes latched a final time.

The two men sitting opposite me were sixty or so, and I'd soon discover they were Franklin Haps and Joshua Daniels on their way back home to the town of Dover in the Colony of Delaware. And sharing my seat were Jonas and Samantha Lee, a young man and his bride taking the coach to the Colony of Virginia to visit his father on his farm outside Richmond. As the carriage bounced, swayed and rolled south along the colonial road those four began to engage in friendly chatter, entwining intriguing stories with fanciful phrases. All the while, amid the hypnotic sound of twin geldings snorting in a galloping trot, I just listened in a hush as a disturbing sense of gloom churned deep inside. I simply gazed through the frost of that little window and quietly withdrew to my twisting emotions and thoughts, searching for answers I prayed awaited just beyond each bend.

As our coach wound about groves of pine, oak, maple and elm, creaking and swaying through wintry fields and scores of hamlets, villages and towns, my thoughts drifted to mother and father, to Franz waiting back home. And although those pressures were tugging and churning my insides, dutiful expectations intensely swirling, the passions gripping my heart would thrust my thoughts back to Boston. I could feel Ethan's tender touch from that night, soft lips pressing mine amid a sensuous warmth flickering from the fire, and as I gazed for hours through the glass of the little carriage window, a fiery clash snapped and flared between heart and mind. I'd desperately listen for whispers of guidance beyond each twisting turn and snowy meadow, only to hear the lonesome sound of galloping hooves as a hushing dark draped each dusk.

Although my unpleasant dilemma seemed to consume me over most of those four long days along the postal road, when we'd stop in a hamlet to rest for a while or sleep for the night at a village inn, the recurring theme discussed by colonists would pivot my thoughts. "Have you heard of the killings in Boston?" a curious looking man spouted to our bundled driver as he halted the stage with a tug of the reins in a village somewhere in the Colony of Connecticut. Still others near the Island of Manhattan insistently asked if any of us knew anything about the "diabolical slaughter by the king's troops?" And when we stopped a bit southwest of the Hudson River, near the village of Bound Brook in the Colony of New Jersey, I could hear huddled merchants angrily whisper, "That damn Governor Hutchinson they have up there!" I suppose in just about every village and town along the road we would heard at least a colonist or two referring to the violence in Boston that March night as "a damn massacre" or "bloody madness."

It was shortly after dusk the second Friday of March when our coach creaked south over the Windrim Road into Germantown, coming to a stop at the office of the stage a mile or so from home. I had just completed the first overland travel in my life, bouncing and swaying through the colonies of Massachusetts Bay, Rhode Island, Connecticut and southern narrows of New York, before ferrying across the icy flow of the Hudson River. Then we rolled through the Colony of New Jersey to the waters of the Delaware, crossing into my Pennsylvania on a rickety ferry several miles north of Germantown. Father was waiting in the shadows just outside the office door, bundled warm in his snow-specked coat amid the yellow glow of a lamp in the nearby window. I jumped to the gravely snow with a tender farewell to my carriage friends and George, our gracious and weary driver, and although it felt so good to finally be home, my thoughts continued to drift north to Boston as my heart yearned for Ethan.

We gently embraced in the chilly night air before father tossed my stuffed burlap bag into the shadow behind our buggy's seat, and as the wheels crunched with each roll toward home, I sputtered of my adventurous sail at sea and some comforting things of his Uncle Jason and Aunt Bea. And for a moment or two I revealed the horrors of my final night in Boston before uttering a few polite words about Ethan, confessing how kind I thought he was to have walked me safely home from the cobblestones of King Street.

As father listened and flicked the reins, as I relaxed now and then amid the cold still of the night, I realized that over those three nights and four days I had come to an internal understand about me. Somewhere along those three hundred miles of snowy ruts and crackling stones I had heard a faint voice wisp from the shadows of the trees while pressing my thoughts near that little carriage window, a soft whisper exposing my desires and limitations. And as our coach wound nearer the Delaware River just hours before that day, I came to frustratingly realize that I would need to keep my true passions for Ethan hidden secretly deep in my heart, at least for the weeks and months to come.

I slowly slipped back to the expectations of my normal life, and to my pleasant surprise, discovered that the pressures from mother and father, from my nursing duties and evolving life with Franz, were mysteriously easing to a more serene place. I was now back home, tending to patients and studying for hours at the Pennsylvania Hospital, seeing Franz a little more each week to mother and father's delight, and snipping and stitching homespun things with Betsy and Lydia some Sunday nights. And even though I had somehow exiled my secret feelings for Ethan to that dark corner of my heart, I'd magically reach for his sensuous touch during the quiet hours of night, feeling his caress in my dreams.

I think it was in early April, perhaps a week or so after I received Ethan's first letter and his precious little poem, not long after my life seemed to unflatteringly settle into a secure, comfortable place, when new rumors began to swirl about Philadelphia and Germantown about those dastardly killings in Boston the month before. Colonists were becoming increasingly disturbed over the terrible deed of that March night, many repeating phrases being printed in pamphlets and papers sweeping across the colonies in the satchels of swift riders.

A few at the hospital were calling the musket fire that night, "the crown's savagery in Boston," a phrase some had read in a pamphlet from the Colony of New York. And Tories more loyal to the king were calling it "the unhappy disturbance in Massachusetts Bay," a rather benign view being spewed by the South Carolina Gazette down in Charles Towne. Still others were selecting more truthful versions with a greater patriot Whig tone, phrases like "the bloody massacre on a Monday night" being printed in Philadelphia's Pennsylvania Gazette, a version Ethan would later say he first read in Mr. Gill's Country Journal.

I remember how the frenzied talk of the "massacre up in Boston" seemed to not only spur gruesome visions by colonists up in Ethan's Massachusetts Bay, but women, children and men in ports, villages and towns throughout all the colonies, awakening what some believed was a slumbering indignation. The smoldering anger about that bloody March night was not only spreading north, south and into the frontier wilderness, but into the home of every royal governor and the hulls of English sailing ships, grisly tales that were spilling across the sea into the halls of parliament and incurious chambers of King George.

It was during that spring that an etching of what happened in Boston that night began to appear in papers and pamphlets throughout the colonies, a revealing design inked to big parchment sheets that were tacked to the walls of taverns and shops, churches and village halls. It was an engraving Ethan would later say was first inked to broadsheets on Mr. Gill's printing press, an image soon repeated in papers across the Colony of Massachusetts Bay and Mr. Giles' Lexington Gazette, an inciting portrait that quickly spread throughout all the colonies.

"I stirred the ink and set the type," Ethan confessed, "for printing that image in the Boston Gazette late that March. And just as Mr. Gill pressed his first sheets, Mr. Edes and Sam Adams came strutting down from the long room while spouting a title for that sketch. Each boldly proclaimed, 'We'll call it, the bloody massacre perpetrated on King Street,' and within moments I had inserted the type for that line into the printing press. And when I galloped to Lexington to visit dad that coming Saturday, with sheets of that broadside twined to my saddle, he nailed a sketch to the tavern wall just left of the barreled bar."

I first set sight on that disturbing image at the Pennsylvania Hospital in early May when some printings of the Evening Post were being slyly passed about rooms and halls among doctors and nurses, visitors and patients. It was a sketch that caused our souls to tremble while gripping the conscious of every women, child and man throughout the colonies, an engraving that instilled a graphic image of muskets blasting death that March night. It was an explosive depiction that enflamed the fiery passions of those of Boston and Ethan's Colony of Massachusetts Bay, and alarmed a wary populace in all the colonies. It was an image some would frighteningly say exposed the fissure erupting on this side of the sea, of the swiftly emerging divide between loyal Tories and patriot Whigs, between King George the Third and his Thirteen Colonies.

Even after all these years, when I gaze deeply into that image I can still feel the frightful tensions that were swirling about the cobblestones of King Street that night, and smell the pungent odor of death oozing to the snow. It was a sketch that looked east over the stones, as if one were standing near Mr. Gill's print shop, and that gibbous moon was dangling high over the statehouse. I can still see those young royal soldiers lined to the right near the crown's customs house, eight exacting men in black boots, bright breeches and crimson coats. Their bayonetted muskets were raised to their shoulders and dark tricorn hats were glaring into the sea of defiant colonists massed on the cobblestones, and their captain commanding just behind his redcoat line, was thrusting his royal sword into the unyielding night air.

Yet I suppose it was the white smoke billowing from those muzzles that truly exposed the gruesomeness of that awful night, for it was the moment streaking lead balls ripped the life from five brave souls. And there were six other Bostonians sprawled about that image, daring men wounded on the stones of King Street that night, scarlet spattered to the snow. It was a sketch which became seared upon the minds of every patriot Whig colonist, even upon the memory of Tories loyal to London and others neutral to it all, merchants like father and Franz who'd disturbingly spout, "They showed disloyal contempt, and met their just fate."

The Pennsylvania Evening Post suggested that the image of that bloody Boston night was an engraving by Mr. Revere, yet I'd later hear that some thought it was the creation of Henry Pelham, another Bostonian said to have frantically sketched that image before any other, something Ethan refused to believe. There were even rumors filtering about Philadelphia and Germantown that the image may have actually been first etched by Jonny Mulliken, a clocksmith from the village of Newburyport some forty miles north of Boston. I've always believed as Ethan, that it was Paul's sketch that I saw printed in the Evening Post that spring, and that the dreadful event on King Street that night was a defining moment of our colonial lives.

"It was around then when you received Ethan's first letter, right grandma?" interrupted Samuel with a gentle nudge of his chair and glance to my eyes. "That first poem too?"

"Yes, it was," I whispered, gazing to those distant rustling leaves, "early that spring at the hospital. I've never forgotten that moment, and of course, still have both in a little box." For a few hushing moments we rocked easy in our chairs amid the warm summer winds, and with each beat of my heart I could sense the confusing emotions that were churning deep inside back then. They were passions for Ethan I struggled to reconcile with a youthful infatuation for Franz, and when I received that letter all those years ago, I could feel Ethan's sensuous knock upon my heart's shuttered door. "Yes, Samuel, that's when I received his first letter."

Then Samuel asked some things I knew he eventually might, questions I had feared would send a twisting surge deep inside, things I was hoping would be gently answered in my own way as my story continued to unfold. "I've got to know, grandma," he inquisitively said with a compassionate glance, "but please, stop me if you want. What happened with you and Ethan? I mean, it's pretty clear how you felt, both of you. I'm wondering why, grandma, why you chose Grandpa Franz?"

"Oh, Samuel," I whispered, staring to his wondering eyes, "don't ever doubt, please, that I cared for your grandfather. He was a kind, honest man, and over time, in my own way, I did find a type of love with him. Life was so different in those days, Samuel, and I suppose I was insecure, rather unsure of myself back then. Maybe I wasn't as strong as I should have been, or maybe I just, sort of let things happen, succumbing to the pressuring wants of others, to things I mistakenly believed were important. I know, it sounds like I'm making excuses, shirking responsibility, and maybe in a way, I am. I've often wondered, Samuel, if things could be magically undone, how my life might have been. I guess I was just too young."

"I think I understand, grandma, really, I do. Even with all the things you're telling me today, I know you loved grandpa."

"It makes me feel good, Samuel, to hear you say that. I know you'll listen to my story, all of it, and hope then you'll understand. I must confess that you've already helped me remember so much, and in a special way, are helping me reconcile my past. I'm truly grateful."

"Awe, grandma," he uttered with a timid glance to my eyes, "I'm just so glad to be here, listening to you." For a moment or two Samuel eased his rock and gazed to the leaves rustling the distant elms, then pivoted his thoughts and said, "Ethan's first letter, that first little poem, must have really changed things in your life."

At that moment I knew that letter and poem were stashed with all the others in that little box hidden in a dark corner of the closet of my bedroom, and as Samuel rocked and stared to the swaying tips of those elms, I wondered how utterly inadequate a simple yes would be. "Yes, Samuel, they did," I whispered, dabbing a tear brimming my eye, "ever more."

I slid my fingers across the ink of Ethan's poem warming in the pocket of my summer dress, caressing passions he quilled all those years ago, and remembered some of the things he confessed in that first precious letter. Yes, he had quilled sweet memories of us nestling before Aunt Bea's fire, but also exposed feelings of what happened on the snowy stones of King Street. "Ethan shared thoughts about the killings that March night," I softly added, caressing his aging words. "There're things I want you to know, Samuel, things that will help you understanding Ethan." As Samuel peered to the summer winds, patiently waiting my coming words with each nudge of his chair, I rocked easy and reached for memories of those days so long ago.

Ethan had quilled about that daring man who expired in his arms on that March night, explaining how he had first seen Mr. Attucks on a muggy July day two years before when Ethan was helping his father in the tavern in Lexington. "I was doing what I normally did on Saturday afternoon," he confided, "brushing tables and washing kitchen things, filling mugs, goblets, cups and tins with ale, wine, rye whiskey and rum. That's when Crispus first came in, Andrea, strutting through the open tavern door with Mr. Jafres and a pair of friends from the Boston docks. They walked right over to dad's table left of the door, in the corner near the bar, and plopped into four slatted chairs."

Crispus' two dock friends looked quite younger than he and Quincy Jafres, perhaps just twenty or so, Irishmen Ethan would learn who had recently sailed to Boston from a village in County Limerick. But the older two had known each other for many years, having first met in the fields of bondage somewhere in the Colony of South Carolina or Georgia. "Quincy and Mr. Attacks seemed to be reflecting on their earlier days," he quilled, "while the two younger ones seemed to be at best, simply curious friends. While scurrying about, I could hear them talking about a few of the disturbing things taking place back in Boston, and sputtering of the disgruntled feelings gripping the docks and spreading across the colony."

Ethan's father brought each their first mug of Boston ale, followed over the coming few hours with refills poured by Ethan, and although Mr. Jafres was the only one who knew Ethan, the other three were always friendly. They displayed courteousness toward other tradesmen, merchants and farmers who came and went that day too, striving in a respectable way to ensure their discussions of ships, wharfs and the sea, of the toils of Mr. Jafres' farm and crops sprouting his fields, were shrouded with civility. And after Ethan's father proudly told them of his son's studious ways and duties at Mr. Giles' print shop, they'd ask inquisitive things each time Ethan brought more ale, especially Mr. Attucks.

Then Ethan's letter started to delve into more sinister things he described as coming from a few unenlightened colonists of Lexington, two men saddled with dim minds shrouded of bigotry, an ugliness dwelling within too many souls wandering the colonies. They were young men sipping Caribbean rum at a little table beneath the rising stairs across the tavern floor, a bit right of the fireplace stones. Ethan had just filled their tins with another splash of rum, when they began to expressively expose their challenged limitations.

Ethan had known Bobby Beatty all his life, who still lived on his father's farm near Mr. Jafres' fields and just west of Ethan's old place, and knew Jimmy Cravitz a little, whose father once helped tend the Beatty farm when Bobby and Ethan were young. It seems Jimmy had recently returned to the Colony of Massachusetts Bay from a rather hazy life down near the port of Savannah, and now tilled his own fields a mile or so south of Lexington. And Ethan knew they could easily spew vile things now and then, opinions much like Bobby's father, and from behind the barreled bar he could hear them whispering disparaging things about Negro women, children and men.

"I was scurrying behind the bar" he quilled, "pouring more ale and wiping some things not far from Mr. Jafres and his friends at the corner table, and dad had just banged through the kitchen door on the other side of the hearth from Bobby and Jim. Their contemptuous whispers were slowly getting louder, ugly words perhaps spurred by the rum, disparaging things that seemed intended to be heard by Crispus and Quincy."

Ethan had just glanced up when young Jimmy rose in his boots with a sliding scrape of his chair, and while gripping his tin of rum, twisted and glared across the tavern at the four harmlessly sipping from frothy mugs. "What the hell is them two doin in here?!" he blurted with an intimidating swagger. "Hey, Bobby, look at em. Negras, thinkins they belong in here, with us."

Bobby twisted right in his chair and gazed across the tavern, clamping his stare upon Quincy and Crispus watching in a startled hush with their two young Irish friends. "Ya, whats the hell?" he predictably slurred. "What's this bloody colony comin to? Hey, Pat!" he spouted with another twist toward Ethan's father near the kitchen door. "Why don't you get them, outta here!"

"That's right, Mr. Sheehan," chimed Jimmy in a rummy tone, "gets them outta here! Or maybes, ya needs some help!"

Ethan quilled that those disgusting bursts, while not surprising, still startled him, and he quickly became concerned about what Crispus and Quincy might do to confront that enflaming nonsense. Yet within moments he could see that those steady men had quickly appraised those two bitter, young dimwitted men, and had quelled any notions of retaliation against the hostility being spewed in the tavern that day. They just remained intelligently calm, and as a tense hush swirled about the room, Ethan's father rushed across the tavern floor with a limp in his scamper and determination in his eyes to confront those two young men, both now rigidly standing with defiant grips of their rum.

"Robert, I've known you since you were a boy," Ethan's father sternly explained, staring into his eyes from a foot or so away, "and your dad was with us at the frontier during the war, when George Pratt was killed. But as God is my witness, I will not allow your mindlessness to threaten anyone in my tavern." Then snapping his glare right, he firmly added, "That goes for you too, Jimmy Cravitz."

They stood in stunned silence as Ethan and others watched with Crispus and Quincy from across the tavern floor, all seemingly waiting for either of those two challenged young men to sputter another word of nonsense. And as they nervously glanced to the glare in Ethan's father's eyes and scanned the others hushed about the room, he calmly advised, "You boys are finished here today. Gather what wits you still have, and walk out of here. And I mean now, Robert."

"Bloody hell we will!" Jimmy defiantly slurred. "We'ves gots just as much rights to be here as them."

"That's right," spouted Bobby, stiffening his stance with a deviant glare as rum trickle his chin. "Just as much, and lots more than them two Negra men."

"Go, Robert," insisted Ethan's father. "Come on boys, put those tins down and leave, now!"

The three just stood and glared for a moment or two while Ethan and the others anxiously waited, and as the tension crackled about the hot summer air, Ethan wondered if he'd need to rush to the aid of his father. Then suddenly grasping their dire situation, Bobby and Jim clicked their rum to the table without uttering a sound and angrily strutted away. And as their boots clumped across the oak slats of the floor, they snapped a menacing gaze to Crispus and Quincy quietly watching their escape out the tavern door.

Ethan's father stood quiet and stern as those two challenged men vanish into the hazy warmth of the summer afternoon, then glanced to the corner as if to reassure Mr. Attucks and Quincy that their discussions with their young dock friends would no longer be disturbed. And as he slowly stepped across the floor to the anxious four, their mugs firmly gripped and eyes snapping to-and-fro the door, he stopped beside their table and calmly said, "Don't pay those bloody dummies any mind. You men are welcome in my tavern, anytime, and don't you forget it."

Crispus and Quincy raised their mugs with a grateful nod, a gesture quickly followed by their two Irish friends. "Thanks, Pat," Quincy respectfully said to his old farming friend. "Yes," Crispus boldly added with a sip of ale, "thank ya, Mr. Sheehan. That was a fine thing you did, takin a stand for us, defendin two black men."

"Hey, there'll be no talk like that in my tavern," Ethan's father uttered with an insistent nod. "To me, to all honorable people around here, my Ethan too, you're simply colonists, fine men. Although I appreciate your thanks, really, there's no need. Believe me, tossing those two was my pleasure." And as Ethan's father stepped closer to the barreled bar, he spun and added with a determined glare, "It wasn't just for you two, but for all colonists striving for their rightful place, only to be subjected to stupid people like them out there. I can't change the entire world, but I can do something right here, in my tavern." Then staring out the panes of the corner window seemingly lost in his thoughts, peering into the haze hovering the village field, he spouted to Ethan watching from behind the bar, "Ethan, please, get these four fine gentlemen another splash of ale, on the Buckman Tavern."

Even after all these years, those thoughts from Ethan's first letter remain vividly etched in my mind, and I remember how he quilled that he was never more proud of his father than that July day. He confided that after starting his Harvard studies he'd see Mr. Attucks in Boston now and then, maybe passing along the docks or walking the expanse of the common, and once when Ethan stepped from that bookstore near Mrs. Davies Tavern. They'd exchange a greeting word, and each time Crispus would give his best to Ethan's father, then gaze into the winds as if reliving that hazy summer day in Lexington.

That first letter also delved deeper into Ethan's emotions about what happened in Boston that March night, feelings of struggling to understand amid a sadness that spurred a tinge of angst inside me. It was as if he were grappling with haunting demons over the madness exposed that night, and maybe dealing with a darkness of his own that dwelled somewhere deep within. "For many days, Andrea," he chillingly quilled, "I awoke in the middle of the night with my stomach angrily churning. I'd search for reasons swirling dreadful dreams, asking God why those brave men lost their lives on the snows of King Street."

I remember struggling, perhaps less intense than Ethan, with many of those same frightful feelings those final days of winter and into spring, just as the others I suppose who witnessed the awful sounds of musket fire on the cobblestones that bloody night. "It was as if I was slipping into the shadows of a melancholy haze," his letter continued to reveal, "as if I were straddling a fine line for control. I even wandered the docks for a while when not at Harvard, or busy studying or tending duties at the print shop. Then after a week or so I began to crawl from the edge of that abyss, soon after many of Boston expressed their solemn respect for those five daring men, laying their souls to eternal rest."

Along with his letter and little poem, Ethan had enclosed a torn portion of Mr. Gill's Boston Gazette and Country Journal, a somber story about the funeral for four of those souls printed shortly after that defiant March night. The port of Boston had bid farewell to the men who had died on the snowy stones that night, patriots joined in a week or so by their bloodied friend, after slowly succumbing to his musket wounds.

The smell of the sea was gently drifting about the harbor that misty morning, a late wintry breeze brushing the waters and swirling about masts of merchant and Royal Navy sailing ships, lingering winds kissing the slats, bricks and panes of churches and taverns, warehouses, shops and homes. "A sullen haze draped our port," the Boston Gazette somberly revealed, "and the March sun, shrouded by layers of roiling grey, desperately sought to soothe the sadness gripping scores of colonists lining the cobblestones."

It was a funeral described as rather public and at times a bit raucous, a ceremony designed by patriot Whigs to honor the victims of that bloody massacre on King Street just days before. Merchants had shuttered their doors and bells dangling throughout the port wept, sullen clacks and dings that sailed with the morning winds into the distant hills and fields. They were somber tolls soon joined by the cries of other bells ringing from steeples and belfries in villages and towns near and far, in Roxbury, Braintree and Ethan's Lexington, in Charlestown, Salem, Concord and Cambridge.

Before being reunited for their somber ride through Boston, those first four to fatally fall had been peacefully at rest in their own sacred places. Mr. Attucks and James Caldwell had been honorably lying within the windows and bricks of Faneuil Hall, just a block or so from where their dreams were shattered on the snowy stones of King Street. The Gazette said they "slept upon a wooden bed of cherry tables draped by bright linens stitched in blue," and for a day or two "Bostonians solemnly prayed as they shuffled past." And Samuel Gray had been resting amid little flickering flames in the parlor of his brother's nearby cottage, while Samuel Maverick had been quietly lying with pillows and blankets in the shadows of pulsating candles in his mother's home just south of the common.

As a chilly mist shrouded the port shortly before noon that second Thursday of March, those four brave souls once again gathered near the spot the king's muskets had fired just days before. Each man was now peacefully lying inside the quiet of a funeral carriage, black pine slats lined by a trio of hallowed windows, and as port bells tolled the hour of twelve and a mysterious man in a dark flowing robe snapped the reins, they began their final journey. The carriage slowly rolled behind a pair of snorting mares, and as a stray redcoat soldier with musket shouldered secretly peered from the shadows, their tan manes danced with each haunting creak upon the cobblestones.

"I watched it all from nearby, just outside the print shop," Ethan quilled in that first letter, "with scores of others lining the stones of King and Queen. There was an eerie hush as that gloomy carriage rolled past, Andrea, creaking west toward the common, and I felt an ugly chill streak my back as its wheels crunched and their iron shoes clacked against the cobblestones. Yet even though those grisly sights and sounds seemed to shroud Boston with death, I could feel a tingling sense of pride as those four patriots slowly passed."

That grim carriage carrying the bodies of those four brave souls to their resting place was trailed by grieving family and friends, followed by a slew of buggies and wagons creaking upon the cobblestones. They were hundreds of mourners bundled in warm scarves, shoes and hats, gloves, boots and coats, colonists silently riding and shuffling close behind, many dabbing tears from sullen eyes. It was a dreary procession taking those men to their final home in the Granary Burying Ground, a cold place near the stones of Tremont Street and snowy grass of the common.

Ethan quilled that he had joined that somber crowd shuffling to that lonesome place, and stood hushed with Boston as those four men were lowered into the ground beneath the weeping limbs of swaying elms. Samuel Gray, James Caldwell, Samuel Maverick and Crispus Attucks had been proudly laid to rest, four souls eternally together in the quiet of the Massachusetts Bay soil. The grisly sound of rocks and dirt striking the stone chamber echoed about the trees, a gruesome sound that reminded

Ethan of that awful day on that Lexington hill with his mother. It was a burying chamber that would soon include young Patrick Carr, the fifth patriot to fatally fall in defiance of the crown that chilling March night.

Looking back after all these years, although Ethan's first letter aroused and thrilled me, it spurred an immerging struggle deep inside, a battle between logic and soul, for my heart screamed to quill a letter right back while my mind grappled with danger. What about Franz, I'd twistingly wonder, and his family and my own, mother and father, and what would those of our Quaker house say? What if my secret was discovered, and my virtue ridiculed and scorned? And I feared that my reply might cast Ethan upon a troubling journey, perhaps even cause his tender dreams to go unfulfilled, and worried that my letters could someday cause him pain. They were fears that constantly tugged my heart and gripped my soul.

During the quiet hours of those first spring nights I grappled with my fears and wondered what I should do, hearing cautious whispers of "no, you mustn't quill!" filtering from the dark while passionate cries of "yes, oh yes!" lingered in the shadows. The flames of my heart were pushing me toward Boston, fiery cries echoing my nights to quill a letter to Ethan, all the while those anxious fears continued to swirl my dreams. I tossed about my pillows and churned about blankets and linens for hours those spring nights, praying to the heavens to tame the struggle between my heart and mind. Then slowly that battle began to be won by the passions gripping my heart, and with tenderness caressing my soul, I quilled my first letter to Ethan.

A chilly drizzle was softly falling from the grey that early Tuesday morning of April, and my stomach was twisting in emotional knots when I dropped the folded parchment into the hospital's mailing box. Although I was a bit nervous, perhaps even frightful to have surrendered to my feelings, even if only for a little while, I recall how my first letter was somewhat mundane, maybe a reflection of the apprehensions swirling my soul. I quilled a few things about his little poem he sweetly called *first night*, confessing how I marveled at his intimacy with words, and like he, relived a few dreadful memories of that bloody March night before expressing my passions about the wondrous moments we spent together near the flames of Aunt Bea's hearth. Yet I suppose I mostly quilled of simple things that kept me away from my fears that continued to churn deep inside, unemotional reflections of nursing at the hospital, of mother and father, and of sewing with Lydia and Betsy on Sunday nights.

Then to my surprise I received another letter from Ethan just weeks after that drizzly Tuesday, folded parchment that had been placed on my hospital nursing desk on a Friday afternoon late that April of 1770. I remember how his second letter was even more passionate than the first, as if he was now letting his inner feelings truly flow. "Dear Andrea," he tenderly began, "It was wonderful to receive your letter, absolute joy! There are some things I've got to tell you. When I wake each morning, my first thoughts are of you, and before drifting to dreams each night, I find myself softly whispering, Andrea. I know we've only just met, yet you are always on my mind."

I wondered of what our fate might be as I read his words and savored each line, and as my tingling fingers pinched the parchment, my anxious emotions were churning deep inside. What am I and Ethan doing, I wondered, and where are we going? There was such great distance between us, Ethan hundreds of miles northeast in Boston, embroiled in studies at Harvard and duties at that print shop. And I was way down here in Philadelphia and Germantown, busy with my nursing training while nestling in another man's arms. I wondered of the many obstacles that were already between us, of Franz and his family, of the expectations of mother and father, and worried of our divergent faiths, pressures that at times seemed too burdensome to bear. And I feared of disapproving taunts that might be spewed by others, wanting desperately to keep such maligning whispers at bay.

Yet as my anxious worries swirled about my mind, my heart would madly race at the sight of each secret letter set to my nursing desk, passions beating wildly with each word as my lips longed for Ethan. But as incredible as my feelings were with every new letter, the complexities entwining my life seemed insurmountable, for no matter how much I struggled, I was still the young women of a Philadelphia merchant whom mother and father continually suggested I would someday marry. During that spring and the many months to follow the pressures of such expectations grew, all the while my passions for Ethan continued to simmer and flare, a fire I mysteriously managed to hide deep inside. While my heart yearned for Ethan, as my skin ached for his sensuous touch, my mind kept tugging me back to the Colony of Pennsylvania, to the realities of my life.

As I continued to read the sweet words of Ethan's second letter, he soon began to delve into things that had taken place in Boston in the hours after the killings on King Street that March night. He quilled about the soldier who wielded the sword near his men, an aging captain named Thomas Preston, and explained how he had been questioned inside that customs house by several Tory and Whig colonists that night, along with a few of Royal Governor Hutchinson's men. Then early the coming morning, soon after I climbed into that carriage and began my ride back to Germantown, the captain was placed under arrest upon the order of judges Tudor and Dania. "Those eight redcoats were soon arrested too," Ethan explained, "and all nine were banished to a stone room on Castle Island in the harbor." It wasn't long before each was charged by Jonathan Sewall in the killings of Crispus and his four friends, accused of five counts of murder by the king's leading lawyer for the colony.

Ethan also quilled that while those nine royal soldiers awaited their fate in that dungeon room east in the harbor, several Bostonians had gathered in that long room up in Mr. Gill's print shop. They were spirited men like Sam Adams, John Hancock and Jim Otis, Whig colonists gathering with others such as Doctor Warren, Mr. Revere and Ben Edes. "They were concerned about the trial for the king's men," Ethan confided, "and according to Mr. Gill, wanted to ensure they were judged by calm, prudent men. They were worried that if the trial were not properly processed, it might be viewed by London and Tories of other colonies as being nothing but a Boston mob condemning those soldiers to the gallows." It was then they realized a Boston barrister known for his adherence to law and honesty would need to be chosen to represent the king's men, and on a bright spring afternoon, they appealed to John Adams to defend those nine redcoats.

"Mr. Adams is viewed by most here in my Colony of Massachusetts Bay," Ethan quilled, "as a lawyer who believes every person, no matter their station, has a fundamental right to a proper defense, regardless of Tory or Whig, colonist or Englishman, even a soldier of London's army. And I've heard he supports that position even when doing so could expose a barrister to misguided punishment by unenlightened women and men. I guess that's why he accepted the challenge, Andrea, even with those kinds of troubles lurking in the shadows, when doing so could cause damage to his practice or anger to be lashed against him or his family. Casting those fears to the winds, Mr. Gill said that within a moment, John Adams agreed to represent Captain Preston and his eight royal soldiers."

Ethan also explained that soon after that bloody March night, the hundreds of redcoats drilling on the common and patrolling the cobblestones, wharfs and docks were swiftly removed from the streets of Boston, thanks to the emphatic insistence of colonists like Mr. Hancock, Sam Adams and scores of sons of liberty men. He revealed that those men had burst into the home of Governor Hutchinson within hours of the shootings on King Street, and expressed their outrage not only with the violence unleashed by the king's men that night, but for an array of disturbing things that had taken place over many months. Then they passionately insisted that every redcoat soldier be removed from the peninsula of Boston.

"Mr. Gill said that when Sam Adams advised Governor Hutchinson," Ethan continued to explain, "and that bloody Colonel Dalrymple, that unruly tempers were flaring high about the port and could spiral from control, those two men suddenly became enlightened with wisdom. They agreed to evacuate the king's troops from Boston east into the harbor, to the aging stones of that fort on Castle Island." Within days hundreds of redcoat soldiers, along with that commander of the king's Boston troops, had boarded a slew of Royal Navy boats and ships, and with muskets shouldered, ferried to new quarters at Castle William on that rocky desolate island.

Even though Captain Preston and those eight soldiers were now securely stowed behind stone walls early that spring, and most if not all of the king's troops had been exiled to that barren island, Ethan revealed that tensions between colonists and the crown continued to simmer along the docks and in churches, taverns and shops. And concern over the impending trial for those nine redcoat men continued to grow, not only in Boston but throughout the colony, in his father's Lexington tavern too. Many wondered if those men could truly receive a just trial, and patriot Whigs worried that with such defiant sentiments swirling against the king, those of Boston might be viewed by outsiders as a rabble of hotheads seeking vengeance. Ethan explained many feared that such a perception could alienate all of Massachusetts Bay, and perhaps even spur colonists still undecided of Tory or Whig, to sway toward the crown.

It seems the colony's royal governor and his loyal Tory allies were worried too, men of power and influence who quietly feared that should those nine men evade the justice many colonists were demanding, they could be seen as indifferent or supporting the violence unleashed by the king's soldiers that March night. Ethan quilled that many loyal Tories could be heard suggesting that such a perception, should it allowed to flourish, could have a devastating effect upon the crown's position in the colony. And the governor was rumored to fear that even more colonists could slide into the clutches of patriot Whigs and their liberty sons.

With those sentiments gripping the thoughts of the royal governor, the king's agents and loyal Tories of Boston, passionate positions intriguingly similar to scores of patriot Whigs like Sam Adams, Jimmy Otis and Doctor Warren, rational minds somehow prevailed. "The governor wanted to ensure that tensions swirling about Boston," Ethan explained near the close of his second letter, "had a reasonable period to subside. And with the support of many colonists throughout the colony, both Tory and Whig, and with a shocking eye upon his fiduciary duties, Governor Hutchinson ordered that the trial of those nine redcoats be delayed until fall. He also insisted that the captain be tried separately from his men, that his fate be decided in late October, and that those eight redcoat soldiers be judged during the early snows of December. I'll be thinking of you, Andrea, each hour of every day," he sweetly concluded, "and will quill another letter soon. I miss you. Love, Ethan."

I can still sense the swirling confusion that suddenly gripped my insides, of the realities of my Philadelphia life, of desperately wanting to reach for Boston, and wondering when I'd find the courage to quill a reply to Ethan. It wasn't until the third Sunday of May that I once again surrendered to my desires, quilling easy thoughts to parchment sheets on a lazy sunny day of spring. I can still see my little desk nestled beneath my bedroom window, and feel that feathered quill thrilling the tips of my fingers, and remember the soothing sounds of sprouting leaves rustling in a soft breeze amid the smell of magnolias blooming in distant Germantown fields. It was a moment I wondered of what my words would be, of the disturbing truths I might unwittingly expose, of my surging passions for Ethan.

I shuttered my eyes for a moment or two and breathed a calming sigh of spring, then gently pinched my quill and began to unleash so many things while desperately trying to soothe notions of pain. I wanted Ethan to know of my feelings for him, simmering emotions that were evolving deep inside, and wanted to be honest with him about the nuances of my life in Germantown and Philadelphia, especially of Franz. And although some of my words were sure to hurt, I wanted to set in motion a lasting bond that could only flourish when bathed in truth.

"Dear Ethan," I hesitantly began, as a flash of insecurity surged my soul, "It was so nice to receive your latest letter. I want you to know that I too think of you, and have every day since our first night. And those feelings, Ethan, seem to flourish a little bit more each day." Yet, as much as I wanted to expose more of me, I realized I wasn't quite sure of my feelings, that I didn't really understand what was happening to me, that maybe I was just too young. All I truly knew, was that a fiery struggled was still raging between heart and mind. "I don't really know what this all means, Ethan, at least right now, but please know that my feelings for you seem to run deeper with each day. I hope with our letters we'll come to know and understand each other, and with our words grow closer in so many ways."

Suddenly, my quill began to dwell upon rather mundane things, questions about his Harvard studies, of his room in Mr. Gill's house and duties at the print shop, of his father and tavern in Lexington. And I revealed tidbits swirling about Germantown and stories of mother and father, and exposed a few things about my nursing duties at the Pennsylvania Hospital. Yet with each stroke I found myself avoiding what I knew was the most difficult to tell, painful things of my Philadelphia life, exposing the truth of Franz. I simply quilled of rumors swirling about my Colony of Pennsylvania, of stories being discussed in the hospital halls and shops of Germantown, troubling things I suppose Ethan already knew.

"The Pennsylvania Evening Post revealed some things about King George the other day," I proudly quilled, "of his displeasure about what happened in Boston that March night, and of the debates that soon gripped parliament." And I confessed how a sense of normalcy seemed to be slowly returning to Germantown and Philadelphia, to all the colonies I suppose, of the resurgence in colonial pride that was spreading to hundreds of ports, villages and towns. "So many are so happy about London coming to its senses a few weeks ago," I added, "by repealing most of those Townshend Acts. Father says it was parliament's way of trying to defuse the ugly tensions that have been flaring in the colonies, especially up in your Boston. But Lydia thinks that the pressures placed upon the crown by the colonies were simply too much for the king to bear, that parliament was compelled to scrap most of those duties and taxes."

I remember the feelings of accomplishment and pride as I quilled those lines about the repeal of those despised acts, and wondered of the thousands across the colonies who had also supported the passionate pleas of the sons of liberty to avoid those London goods. And I felt a patriot warmth surge inside when recalling snipping and stitching scores of homespun stockings, coats, breeches and shirts with Betsy and Lydia all those Sunday nights. It was something hundreds of others had also done over the past several years, something the three of us had already determined to continue.

I dipped my quill in my tin of dark ink and gazed to the sights and smells flourishing outside my window, and wondered how it seemed that parliament had been the first to nervously twitch, that the king had blinked. Perhaps London had been nudged to the edge of its royal cliff by the mayhem that had exploded on the cobblestones of Boston that March night, or maybe it was the surge of colonial unity to shun those malicious acts, to oppose the increasingly encroaching authority of the crown. Regardless of what had truly caused that royal reversal, for many it seemed, at least for a little while, that the perseverance of the colonies had prevailed.

As I breathed sweet aromas drifting about the brisk spring air, I wondered of another action recently taken by London, declaring that its quartering acts imposed upon the colonies for several years had finally run their course. Although parliament had delegated those intrusive policies to the embers of history, the Evening Post soon revealed that London had refused to fully renounce every aspect of those bloody Townshend Acts, declaring it retained the authority to tax the colonies whenever it deemed appropriate. It seems that King George and his newest prime minister, the Earl of Guilford, Lord Frederick North, insisted upon keeping a dangling remnant of those laws. Parliament had refused to repeal or rescind all of the crown's powers, choosing to retain its taxes and duties on tea sailed into the colonies, clinging to a perennial vestige of those despised acts.

While gazing through the open panes and pondering all those things, my thoughts began to slowly slide toward my simmering quagmire of Ethan and Franz. I knew I hadn't whispered a word of Franz before the fire that March night nor quilled an inkling of him in my first letter, then dipping and pressing my feather to the parchment, I knew honesty must prevail. And although I was struggling with just how to expose my entangling life with Franz, explain the pressures I felt from all around, I was determined to cling tight to my resolve. With a tinge of fright swirling deep inside, with fears of causing Ethan disappointment and pain, of being misunderstood, I began to stroke the truth as gently as I could.

"I must tell you something, Ethan," I nervously quilled, "and pray that somehow, you'll find a way to understand." Then I revealed the many things of Franz, of us, of his family and faith, and delved into the expectations of mother and father, the pressures I felt here in Philadelphia and Germantown, at times smothering me. "But please, Ethan, know that my feelings for you are strikingly real. As crazy as this may sound, even though I've been seeing Franz for many months, and all these weeks since that night in Boston, my feelings for you astound me, and continue to grow. I reach north for your touch each night, and search for us in my dreams."

With each slide of my quill I could sense feebleness surging within, and for a moment I wondered if I could go on. "How can I explain the guilt that grips me deep inside," I confessed, "of seeing Franz when my passions are reaching for you, when my heart pounds to be with you, Ethan, in the quiet of night?" And I touched upon my selfish fears of being exposed by the truth, of the rumors I've imaged being whispered in the hospital halls or our Quaker house. They were revelations I desperately hoped Ethan would understand, of a situation that was starting to transcend my own entwining beliefs.

An ugly chill of confusion began to race my skin as I wondered of my disheartening faults, then with a daring brush of my quill, I surrendered once again. "Oh, Ethan, know that my feelings for Franz are not like those I have for you. They're different, and in an unsettling way, is what many here expect of me. Just know that how I feel about you is much more, emotions I never dreamed I'd have for anyone. But I'm confused, and wonder if it's possible for a woman to have feelings for more than one man, not the same type, but maybe, in an unflattering way, emotions seeking acceptance while grappling for material things. Maybe my situation is simply a reflection of my own limitations, my troubling frailties. Oh, Ethan, I just don't know." I dabbed my eye and breathed a wisp of spring air, then brushing a tear trickling my cheek, timidly added, "I'm sorry for not having told you before, and pray, you'll forgive me."

I once again dipped my quill and began to peruse each line over and over again, for I desperately wanted to ensure that my words were not only forthright, but were quilled in a way to cause Ethan the least harm, pain than often comes with truth. Then I realized that although my letter seemed to logically expose the realities of my life, perhaps more depressingly than I'd hoped, maybe I hadn't fully conveyed how intense my struggling emotions were reaching for Ethan.

"I pray my honesty has not hurt you," I tenderly continued, "for I never want to cause you pain. All I can do, Ethan, is be truthful, and hope you'll find a way to understand my situation. I began seeing Franz many weeks before you and I met, and our relationship has evolved to what it is today, for all kinds of reasons. I admit to having feelings for Franz, strangely safe kinds, emotions that I selfishly say are spurred by so many pressures I feel from mother, father and others. But never doubt, Ethan, that my feelings for you are deep, strong and real. The hours we spent before Aunt Bea's fire that night were wonderful, the most arousing moments of my life, and as confusing as this must seem, my heart longs for you. I'm torn, Ethan, by an entangling relation down here with Franz, while my thoughts constantly swirl of you. I don't want what we have, what we're slowly discovering, to come to an end. Maybe, I just can't stop."

I gazed out my window for a moment or two and breathed sweet scents of spring blooms, then began closing my intricate letter with confessing strokes of my quill. "I hope my frankness doesn't cause our letters to stop, for I want us to continue to quill to each other, nurture this wonderment we've found. Although my words surely sting, and I'm sorry for that, I pray you'll understand and write to me soon. And for my sake I suppose, and maybe yours too, please, Ethan, let's keep our letters our secret, at least for now. I'll continue to send my letters to your father's Lexington tavern, and you can mail yours to the hospital in Philadelphia. In the meantime, Ethan, remember how I feel about you, and even though many miles separate us, know my heart reaches for you. I miss you. Love, Andrea."

I creased the parchment and sealed my letter with a drip of candle wax and tender kiss, and after secretly mailing it during my nursing duties at the hospital early the coming morning, began my tortuous wait for a reply. May slowly passed and spring surrendered to summer without a letter from Ethan, and when I turned twenty on the Third of July, I began to nervously wonder if I'd ever hear from him again. Distressing visions were soon swirling my mind as those warm summer days drifted to the hot August haze, fears that I had crushed Ethan with the truth of my letter. I was gripped with despair that my honesty had doused the embers of our flame, and was fraught with thoughts that maybe he shuttered his heart with feelings of being rejected or betrayed. No matter what I was doing those weeks and months of anguishing wait, whether scampering among patients at the hospital or scurrying about Philadelphia with Franz, or home with mother and father, my thoughts of Ethan were consuming, and every moment I depressingly wondered if I had destroyed our beauty before it could truly bloom.

Soon a confusing sense of sorrow began to creep into my soul, a painful revelation of my own selfish plight, unfounded doubts that Ethan had never really felt for me as I did for him. At times I'd drift with emotions which seemed unstable, somber thoughts that gripped my heart each hour of each night, squeezing each beat from dusk to dawn. And I'd wonder if others knew, if mother and father somehow sensed the unhappiness wrapping me, and feared that Franz might discover my secret, yet no one unveiled the truth. Perhaps they were unable or unwilling to search for the real me, or maybe I had become so good at hiding my true emotions, of stashing my passions into that corner deep in my heart, that no one could possibly see.

I missed Ethan terribly, the softness in his eyes and gentleness of his words, and fearing I might never see him again, never feel his sensuous touch or his tender lips pressing mine, could sense desperation beginning to take hold. Then as if by magic or the mercy of angels, on a muggy summer day I was whisked from my sorrows, could taste the sweet scents sprouting distant meadows once again as my soul soared and heart beat wildly. I can still smell the river wafting through the open panes of the hospital windows, and feel the sticky Philadelphia air drifting the rooms and halls that late Thursday of August, 1770. I had just finished my early nursing duties a bit before noon, and as I stepped near the hospital door and down the hall to my little nursing desk nestled to the wall, I could see the creased parchment resting the center of my desk, its tan folds sealed with a waxy kiss.

For a desperate moment I wondered if it was what I had been waiting for, then my eyes fixed upon "Buckman Tavern, Lexington" scrawled to the upper left corner, and my heart fluttered wildly. At that moment it was as if the numbing haze that had shrouded me all those weeks suddenly vanished with mystical winds, for I knew the parchment had been touched and folded by Ethan, was a letter from the north, a gift from heaven. I rushed to my desk and nestled to the oak slats of my chair, and as arousing anticipation surged within, just gazed to his letter for a moment or two. And with a relieving sigh, I pinched the parchment and anxiously flicked open its seal, then unfolded five sheets quilled with sweet words from my Ethan.

"Dear Andrea," he tenderly began, just two little words that mercifully vanquished the fears which had taunted me since spring, "You've been on my mind all these weeks, and now more than ever, each thought of you warms my heart." I could feel the joy unleashed deep inside as a tear trickled my cheek, and could sense happiness wrapping my heart with each rapturous beat.

"Please forgive me, Andrea, for staying silent all these weeks. Your letter struck me hard, and for a long time I struggled to cope, found it difficult to accept. I guess I slipped into a kind of gloomy, melancholy haze for a little while, and maybe even felt sorry for myself, a rather pitiful state. I discovered some unflattering traits about myself too, things like misplaced anger and ugly jealousy, dreary feelings that spurred suspicious dreams. Then while helping dad in the tavern and strolling about the grass of our Lexington field, I began to understand things more clearly, began to see what was truly important in life. And one day while lying with mom on her Lexington hill, I began to realize the beauty of your letter, began to see the honesty that bathes your soul.

"Maybe it was your compassion that helped me see that I don't have control of what happens to others in life, that the only true powers I have are over me, and even that at times, can be daunting. But more importantly, over these many summer weeks I've come to realize how much you mean to me, bubbling emotions that cry for you as if I had been struck by a mystical bolt from the heavens that March night. The panes of my heart have swung wide, Andrea, and my passions for you are oozing.

"After searching for answers deep inside for several weeks, I finally understood the nature of your life, found a way to feel the true situation that entwines you in Philadelphia and Germantown. It was your compassion and honesty, Andrea, that led me to that relieving place, and for that I'm truly grateful. I too believe you and I should be truthful with each other, about our desires, lives and dreams, for without such, we'd never survive. You helped me see that what's important is how we feel about each other, not how much we control. I need you, Andrea, and want to be with you in any way, sharing our passions and thoughts with words. And when we can, we'll find wondrous moments together, if only for a little while. We don't know what the future holds, nobody can, yet I sense ours is filled with happiness and hope."

For a few hushing moments I reread those lines several times, captured by the depth of his feelings while sensing his passions with each stroke, and I could feel my heart reaching for his, as if upon a sea drifting to his shore, and wanted more. And with each thrilling word I realized how special Ethan truly was, for he was seeking my forgiveness, when it was I who needed to be forgiven. Then sliding my fingertips across the lines of that first sheet I began to feel the pressures of my distressing situation, and wondered of the dangers that lurked in the waters for both of us. What of the pain that could be cast upon the innocent I wondered, should our secret be exposed before mother and father, and most disturbingly, Franz? Oh how I desperately wanted to keep such things from becoming real.

As I grappled with those twisting thoughts I came to understand that denying my true feelings would simply embolden my limitations, and realized it was becoming impossible for me to keep my distance from Ethan. I guess I finally knew I couldn't just stuff my emotions into a French bottle and toss them into the sea to aimlessly drift the rest of my life, and that my feelings for Ethan were as his were for me, knew I too desired us so. Yet I wondered if all we'd ever have were words quilled to parchment sheets, wondered if we'd ever see each other again, even if only for a few sweet hours or sensuous day. As I dabbed a tear and read those alluring lines once again, I somehow knew what I felt for Ethan would caress me throughout my life, knew our passions for each other would never wither and die.

I don't think I had ever really understood until that moment what notions of absolute love truly entailed, not the deeply passionate kind that flames deep inside, and realized that I had never felt such things with Franz, and never would. Was the intense passion erupting deep inside for Ethan that true thing, I wondered? I didn't really know the answers in those early days, and perhaps if I had I might have denied such a thing, for to admit so, to quill or whisper such things, could cause pain in lives. Although my heart was flaring wildly that moment, my mind was able to damp those flames with splashes of logic, and as I slid my fingers across Ethan's words, I knew my passions would need to stay stashed deep inside, until such time God deemed it right.

As I slowly read the rest of Ethan's letter, sheets sprinkled with passionate words and comforting truths which soothed my heart, he began to slide from intimate thoughts to troubling things brewing in Boston and Massachusetts Bay, and simmering about all the colonies. And with each intriguing line I came to realize he was exposing his soul to me, not only revealing how much I meant to him, but his humanity, expressing his desires, fears and frailties.

He confided how he had struggled for months since that bloody March night about his true feelings, not only pondering the fate of those five brave men but wondering what he should do in response to the dastardly deed of the king's soldiers. "I've always thought myself to be somewhat passive, Andrea," he gently confessed, "dousing anger by reading words of others or just thinking for hours, or maybe expressing my troubles with lines of poetry. Perhaps I don't quite understand the truth of such terrible things, maybe I'm still a bit too young, but I find myself wanting to retaliate with empathy and kindness, things I suppose are lacking in our changing world. For so long I've believed that we need more compassion, not a compulsion toward violent acts which simply spur tensions, notions I could sense slowly dwindling inside."

Then Ethan revealed he was becoming more confused as the weeks of spring begot summer, admitting that although he had been holding onto the ideas shrouding kindness, the memory of Mr. Attucks and all the others lying bloodied and dying on the snowy cobblestones that wintry night had truly jolted his core. "It was as if I was compelled," he reluctantly quilled, "to fully reexamine just what type of lives we truly have here in the colonies." And shortly before the close of his Harvard studies for the weeks of summer, visions of those horrid killings and reports of unjust events continuing about the colonies instilled a sense of clarity to his swirling thoughts, helping him make a pivotal decision.

"Freedom, Andrea," Ethan passionately added, "is of the most precious of things, something some are saying that only our Creator can provide, not some Tory committee or royal governor, not parliament across the sea, and certainly not the king. I've come to believe like a growing number of others, that no monarch or group of men should have the power to give or take freedom, that such a right is fundamental for every woman, child and man. And maybe, Andrea, should God deem it so, we colonists may need to till the soil for sprouting such things.

"It was those things, Andrea, spurred by the courage of Crispus and the others that night, which propelled me to begin taking an active part in the sons of liberty. I joined Henry's group in Boston on the final Saturday of May, as zillions of stars twinkled upon the common, and a few weeks later became a full-fledged member of our Lexington group, accepted in June by dad, Mr. Giles and a dozen others in the tavern. Henry invited me to the common shortly after dusk that brisk night, to a big gathering near the port's liberty tree, and we listened to James Bowdoin snap an inspiring speech from atop a crate hauled from the docks. I had never seen him before, but his words were fiery, Andrea, declaring the need for 'colonial unity to resist the bloody intrusions of Governor Hutchinson, parliament and the king.' He insisted Whig colonists must 'band as a single patriot force' to express their disgust at the killings on King Street that awful night, and bond as one to oppose London's encroaching tyranny.

"His emphatic appeals and determined stance inspired me that night, dousing my fears with notions of colonial unity, and as Henry, I and scores of others watched Mr. Bowdoin flail his arms with each pleading cry, I came to realize that the moment had come for me to finally take an outward stand. In an eerie way, Andrea, it was time for me help carry on for those five brave souls killed that bloody March night, accepting some responsibility, in my own little way, for our freedom. That's when I whispered my pledge, and became a true member of the sons."

As I read those determined lines, my stomach began to twist and churn with concerns of what such devotion might truly mean, not just for all the colonies but for my Ethan, and I worried he could become involved, surely in an unwitting way, with sons more inclined to delve into questionable deeds. After all, many of the troubling stories and rumors I'd heard over the past few years about segments of the sons were still fresh on my mind, of fiery events that exploded in villages and towns throughout the colonies, at the docks of the Island of Manhattan or along the river right here in Philadelphia, especially up in Ethan's Boston. But as I continued to read, his rational words began to ease my mind and calm my heart.

"I insisted and they agreed," he continued with words that dampened my fears, "that my role with the sons be less assertive and more passive, that my functions be what many might say, unexcitedly mundane. I'm to dwell in the areas of ideas, of expressing Whig visions and thoughts with words by helping to prepare printed opinions in Mr. Gill's Boston Gazette and County Journal. Someday, Andrea, in my own limited way, I might even help craft those views too, when they think the time is right. And now that I'm here in Lexington, between Harvard studies for the summer, I'll be doing those very things for Mr. Giles and his Lexington Gazette. For the coming weeks I'll be able to help expose the positions of the sons for all of Middlesex County to discuss and debate, just like the tradesmen, merchants and farmers sipping spirits in dad's tavern Saturday nights."

Even after all these years I can still feel the tingling sensation that raced my skin as I read Ethan's words, of the pride that surged my body knowing of his passion for the convictions of the sons and what patriot Whigs truly believed. And there was a warming comfort that deeply flowed during those moments, for now I truly knew how he and I felt about those spirited things, knew we had such similar intimate beliefs. We both supported the simmering cause in a quiet way, he with parchment and ink in the Colony of Massachusetts Bay and I snipping and stitching homespun things with Lydia and Betsy here in Pennsylvania.

"I just know the time is right," Ethan confessed, "for me to carry my weight. I can't simply watch anymore as events unfold, without doing my part for our patriot cause here in Massachusetts Bay. Maybe it's the least I can do, any of us can do, to honor the memory of those five brave souls. I hope you understand my reasons, and in your own way, support what we must do. I miss you, Andrea, and impatiently wait for your letter. Love, Ethan."

Oh yes, I understood his reasons more than he knew, and feeling that sense of pride surging once again, wanted to quill a letter as soon as I could. Then I shuffled the parchment to his letter's final page, a sheet that reflected some of the passionate things that attracted me to Ethan so. It was a little poem he had quilled for Crispus, Mr. Jafres and others who found themselves exposed to the ugliness of bigotry, stanzas spurred by what he had witnessed in his father's tavern that summer afternoon many months before. And he explained it had also been inspired by the odor of hypocrisy that wafted about some in the colonies now and then, things he'd see and hear from a few strolling about the cobblestones of Boston on Sundays, women and men who seemed to wrap within the cloth of faith while foundering in the waters of self.

"Some colonists profess kindness while in their Sunday pews," he quilled in an introductory way, "whether shopkeepers or doctors, wheelwrights, seamstresses or lawyers, even students of Harvard and loyalist Tories and patriot Whigs. Yet once beyond those steeple doors, Andrea, some expose unkind views hidden within. I've heard despicable things whispered about good men, hateful words about people who simply look different than they. But when some spewed mendacious things about Crispus this spring, I felt a burning compulsion to quill my disgust, expose the wickedness of such things." Then he added with a dash of frustration, "Although Mr. Gill thought of printing my poem in his Boston Gazette, he believed the moment was not right, that it might be unwise to stir the hornets from their nest. I call it *false faces*, Andrea, and hope it arouses your senses as it does mine."

> *spring rains gently shower steeples, cleanse spires rising our land*
> *worshiping knees, forgo our trespasses, scriptures gripped in hands*
> *faithful pews filled, preachers dripping dark robes, women in song*
> *whispers of kindness and peace, our righteous lord, holiness drawn*
>
> *colonists shuffle among fading chimes, beyond tales, sculptured glass*
> *a few spew vile views, masked by cries blessed are we, a chosen caste*
> *some gather for perusing lines, failing to see, struggle to understand*
> *bigotry dwells, opulence bewilders, blinded pleas twist souls of man*
>
> *dark colonists seek farms and homes, strive for happiness, to live free*
> *crispus once bound, unleashed from bloody chains, dreams of diversity*
> *men of dull minds, bright skin spout wickedly, jesting of negra bones*
> *misguided sputter god mendaciously, seek to banish them from homes*
>
> *intolerance wafts about the winds, stench swirling shadows exposed*
> *indulgence destroys humanity, strays some from the love jesus shows*
> *hearts bathed of virtuous intents, truth shrouded by hateful hypocrisy*
> *protect us from masks shielding perfidy, from treachery of false faces*

"Ethan has a way of turning a candle to rather dark things," snapped Samuel, interrupting my thoughts in a reflective tone, "perhaps on things few truly see, or maybe just want to hide. To me, that little poem is a bit depressing, yet in a strange way, appealing. I can sense his deep displeasure of those who show to be one thing, then act in a conflicting way, and see why he attracted you so."

"Yes, Samuel," I whispered, slowing my rock while gazing to the summer winds, "he did. I think Ethan really did have a delicate sense about many things, more so than most. I wish more colonists had felt as he, and those attitudes he exposed no longer existed, but I suppose such notions will just remain a wish. His words may have been quilled many years ago, Samuel, but I still hear talk like that from some of Germantown and Philadelphia, ugly whispers of those who look different. Why do such things remain so?"

"I wish I knew, grandma," Samuel softly replied while nudging his chair into an easy rock and glancing to my eyes. "Maybe someday things will be different, if more kindness is out there, like Ethan says. But I'm afraid it might be a fear that some will never be able to shed."

"What a nice thing to say about Ethan," I gently uttered, gazing to Samuel's eyes. "You know, Samuel, in a way you sound like Ethan. Maybe there's a poet lurking inside you, burrowing about, just waiting to burst free."

"Maybe there is, someday," he said, snapping his stare to all those leaves gently rustling in the warm summer breeze. "I've been thinking, grandma. If you don't want to tell me everything about Grandpa Franz and Ethan, rather delicate things of your life, then don't. Do I want to know it all, yes, but not at your expense. I don't want to impose, grandma, just want you to do what you feel is right."

I could feel my stomach anxiously churn as memories swirled amid emotion and reasoning, for I knew I had failed to truly grasp the longings gripping of my heart in those days. As I rocked and glanced to Samuel gazing to those distant trees, I remembered those lonesome summer and fall nights of 1770 and beyond, of the hours tossing about blankets and pillows with a tear trickling my cheek. I'd wonder of the two men now entwining my life while peering through panes into the dark, struggling during those hushing hours with what I should do. Then shortly before each dawn I'd subdue the passions beating my heart with logic chilling my mind, and once again stash my desires for Ethan deep inside.

Perhaps it was fear that tamed my struggles each night, or panic of causing pain to Franz, or in a strange way, a desire to protect Ethan. I suppose I was torn with frightening thoughts of change too, and with each tear I came to reluctantly understand I was choosing to sacrifice my passions to please those of Philadelphia and Germantown. I was a conflicted young woman in those days, with what I now see were unflattering reasons for choosing a man of station in my Colony of Pennsylvania while shunning my fiery passions for another far away in the Colony of Massachusetts Bay.

Those tears and fears have long since passed, and the girl beguiled by perception and innocence has greyed with fleeting memories of those years, yet I knew Samuel must hear it all, of his Grandfather Franz and Ethan, must come to understand what truly happened back then. And I suppose in a mysterious way, telling my story was the penance I owed to those two men, to all those of a generation that sacrificed so much, even myself, to patriots who've been resting all these years in the soil of colonial fields.

"It's alright, Samuel," I whispered, rocking easy as a wisp of warm wind gently kissed my cheeks. And while he quietly gazed to the tips of distant elms lazily swaying in the afternoon breeze, I slid my fingers back into the pocket of my summer dress and caressed the parchment of Ethan's poem. "I want you to know those things, want you to better understand your grandfather and me, and most of all, Ethan. You know, Samuel, the world has turned so many times since then, yet the realities of those days remain, and always will." As he pressed to the slats of his chair and pushed to a steady rock, I softly stroked the passions of Ethan's poem, and remembered.

I quilled my reply to Ethan within days, shortly after I began the third year of my nursing training at the hospital near the close of that August, 1770, then soon received another letter from Ethan. He quilled of printing shop things and about classes he'd just started that third year of his studies, even revealing a tidbit or two about Harvard's new president, Samuel Locke, all the while exposing his pleasing feelings for me. We exchanged a few rumors of troubling events happening about the colonies in those days too, Ethan explaining some things he'd seen or heard in Boston and Lexington, of tensions brewing in his Colony of Massachusetts Bay, and I quilling of stories I'd heard in Germantown and Philadelphia, of revelations printed in my Pennsylvania Gazette or Evening Post, and of how I missed him so.

We seemed to settle into that type of life in those days, when exchanging letters became our norm, when Ethan and I quilled of colonial things while exposing our brewing feelings. Yet when looking back, I think Ethan may have been more candid in his expressions about me, of us, and I may have been slightly reserved, shielding my passions just a bit, for an array of pressing reasons. With each new letter I could feel his understanding continue to grow of the struggle that swirled deep inside me, and with each compassionate word I could sense he was becoming increasingly sensitive of the realities that gripped my life. And seeing the sweet evolution of his letters, sensing how his patience calmed the anxious fears that always seemed to drape me, I could feel my heart gently nudging closer and closer to his soul.

I remember one such letter that arrived at the hospital on a Thursday in late November, several weeks after the Pennsylvania leaves had settled to their rest that fall, a letter which Ethan lovingly began, "My Dear Andrea. If you only knew how I long for you each night, how I miss you so." I can still feel the sensuous tingle that raced my body as I brushed my fingers across his words, and hear the chilling autumn winds gently whistling into the hospital halls from tiny fissures near windows, icy wisps that frosted panes and cooled my skin as I nestled at my nursing desk. A thin layer of snow had blanketed the cobblestones of Philadelphia by noon that day, dusting shops, steeples, docks and homes in soft white, and the hills and fields of Germantown, its fence posts, cottages and trees now sparkling bright, awaited in the cold for my return home near dusk that night.

"My feelings for you grow every hour of each day," he tenderly spilled with his quill, "so much so, that I find myself wondering what is happening to me. I don't really understand what's swirling inside me, Andrea, such emotional intensity, yet know my heart passionately pounds each night for you. Many months have passed since our wondrous March night, and we've exchanged so much of each other in many letters, and although we're closer now than ever, I lie in the quiet of night and wonder what will become of us. I ask myself, Andrea, when will we see each other again?"

I just stared at his honest words for a moment or two, feeling an anxious rumbling stirring deep inside, and read his innocent question over and over, words that had a profound effect upon me. Ethan's desires for us to meet again sparked the simmering embers striving to flare in my life, releasing so many feelings I protectively kept stashed deep in my heart. Yet as frightening as his arousing query was, it sent a fiery passion surging within, for I too had wondered such things many times, and searched for answers I had yet to find.

Ethan's alluring question had caused my thoughts to sail for several fanciful moments to a sensuous place oozing desires, and then his words began to quickly change, sliding from passions to colonial intrigues. He began to explain nuances of the trials in Boston for those nine soldiers who doused the lives of those five brave men months before, judicial proceedings which most of Philadelphia and Germantown were striving to know, drama swirling rumors and being revealed in our Evening Post and Pennsylvania Gazette. And he included a few columns snipped from Mr. Gill's Boston Gazette and Country Journal, which helped me understand what happened in that first trial of Captain Preston in late October. "It took place just off the cobblestones of King Street," he excitedly quilled, "not far from Mr. Gill's shop, the same room that will hear the coming trial for those eight redcoats who blasted their muskets that bloody night."

The parchment clips from the Country Journal revealed that John Adams had been assisted in Captain Preston's defense by young Boston lawyers named Auchmuty and Quincy, barristers who judiciously explained that the crown's captain never ordered his redcoats to fire. "Therefore," Mr. Adams was said to have spouted, "this dutiful soldier must be exonerated of guilt to the unfounded charges of murder in the unfortunate deaths of those five Boston men." And the crown's prosecution had been guided by another Quincy, a loyal Boston Tory named Sam, a friend of the royal governor who whimsically decreed the captain's defense to be "malicious humbug!" It was an accusing indictment repeated by Robert Paine in various legalese ways, a Boston barrister some suggested was assisting the prosecution at the behest of colonists seeking to tame the loyalist zeal of Sam Quincy.

It seems the captain supported his contention that he never told his men to fire by testifying that those eight redcoats "were upon the half cock and charged bayonets, and my giving the word 'fire' under those circumstances would prove me to be no officer." Then he nervously added that one of the soldiers had instinctively blasted his musket after a club struck his arm with a thunderous whack, and said that when he asked that soldier why he fired, the redcoat explained, "Had it been placed on my head, it most probably would have destroyed me." Aside from what Ethan described as the captain's persuasive testimony, Mr. Adams had also paraded a trio of witnesses before the crown's court, each distinctively repeating having heard Captain Preston shout "Don't fire!" to his men.

The Boston Gazette also revealed how the prosecutor Quincy countered Mr. Adams' impassioned defense with several witnesses of his own, each in various ways suggesting that the captain's recollections bordered on "fanciful nonsense." Yet it was the testimony of Danny Calef which perhaps supported such a notion the best, for after promising to speak the truth, he explained how he listened and watched the ugly rattle of musket fire on King Street. "I was standin just right of that redcoat line," he bluntly said, "watchin em pointin them muskets into the crowd, and heard that captain shout 'Fire!,' not once, but twice. I could see his sword shinin in the glow of the moon, and watched his lips movin each time he barked that order."

Ethan confided that he was in the courtroom during the final hours of the captain's trial, hushed with scores of others after classes on the final Tuesday of October. "That's when I discovered how intense Mr. Adams can truly be," he quilled, "and found his barrister style rather compelling. It was the words he chose, Andrea, and the legal phrases he strung so easily together in a powerful, hypnotic way, that were so impressive. And along with all the others watching and listening from the gallery, I could see how his emphatic summation captivated the jury. They weren't colonists from Boston, but twelve men from nearby villages and towns sitting in judgment of the captain's fate, merchants and farmers like Joe Mayo from Roxbury."

Then an hour or so after the barristers of prosecution and defense fell silent, that jury of Massachusetts Bay men, swayed by the persuasive oratory of Mr. Adams, declared that redcoat captain, "Not guilty." Ethan quilled that many in the courtroom were stunned, and in the days that followed he could hear professors and students at Harvard shockingly sputter "that dimwitted jury!" And when colonists stopped by Mr. Gill's print shop, patriot Whigs like Doc Warren, Mr. Revere and Henry, or gathered in taverns and shops of Boston and nearby villages such as Lexington, they could be heard grumbling that the captain's royal trial would "forever be shrouded by the unjust odor of treachery."

I remember how scattered reports of Captain Preston's trial were soon sweeping across the colonies in leather satchels of swift riders, and of wild rumors filtering into the shops and homes of Germantown and the halls of my hospital in Philadelphia, some tinged of confusion and others spewing angry contempt. There were theories by those struggling to understand soon being printed in pamphlets and papers in hundreds of ports, villages and towns throughout the colonies too, including what Ethan described as "Mr. Giles' personal renditions of that questionable verdict so eloquently espoused in his Lexington Gazette."

Ethan closed his final November letter as he always did, with tender words that made me feel so special and good, "Quill soon, Andrea, and remember, you're on my mind every moment of every day. Love, Ethan." Within days I stroked my reply, quilling of reports about that trial being printed in the Pennsylvania Evening Post and rumors swirling about Germantown and Philadelphia. And even though I tended to shy from dwelling too deeply into my feelings about us in those early days, I strayed and surrendered for a magical moment. "I miss you, Ethan, something I still find difficult to confess." Then in a surprising way, in a conflictingly confusing, perhaps uncontrollable way, I found myself addressing that arousing question. "I don't know when we'll meet again. But know this, Ethan, I think about that too, often every day, and wonder how, where and when. I passionately wait for your next letter. Love, Andrea."

Wintry flurries had gripped the northern colonies by the time I received another letter several weeks after Christmas, folded tan parchment with tiny spotty stains placed to my hospital nursing desk shortly after noon the second Friday of January, 1771. My eyes clamped upon those three thrilling words, "Buckman Tavern, Lexington," and sliding to the slats of my oak chair, I pinched the parchment in my fingertips as snowy flakes whisked past the frosting panes of the window in a nearby room. I glanced about the chilly hall to ensure I was alone, raising Ethan's letter to my tingling lips, then lowered his folded sheets to my lap, flicked its waxy seal, and began to read. "Dear Andrea," he sweetly began, "I hope my words find you happy. Oh, how I've missed you so."

Ethan explained he was once again back in Lexington with his father at the tavern, having arrived shortly before Christmas, and would stay into the first few weeks of the new year, during the wintry break of his Harvard studies. And although his quill seemed to stroke notions of contentment, at times his words seemed brushed with a tinge of loneliness. "I've missed dad, Andrea, more so than ever before, and it feels so good to be home, helping dad in the tavern and sleeping in my old bed. I was starting to forget how peaceful Lexington truly is, how a hush settles upon the village each night. Sometimes, Andrea, I wonder how I will survive over another year at Harvard. There's just so much commotion swirling Boston these days, a bustling amid cobblestones, warehouses, wharfs and shops that seems to drift the night."

Uneasiness began to surge within while reading his worrisome words, wrapping my vulnerabilities with an anguishing twist, then Ethan suddenly tamed his tone in a way that seemed intended to calm me, as if he could sense how his words might affect me so. "I suppose I sound a bit disgruntled, Andrea, but please, don't worry. I'm just releasing some of my pent frustrations, that's all. I'll be alright, truly I will. I'll just keep doing what I must at Harvard, studying hard, and continue learning new things in my duties at the print shop. I guess the real truth is that I feel I can expose things to you, Andrea, share my feelings about anything, and know you'll listen, know you care."

Then as if he dipped his quill into a tin of gracious ink, his words began to stroke feelings and visions of serenity. "The snows blanketing the hills and dusting the trees is beautiful. From my bedroom panes I can see crystals shining bright on rooftops from the glow of a midnight moon, and watch lamps and candles glisten against frosting windows of cottages and homes across the snows of the village field. And the wonderful smells, Andrea, are alluring, the enticing odors of baking breads, pies and treats filtering from windows, the smell of dad's special stew simmering over a fire down in the kitchen hearth, and the aroma of spirits, ales and wines wafting about the tavern, soothes me. Maybe, in an aging way, I'm beginning to understand the folly of youth, and coming to realize the powerful emotions which entwine me to Lexington. Oh, Andrea, how I do miss this place so."

I could sense Ethan's passions with each stroke of his quill, and soon he began to slide toward feelings of his mother, a tranquil place I knew he loved to dwell, and could feel being pulled closer to him. "As good as it felt to be home, in the tavern with dad and so many comfortable things, perhaps what draws me back to Lexington the most, is knowing I'll be nearer mom. I miss her, and just being closer makes me feel good, as if she's wrapping me in one of her blankets again. I feel safe, and in a serene way, truly home. It's strange, Andrea, but no matter what I do each day that I'm here, regardless of darkness, snow or chill, sooner or later I find myself with mom on her hill, feeling her warmth while whispering longing things to the winds."

He confided about one of those moments up on her hill the day after Christmas when he turned twenty, a night which began with a birthday supper specially prepared in the tavern by his father. "Nathan Giles was there too," Ethan quilled, "for a bowl of fowl and beet stew and a few cups of rum, and so was Reverend Clarke and Mr. Parker, for some rye whiskey, and all wishing me the best." They talked with Ethan about his Harvard studies and discussed troubling colonial things with his father, and after finishing several mugs of birthday ale, his bowl of stew and crusted roll too, Ethan felt the tug of his heart toward the slopes of that burying ground hill. "I felt compelled toward that sacred place, Andrea, and thanking dad and the others, rushed out the tavern door into the chill." The Lexington air was briskly cold that December night, with mist billowed with each breath as Ethan trudged up the hill, then he dropped to his knees beneath the wintry moon upon the snow of his mother's grave.

I've always believed that what Ethan quilled next was such a reflection of his tender soul, sentiments which to this day still move me so, passionate words, which in a spiritual way, exposed the simmering emotions swirling inside him, a place from whence his poetry surely flowed. "A soft crystal sheet had settled upon the grass of mom's resting place, and the top edge of her stone was sparkling with a dust of white. I bowed for a solemn moment or two, whispering a few wishing words to the snows, then glanced to her stone and gazed to the symphony of pulsating stars. I just peered into the night with thoughts of you, Andrea, and pondered the many things I wanted to say to mom, wondering of my life."

He quilled how he missed his mother, perhaps more so on that special night, and how he thought of the many things they had talked about while alone on the farm when his father was away during that frontier war years before. "As I gazed into the quiet of the night, toward a place where memories are stored, I began to whisper to mom as if she were lying on the snows beside me. I told her things about my life in Boston, of my Harvard studies, but most of all, Andrea, I whispered of you, of how much I feel for you, how I love you. This might sound strange, but in a spiritual way, I could sense she fondly approved of you, of us, and wants you in my life."

My heart was madly pounding as I reread his words, "I love you," and my imagination sailed north with the wintry winds to Massachusetts Bay and those arousing hours with Ethan, to that enchanting Boston night a year before. I knew the feelings warming my soul were bathed with similar emotions, yet couldn't find the courage to speak or quill those three frightening words, at least not as of that winter of 1771. Confusion swirled my mind for several moments as I slid my fingers across the ink of Ethan's tender line, all the while I could feel the twisting struggle that had consumed me all those months, fears of setting my passions free. I knew I couldn't release my desires, had coldly convinced myself I mustn't, at least not then, not completely.

Then slowly, Ethan pivoted his thoughts from his mother and me, from memories, passions and desires to tensions and troubles brewing not only around Boston but in villages and towns throughout the colonies, in ports such as Charles Towne, New York and Savannah. Yet he mostly dwelled upon that second trial up in Boston for those eight soldiers who fired their muskets that March night, a judicial reckoning that seemed to have captured the imagination of colonists everywhere. Although I already knew some things about that trial from rumors that had swept into Philadelphia in the days before Christmas and sporadic reports printed in the Evening Post, Ethan's reflections were insightful. Doctors, patients and nurses were talking about it at the Pennsylvania Hospital too, and father would sputter with Quaker friends at our Germantown meeting house and Franz with merchants along the Delaware River docks. Women, children and men in all the colonies had become wrapped in its royal legalese and defiance, children during play at school and loyal Tories and patriot Whigs in village churches, taverns and shops.

I remember that the jury for that second trial had been assembled in a way much like the first, a dozen colonial men from villages and towns near Boston, and that the barristers remained the same for the king and those defending his soldiers. It lasted some three weeks too, coming to a close soon after Mr. Adams' final defensive words on a cold Friday afternoon, the Fourteenth of December. And although vague rumors had filtered about the colonies of the identity of those eight redcoat men, most brushed with vicious contempt, Ethan revealed their true names as exposed by Mr. Gill in his Boston Gazette. Perhaps the youngest was Corporal Billy Weems, followed closely by privates McCauley, Warren and Penny, Killroy, Montgomery, Stevens and White, royal soldiers some colonists could be heard vengefully whispering, should be hanged.

Ethan revealed that Mr. Gill and Ben Edes had been in the courtroom on many days of that trial, and on several occasions had printed in their Boston Gazette that those eight soldiers were "attempting to deceive the good citizens of Boston, pleading that they blasted their muskets without a whiff of spite." And they reported that Mr. Adams had supported such claims while admonishing the court, "These loyal soldiers cannot be guilty of the heinous crime of murder, for each fired his weapon in defense of self. By any norms cherished by civilized people, surely, gentlemen of this honorable court, every man has the right to protect his life!"

Mr. Adams was said to have paraded a slew of witnesses before the court too, Bostonians like Jimmy Bailey, a maker of ropes who had been standing near the statehouse as the colonists surged toward the soldiers on the cobblestones of King Street that chilling night. "I'm sorry to say," he hesitantly declared while glancing now and then to jurors' eyes, "but they were a brawling band of unruly people, a rabble spewing taunting things. I just watched as many pelted those young scared soldiers with bits of coal and chunky balls of ice and snow, and remember seeing a big Negro man angrily hurl a knotty stick at that redcoat line. It struck who I learned was Private Montgomery, knocking him to the stones with a mighty blow."

Ethan also quilled about something barristers of Boston were saying was questionable testimony being presented to the court by Mr. Adams and his team in defense of the king's soldiers, candid recollections by a colonial surgeon. "Charles Wilson was the doctor tending to Patrick Carr," Ethan carefully explained, "that poor soul from Ireland who was the last of the five to succumb to his musket wound. Mr. Gill said it was being described as a dying declaration, a concept some believed would taint the judgment of the jury by forging a dangerous exception to the legal notion of hearsay."

The Boston Gazette had revealed most of Doc Wilson's testimony, reporting how he told the court, "Shortly before Mr. Carr's unfortunate demise, he whispered to me in a struggling wheeze, 'I am a native of Ireland. Too often I witnessed mobs and the crown's soldiers called to quell them, at times firing their muskets. But never did I see soldiers bear half as much before they fired, as those redcoats did on King Street.'" Then spurred by Mr. Adams to enlighten the court, he summed his story by revealing, "Mr. Carr, gasping for breath, told me he forgave the soldier who fired upon him, saying, 'He could not have borne me malice, but fired to defend himself.'"

One of the prosecuting lawyers was reported to have leapt from his chair to disclaim such a defensive tactic, then presented a string of witnesses to dispute what he scornfully described as the good doctor's fanciful memories. "Private Killroy would never miss a chance to fire on a Bostonian," Sam Hemmingway declared to the court, an aging seamstress with a shop by the ferry near Copp's Hill. "To me, he had always wanted such an opportunity, ever since he strutted into our port from one of the king's bloody warships."

As I read Ethan's letter I could sense how he seemed rather intrigued with that second trial, and in an emotional way I understood why, for it was about something that happened the night we met. And even though it was an awful event, it was something that brought us together, drew us to Aunt Bea's fire that night. I suppose it was a trial that not only impacted the colonists of Boston, but would rumble with consequences through ports, villages and towns in all the colonies. "By the end, Andrea," Ethan continued with his quill, "Mr. Adams had presented some forty witnesses to convince the court that the king's eight soldiers had fired their muskets in self-defense. And Mr. Edes said his closing summation seemed to impress the twelve men of the jury, and I heard Doc Warren say that Mr. Adams' final words were mesmerizingly brilliant."

One of the snipped slices from the Boston Gazette that Ethan had folded with his letter included many of the phrases Mr. Adams had bellowed to the court in its closing moments, gripping words intended to save those soldiers. "If an assault was made to endanger their lives," he passionately said, "the law is clear, they had a right to kill in their own defense. If it was not so severe as to endanger their lives, yet if they were assaulted at all, struck by blows of any sort from clumps of ice or balls of snow, oyster shells, cinders or sticks, it was a provocation. For such, the law reduces the offence of killing down to manslaughter, in consideration of those passions in our nature."

It seems Mr. Adams also reminded the hushed jury about the colonists they had heard bear witness to the "menacing mob that taunted and surged toward those eight young soldiers who were simply doing their duty for the crown." And while the jury was grasping each word being spewed in defense of the king's men, he rattled off a few intriguing queries for those twelve to ponder. "It was in the power of those sailors and men to kill one half or whole of the king's party, if they had been so disposed. What had the soldiers to expect when persons armed with clubs were daring enough, even at the time when they were loading their guns, to come up with their clubs and smite on their guns? What had eight soldiers to expect from such a set of people? Would it have been a prudent resolution in them, or in any body in their situation, to have stood still, to see if those men would knock their brains out or not?"

Ethan quilled that the conclusion of the jury "stunned a lot of colonists in Boston," even filling scores of women and men with "anger and spite," yet I could sense in his words that in an enlightening way, he understood the justness of their verdict. I suppose in truth I did too. I mean, after all, he and I had been there that night, watched those frightened young soldiers being unruly confronted by so many fiery colonists, Bostonians I now understand were spurred by righteous reasons. Yet Mr. Gill suggested in his Boston Gazette, "The jury, in its misguided perception of justice, declared six of the king's men innocent of all charges, while finding that just two of those bloody redcoats were guilty. But alas those of Boston, of all the colonies, they are not guilty of murder so say those jurors, but of simply killing our five brave men without malice."

Mr. Adams had held true to his belief that the accused have a fundamental right to a meaningful defense, even when providing such might unleash the wrath of colonists who disagree, and at the hour of sentencing, appealed for the court to show leniency. "Those two killing soldiers," spouted the Boston Gazette, "redcoats Montgomery and Killroy, were shown mercy by the court, each being allowed to wrap themselves about the crown's benefit of clergy." Ethan quilled they were thus shielded from imprisonment or death, and after the court branded each man's right thumb with a tiny crimson seal of the crown, those two loyal soldiers were summarily released.

Ethan explained how some in Boston and in villages and towns throughout the Colony of Massachusetts Bay, in his Lexington too, seemed quietly consigned to the jury's verdicts and the court's display of leniency, while loyal Tories were rather pleased. "But others," he confessed near the close of his letter, "many patriot Whigs and members of the sons, were fit to be twined. Some in Mr. Gills' print shop and others in the halls of Harvard have been voicing troubling concerns that Boston had shown a disgusting sense of appeasement toward London, a view sure to sweep the colonies. I wonder just what kind of legacy that verdict will truly have on thousands of colonists, oh, not only up here, but everywhere. Write to me soon, Andrea, and remember, you are always on my mind. Love, Ethan."

Even after all these years, I can still see Ethan's letter pinched in my fingers and feel the sensuous tingles that surged my body back then. Sometimes it feels like those Boston trials took place only yesterday, that those verdicts had just been rushed about the colonies in the satchels of swift riders, and sometimes I wonder how such things could have happened over fifty years ago. Most loyal Tories thought those verdicts righteous while many patriot Whigs vehemently disagreed, and some colonists continued to show indifference to it all, colonists like mother, father and Franz. Some said civility had triumphed that fall, a view Ethan struggled to accept and I tried to believe, for we were young colonists who hoped justice had prevailed, yet had witnessed the truth of it all.

Although the trials for that bloody massacre on King Street had begun to fade as 1771 began, and the bulk of those Townshend Acts had been repealed, tensions between the colonies and London continued to fester while thousands of redcoat troops remained quartered on that Boston island and continued to roam ports like Charles Towne, New York and Savannah. And even though frictions sporadically flared about the colonies from time to time, most women and men simply carried on with their lives, loyal Tories and patriot Whigs and those indifferent, tradesmen, doctors and seamstresses, lawyers, merchants and wheelwrights, and farmers toiling their fields and tavern men like Ethan's father pouring ale, wine, rye whisky and rum while simmering tasty stews. Ethan continued his Harvard studies and printing duties that winter and spring too, and I carried on with my nursing training and patients at the hospital, all the while we continued to exchange letters strewn with colonial things and words bathed of passions.

I quilled a letter right back to Ethan that very Friday of January, stroking my words at my nursing desk shortly before dusk that wintry afternoon, then sealing the folded parchment with a kiss and drip of candle wax, dropped it into the little pine box near the hospital door for mailing the coming morn. Only this time, I had once again quilled some lines I feared might cause Ethan pain, if only for a little while, something that happened that I knew he must be told. I believed in our views of honesty, and that if he felt for me as he had quilled so many times, then his heart would continue to hold me. "Dear Ethan," I nervously began, "As you read this letter please know that my feelings for you remain the same, deep and real."

In a feeble way I suppose, I eased into the fray by beginning with harmless words, mundane tales of simple life with mother and father, of nursing at the hospital and sewing homespun things with Lydia and Betsy some Sunday nights. Yet with each delaying word a fretful gloom was spritzing deep inside amidst a frantic desire to passionately wrap Ethan in my arms, for I knew what I was about to quill would painfully expose the complexities of my life.

I still believed that without honesty there could never be real understanding or the truest passion between us, a truth I was determined to reveal with caring tenderness, and maybe, in a selfish way, I wanted Ethan to understand the real me. He had once quilled that without honesty we'd never survive, and without open hearts we'd never feel the true passion of absolute love. I too believed those things and clung tightly to his visions of us, to his words that brought comfort to my soul and wisdom to baseless fears that roamed my heart.

"Before I drift to sleep each night," I continued, slowly pivoting my words with each stroke of my quill, "my thoughts are consumed of you, all the while my heart struggles mightily with my mind. The pressures and expectations with Franz tug me one way, Ethan, while the fires of my heart reach for you, and sometimes, the realities of my life overwhelm me, causing tears to drip to my pillows. At times I think I have two lives, one tender with you and one more frigid with Franz, as if my heart has two rooms, one oozing warm passions while the other seeps an uneasy etiquette. I have an unflattering ability to latch one door tight and creak the other open, and sometimes, I'm awash with fright, yet don't want to let you go. Oh, how I miss you so."

I could feel the guilt surging inside with each word as I desperately tried to avoid the disturbing realties about to unfold, yet I knew the moment had come for that anguishing truth to flow. "There's something I must tell you, and pray you'll understand, not think too harshly of me. A few weeks ago Franz asked me to marry him. Oh, Ethan, the expectations I feel can be so heavy, not only from Franz, but mother and father, from our Quaker faith, gripping pressures that seem to constantly nudge me toward him.

"I'm sorry, Ethan, but this is just the truth of my life in Pennsylvania, and there's more. I've been forbidden by mother and father to marry outside our faith, a position they've instilled in me for years. And mother has whispered many times how she and father hope I'll wed Franz, insisting his faith and position in Philadelphia society are what they see as best for me. She's always saying how he can provide so many things for me, just as Franz too has told me many times. Sometimes I feel confused, and wonder if perhaps they're right, that my life truly belongs here in Philadelphia, near mother and father, with Franz. Oh, Ethan, sometimes I want to scream, and in an anguishing way, wonder during the quiet hours of night whether I too desire those things, not just for me, but for my children. I fear I lack the courage to resist their wishes, and wonder if I'm brave enough to survive without the blessing of our Quaker faith, without the acceptance of mother and father."

Then sensing Ethan's tenderness and gloom sure to grip his soul while grappling with the truth of my words, I desperately wanted to calm him. "I told him no," I quickly quilled, "told Franz I would not marry him, at least for now. But I must be honest, and confess there might come a day when my mind prevails, when those unflattering needs I feel at times say yes. Oh, not because my passions for you would somehow dwindle, but because I've surrendered to the expectations tugging inside, to the pressures wrapping me all the time. Sometimes I just don't know, don't understand myself, and pray that God will show me the way. Yet no matter what, Ethan, my heart always reaches north for you.

"Please remember that I haven't said a word to anyone about us, especially to Franz, and plan never to do. You and I, we, are our secret, at least for now. I just told Franz I wasn't prepared to marry, that I needed to finish my nursing training before thinking of wedding anyone. Maybe, I just felt too young. He sputtered a few disappointing words, even becoming frustrated for an angry moment or two, then insisted he would ask again when the season was right. I'm sorry, Ethan, but we're still seeing each other, and as difficult as this must be for you, know that it's confusing, anguishing for me, and I don't know when things will change. Sometimes, in a mysterious, fateful way, I feel like my life is shackled to Philadelphia, at least for now, and maybe, forever. I just don't know."

As I dipped my quill a final time, that enticing notion Ethan proposed weeks before began to once again swirl my mind, that alluring question of whether, how and when we'd see each other again. I could feel my heart pounding wildly, in a frighteningly anxious, rather excited way, and wondered of how perplexing I must seem to Ethan, a puzzling bewilderment churning inside. Yet I also knew that no matter how entwined my life was becoming with Germantown, Philadelphia and Franz, a life wrapped by conflicting emotions and pressuring expectations, my desires for Ethan would continue to burn deep in my heart, flames I was coming to understand, could never be doused.

"Maybe, we've got to just let life naturally flow, like a stream," I continued with a stroke of reasoning, "leave our fate in our Creator's hands, let things unfold in their proper time, as God deems fit. But know,

Ethan, my wish is for us to meet again, I just don't know where, how or when. I miss you, and anxiously await your next letter. Love, Andrea."

Soon a month had passed without a letter from Ethan, then two, all the while an agonizing fear was wrapping my insides that once again I had hurt him, maybe even destroyed the intimacy we were discovering with our words. For weeks I feigned a semblance of emotional normalcy, tending to my nursing duties at the hospital, mingling with colonists in Germantown and living with mother and father, and seeing Franz in Philadelphia as winter snows trickled to spring. But each morning my heart cried to know what Ethan was thinking and feeling, and each night I'd dream of his sensuous touch and pray for his return. And I wondered every anguishing day, if my honesty had forever pushed Ethan away.

When with Franz, I had discovered a way to stash my fears into lonely recesses of my mind, giving an impression that my life was calm and properly flowing, as if I hadn't a trouble of any sort in our crafted world. I was honing an essential talent of masking my innermost feelings, of hiding the truth of my passions in a dark secret place, and found myself uttering deceiving words in hopes of allaying Franz's desires. I'd magically summon threads of emotions and surrender those to him, all the while wondering if he sensed the truth gnawing within. And when he'd ask of my concerns now and then, inquire how I felt about us, I'd reach for the logic that dwelled inside and assure him everything is alright. He seemed to accept my drab expressions brushed with rational words, yet I suppose, I'll never truly know.

Then after waiting all those tormenting hours, days and weeks, and just before riding back to Germantown at the end of my nursing duties on a rainy spring day in April of 1771, a letter from Ethan finally came. I can still hear the drops tapping the leaves of oak and elm that cool Wednesday afternoon, see the water dripping the panes and splashing the windowsills, and feel the excitement surging within as I rushed down the hall to the parchment quietly folded on my nursing desk. "Boston, Colony of Massachusetts Bay," was stroked to its upper left, with "Andrea Van Dijk," quilled below in smudging ink, "Nurse Trainee, Pennsylvania Hospital, Philadelphia."

My heart was racing wildly as I dashed to the slats of my chair, thumping as if it might leap from my chest, and I could feel the joy madly rushing through my body. Then pinching the parchment in my fingertips and envisioning unfolding Ethan's letter, a chilling fear of rejection gripped my soul. What if these are his final words, I desperately wondered, and my agonizing thoughts all these weeks were not delusional follies but devastating premonitions? I wondered of the lines quilled inside as I pinched those folded sheets, and whispered a pleading prayer they were from his heart, not his mind. Then closing my eyes for a moment or two, hoping and wishing, I breathed some calming spring air, snapped its waxy seal, and began to read.

"Dear Andrea," he tenderly began. "I struggled for many weeks with what to do after getting your letter, and every minute of each day, I've missed you so. I wasn't sure if I should or could write back, or whether it was even proper to do so. There was a battle going on inside me, Andrea, with my mind shouting it would be best for you if I removed myself from your life, while my heart cried to be near you. An ugly guilt began to grip me too, sad notions that I was a source of trouble for you, that because of me, your life in Pennsylvania was even more stressful. Yet, as unsettling as those things were, I'd recall the honesty of your caring words and our first wondrous hours before that fire, and could feel my heart reaching for you each night."

I dabbed my eyes and brushed a tear trickling my cheek, and as the spring rains tapped the leaves and danced the sills, I breathed a sigh of relief, glanced about the hall and continued to read Ethan's words. "Many times I wanted to write, Andrea, tried to at the little desk of my Boston room many nights, and would even have the quill pinched in my fingers. Then all those twisting thoughts would overwhelm me, and I'd slide my quill into its cup and wonder why our lives have to be so. Sometimes, I'd battle ugly visions of you and Franz too, and find myself sinking into a selfish, melancholy place. And I'd struggle to refute the painful notions that perhaps your mother and father were right, wonder if it were true that you belonged in Philadelphia. I didn't want to, but I'd wonder if your life would indeed be best, if twined to a merchant like Franz."

I remember how startled I was that Ethan's words eerily conveyed so many feelings I too was grappling with, sentiments which pulled me even closer to him, and as I gazed to his lines, I realized I understood his struggles, doubts and fears. "Then I recalled something mom whispered to me on the farm a long time ago," he reflectively quilled, "while we bundled near the fire on one of those wintry nights when dad was away at the frontier. 'Life will not always be easy,' mom sighed as flames flickered and snapped, 'and sometimes, Ethan, we become confused. When you find yourself struggling, searching for answers, try to hear the whispers warming your heart. It might be difficult to do, and some might even disapprove, but listen to its song, and find the courage to pursue your dream.'

"I knew right then, Andrea, that mom was right. No matter what hardships may come, what troubles or unkind words, I know my path leads to you. I want to be in your life, somehow, anyway I can, and hope you feel the same too. I love you, Andrea, and circumstances and distances will never change that. Quill to me soon. Love, Ethan."

Joy surged my body as I pinched the parchment and reread Ethan's affections several times, and although I now realized our path would not come easy, understood the expectations and pressures of mother, father and Franz, the magic of Ethan's tenderness had touched me in a way no other man possibly could. I folded his letter to its weathered creases and pressed my lips to the parchment, and as my skin tingled, placed it safely with all the others in the lower right drawer of my nursing desk. The truth of my life was that Ethan was on my mind every day and through the night, even when pressed in Franz's arms, and although I wasn't sure, I wondered if what I felt were the passions of absolute love.

Yet my mind would unsettling shout "no!" from time to time, for to admit such feelings would cause danger to hover my Pennsylvania life, all the while the flames flaring my heart would cry "yes, oh yes!" Maybe I had come to accept the numbing contentment that seemed to wrap me in those days, protection from hateful scalds or frightful banishment, or maybe I understood my dismal struggle for courage, and had come to accept the limitations imposed on my life. Nevertheless, amid such imaginative feelings and troubling thoughts I could feel the joy Ethan brought to me, and as I gazed to the scuffed little nob of my special desk drawer, I knew even more that I could not, would not, ever let him to go.

We continued to exchange letters that spring through summer of 1771, Ethan now finished with his third year of Harvard studies and me my third of nursing training at the hospital. He rode back to Lexington to be with his father and nearer his mother during those muggy summer weeks, to help about the tavern and just feel home, and I continued to hone my nursing skills at the Pennsylvania Hospital. And between our letters filled of surging passions and colonial things, I continued with Franz in

Germantown and Philadelphia, suppers with mother and father or dining in taverns and inns, or strolling along the cobblestones and river docks, all the while reaching for Ethan. I suppose I gave as much of myself to Ethan as a quill possibly could, knowing my words could never replace a sensuous touch, and Ethan exposed the depths of his heart with each thrilling letter, perhaps more than I deserved.

Soon the chill of fall swept the colonies and Ethan was back in his little Boston room at Mr. Gills' house, returning to his duties at the print shop and his final year of Harvard, an autumn of extended learning that excited him so. "I'm reading words quilled by men across the sea," he gushed in a November letter, "studying the ideas of Voltaire, Burke and Lock, and really like the challenges my final year presents. Some say Mr. Burke's thoughts are spurring a nervous angst in the halls of parliament, Andrea, what with all his talk of reigning in the powers of the crown. But here in Boston and over at Harvard his ideas of freedom are intriguing many, and Mr. Gill said he's inspiring patriot Whigs like Sam Adams and others throughout the colonies, men like Patrick Henry and Mr. Jefferson in the Colony of Virginia."

Ethan also expressed other fascinations about that Edmund Burke, quilling that he was igniting anxious fires about the streets of London with passionate speeches about how every man has a right to be part of his own governing. "Some say he supports views being expressed by Whigs in the colonies," Ethan continued, "boasting ideas many at Harvard believe are at odds with Prime Minister North and King George. But I think what he said to a group of parliament peers is what gripped me the most, words reprinted in Mr. Gill's Boston Gazette that went something like this, 'The only thing necessary for the triumph of evil, is for good men to do nothing.'"

And he delved into spirited ideals being espoused about Paris by the Baron de Laune, a Frenchman most simply called Turgot, quilling about his views of tolerance for those of faith and support of theories that espouse things like natural laws and individual liberties, rights he'd say are passed to us by our Creator. "He thinks a lot like some right here in the colonies, Andrea, saying the rights of people sprout from God, not from men, governments or other such things." Yet, no matter what rumors, studies or theories Ethan would quill about in his letters that fall, winter and coming year, he'd always return to his passions for me and hopes for us. "I miss you, Andrea, and think of you every hour of every day. Love, Ethan."

Ethan and I were now both twenty-one by the first chilling weeks of 1772, and as wintry winds swept across farmers' fields to hamlets, ports, villages and towns throughout the colonies, swirling about Ethan's Boston and my Philadelphia too, we continued to wonder when we'd see each other again. And as our anticipation swelled, Franz sought my hand in marriage once again, a flattering plea I gently declined, conveying once again that I was not ready. It was a truth I quilled to Ethan as tenderly as I could, and although I knew my honesty would sting, I no longer feared his passions would waver. With each new letter we continued to exchange wishful hopes and colonial intrigues, and each lonely night our lips tenderly pressed in sensuous dreams.

Chapter XI

Golden Gardenia

The spring of 1772 was one of the more pleasing seasons to come, for the harsh howls of that winter had quickly vanished, its snows trickling to cool flowing streams, and the April rains seemed to bring a refreshing resurgence to the hills and fields, forests, shops and homes, and perhaps a few wandering souls. They were mystical showers that brought a fresh scent of beauty about the colonies, sprinkling an innocence which had been tainted for several years. And there was an aura of optimism filtering about the air that spring, a wishful sense that the worst of times were fading, surrendering to a dawn bathed of tranquil goodwill. Or perhaps those feelings of hope were simply my youthful cries for calming serenity, an awakening of desires, a yearning for the joy of true passion, a love that seemed so near yet beyond my desperate reach.

Those fleeting rains stirred my simmering emotions a bit more intensely that spring, and at times I found myself fancily gazing to tiny leaves sprouting groves of maple, birch, oak and elm, soft shades of green hovering bushy shrubs spritzing dainty blossoms of lavender, white and pink. The cool air once icy crisp was beginning to warm with a season of hope now brushed by little petals of clover, sundew and rue blooming Pennsylvania meadows in yellows, reds and blues, and the sweet scents of crimson roses dangling mother's porch in thin quaint boxes and mountain laurels sprouting about the colony wisped through the open panes of my window. I remember gazing to the life erupting beyond the glass while lazily lying upon my bed those spring mornings, and watching bright puffy clouds drifting the horizon amid enchanting colors spraying the dawn. And I'd listen to the tender coos of innocent little finches as they danced about the trees, and the song of thrashers and sparrows prancing about flowery Germantown fields.

Sometimes on those early spring morns, as I gazed and listened to all those wonders stirring beyond my window, I could feel Ethan tenderly touching me, sense my tingling passions wanting to burst deep inside, arousing desires my mind grappled to explain. Although I understood those fiery sensations less in those days, I knew what I was feeling was real, and could sense that Ethan was simmering with the same when reading his letters. And even though the emotions erupting between Ethan and I were thrilling, they continued to cause my spirit to twist and churn with an uneasy anxiousness those weeks of spring. They were exhilarating desires that overwhelmed me at times, frighteningly so, yet I knew we'd continue to wrap ourselves within the passions entwining our lives.

While Ethan and I were exchanging feelings and thoughts with quills, learning more of each other with each passionate word that spring, the embers of colonial discontent continued to smolder. As shopkeepers, doctors and tradesmen, seamstresses, farmers, merchants and lawyers went about their lives, colonists like Mr. Revere and John Gill, mother, father and Franz, tensions continued to fester between King George the Third and his Thirteen Colonies. There was a brewing stench beginning to waft the air amid beauty sprouting that spring, an ugly smell slowly dividing Tory and Whig, a dangerous era emerging between the colonies and London. It would be a time many patriots would welcome with an undaunted spirit while others would fear as unimaginable, an era that was slowly approaching upon fractious winds from across the sea.

It had been two years since the king's muskets bloodied the cobblestones of Boston that frightful March night, and perhaps in the eyes of many colonists those kinds of deadly clashes were over, safely shelved to memories. Yet some seemed to keenly sense that such divisiveness had not been truly tamed, that those fiery flames continued to spritz from just beneath our colonial soil. There was a feeling among some that unresolved troubles continued to lurk about roaming shadows, vexing frictions quietly waiting to erupt at any hour upon some royal provocation.

In many of Ethan's letters he quilled about troubling things being talked about in the halls of Harvard and Mr. Gills' shop that spring, confiding how he'd hear Mr. Edes whispering with others about discontenting things occurring about the colony. They'd secretly meet upstairs in that long room too, men like Sam Adams and Jimmy Otis, and discuss what Ethan heard Doc Warren say were the latest unjust actions being thrust upon the colony by Royal Governor Hutchinson. There were others who would meet and talk about the brewing tensions too, not only patriot Whigs in Boston and Lexington but in the places like Williamsburg, Dover, Charles Towne and New York, in Philadelphia and Germantown too, spirited men who believed it their duty to keep the colonies appraised of royal misdeeds.

I remember how pamphlets and papers throughout the colonies, Philadelphia's Evening Post and Pennsylvania Gazette too, were printing insights espoused by spirited men that spring and summer of 1772, even into fall and beyond. Those publications were alerting colonists to disturbing royal actions being unveiled by men with courageous quills, patriot Whigs like Lyman Hall of the Colony of Georgia expressing views some say were unflattering toward the crown, and the barrister Thom Lynch from the Colony of South Carolina, a farmer quilling things detrimental to the king.

Ethan quilled that the beliefs of Whig men were being reprinted in Mr. Giles' Lexington Gazette and Mr. Gills' Country Journal too, ideas such as the scathing remarks about the policies of London being expressed by Joe Hewes in the Colony of North Carolina. His opinions were first printed in the village of New Bern, thoughts quickly whisked north to places like Boston, Philadelphia and New York in the satchels of swift riders or hulls of colonial merchant ships. Yet Ethan confessed that most things being printed in Boston were from Massachusetts Bay men like Mr. Adams, Jim Bowdoin and Artemas Ward.

An array of Whig men throughout the colonies were quilling their disapproval of the crown in those days, patriots such as that Mr. Henry over in the Colony of Virginia, along with brothers Francis Lightfoot and Richard Henry Lee. Thom Jefferson of their House of Burgesses was also quilling his thoughts, one of their younger peers from the County of Albemarle northwest of Williamsburg. A few at the hospital were talking about the writings of Samuel Chase in the Colony of Maryland too, along with Thomas McKean down in Delaware and Robert Morris from my Colony of Pennsylvania. And some were reading the opinions of Johnny Witherspoon from the Colony of New Jersey printed in the Evening Post, or perhaps Philip Livingston from the Colony of New York, Oliver Wolcott up in Connecticut, William Ellery in Rhode Island and Josiah Bartlett from the Colony of New Hampshire.

While those patriot opinions were being espoused by many throughout the colonies, I remember father sputtering, "Those misguided men are spewing humbug!" along with other disgruntled things. There were disapproving bursts from others of our Germantown meeting house Sunday mornings too, Quaker women and men vowing to remain loyal or quietly uninvolved. And I'd hear Franz and his merchant friends angrily utter in Philadelphia taverns and shops that what they valued most was unimpeded trade with London, saying those patriot men were "exposing the colonies to ruinous despair by quilling disloyal treachery."

Amidst all those evolving things were the steadily quilled thoughts of a colonist not living in the port of Boston, New York, Philadelphia or Savannah, but rather across the sea in London. They were enlightening reports being printed in the Pennsylvania Gazette, spirited opinions I'd read at my hospital nursing desk that spring, summer and into fall. Doctor Franklin had been at his post in England for several years by that spring, enmeshed with his diplomatic duties of carefully observing on behalf of the colonies the encroaching mischief of parliament and the crown. The Gazette explained he was providing King George and his ministers with his colonial views too, insightful opinions about laws, policies and acts being debated that would affect the colonies, especially those he called "unjustly egregious."

The revelations of Mr. Franklin's opinions being expressed in the halls of London, insightful impressions some described as colorful oratory bathed with devious prose, and reports of his expressive deeds inspired by his devotion to the colonies, were being quilled to parchment and safely stuffed into leather satchels, then sailed across the sea. Those revealing accounts were being shipped to an array of colonial ports, Ethan's Boston and my Philadelphia too, and being printed in papers and pamphlets like the Evening Post and Mr. Gills' Country Journal, then raced to hundreds of villages and towns by a slew of patriot riders.

Meanwhile, the soothing monotony of ordinary life was being savored by most throughout the colonies that spring, summer and beyond, reassuring events and calming deeds taking place on thousands of farms and in taverns, homes, churches and shops. Women and men carried on as generations before, bartering for goods, toiling for shillings and pounds and gathering with family and friends, while the young snuggled and passionate lovers nestled on the sensuous grass of cool meadows. And there were less tender affinities unfolding in those days too, some rather entangling I must say, such as my impassive courtship with Franz.

I can still feel the outside pressures and inner struggles of becoming increasingly involved with Franz, a good man with faults not unlike every woman, child and man, a Quaker man I continued to see for reasons I'd someday come to realize were flawed. And looking back after all these years, I suppose our moments together were sometimes awkward in those days, a feeling I must admit shrouded our relations over the years. There were times we'd spend our moments rather casually, in innocent public ways, and other times we seemed to gasp for calm. For reasons I still struggle to fully understand, I'll never forget one such evening back then, a night my two lives came frighteningly close to bashing together.

It was a bit after dusk the last Friday of April, shortly after an alluring shower and the close of my training duties at the hospital that brisk spring day. Just moments before I had reread the passions of one of Ethan's letters, and in the twilight of the hour had pressed my lips to his tender words, creased the parchment and slid it back to the solitude of that secret drawer of my nursing desk. As I gazed down to that dull little knob for a few reflective moments, wondering of all his letters lying in the darkness, quietly feeling his caress, I suddenly heard the hospital door creak open then close with a latching clack. An anxious chill surged my body as I snapped a nervous glance down the hall, for it was Franz strutting toward my desk, his muddied shoes scrapping the oak slats.

"You look, surprised, Andrea," he whimsically quipped with a piercing gaze to my startled eyes. "And your cheeks, why, are so flush. Have I interrupted something?"

"No, of course not," I clumsily sputtered as an anxious chill raced my skin, "I'm just finishing up." I nervously shuffled a few parchment sheets into a little stack as he stepped to the edge of my desk, then snapping a glance to that tiny knob, I calmly added, "I must say, Franz, I am a bit surprised to see you here. Are things alright?"

"Yes, everything is fine, Andrea, just fine," he curtly replied while stepping and snatching my coat hanging from a thin spindle of a tall pine rack nudged against the wall just beyond my chair. "Come," he briskly commanded with a tap of his lips to my cold cheek, "let's go. We're dining at Tun Tavern tonight."

"Oh," I timidly whispered while rising with a scrape of my chair, eager to distance Franz from the secrets hidden in the shadows of my nursing desk, "that sounds nice."

He helped slide the dark blue wool over my arms while I guided little buttons through tiny loops, then with his hand clutching mine, we stepped the hall and out the hospital door into the brisk spring night. The earlier clouds had vanished to expose a spray of brilliant stars, and as we strolled several blocks east along the cobblestones to a corner near the docks of the Delaware River, a feeling of anxious unease began to grip my soul. My thoughts had been of Ethan for so much of that day, having reread many of his tender lines, yet there I was awash in the reality of my life, walking with Franz in Philadelphia while my emotions twisted inside. I nodded with agreeing sighs now and then as he told me of his merchant day, and as our shoes scraped the gravely stones, I'd gaze to the stars twinkling toward Boston and wonder of Ethan.

Franz and I had dined at Tun Tavern several times since we met, and every now and then I'd hear a doctor, patient or nurse whisper of its fine ales, spirits and wines and say alluring things about the tavern's scrumptious beef and tasty lobsters and stews. And I remember Lydia, Betsy and I talking about the tavern on Sunday nights too, confessing how it might be nice to meet for a few goblets of wine on a quiet evening, something we never seemed to do.

Franz said that the tavern had been near the river for many years, and for a while colonists knew it as Peggy Mullan's beef steak club, yet by the spring of 1772 most in Philadelphia were simply calling it the Tun Tavern. I suppose it had always been a place for colonists to gather to dine or just talk of farming and merchant deals, of the river and trades, and perhaps the latest rift between the colonies and London while sipping spirits, ale and wine. And I once heard that sometimes men would gather in the tavern upon their militia's muster call, aging colonists who now exchanged intriguing stories about that frontier war years before.

The tavern looked as it had for many years that April night, resembling a big farmhouse nestled near the woods north of Germantown, with three little windows crowned by quaint gables peering from its upper floor toward the alley by the river. As Franz and I stepped the stones I could see the silhouette of a chimney rising at each end, crimson bricks with a thin grey stream lazily twisting toward the stars. The tavern was pulsating with life that brisk night, with lamps and candles glistening off an array of panes in shades of yellows, oranges and reds. And as we stepped up a few slats and past elm spindles and rails to the tavern's twin doors, the tantalizing aroma of simmering stews and roasting fowl and beasts filtered about the spring air.

I suppose that evening was not unlike others Franz and I had experienced together that winter, spring and beyond, and perhaps I truly did find his company mostly easy and pleasing. After all, we did seem to enjoy strolling upon the cobblestones or along the river now and then, and having supper with wine in taverns or inns. I think such public displays were more expressive for him and comfortable for me, for I felt less pressure then. And I already knew of his feelings for me, for Franz had told many times how he cared, and in his own convoluted way, how he loved me.

That spring night we'd share a dish we had come to enjoy, crusted soft rolls and thin strips of meat fired over the bricks of the kitchen hearth just beyond the western wall, tender beef bathed with steamy little chunks of orange, red and green beans, carrots and beets. And even though mother and father knew Franz and I honored our Quaker faith traditions, we strayed that chilly night from those sacred rules, as we had other times too, indulging in a few secret goblets of wine. It was a rather spacious tavern bustling with colonists that night, and as we stepped to a little round table, its polished maple shining near the corner panes right of the door, my thoughts drifted to Boston and Ethan before snapping back to Franz and Tun Tavern.

"This table alright?" Franz politely asked while sliding off my coat and laying it easy upon the back of a cushioned maple chair.

"Yes, I like it," I whispered with a nod, nestling to my chair and glancing about the tavern as a little flame danced the candle of our table. "It's quaint, Franz, near the window, and off from others, just enough."

While Franz casually waved to a waiter, I slowly scanned the tavern abuzz with colonists nibbling, talking and drinking at a slew of scattered tables. They were a rather polished assortment of men in ruffled shirts, stylish coats and tan, blue and bright breeches, and the women were prim, adorned with smoothly wrapped hair, elegant dresses and precious metals and jewels. And then there was me, tired and unpolished in my blue nursing dress with no diamonds, emeralds or pearls, wondering whether I truly belonged. Oh, I knew Franz was in his niche when mingling with those of abundance, doctors and shipping men, merchants and lawyers both Tory and Whig, surrounded by such opulence. But was I? Then I'd remember something Ethan once said that night we first met, "We're all equal in our Creator's eyes, Andrea, each of us simply doing our best."

As I gazed to the flicker of our candle's little flame amid snapping glances to Franz, I felt an unflattering queasiness swirling inside, a realization that the opulence assembled in Tun Tavern that night was in a nauseous way, what I wanted. Yet now, as I rock easy in my chair and Samuel peers to elms swaying in the warm summer winds, I depressingly realize how utterly mistaken I had been. Perhaps I was simply too young in those days, failing to listen to my heart and search my soul, and had deceived myself that such nonsense was needed for my life, for my children yet born. I had believed such folly, and that those things would be realized with Franz.

"I'm a bit fond of this table too," Franz softly muttered with another snapping wave to our aging thin waiter. "Two cabernets, Hans, and two plates of beefsteak, not bloody, with all the trimmings."

"Yes sir, Mr. von Handel," he dutifully replied while slinging a thin white cloth over his wrist and patting back a string of straying grey hair. "I'll bring your wine right now."

"Yes," I whispered as Franz pressed his right hand upon my left, gently caressing my skin, "wine sounds nice. Thank you, Franz."

We began to softly talk of rather innocuous things, Franz of his hectic merchant day once again as I quietly listened, perhaps sputtering a word now and then about a patient or two at the hospital. At times his voice would seem to fade as my eyes wandered to all the little flames flickering on tables, and for a brief moment I'd sense the door of that little room hidden deep in my heart gently nudge open, feel Ethan for a sensuous moment. And amid our easy words and my tantalizing thoughts of Boston, I'd glance about and listen of lives and events being discussed throughout the tavern.

At a table off to our right I could hear colonists talking about Ethan's Massachusetts Bay, could see four men involved in an intense discussion of what they said was that colony's recent attempt to banish from its shores any links to that devilish trade of buying and selling Negro women, children and men. "The king's shredding of our colonial rights is preposterous!" growled a disgruntled rotund man as Hans clicked our goblets of cabernet to our table. "How dare London strike down the will of the Massachusetts Bay people!"

As Franz whispered a pleasant "to us" and we pressed our wine to our lips, another one of those four men boisterously countered, "Rightfully so, Sam. That's what kings are born to do. They must maintain control, keep discipline over their lands." I watched as the least intimidating of the four added his support, a petite man who thrust his mug of ale over their flickering candle and chimed in a slurring way, "Hear, hear, Homer! No doubt, parliament and the crown must keep control, and that includes the power to determine the validity of colonial laws. And that, Josh, my dear old friend, is just what the king did."

Nearer the tavern door was an elderly man sputtering to a gracefully dressed woman seated beside a younger man, perhaps her brother. "Those blasted demigods over there in London!" the older man spouted, grumbling about shillings, pounds and the crown. "Why, with all their bloody meddling over here, they're sure to cause a fiscal mess." I watched in a secret hush as she snapped a nervous glance about the tavern, then calmly reaching and pressing her hand to his, whispered, "John, this isn't the time, or the place. Please, let's just enjoy our supper."

"What we need," he spiritedly snapped in an impatient tone, "is our colonial scrip back. We should have the right to print our own currency to deal with this blundering mess, like we used to do." Then he gripped his goblet, glanced left and right, and firmly whispered, "What we need is parliament and the king off our backs!"

"I'm not so sure I agree, John," the younger man chimed in a cautious tone. "After all, to me, it does seem London has the interests of the colonies at heart, and we are an inseparable part of the empire. I truly believe the crown is looking out for our interests over here, John, and parliament is doing its best."

"Humbug!" he curtly replied. "All I can say is, God help us."

Closer to the center of the tavern and surrounded by a scattering of colonists sipping spirits and nibbling tasty bits at tables from fine leathered chairs, was a pair of intriguing men and two younger women dressed in silky shades of blue pressing bosoms rather endowed. Their demeanor lured my attention while their goblets glistening candle flames grasped my eyes, and as I pinched the stem of my crystal and nodded to Franz explaining the numbing nuances of the merchant trade, I strained to hear and secretly watched.

"We just produced hundreds of granite blocks for that new Fort Mifflin," the older looking man in dark breeches and bright ruffled shirt boasted to the other sipping wine across the table, "some fifteen tons. And I'm expecting another demand from Governor Penn soon, an order for some sixteen more."

I had heard Franz and some of his merchant friends speak of that fort before, and was vaguely aware that it was rapidly being assembled a bit south of Philadelphia, on my colony's shore of the Delaware River. They said it was needed as a defense from an attack by an enemy from the south, a foe I could hear some at the hospital sputter, was who or what? "Good for you, Henry," the younger man uttered while glancing to their sultry friends. "I'm sure it will be a mighty fort, solid and strong. But tell me, Henry, from whom do we need protection?"

"That's a fine question, Jim," he whimsically replied. "To tell you the truth, I'm not sure. But with so many merchants struggling around here, my granite trade is doing pretty well. I just hope Governor Penn keeps those orders coming. There's some talk of a second fort too, Mercer, if I recall, being planned on New Jersey's side of the river."

"Andrea?" Franz softly sputtered as Hans slid our steaming dinners to the table. "Andrea, do you mind if we talk about something during supper? Maybe this isn't the perfect time, but it's been on my mind for a while."

"I suppose so," I whispered as an anxious feeling began to twist inside. Then slicing and scooping a tiny bite, I nervously added, "No, I don't mind. What is it?"

He sipped more wine and stared to his platter in a contemplating hush, then clicked his goblet to the table and nervously spun its crystal stem. "I think it's time you stopped that homespun stuff," he insisted, "stopped sewing with your two friends Sunday nights."

"What?" I instinctively snapped with a contemptuous glare. Then tapping my crystal and pressing to the back of my chair, I reached for calm with a breath of tavern air and softly added, "What do you mean? I don't understand?"

"We're Quaker people," he discreetly advised while peering to my eyes with an intensity I had never seen before, "you, me, my mother and father, yours too. Those clothes you three sew Sunday nights, garments you call homespun, run afoul of what our society of friends believe, in Philadelphia and Germantown. What you are doing, Andrea, is an affront to our fundamental faith, to our notions of loyalty to the crown, or impartiality to such things. And I do wish you'd have consideration for my merchant trade. Why, just being associated with those two, making all those homespun things, can only stir trouble, and harm my business in the colony. Some might even come to think we're disloyal, Andrea, and that would not be good. I want you to stop."

I could feel my insides twisting with betrayal as I stared to my wine and painfully held my silence, snapping a piercing glance to Franz once or twice, and amid the bustle of the tavern I struggled to compose my anger and cling to my wits. Although I felt attacked, as we gazed to our goblets in an eerie hush I slowly began to understand the reasons why he was so concerned. I knew he wanted to remain in our governor's favor, with London and Tory merchants, with shipping men in Philadelphia and the colony, and feared being viewed as disloyal. And as we exchanged anxious looks and fiddled with our wine, I came to understand myself in an unflattering way, realizing I might someday share what Franz desperately sought to hold. In a shameful way I too desired such earthly things, or at least I believed I did in those days, when I was confusingly young.

Yet I also knew I supported the ideals of thousands of patriot Whigs like Sam Adams, John Gill and Mr. Henry, Ethan and his father too, and realized I'd continue to stray from the loyal or neutral views of my society of friends. And by that spring some were referring to society women who strayed from the faith as freedom seeking Quakers, patriot women like Lydia, Betsy and me, a growing group of spirited colonists Franz, father and others scorned as "misguided renegade friends." Yet from the shadows of meeting houses throughout the colonies such freedom views were immerging from villages in the Colony of Georgia to towns in the colonies of New York, Connecticut, Virginia and New Hampshire. Looking back after all these years, most now know we were simply Quakers who were compelled to partially shun the pressures of our faith for a greater sense of liberty, choosing to veer from silent loyalty toward a cause we held dear.

Franz quietly stared and fidgeted in his chair, impatiently waiting for my words, then motioned toward Hans for more wine as my anguish began to ease. I now knew no matter what our relation was becoming, a struggling bundle of contradictions and feelings, I would continue to do what I believed right, would continue to snip and stitch homespun things with Lydia and Betsy Sunday nights. I had come to realize I would never betray the patriot ideals Ethan and I both held, not for my society of friends or any other group, not for mother and father, nor for any notion of harmony with Franz. Maybe it was the bond Ethan and I had found on the cobblestones of Boston that March night, or the crimson courage that slowly oozed to the snows from those five brave souls. Or maybe it was the patriot zeal being stroked by Ethan's quill in those days, and the magic of his passions that had captured my heart. No, I knew I would never abandon him, knew I'd remain with Ethan and our patriot cause, forever.

"I understand how you feel," I finally whispered in a conceding way, "truly I do. I'm sure others in this tavern feel the same, and know mother and father do too." I nervously paused for a tense moment and sipped more wine in hopes of easing my mind, searching for perfect words while glancing about the tavern, then stared to his glaring eyes and gently added, "I know you love me, Franz, and hope you'll try to understand. I'm proud of myself, studying with my nursing, helping others where I can, and have my own views on things, beliefs I've got to honor. Although causing you trouble is not what I want, and will do my best to avoid such things, I must be who I am. I'm sorry, Franz, but I can't do that, won't do what you ask. Betsy and Lydia are my friends, and we find joy in sewing all those homespun things. It's compelling for us, fulfilling too. I intend to keep snipping and stitching with them, quietly, I promise."

He tensed and leaned to the table as I escaped into my wine, then tightly gripping his goblet near our candle's flame, glared and asked, "Why do you insist on doing this to me?"

"Franz, please," I whispered, tapping my crystal and nervously glancing about the tavern, "I'm not trying to do anything to you. If you love me, and you say you do, then please, let me be who I am."

He pressed to the back of his chair and just stared to my eyes for a gripping moment, then snapping glances left and right and snatching another taste of cabernet wine, softly pled, "Please, Andrea, think of what's at stake here. When you three sew those homespun clothes, when you gather with anyone who does those kinds of disloyal things, spurring frictions with London, it puts us both in danger. It can only bring harm to my merchant trade, and maybe even destroy it, a livelihood that could be yours too someday. And I'm afraid, Andrea, such troubles will come sooner rather than later."

"I'm sorry, Franz," I hushed in a consoling way, "I can't do what you want. But what I can do, promise to do, is keep my involvement quiet."

"Damn these bloody troubles I see coming!" he frustratingly sputtered while sipping more wine. Then reaching and touching my hand, he softly added in a surrendering tone, "Alright. I'll try to understand, I doubt I will, but will try. But I don't want to hear any rumors, understand. So please, Andrea, keep your homespun mischief quiet."

"I will," I whispered. "I'll even talk with Lydia and Betsy about it this Sunday. Everything will be alright, Franz, you'll see. Thank you."

"I sure hope so," he wearily uttered while snatching his silvery fork and slicing blade. "Now, let's finish our supper, and I'll have Hans pour more wine."

We immersed into clicks and slices of juicy bits as a tense hush settled over our table, and as candles flickered amid spirited discussions swirling about the tavern, I could feel the chill that had descended between us. With each nibble and sip of cabernet wine I wondered if others could feel the strain shrouding our little corner table, see the stoic expression splashed upon Franz or sense the anxious resignation surging my soul. And with each pulse of our candle's flame my thoughts slowly drifted to Boston and Massachusetts Bay, and for a few wondrous moments, I could feel the serenity of Ethan's sensuous touch.

"Philadelphia sounds like a pretty loyal place in those days, grandma," Samuel suddenly interrupted in an inquisitive way, taming a sense of loneliness and guilt that was beginning to stew deep inside me. "I mean, many seemed to support parliament and the king. But I guess there was a growing group with different thoughts, colonists like you and your sewing friends."

"I suppose that's the way it was, Samuel," I whispered, nudging my chair into an easy rock while brushing of a tear trickling my cheek, "at least in a simple way. But in truth, it was much more complex than that. Sure, there were many supporters of the crown, thousands of loyal Tories, yet there were a growing number of colonists aligning with the ideals being espoused by thousands of patriot Whigs, women and men who disapproved of parliament and the king. It wasn't just in Philadelphia either, but was brewing in villages and towns across our Colony of Pennsylvania, just like up in Ethan's Massachusetts Bay, and in the colonies of New Hampshire, Delaware, Georgia and Virginia. But I guess showing loyalty to London, or at least muzzling ones' opinions, was pretty common in those days, especially by our Quaker friends before the war, colonists like mother and father, your Grandfather Franz too."

"I don't think you've ever told me, grandma," Samuel confessed with a caring glance and robust rock of his chair, "how Grandpa Franz felt in those days. I never knew of the divide of ideals between you and grandpa, what with his sentiments of loyalty and your patriot leanings."

"No, I never have," I softly sighed while dabbing my eye, "so you couldn't have known. I guess I've never really spoken of these things before, to anyone."

"Are you alright, grandma?" Samuel tenderly asked as I brushed another trickling tear. "Do you want to stop? Can I get you anything?"

"I'm fine, Samuel," I whispered as a tinge of melancholy oozed my soul, "really. No, I don't want to stop." For a few quiet moments we just rocked in our chairs, Samuel peering to those distant elms swaying easy in the July breeze and I recalling all those things just told. The air was still warming as my mantel clock chimed one, and although a sense of sadness surged now and then, each caress of Ethan's poem nestled in the pocket of my summer dress brushed my memories with joy. "It's awfully warm. Maybe we need something to cool us down, and soothe our souls. There's a bottle of wine on the far counter in my kitchen. How about filling these goblets, Samuel, please?"

"I sure will," he gladly uttered before snatching our goblets from the little table, swinging open the door and dashing into the house. I slid my fingers across the parchment of Ethan's poem and gazed to the pink petals of mountain laurels fluttering in the afternoon hush, and with each stroke of his tender words, I felt the calm of being home, safe and loved. Another tear spilled as I rocked and remembered Ethan's sweetness all those years ago, then I dabbed my eyes and brushed my cheeks as Samuel burst through the door and clinked our goblets to the table. Caressing Ethan's words once more, I reached for my wine as his passions wrap my heart.

"Thank you," I whispered, twisting and dabbing my eye a final time, then sipping wine. "Oh, that's tasty. Now, Samuel, you just sit there and relax, enjoy your wine, and I'll tell you more."

He nudged his chair into an easy rock, sipped his wine and cupped his goblet in his fingers, then gazing back into the gentle summer winds, softly professed, "There, now I'm ready, grandma. Tell me everything. Help me understand what happened back then, with the colonies, grandpa and you, with Ethan. Take me back to those years, to the war."

I nestled my hand back into the pocket of my dress as Samuel gazed to those distant elms, and sliding my fingers over Ethan's aging words, reaching for the past, I confessedly said, "I want you to know, Samuel, no matter what your Grandfather Franz said that night in the tavern, or my feelings for Ethan, I truly believed in the ideals espoused by patriot Whigs in those days."

"I know, grandma, and I'm proud of you. You didn't just watch things happen, but helped spur patriot beliefs in your own way, like sewing homespun with your friends."

"But remember, we weren't the only women doing things in those days. Why, there were many patriot women daring to defy the crown in all sorts of little ways." I pushed my chair easy and caressed the lines of Ethan's poem as Samuel peered into the summer winds, and while those tiny pink petals quivered in the breeze, I breathed a calming sigh and reached for memories.

I met Lydia at Betsy's house the last Sunday night of April, 1772, gathering to sew homespun things just as we had many times over the years. I had walked several blocks east on Philadelphia's cobblestones shortly after my nursing duties at the hospital that spring day, arriving at her parent's home at the corner of Bread and Arch as dusk quietly settled. She said the three of us would be alone most of that night, for her mother and father were visiting an aunt in Mount Holly, a village some twenty miles east of the river in the Colony of New Jersey.

We sewed a slew of grey and blue shirts for several hours that chilly night, with tiny loops and little buttons, and just below the collar on the back of each, *homespun* was stitched with crimson thread on a little tan patch. And as we measured, snipped and stitched near a crackling fire in their gathering room, we sipped white wine from goblets of crystal, spirits unleashed from a French bottle or two Betsy kept stashed in a dark closet corner of her bedroom.

"To the three of us," Betsy boasted with our goblets thrust high, something she liked to infuse once or twice those Sunday sewing nights.

"To the colonies," Lydia would jovially chime, tossing her cloth, needle and thread to the cherry shine of a nearby table. "May we someday be free from the unjust whims of monarchy."

"To friends," I'd calmly add as we pressed our wine to our lips, "and to love."

I remember how our words seemed to mysteriously vanish with each flicker of those snapping flames that night, and as we relished our sweet wine and poured a bit more, how our talk would expand as it often did those sewing nights. With each spirited stitch and liberating sip we'd reveal a little more of our hidden truths, exposing rather delicate things as if lured by the shadows dancing the room.

After a fresh splash of wine Lydia began to talk kindly of her husband William, revealing simple things about what he had done and how he enjoyed teaching children of Philadelphia, mainly through tutoring young colonists in their homes. With each snip, stitch and sip I found myself admiring the fondness she showed toward William, never grumbling about this or spewing a disparaging word about that, things I'd too often hear from other women of Germantown and Philadelphia. It was refreshing to hear her express such an affection for a man she surely cared for deeply, and knowing that made me feel good, and happy for her.

After a while Betsy began to expose a few of her own tender things, confiding in a rare shy way that she was now seeing someone, had "innocently met" a young man of twenty at a social at Christ Church near the river, just a block or two south of her home. "Mother and father don't know," she nervously confessed with another sip of courage, "and I want to keep it that way. So please, both of you, please don't tell anyone. Father just wouldn't understand, and mother, well, she'd think the worse. They both have said some rather unflattering things about the king's church, and just the other day mother sputtered, 'they're just not the same as us friends.'"

Betsy pressed her homespun cloth, needle and thread to her lap and reached for her goblet once again, then glancing restlessly to the flames snapping in the hearth, peered to Lydia and I and nervously said, "He's of the Anglican faith, and his father is a clergyman at the church. Well, don't you see? My parents have forbidden me from seeing a man not of our Quaker faith. So please, this has to stay a secret."

I pinched my homespun cloth more tightly while listening to her revealing words, then resting my half-stitched shirt to my thigh amidst an eerie hush, stared to the flickering fire for a moment or two. I understood why Betsy was frightfully nervous, worried what her parents would do and what others might think, and as I reached and sipped my wine, I knew why she begged for our silence. And I was sure Lydia grasped those things too, for she was some twenty years older than Betsy and me and seemed so much wiser, always accepting us for who we are, and never wavering from being our friend. "I understand, Betsy," I uttered with a caring gaze to her eyes, "I really do, and won't say a word to anyone. Promise."

"That goes for me too," Lydia softly chimed, "I won't say a word. Your secret is safe with us." Then tossing her homespun things to pillows of the couch near the fire, she reached for her crystal brimming of French wine and playfully added, "Now, Betsy, tell us, who is this man? Does he have a name?"

"I'm so relieved to hear both of you say those things," Betsy gratefully sighed. "I've wanted to say something for weeks, but each time I came close these past Sunday nights, I couldn't do it. I don't know, maybe I just wanted to wait a little longer, see how things went, and maybe I was afraid of what you might say." Lydia and I quietly watched as she spread her final shirt with the others lying with pillows on the couch, then sipping her goblet and staring to the flames, softly confessed, "His name is John, John Ross. He's an upholsterer, and loves to sew things just like us. Oh, but there's so much more about John, his calm demeanor, and the gentleness that sparkles the blue of his eyes when he gazes to me. Sometimes I think he can see right to my soul, as if he's searching for the real me. And I just love the affection he pours over me. I guess for weeks now, he's all I've been able to think of."

"Oh, Betsy, he sounds divine," Lydia softly gushed. "Maybe I'm wrong, but it sounds as if you're smitten with him, maybe even in love. I'm so happy for you."

"I'm happy too," Betsy confessed as her cheeks blushed a tender rose, "almost giddily so. I have to admit, I don't know much about love, don't really know how it's supposed to feel, but do know how wonderful he makes me feel. It's only been a few weeks, yet in a comfortable way, it feels so right. Oh, maybe I am, Lydia, I don't know. Help me, Andrea."

"I don't know, Betsy," I sputtered with a dash of trepidation, knowing how I too grapple with such things. "I'm not very good at this, but I suppose, only you can truly know if what you're feeling is real love. I don't know. Maybe it doesn't matter, what Lydia or I think, or anyone else. What counts is how your heart feels. But I must say, Betsy, from what you've said, you just might be in love. He sounds so nice. I'm happy for you."

"You know, Betsy," Lydia wisely conveyed, "Andrea is right. You'll know if you are truly in love with John." Then touching Betsy's shoulder with an affectionate caress, she tenderly added, "Just let things naturally flow, happen in their own time."

"Where did you two find so much wisdom?" Betsy whispered, sipping her wine and gazing to the crackling fire. "I feel like I am, in love, with John. But I think I'll take your words to heart and slow down a little, let our emotions unfold in due time."

"Now who's the wise one?" asked Lydia in a motherly tone. "Tell us some more about him. What's he really like?"

"Oh, forgive me, please," Betsy pleaded while twisting from the dwindling flames, snatching a French bottle and pouring more wine. "I'm sorry to sound so mysterious. Maybe you've heard of John's uncle, George?"

"I think I have," I sputtered with a tinge of doubt. "Yes, I heard some at the hospital say something once, and a while back, Franz might have mentioned his name. I guess I really don't know much."

"Oh yes, I have," Lydia quickly revealed. "Your John has a rather intense uncle, a man who's delved in Philadelphia affairs for quite some time. If I recall, George Ross did some special things for our royal governor a few years back, as a royal barrister, and served as one of the king's colonial prosecutors for a while. He's in our colony's assembly now, and even though some say he was aligned with loyal Tories for years, supporting the acts of London and policies of Governor Penn, it seems he's shifted toward patriot Whig views."

"Gosh, Lydia, I guess you do know of George," uttered a surprised Betsy. "And you're right about his views, moving from Tory to Whig, John's told me so. He said his uncle supports the little things patriot colonists are doing too, people like us, opposing the intrusions of London by making all these homespun things."

"I've heard some right here in Philadelphia," Lydia replied, "talking about those very things about George, other patriots too. And I can tell by what you say, Betsy, that John has those same views, supports you and us."

"You're right, Lydia, he does," Betsy whispered. "But wait," she quickly added, sipping more wine with a sparkle in her eyes, "there's more. I'm going to start sewing things at his upholstery shop, not far from here, on Walnut Street. I'll be a seamstress for him, and even be paid a few shillings and pounds each week."

"That's wonderful," I excitedly snapped, spilling a drop or two of wine. "You two will see each other an awful lot, almost every day. How intriguing."

"Yes, isn't it," Betsy giddily sputtered. "I'll be paid to snip and stitch, while cuddled in his arms, bathed with kisses."

"Oh, Betsy, we're glad for you," Lydia affectionately assured as I nodded and said, "Yes, we really are. You just look so happy. Here's to you and John," I wishfully added as we clicked our crystals near the fire, "to happiness."

A hush settled over the calming sounds of fiery crackles and snaps as Betsy gleamed and we tipped our wine, then she breathed a relieving sigh, spun toward Lydia and me and gratefully whispered, "Thank you. But I've got to add one more thing, to us, to our cherished friendship, to our sewing these Sunday nights." As the fire flickered and shadows danced the walls of the room, we tapped our goblets and sipped our wine.

With each sweet sip I could sense truth being stirred by a mysterious serum flowing to every crevice of my body, and soon I realized we had yet to speak much of me, that I had not revealed what was always simmering deep inside. Sure, I had talked some of Franz, that we continued to court and for months he had not pressed me to marry, but it was what I had not spoken of, and had never before, that was spritzing to a boil. I felt a compulsion to expose my secret as if I were about to burst, to share my dilemma just as Betsy had done. Maybe I needed to release the pressures that had been building for so long, or maybe I just needed to talk truth with my two dearest friends. I suppose I just felt the moment had come to expose the web I had spawned, hoping that maybe, it might make Ethan more real, bring him closer into my life.

I pressed my lips to my crystal once again, sipping more courage as that door deep in my heart crept open, then tossing my fears into the dwindling fire, began to expose my secret to Lydia and Betsy. I confided his name and where, why and when we first met in Boston that chilling March night, of his Harvard studies and duties at Mr. Gill's print shop, and some gentle things of his father and tavern in Lexington. And in a liberating way, I confessed about all the letters we had quilled the past two years, and of that special little drawer of my nursing desk. "I'm not exactly sure," I finally sighed, "but I might be in love with Ethan. Oh, Betsy, Lydia, I'm thrown into heavenly heights, just thinking of his sensuous touch." Then gazing to their eyes, I explained why my life in Germantown and Philadelphia must go on unchanged, and that Franz must never know, that Ethan must remain my secret.

Lydia stared at me for a bewildering moment as if trying to understand my revelation, fiddling with her goblet and sloshing its nectar to its rim, while Betsy sipped her wine and escaped into those little flickering flames. "If that's how you feel about this Ethan," Lydia questioned in a puzzling tone, "then why, my dear, do you remain with Franz?"

"Lydia, please," I anxiously pled as my stomach churned and Betsy gazed to my eyes in a sympathetic way, "I explained why. Maybe they're not very good reasons, unacceptable to most, but they're real, Lydia, and mine. Oh, I know this whole thing sounds so un-noble, but please, don't judge me, just try to understand, both of you. I guess I just had to tell you, share my secret with my only true friends, wanted you to know about Ethan, and the burden I bear. Know this too, I don't ever want to release him."

They stared at me for a moment or two, pressing their goblets in hands as the snapping fire blushed our cheeks, then I watched as compassion brush their eyes and sensed the tenderness in their hearts tame doubts swirling their minds. "I'm sorry, Andrea," Lydia caringly whispered, reaching and caressing my hand, "You're right. We're not here to judge. We're your friends, we care about you, want to listen, understand."

"That's right, Andrea," Betsy sighed, "I'm sorry too."

"Oh, it's alright," I uttered in a forgiving tone as a mist sprayed my eyes, "really, I understand. I'm just so grateful you both care. I've been carrying this around with me for so long, this situation, this dilemma, and so relieved to finally confide it all to you two."

"We do care, Andrea," Betsy softly added while touching my hand. "And your secret will remain so with us."

"Of course," Lydia caringly chimed, "your Ethan will remain our secret too. We just want you to be happy, Andrea. That's all that matters."

"Oh, I'm so grateful for you two," I sighed while brushed a trickling tear, "so blessed to have your friendship." Then gasping a weary breath, I despairingly released, "Sometimes I feel helpless, as if I'm all alone, yet living two lives. One is with Franz here in Philadelphia, a life of pressures by others, a life I've allowed to become beholden to my own wants and needs, my own limitations. And one is controlled by my heart, each beat exploding with desires for Ethan, a life of tender letters traveling hundreds of miles to-and-fro Boston. Sometimes I feel like I want to scream into the night, then I find a way to calm myself, and carry on. Oh, Lydia, Betsy, I do have feelings for Franz, I truly do, maybe even a strange kind of love. But I must confess, those feelings are nothing like my passions for Ethan."

"You poor dear," Lydia whispered while brushing my hair with her fingers, "you really are struggling with this. Come now, it's going to be alright. You know, Andrea, in a way I do understand why things are the way they are for you, and see the reasons why you don't want to change things, can't change things, at least not now. Just know I'm here for you."

"Thanks, Lydia," I sighed, "that means so much."

"Do you truly love this man," Betsy asked, delving to my core, "this Ethan? I mean, are you really sure?"

"I think I am, Betsy," I uttered in a befuddling way, "at least I'm pretty sure. Yet I must admit there are times I don't allow myself to truly know, as if I'm afraid to search deeply, discover the unflattering contradictions that grip me. Ethan and I quill to each other with such passions, feelings I've never known with Franz. I can't seem to stop thinking about Ethan, as if I've been consumed by some thrilling obsession. At times I feel so guilty, but I simply can't stop, don't want to stop." Then glancing to Lydia and Betsy listening with dazzled stares, I sipped another dash of courage and confessed, "Yes, I guess I am. I must be. I must be in love with Ethan."

With compassion in their eyes, they told me they supported me, would be there to listen whenever I needed, and for the remainder of that April night we talked a little more of our lives, of William and John, of Franz and Ethan. And somewhere amid our words and wine I told them about what Franz had said at the Tun Tavern a few days before, of his unpleasant remarks about patriot Whigs, of his disapproval of our homespun sewing Sunday nights and demand that I, that we, keep our actions quiet. Then as he often did in those days, shortly after ten Franz arrived to take me home to Germantown, and Lydia, Betsy and I bid our farewells to another evening of needles and threads, snipping, stitching and wine.

Franz and I talked now and then as we creaked through the chilly night air some five miles north along the ruts and stones of the road to Germantown, Franz gripping the reins as the buggy swayed, bounced and rolled. I could feel his chill as we crunched the soil beneath the sparkling stars, perhaps displeased that I had defied his wishes by continuing to sew homespun things with Lydia and Betsy, and sense the strain in his voice while talking of his day. And as the lonely sound of clumping hooves and creaking wheels vanished in the dark, my thoughts drifted north to Boston, to tender visions of my Ethan, then the buggy came to a tugging halt in Germantown. I remember how Franz walked me to the door in an eerie hush before tapping his cold lips to mine and whispering "goodnight," and how I twisted about my blankets, linens and pillows before escaping to sleep. I tossed and drifted to conflicting dreams that spring night, then woke the coming morn to the truth of my life, to the reality I had created with two men.

Over the coming weeks I quilled several times to Ethan about nuances at the hospital and my nursing training, and revealed some simple things about Germantown, of mother and father, and of Sunday sewing sessions with Betsy and Lydia, of intimacies being told. With each letter stroked by candlelight in my bedroom those lonely May nights or at my nursing desk at the hospital during a tranquil afternoon shower, I never failed to confess to Ethan how I missed him so. And even though Ethan's letters were a bit sporadic those weeks, what with all the hectic hours of studying and testing for his liberation from Harvard that spring of 1772, his quill always confessed of his arousing passions for me.

I found one of Ethan's letters innocently resting on my nursing desk on a sprinkling Thursday afternoon in early June that spring, and I can still feel the pounding of my heart as my eyes fixed upon those wondrous words, "Colony of Massachusetts Bay." I excitedly glanced about the hall to ensure I was alone, then darting to the slats of my chair and pinching the parchment in tingling fingers, unfolded his words stroked many days before. "My dear Andrea," he tenderly began, "I've begun to quill many times these past several weeks, only to be interrupted with Harvard challenges and frustrating delays. Please forgive me for not writing as much as I wanted, but know that I intend to make it up to you. I've missed you, Andrea, terribly, and have thought of you every day and lonely moment each night." I could feel his passions pulling me to Boston as I slid my fingers across his alluring words, and feel my heart being swaddled in his sensuous arms.

He confessed of his erupting emotions for me as he always did, sentiments which attracted me so, and quilled of some colonial issues simmering about Boston, then began to expose other personal things, especially his elation at finishing Harvard College on the Ninth of May, a Saturday afternoon misting from a briskly grey. "It felt so fulfilling, Andrea," he confided, "to have all my years of study come to fruition. I could see in dad's eyes that he was proud of me, and in a mystical way, I knew mom was too." With each word I could sense pride simmering within me too, for I knew the dedication he had shown not only to his studies, but his printing duties at Mr. Gill's Boston shop. Ethan had attained his personal goals, had persevered with dreams and grit, and done so not only for himself, but for his father and mother. He had received a bachelor's degree in enlightening fields, a crowning achievement of four long resolute years.

Ethan quilled that with the help of Ben Edes and John Gill, his father had secretly arranged a celebration that night up in the long room of their print shop, and explained how his four Junto friends from Harvard were there too, along with Mr. Revere, Henry Knox and several others he had come to know at the print shop. There were some from the Green Dragon Tavern and a few sons of liberty men there too, and even Mr. Giles galloped in, his old printing boss of the Lexington Gazette. He confided that Mr. Hancock came by for a moment as well to confer with Mr. Edes about some colonial vex, and just before leaving with a tin of rum in hand, told Ethan, "Well done." Ethan's father then arranged a more personal festivity in Lexington several days later, a little celebration at the Buckman Tavern with villagers he'd known for years, spirited men like Doc Newman, Mr. Jafres, John Parker and Reverend Clarke.

Ethan revealed a few fascinating things too about the final gathering of his little Junto group at the Green Dragon Tavern a few weeks before, shortly after his duties at the print shop the last Saturday night of April. There was a chilly mist sprinkling the port when he rushed to meet Benjamin, Josiah, Samuel and Myles already waiting at their favorite table right of the tavern door, near the corner and panes facing the stones of King Street. Mr. Gill dropped by for a moment too, something Ethan said he often liked to do, and before dashing back to his shop, handed Thom the barkeep several dinged shillings with instructions to fill their mugs now and then with frothy ale.

For a while they talked about what each was planning to do once their Harvard studies came to a close, and although Ethan confessed how happy he felt for all of them upon achieving such a milestone, he couldn't help but feel an uneasy sense of loss knowing that the youthful camaraderie with his Junto friends was coming to an end. "Ben Loring isn't going back to Concord," he slowly quilled, "but leaving Massachusetts Bay, altogether. He's decided to study colonial law, Andrea, with his mother's uncle on the Island of Manhattan in the Colony of New York."

He explained that Myles Whitworth was returning north to the village of Salem to help his father in his shipping and mercantile trade, while Samuel Haven intended to gallop back to his Colony of Connecticut sometime in early June. "Only Sam's not going home to Milford," Ethan confided, "but riding to the village of New Haven a bit northeast to do what his father insists he do, study the legal profession at Yale College. I guess the only one staying on here in Boston is Josiah Badcock, to help his mom and dad in their merchant shop over by Hutchinson's Wharf. Yet Josh did say that in a year or so he hopes to travel down to your Philadelphia, Andrea, become a partner with his brother George in his shipping trade along the river."

Then Ethan began to reveal something strikingly different from what he normally quilled, straying from comfortable things of Harvard and Mr. Gills' print shop, of his father and tavern in Lexington, of his sensuous feelings for me, of us. He confided about a stranger who had galloped into Boston earlier that evening, and the explosive episode that occurred at the Green Dragon Tavern that night. Ethan and his four Harvard friends had been sipping mugs of ale and chatting of their futures for an hour or two, then slowly began to wade into the various frictions continuing to stew between the colonies and London. They discussed that despised tax on tea shipped into the colonies, a duty parliament and the king refused to repeal. And they talked of the tensions brewing about Boston once again, now that hundreds of redcoat troops had returned from their haven on Castle Island to drill on the grass of the common and patrol the port's cobblestones, wharfs and docks.

He explained that Ben and Myles continued to lean toward the positions of the crown that night, just as they had most times their Junto group gathered, somehow believing that relations between the colonies and London would begin to improve as differences slowly dissolved. They'd say colonists must maintain faith with the king and show loyalty to his royal governors, while Ethan, Josiah and Sam failed to be swayed by such convictions, voicing their opinions too. I knew Ethan believed supporting the positions espoused by most patriot Whigs over the past several years was the proper course, and he quilled how the three unsuccessfully tried to convince Benjamin and Myles to support such views.

"I tried to explain how the cries of the sons of liberty were becoming more righteous with each passing year," Ethan revealed in that June letter, "not only here in Boston, but throughout all the colonies. I told them I believed it just for colonists to heed the sons' plea to avoid all those London goods too, and that I supported women like you and your friends, Betsy and Lydia. I'm proud of you, Andrea," he tenderly added, making me feel good while bringing me closer to him, "for supporting our patriot cause by sewing homespun clothes."

Even though Benjamin and Myles refused to stray from their loyal beliefs that spring night, Ethan's Junto group came to agree that every colonist has a fundamental right to his or her opinion, and that the colonies should strive to bring about change peacefully. Then the tone of Ethan's lines began to expose that fiery event in the tavern that night, a place bustling with shopkeepers, tradesmen, lawyers and merchants, along with a few weary men from the docks and two strangers from a village somewhere north of Boston. Yet it was one of those strangers near the rear of the tavern, standing confident and strong at the barreled bar just right of the fireplace bricks, who snatched the attention of Ethan and his Junto friends. He stood straight with his back to the tavern, a mug of foaming ale gripped in his hand as he pressed to the bar, and seemed comfortably in his element.

He was several inches above his nearest competitor and seemed boldly fit for a man Ethan believed middle-aged, and a dirtied shirt wrapped his thick arms, tan breeches hugged bulging thighs and grey stockings vanish into dark muddied boots. His features were sculptured by the toils of Irish and Scottish descent, and whenever he twisted his sepia tan eyes seemed to glare about the tavern in a stoic stare as his soft brown hair twined to a tail brushed his neck. From across the room Ethan could see a dark tricorn hat set on a rustic coat resting to his left on the barreled bar, and nearby was a long black musket leaning to the fireplace bricks, its weathered elm butt harmlessly nestled to the oak slats of the tavern floor. "That stranger looked almost like an ancient Roman warrior," Ethan quilled, "as though he could slay beasts of the frontier with wicked blows, then wrestle a snorting ox from its plow."

Amid the glow of a barreled bar lamp and the flicker of table candles, Ethan would glance from time to time to that intriguing stranger from his table near the corner window peering over King Street, even staring now and then as his Junto friends delved into troubles simmering about the colonies. "Sometimes I could even hear what he was saying to his friend on his right," Ethan explained, "and thought I heard them say things about the town of Epson, some eighty miles north in the Colony of New

Hampshire. Myles said he and his father once traveled to that place, a farming village nestled in the Suncook Valley several miles northwest of Portsmouth."

Soon Ethan and his friends could hear that man voicing disparaging things about the king's soldiers roaming Boston, belittling remarks the crown's Tories would surely view as disloyal. And as Ethan nervously glanced about the tavern, wondering of the sentiments of others who might be listening, he began to hear more unflattering things about parliament and King George. "He sounded like a colonist who had experienced some ugly things," he quilled, "troubling assaults upon his property and beliefs, while expressing in rather clear terms just what his views truly were. He spouted what he thought was best for all the colonies, Andrea, especially his New Hampshire, and his opinions oozed patriot Whigs ideals. And the more I listened, the more I realized, his views were much like mine."

As that stranger continued to softly spew contempt for royal governors and the crown, a burst of cold night air surged into the tavern as a trio of the king's soldiers clumped inside with a latching swing of the door. Many in the tavern, including Ethan and his Junto group, and that man and his friend from the Colony of New Hampshire, spun, twisted and stared to those royal troops in dark tricorn hats and crimson coats, menacing muskets dangling shoulders. For an eerie moment a strange hush hovered over the room, as if a malicious chill had swept through the tavern, then glancing about gleaming lamps and pulsating candles, they strutted in muddied boots across the oak slats to a table between Ethan's and that spirited man from the village of Epson. Ethan watched as they carefully placed their muskets against a nearby chair and tossed their tricorns to the table, and as the little flame of their candle anxiously fluttered, each slid to the haven of a chair with scratching tugs and scrapes.

Soon most in the tavern resumed their discussions with spirits, wine and ale amid tiny flames flickering candles, delving into the nuances of merchant deals or exchanging beliefs about colonial events and Tory and Whig views, rather expected things for a Saturday evening at the Green Dragon Tavern. But that stranger's stare never wavered from those three young redcoats, an intense glare that seemed to enhance as one of those soldiers spouted to the barkeep, "Hey, how's bout three ales over here." And while Josiah and Myles snapped a glance and continued their Junto discussion with Benjamin and Sam who hadn't flinched, Ethan watched and listened to the king's men and that intriguing man at the barreled bar, wondering what was to unfold.

"This damn Boston is startin to get under my skin," the bulkier of the three sputtered in a tone most of the tavern were sure to hear. And with his back to that stranger watching and listening from the barreled bar, he pressed back to the slats of his chair and tauntingly added, "These bloody farmers around here, whys, theys nothin but blooming dopes, each one of em of Cambridge, Somerville and Medford, all those filthy towns! If only those back home in Shrewsbury could see."

"Come on, Charlie," the slimmest redcoat nearer Ethan insisted from across the table, "keep it down. We don't know who's in here, and we don't want trouble. Remember what the captain said. Let's just drink our ale and mind our own business."

"Aw, horse dung!" Charlie spouted before tipping his mug and gulping more ale. "To the devil with trouble! To the devil with Boston too, with this whole damn Massachusetts Bay, all the colonies! Just put me on a ship bound for home, to England, to civility, and I'll be a jolly soldier." As he chugged more ale and his pair of redcoat friends fiddled with their mugs while snapping nervous glances about the tavern, that New Hampshire stranger, standing stoic with his back pressed to the barreled bar, glared to the back of Charlie.

Then suddenly, as if Charlie had mysteriously sensed that stranger's eyes slicing contemptuous glares into his back, the king's soldier spun in his chair and angrily stared to the man from Epson. "What the hell do you think you're lookin at?!" he blasted. And as Ethan and his Junto friends watched those two men grip their ale with defiant glares, that redcoat blasted once again, "Well, you bloomin dope, what the hell you lookin at?!"

Ethan and his Harvard friends, and all those colonists scattered about the tavern, watched in a nervous silence as the farmer from Epson stood stoic and hushed, glaring to Charlie's eyes for a moment or two. Then spinning and pressing his belly to the barreled bar, turning his back to the king's soldiers, that farmer and his friend whispered a few scornful words amidst taunting laughs, then tipped their dripping mugs and swigged more ale.

"Hey you!" blurted Charlie in an intimidating tone. "Ya you, bloody farmer, I'm talkin to you! Turn around!"

Every colonist about the tavern could sense the fiery intensity snapping between that redcoat and Epson man, and as frictions crackled the air, the third soldier pressed back into the slats of his chair and spouted a surprising royal jab of his own. "Hey, farmer man, we're talkin to you!"

Ethan watched as that New Hampshire man slowly spun, pulled back his shoulders with a bold swoosh while balancing strong in his boots, and with his mug gripped tightly, stood stoic and glared to the king's three men. As an anxious hush once again befell upon the tavern for a moment or two, that farmer's friend didn't move, just kept his belly pressed to the bar while nervously vanishing into his ale.

"Well, you bloomin farmer," that bulky redcoat clumsily blasted, still twisting and glaring from his chair, "or whatever you are, I'm waitin. What the hell do you think you're lookin at?!"

Without so much as a flinch, blink or nod, that Epson man gently clicked his ale to the barreled bar and pulled back his shoulders once again, and with a firm demeanor and icy stare, calmly said, "I'll tell you, son, all three of ya, and I'll make it real simple so you'll understand. I've seen stupid boys before, but I must say, I do believe I'm looking at three of the dumbest, bloody damn redcoats I've ever seen. Now, why don't you, royal soldiers, put those mugs down and get! Go back to your warehouse, to your barracks or that bloody island, or wherever you vermin burrow each night, and sleep this one off."

Ethan quilled that he could see an angry shock spray across the faces of the crown's soldiers, perhaps a display of ruffled egos or defiance of such daring colonial words, yet each simply stared in a bewildered hush. And after a moment or two of inflaming glares, that Epson farmer insisted once again in an intimidating tone, "Well, you dumb redcoats, you heard me. Get your royal arses out of them chairs, and get the hell out of this tavern, now. I want to drink my ale without your royal stench fouling the air."

That burly redcoat suddenly scraped back his chair with a scratching screech and sprang to his muddied boots, then spun and stood hushed in a defiant glare just a few feet from that New Hampshire farmer. Then as candles anxiously flickered and frictions snapped about the tavern, his two royal friends popped up in their boots and joined that daring stare. "You bloody farmer!" Charlie boldly spritzed. "You the one who's gonna make sure we get from this place?"

"Son," that Epson man spritely replied, his arms pressing to his sides, "if you three, soldiers, do anything but leave, and I mean now, if you utter just one more royal word, that's precisely what I intend to do."

"You damn tiller!" that redcoat Charlie brazenly blasted as his two friends rushed to his side.

Ethan and his Junto friends, and all those Bostonians gathered in the tavern, would forever wonder of what they had witnessed that spring night. "Nobody could have predicted what happened next," Ethan quilled in his June letter. "It was as if that Epson man had waited his entire life for that very moment, springing into action as if inspired by some mythical spirit, while the rest of us simply gripped goblets, tins and mugs and watched amid a throng of oohs, awes and gasps." With bravado spraying his eyes, that farmer lurched and snatched the back of Charlie's neck with his left hand, and before the king's soldier could fathom his fate, he clutched the behind of that redcoat's breeches with the other and hustled toward the tavern door.

"He rushed with the force of an ox, Andrea, racing that redcoat across the tavern floor before ramming his royal hair with a crashing bang through the door. Shards of splintering oak went flying into the night, and we watched as that redcoat wildly tumbled down the planks into the dark, finally coming to a dazed rest on the cold damp stones of King Street."

Amid an array of stunned stares, that banished soldier's two redcoat friends rushed toward that Epson farmer still gazing through the shattered door, and before realizing their royal zeal, the thinner of the two struck a mighty blow to the side of the farmer's neck. As if simply nagged by a tiny pestering beast, without a burly moan or whiff of fright that New Hampshire man twisted, and with the might of a frontier bear, whacked his fist into the nose of that young redcoat. Ethan and the others watched as the soldier sailed through the panes right of the tavern door, crashing down planks to the cobblestones as pieces and shards of glass sprayed into the night and crackled to the slats of the tavern floor.

Suddenly the third royal soldier, who had yet to experience the sting of battle and the cold cobblestones of King Street, abandoned his zeal, raised his hands with a yielding swing and surrendered. "Alright, stop! That's it, we're done!"

"Damn right you boys are done," that Epson man calmly replied with an insistent stare before glancing to the two dizzily rising in the dark from their dazed sprawl on the stones. Then spinning his gaze back to that yielding redcoat and glancing to their muskets and tricorns resting at their table, he added with an emphatic glare, "Now get! And take that royal junk, and those two bloody dummies out there, with you."

Some in the tavern quickly erupted in supportive bursts of "hear, hear!" as others perhaps more loyal to the king simply watched and quietly sipped spirits from goblets, mugs and tins, while that Epson man brushed his breeches and shirt and returned to his ale waiting at the barreled bar. Ethan and his Junto group gazed with fascination as that farmer calmly tipped his mug and sputtered a few whispers to his friend, then watched through the corner window as that trio of royal men mustered their remaining wits. They flicked the humiliation from their crimson coats and donned their tricorn hats, and with muskets dangling shoulders, retreated on the cobblestones into the night toward the eastern docks of King Street.

Without muttering a disparaging word, the barkeep gathered and swept the bits, pieces and shards of the shattered panes and tavern door, and Ethan and his friends humbly discussed what they had just seen while darting anxious glances to that Epson man sipping ale at the bar. For a while they pivoted their thoughts to less fiery things, slowly taming the excitement that had erupted that April night, and then their little Junto group disbanded for the final time. Ethan stepped through the dark back to his room at Mr. Gills' house, and as a foggy mist gently shrouded Boston, he wondered of what he had witnessed that chilly spring night.

"Although I was a bit stunned at first," quilled Ethan about what he had seen, "I was impressed with the daring actions of that stranger from the Colony of New Hampshire, and the patriot Whig positions he espoused. The determination he displayed in the tavern that night, his courage and resolve, made me, and I suppose all of us, feel rather feeble." Ethan would later discover that the name of that farmer was McLaughlin, or perhaps it was McElroy, Kelly or McClary, and like his father in Lexington, was the proprietor of a tavern in the village of Epson.

Near the close of Ethan's June letter he explained how he too told his Junto friends earlier that night of his plans once his studies at Harvard were done. "I'm going back to Lexington, Andrea," he gently quilled, "got to, at least for a year or so, maybe more. I've watched how dad's been slowing down, how his ability to keep up with the strains and chores of the tavern are becoming more and more limited. His wounded leg seems to be getting a bit worse, little by little, making things difficult, what with all those sacks and crates of supplies, carting and lifting barrels and bags. I know I can help."

Ethan also confided that Mr. Giles said he could return to his print shop, doing more creative things while expanding his duties with the Lexington Gazette, even suggesting he might want to come in as a partner someday. It would be an opportunity to escape from the tavern too, at least for a little while, and utilize the printing technics he learned at Mr. Gill's Boston shop, as well as the enlightening ideals honed at Harvard the past four years. As I read Ethan's words I could sense his happiness at being given hope of quilling articles of his own about the frictions stewing about Boston and Massachusetts Bay, all the colonies, of the tensions being spurred by London. And I knew of his desire to see his creations printed in Mr. Giles' Gazette, especially the passions of his poems.

"I don't know what the future holds," he confessed, "but no matter what might happen in the weeks, months and years to come, know I love you. Wherever I might be, Andrea, whatever you might be doing, remember always that I miss you, want you. If you only knew how desperately I wish to could gallop to Philadelphia this very moment, wrap you in my arms, be with you, but I can't. The time just isn't right. I'm compelled to go home to Lexington, feel a responsibility to help dad. Maybe the coming months at Mr. Giles' print shop will open new frontiers for me, bring a future I hope will someday be yours and mine.

"But no matter my course, Andrea, know that I need you in my life, even if only with passions stroked with our quills. Maybe, and I'm simply wishing, you'll find your way back to Massachusetts Bay, perhaps to visit your aunt and uncle in Boston, and if you do, I'll bring you to Lexington. I've told dad about you, about us, and many times he's said how much he hopes to meet you someday. There's a tranquil hill nearby, Andrea, and on summer nights the sky is sprayed with bright twinkling dots. We can just lie on the grass together, touching and talking about anything, and count all those stars. I miss you, and wait for your next letter. Love, Ethan."

His words laced with feelings of anticipation and joy were brushed with a tinge of disappointment, for I desperately wanted to see him, hoped he might find a way to gallop to Philadelphia once his Harvard days were done, yet I frustratingly understood. Ethan loved his father so, and saw his duty with him, at the tavern in Lexington, and seeing such tenderness, knowing how deeply he cared, warmed my heart even more. I slowly succumbed to the notion that at that moment our lives were not supposed to align, and realized, vexingly so, that our future would need to continue to be entwined with parchment and quills. Yet as I pinched Ethan's letter, folded it to its creases and laid it easy in that secret drawer of nursing desk, I could sense apprehensions set free by the enticing thoughts of traveling to Boston and Lexington, feelings and visions that thrilled me. And before I drifted to fanciful dreams that early June night, I quilled a letter back to Ethan stroked with hopes of all those alluring things.

While we exchanged passions and plans with quills that spring and into summer of 1772, the tensions that had existed between King George and his colonies seemed to ease for a moment, or perhaps they were simply being ignored. Yes, it had been two years since that awful Boston night, and such dreadful encounters had since been avoided, yet there remained many who disapproved of the ways of London and the presence of the king's troops, spirited men like that Epson farmer from the Colony of New Hampshire. Maybe there was a delusional sense of calm in those days, for discontent seemed to continue gathering in the shadows, a quiet struggle manifesting in unseen ways, such as those like Lydia, Betsy and me stitching homespun things Sunday nights. But sometimes the winds of discontent would howl about the colonies for all women, children and men to see, whether patriot Whig, loyal Tory or otherwise, and cause the sea to surge east and crash upon the rocks of England.

There were rumors of patriot events and activities taking place in villages and towns throughout the colonies that spring and summer, stories I'd hear in the hospital halls, and there were opinions being voiced in newspapers in Dover, Savannah, Williamsburg and the port of New York, here in my Evening Post and Pennsylvania Gazette too. Pamphlets and papers were printing the defiant words of colonists up in Ethan's Boston too, spirited opinions of men like Doctor Warren and Sam Adams. They were Whigs continuing to expose the simmering disagreements between the colonies and London, revealing what they viewed as unjust actions from parliament and the crown, such as laws and policies that denied our colonies "the fundamental right to pay our own judges with our own shillings and pounds."

Some believed that rulings from our colonial courts were being skewed by such policies, judicial findings that favored the king and his royal governors, and some lawyers, shopkeepers, merchants and tradesmen were voicing concern of improper settlements and unjust sentences. Most were colonists with an entrenched stake in the fiscal interests of the colonies, some loyal Tories and their friends like Franz, while most if I recall were patriot Whigs. And near the end of spring the Pennsylvania Evening Post printed another appeal by that association created by Mr. Adams up in Boston years before, fresh pleas for non-importation of English goods. It was a letter being distributed throughout the colonies that urged women and men to express disapproval of the disturbing policies still being spewed from London, laws and acts it described as "infringements of our liberties, of our sovereign rights to live free."

And I remember a story Ethan conveyed in a letter earlier that spring, of a gathering of women, children and men on the grass of the common near that special Boston tree shortly after dusk on a chilly Saturday night. He explained that his friend Henry told him about the gathering a day or two before, having come by Mr. Gill's print shop after drills with his special grenadiers, a militia comprised of sons of liberty and other Whig men, a patriot group he hoped Ethan would someday join.

Ethan left the print shop after finishing his printing chores a bit after seven that spring night, leaving behind Mr. Gill busy setting type, and quilled that Henry was already at the common, along with Mr. Edes. As Ethan neared the darkness of the field from the cobblestones of Queen Street, he could see scores of colonists milling about the shadows near that liberty tree, Bostonians bundled in coats, scarves and hats amid the glow of torches, lanterns and candles flickering about the night.

Aging men were gathering with the young, some gripping sticks with fiery tips dipped in tallow, and there were many boys of perhaps eight, ten or twelve who would someday become entwined in it all. Scores of women in dainty bonnets were massing too, and a few of the younger ones were mingling close by, little girls and boys clinging to their mothers. And in the shadows Ethan could see an array of smaller children scampering at play, oblivious of the night's reasons, little silhouettes frolicking about the flickering flames and dangling free of fright and harm from twisting limbs of oak and elm.

As Ethan stepped from the cobblestones into the shadows roaming the grass from all those pulsating flames, carefully maneuvering through the throng toward that liberty tree, he spotted Henry standing alone, quietly watching as a man stepped onto an elm box. Ethan waved and joined his friend as their eyes latched upon that man balancing in muddied shoes atop that rickety crate in tan breeches and coat flaring blue. He stood over the crowd by a foot or two just beneath a dangling liberty limb, and standing stoic, straight and strong, scanned the gathering of women, children and men in a searching gaze. And as Ethan, Henry and all those colonists whispered and watched, he signaled for quiet and calm with an easy sweep of his arms and pat of his hands in the cooling mist of the night air.

"That's James Otis," Henry whispered with a nudge to Ethan's side just before Mr. Otis began to speak, not knowing that Ethan had briefly met him in the print shop many months before. Mr. Otis spoke for several minutes that night, emphatically spouting of what he viewed as an assortment of unjust actions by parliament and the king, many of the things Mr. Adams and others were exposing in those days. "He was adamant in his words," Ethan quilled, "and with fire in his eyes, alerted the crowd of the many concerns and troubles brewing about the colonies as a result of the nonsense coming from London."

Soon more spirited men climbed atop that rickety crate to express their opinions of the disturbing frictions simmering between the colonies and the crown, doctors and lawyers like John Adams and Mr. Warren, and printers and merchants like Ben Edes and Mr. Hancock's friend, Joseph Barrell. Ethan confided how the crowd seemed strangely polite, staring in a hush as if captured by some mystical spell, and that even some of the children quieted their play to watch and listen. Yet he confessed that it was Mr. Otis who truly mesmerized the throng of Bostonians gathered on the common that spring night, women and men clutching every word being expressed with a dignifying grace from atop that crate. Then after an hour or two of spirited bursts amidst all those lamps, candles and flames, everyone dispersed to taverns, shops and homes, Henry to his bookstore and Ethan to the haven of his bedroom.

While those types of stirring gatherings were taking place up in Boston and rumored to be happening throughout the colonies, another story began to swirl with the northeast winds early that summer of 1772. It was an encounter that sent frightening chills surging my skin, a dangerous event that caused colonists everywhere to tremble, even loyal Tories and patriot Whigs of Philadelphia and Germantown, mother, father and Franz too. Ethan would later say that his Lexington Gazette exposed the destructive violence in the Colony of Rhode Island in late June, repeating the fiery tale of the king's *HMS Gaspee* first revealed by that colony's Newport Mercury news. And if I recall, by the first hours of summer the Pennsylvania Evening Post was saying that incident between spirited colonists and that royal ship was an unfortunate yet predictable affair, an alarming story that swept to villages, ports and towns in leather satchels of swift riders and weathered hulls of merchant ships.

Some said that the fate of the *HMS Gaspee* was simply the latest incident to erupt in those days about Rhode Island's Narragansett Bay, a small sea of turbulent waters some fifty miles south of Ethan's Boston. It seems the king's customs agents had been assaulted several times near those chilly waters, attacked by disgruntled shippers and merchants bent upon destroying property of the crown, angry patriot Whigs rumored to have burned an array of royal boats while tossing London goods into the roiling bay.

When revelations of those destructive events reached the chambers of Joseph Wanton, the colony's aging royal governor, and began to sweep across the sea into the halls of London, the crown's initial reaction was viewed by many loyal Tories as rather timid. But not so with the *HMS Gaspee* they say, for many would boast that parliament and the king were viewing that troubling affair in an increasingly dangerous light. "This is not only an assault upon His Majesty's Royal Navy," many of the crown's loyal allies were heard to spew, "but a bloody assault upon the King himself. As such, this mandates a proper royal response!"

The Evening Post suggested that a slew of royal actions had been taking place about Narragansett Bay for months prior to that assault upon the *Gaspee*, intimidating things that were spurring frictions already simmering about the colonies. "Recent proclamations have authorized the king's navy," exposed the Post, "to support functions of the crown's customs agents in unjust activities like confiscating merchant goods." They were spirits, fabrics and wares Franz and loyal Tories would angrily say had been secretly unloaded by patriot Whigs upon colonial docks without proper payment of taxes and duties to London. Royal sailors were rumored to be assisting too, disembarking warships to arrest colonists royal governors believed had slighted the king's agents or committed disloyal acts against property of the crown.

In the midst of such escalating things, parliament also unleashed a new troubling assault upon the colonies it called the Dockyard Act. The Post described it as "an appallingly vile, unjust law" that authorized customs agents to not only arrest and punish those deemed to be violating London's positions, but to shackle such colonists in the hulls of royal ships and sail them for trial three thousand miles across the sea in England. Many about the colonies were said to be viewing the increasingly intrusive actions of the crown as unreasonable infringements on the liberties of every colonist, particularly it seems, the seaman of Narragansett Bay. And some who opposed the king's agents in the Colony of Rhode Island chose to increasingly display their brewing displeasure not only through boisterous speeches of disobedience, but through fiery acts of patriot defiance.

Some said the crown's *HMS Gaspee* was a sleek schooner of three masts under the helm of a young officer named Dudingston, a Royal Navy vessel that first sailed north from the chilly waters of Rhode Island Sound into Narragansett Bay months before. The Evening Post would later propose, "Lieutenant Dudingston had been personally sent to those waters by King George the Third, authorized to enforce the despicable regulations that our shackling our colonial trade." He'd been ordered to collect the crown's unjust duties and taxes they'd say, and arrest any colonist viewed to be disobeying London's intrusive maritime rules. It was a bay stretching some thirty miles north from the docks of Newport, a village on the Island of Providence some fifteen miles wide edged by an array of rocky crevasses and fingers near the sound. And although the waters of the bay were scattered by a slew of little islands with quaint names like Conanicut, Gould, Prudence and Hope, the lieutenant was said to be intent upon patrolling every jutting rock and watery nook.

I remember how loyal Tories of Germantown and Philadelphia that spring and summer were saying troubling things about Narragansett Bay, calling those waters "the disloyal center of contraband goods being sailed to-and-fro the colonies." Many loyal merchants like Franz were voicing what seemed selfish concerns too, and spouting dangerous things like "justice must be done!" And the Earl of Dartmouth, the king's minister assigned to keep watch upon the colonies, a loyal man most of London knew as Viscount Lewisham and many in the colonies simply called William Legge, was rumored to be inciting retaliation by the crown. "Narragansett Bay seethes with treacherous rebels," he was reported to have informed the king, "a disloyal rabble intent upon flaunting our laws and denying England its rightful duties and taxes. The hour is now, for the crown to act boldly!"

Then shortly after dawn on the second Tuesday of June, a cool spring morn shrouded by mist, those simmering beliefs, fears and scorns came to fruition on the chilly waters of Narragansett Bay. Royal sailors of the *HMS Gaspee* were said to have spotted the colonial boat *Hannah*, a smaller lone-mast vessel known to sail up and down the bay carrying sacks and bags stuffed with packages and letters, and crates brimming an array of precious goods. The Evening Post suggested that the king's lieutenant viewed the *Hannah* through the lifting fog, and within moments was "spouting nonsensical beliefs that her hull was bulging with contraband, that her disloyal crew was thieving from the crown." His sailors dutifully turned the *Gaspee* upon his command, and with her sails bulging in the morning winds, sliced north in chase of the *Hannah,* a maneuver quickly discovered by an alert patriot helmsman. "In a frantic attempt to escape into the bay, that Rhode Island vessel swiftly sliced north past the docks of Newport and through the waters off little Gould Island and the narrows between the islands of Conanicut and Prudence."

There were rumors that soon colonists along the western shore of the bay became aware of the unfolding chase, woman, children and men watching as swift riders, with snapping glances and alerting hollers, trailed that nautical race along the ruts and stones of the winding road north. They watched as the *Hannah* cut through the icy waters past tiny Hope Island, and as the *Gaspee* sliced the blue in chase, the patriots sailed toward a rocky point jutting from Patience Island near a little inlet south of the village of Warwick. After several hours of hectic chase, the king's young officer found his royal ship slowing in the shallows near that point, waters known by colonists to be scattered by hidden sandy mounds. And as the *Hannah* continued her dash north to the haven-docks of Providence, the *Gaspee* became frustratingly mired in the clutching muck south of those jutting rocks.

By late afternoon stories of the chase were swirling about the docks of Warwick and Providence and villages and towns dotting the northwest shores of Narragansett Bay, and the *HMS Gaspee* remained stuck in the muck as the waters of the bay lapped the elm slats of her hull and gulls sailed the fading blue. Colonists could see her crew scampering to release the king's ship from that sandy grip, tugging ropes from little boats and splashing oars upon their lieutenant's command, and watched as the king's men slowly realized their fate rested with the tide. And while dusk sprayed its colors over the frontier that brisk spring night, the crown's crew began its nervous wait to be set free as an anxious hush settled upon the *Gaspee*.

While those royal sailors remained embedded in the sands off that point that spring night, it seems that defiant winds were beginning to stir the patience of nearby patriot Whig men. The Evening Post revealed that dozens of dockworkers, tradesmen, merchants and seamen, many believed to be from that colony's spirited sons of liberty, gathered to talk of resistance shortly after dusk in the Sabine Tavern a bit south of Providence. They were an array of daring men with intriguing names like Ephraim Bowen, Abe Whipple and Doc Mawney, Aaron Biggs, Joe Bucklin and Johnny Brown.

Most were said to have discussed for several hours what to do about that royal ship while others assembled a small fleet of tiny crafts, then finalizing their plan in the quiet hours of early morn, around three they boarded all those little bobbing boats. One of the men would later say they gently stroked the oars under the gaze of a crescent moon, slowly creeping south toward the *Gaspee* in an easy row, and after an hour or so of quietly skimming the bay, her shadowy figure sprouted from the dark. As the colonists slithered closer to her hull, her trio of masts eerily pitching toward the dawn soon to creep from the sea, Abe Whipple shattered the hush with a cry to a royal sailor wearily leaning to a rail. "Ahoy, lad," he hollered in feign, "I'm the sheriff of County Kent. We've come to help."

As that royal sailor gazed with a puzzling squint down to the dark waters, those quietly skimming boats began to gently tap the hull of the *HMS Gaspee*, and without uttering a sound, those Rhode Island men sprang in their soggy boots and swiftly scaled the hull of the king's ship. "We sprayed across her deck," that witness would confide, "most gripping muskets and some clutching flintlock pistols, and within minutes we had subdued dozens of dazed royal men, their stunned Lieutenant Dudingston too." Although muskets and pistols, both royal and patriot, were fired on her deck early that morning, it seems the only true wound was sustained by the king's lieutenant. Some would say it was a musket blast by Johnny Brown that ripped through his thigh, but most would come to believe it was the pistol of Abe Whipple that bloodied those royal breeches, wounding the heart of the crown.

"Soon after the daring assault by the raiders of Sabine Tavern," the Evening Post revealed, "and after the lieutenant's painful wound was dutifully tended, the king's men were afforded safe passage to shore, herded into little boats and set free." But some of those spirited Sabine men were not finished with their defiance against the crown, and as the new day began to spray glistening rays upon the calm waters of the bay, they unleashed their remaining rage upon the *HMS Gaspee*. "Those Rhode Island men torched her royal ropes, sails, hull and deck," continued the Post, "engulfing the king's ship in an inferno of rebellious flames. Within the hour only darkened ribs could be seen smoldering her keel, and ashen shards and charred little bits were slowly floating away, spirited remnants doomed to roam the waters of Narragansett Bay."

"Hum, the *Gaspee*," Samuel suddenly sputtered with a quizzical look, "I don't think I've ever heard of that ship, grandma, or what those patriots did. What happened to those Rhode Island men? I mean, what did the king do?"

"I'm not surprised you haven't heard of the *Gaspee*," I whispered, caressing the words of Ethan's poem as Samuel peered to the swaying tips of distant elms and rocked easy. "I suppose many of my generation have forgotten about that ship too, or maybe, Samuel, they never really understood. The stories about that frightening event started to fade after a year or so, cast aside by more unsettling things soon to erupt in those years just before the war. But for me, Samuel, I'll always remember that fiery affair."

"Of so many things that happened back then," he gently asked with an attentive glance, "why do you remember that so well?"

"I think many colonists began to see things differently," I reflected as a warm summer wisp tossed the silvery strands of my thinning hair. "The *HMS Gaspee* wasn't a merchant ship or some private boat, Samuel, but one of the king's own, a Royal Navy vessel, and its burning caused a change in the relations between the colonies and London. Although it was daring, it was such an abrasively defiant act against the crown, that I guess things could never truly be the same. And that event seemed to dim the views of many colonists, especially patriot Whigs, about all the king's warships and royal crews over here, as well as our already strained relations with the increasing numbers of redcoat troops. Some throughout the colonies, woman and men of Germantown and Philadelphia, Ethan's Massachusetts Bay too, were also saying that the destruction of the *Gaspee* simply spurred more unflattering views some of England already had about the colonies. Many wondered, Samuel, even mother and father, Ethan and I, your Grandfather Franz too, what nasty things the king and parliament might now do."

I stroked the passions of Ethan's poem nestled in the pocket of my summer dress and listened to the soothing sounds of rustling leaves, while Samuel tapped his fingers to the arms of his chair and gazed to those distant trees. "But, grandma," he inquisitively asked while nudging his chair into a robust rock, "what happened to those Rhode Island men? Did they just return to their normal lives, or did the king come after them?"

I released my caress of Ethan's words, slowed my rock and snatched another sip of wine, and as Samuel gazed into the warm afternoon winds, I clicked my goblet to our little table and returned my fingers to the haven of my summer dress. "It's been over fifty years," I softly confessed, sliding my fingers and reaching for memories, "and sometimes, Samuel, things fade. Yet I can still smell the scent of spring flowers, and feel the emotions that gripped me in those days. I remember that a special panel was eventually created to review what happened to the *Gaspee*, a commission of inquiry assigned to decide the fate of those patriot Whigs, a tribunal of the king's men like that royal governor of the Colony of Rhode Island and Judge Horsmanden of the Colony of New York, and Peter Oliver, a loyal Tory from Ethan's Massachusetts Bay."

"What happened, grandma?" Samuel sputtered impatiently. "What happened next?"

"To the dismay of many loyal Tories, Samuel, that panel dismissed the dreadful accusations, many saying that the royal governor of Rhode Island betrayed his duties to London by showing sympathy for those patriot men. Some believed that pressures by colonial Whigs were also brought to bear, rumors which have lingered through the years. And even though most knew that the king and many of parliament insisted on charges of treason, loyal men like Prime Minister North and that Mr. Legge, that commission rejected those demands. To the elation of patriots throughout the colonies, of Lydia, Betsy and I, and Ethan too, damning action against the raiders of Sabine Tavern was mercifully rejected."

"So that was the end of it?"

"Yes, Samuel, that was the end of it," I whispered with another tender caress of Ethan's poem, "at least for those Sabine men. But that episode seemed to ignite a rebellious sense of colonial dismay. Some in the colonies were soon expressing concerns about that troubling affair, not of that panel's mercy, but of the notion that the fate of those men could have turned out differently, reminding colonists that those daring men could have just as easily been shackled in the hull of a king's warship and sailed to London for trial. I think it was the reality of that, along with a growing number of other disturbing things in those days, which spurred some patriot Whigs in Boston to reform its committee of correspondence, colonists like Sam Adams and Doctor Warren. Ethan quilled in his letters back then that smaller committees also began to sprout in villages and towns throughout the Colony of Massachusetts Bay, including one reformed by Nathan Giles in Lexington."

"I know you said something about those committees before," Samuel uttered as a blush brushed his cheeks, "but, what were those committees again?"

"They were groups of colonists wanting to communicate," I gently reminded in a grandmotherly way, "to discuss increasing tensions between the colonies and London, and first sprouted throughout the colonies several years before to talk about the unjust policies and laws of the king and parliament, like that despised Stamp Act. Only now, it was that *Gaspee* affair that spurred the resurgence of those committees."

I slowed my rock and glanced to Samuel gazing to a puffy string of bright little clouds slowly drifting toward the sea, his chair in a hypnotic rock and peer reaching for the past, then reflectively added. "Once that committee in Boston was resurrected after that Rhode Island affair, and spread about the Colony of Massachusetts Bay, others were reborn in ports, villages and towns throughout the colonies, in Charles Towne, Dover and Savannah, over in Williamsburg and up in the Colony of New York, here in Philadelphia and Germantown too. Ethan once quilled that those committees were vital for ensuring proper correspondence not only between villages and towns, but patriot Whig groups throughout the colonies, helping to coordinate a colonial approach to London's increasing encroachment upon our rights and liberties. If I recall, most colonies had formed a core committee within a year or two after that affair, and all the groups were exchanging thoughts and plans carried by swift riders or stuffed in the hulls of colonial merchant ships."

"It sounds like the rebirth of those committees," Samuel proudly concluded, "was a rather significant effect of the torching of that ship."

"I suppose so, Samuel," I whispered, softly stroking Ethan's words, and remembering. "Yes, it probably was. In fact, those committees never stopped meeting after that, delving into the increasing troubles brewing about colonies. And Ethan would soon quill that Mr. Revere was once again corralling a slew of special riders at the behest of the committee in Boston, and forging new riding routes not only in the Colony of Massachusetts Bay, but stretching to all the colonies, down here to Philadelphia too. It was during those days, Samuel, when Ethan became even more involved, agreeing once again to ride patriot Whig messages for Mr. Giles to-and-fro Boston, as well as other villages and towns too, and sometimes, for Mr. Revere."

"Those days seem so trying," Samuel muttered in a reasoning way, "so entwined with difficulty. But what about of you, grandma? What were you doing that spring and summer of 1772?"

"They were, Samuel," I sighed, gazing to silky petals of crimson rose fluttering in the warm summer winds, "truly challenging days, with many more yet to come. I was always busy at the hospital, just finishing my training that June and beginning normal nursing duties. And of course, I was still with Franz. But for me, those days were in truth like so many wonderful weeks and months before, filled with passionate letters between Ethan and me, and with each passing day, my desires to be with him consumed me. Then I awoke one June morning and knew what I had to do, that I had to see Ethan, and began planning my sail to Massachusetts Bay."

Samuel glanced to my eyes and reached for a sip of wine as a whimsical expression brushed his face, then pressing back in the slats of his chair and slowing his rock, he tenderly said. "You know, grandma, in a strange way,

I've always felt you were hiding something special deep inside, memories you've never told another soul. You've made me feel special, telling me your secrets about Ethan today. I suppose I don't often say this, grandma, but I love you."

"Oh, Samuel," I pleasingly gushed, "I love you too." We just rocked our chairs and looked into each other's eyes for a tender moment or two, and as he blushed a bit more I softly added, "I've always wanted you to know these things, Samuel, of the colonies in those days, of the war and so many people, your Grandfather Franz too, but especially, Ethan. I guess after all these years, today just seemed right."

We gazed into the warm summer winds and snapped an affectionate glance to each other's eyes now and then, tender peers which spurred so many reasons why I knew Samuel was so special to me. His tenderness reminded me of Ethan so, his compassion and understanding too, impressions that seemed to erupt from my past to brush a tranquil calm upon my soul. I pressed to the slats of my chair as we rocked and listened to distant leaves rustling in the afternoon breeze, and with each tingling caress of Ethan's poem, I reached for precious memories.

I could sense the displeasure in Franz's tone when I told him of my plans to travel to Boston in early August, to visit Uncle Jason and Aunt Bea, and could feel a tinge of his insecurity when he snatched me into his arms and insisted I not go. Yet I knew I would go, knew I must, and in an uncommon moment of courage, told him so. I desperately wanted to go to Boston to be with my Ethan, if only for a little while, a passionate affair I'd share only with Betsy and Lydia, a twisting secret I'd forever keep from mother, father and Franz. And in a deceiving yet reasoning way I explained why I wanted to go, to unleash some of the strains of four years of nursing duties, if only for a week or so, to ease my mind with Boston air and regroup my energies.

At times there was a telling tremor in Franz's voice when I'd speak of Boston in those days, as if he sensed my secret of Massachusetts Bay, and his demeanor would mysteriously pivot and eyes nervously quiver whenever the notion of Boston was heard. All the while, I strove to keep harm from Franz at bay, to not hurt him in any way, while struggling with an unflattering guilt that would anxiously gnaw my soul. It was a remorseful feeling I was somehow able to stash deep within, a torturous emotion I was able to tame in my own numbing way. Yet as I grappled with dreams those lonely summer nights I was confronted with a twisting truth, that I was a duplicitous woman struggling with intricate expectations, passions and fears. I was clinging to the pressures of an analytical love of diluted emotions for Franz, while bathing in the fiery passions for another man, a magical love for Ethan.

Father soon arranged passage for me on the very tri-masked schooner that sailed me to Boston over two years before, an English vessel scheduled to depart Philadelphia shortly after dawn the last day of July. After sailing down the river and out Delaware Bay, we'd slice the sea north once again past the sands of Long Island and jutting arm of Cape Cod Bay, then moor at a Boston dock on a Tuesday afternoon a bit before dusk, the Fourth of August, 1772. I quickly quilled to Ethan and passionately revealed that I'd be seeing him soon, and asked that he meet me at Aunt Bea's around noon the day after the *Dorchester* docked. I'd be waiting for him up on Beacon Hill, where we first nestled and talked for hours before a crackling fire that enchanting March night, where we last touched, where Ethan pressed his lips to mine.

Although my letter explained that my journey to Boston was being viewed by others as simply a respite from nursing entwined with a caring visit with my aunt and uncle, I gleefully confessed that my true intentions were to spend as much time as possible with Ethan. We could be together in Boston for days, and I desperately wanted to go with him to Lexington, to see his tavern, his home, and finally meet his father. I wasn't truly sure of all the things Ethan and I would do those ten wondrous days we'd have together, but as I pondered the fancies of my coming journey, I knew it really didn't matter. We'd be able to see each other again, touch until those agonizing moments that the *Dorchester* would sail in the hush of an early Saturday morn. That's when I'd leave Boston and my Ethan once again, begin to shutter my passions into that room deep in my heart once again, when I'd begin a somber journey back to my entangling life in Pennsylvania.

On the outside I continued a normal life those remaining days of July, mending patients at the hospital and seeing Franz, while on the inside my passions flared, and when alone in my Germantown room I began to make a special gift for Ethan, a quilt blanket to commemorate his completion of Harvard studies. I suppose a silvery trinket from a Philadelphia shop might be appropriate for most men, but I'd have no such thing for my Ethan, for his gift had to come from my heart, be something more intimate, from my hands to him. At times those sewing nights I'd envision my blanket wrapped about his body, a quilt adorned with my caresses to warm his tender soul, and recall how he once confessed how the shades of autumn soothed him so. I creased and snipped fabrics of greens and browns, yellows, oranges and reds in the solitude of my bedroom during the still of night and before rising for nursing duties, and stitched each tantalizing piece of Ethan's gift in the flickering flame of a lonesome candle.

A little basket of sewing things always rested near the window in the corner of my room in those days, wicker stuffed with little shears and shards of cloth, spindles of colorful thread and thin prickly needles, a sewing basket nudged near my precious quilting frame. It was some four feet high with maple legs and a polished top that curved in an easy arch, a gift from father many years before, and I can still see the proud gleam in his eyes explaining how he finagled it from a London merchant on a Philadelphia dock for just a few shillings and pounds.

I remember how that special quilting table warmed my soul simply upon its sight, nudged close to the window near my little desk, and how good I felt gazing through the panes while pressing a blanket, listening to the patter of a spring shower or watching the swirling snow on a winter day. I could somehow sense a wondrous serenity of life whenever my fingers gently slid its curvy arch, and sometimes my thoughts would wander on wintry nights, escape to the woods and Gunter's Pond glistening of snow and ice.

After a slew of sewing nights Ethan's special quilt was finally finished, three layers of tender fabric intimately entwined. Its upper cloth of emerald green was smothered by an array of snipped autumn leaves and golden soft fleece was pressed to its underside, and hidden within was a padding of silky fibers Betsy had procured, delicate fabric sailed to the colonies from a little island of the Caribbean Sea. I've always thought it my most enchanting blanket, a quilt passionately stitched seven and five feet by caring fingers, a gift I hoped Ethan would find serenely pleasing.

I can still feel the elation that surged my body when I sewed the final stitch just before midnight that last Thursday of July, only hours before the *Dorchester* would sail. The air was warm and muggy after a summer rain, hushed and still that night, when my fingers twisted the needle's final loop along the edge of a little square cloth. Just a moment before I had pressed my lips to that tiny tan patch, a small snip of my childhood now embroidered with caring words scripted with golden thread and stitched to the low right corner of his quilt's tender side. I prayed that from across the miles Ethan would feel my caress when warmly wrapped on snowy winter nights, and hoped that each time he touched that little patch he'd hear me whisper those words stitched in gold: *For Ethan. Congratulations. All my love, Andrea. July 30, 1772.*

I pressed a final kiss to that little patch, folded Ethan's blanket and carefully stuffed it into the largest of my two deerskin bags, and before twisting and turning the remaining hours that night, mercifully dozing now and then, I packed those bags with a few belongings and secured their leather straps into little iron loops. Then shortly after dawn that final day of July, I hugged mother and father and bid them a tender farewell, and as my stomach churned in anxious knots and dew dripped Germantown petals, I climbed to the damp cushion of Franz's carriage for our five mile ride to Philadelphia.

Franz tossed my bags to a little spot just behind the seat and climbed into the buggy, and as he flicked the reins and his mare snapped into an easy trot, I sighed a tender goodbye and softly waved to mother and father watching from the door. We spoke of rather innocuous things as we swayed, bounced and rolled south along the stony ruts of the winding road, and from time to time I'd sneak a glance to that bag secretly stuffed with Ethan's quilt. And as the sound of clumping hooves and creaking wheels faded in an eerie morning mist brushing the trees, hills and fields, an anxious guilt would surge deep inside now and then, only to subside with visions of what might be, of the bliss which awaited me.

I could hear the crunch of tiny pebbles as we scraped the cobblestones of Philadelphia, rolling east past the hospital and Betsy's place, then we came to a stop with a tug of the reins near the *Dorchester* moored along the river. Her bow was thrusting south as her crew unfurled sails and scampered about, and Franz gripped my bags and walked with me up her rigid elm plank. I can still see him handing my bags to a young sailor adorned in maritime white and blue, then leaning and kissing my lips as we each whispered, "I'll miss you." As Franz began to descend he twisted, and with a forlorn glance, sputtered "be safe," then turned and strutted to the dock while I gripped the starboard rail and sailors tugged the plank to her deck. And while some on the dock began to unravel the *Dorchester* from her ties, I gently waved to Franz gazing up, and as she began to slowly flow the waters of the Delaware, we bid each other a soft, "goodbye."

I followed that young sailor still gripping my bags toward the *Dorchester's* stern as her sails, flapping in the summer winds, were tautly tied, then watched as he clicked open the door of my small starboard cabin and plopped my bags at the foot of a quaint little bed. "We trust these accommodations please you, miss," he shyly uttered while stepping out the door, "and please, let us know if you should need anything as we sail." I thanked him for his kindness and closed the door with a snapping click, then stared at the small round window embedded in the hull, its glass swung open near the head of the bed. And as I glanced about my little room and breathed the warming river air, I could feel a sense of liberating relief from the expectations binding me to Philadelphia and Germantown.

Yet my relief was tainted by an unsettling sense of deception that taunted my thoughts now and then, feelings I had come to realize would soon pass, for even though I knew others would disapprove, I had come to believe it was the only path I could follow in those days. Soon the sound of splashing water helped soothe my mind, and glancing to my bag bulging of Ethan's quilt, I could feel its serenity resonating inside. I closed my eyes for a moment and felt a wisp of summer air brush my cheeks, then stepping from my little room and bounding up elm slats to the *Dorchester's* deck, I clutched the stern rail and watched my colony slowly drift past.

Her sails were taut as I watched the spires of Philadelphia fade in the summer haze, and while the warming breeze gently tossed my hair, I could sense the anticipation surge, a joyous feeling I had never known before. Although I knew that sleek ship would slice the waters as quickly as any vessel could, and believed her crew to be confident and strong, I could feel impatient pangs and realized she wasn't swift enough to calm the anxiousness twisting inside. As the waters of Delaware Bay slowly crept toward the bow, I knew I wanted to be in Boston that very moment, not days from then. And as I clutched that rail I could feel Ethan's tender embrace, yet knew we'd have to wait, knew I'd need to tame my flaming desires for many lonely hours.

Over the coming days the *Dorchester* sliced the waters some five hundred miles in its northeast sail to the Colony of Massachusetts Bay, and as the sea sprayed over her bow with each splashing toss, I'd often lie on my cabin bed and nervously wonder what Ethan would think of me. And sometimes while strolling about her deck those warm summer nights, peering into the blackened sea and gazing to pulsating stars, my stomach would twist in anguishing knots with thoughts of, what if he rejects me?

Yet deep inside I knew my doubts weren't truly real, for Ethan and I had exposed our hopes and desires in many letters since that March night. Still, at times I couldn't seem to tame my fears while lying on my little bed and peering to the summer sky through that quaint cabin hole, and would continue to grapple with nonsensical thoughts of what if this, what if that. Then I'd slide my fingers over Ethan's quilt spread over my skin each night, and slowly drift to calming dreams as those troubling doubts faded.

After five long days and four anxious nights, shortly after dawn on the fourth day of August the *Dorchester* sailed north along the eastern shore of that strip of hooking land corralling the waters of Cape Cod Bay. Then a bit past noon she pivoted northwest and began her final leg through Massachusetts Bay and into the waters to Boston Harbor. I gripped the port rail near her bow and gazed through the summer haze as we sliced our final fifty miles of sea, and watched little islands pass as we sailed toward a string of puffy clouds drifting the western horizon.

"They call those islands Raynsford and Gallops, Miss Van Dijk," a dutiful sailor kindly revealed with his hand pointing south, a young man I had come to know as Seaman McGuire, "and that's Lovell Island." Then he confidently swung arm over the starboard rail and proudly added, "Over there, by all those rocks and sandbars, is an island they call Deer."

He proudly pointed to another rocky patch in the distance off the starboard rail, an island in the eastern waters of the harbor he called Little Brewster, and said a few intriguing words about the white tower rising in stone, confiding it was known as Boston Light. "She's guided many a weary sailor into the harbor, miss," he explained, "brought hundreds of ships through a milky fog or mist of a dark night." Ethan once said it was the first lighthouse in all the colonies, mortared some sixty years before, and that its' flaming light was a calming beacon that could be spotted for many miles. I could see two little cottages nestled to the base of the tower's stones, quarters it seems for the keeper and his family, and an iron cannon, its barrel thrusting toward the sea, was perched between elm wheels. "She's not for battle," Seaman McGuire advised before returning to his duties, "but simply to guide. They fire her off on the half hour during a fog, helping to bring ships safely into the harbor."

As we sailed further west I began to realize I was no longer in Germantown or Philadelphia, for anchored about the harbor and moored in the distance at Boston docks was a small fleet of the king's Royal Navy ships. Three or four sturdy masts rose from each royal vessel, most with its sails tightly furled, and each had little round holes carved into its hull, starboard and port, gaps for menacing cannons to thrust and blast in battle. And dangling a thin pole of each stern was a flag of white, red and blue fluttering in the afternoon winds, the symbol of an empire that had ruled the colonies for over a hundred years, the crown's Union Jack.

Yet it was one of the little islands off the port bow as we sliced through the harbor that sent an eerie chill rushing my skin, a gloomy looking patch of sand and grey stones rising from the waters a mile or so from Boston's eastern docks. I could see a strange tan structure that resembled a medieval fort spread about in beige stone, and a string of little buildings lined with small panes that a *Dorchester* sailor said were the soldiers' barracks.

It was that Castle Island Ethan had quilled about in some of his letters, and that fort was the one he called Castle William, the place many of the king's soldiers had been quartered since that bloody night on King Street over two years before. I could see scores of royal soldiers strutting about the island, little figures in dark boots and bright breeches milling about the haze, troops with black tricorn hats and long musket guns slung over crimson coats.

And there was a soldier standing in the summer haze who grabbed my attention more than any other, drawing my eyes to his mystical stance. He seemed several years younger than Ethan and me, not much older than a boy, and stood near a rickety dock that twisted into the bay from piles of rock, his red coat flaring over breeches and musket dangling his shoulder. He was watching the *Dorchester* slicing toward the Boston docks, with one boot perched upon a big stone and his eyes in a stoic gaze, and I wondered what he was thinking as our lives slowly passed. His stare stayed steady as we sailed, as if he were looking deep into me, and after a while he began to vanish in the encroaching dusk and misty haze.

As the August sun slowly succumbed to its fate, brushing strings of clouds drifting the western sky in shades of yellow, orange and red, the *Dorchester* eased into Scarlet's Wharf and quickly moored to a Boston dock. My two bags were resting at my feet, and as I gripped her starboard rail near the bow, I smiled and waved to Uncle Jason and Aunt Bea patiently waiting on the dock. I could see the shadowy spire of that north side church reaching for the emerging stars while dozens of men scurried about the wharf strewn with bags and crates waiting for merchant boats, and watched in an eerie hush as the king's soldiers strutted about the cobblestones and docks in little groups of twos and fours.

Suddenly Seaman McGuire graciously clutched my bags, Ethan's quilt secretly stashed inside once again, and I carefully followed him down that elm plank to the safety of Scarlet's Wharf. Uncle Jason snatched my bags and tossed them to the rear of their buggy as he and Aunt Bea greeted me with caring hugs and loving words, then we rolled through the Boston twilight toward their home just north of the common. Little flames flickered lamps as our mare's iron shoes scraped and clacked the cobblestones, and as candles glistened windows of shops and homes and we creaked up Beacon Hill, I could hear the chilling sound of redcoat troops finishing royal drills on the grass of the common.

"I bet you don't have those bloody redcoats down in Philadelphia!" Uncle Jason surprisingly blustered with a flick of the reins and snapping glance toward the shadows of the common.

"No, not really, Uncle Jason," I timidly replied as Aunt Bea pressed her hand to mine and calmingly glanced to my eyes. "There just doesn't seem to be a lot of royal soldiers around Germantown and Philadelphia. Oh sure, there're some, but not many."

Before Uncle Jason could sputter another word, Aunt Bea pivoted our thoughts back to more pleasant things, to their lives in Massachusetts Bay and mine in Pennsylvania, to my nursing, to mother and father, even Franz. And as we crested the gravel of Beacon Street and came to a crunchy halt outside their home, I could hear the faint sound of water lapping rocks of the Charles River just a bit west. Even in the shadowy twilight the sight of their home comforted me, its shutters wide and panes swung open as if reaching for a whiff of the summer sea, spurring memories of Ethan and me before the fire that wintry night many months before.

After a short while Aunt Bea showed me to my room just beyond the hearth and kissed me goodnight, the same room I had before. I unpacked some things from my bags and slid my clothes from my weary body, tossing my rumpled dress to a corner chair, then nestled to the linens of my bed after dabbing my cheeks and skin with a cloth dripping cool basin water. As I pressed to my pillow with Ethan's quilt unfurled at my side, my mind began to wander to Harvard College and Cambridge just beyond the river, sailing northwest past the villages of Somerville, Medford and Menotomy to the hills, trees and fields of Middlesex County and Ethan's Lexington. As shadows from a flickering candle roamed my room, I slid Ethan's blanket over my skin and wondered what he was doing that very moment just a dozen miles away. Perhaps he was scampering about the tavern with his father, or strolling on the grass of his village field and wondering of us beneath the gaze of summer stars. Or maybe, he was lying on his bed like me, with sensuous visions swirling of intimacy.

I snuffed my lone candle, and after a while wondered if my first night in Boston would ever come to an end, as an hour then another slowly trudged by. As I rolled and twisted about my linens and caressed Ethan's blanket, at times feeling as though my body might burst with anxious anticipation, I'd gaze out my room's open panes to all those stars twinkling the night. It was quiet and still, and the air was scented with a salty smell of the sea, an aroma that seemed to tame twinges of disturbing guilt that would grip my soul now and then. Then perhaps an hour or so past midnight, as the lamps and candles flickering about Boston faded and dwindled, I mercifully drifted to dreams of morrow.

I snapped from my sleep a little after dawn, and with anxious thoughts, cuddled with Ethan's blanket for hour or so, then about eight washed and dressed and joined Uncle Jason and Aunt Bea in the kitchen whispering and sipping tea. "We wanted you to sleep as long as you could," she caringly said as I slid to a chair and they nibbled biscuits spread with a sweet reddish jell, "so didn't want to wake you." I sprang from my chair and grabbed the kettle brewing over a flame in the kitchen hearth, then refilling their cups with steaming tea and one for me, nestled back to the table. We began to talk of events that had flared about the colonies the past couple years, of Boston and Philadelphia, then of easier things like their lives on Beacon Hill and mine at the Pennsylvania Hospital, and stories of mother and father in Germantown. Then a nauseous angst raced my body when they asked of my plans while in Boston.

I innocently sipped and explained how I simply wanted to rest from the pressures of nursing, then springing from the table once again, nervously wondered how to broach the notion of Ethan while they watched and listened and I refilled our flowery cups. Then I uttered Ethan's name in an unsuspecting tone and confided a harmless tidbit or two, and after another sip of steamy tea, casually revealed that around noon he was coming to see me. They sipped and twitched while asking a few intriguing questions, then eased my twisting tensions by reflecting upon meeting Ethan that snowy March night. "I thought he was a fine young man," Aunt Bea pleasingly said, "and look forward to seeing him again." "So do I," sputtered Uncle Jason with an agreeing nod.

Sensing concern in their tone, I tried to calm their apprehensions without revealing my true desires. I confided of more things in Philadelphia and Germantown, of my nursing and sewing with Betsy and Lydia too, and explained my continuing courtship with Franz. Then hoping to ease what seemed a stirring imagination with each sip of tea, I tried to convince them that everything was in its proper place in Pennsylvania, saying my life was doing just fine. "Please," I implored Aunt Bea and Uncle Jason while tapping my cup, "don't judge me too harshly for seeing Ethan while I'm here. He and I have quilled many letters over these past two years, and have simply become good friends. But you know how people can talk, and not even try to understand. So please, both of you, for my sake and Ethan's, please keep this a secret."

"We love you, Andrea," Aunt Bea tenderly whispered, reaching and caressing my hand while glancing to Uncle Jason nodding in accord, "and want you to be happy. And who are we to judge, anyone. Don't you let this worry you, not one bit, cuz we'll do what you wish. We'll keep your friendship with Ethan our little secret."

"Bea's right," Uncle Jason added with a twinkle in his eye, "we want you to be happy. Ethan is welcome in our home, Andrea, anytime. And if you need, I'll take you to see him. So don't you worry, about anything."

"Oh, thank you," I gushed with relief, "both of you, for being so understanding. You're the best aunt and uncle anyone could ever have. I love you."

"If you like," Aunt Bea tenderly advised, "Ethan can stay for supper. Say, around seven?"

"Yes, Aunt Bea," I spouted with glee, "oh yes, I'd like that, and just know Ethan will too. Thank you so much. I'm hoping we'll just stroll about Boston this afternoon, see some of the places Ethan quilled to me about. We should be back around dusk, just in time."

Aunt Bea and I continued our intimate talk for another hour or so in a quaint little nook in her kitchen corner, then desperately wanting to tame my spiraling emotions, I returned to my room to calm for a while and change into a blue summer dress. And when the mantel clock chimed half past eleven that morning, just thirty arousing minutes before I'd finally see my Ethan again, I fluttered from my little room and nervously settled to the cushion of a chair facing the cold fireplace stones. With my hands pressed to my lap in an anxious clasp and my eyes fixed upon the thin little arms of that clock, I began the final moments of my impatient wait. Aunt Bea sat quietly nearby, steadily transforming strands of wool into a shawl of autumn colors, and from his favorite chair Uncle Jason perused the latest printing of Mr. Gill's Boston Gazette, devouring parchment sheets exposing colonial troubles and views.

I nervously flicked my hair flowing easy to my shoulders, twisting my fingers about strands now and then, then clasped my hands once again as twelve chimes echoed the room, causing my skin to tingle. I quietly watched those thin little hands continue to tick while snapping anxious glances toward the door, and as my fingers twisted and stomach churned, the most exciting sound I could have ever imagined began to filter through the windows. It was a steady gallop that came to a frantic halt on the dusty pebbles of Beacon Street, a sound quickly followed by boots scrapping the stony path to our front door. My heart began to beat wildly as I stared to the door left through the foyer, then began to thump and pound when I heard its brass ring clank two rapping taps, followed by an arousing three more.

Aunt Bea and Uncle Jason caringly glanced to my eyes, then as joy surged my body, he rose and shuffled through the foyer as I stared from my chair. "Mr. Sheehan," Uncle Jason tenderly greeted, "it's good to see you again. I do hope your ride from Lexington was good. Please, come in, Andrea is expecting you."

"Thank you, Mr. Van Dijk," Ethan respectfully replied as their hands firmly clasped. "It's good to see you again, sir."

"Please, call me Jason," he quickly added as Aunt Bea stepped to his side. "I'm sure you remember Mrs. Van Dijk?"

"Yes, of course," Ethan nervously said, reaching and patting his lips upon the back of her outstretched hand. "Good afternoon, Mrs. Van Dijk. It's nice to see you again. Please, call me Ethan, both of you."

"Alright, Ethan," she replied with a blush, "and I insist you call me, Bea." Then glancing and twisting toward me as I anxiously watched from my chair, she enticingly added, "There's someone here, Ethan, whose been waiting for you. Andrea, you have a visitor."

Our souls seemed to entwine as our eyes fixed upon each other, and springing from that cherry chair, my heart pounding as Ethan tenderly stared, he nervously grinned as I stepped toward the door. Without uttering a word we reached for each other's hand, and as if all alone in the foyer we gazed into each other's eyes for a sensuous moment, as if reaching for passions that had been simmering for weeks, months and years. "It's wonderful to see you again, Ethan," I clumsily sputtered as his fingers began to slowly caress mine.

"It's so good to see you, Andrea," he serenely whispered, leaning and pressing his lips to my tingling skin. "You look wonderful, strikingly so." We just gazed into each other's eyes, his fingers thrilling mine, a tantalizing touch that seemed to banish the entire world for a magical moment.

While we touched and gazed near the door, Uncle Jason quietly shuffled back to his Boston Gazette and chair while Aunt Bea began to fiddle with her knitting needles and little bundles of yarn once again. "Ethan," she softly chimed, shattering our intimate moment, "why don't you stay for supper tonight. Please, after you two come back from your day. Say, around seven?"

Ethan flashed a tender gleam to my eyes while his fingers caressed my skin, then glanced to Aunt Bea and said, "Why, yes, I'd be delighted. That's very kind. Thank you."

"Good," she snapped in a comforting way. "Now, you two enjoy your day."

"We won't be going far, just walking about Boston," I confided with a gentle squeeze of Ethan's hand, "and will be back before sunset. Won't we, Ethan."

"Yes, we will, Mrs. Van Dijk," Ethan softly confirmed as his fingers thrilled mine.

Following a few departing words, Ethan and I clicked the door and escaped into our own tantalizing world, leaving Aunt Bea and Uncle Jason to the peace of their day, and slowly stepped in the warm summer breeze to the gravelly stones of Beacon Street. And with my left hand now gently nestled in his right, Ethan twisted, gazed to my eyes and softly said, "I've waited for this moment for over two years, Andrea, just to hold your hand. It feels so good to finally touch you again. You make me feel like I've been blessed with a slice of heaven."

"Oh, Ethan," I whispered, peering deep into his eyes, "I feel the same way." As we gazed in a magical way and our fingers softly caressed, I came to finally realize that what I was doing was right for Ethan and me, and could sense the lingering pressures and guilt of mother and father, of Philadelphia and Franz, slowly vanish. For at least one joyous moment my true passions were overwhelming the repressive logic of my analytical mind, and the dreams I had stashed deep inside for so long were magically being unleashed.

Suddenly, Ethan looked about as I anxiously glanced toward the panes of the house, then returning our gaze to each other's eyes, he tenderly pressed his lips to mine for a long wondrous kiss. "Oh, Andrea," he whispered, "you feel so good. Come on, let's walk down to the river. We can find a little spot to sit and talk for a while, just be."

"Mmm," I thrillingly sighed, "that was so nice. Yes, let's, that sounds good. I just want to be with you, Ethan, anywhere."

While the warm rays of the August day vanished behind bundles of grey drifting out to sea now and then, Ethan and I began our westward walk down the dusty pebbles of Beacon Street, my hand tenderly nestled in his. We talked of simple things as we neared the murky waters of the Charles

River a bit north of the common, then confessed intimate desires, thoughts and dreams as we pivoted along a stony path running north along the water. I remember how relieving it was to utter anything that came to mind without fear of hearing a snide reply or belittling taunt, how good it felt to speak without being judged, hurtful things sometimes muttered by Franz.

Ethan told me more things of his final years at Harvard and Whig events not quilled in his letters, and explained the gratitude he felt toward Mr. Gill and Ben Edes for all the things they had done for him. And he became a bit excited when revealing the printing things he learned those years at their Boston shop, and of his intriguing new duties with Mr. Giles and his Lexington Gazette. "Even though I miss things of Boston and Harvard," he whispered, our fingers entwining as we continued to walk, "it feels right to be home. Dad struggles more each day too, Andrea, what with his leg. But now that I'm back, helping at the tavern, things will be easier for him."

And I told him of Philadelphia and Germantown, of my new nursing duties at the hospital, of mother and father, and of my sewing sessions with Lydia and Betsy Sunday nights, talking, snipping and stitching with goblets of wine. Yet, I nervously shied from any mention of Franz, and to my joyous relief Ethan seemed to understand how hard it was for me, resisting any urge to delve into those troubling emotions challenging me. As we walked and talked while resting now and then, Ethan showed an interest in the things I was saying with a brush of tenderness that helped soothe me so, patiently listening to every word, showing how much he truly cared.

The sounds of carriages, horses and wagons clacking and creaking upon the cobblestones was rather pleasing as we neared the slopes of Copp's Hill, and as the smell of the sea wafted about Boston, Ethan showed me the bricks of Harvard College rising in the village of Cambridge southwest across the river. And with our fingers tenderly entwined, we watched an array of colts, mares and buggies scamper from the slats of that Charlestown ferry, then continued our stroll east on the wharfs and docks along the waters of the harbor.

Our easy talk began to slide toward more unpleasant things, of contentious events happening about the colonies, like the torching of that royal ship just weeks before and the resurrection of those colonial committees to spur

Whig correspondence. We even returned to that awful clash nearby on King Street two years before, and whispered a soft condolence for those five courageous souls. But soon we released those challenging memories and began to reminisce of the wondrous moment when our eyes first met that March night, when we touched and talked for hours before Aunt Bea's crackling fire.

We'd stop and softly kiss many times along our stroll, press our lips and listen to the alluring sounds of the day, then near three we rested once again near the waters of Scarlet's Wharf. I remember how a gentle breeze tossed our hair as we nestled to an intriguing bench sliced into the aging trunk of a fallen tree, a quaint spot peering east over the water, and how Ethan caressed my hand pressing his thigh as we snuggled and gazed out to sea. Scores of royal ships and merchant boats were moored at wharfs and quietly anchored in the harbor, and sweating men along the docks were tossing and tugging bags, sacks and crates as redcoat soldiers mingled about in tiny menacing groups. "There's my ship, Ethan," I whispered as we gazed through the afternoon haze at little islands dotting the distant waters, "the *Dorchester,* right over there."

Ethan nodded and softly squeezed my hand, then we began to expose more calming thoughts as I nestled my cheek into his shoulder. He seemed so content that very moment, having shown me much of his Boston, places which had come to be dear over the past several years, while proudly describing many of those little islands too. And I felt a wondrous joy simply being with him on that old rickety bench, his hand caressing mine as we tenderly pressed our lips now and then. We whispered of intimacies held in a secret place while peering out to sea, and talked of desires, hopes and feelings, of the beauty of the morning sun and magic of dusk. As we snuggled and caressed we discovered a serenity we both yearned, as if bathed in the sweet scent of a flowery spring meadow, or gazing into a gentle wintry snow or spray of summer stars, a tranquility we found in the smell of the sea that soothed our hearts and swaddled our souls.

After an hour or so of tenderly touching, exposing thoughts and dreams on that special bench, gazing at islands and ships and watching gulls sail about masks and swoop the waters, Ethan reluctantly whispered, "Maybe we should be making our way back." I didn't want to leave our little spot of heaven, wanted to stay there forever, yet with a squeeze our hands and press of our lips, one more taste of true bliss, I knew it was time for us to go.

The August sun was slowly creeping toward the frontier, perhaps an hour or two from slipping beyond those forests and hills, as we rose from our haven at Scarlet's Wharf and continued our stroll back to my interim home atop Beacon Hill. With Ethan's hand tenderly caressing mine, we stepped south along the dusty stones of Fish Street edging the docks, then glancing right, Ethan muttered in a strangely contemptible tone, "See that big house over there, Andrea, near that distant corner, that's the governor's place. And down there, that little grey building by the water, is Paul's silversmith shop." Then an expanse of mortar, panes and bricks came into view, an impressive place Ethan said was Faneuil Hall.

Soon the harbor, wharfs, ships and docks were left behind, and as we began to stroll west on the cobblestones of King Street, Ethan nodded a bit left to a place that looked like a quaint home or little shop. "Remember the trial of those redcoats, Andrea," he asked, "of those soldiers from that March night? Well, that's Mr. Adams' office, John, the one I quilled you about, the lawyer who defended those men." Then suddenly I began to recognize another building approaching on the right, the one Ethan said was his colony's statehouse, and just a bit further was the spot where Ethan and I first met, where those patriot men lost their lives that wintry night.

"Do you think about them, Ethan," I whispered, entwining our fingers a bit tighter while nudging closer to his side, "those poor men?"

"Oh yes, I sure do," he solemnly uttered, "often, and every time I pass."

"I do too," I sighed, dabbing an eye. "Sometimes, it's like an awful, dreadful dream."

We slowly stepped past those sacred stones in a respectful silence, then snapping our reverent hush, Ethan spiritedly said, "There it is, the Green Dragon Tavern. You know, I sure miss gathering in there with my Junto friends." Then Ethan paused for a moment, and with a mischievous grin and stutter in his step, added, "I'll never forget that New Hampshire farmer, Andrea, and what he did to those redcoats that night."

As we approached the stones of Queen Street, with the shop where Ethan had apprenticed the past four years up on the right, he realized I hadn't seen his room at Mr. Gill's house. "Come on, let's swing over to Spring

Lane," he excitedly said as we pivoted south past that old Boston church, "it's not far from here." And after pointing to the panes of his room and having his raps upon the door go unanswered, we walked back to Queen Street and entered the print shop.

Ben Edes was at his desk intently quilling thoughts to parchment when Ethan introduced me, and John Gill was busy arranging little iron bits at his press when he kindly said, "It's very nice to meet you." Then Ethan showed me about the shop for a little while, even taking my hand as we stepped up those elm steps to that long room for a moment or two. And when we bid our goodbyes and started back to the stones of Queen Street, a feeling of acceptance soothed my soul when I heard Mr. Edes whisper, "Ethan, she's lovely."

We strolled west on the stones of Queen Street and a bit north near the grass of the common, then pivoted west once again up Beacon Hill as the sun began to fade beyond the frontier amidst a spray of enchanting summer colors. Aunt Bea was stirring a special stew simmering in a kettle dangling over flames of the kitchen hearth when Ethan and I shuffled in, and Uncle Jason was slicing a crusty loaf of still warm bread. Four flowery plates were perfectly arraigned about the table, and six little flames from thin candles glistened off crystal waiting the flow of French wine. As we sipped and dined, Ethan and I revealed many of the nuances of our day, while Aunt Bea and Uncle Jason attentively listened and offered a few intriguing words of their own. "It's so good to have you here, Andrea," they both would sputter in their own way. "And we're so glad you could join us tonight, Ethan." I'll always remember the kindness they showed Ethan and me that night, and the sense of peace I felt watching them make us feel so welcomed, home.

Ethan and I cuddled on the rug near the cold stones of the fireplace for an hour or so after supper, nestling with a blanket and pillows just as we had done that March night. We talked of sweet things of our day while touching and pressing our lips now and then, dreading the moment he'd need to gallop back to Lexington. And although he said he'd return the following day, he explained he could only come for a short while that afternoon, for he needed to be at Mr. Giles print shop all morning and help his father in the tavern by dusk. Then sliding his lips about my hands, he tenderly whispered, "But I'll be back on Friday, Andrea, in the morning, and we'll ride back to Lexington for the entire day. I promise." Ethan was excited about showing me the wonders of his village, and I'd finally meet his father too, and have supper at the tavern. My heart pounded with anticipation as I agreed to be ready at ten, just two short days from then, and trying to tame their instinctive fears, I assured Uncle Jason and Aunt Bea I'd return to Boston by the chime of midnight.

The few hours we spent together that Thursday afternoon were tantalizing, and as I fidgeted about my sheets and pillows, gazing to the summer stars through the open panes of my bedroom window, my mind swirled with arousing anticipation. And as my skin tingled with desires, I drifted to sensuous dreams shortly after Aunt Bea's clock chimed one from the mantel that night.

It was a bit past eight when I crawled from my bed, dabbed my skin with a damp cloth and slid into a tan and yellow dress, then folded Ethan's quilt and hid it safely in my big rumpled bag. I gripped its thin leather strap and scampered past the hearth into the kitchen, settling into that little nook with Aunt Bea, and for an hour or so we talked as I anxiously waited, gazing through the panes of her corner retreat. Then as a string of clouds drifted toward the sea shortly after her clock chimed ten, a snorting brown colt and dark buggy crunched to a halt on the pebbles of Beacon Street. I leapt from that nook in what seemed a mystical haze as a thrilling chill raced my skin, and with a sweeping swoosh and snatch of that bag, dashed out the door with a fading goodbye.

Ethan was still gripping the thin reins when I rushed to the dusty street, then twisting with a smile, he jumped from the buggy and greeted me tenderly. "You look wonderful, Andrea," he sweetly whispered, gently holding my hand and helping me up the right side of the carriage. "I like your dress," he nervously added, setting my bag just right of my shoes, "very nice, so soft. What's in the bag?"

I settled to the buggy's cushioned board as Ethan scurried about the rear in dark scuffed shoes, tight tan breeches and bright fluttering shirt. "Thank you, Ethan," I anxiously said as he climbed into the buggy, snatching and reins and nudging closer to me. "I stitched this dress just last spring. And you, why, you too look awfully nice." Then he glanced to my bag with a puzzling look, and I quickly assured him, "I made something for you, Ethan, something special. But please, let's wait a little while, until tonight, at supper."

Ethan leaned and pressed his lips to mine as I nestled to his side, my hand resting his thigh, and with a tender sparkle in his eyes, he snapped the reins and demanded, "Get! Get, get!" I could feel his sensuous touch as that colt's iron shoes dug into the gravel and the buggy lurched, and as we began to creak east down Beacon Hill, I flicked a tiny wave to Aunt Bea peering from the panes of her little kitchen nook. We talked of easy things as the buggy bounced and rolled, then we crossed the waters of the harbor on that Charlestown ferry and began to creak west toward the narrows of the peninsula.

"The village of Cambridge is just beyond those distant trees, Andrea," Ethan proudly explained with a glance south as we rolled through the narrows, "and those halls of Harvard I've told you so much about." I gazed through the warming haze and smiled, and as a dusty plume followed the buggy along the ruts and stones of the Massachusetts Road, I could feel a tantalizing tingle with each press of our thighs and flick of the reins. We softly talked of various things amid sweet scents drifting the summer breeze, bouncing past farmers' fields sprouting in yellows, browns, reds and greens. We wound through the villages of Somerville, Medford and Menotomy, creaking past grassy hills and swaying meadows, and as we approached groves of oak, birch and elm just east of Lexington, I pressed my cheek to Ethan's shoulder.

Then suddenly my stomach began to nervously twitch as we rolled nearer the edge of his village, a nauseous sensation spurred by my own apprehensions of meeting Ethan's father. What will he think of me, I tortuously wondered? "Ethan," I anxiously uttered with a tense press of his thigh, "what have you told your father about me? Will he like me?"

"Yes, he'll like you," Ethan caringly whispered, pressing his lips to my hair while flicking the reins. "He already likes you. Dad knows quite a few things about you, and is impressed with your nursing at the Pennsylvania Hospital, telling me so. I've talked about your home in Germantown too, and a few things about your mother and father, even about your sewing Sunday nights with your friends, and why. I think he's proud of me, for feeling so deeply for you. So please, Andrea, there's no reason to worry."

I glanced to my bag and stared to a grove of passing elm, then grasping for courage, nervously delved into a subject we had managed to avoid for days. "What about Franz? Does your father know? Please, Ethan, tell me. Have you told him?"

"No," Ethan uttered, sliding his hand from me for a moment. Then as if sensing his own dwelling fears, he pressed his hand back to mine and said, "Some things are just between you and me, Andrea. I haven't talked to dad about Franz, nor to anyone else, and don't plan to either. I've just told him about the passion you feel for your nursing at the hospital, and maybe of some of the commitments you have in Germantown and Philadelphia, personal responsibilities you hold important. I think we should simply leave things that way. Of course, you can tell him if you want. I just hope someday, Andrea, our lives will be different. But until such time, I'll respect your wishes, as I always have. I think dad understands too, in his own aging way."

I tipped my head to Ethan's shoulder and nervously twisted my fingers about his in soft stroking swirls, then gently whispered, "Thank you, Ethan, for understanding, for caring the way you do. But, there is something else. Does he know about my Quaker faith?"

"Yes, he does," Ethan confessed while caressing my hand, easing my tensions. "You don't know dad, Andrea, but you will. Like you and me, he's not concerned with how someone worships their God. He says it's nobody's business, that it's personal liberty. So don't you worry, Andrea. Just remember, dad likes you, and knows how I feel about you."

Sensing an unease that kept flaring deep inside me, Ethan brought the buggy to a creaking halt with a tug of the reins near Lexington's little belfry hill, then holding my hand with his gentle fingers, gazed to my eyes and said, "I love you, Andrea, for who you are, just the way you are, and I know you feel the same. That's all that really matters."

I could feel the joy erupting inside hearing his caring words, and as a tear began to trickle my cheek, I thrust my arms about his neck and pressed my lips to his. "You've made me feel so good, Ethan," I sighed, sliding to his shoulder and entwining my fingers with his, "so welcomed, comfortable, loved. Now, take me to your home, Ethan, to the tavern. Let's go see your father. Show me all of Lexington."

Ethan kissed me tenderly, then with a snap of the reins, we lurched into our final roll into Lexington. Off to the right I could see the spire of the king's church reaching into the warming haze, and in the distance straight ahead were the slopes of his mother's hill. As we creaked and swayed about the bend just past that little belfry, an array of chimney stacks, shops and homes came into view amid scattered birch and pine, maple, oak and elm. That's when I saw that grassy space spreading about the core of Lexington, a spirited expanse Ethan many times quilled was his village field.

"There's dad's competition," Ethan muttered in a playful tone as the Munroe Tavern passed on the right. "And that's Doc Newman's place, his apothecary shop," he quickly added, glancing left with a flick of the reins. My gaze snapped left and right as Ethan pointed to this and that, and I could see the joy in his eyes with each clump and creak of hooves and wheels. "Our little schoolhouse is tucked up there, Andrea," he excitedly revealed as I glanced to a quaint white place near an intriguing oak on the slope of a small hill, "and that's Ernie Wilson's gun shop."

Several horses were lazily meandering in corrals near weathered barns on the southern edge of that village field, and I could hear clucking hens scampered about a few goats and cows roaming that expanse of green. Then Ethan tugged the reins as we rolled past a cabinet shop and wheelwright, and gazing toward that burying ground hill, somberly said, "Mom is up there, near that far right tree." I leaned to his shoulder and wrapped my hand about his, and as we stared to the tips of that solemn tree gently swaying in the summer breeze, he whispered, "We'll walk up there, Andrea, later today. You'll see what a serene place she has."

We pivoted north with a twitch of the reins and creaked onto the dust of Bedford Street, rolling along the western edge of the village field past the general store and postal place, and rising a bit back off on the left was the steeple of Ethan's mother's church. That's when I saw the Buckman Tavern, panes, slats and chimney stacks nudged among a few trees, its door invitingly open. And across the ruts and stones was that liberty oak Ethan had quilled about, its twisting limbs spraying a spirited shadow upon the grass of his Lexington field.

It was around noon when Ethan stopped the buggy not far from the tavern door, and as our little trailing plume began to settle, I could sense a peaceful hush brushing the village. "Your tavern has a majestic look," I whispered as the sweet aroma of farmers' fields drifted the warm summer air, "and Lexington is so quaint, with a calming feel of home." Ethan tenderly squeezed my fingers, then leaping and dashing around the rear of the buggy, took my hand, snatched my special bag and caringly guided me to the dusty stones of Bedford Street.

"There you two are," spouted an intriguing looking man stepping from the tavern with a tiny limp in his gait. "Welcome to Lexington," he softly added, staring to me as he strutted to the dust of the street. And before I could utter a word, he rubbed Ethan's shoulders in a fatherly way, then spun and gently hugged me. "It's good to finally see you, Andrea," he whispered, "good to have you here. Ethan's told me so much about you."

His tender greeting doused awkward notions and surged a soothing calm through me, and the warmth I could sense flowing from his heart showed me how much he cared for Ethan. I squeezed him gently and slightly pulled back, and as his hands slowly released mine, I gazed to his azure-blue eyes and softly said, "Thank you, Mr. Sheehan. You've made me feel welcomed."

"Good," he gushed as Ethan gently took my hand and we began stepping toward the tavern, "but please, Andrea, call me Patrick."

"Alright," I nervously replied, "thank you, Patrick." And as we bound through the tavern door, I twisted and added, "Ethan has told me so much about you. I feel like I already know you, and your tavern and Lexington. I'm so happy to be here, and finally meet you."

"You must be tired," he said with a caring glance while shuffling toward a pair of merchant men sipping ale at the barreled bar, "and I'll bet would like to rest a bit. Ethan, why don't you show Andrea to your room? There's a little breeze coming through the windows, and fresh water in the basin. I suppose you'd like to show Andrea some of Lexington too, and maybe take the buggy out to the old farm. We'll have supper around five, Ethan, one of my special stews."

"That sounds nice, dad," Ethan shyly uttered, gently squeezing my hand. "What do you think, Andrea?"

"Yes, I'd like that, very much" I softly replied with a glance toward the bar. And with my hand caressed by Ethan's, we began to step to the stairs rising along the right wall. "Thank you, Mr. Sheehan, Patrick."

"Good," Ethan's father spouted in a satisfied way while shuffling behind the barreled bar toward the kitchen door.

"Thanks, dad," Ethan graciously added as our fingers entwined. "I think we'll ride out to the old place, and maybe see mom too. We'll be back by supper."

Ethan and I dashed past a spirited farmer and what seemed his loyal son tipping cups of rum at a little table, then I twisted and thanked Mr. Sheehan once again as we bound up those steps to the privacy of his room, Ethan gripping my bag and hand.

He tossed my bag near the cold fireplace stones left of the door as I stretched upon the blanket of his bed, then he quickly joined me as I pressed my hair to his pillow. We simply rested for a while, his side sensuously pressed against mine, and listened to leaves rustling in the summer breeze. "It feels so good to be here," I sighed as we gazed through the open panes and bathed in magical sounds filtering into the room. Then I entwined my fingers about his and softly added, "I love lying beside you, Ethan. And am so happy, to finally meet your father."

"I love lying here with you too," he whispered with a tingling caress of my hand, "and have dreamed of this moment a thousand times. I know dad's glad you're here too."

We rested on his bed for another hour or so, caressing and snuggling amid soothing sounds of the summer winds, and with a tender kiss now and then, whispered thoughts about an array of passionate things. The world seemed right for perhaps the first time, for Ethan was safe in his home and I was lying with him. Then after our bodies, minds and souls had been tantalizingly revitalized, we grudgingly slipped from our tranquil cocoon and quietly fled the tavern, climbing back into his buggy and riding to Ethan's old place.

I nestled to his side and pressed my hand to his thigh as he gripped the reins, and as we trotted north and east around that village field and onto the ruts and stones of the Billerica Road, he gleefully revealed intriguing things to me. "That's George Pratt's old place," he reflected in a somber tone while glancing to the first farm on the right. "He was killed in that frontier war. And that house up there, with those fields sprouting corn, cabbage and greens, belongs to Andy Beatty." As we slowly creaked, swayed and rolled past that farm, Ethan snapped the reins and grumbled, "Dad says Andy, and that son of his, are Lexington's village bigots."

I could sense that Ethan missed his years on the land as we neared the old Sheehan farm on the right, and could see in his eyes how the sweet aroma oozing the soil was spurring precious memories. And as their little house shaded by oaks and elms came into view, its quaint windows swung wide gasping for a wisp of summer wind, Ethan pressed my hand and whispered, "There it is, Andrea, our place." I peered to its fading yellow slats for a moment or two and glanced back to Ethan, then tenderly squeezed his hand as tears swelled his eyes. "Mom took her final breath that awful night right there, Andrea, in that old house. It belongs to the McElroy's now, Jim and Nancy, has for some ten years, since dad swapped it for the tavern."

We continued our ride a bit further east before Ethan tugged the reins and spun the buggy around, then we swayed and creaked past the Hosmer place and Spoons farm on the north side of the Billerica Road in our roll back to Lexington. With each clumping dig into the dusty path I could see in his eyes how proud Ethan was of his farming past, and as I listened to him confide tender memories of his youth, I knew he wanted to show me more, wanted to show me everything in a slow stroll about Lexington.

Ethan hitched the carriage and colt to an oak behind the tavern, and with his hand gently holding mine, we stepped the ruts of Bedford Street in the warm afternoon winds and strolled across the grass of the village field toward the dusty stones of Hancock Street. "Over there," he whispered, his fingers entwining mine, "is Nathan's place." We pivoted north past a grunting goat and walked to the print shop, surprising Mr. Giles arranging hundreds of little iron bits for his coming Gazette. Ethan showed me about the shop too, explaining intriguing things about his printing trade, and as we bid goodbye and began to step back into our summer day, Mr. Giles told me how pleased he was that we'd finally met.

For an hour or so we strolled about Lexington's dusty paths and stony roads and softly talked of colonial things, and desires, hopes and dreams. Ethan pointed to quaint little homes and merchant shops too, and introduced me to an inquisitive villager now and then. "We'll visit mom a little later," he whispered as our fingers entwined and hair gently tossed in the warm winds, "after supper." And as the summer sun slowly drifted toward the frontier, we returned from whence we'd come, bounding through the tavern door a bit before five.

Ethan's father had already prepared one of the tavern tables just for the three of us, a small round oak near the fireplace right of the barreled bar and kitchen door. I could see three glossy plates with bowls set perfectly about the table, bright porcelain scattered with little blue flowers, and a trio of crystal goblets nestled near silvery spoons, knives and forks. A pair of elegant thin candles rose near the center from two polished holders too, and set before the front unclaimed chair was a slender bottle of wine patiently waiting for Ethan, his father and me.

"I want to help dad," Ethan whispered with a gentle squeeze of my hand.

"Yes, do, Ethan," I uttered with a kissing glance. "I'm going up for a moment, freshen up a bit, and will be right back." After a splash of water and brush of my dress, I snatched my bag with Ethan's quilt, rushed down the stairs and shuffled toward our special little table, passing a few Lexington men sipping cups of rye whiskey and rum. There were other villagers in the tavern early that evening too, weary farmers gripping pewter mugs at the corner table near the panes peering over the village field, and a couple tradesmen sipping ale at the barreled bar. I carefully set my bag beside a chair facing the bar and kitchen door, then slid to its slats and waited near the ashen fireplace stones, watching and listening.

After a moment or two the kitchen door swung with a crackling squeak and Ethan spritzed into the room, and shuffling between the table and wall, set a little basket of hot crusted rolls to our table and nestled to the chair just right of me. And before we could delve into a few tender words his father quickly followed, clicking a flowery bowl brimming tasty stew between that bottle of wine and flickering candles. "Here we are," he proudly proclaimed, sliding to the chair nearest the kitchen door. "Now, let's enjoy our supper."

While Ethan scooped steamy chunks of chicken and creamy bits of beets, potatoes and corn into my bowl, then spooned stew to the other two, his father snatched that French bottle, pried its cork with a special twist and quietly poured our wine. I remember how Ethan's father was so attentive while we shared things of our day, and as we sipped, dined and talked he added a few tender thoughts of his own. "Here's to your visit to Lexington, Andrea, being here with us." And as we clicked our goblets near our candles' little flames, he glanced to Ethan, gazed to me and said, "May you be back, soon."

His father had to slip away now and then to tend to a villager's spirits or a steaming kitchen kettle, and each time he did, Ethan and I sipped our wine and tenderly whispered. "To us," I'd sigh, sliding my hand to his, "and tonight," and he'd glance about the tavern carefully, then sensuously whisper, "To you, Andrea, and your alluring pearl-green eyes." Then we'd scan the others sipping at tables and the barreled bar, and when the moment was right, seal our simmering desires with a tantalizing kiss.

Soon we neared the end of our supper of intriguing talk, tender words and soothing wine as the August sun succumbed to its daily fate, and as Ethan's father filled our crystals a final time, I began to anxiously glance to that special bag patiently waiting near my feet. "I have something for you, Ethan," I excitedly said, "something I made, special." And as his father hushed and Ethan fidgeted with anticipation, I reached and snatched my bag and settled it to my lap. "There's something inside, Ethan, in honor of your graduation from Harvard. I hope you like it."

I unlatching its strap, reached inside and snagged his folded gift, and tugging it easy into the candlelight, proudly confessed, "It's a blanket, Ethan, a special quilt just for you." Then rising from my chair as Ethan's eyes sparkled to mine, I unfurled its autumn colors.

"Andrea," Ethan passionately gasped, "it's beautiful."

I shuffled right as Ethan slowly screeched back his chair, then gently spread the blanket about his lap and chest as some sipping ale, rye whiskey and rum sputtered little cheers and his father pleasingly stared. Ethan pressed his blushing cheeks to those soothing colors and slid his fingers across his quilt, then I rested my hands to his shoulders and leaned from behind. "How does that feel, Ethan," I whispered, tenderly brushing my lips to his cheek. "Do you like it?"

"My blanket," he sighed in jest, "or your lips?"

"Oh, Ethan," I friskily sputtered, hearing a chuckle from the barreled bar as Ethan blushed a bit more, "your blanket of course. Do you like it?"

"I love it," he sighed while twisting and sweetly hushing, "and your kiss," before brushing his lips to mine. "It's beautiful, Andrea, so soft. Most of all, I love it because you made it, snipped and stitched it all with your caring hands." Then pausing for a moment and glancing to his father as a mist sprayed his eyes, Ethan pressed his cheek to mine and tenderly said, "Thank you."

"You're welcome," I whispered with another slide of my lips to his cheek. "I'm so proud of you, Ethan." Then remembering that special tan patch, I excitedly exclaimed, "There's a little message stitched to a corner. Please, Ethan, read it."

Ethan quickly searched his blanket, pinched that corner and spun it up closer to the candles flickering on the table, then I watched his lips as he quietly read each word. And after glancing to his father and others about the tavern, he gazed back to that tiny patch and slowly recited, *For Ethan. Congratulations. All my love, Andrea. July 30, 1772.*

"I wanted this to be very special, Ethan," I softly sighed, "from me, to you."

As his father gleamed and spirited patrons of the Buckman Tavern watched, Ethan twisted and pressed his lips to mine, then softly whispered, "I love you, Andrea."

"That was awfully nice of you, Andrea," Ethan's father gracious proclaimed. "Such a beautiful blanket, and caring words. Ethan was right, you are a very special woman. And it seems rather clear, you bring him happiness."

"You're right, dad," Ethan softly insisted, "Andrea is very special."

"Thank you, Patrick," I shyly replied as a blush brushed my cheeks, "for those kind words. I'm truly flattered." Then pressing my fingers about Ethan's shoulders, I leaned to his ear and whispered, "Thank you, Ethan. You're special to me too."

Ethan and I soon realized it was close to half past seven, and with each passing moment we knew our precious hours together were quickly dwindling. "It's getting late, dad," Ethan explained as I settled back to my chair for a final sip of wine, "and Andrea needs to be back to Boston by midnight. We're going to take a walk up the hill and visit mom for a while. It's so pleasant up there these summer nights. Then I'll take Andrea home."

"Yes, of course," his father concurred, "should be nice up there tonight. You two go, enjoy the evening. And don't worry, Ethan, I'll be fine here." Then gazing to me while rising from his chair, he tenderly added, "It's been so nice to have you here, Andrea. If we don't see each other before you leave, goodbye, and be safe."

Suddenly I was gripped by an urge to show Ethan's father how much his kindness and love meant to me, and clicking my goblet to the table, I dashed toward the kitchen door. "Thank you so much," I whispered, wrapping my arms about him and feeling his fatherly squeeze, "for this wonderful evening, for being so caring. You've made me feel so good."

"It's been my pleasure, Andrea, truly," he whispered, gazing to my eyes while tenderly releasing my hands. "Please, I want you to come back, soon. Whenever you can."

Ethan rose from his chair and carefully folded his blanket, then wedging it beneath his arm, uttered to his father as I reached for his hand, "Thanks, dad, for everything." We stepped from the tavern into the warm summer night, walking south on Bedford Street under a spray of stars and fading gibbous moon, then pivoted right on the dusty ruts of the Massachusetts Road. I could see the silhouette of his mother's church off to the right, and as Ethan tenderly caressed my hand, we started our easy assent up the grassy slope of Lexington's burying ground hill. Soon the slats of that cemetery fence came into view in the shadowy light of the night, and as we slowly walked through its little gate and passed cold crosses and stones, Ethan nudged a bit right and whispered, "Mom is over there."

I could see candles and lamps glistening off windows of village shops and homes as we carefully stepped the soil swaddling Lexington's past, and amid the tranquil sounds of the summer night, we stopped at a special stone rising from the grass. We just stood and quietly gazed for a moment or two, and as Ethan tenderly squeezed my hand, we lowered to our knees on the grass of his mother's grave. In the faint starry light I could see four angels etched in her stone, their wings nursing his mother's soul, and read the words comforting her eternal sleep: *Elizabeth McCully Sheehan, Loving Wife & Mother, October 5, 1725 - November 20, 1761.*

"Her stone is lovely, Ethan," I whispered. "What a peaceful place."

"I miss her," he sighed with a caress of my hand, "a lot, every day. It's strange, Andrea, how powerful feelings can be after so many years."

"I don't know how you feel, Ethan," I confessed, trying to ease his pain as a sorrowful mist sprayed his eyes, "not really. I've never lost someone so close. But I do believe your mother is with you, somehow, and that she's found a comfort up here, resting in peace."

Ethan set his folded quilt to the grass and softly whispered while sliding his hand across those tender words etched for his mother, then leaned and pressed his lips to the wings of an angel. And as he strummed the top of her stone with his fingers and silently bowed amid the lonely sound of leaves fluttering in the night winds, a tear slowly trickled my cheek and spilled to her grave. "If it's alright with you, I'd like to go," he softly said, glancing to my eyes. "Let's try my new blanket for a while. I know a perfect spot, over there, on that hill. We can just lie and count all those stars, and savor the night."

"Yes, let's" I sighed with a tender squeeze of his hand. "That sounds so nice."

He brushed her stone a final time and snatched his quilt as we rose to our feet, and gently holding my hand, we stepped past his mother's sacred tree and through a creaky little gate. We slowly walked down the grass and up the coming slope toward a trio of elms arching toward the setting moon, and as we reached the peak of that western hill, Ethan spread his blanket about the cooling grass. I sensed we had found our intimate place amid all those alluring sounds, and beneath a spray of twinkling stars, we'd discover the magic of our summer night.

"What do you think, Andrea?" Ethan softly asked as we settled our knees to his quilt, his hand wrapped about mine. "Do you like my hiding place?"

"Oh, yes," I sighed, gazing to all those stars and tiny glows glistening distant panes of the village. "It's so peaceful, Ethan, as if we're the only two people in the world."

As our fingers enticingly entwined we nestled closer upon Ethan's blanket, lying on our backs and gazing into the depths of our August night. We just peered into the darkness bathed with all those pulsating stars amid the fading glow of the dwindling moon, and as Ethan's hand caressed mine, our sides sensuously pressed. I could smell the alluring aroma of nearby farmers' fields and the sweet fragrance of azaleas drifting to dreams just beyond the hill, and gently stroking Ethan's skin, softly said, "I love this hill, Ethan, lying with you. It's so calming."

"Lying here with you, Andrea," he whispered, "beneath all these stars, your hand with mine, is heaven."

I nudged a bit deeper into Ethan's left side, and as we gazed into the night and listened to the summer winds gently brushing trees, I stroked my tingling fingers about his hand, thrilling our skin. We began to confess special thoughts, whisper of hopes, desires and dreams, and sputter of life and the stars, of his Harvard days and my hospital nursing, of the challenges flaring about the colonies. And when Ethan exposed tender things of his mother, we wondered what await us all after life. It felt so good to lie with Ethan without conditions, whisper intimate things while peering into the night.

"I cherish this," Ethan sighed, "touching you, talking. It's a dream."

"I've never felt so calm," I softly said, rolling to my side and gazing to his eyes while sliding my arm across his chest. "I love being here, Ethan, with you, like this."

Ethan gently pulled and pressed his lips to mine, sending a surge of passion exploding through my body, then sliding our lips a few more thrilling times, tenderly said, "You've been on my mind every day, Andrea, for over two years, since that March night. I've been desperately waiting to see you again, somehow, somewhere, and now, here we are."

"Oh, Ethan," I sighed, pressing my lips back to his, "what a nice thing to say. I feel the same, and love your kiss."

"Never before, Andrea, have I felt like this," he whispered with another sweet slide, "never. The hours between your letters are anguishing, all the while my heart cries for you. I guess, what I'm saying is, I love you, more than I ever thought I could."

I remember how wonderful it felt to hear Ethan's words, feelings just like mine, and even though resistant thoughts oozed to the surface from time to time, of my life in Philadelphia and Germantown, of mother, father and Franz, I was able to cast my fears and guilt from that Lexington hill and surrender to the passions of my heart. "I have those same feelings too," I softly confessed as a starry glow brushed his lips, "and have for a long time. Oh, Ethan, if you only knew how my heart pounds wildly whenever one of your letters is set to my nursing desk. I love touching your words, and kissing the parchment too, as if it were you." Then I hushed for a moment and wondered of the apprehensions that too often flared inside, and grudgingly said, "But then, Ethan, I'm gripped by reality, the truth of my Pennsylvania world roaring to life."

"I think I understand," he caringly said, "really I do. I guess I just wish things were different. I'm human, Andrea, and have struggled with jealousies, frustrating thoughts, yet have found a calm acceptance of it all. I can't help it, I just want to be close to you, be part of your life somehow, in whatever way you're willing to give me. But I don't want to cause problems for you, don't want to bring you stress, just want you to be happy."

"We don't know what the future holds," I whispered, gliding my fingers across his lips. "Sometimes, Ethan, I feel so torn, in an exhausting struggle between my heart and mind, but every night you're with me in my dreams. Oh, Ethan, hold me tight." I could feel the passions bursting inside as Ethan rolled, sliding his fingers across my cheek and sensuously down my side, and beneath the magic of our celestial spray, we tenderly pressed our lips.

Even after all these years I still recall the wondrous passion that erupted on that Lexington hill, and feel the tender magic that flowed on Ethan's blanket that summer night. Our hearts pounded with rapturous beats as we entwined amid slides of our lips, and beneath all those pulsating stars, Ethan and I escaped from the limits of our world to revel in intimacy. I had never known such passion before, and would later grapple with the challenge of stashing such memories deep in my heart. We had found a bliss most would only find in wishful dreams, a precious love I'd hold dear throughout the years, a memory I'd caress the rest of my life.

"I love you," Ethan whispered, strumming his fingers through my hair as his racing heart began to ease.

"I love you too," I sighed, pressing my cheek to his chest.

Ethan wrapped me in his arms for several precious moments, and as a gentle summer wind brushed our skin beneath all those twinkling stars, I pressed my lips to his and rolled to his side. "Oh, Ethan," I gushed, "just look at the night, it's beautiful." And as we nestled upon his blanket and entwined our fingers once again, gazing to all those pulsating wonders, I breathed an anxious sigh and confessed, "You know, Ethan, things have just gotten more complicated. Yet, as those stars are my witness, I don't seem to care."

"Ya, I suppose they have," Ethan hushed, softly caressing my skin. "But just like you, I too don't care. You know, Andrea, I wouldn't change a thing about our perfect day and incredible night. I guess all we can do is just keep quilling our letters, at least for now."

"I'm so glad to hear you say that," I whispered as he pressed my fingers to his lips. "I want that too. Yes, we'll simply keep writing, for now." Then nudging my cheek back to his chest and kissing his skin, I softly confided, "I love the way you feel about me, Ethan, everything you say. You make me feel so good, about myself. Just remember, even though you'll be up here and I'll be down there for months to come, separated by hundreds of miles, my feelings for you could never change. The way you understand me, your acceptance of my life, our situation, at least for now, shows me how much you truly care."

"I love you, Andrea," he tenderly sighed, kissing my fingers once again. "Everything's going to be alright."

We gently nestled on Ethan's blanket for another hour or so, caringly touching and softly talking while gazing to the twinkling wonders of the sky, then that dreaded moment when we'd have to leave our sensuous hill finally arrived. We held each other close for one last moment, then beneath all those witnessing stars, quietly dressed, furled his quilt and stepped through the dark back to the tavern, my hand wrapped by his. And as the final hour of our wondrous day crept near, we creaked, swayed and rolled to Boston in the hush of the night.

Ethan and I would meet in Boston for a few hours each day after that magical night, then as a lazy mist roamed the port shortly after dawn the third Saturday of August 1772, I boarded the *Dorchester* once again and sailed south for the Colony of Pennsylvania. As she sliced through the waters the coming days my thoughts were consumed of my two lives, of the pressuring expectations entwining my life with Franz in Philadelphia and the fiery passions I held secretly inside for my Ethan in Lexington. It was an anguishing battle that raged as we tossed and splashed about the sea, and as tears of dismaying guilt dripped to my pillow those daunting nights, I realized I was reluctantly accepting the limitations gripping my life. Upon my return I resumed my nursing duties at the hospital, and as if doused by a numbing potion, continued to forge a life with Franz, all the while my heart pounded for Ethan.

I remember how my thoughts often wandered those first few weeks, anxious hours waiting for another letter from Ethan, then around noon the first Wednesday of September a young postal rider slid creased parchment to my nursing desk. Ethan had quilled of my visit to Boston and time in Lexington, of the tavern and his father, and stroked sweet memories of our intimate hours on our special hill. And he closed his letter with a tender poem quilled just for me in the glow of a candle, emotions he had caressed since our wondrous night. They were passionate words quilled during the lonely hours of his little room, enchanting lines he called, *blissful dreams.*

> *tantalizing movements in darkness, heaven's mystical symphony*
> *stars streak about the night, bewitching trails flaming serenity*
> *galaxies spinning endlessly, mozart strings swirling about time*
> *two souls touching tenderly, enchanting flames surge my mind*
>
> *aroma of distant blooms, glistening grass swaying tranquilly*
> *summer leaves fluttering the dark, sounds soothing rapturously*
> *stardust blesses our lexington hill, sprinkles our precious night*
> *gentle green eyes arouse, andrea's skin aglow in our moonlight*
>
> *beneath a pulsating spray we lay, her tender touch thrills me*
> *sensuous lips erupting passions, spurring hopes and fancies*
> *alluring glances captivate my soul, her luscious pearl beams*
> *two lives bathed of intimacy, hearts adrift in blissful dreams*

Made in the USA
Middletown, DE
18 January 2017